Trusts and Equity

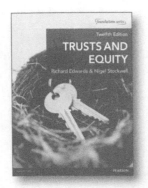 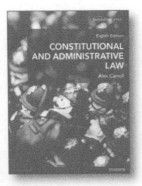  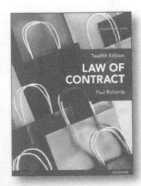

Twelfth Edition

Trusts and Equity

RICHARD EDWARDS LLB, LLM
Formerly Principal Lecturer in Law, APU
(now Anglia Ruskin University)

NIGEL STOCKWELL BA, LLB
Barrister, Visiting Fellow, and formerly Senior Lecturer in Law
Anglia Law School, Anglia Ruskin University

PEARSON

Harlow, England • London • New York • Boston • San Francisco • Toronto • Sydney • Auckland • Singapore • Hong Kong
Tokyo • Seoul • Taipei • New Delhi • Cape Town • São Paulo • Mexico City • Madrid • Amsterdam • Munich • Paris • Milan

Pearson Education Limited
Edinburgh Gate
Harlow CM20 2JE
United Kingdom
Tel: +44 (0)1279 623623
Web: www.pearson.com/uk

First published 1992 (print)
Second edition 1995 (print)
Third edition 1997 (print)
Fourth edition 1999 (print)
Tenth edition 2011 (print)
Eleventh edition 2013 (print and electronic)
Twelfth edition 2015 (print and electronic)

© Longman Group UK Limited 1992 (print)
© Pearson Professional Limited 1995 (print)
© Financial Times Professional Limited 1997 (print)
© Pearson Education Limited 1999, 2011 (print)
© Pearson Education Limited 2013 (print and electronic)
© Pearson Education Limited 2015 (print and electronic)

ISBN: 978-1-292-01705-1 (print)
    978-1-292-01710-5 (PDF)
    978-1-292-01706-8 (eText)

British Library Cataloguing-in-Publication Data
A catalogue record for the print edition is available from the British Library

Library of Congress Cataloging-in-Publication Data
A catalog record for the print edition is available from the Library of Congress

ARP Impression 98

Cover image: Getty Images/Jamie Grill

Print edition typeset in 9/12pt StoneSerITCStd by 35
Printed by Ashford Colour Press Ltd

NOTE THAT ANY PAGE CROSS REFERENCES REFER TO THE PRINT EDITION

Brief contents

Contents

14 The office of trustee: appointment, retirement and removal   393

15 Trustees' powers   426

Preface

Many students come to the subject of trusts and equity with a lack of enthusiasm, having little idea of what it covers, but believing it to be complex and difficult. As a result it is (at least to us) an unpalatable fact that many students do find the subject less than easy to get to grips with, especially during their first few weeks of study.

We had these issues in mind when we wrote the first edition of *Trusts and Equity* in 1992. One of our aims then was to try to demystify the law of trusts and equity without any undue oversimplification. Over the intervening years the law has become very much more complex and the trust is being used in an ever-increasing variety of situations. We see no reasons why that initial aim is any less important now than it was in 1992.

One of the reasons why students may find the subject 'challenging' is because they say that they find the subject mundane and remote from their lives. In fact trusts and equity is a branch of the law which, although having ancient origins, has the flexibility to lend itself to providing solutions to many problems of the twenty-first century, impacting on the lives of many, if not all, of us. A short perusal of some of the cases can show that the facts involved often entail common situations in personal, domestic and commercial life with which it is not difficult to identify. The challenge for teachers is to communicate this to their students and to fire their enthusiasm. The challenge for students is to see the subject as dynamic and relevant.

We have made some structural alterations which we hope will aid this process. We have expanded our statements of aims and objectives for each chapter and linked these to the main text, in order to make it easier to identify particular topics within each chapter. We have adopted a policy for new cases of including the neutral citation, as well a citation to one of the leading reports, as we feel this more accurately reflects the modern student experience where cases are as likely to be read online as in hard copy. We have also created a new chapter dealing with unlawful trusts which places emphasis on the problems associated with the time that a trust can last.

Once again for this new edition we have included a number of new cases and statutes as well as updating the sections on taxation. Some chapters have undergone a more radical overhaul than others.

Statutory changes, both recent and prospective, include the Trusts (Capital and Income) Act 2013 (in force 1 October 2013) which affects the apportionment of capital and income in trusts, and the Inheritance and Trustees' Powers Act 2014 which, amongst other things, made changes to the statutory powers of advancement and maintenance and came into force in October 2014. We also make reference to the Marriage (Same Sex Couples) Act 2013, redefining marriage to include marriages between same sex partners. Possible future legislation referred to includes a cohabitation bill, currently being debated, which if implemented would give cohabitees the same rights as married couples on divorce, and the EU Anti-Money Laundering Directive which may require trusts to be publicly registered.

Recent case law we have referred to includes *Futter* v *HMRC, Pitt* v *HMRC* [2013] UKSC 26, [2013] 3 All ER 429 which re-states the rule in *Re Hastings-Bass* and also deals with when trustees' decisions can be overturned on the ground of mistake; *Keene and Phillips* v *Wellcom London Ltd and others* [2014] EWHC 134 (Ch), [2014] All ER (D) 241 (Jan) concerning the winding up of unincorporated associations; *FHR European Ventures LLP* v *Cedar Capital Partners* LLC [2014] UKSC 45, on the application of proprietary remedies to improper profits by fiduciaries; *Central Bank of Nigeria* v *Williams* [2014] UKSC 10, [2014] All ER (D) 172, *Novoship (UK) Ltd* v *Mikhaylyuk* [2014] EWCA Civ 908 on the use of the duty to account for profits imposed on intermeddling strangers; and *Coventry (t/a RDC Promotions)* v *Lawrence* [2014] UKSC 13, [2014] 2 All ER 622 on the relationship between injunctions and damages in lieu; and *O'Kelly* v *Davies* [2014] EWCA Civ 1606 where it was held that there is no distinction between a resulting and a constructive trust that is sufficient to make a resulting trust enforceable in the face of an illegal purpose and a constructive trust unenforceable.

We still hope that the text will be used in two ways: first, as a reference to dip into for help with particular aspects of the law and, secondly, to obtain an understanding and appreciation of a particular area of the law. To this end we have included the details of the facts and decisions of the most important and/or the most recent cases and extracts from relevant statutes. Again, because we hope that *Trusts and Equity* will be used as a reference, we have occasionally included key extracts from cases or statutes more than once. This is deliberate and is aimed at reducing the need to refer readers back and forth for information.

We could not end this Preface without again thanking Anne, M and m for their continued understanding and support, and H, B and m for sometimes providing a much needed excuse to take a break from writing.

RE and NBS
November 2014

Publisher's acknowledgements

We are grateful to the following for permission to reproduce copyright material:

Text
Extracts on pages 11, 16, 22, 114, 166, 218, 240, 245, 249, 256, 372, 375, 382, 388, 469, 482, 500, 521, 551, 559, 560 and 585 contain public sector information licensed under the Open Government Licence (OGL) v3.0. **http://www.nationalarchives.gov.uk/doc/open-government-licence**; Extract on page 26 from *The Times*, 04/11/1997, © News Syndication; Extract on page 380 from *Le Foe* v *Le Foe* [2001] 2 FLR 970, © Jordan Publishing.

In some instances we have been unable to trace the owners of copyright material, and we would appreciate any information that would enable us to do so.

Table of cases

Table of legislation

Growth of equity and the evolution of the trust

Objectives

After reading this chapter you should:

1. Understand and appreciate the main stages in the growth of equity and the evolution of the law of equity, a body of rules created by the Court of Chancery, initially presided over by the Lord Chancellor, and understand that the origins of equity and of the trust lay in overcoming shortcomings of the common law.

2. Understand and appreciate that the initial flexibility of equity resulted in uncertainty and unpredictability and that this led, in the late seventeenth and eighteenth centuries, to a body of precedent used in deciding cases, while preserving the discretionary nature of equity.

3. Be aware of how the conflicts between equity and the common law were addressed.

4. Be aware of the way in which the trust concept evolved.

5. Be able to describe the trust concept and identify the key elements of a trust, particularly of an express private trust.

6. Understand the nature of a beneficial interest.

7. Be aware of the concept of the *bona fide* purchaser principle and its reduced importance following the 1925 property legislation.

8. Be able to identify the main types of trusts both private and public.

9. Be aware of the distinction between a trust and other concepts.

10. Understand that tax avoidance or reduction is a reason for the creation of many trusts (or the form that the trust takes) and appreciate that the main taxes that are relevant are income tax, capital gains tax and inheritance tax.

The title of this text is *Trusts and Equity*. It deals with the most important principles and doctrines of equity and the main equitable concepts. It covers the trust at length. Maitland, in his *Selected Historical Essays*, said: 'If we were asked what is the greatest and most distinctive achievement performed by Englishmen in the field of jurisprudence I cannot think that we should have any better answer to give than this, namely, the development from century to century of the trust idea.' As Maitland points out, the 'greatest and most distinctive

1

achievement' of English law is not merely the 'invention' of the trust but also the fact that the concept has been developed and refined over time to meet new demands and to provide solutions to new problems. It is this ability to adapt to new needs and circumstances which has led to the trust being so widely and inventively used. The trust was created and developed by equity, and in order to appreciate the modern law of trusts it is necessary to outline the evolution of equity and the manner in which the trust concept has grown.

As Maitland indicates, the trust is the invention of English law and, while it is a feature of other systems of law based on the common law, it is not normally found in civil law systems.

Although this text concentrates on the trust, it must not be thought that this is all that equity is, or has been, concerned with. Its field is very wide, and equitable jurisdiction includes certain probate business, patents, trademarks, copyright, the appointment of guardians for minors, partnership matters, companies and mortgages.

See Chapter 19 (p. 545) for a discussion of equitable remedies.

Equity has also developed a number of 'equitable' remedies, such as specific performance, the injunction and the remedy of account. Remedies will be discussed later.

Many of the concepts developed by equity are now, at least partially, covered by statutes which usually draw on the principles and rules developed by equity and also introduce additional material. One example where statutory intervention has taken place is in the area of trusts, where, in particular, the Trustee Act 1925 and the Trustee Act 2000 now contain a good deal of the relevant law.

Development of equity

Origins

Objective 1

The word 'equity' has a wide range of meanings and to many people it is a synonym for 'fairness' or 'justice'. To a lawyer, however, equity has a very special and narrow meaning: that body of rules originally developed and applied by the Court of Chancery. This court was presided over by the Chancellor and the rules were developed under his authority.

The origins of equity lie in deficiencies in the common law. The common law had gaps where a remedy was not available or where a remedy was available but was not appropriate to the particular loss of a plaintiff. The Chancellor was responsible, among other things, for the issue of writs and all actions had to be commenced by the issue of a royal writ. If there was no writ appropriate to a claim, there could be no action and thus no remedy. To some extent the severity of this was tempered by the Chancellor's willingness to develop new writs, but this came to an end when the Provisions of Oxford 1258 stopped the issue of writs to cover new forms of action without the consent of the King in Council.

Another problem of the common law lay where a plaintiff may have had a common law remedy but he was prevented from enforcing it because of the power or influence of the other party to the case. Or a plaintiff might be the victim of the corruption of the jury which heard his case.

Additionally, the common law was preoccupied with formality. For example, if two parties tried to enter into a verbal contract which was required, at common law, to be in writing the result would be that the common law would not recognise the contract nor grant any remedies on it. This was the case whatever the situation, whatever the merits of the case and irrespective of how the parties had behaved. In some of these situations equity would step in and provide a remedy despite the lack of formality.

The original role of equity was often as a 'gloss on the common law'. Equity might well provide a remedy where the common law provided none or provide a more suitable remedy than the common law. Equity might also intervene to ensure that the available common law remedy was actually enforceable. In other words, equity worked alongside the common law and provided different solutions to problems.

It was considered that a residuum of justice resided in the King, and petitions were directed at tapping into this as a last resort if the common law had not provided justice. If a subject believed that the common law would not provide an appropriate solution to his case, he could petition the King and the Council asking that justice be done and that a remedy should be ordered. These petitions were referred to the Chancellor and eventually the Chancellor was petitioned directly. Cases brought before the Chancellor were called 'suits'. The Chancellor was making decrees by the end of the fifteenth century. The Chancellor was a very important figure, perhaps second only to the King, not least because he was responsible for issuing the royal writs. The Chancellor was, in effect, at the head of the common law and what he did was to ensure that the common law worked in an acceptable way. Initially, he was not creating a separate system but was dealing with the faults of the common law.

It was not until the end of the fourteenth century that it could be said that a Court of Chancery, in any real sense, came into being. Up until that time the Chancellor simply responded to petitions by issuing a decree without the procedures usually associated with a court hearing. It was only very gradually that equity developed and came to be regarded as a separate and, in some ways, a rival system of law.

Originally, Chancellors, though generally well versed in the law, particularly the canon law, were ecclesiastics rather than lawyers. They were sometimes referred to as the keepers of the King's conscience. Early decisions tended to be idiosyncratic and to be based on the ideas, beliefs and conscience of each particular Chancellor. John Seldon the seventeenth-century jurist illustrated this by saying it was as if equity varied with the length of the Chancellor's foot. In other words, the decision in any particular case would be relatively unpredictable and uncertain. This may be an acceptable approach in single isolated cases, but the uncertainty meant that the rights of individuals were impossible to assess without the trouble and expense of going to court.

Introduction of rigidity

Objective
2

The appointment of Lord Nottingham as Chancellor in 1675 marked the start of the systemisation of equity. He was responsible for setting down the principles upon which equity operated, thus moving away from the era of idiosyncratic, unpredictable decisions. He also laid out the boundaries within which equity functioned. Lord Nottingham was also instrumental in developing the law of trusts. The next important Chancellor was possibly Lord Hardwicke, who was first appointed in 1737. Lord Hardwicke further developed the principles of equity, and many of his decisions demonstrated the fine balance that had to be held between certainty and the flexibility needed to allow both 'justice' in a particular case and also the evolution of the law. Lord Hardwicke often emphasised the function of equity to provide a remedy in the case of unconscientious conduct.

The last great Chancellor involved in the development of equity into a modern system of law was Lord Eldon, who was first appointed in 1801. Lord Eldon was twice Chancellor, for a total of almost a quarter of a century. He stressed that decisions must be based on precedent (perhaps applied in a flexible and creative manner) and he consolidated the principles previously developed. Since the Chancellorship of Lord Eldon the principles and scope of equity have gradually evolved, adapting to new and changing situations.

Lord Nottingham has been described as the father of equity, while Lord Hardwicke was responsible for laying down the general principles upon which equity operated.

Lord Eldon was the consolidator, who worked on the application of the rules and principles of equity which he inherited from Lord Nottingham and Lord Hardwicke.

Gradually, decisions began to be based on precedent. This development took place at the same time as lawyers began to be appointed as Chancellors. Eventually a body of law evolved which was a more predictable, precedent-based system. This move started at the end of the seventeenth century and coincided with the refinement of the reporting of cases heard in the Chancery courts.

Trusts, which began to be developed to address family/domestic matters, gradually began to be used in a commercial/business context and here certainty and effective law reporting were particularly important.

Conflicts between equity and the common law

Objective 3

The general approach of equity was to follow the common law unless there was a sound reason to do otherwise. So, equity recognised and protected those estates in land and those interests in land that were recognised and protected by the common law. In fact, as well as recognising the common law estates, equity recognised other estates too.

But in a legal system where two bodies of law existed, there were bound to be occasions when there was a conflict. If conflicts arose between equity and the common law, equity would use the common injunction, which had the effect of preventing the common law action from proceeding or preventing the common law judgment from being enforced. This was clearly not acceptable to the common lawyers and for many years there was very active conflict. This was not resolved until the reign of James I when it was decided that equity should prevail.

The Supreme Court of Judicature Act 1873 s 25(11) provided that in cases of conflict between the rules of equity and the rules of the common law, equity shall prevail (now the Senior Court Act 1981 s 49).

Nature of the Chancellors' interventions

There are a number of very important underlying principles which relate to the ways in which equity intervened.

Equity acts *in personam*

See Chapter 19 (p. 545) for a discussion of equitable remedies.

The main remedy available at common law is damages. Equity, however, acted against the person and ordered him to do something. For example, a decree of specific performance ordered a party to a contract to fulfil his promises. An injunction ordered that something was not done or, sometimes, that something was done. Other equitable remedies are **rescission**, **rectification** and account. If the order of the court is not obeyed, then imprisonment may follow.

Equitable remedies are discretionary

A common law remedy can be claimed as of right. For example, if a breach of contract is proved, the victim can demand an award of damages. However, the award of an equitable remedy is at the discretion of the court. The victim of a **breach of contract** to transfer property can only ask the court to exercise its discretion and award a decree of specific performance ordering the transfer of the property. There are now clear principles governing the exercise of the discretion and these will be discussed in detail
See Chapter 19. later.

The *bona fide* purchaser

Whereas a legal right may be said to be enforceable against anyone in the world, an equitable right is enforceable against anyone except a *bona fide* purchaser of the legal estate for value and without notice of the prior equitable rights. (This principle is of less importance following the introduction of registration of rights over land but is nevertheless a basic principle of equity.)

Judicature Acts 1873–75

It is clear that although equity started life as mere supplement to the common law it developed into a separate system. Equity was administered by the Courts of Chancery, which were separate from the common law courts. This caused many problems. For example, it was often necessary to use both the common law courts and the court of equity in the same dispute. There were some improvements but it was not until the Supreme Court of Judicature Acts 1873–75 that the position changed significantly. This legislation provided for the creation of one single Supreme Court to replace the separate courts that existed previously. The Courts of Exchequer, Queen's Bench, Chancery, Common Pleas, Probate, Admiralty and the Divorce Court were abolished. In their place was one court, divided, for convenience only, into three Divisions of the High Court (Queen's Bench, Chancery and the Probate, Divorce and Admiralty Divisions, the latter being renamed the Family Division in 1970). In practice, matters are allocated to the most appropriate Division but in fact any Division can adjudicate on any matter and both common law and equitable remedies can be awarded in any Division. As mentioned above, it was specifically provided that, if there was a conflict between the rules of the common law and the rules of equity, equity shall prevail (Supreme Court of Judicature Act 1873 s 25(11); now the Senior Courts Act 1981 s 49).

There is no doubt that this legislation merged the administration of the two systems of law. There is, however, some debate as to whether the two systems of law themselves have been fused into one. Ashburner, in *Principles of Equity*, expressed his view by saying that 'the two streams of jurisdiction, though they run in the same channel, run side by side and do not mingle their waters'. There have been judicial and academic statements to the effect that there is a fused system of law. For example, in **United Scientific Holdings Ltd v Burnley Borough Council** [1977] 2 WLR 806, Lord Diplock said:

> The innate conservatism of English lawyers may have made them slow to recognise that by the Supreme Court of Judicature Act 1873, the two systems of substantive and adjectival law formerly administered by courts of law and Courts of Chancery (as well as those administered by Courts of Admiralty, Probate and Matrimonial Causes) were fused.

The prevailing view appears to be that, although the two systems operate closely together, they are not fused. In **MCC Proceeds Inc v Lehman Brothers International (Europe)** [1998] 4 All ER 675, Mummery LJ said that the substantive rule of law was not changed by the Judicature Acts. These were intended to achieve procedural improvements in the administration of the law and equity in all courts, not to transform equitable interests into legal titles or to sweep away the rules of the common law.

However, Lord Browne-Wilkinson, in **Tinsley v Milligan** [1993] 3 All ER 65, appears to take a different view. He said:

> More than 100 years has elapsed since the fusion of the administration of law and equity. The reality of the matter is that, in 1993, English law has one single law of property made up of legal estates and equitable interests.

The distinction still remains between equitable and common law remedies. There remain important differences between common law and equitable rights.

Evolution of the trust

Objective 4

Tracing the development of the trust by equity is to discover a series of problems looking for answers: the answers being provided by the trust. It is a concept which began as the solution to some relatively simple and straightforward problems and then just grew and grew. Its great merit was and still is its adaptability, its ability to evolve and to solve new and different problems.

The modern trust has its origins in the use (from the Latin *ad opus*) which was developed as the response of equity to the shortcomings of the common law.

The development of the trust began even before the Norman Conquest in 1066, when land was transferred 'to the use' of other people or purposes. At first the problems for which uses provided a solution were often short term and rooted in a family or domestic setting, rather than in a business or commercial context. For example, the owner of land was planning to be away for some time (perhaps on a crusade) and he transferred the land to a friend (the transferee) who it was understood would take the land not for his own benefit but would hold it for the family of the owner. Often the arrangement was to last only until the owner returned. In most cases there would be no problem: the friend would honestly and faithfully carry out his promise and would ensure that the benefits of the land flowed to the family. However, there were occasions when the promise was not kept or a disagreement arose over the manner in which the land was administered. In such cases the common law would recognise only the ownership of the transferee. The family was considered to have no rights in the land at all. In other words, the family had absolutely no legal redress if the transferee simply ignored his promise and administered the land for his own benefit. The promise was binding in honour only and the family had to hope that a wise choice had been made and that the transferee was a man of honour.

In the fourteenth and fifteenth centuries the Chancellor began to protect the family and would order the transferee to carry out the terms of his promise. As equity acts *in personam*, the protection took the form of ordering the transferee to act in a particular way to accord with the terms of his agreement. Soon, however, equity allowed the family to enforce their rights not only against the original transferee but also against third parties who had received the property from the original transferee. However, it was always accepted by equity that the legal owner of the property was the transferee. So, gradually, over a period of many years, the attitude of the Chancellor evolved into the recognition of separate rights of the family, and eventually it was accepted that two types of ownership could exist in property at the same time. One was recognised by the common law and the other by equity.

The terminology used was that the transferee (now called the trustee) was known as the 'feoffee to uses' and the people for whom he held the property (now called the beneficiaries) were called the '*cestuis que use*'.

Another classic reason for employing the use was to enable property to be held for an individual or body which was not itself allowed to hold property. For example, Franciscan friars took vows of poverty and were not allowed to hold property and so land would be conveyed to an individual to hold to the use of the community of friars.

Again, the use was applied in order to sidestep the common law prohibition on disposing of land by will. The would-be testator would transfer the land during his lifetime to a number of his trusted friends and then nominate to whose use they were to hold the land after his (the transferor's) death, and in the meantime until his death the property would be held for the transferor. Once more, the use was being employed to overcome what many saw as a defect of the common law.

However, perhaps the most common application of the use was to avoid feudal dues. It will be recalled that since the Norman Conquest the Crown owns all land. Under the feudal system all land was held under the Crown in exchange for the provision of money or services. The Crown granted estates in land to certain lords who in turn could allow others to hold from them, again in return for money or services.

Over a period of time the obligations to provide services were converted into money, but with the effect of inflation these payments lost their value and were often not collected. The Tenures Abolition Act 1660 abolished most of the remaining dues.

However, although the dues became less and less important there were incidents which often attached to land and which could be very valuable. A lord was entitled to a payment if land was held by a minor, and if a tenant died without leaving an heir the lord was entitled to the land under the right of escheat. It was common to employ the use to avoid these feudal incidents. If a tenant feared that he might die leaving his minor son as his heir he might decide to transfer the land to some trustworthy adults who would hold to the use of the son. If the tenant died before the heir was adult, no feudal dues were payable as the land was, according to the rules of the common law, held by the adults.

It is clear that, since all land was held from the Crown, it was the Crown which suffered most from the employment of uses to avoid the feudal dues.

The response of Henry VIII to this loss of revenue was the Statute of Uses 1535 which was initially intended to apply to all uses but was, in the event, modified so that it affected only some of them. The Statute was one of the first examples of anti-tax avoidance legislation. The Statute simply executed uses to which it applied. If, for example, land was held by Arthur to the use of Ben, the Statute of Uses caused the use to be executed or ignored, and the feoffee to uses disappeared and the legal estate was considered to be vested in the *cestui que* use. The end result was that the legal estate was vested in Ben, the *cestui que* use. When Ben died feudal dues would become payable. In this way the Statute of Uses prevented the avoidance of taxes on the death of Ben.

The Statute did not apply to uses where the feoffee to uses had active duties to perform such as the collection and distribution of profits from the land. Nor did the Statute apply if the property subject to the use was held only for a term of years.

For some time the Statute was effective in restricting uses to active uses or uses covering only a period of years, but attempts to have recourse to the passive use, which was the use normally employed to avoid feudal dues, were no longer profitable.

This remained the situation until about 1650 when a device known as a use upon a use was found to be an effective way round the Statute. The solution involved a double use. Land would be transferred to Arthur to the use of Ben to the use of Charles. It was eventually accepted that only the first use was executed under the Statute of Uses leaving the second use intact. The phraseology altered and the second use began to be described as a trust and the common form was to transfer land 'unto and to the use of Ben in trust for Charles'. The effect was that the legal estate was vested in Ben, and Charles owned the land in equity. Eventually the terminology was refined even more and land would simply be conveyed to Ben on trust for Charles.

Definition/description of the trust

See Chapter 9
(p. 199) for a
discussion of
purpose trusts.

See Chapter 10
(p. 216) for a
discussion of
charitable trusts.

**Objective
5**

A trust is very difficult if not impossible to define, but its essential elements are reasonably easily described and readily understood. There have been very many attempts to produce a definition of a trust but such definitions are either long, amounting to descriptions rather than definitions, or shorter but susceptible to criticism, often as not being comprehensive. It is not considered worthwhile either to attempt yet another definition or to criticise existing definitions; rather the concept of a trust will be described.

If a settlor, Simon, transfers property to trustee 1 and trustee 2 (Tim and Tom) to hold on trust for Ben, the legal ownership of the property is vested in Tim and Tom and the equitable (or beneficial) ownership is vested in Ben. It will be recalled that this division of ownership was the invention of equity and is the basis of the trust. Tim and Tom hold the property not for their own benefit but for the benefit of Ben. Tim and Tom's technical, legal, ownership brings only burdens and responsibilities which can make their position very onerous. The duties and responsibilities of Tim and Tom will be imposed by the settlor, by statute and by the general law of trusts. The beneficial ownership which rests with Ben brings with it, as the name suggests, the positive advantages of ownership. Any income which the trust property generates will belong to Ben. Any profit made from the trust property will accrue for the advantage of Ben.

Generally speaking, it is not possible to create trusts for purposes rather than to benefit human beneficiaries (see p. 200). The law generally requires there to be human beneficiaries who can enforce the trust or who can apply to the courts for enforcement. The most important exception to this general rule against purpose trusts is the charitable trust which will be dealt with at length later.

Charitable trusts cannot be enforced by beneficiaries because there are none, but are enforced by the Attorney-General. It is also possible to have a trust for a purpose which is to provide a direct benefit to a group of people. For example, in **Re Denley** [1968] 3 All ER 65, the court found that a valid private trust came into existence when land was given to be used as a sports field primarily for the benefit of the employees of a specified company.

In most trusts the settlor will transfer the trust property to others to hold as trustees, but it is perfectly possible for a trust to be created by the owner of the property declaring that he holds it henceforth on specified trusts for the beneficiaries. (See Figures 1.1 and 1.2.)

It is also possible for a settlor to be a beneficiary under a trust he has created. For example, Arthur might decide to transfer a block of shares to a trustee to hold on trust for himself for life and then the remainder for his son, George.

Any property may be the subject matter of a trust, and, although the nature of the property may affect the formalities for setting up or running the trust, the essential elements remain constant whatever the type of property involved. Property both real and personal can be the subject matter of a trust. The property may be tangible or intangible. Choses in action such as shares in companies can as readily be trust property as land or money. It is even possible to create a trust of an interest under an already existing trust. This is called a sub-trust.

An example of the breadth of the categories of property that may be the subject matter of a trust is **Don King Productions Inc v Warren** [1998] 2 All ER 608, in which contracts expressed to be non-assignable were the subject matter of a valid trust. The case concerned two partnership agreements which were intended to deal with the boxing promotion and management interests of two leading promoters. One of the agreements stated that the two parties would hold all promotion and management agreements relating to the business

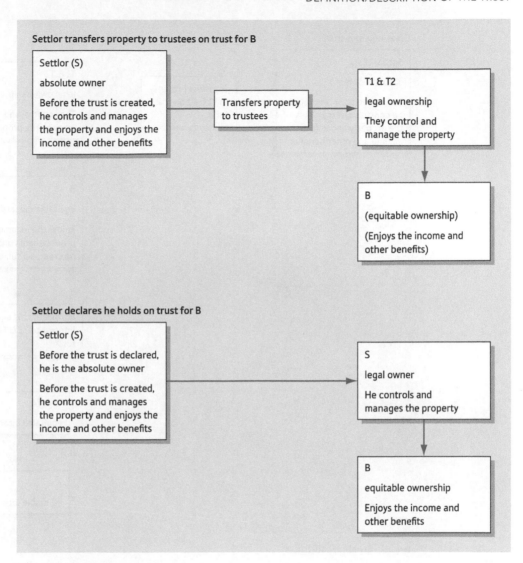

Figure 1.1 Creating trusts

for the benefit of the partnership. Some of the promotion agreements and all the management agreements contained non-assignment clauses. However, none of the contracts (promotion and management) contained a prohibition on the partners declaring themselves as trustees. Lightman J considered that a trust of the benefit of a contract was different in character from an assignment of the benefit of a contract. The Court of Appeal upheld the decision of Lightfoot J at first instance ([1999] 2 All ER 218). (Further discussion of transfer formalities may be found at pp. 104–07.)

See Chapter 17 (p. 492) for a discussion of remedies for breach of trust.

If the trustees deal with the trust property in a way that is contrary to the terms of their trust this will constitute a **breach of trust**, and the beneficiary will be able to seek various remedies through the courts, including damages. If trust property has improperly been transferred to a third party, it may be possible for the beneficiary to 'follow' or trace the trust property into the hands of third parties and recover it.

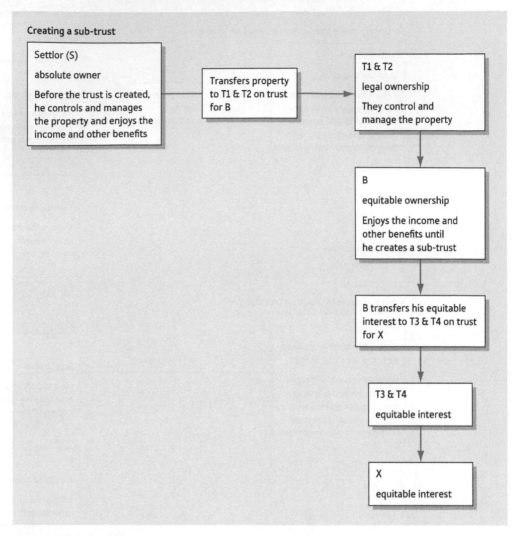

Figure 1.2 Creating sub-trusts

Westdeutsche Landesbank Girozentrale v *Islington London Borough Council* [1996] 2 All ER 961

In this case, Lord Browne-Wilkinson made a number of points that relate to the underlying nature of the trust and of equitable interests:

(i) Equity operates on the conscience of the owner of the legal interest. In the case of a trust, the conscience of the legal owner requires him to carry out the purposes for which the property was vested in him (express or implied trust) or which the law imposes on him by reason of his unconscionable conduct (constructive trust).

(ii) Since the equitable jurisdiction to enforce trusts depends upon the conscience of the holder of the legal interest being affected, he cannot be a trustee of the property if and so long as he is ignorant of the facts alleged to affect his conscience, i.e. until he is aware that he is intended to hold the property for the benefit of others in the case of an express or implied trust, or, in the case of a constructive trust, of the factors which are alleged to affect his conscience.

(iii) In order to establish a trust, there must be identifiable trust property. The only apparent exception to this rule is a constructive trusts imposed on a person who dishonestly assists in a breach of trust who may come under fiduciary duties even if he does not receive identifiable trust property.

(iv) Once a trust is established, as from the date of its establishment the beneficiary has, in equity, a proprietary interest in the trust property, which proprietary interest will be enforceable in equity against any subsequent holder of the property (whether the original property or substituted property into which it can be traced) other than a purchaser for value of the legal interest without notice.

These propositions are fundamental to the law of trusts and I would have thought uncontroversial. However, proposition (ii) may call for some expansion. There are cases where property has been put into the name of X without X's knowledge but in circumstances where no gift to X was intended. It has been held that such property is recoverable under a resulting trust (see *Birch v Blagrave* (1755) Amb 264, 27 ER 176, *Childers v Childers* (1857) 1 De G & J 482, 44 ER 810, *Re Vinogradoff, Allen v Jackson* [1935] WN 68 and *Re Muller, Cassin v Mutual Cash Order Co Ltd* [1953] NZLR 879). These cases are explicable on the ground that, by the time action was brought, X or his successors in title have become aware of the facts which gave rise to a resulting trust; his conscience was affected as from the time of such discovery and thereafter he held on a resulting trust under which the property was recovered from him. There is, so far as I am aware, no authority which decides that X was a trustee, and therefore accountable for his deeds, at any time before he was aware of the circumstances which gave rise to a resulting trust.

Lord Browne-Wilkinson places a good deal of emphasis on trusts being founded on the conscience of the supposed trustee. This, except in the case of constructive trusts, requires the supposed trustee to have knowledge of the fact that he is to hold property on trust and not beneficially. In such cases the fact that the 'trustee' had no relevant knowledge would mean that there is no reason why his conscience should be affected. This case will be referred to in other points of this text (and, in particular, will be discussed at pp. 264–5).

A statutory provision which is helpful in appreciating the nature of a trust is contained in the Recognition of Trusts Act 1987 (enacting the terms of the Hague Convention on the Recognition of Trusts). The provision focuses on the characteristics of the concept rather than attempting a definition. Article 2 provides:

For the purpose of this Convention, the term 'trust' refers to the legal relationship created – *inter vivos* or on death – by a person, the settlor, when assets have been placed under the control of a trustee for the benefit of a beneficiary or for a specified purpose. A trust has the following characteristics –

(a) the assets constitute a separate fund and are not part of the trustee's own estate;

(b) title to the trust assets stands in the name of the trustee or another person on the behalf of the trustee;

(c) the trustee has the power and duty, in respect of which he is accountable, to manage, employ or dispose of the assets in accordance with the terms of the trust and the special duties imposed upon him by law.

See Chapter 9 for more on purpose trusts. See Chapter 10 for more on charitable trusts.

The statement that trusts may be for 'a specified purpose' requires qualification.

Nature of equitable rights

Objective 6

There is a great deal of discussion and confusion surrounding the precise nature of equitable interests. Indeed there is often disagreement over the terminology to be used in a particular situation. The debate has been especially lively in the context of the interest of a beneficiary under a trust. The main dispute is as to whether his interest can be described as a right *in personam* or a right *in rem*. One difficulty is that these concepts, rights *in personam* and rights *in rem*, are used with different meanings by different commentators in different situations. However, in the context of the analysis of the nature of the interest of a beneficiary under a trust, it should be recalled that these rights were developed by equity acting *in personam* and every beneficiary will have a chose in action, a right against the trustee to compel the due administration of the trust. But the evolution of the protection provided by equity eventually gave the beneficiary the right to trace the trust property into the hands of third parties (except into the hands of a *bona fide* purchaser of the legal estate for value without notice of the equitable interest). This, it has been argued, means that the beneficiary has a right *in rem*, a right against the property itself. This is a right of a proprietary, rather than a personal, nature. The problem then is to decide if the right of the beneficiary is actually a right *in rem* or simply a right that is almost, but not quite, a right *in rem*! The fact that the right is not enforceable against the whole world (it cannot be enforced against the *bona fide* purchaser of the legal estate for value without notice) is said by some to mean that the right cannot be a right *in rem* as enforceability against the whole world is a key requirement of such a right. This may well be an unsound argument as in a number of cases a person who owns the legal estate in property (the possessor of a right *in rem*) is unable to enforce the right against the whole world.

There is some evidence from statutory provisions that equitable interests are interests in property. For example, under tax law, one who is entitled to shares under a trust is considered to be the owner for the purpose of liability to income tax on the dividends (*Baker v Archer-Shee* [1927] AC 844). Lord Tomlin said in *Archer-Shee v Garland* [1931] AC 212, commenting on *Baker v Archer-Shee*:

> I do not think that it can be doubted that the majority of your Lordships' House in the former case *Baker v Archer-Shee* founded themselves upon the view that according to English law . . . [the beneficiary] had a property interest in the income arising from the securities . . .

It is also possible to find support for this view in the judgment of Lord Browne-Wilkinson in *Tinsley v Milligan* [1993] 3 All ER 65. Having said that it was more than 100 years since the administration of law and equity was fused (see discussion of the Judicature Acts 1873–5 earlier in the chapter) he said:

> The reality of the matter is that, in 1993, English law has one single law of property made up of legal estates and equitable interests. Although for historical reasons legal estates have differing incidents, the person owning either type of estate has a right of property, a right *in rem*, not merely a right *in personam*.

Again, in *Westdeutsche Landesbank Girozentrale v Islington London Borough Council*, Lord Browne-Wilkinson made it clear that in his view the interest was a proprietary interest. He said:

> The Relevant Principles of Trust Law
> . . . (iv) Once a trust is established, as from the date of its establishment the beneficiary has, in equity, a proprietary interest in the trust property, which proprietary interest will be enforceable in equity against any subsequent holder of the property (whether the original property or substituted property into which it can be traced) other than a purchaser for value of the legal interest without notice.

The best conclusion may be to say that a beneficiary does have a proprietary right against the trust property but that it is not identical to the proprietary right of the owner of a legal interest.

An additional source of difficulty is that a person is sometimes described as having an equity or an equitable right when that person possesses something of a different nature to the rights of a beneficiary under a trust. Often these rights, initially created by the Court of Chancery, are called 'mere equities' to distinguish them from equitable interests proper. They are rights which, in most cases, are not assignable, and the benefit of a mere equity cannot run with the property. It is sometimes said that a mere equity is the right to seek an equitable remedy.

Equities are often categorised as proprietary rights. While the purchaser of an equitable interest without notice takes free of any equities, only the purchaser of the legal estate without notice takes free of equitable interests. The right to rescission on the ground of fraud or undue influence, the right to have a document rectified and the right to the consolidation of mortgages are examples of mere equities. The right of a deserted wife to occupy the matrimonial home was thought to fall within this category, but in **National Provincial Bank Ltd v Ainsworth** [1965] 2 All ER 472, the House of Lords categorised this as a personal right against the husband.

Bona fide purchaser principle

Objective
7

When the concept of the trust was being developed by equity, one of the problems that had to be addressed was what rights did a beneficiary have if the trustee transferred trust property to a third party in breach of trust. The solution that equity imposed is not surprising when it is recalled that the courts proceeded on the basis of principles of conscience. If the trustee transferred the trust property to a purchaser who was acting in good faith, who gave value for the property and who had no notice of the equitable interests existing in the property, equity saw no reason why the purchaser should be treated as having acted unconscionably and so there was no reason why equity should allow the claim of the beneficiary to prevail. It can be said that the claims of the beneficiary and of the third party are equally valid and that in such a case the equitable maxim 'where there is equal equity, the law prevails' is applicable to protect the third party. In other words, the purchaser's legal estate is allowed to prevail over the equitable interest of the beneficiary.

An example of the *bona fide* purchaser rule in action is to be found in **MCC Proceeds Inc v Lehman Brothers International (Europe)** [1998] 4 All ER 675. Macmillan Incorporated (M) was a company taken over and controlled by Robert Maxwell and members of his family. The company placed shares in Berlitz International Inc, a wholly owned subsidiary, together with the share certificates in the name of Bishopsgate Investment Trust plc (a nominee company controlled by Robert Maxwell). An agreement declared that Bishopsgate held the legal title to the shares as nominees for M, which retained the beneficial ownership in the shares. The agreement stated that Bishopsgate Investment Trust plc would immediately transfer the shares to M on M's written demand. Bishopsgate then, in breach of trust, pledged the certificates with the defendants as collateral under a stock-lending scheme. M knew nothing of this. The defendants were unaware of the interest of M. The shares were later sold by the defendants. The Court of Appeal said that, as the defendants were *bona fide* purchasers of the legal interest in the shares and had no notice of the claim of M or of the breach of trust by Bishopsgate, the interest of M was overreached and the defendants took free of any interest of M.

The *bona fide* principle is obviously important but it is limited. It does not apply if the trust property is acquired by a volunteer or by a purchaser of an interest other than the legal interest. In this context the consideration provided can either be money or money's worth

13

or marriage consideration, which is recognised by equity, but not the common law, as being consideration. In these cases the claim of the beneficiary prevails and he is able to assert his rights against the third party. These situations are resolved by applying the maxim 'when the equities are equal the first in time prevails'.

The *bona fide* principle only applies if the purchaser has no notice of the equitable interests. Notice can include actual and constructive notice. A person has constructive notice of matters of which he would have known had he made those inquiries which a reasonable man would have made. A purchaser will also be fixed with notice of facts known to his agents (e.g. his solicitor). This is called imputed notice.

Impact of the 1925 property legislation

The 1925 property legislation attempted to make the transfer of real property simpler and is important in the area of trusts for two reasons.

Fewer legal estates

The Law of Property Act 1925 s 1 reduced the number of legal estates in land to two. These are the fee simple absolute in possession and the term of years absolute. Any other estate can now exist only in equity. For example, any future or life interests cannot exist as legal interests but can be equitable interests.

Modification of the *bona fide* principle

The importance of the *bona fide* purchaser principle was much reduced as a result of the 1925 property legislation. In many cases the *bona fide* principle was replaced with registration. Many equitable interests are registrable and registration is deemed to be actual notice to all persons. In other words, whether a third party takes subject to, or free from, an equitable interest depends on whether or not the interest has been correctly registered. If the interest has not been registered, then a purchaser takes free of it even if he has actual knowledge: **Midland Bank Trust Co Ltd v Green** [1981] 1 All ER 153.

There were a number of difficulties with the *bona fide* principle which it was hoped would be overcome by registration. For example, the owner of an equitable interest could find that he had lost his interest, through no fault of his own, to a *bona fide* purchaser for value who had no notice of the equitable interest. Under a system of registration the owner of the equitable interest is able to protect himself by registering the interest. Purchasers could never be absolutely certain that they had undertaken a thorough enough investigation in order to take free of any interest which had not been revealed by their searches. The system of registration means that the purchaser simply has to inspect the register to know what interests will bind him.

The provisions relating to unregistered land were contained in the Land Charges Act 1925 (now the Land Charges Act 1972). Registered land is now dealt with by the Land Registration Act 2002.

Classification of trusts

Objective 8

There are several ways in which trusts can be classified, all of which have some value (see Figure 1.3). However, it is not proposed to discuss every possible method of classification but rather to concentrate on some of the more important categorisations. The reason for

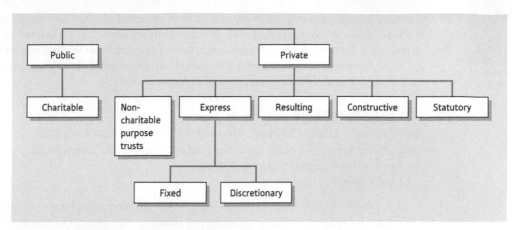

Figure 1.3 Types of trusts – public and private

discussing classification at this point is primarily to introduce a number of terms and ideas which will be encountered throughout the text.

By method of creation

This method classifies trusts according to their method of creation. The majority of trusts discussed in this text are express trusts, i.e. trusts in which the settlor expresses an intention to create the trust. In the course of the text a number of trusts will be encountered which come into being without the express intention of the settlor.

Express trusts

These trusts are the product of the express and expressed intention of the settlor to create a trust. It may be that the potential settlor has not expressed himself as clearly as he might and that the court has to decide if a trust is actually intended; nevertheless, if the court finds that a trust is intended, it will be an express trust.

Resulting trusts

This type of trust comes into being when a settlor has set up a trust but the beneficial interest (or part of it) results or returns to the settlor. An example would be if a settlor transfers property to trustees but fails to name or describe the beneficiaries.

Another illustration of a resulting trust occurs if property is bought and conveyed into the name of someone else. Again, if property which is owned is conveyed into the name of another a resulting trust may arise. In both of these cases the person in whose name the property stands holds it on resulting trust for the purchaser or owner. In both of the examples in this paragraph a resulting trust will exist unless it can be proved that the transferor intended to make a gift to the transferee. For completeness it should be added that there are some situations (e.g. husband transferring property or having property conveyed into the name of his wife, and father transferring property or having property conveyed into the name of his child) where the presumption of advancement displaces the presumption of resulting trust and the law presumes that a gift was intended, and so in these cases there will be a resulting trust only if the presumption of gift is rebutted. Section 199 of the Equality Act 2010, when in force, will abolish the presumption of advancement. Under 199(2) the abolition will not have any effect on anything done before the commencement of the section,

For further discussion on resulting trusts, see Chapter 11.

or anything done pursuant to any obligation incurred before the commencement of the section. So for many years the presumption of advancement will still need to be considered in relation to trusts that came into being before the date that section comes into force.

Many resulting trusts may also be argued to arise as the result of the presumed intention of the settlor and are described as implied trusts.

Constructive trusts

In *Williams* v *Central Bank of Nigeria* [2014] UKSC 10, [2014] All ER (D) 172, a recent decision of the Supreme Court, the often confusing use of the description 'constructive trust' or 'constructive trustee' was highlighted.

Lord Sumption said:

> 7 . . . there are few areas in which the law has been so completely obscured by confused categorisation and terminology as the law relating to constructive trustees.

In his judgment, Lord Sumption sets out two categories of constructive trust. The first is what many people would regard as true constructive trusts. An example would be where an individual is a trustee under trusts implied from the common intention to be inferred from the conduct of the parties, but where a trust is never formally created as such. Lord Sumption described such people as '*de facto*' trustees. The second category covers situations where a person is not a trustee of an express or other trust that has been created or found to exist, but is a person who has exposed himself to remedies having either dishonestly assisted in a misapplication of the funds by the trustee, or having received trust assets knowing that the transfer to them was a breach of trust. In these cases, they may be required by equity to account as if they were trustees or fiduciaries, but, says Lord Sumption, they are not trustees.

He said:

> 8 The starting point for any consideration of this subject remains the well-known statement of principle of Lord Selborne in *Barnes* v *Addy* (1874) LR 9 Ch App 244, 251: 'Now in this case we have to deal with certain persons who are trustees, and with certain other persons who are not trustees. That is a distinction to be borne in mind throughout the case. Those who create a trust clothe the trustee with a legal power and control over the trust property, imposing on him a corresponding responsibility. That responsibility may no doubt be extended in equity to others who are not properly trustees, if they are found either making themselves trustees de son tort, or actually participating in any fraudulent conduct of the trustee to the injury of the *cestui que* trust. But, on the other hand, strangers are not to be made constructive trustees merely because they act as the agents of trustees in transactions within their legal powers, transactions, perhaps of which a Court of Equity may disapprove, unless those agents receive and become chargeable with some part of the trust property, or unless they assist with knowledge in a dishonest and fraudulent design on the part of the trustees.'

> 9 . . . The problem is that in this all-embracing sense the phrase 'constructive trust' refers to two different things to which very different legal considerations apply. The first comprises persons who have lawfully assumed fiduciary obligations in relation to trust property, but without a formal appointment. They may be trustees de son tort, who without having been properly appointed, assume to act in the administration of the trusts as if they had been; or trustees under trusts implied from the common intention to be inferred from the conduct of the parties, but never formally created as such. These people can conveniently be called *de facto* trustees. They intended to act as trustees, if only as a matter of objective construction of their acts. They are true trustees, and if the assets are not applied in accordance with the trust, equity will enforce the obligations that they have assumed by virtue of their status exactly as if they had been appointed by deed. Others, such as company directors, are by virtue of their

status fiduciaries with very similar obligations. In its second meaning, the phrase 'constructive trustee' refers to something else. It comprises persons who never assumed and never intended to assume the status of a trustee, whether formally or informally, but have exposed themselves to equitable remedies by virtue of their participation in the unlawful misapplication of trust assets. Either they have dishonestly assisted in a misapplication of the funds by the trustee, or they have received trust assets knowing that the transfer to them was a breach of trust. In either case, they may be required by equity to account as if they were trustees or fiduciaries, although they are not. These can conveniently be called cases of ancillary liability. The intervention of equity in such cases does not reflect any pre-existing obligation but comes about solely because of the misapplication of the assets. It is purely remedial. The distinction between these two categories is not just a matter of the chronology of events leading to liability. It is fundamental. In the words of Millett LJ in *Paragon Finance Plc v DB Thakerar & Co (a firm)* [1999] 1 All ER 400, at 413, it is 'the distinction between an institutional trust and a remedial formula – between a trust and a catch-phrase.'

Williams v Central Bank of Nigeria is discussed in more detail in Chapter 12 (p. 341).

With the two meanings of constructive trust as set out by Lord Sumption in mind, the general characteristics and consequences of a constructive trust coming into being will be discussed briefly.

Constructive trusts arise by operation of law. They are imposed irrespective of the intention of the trustee and in many cases it is clear that a trust was the last thing that the trustee contemplated. For example, a constructive trust may arise if a trustee uses his position as a trustee to acquire property or to make a personal profit. The property or profit will be held on a constructive trust for the beneficiaries. Clearly, the intention of the person obtaining the property or profit is to keep it for himself.

There is a wide range of other situations where the courts have been willing to impose constructive trusts, but the accepted view is that in order to impose a constructive trust in a given case the courts need to find that the situation comes within the accepted, existing circumstances where a constructive trust can be imposed. In other words, although the courts are seeking to remedy unacceptable conduct, they must work within the limits defined by precedent cases.

There are a number of issues still at large in the area of constructive trusts.

First, the courts do not currently claim the power to impose a constructive trust every time there appears to be an injustice looking for a remedy. In *Eves v Eves* [1975] 3 All ER 768, Lord Denning asserted that the courts had such a power when he described a 'new model' of constructive trust. In *Hussey v Palmer* [1972] 3 All ER 744, he said it was a constructive trust which may be imposed 'whenever justice and good conscience require it'. He said that this would enable the courts to provide a remedy allowing the aggrieved party to obtain restitution. This, in many ways, reflects the American view that constructive trusts are a remedial institution. The American courts will impose a constructive trust when they perceive an unjust enrichment in order to allow the benefit to be reclaimed by the person at whose expense it was obtained. In English law the constructive trust has traditionally been regarded as just another type of trust which comes into being in a different way from other trusts. At root it is just another form of the accepted 'normal' institutional trust. The view of Lord Denning has been rejected in a number of cases both on the ground of the uncertainty that such a power would bring, and also because in many cases a constructive trust might be accompanied by unforeseen and unconsidered consequences. For example, the imposition of a constructive trust on a piece of property will remove it from a trustee's creditors in the event of his later bankruptcy. This appears to many to be a rather unacceptable by-product of a desire to give one aggrieved individual a remedy, the burden of which will be felt by the remainder of the trustee's creditors.

See Chapter 12 for a discussion of constructive trusts.

So it may be said that the remedial nature of the constructive trusts in the event of a finding of unjust enrichment is not presently accepted in the domestic courts although it is possible to argue that recent Commonwealth decisions indicate that this is a potential avenue of development for the near future.

Similarities between resulting and constructive trusts were highlighted in *O'Kelly* v *Davies* [2014] EWCA Civ 1606 where the Court of Appeal held that there is no distinction between a resulting and a constructive trust that is sufficient to make a resulting trust enforceable in the face of an illegal purpose and a constructive trust unenforceable.

Statutory trusts

A number of statutes impose trusts. Perhaps the most important examples of these statutory trusts arise in the context of the 1925 property legislation. The Law of Property Act 1925 ss 34–36 imposed a statutory trust for sale whenever land is co-owned. Also the Administration of Estates Act 1925 s 33 imposed a statutory trust for sale on the property of a person dying intestate.

The Trusts of Land and Appointment of Trustees Act 1996 (which came into force in January 1997) modifies that law in both these situations. Where land is co-owned, the property will be held on a trust of land under which there is a power (not a trust) to sell coupled with a power to retain (Schedule 2 paragraphs 3 and 4).

The Administration of Estates Act 1925 s 33 has also been amended by the Trusts of Land and Appointment of Trustees Act 1996. Any property that is not effectively disposed of by will is now held by the personal representatives on trust under which the personal representatives have a power of sale (Schedule 2 paragraph 5).

By type of beneficiary

Private trusts

Most of the trusts discussed in this text are private trusts in that they are set up to benefit either a single individual or a class of specified people.

Public trusts

Charitable trusts are discussed in Chapter 10.

These trusts are intended to benefit the public at large or at least a section of it. One of the commonest examples of a public trust is the charitable trust. One of the conditions for validity as a charitable trust is that it bestows a benefit on the public or a section of the public.

By nature of beneficiaries' interest

Fixed trusts

In a fixed trust the settlor states in the trust instrument the exact interest or share that each of the beneficiaries is to have. For example, if the settlor, Sam, transfers property to trustees to hold for his two children, Ben and Bill equally he has created a fixed trust. The shares of Ben and Bill have been precisely defined by Sam. The result of creating a fixed trust is that the beneficiaries have the beneficial ownership of property. Bill, for example, will be the owner of an interest equal to his share in the trust.

Discretionary trusts

Under such a trust the trustees are given the discretion to decide the extent to which beneficiaries are to benefit. For example, Sam may decide to transfer property to trustees to hold on a discretionary trust for his two children, Bill and Ben, giving the trustees the discretion to decide how Bill and Ben are to benefit from the income and/or the capital of the trust fund. Neither Bill nor Ben has any interest in the trust property unless and until the trustees exercise their discretion in their favour. A discretionary trust may be exhaustive or non-exhaustive. Under an exhaustive trust the trustees are under an obligation to distribute all the trust property; their discretion extends only to deciding which of the beneficiaries are to benefit and the extent of their individual benefit. If the trust is a non-exhaustive trust, the trustees also have a discretion to decide how much of the trust property is to be distributed as well as determining what is to be allocated to which beneficiary.

According to trustees' duties

Simple trusts

A simple or **bare trust** exists where the trustees have no active duties to perform. The trustees are simply the holders of the legal estate. An example of a simple trust is if property is transferred into the name of a mere nominee for the 'real' or beneficial owner.

Special trusts

These are trusts where the trustees do have positive active duties to perform. Unlike the simple trust, the trustees have a responsibility which goes beyond merely holding the legal estate. This type of trust can be divided into ministerial and discretionary trusts according to the duties which the trustees have. If the trustees have merely routine, administrative duties, such as the collection of rent from trust property and holding it on a fixed trust, a ministerial trust will exist. By contrast, a discretionary trust will exist if the trustee has to exercise his discretion or judgment in fulfilling his duties. For example, a trust which requires the trustees to make decisions as to whether or not to sell trust property will be classed as a discretionary trust.

By whether or not the trust property is vested in the trustees

This is a classification often used in texts but in fact is not a way of classifying trusts at all. It does in fact distinguish between trusts and non-trusts. If the trust property is vested in the trustees, the trust is said to be completely constituted. This constitution can take place either by the property being legally transferred to the trustee or by the settlor declaring himself to be a trustee over the property. In either case, assuming no other vitiating factor exists, the trust will be completely constituted with the very important consequence that the beneficiaries have enforceable rights against the trustee and the trust property. If the trust is not constituted, because the trust property has not been transferred to the trustee (or the settlor has not effectively declared that he holds the property as a trustee), there will be no trust. All that will exist is the promise of the 'settlor' that he will create the trust. This

See Chapter 4 (pp. 104–07) for a discussion on the formalities of transfer.

promise may be a contractual promise or perhaps contained in a **covenant**. The would-be beneficiaries cannot sue on the promise unless they have provided consideration. As few would-be beneficiaries provide consideration, this means that in the majority of situations the 'settlor' can ignore his promise and refuse to constitute the trust.

Distinction between a trust and other concepts

Objective 9

It is often important to decide in a given situation whether a trust or some other concept has been created. There are several concepts which, at least superficially, are similar to a trust and it is necessary to identify the characteristics of each of these concepts in order to be able to verify that it is a trust which is being considered and not something else.

Contracts, debts and *Quistclose* trusts

It is sometimes difficult to decide if a trust or a contract has been created. Of course the concepts are in theory totally different but in practice there is a grey area where classification causes problems, particularly in the area of debts.

Example

A situation where it could be difficult to determine if a trust or a contract exists might arise in the following example. Simon may transfer some shares to Tim and Tom with the object that the dividends on the shares will be applied for the benefit of Ben. There are (at least) two possible mechanisms that could be adopted to achieve this purpose but the legal implications of each would be different. There could be a contractual relationship between Simon, Tim and Tom under which Tim and Tom agree to look after Ben, or Simon could be the settlor of property, vesting the legal title to the shares in Tim and Tom who hold on trust for Ben.

The origins of the concepts are different, trusts being a creature of equity whereas contract was a development of the common law. This distinction is, however, of very little use in attempting a classification. It is probably most useful to examine the characteristics of the two concepts and then to see which most closely resembles the issue being considered.

Perhaps the most important feature of a contract is that it is usually the product of an agreement between the parties whereas a trust can be and often is the result of a unilateral decision by the settlor. No one's agreement or consent is needed to create a trust and indeed it is quite possible that no consultation takes place between the trustees, the beneficiaries and the settlor.

In the law of contract the common law doctrine of privity prevents enforceable rights being acquired by those not parties to the agreement. However, in the law of trusts beneficiaries always obtain enforceable rights whether or not they are parties to the agreement creating the trust. This is perhaps the single most important characteristic of the trust and has been used as the basis of attempts to circumvent the contractual rule of privity of contract. It has been argued that it is possible to contract as the trustee for a third party and that a trust is created of the promise. This would then entitle the beneficiary to enforce the promise if the trustee will not. It is beyond doubt that it is possible to create trusts of promises, but the difficulty in this attempt to override the privity rule is that in order for a trust to exist there must be a clear intention to create a trust. In many contractual situations it has proved impossible to satisfy the courts that this intention existed. This attack has been of very limited success and is generally thought to have an unpromising future.

The common law doctrine of privity of contract has been modified by the Contracts (Rights of Third Parties) Act 1999 under which a non-contracting party is able to enforce a contractual term if the contract expressly allows him to do so or a term purports to confer a benefit on him (unless the contracting parties intended otherwise). The Act applies to contracts made after 11 May 2000. If the Act applies to contracts to create trusts (the wording of section 1(1)(b) and section 1(1)(3) seems to apply to beneficiaries under a trust) third parties will have a right to a remedy. But, the right given under the Act is a common law remedy in contract. In some cases this may not be of much help, where the third party wishes to assert a right in equity. To the extent that the Act does apply, it will reduce the need to seek ways of circumventing the rule of privity of contract and thus the need to seek the aid of the trust.

Another distinction between the two concepts is that a contract creates rights which are merely personal whereas a trust can create property rights. The remedy for a breach of contract is the personal remedy of damages. A breach of trust renders the trustee personally liable to compensate the trust for any loss suffered but additionally proprietary remedies may be available. (See p. 493 for further discussion of personal liability and p. 504 for further discussion of proprietary remedies.)

Particular problems of classification occur if Arthur, for example, transfers money to Ben. Of course the transfer may be intended to be an outright gift, but if the transaction simply creates a debt, then the rights of both parties are regulated by the law of contract and, subject to the terms of the contract, the debtor is under an absolute liability to repay the loan. The fact that the debtor no longer has the money is irrelevant. He may have had the money stolen or the money may have been lost as the result of an unfortunate investment but nevertheless the obligation to repay remains. If the debtor becomes bankrupt, Arthur will have to reclaim the money as one of Ben's creditors and will be competing with all the others to whom Ben owes money. So it is probable that Arthur will be unable to recover more than a small proportion of what Ben owes to him.

However, if the transfer of the money creates a trust the position is rather different. It may well be that, if the money is lost without any fault on Ben's part, he will not be liable to repay. Also, the money will be 'safe' if Ben becomes a bankrupt as property held as a trustee does not pass to the trustee in bankruptcy and is not available to the general creditors. Instead, the property remains available (only) to the beneficiaries under the trust.

However, confusion may arise from the fact that a loan and a trust may exist side by side! This is often regarded as an opportunity for a well-advised lender to protect himself against the possible bankruptcy of the borrower. While this is obviously advantageous to the lender in question, it is disadvantageous to other creditors as it removes a possible source of funds against which they could claim.

Barclays Bank v *Quistclose Investments Ltd* [1968] 3 All ER 651

In this House of Lords case, Lord Reid, Lord Morris of Borth-Y-Gest, Lord Guest, and Lord Pearce all agreed with Lord Wilberforce, who delivered the only judgment.

In this case the court found no problem in finding that there was both a debt and a trust involved in the same transaction. A company, Rolls Razor Ltd, declared a dividend but there were no funds from which to make the payment to shareholders. A loan was negotiated from Quistclose Investments Ltd which was made on the condition that 'this amount will only be used to meet the dividend due'. The cheque was paid into a separate account with Barclays Bank and the bank agreed that the money was only to be used to fund the dividend payments. Rolls Razor Ltd went into liquidation before the dividend was paid and the question that the House of Lords had to decide was whether a trust had come into being with the lender as the beneficiary, because if it had the lender would be able to reclaim the money. If only a debt existed, the lender would have no special claim and would have to compete with all the other creditors. The court held that the essence of the bargain between the lender and the borrower was that the money would not become part of the general assets of the borrower but that it should be used only to pay the dividend and for nothing else. The fact that the loan was to be 'only' for the purpose of paying the dividend could only mean, in the view of the court, that if the money was not so used it was to be returned to the lender. The way in which this intention would be implemented was via the creation of a trust. The money was received on trust to apply it to the payment of the dividends, and when that purpose failed the money was held on trust for the lender. The initial trust, in favour of those entitled to a dividend, was described as the 'primary trust' by the court. The trust in favour of the lender that arose when the purpose was not carried through and which then replaced the primary trust was described as the 'secondary trust'.

(See also below and pp. 84, 99 and 266 for further discussion of *Quistclose* trusts.)

In the recent case of *Bieber* v *Teathers Ltd (in liquidation)* [2012] EWCA Civ 1466 the court discussed *Quistclose* trusts and set out the basic requirements of their existence.

Bieber v *Teathers Ltd (in liquidation)*

Teathers had marketed an investment vehicle in which the claimants invested. The aim was to take advantage of a tax concession. The vehicle made no money and also often the claimants were not allowed to qualify for tax relief. Teathers then became insolvent. It was claimed that a *Quistclose* trust had arisen under which the defendants held the investments on trust. If this claim was successful Bieber could recover the investments before the other creditors in the insolvency. The claim that there was a *Quistclose* trust was upheld.

In the case the characteristics of and pre-requisites for a *Quistclose* trust were examined. Patten LJ:

These principles [for the establishment of a *Quistclose* trust] were reviewed by the House of Lords in *Twinsectra Ltd* v *Yardley* [2002] AC 164 and the judge [at first instance in *Bieber* v *Teathers*] directed himself in accordance with the following summary of the law:

'16. First, the question in every case is whether the payer and the recipient intended that the money passing between them was to be at the free disposal of the recipient: *Re Goldcorp Exchange* [1995] 1 AC 74 and *Twinsectra*. . . .

17. Second, the mere fact that the payer has paid the money to the recipient for the recipient to use it in a particular way is not of itself enough. The recipient may have represented or warranted that he intends to use it in a particular way or have promised to use it in a particular way. Such an arrangement would give rise to personal obligations but would not of itself necessarily create fiduciary obligations or a trust: *Twinsectra*. . . .

18. So, thirdly, it must be clear from the express terms of the transaction (properly construed) or must be objectively ascertained from the circumstances of the transaction that the mutual intention of payer and recipient (and the essence of their bargain) is that the funds transferred should not be part of the general assets of the recipient but should be used *exclusively* to effect particular identified payments, so that if the money cannot be so used then it is to be returned to the payer: *Toovey* v *Milne* (1819) 2 B&A 683 and *Quistclose*. . . .

19. Fourth, the mechanism by which this is achieved is a trust giving rise to fiduciary obligations on the part of the recipient which a court of equity will enforce: *Twinsectra*. . . . Equity intervenes because it is unconscionable for the recipient to obtain money on terms as to its application and then to disregard the terms on which he received it from a payer who had placed trust and confidence in the recipient to ensure the proper application of the money paid: *Twinsectra* at [76].

20. Fifth . . . It is not as such a "purpose" trust of which the recipient is a trustee, the beneficial interest in the money reverting to the payer if the purpose is incapable of achievement. It is a resulting trust in favour of the payer with a mandate granted to the recipient to apply the money paid for the purpose stated. The key feature of the arrangement is that the recipient is precluded from misapplying the money paid to him. The recipient has no beneficial interest in the money: generally the beneficial interest remains vested in the payer subject only to the recipient's power to apply the money in accordance with the stated purpose. If the stated purpose cannot be achieved then the mandate ceases to be effective, the recipient simply holds the money paid on resulting trust for the payer, and the recipient must repay it: *Twinsectra* at [81], [87], [92] and [100].

21. Sixth, the subjective intentions of payer and recipient as to the creation of a trust are irrelevant. If the properly construed terms upon which (or the objectively ascertained circumstances in which) payer and recipient enter into an arrangement have the effect of creating a trust, then it is not necessary that either payer or recipient should intend to create a trust: it is sufficient that they intend to enter into the relevant arrangement: *Twinsectra* at [71].

22. Seventh, the particular purpose must be specified in terms which enable a court to say whether a given application of the money does or does not fall within its terms: *Twinsectra* at [16].

23. It is in my judgment implicit in the doctrine so described in the authorities that the specified purpose is fulfilled by and at the time of the application of the money. The payer, the recipient and the ultimate beneficiary of the payment (that is, the person who benefits from the application by the recipient of the money for the particular purpose) need to know whether property has passed.'

Both sides accepted this as an accurate statement of the relevant principles. I would only add by way of emphasis that in deciding whether particular arrangements involve the creation of a trust and with it the retention by the paying party of beneficial control of the monies, proper account needs to be taken of the structure of the arrangements and the contractual mechanisms involved. . . . It is . . . necessary to be satisfied not merely that the money when paid was not at the free disposal of the payee but that, objectively examined, the contractual or other arrangements properly construed were intended to provide for the preservation of the payor's rights and the control of the use of the money through the medium of a trust.

Advantages to the payer

The main advantage of a *Quistclose* trust to a payer is that the money paid over does not become part of the general assets of the payee and so, for example, is not available to pay creditors generally should the payee become bankrupt. The payer can claim the money under the resulting trust.

Again if the payee uses all or some of the money for a purpose other than that agreed, the payee can claim the money as the beneficiary under a resulting trust. This is illustrated by the first instance decision in ***Templeton Insurance Ltd* v *Penningtons Solicitors LLP*** [2006] All ER (D) 191 (Feb).

A company agreed to provide funds for the purchase of land. It was planned that the land would be quickly sold and that the company would take a share of the profit. The company insisted that a solicitors' undertaking was provided under which the solicitors undertook to use all reasonable efforts to buy the land and that the money would be placed in its client account. The solicitors further undertook that, if the purchase was delayed, the money would be placed in an interest-bearing account. In the event, the purchase price was less than half of what had been provided by the company. Some of the money was used for purposes that were not connected to the land purchase.

It was clear that the parties had not intended that the solicitors would be free to dispose of the funds without restriction. It was clear that the solicitors were to have limited use of the funds for the stated purpose.

The money was thus held on a *Quistclose* trust and so it was a breach of trust when part of the money was used for purposes unconnected with the land purchase. The company successfully claimed compensation and a proprietary interest in the balance in the solicitors' client account.

The solicitors conceded (following an earlier hearing) that when the money was paid over by the company, it was held by them on trust for the company with the company retaining beneficial ownership. There was a resulting trust in the company's favour only, subject to a power for the solicitors to use money to buy the land. As the solicitors' use of the money was limited, when they used part of the funds for purposes unrelated to the purchase it was a breach of trust. Thus the company was entitled to judgment for the sums listed in its particulars and for the balance held in the client account.

The current position of *Quistclose* trusts

The current position has been arrived at through a series of cases. In the following cases only the key points that relate to *Quistclose* trusts are mentioned. As well as *Quistclose* trusts being found to exist in a wide variety of situations, the courts have reviewed the basis of a successful claim under a *Quistclose* trust and in particular Lord Wilberforce's 'primary and secondary' trusts have given way to the claimant being entitled under a resulting trust. (These latter two points are discussed below at p. 29.)

The discussion that follows is to a large extent based on the principles set out and approved of by Patten LJ in *Bieber* v *Teathers Ltd* discussed above.

Funds must not be intended to become part of the transferee's assets and also that they must be used exclusively for the agreed purpose.

A key requirement of a *Quistclose* trust is that the parties do not intend the money paid over to become part of the assets of the payee whereby the payee is entitled to use the money as he pleases. But additionally it is necessary that the parties are seen to agree that the funds should *only* be used for the agreed purpose(s). This was discussed by Roch LJ, along with other central requirements in *R* v *Common Professional Examination Board, ex p Mealing-McLeod* (2000) *The Times*, 2 May. In the case the Court of Appeal found that there was a *Quisclose* trust.

A litigant was required to pay money into court as security for costs in relation to an action against the Common Professional Examination Board. She borrowed £6,000 from Lloyds Bank. Clause 2(c) of the loan agreement stated: 'You must use the cash loan for [the] purpose specified . . . You will hold that loan, or any part of it, on trust for us until you have used it for this purpose.'

In the event the action was settled. The issue was who was entitled to the £6,000 paid into court. The litigant was already indebted to the Board in respect of the costs of earlier cases to the extent of about £20,000. The Board wished to be able to set the £6,000 against the £20,000 debt.

The court held that a *Quistclose* trust had been created with respect to the £6,000.

Roch LJ stated that in *Quistclose*, Lord Wilberforce had based the finding of the '*Quistclose*' trust on the mutual intention of the parties, and that the essence of the agreement in that case was that the sum borrowed should not become part of the assets of the company. It was intended that the loan should be usable only for a particular purpose – the payment of a dividend to the shareholders. If the money was not so used, then the clear consequence was that the money should be repaid to the lender (under a resulting trust).

Roch LJ considered that in the instant case the language used in clause 2(c) was imperative. It was clear that the parties to the loan intended that the money should be subject to a trust (which did not end when the money was paid into court). (See p. 25 for more on the requirement that a trust must be intended.) The loan agreement – either expressly or by implication – provided that if the money was not used to satisfy an order for costs, then the money would be held on a resulting trust to repay to the bank. If the appeal had failed and the money had been used to satisfy an order for costs, the matter would be one of loan only and not of trust. It was held that the bank was entitled to be repaid the £6,000.

The requirement that the funds are not intended to become part of the payee's general assets was central in *Freeman* v *Customs and Excise Commissioners* sub nom: *Margaretta Ltd (in liquidation)* [2005] EWHC 582, [2005] All ER (D) 262 (Feb). The case does not appear to make any new points, but it is an illustration of when *Quistclose* trusts arise and the effect of such a trust.

A company had sold a property to a purchaser for £3.96 million plus VAT if payable. The purchaser was not willing to pay VAT to the company before it had been decided if, in fact, VAT was payable. An agreement was made under which money to cover the possible VAT bill was held by the company's solicitors on terms set out in a letter from the solicitors which stated that the VAT money would be held by the firm until a VAT invoice had been issued and the appropriate payment to the commissioners had been negotiated and paid. The solicitors advanced the money to an accountant to deal with the VAT issue. The accountant misappropriated the money. As a result VAT due was not paid and as a consequence of this the company was wound up following a petition by the commissioners. Was there a *Quistclose* trust?

The court stated that a *Quistclose* trust does not arise unless the person advancing money clearly intended to restrict the freedom of the recipient to dispose of the money being advanced to discharging the stipulated purpose: *Barclays Bank Ltd* v *Quistclose Investments Ltd* [1970] AC 567 applied. In the instant case, it was clearly intended that the money should not be at the free disposal of either the solicitors or the company. In the circumstances, the solicitors could only have received the money as trustees and the company had no beneficial interest in it.

Thus it was decided that the money was held on a *Quistclose* trust. Money recovered from the accountant (who was acting as the agent of the solicitors) was payable to the Customs and Excise Commissioners to cover the VAT liability. It was not available for distribution on the liquidation of the company.

Intention to create a trust

In *Bieber* v *Teathers Ltd* Patten LJ stressed that it is necessary that there is an intention to create the trust. The subjective intentions of the parties are not relevant. The court will examine if the terms of the transaction, properly construed, have the effect of creating a trust or alternatively if the objectively ascertained circumstances in which the parties enter into the arrangement have the effect of creating a trust.

Need for certainty

With *Quistclose* trusts, as with trusts generally, there must be certainty of the terms of the trust. Certainty was the key issue in *Re Challoner Club Ltd* (1997) *The Times*, 4 November. The court was not willing to find a *Quistclose* trust on the ground that the terms of the proposed trust were not sufficiently certain.

In the case a club (operating through a company) was in financial difficulties and its members agreed to pay extra contributions and the board was empowered to take steps to ensure the continuation of the club. The board stated: 'As members will naturally want to know the position regarding the payments being made for subscriptions and donations, the position is that a separate bank account has been brought into being for these monies. They will remain in that account until the club's future is decided.'

Lloyd J said:

> The difficulty, it seems to me, that is faced by the argument in favour of a trust is to know what the terms of the trust are. In *Re Kayford* it was clear what was the event on which the company was able to draw on the money in the special customers' trust deposit account, namely the company satisfying the order in respect of which the payment was made.
>
> In the other cases that were cited to me . . . again it was clear that there was an event on which the payment would become, as it were, unconditional.

In the instant case the circumstances in which the payment would become unconditional were referred to in a number of different ways. During argument counsel submitted that the purpose of the payment – and the only purpose for which the payment could be used – was to help the club in the event that it was able to continue. Then counsel put it slightly differently in that the money could only be spent for the saving of the club. In a circular of

24 September the phrase 'the money in the special account will not be touched until the future is known' was used. In an affidavit, the phrase 'these donations are in an escrow account and are only available to the club if it is able to utilise the monies to survive' was used.

Lloyd J said:

> If these monies were to be held on a valid and binding trust, it must have been possible to spell out with certainty the circumstances in which the money became available to the club to be used for its general purposes; and conversely the circumstances failing which their being satisfied the money became repayable to the member who had provided the money. It seems to me that what the directors were doing was entirely commendable in attempting to segregate the fund and to create a ring-fenced fighting fund or rescue fund, but it seems to me that they did not succeed in that attempt because there is no adequately precise definition of the circumstances in which the company was to be able to use the money.
>
> *Source*: *The Times*, 4/11/1997, © **TheTimes/newssyndication.com**

The result was that the funds were available for the creditors of the club generally, and not only to the members as would have been the case had a trust been established.

Wrongly applied funds

Freeman v *Customs and Excise Commissioners* **sub nom:** *Margaretta Ltd (in liquidation)* (above) deals with wrongly applied funds as does *Twinsectra Ltd* v *Francis John Yardley* [1999] Lloyd's Rep Bank 438. *Twinsectra* involved another, though perhaps unusual, example of a *Quistclose* trust. The following account relates only to the *Quistclose* issue in the case and it is debatable whether the decision on this point is correct. Twinsectra provided funds to companies owned by Yardley. The purpose of the loan was to acquire specific property. Yardley's solicitor would not give Twinsectra an undertaking that the funds would be released for that particular purpose only. However, the solicitor passed his client on to a second solicitor, who did give the undertaking. On the basis of the undertaking, Twinsectra transferred the funds to the second solicitor. The funds were then paid to Yardley's companies on the direction of the first solicitor. The first solicitor knew that the funds were not going to be used for the specified purpose. Some of the funds were used by the second solicitor to settle the first solicitor's bill for work done for Yardley. As soon as Twinsectra found out about the fraud, they started an action against Yardley in deceit and in contract, and against the first solicitor for knowing receipt and knowing assistance. Success of the claims against the first solicitor depended on finding a breach of trust or fiduciary relationship by the second solicitor. Part of the finding of the Court of Appeal was that there was a *Quistclose* trust under which the second solicitor owed Twinsectra a duty not to release the money save for the agreed, specified, purposes. The trust arose through a combination of factors: the agreed specific purpose and paying the funds into a separate bank account. When the first solicitor instructed the second solicitor to release some of the funds, he had acted dishonestly. The first solicitor was thus liable for knowing receipt of that part used to pay his bill and for knowing assistance in respect of the rest of the fund.

The difference between *Twinsectra* and *Quistclose* was that in *Twinsectra* the funds were wrongly applied, whereas in *Quistclose* the purpose for which the loan had been obtained could not be achieved and the funds remained unused. Potter LJ stated that the interest of the lender arose under a 'quasi' trust. Under this trust the lender's rights were (he said) only to prevent the fraudulent use of the fund. So long as the primary purpose was capable of being carried out, the equitable interest in the fund was in suspense. If the purpose had failed (as in *Quistclose*), there would be a resulting trust under which the lender would hold the equitable interest. But here the money had been misapplied. Potter LJ said that in this situation the equitable interest passed to the transferee. It may be argued that this may not be correct. It may be argued that, in cases of misapplication (just as in cases of the failure of the purpose), the secondary (resulting) trust should have sprung up.

The House of Lords (*Twinsectra Ltd* v *Yardley and Others* [2002] 2 All ER 377) unanimously confirmed the Court of Appeal decision that a trust did exist. However, four of the Law Lords did not mention *Quistclose* in their judgments – although, to be fair, only two of them delivered judgments of any length.

Where there is a pre-existing debt

In *Carreras Rothmans Ltd* v *Freeman Mathews Treasure Ltd* [1985] 1 All ER 155, the court found that a trust had been created in respect of a debt that already existed, and Peter Gibson J accepted that those who were intended to benefit had the right to enforce the trust but were not beneficiaries under the trust in the normal sense of the word.

Trust imposed by the debtor

In *Re Kayford* [1975] 1 All ER 604, the trust was imposed by the debtor whereas the trust was imposed by the creditor in *Barclays Bank* v *Quistclose Investments Ltd*. The court decided that a trust had been created when deposits for goods ordered by post were placed in a special 'Customers' Trust Deposit Account'. The intention was that the money was to be used for the prescribed purpose and no other. The key factor to establish that the money was not intended to form part of the general assets of the borrower. It appears that this is the vital element that the court will look for before deciding that a *Quistclose* trust has been created. It seems that while the setting up of a special fund, as happened in both *Quistclose* and *Re Kayford*, does help to establish that the money was not to become part of the funds of the borrower, it is not essential to create the separate fund in order to persuade the court that a trust has been created. In Re *Kayford* Megarry J, having found that a *Quistclose* had arisen, sounded a warning where the creditors are trade creditors.

> Different considerations may perhaps arise in relation to trade creditors; but here I am concerned only with members of the public, some of whom can ill afford to exchange their money for a claim to a dividend in the liquidation, and all of whom are likely to be anxious to avoid this. In cases concerning the public, it seems to me that where money in advance is being paid to a company in return for the future supply of goods or services, it is an entirely proper and honourable thing for a company to do what this company did, upon skilled advice, namely, to start to pay the money into a trust account as soon as there begin to be doubts as to the company's ability to fulfil its obligations to deliver the goods or provide the services.

Some issues raised by *Quistclose* trusts

The *Quistclose* case raises several issues and problems.

Purpose trusts?

See Chapter 9 for more on purpose trusts.

The law does not generally permit trusts for purposes as opposed to trusts with human beneficiaries, yet the trust in this case appears to be a trust for a purpose – to pay a dividend. Perhaps the shareholders in *Quistclose* were the beneficiaries. If so, what would be their rights? Perhaps the trust resembles that accepted as valid by Goff J in *Re Denley* [1968] 3 All ER 65 under which ascertainable human 'beneficiaries' received a sufficiently direct and tangible benefit so as to give them a *locus standi* to enforce the trust. This was the attitude taken by Megarry V-C in the unreported case of *Re Northern Development (Holdings) Ltd* (6 October 1978) which was discussed by Peter Gibson J in *Carreras Rothmans Ltd* v *Freeman Mathews Treasure Ltd* [1985] 1 All ER 155. Again, it is not clear exactly what rights such 'beneficiaries' would have under the trust. Such beneficiaries clearly would not obtain a full beneficial interest. What they do have is the right to compel due administration of the trust. By this means the trust can be controlled by the courts.

In *Bieber* v *Teathers Ltd* (above) Patten LJ said that the trust was not a purpose trust where the recipient is trustee with the beneficial interest going back to the payer if the purpose cannot be achieved. Instead there is a resulting trust under which the payer is entitled, coupled with a mandate granted to the recipient, to apply the money for the agreed purpose.

Where the loan is used for the intended purpose

What would have happened if a loan is used for the intended purpose? Presumably the relationship would be that of creditor/debtor and the lender would rank as a 'normal' creditor. In *Re EVTR* [1987] BCLC 646, Dillon LJ opined that in such a case the lender would indeed be in the position of an unsecured creditor.

It is open to doubt as to who can enforce the *Quistclose* type of trust, but it seems probable that only the provider of the money may enforce.

Why the courts recognise a *Quistclose* trust

In *Bieber* v *Teathers Ltd* Patten LJ said:

> Equity intervenes because it is unconscionable for the recipient to obtain money on terms as to its application and then to disregard the terms on which he received it from a payer who had placed trust and confidence in the recipient to ensure the proper application of the money paid.

Under this approach, if a person knows that property is to be held on trust it would be unconscionable for him to use or apply the money in ways other than those agreed or at least known to him.

Nature of a *Quistclose* trust

It is not absolutely clear from *Quistclose* what type of trust came into existence. Express or resulting? Discussions in *Westdeutsche Landesbank* v *Islington London Borough Council* [1996] 2 All ER 961 and *Twinsectra* may help to throw some light.

In *Westdeutsche Landesbank* v *Islington*, Lord Browne-Wilkinson regards the trust as a resulting trust and the generally agreed analysis is that it is such a trust, rather than, for example, a constructive trust that arises when the help of the court is sought by the borrower.

In *Twinsectra*, although other Law Lords did not, Lord Millett did discuss *Quistclose* and subjected the issue to detailed analysis. Although Lord Millett did agree with the Court of Appeal that a trust was created, he disagreed on the Court of Appeal's analysis of the trust that was created.

Lord Millett emphasised that in order to create a trust, it was not necessary for the parties to explicitly think or believe that they were creating a trust. Subjective intentions are not relevant. What is needed is that the parties enter into an arrangement that has the effect of creating a trust. He went on to say that arrangements of the kind made in the instant case are not intended to provide security for repayment of the loan, but to prevent the money from being applied otherwise than in accordance with the lender's wishes.

Lord Millett stated that the essence of a *Quistclose* trust is not that there is *merely* a situation where money is paid for a particular purpose. The key question in every case is whether the parties intended the money to be at the free disposal of the recipient.

In the present case, Lord Millett said, the undertakings were crystal clear. The money was taken on the basis that it would be used *solely* for the acquisition of property and for no other purpose, and was to be retained by the firm until so applied. Any payment otherwise than for the acquisition of property would constitute a breach of trust.

On the 'loan/trust' issue, Lord Millett said:

> Money advanced by way of loan normally becomes the property of the borrower. He is free to apply the money as he chooses, and save to the extent to which he may have taken security for repayment the lender takes the risk of the borrower's insolvency. But it is well established that a loan to a borrower for a specific purpose where the borrower is not free to apply the money for any other purpose gives rise to fiduciary obligations on the part of the borrower which a court of equity will enforce. [In other words a '*Quistclose* trust' is created.]
>
> The lender pays the money to the borrower by way of loan, but he does not part with the entire beneficial interest in the money, and in so far as he does not it is held on a resulting trust for the lender from the outset . . . , it is the borrower who has a very limited use of the money, being obliged to apply it for the stated purpose or return it. He has no beneficial interest in the money, which remains throughout in the lender subject only to the borrower's power or duty to apply the money in accordance with the lender's instructions. When the purpose fails, the money is returnable to the lender, not under some new trust in his favour which only comes into being on the failure of the purpose, but because the resulting trust in his favour is no longer subject to any power on the part of the borrower to make use of the money.

In other words, the 'primary trust' that Lord Wilberforce described in *Quistclose* is not really a trust at all. The lender retains a right or interest in the money. If the purpose fails, the lender's claim is rooted in the resulting trust (see below).

Lord Millett then examined the nature of the *Quistclose* trust and the several competing theories.

Having referred to Lord Wilberforce's judgment in *Quistclose*, he said that the passages suggest that there are two successive trusts – a primary trust for payment to identifiable beneficiaries, such as creditors or shareholders, and a secondary trust in favour of the lender arising on the failure of the primary trust. In many ways this is the normally accepted analysis.

However, Lord Millett raised a number of problems with this solution and said: '. . . there are formidable difficulties in this analysis, which has little academic support. What if the primary trust is not for identifiable persons, but as in the present case to carry out an abstract purpose? Where, in such a case, is the beneficial interest pending the application of the money for the stated purpose or the failure of the purpose?'

Lord Millett listed and discussed four possible solutions – (i) in the lender; (ii) in the borrower; (iii) in the contemplated beneficiary; or (iv) in suspense – before stating that in his view solution (i) is correct.

> Like all resulting trusts, the trust in favour of the lender arises when the lender parts with the money on terms which do not exhaust the beneficial interest. It is not a **contingent** reversionary or future interest. It does not suddenly come into being like an eighteenth-century use only when the stated purpose fails. It is a default trust which fills the gap when some part of the beneficial interest is undisposed of and prevents it from being 'in suspense'.

In *Bieber* v *Teathers Ltd* (above) Patten LJ clearly set out what he accepted as the underlying basis of the *Quistclose* trust. He thinks that the beneficial interest remains with the payer and the payee simply has a mandate to use the money in the agreed way and only in the agreed way. Patten LJ said:

> It is not as such a 'purpose' trust of which the recipient is a trustee, the beneficial interest in the money reverting to the payer if the purpose is incapable of achievement. It is a resulting trust in favour of the payer with a mandate granted to the recipient to apply the money paid for the purpose stated. The key feature of the arrangement is that the recipient is precluded from misapplying the money paid to him. The recipient has no beneficial interest in the money: generally the beneficial interest remains vested in the payer subject only to the recipient's power to apply the money in accordance with the stated purpose. If the stated purpose cannot be achieved then the mandate ceases to be effective, the recipient simply holds the money paid on resulting trust for the payer, and the recipient must repay it.

Bailment

If goods are delivered to a bailee, they will be held for a particular purpose after which they will be re-delivered to the bailor. Depositing goods for repair or for safe keeping are examples of bailments.

There is a clear but superficial similarity between a trust and a bailment. In both cases property may be 'handed' over and the recipient takes the property subject to certain duties and responsibilities. However, there are a number of crucial differences between the two concepts, perhaps the most important being that a trustee does, but a bailee does not, obtain full legal ownership of the property. This means that while a trustee can pass good title to any third party (other than a *bona fide* purchaser for value of the legal estate) a bailee cannot. There are other differences: for example, bailment is the creation of the common law while the trust was developed by equity. Also, while any type of property can be made subject to a trust, only personalty can be bailed.

Agency

While there may be similarities between an agent and a trustee, there is at least one important distinction. A trust creates proprietary rights whereas agency creates only personal rights. This will be important if it is sought to recover money or property. Under a trust, there will be rights created against the property itself, while only personal claims against the agent can be made. This can be particularly important if the one against whom the claim is being made has become bankrupt. In cases of trust a claim can be made against the trust property whereas it is only possible to make a claim against an agent personally, which may have little chance of success if the debts of the agent greatly exceed his assets.

The office of trustee and agent are similar in that both have to be performed personally and often an agent, like a trustee, is in a fiduciary position.

Administration of estates

At first sight there would seem to be a similarity between the position of those administering the estate of a deceased person and trustees. The persons administering the estate of a deceased are called 'personal representatives' which includes both executors and administrators. An executor is appointed by a testator in his will. If there is no executor, perhaps because the deceased died intestate, the court will appoint the personal representatives, who are called administrators.

Both trustees and personal representatives hold property, not for themselves but for other people, and both are under a fiduciary duty. These factors point towards similarity between the two offices.

The apparent similarity between trustees and personal representatives is partly due to the fact that in many cases a deceased will appoint the same persons to be both his executors and his trustees. In this type of situation it is often rather difficult to determine when the changeover from personal representative to trustee takes place. The generally accepted view is that once all the assets have been gathered in and the debts paid the residue will be held *qua* trustees. This means, for example, that from that date the powers contained in the Trustee Act 1925 to appoint new trustees can be used. However, it seems that the office of personal representative does not totally disappear once the residue has been ascertained but rather it fades into the background. The appointees remain liable for any breaches of duty committed while acting as personal representatives.

Also the apparent similarity of the two offices is indicated by the Trustee Act 1925 s 68(17), which states that 'trustee' includes 'personal representative' where the context permits.

There are differences, however, between personal representatives and trustees. The main objectives of personal representatives are to gather in the assets of the deceased, to pay off debts and to distribute whatever remains to those entitled under the will (or the intestacy rules if there is no will). In other words, the personal representative aims to deal with the property and to pass it on as quickly as possible. The role of a trustee is in many cases a longer-term one. He may well be expected to hold and manage the trust property for many years. For example, if the property is to be held on trust for Arthur for life, remainder to Ben, the trustee would expect to be involved with the trust until Arthur dies and even then the responsibility will continue unless and until Ben calls for the trust property to be transferred to him.

Another important difference lies in the power to dispose of personal property. One of several personal representatives can pass title to personalty but all trustees must join in if the sale is to be effective.

As mentioned above, it is not uncommon to appoint the same persons as personal representatives and trustees and it may be important to determine in which capacity property is held, and at what point the property is no longer held *qua* personal representatives but is held *qua* trustees. If a transfer is purported to be made by trustees, the purchaser must assure himself that the property has been vested by the personal representatives in the trustees, otherwise he will not receive good title. If the property is personalty, the courts appear to be prepared to find an implied assent (transfer from personal representative to trustee) by reference to conduct. This can sometimes work to the disadvantage of one acquiring property.

In *Attenborough & Son* v *Solomon* [1911–13] All ER Rep 155, Moses Solomon appointed his two sons, A A Solomon and J D Solomon, to be his executors and trustees. He directed that the residue of his property should be held on specified trusts. All the debts and expenses were paid within a year of the death. Some silver plate, which formed part of the residuary estate, remained in the possession of A A Solomon. Some 14 years after the death of the testator, A A Solomon pledged the plate with Attenborough & Son for £65 and used the money to pay off a personal debt. The House of Lords held that Attenborough & Son had no title to the plate and must return it. The House inferred from the fact that the general administration had been completed, and that no attempt had been made to do any act under their powers as executors since that time, that the executors had assented to the vesting of the property in themselves as trustees. As trustees must act together to deal effectively with personalty, the title to the plate remained with the trustees.

However, if the property is land then the provisions of the Administration of Estates Act 1925 s 36(4) states that any assent to the vesting of the legal estate in land must be in writing, signed by the personal representative and must name the person in whose favour it is made. This means that even if the same people are appointed to act as personal representatives and trustees the legal estate will not vest in them *qua* trustees unless they have signed a written statement naming themselves as those in whom the legal estate is to vest: *Re King's Will Trusts* [1964] 1 All ER 833.

There is also a very important difference between the rights of beneficiaries under a trust and beneficiaries under a will. A beneficiary under a trust has an interest in property, an equitable interest, but a beneficiary under a will has no such right while the estate is being administered. On death the property of the deceased passes to his personal representatives who hold the property subject to the obligations imposed upon them by their office. They do not hold as trustees on trust for those named in the will.

In the case of *Commissioner of Stamp Duties (Queensland)* v *Livingston* [1964] 3 All ER 692, the Privy Council decided that while the estate was being administered a residuary beneficiary had no legally recognised right to any particular piece of property that formed part of the deceased's estate. The main reason given for this decision was that to create a trust there must be certainty of the property within the trust and that the residuary estate was a constantly fluctuating body of property. The property comprising the residue was liable to changes as more property was gathered in and property was transferred out or sold to raise money to pay debts. The court did state that beneficiaries did have a chose in action, a right to compel the due administration of the estate, and this provides an indirect way for beneficiaries under a will to ensure that any property is properly dealt with, including its transfer to those entitled to it.

It is probable that once the residue has been ascertained the personal representatives do hold the property on trust for the residuary beneficiaries. The residue is ascertained once all debts and other liabilities have been provided for and when it is clear exactly which property will be available for the residuary beneficiaries. At this stage it is possible to say, with certainty, what property is within the residue and so within the trust.

The case of *Commissioner of Stamp Duties (Queensland)* v *Livingston* (1964) concerned the position of a residuary beneficiary, but it is generally agreed that the same principles also apply to the case of specific beneficiaries under a will.

Conditions

If Arthur receives a legacy under a will 'to pay Ben £200' it is necessary to decide whether a trust has been created or if Arthur takes a conditional gift.

It is a matter of construction whether a trust or a conditional gift has been created. As usual with equity, the words used are not necessarily conclusive. For example, in *Re Frame* [1939] 2 All ER 865, Simonds J decided that a trust had been created despite the fact that the testator gave property to Mrs Taylor, his housekeeper, 'on condition that she adopt my daughter Alma Edwards and also gives my daughters Jessie Edwards and May Alice Edwards the sum of £5 each'. Simonds J said:

> The question is what those words mean . . . As I listened to that argument it impressed itself more and more on me that, after all, this was not a condition at all, for in my view, on the

true construction of this clause, the word 'condition' is not used in its strict legal sense. It is a gift to Mrs Taylor on condition, in the sense of on the terms or on the trust that she does certain things, and that, I think, becomes clearer when it is realised that the condition relates not only to the adoption of one daughter, but to the payment of certain sums to other daughters. A **devise**, or **bequest**, on condition that the **devisee** or **legatee** makes certain payments does not import a condition in the strict sense of the word, but a trust, so that, though the devisee or legatee dies before the testator and the gift does not take effect, yet payments must be made; for it is a trust, and no trust fails for want of a trustee.

In the example above, if a conditional gift has been imposed, Arthur has the choice either to take the gift subject to an obligation to pay £200 to Ben or to refuse the gift. In the latter case Arthur will not receive anything, but neither will Ben as his £200 can only flow from Arthur's gift, which he has declined. Even if Arthur accepts the gift, Ben will have no interest in property.

If the will imposes a trust then Arthur will take the property as a trustee and Ben, as the beneficiary, obtains an equitable interest under the trust that he can enforce in the usual ways. If there is a surplus after Arthur has paid Ben his £200, it is a question of construction if Arthur is entitled to keep it or if he holds it on a resulting trust for the deceased's estate. If Arthur refuses to act as trustee, the trust will not be allowed to fail for lack of a trustee, and in the last resort the court will ensure that a trustee is appointed.

Powers

See Chapter 15 (p. 426) for a discussion of trustees' powers. See Chapter 5 p. 132 for a detailed discussion of powers and discretionary trusts.

It is often necessary and sometimes difficult to distinguish between trusts, particularly discretionary trusts, and powers. We are not discussing here the powers a trustee may have to administer and manage the trust property. The discussion rather relates to the situation when the owner of property gives the power to another to decide on the distribution or destination of that property. In other words, the powers we are addressing are **powers of appointment**. Since 1925 most powers of appointment can exist only in equity: that is, they must be contained within a trust or **settlement**.

Example

If property is left by will, the testator may direct that Arthur is to decide who is to take the testator's land, Greenacre. The testator may direct that Arthur is to select one of his (the testator's) three children as the recipient of the land. It is very important to be able to decide if the testator has given Arthur a power of appointment or if a trust has been created. The obligations of Arthur, the rights of the children and the degree of certainty with which the objects or beneficiaries must be described all vary depending on whether a trust or a power has been created. (The issue of certainty will be discussed at pp. 98 and 140.)

The key point when distinguishing trust and powers is that trusts are imperative while powers are discretionary.

If Arthur has been given a power to appoint property between named children, he is under no obligation to exercise the power and to make a decision as to which child shall receive the property. Often there is a gift over in default of appointment which names the people to whom the property will pass if the power is not exercised.

There are three types of powers of appointment. A general power exists where there is no restriction as to whom the property may be appointed. It is even possible for the property to be appointed to the person exercising the power. A special power describes the situation where the property can be appointed only among specified people or among a specified group or class of people. A hybrid power exists where the property may be appointed to anyone except specified people or a specified class of people.

Trusts

Many, if not most, trusts are fixed trusts: that is to say that the settlor stipulates or fixes the extent of the interests of the beneficiaries. For example, the settlor may transfer property to trustees to invest and to distribute the income produced equally between the settlor's three children. Here the trustees have no discretion; the settlor has mapped out exactly the interests of the three children. This type of trust causes no confusion with powers of appointment.

It is with discretionary trusts that there may be an apparent similarity to powers of appointment. (See p. 132 for more on discretionary trusts, including exhaustive and non-exhaustive discretionary trusts.)

If Arthur holds property on trust to divide all the property (or perhaps all the income from the property) between three named children in such shares as Arthur sees fit, the trust must be performed. An exhaustive discretionary trust has been created and Arthur is under an obligation to ensure that the property is allocated to the children. Arthur has to exercise his discretion as to how much, if anything, will go to each child. If Arthur fails to perform his duty, in the last resort the court will step in and decide how the property shall be distributed. The court will keep in mind the wishes and intentions of the settlor or testator. In the context of a family trust this *may* involve equal division between the members of the class if this is thought to reflect the settlor's intention. In other cases the court may decide that equal division would be the last thing that the settlor would want and so equal distribution would not be appropriate (see e.g. ***McPhail v Doulton*** [1970] 2 All ER 228).

Trust and powers – terminology

There is a difference in terminology between powers and trusts. Under a trust, the settlor transfers the property to trustees who will hold for the benefit of beneficiaries. Under a power of appointment, the power is given by the donor of the power to the donee who has the power to appoint the property to the objects of the power. In many cases the objects of powers of appointment are individuals but it is possible to create powers in favour of purposes. Law of trusts generally does not permit trusts to be set up for non-charitable purposes but powers in favour of purposes are allowed.

See Chapter 9 for more on purpose trusts.

Creating a power of appointment among a range of purposes may be an attractive alternative to one who wishes to benefit purposes but wishes to 'delegate' the decisions as to the precise purpose to benefit and the extent of any benefit. The problem in creating a power is that there is no possibility of the objects seeking the aid of the court if appointments are not made.

Position of the beneficiaries under a trust and the objects of a power

If the trustee does not exercise his discretion and distribute the property, then, as seen above, the beneficiaries can seek the help of the court and in the last resort the court will order the manner in which the property is to be distributed. In the case of a power of appointment, if the donee simply does nothing the objects of the power have no redress. If the power is never exercised the property will either revert to the donor (or his estate if he is dead) or will pass to those named by the donor as being entitled in default of appointment. The only time that the objects of the power can expect the help of the courts is if the donee makes an appointment outside the terms of the power.

Both the beneficiaries under a discretionary trust and the objects of a power of appointment have no guarantee that they will receive any benefit but there is a difference between their respective positions. Under a power, the equitable ownership of the property is in those entitled in default of appointment whose interest is liable to defeasance if and when the power is exercised. An object of a power of appointment has no interest at all until the power is exercised in his favour. The precise nature of the interest of a beneficiary under a discretionary trust was considered in *Gartside* v *IRC* [1968] 1 All ER 121. The House of Lords stated that the beneficiaries under a non-exhaustive discretionary trust were in competition with each other and had individual rights. Anything given to a particular beneficiary was his and his alone. This also appears to be the position in the case of an exhaustive discretionary trust. All a beneficiary has is the right to be considered and the right to seek the assistance of the court in the event of the trustees' maladministration of the trust. A beneficiary may also apply to the court if the trustees refuse to exercise their discretion or exercise it improperly. It is very difficult to see where the equitable interest in the trust's property is, pending the trustees exercising their discretion and passing it to one of the beneficiaries. What is clear is that no single beneficiary has an equitable interest pending allocation to him, nor do the beneficiaries collectively own the beneficial interest. Perhaps it is simply in suspense pending the trustees exercising their discretion. (See also p. 135.)

Trust or power?

Whether a trust or a power of appointment has been created is a matter of construction for the courts.

As stated above, the key characteristic of a trust is its mandatory nature. Thus, the conclusive indication of an intention to create an exhaustive discretionary trust is that the beneficiaries are to benefit in any event. A trust involves the clear intention that the property *will* be distributed among the beneficiaries and the only uncertainty pertains to which of the beneficiaries it will be given. The absence of this mandatory element necessarily means that a trust has not been created. One indication of an intention to create a power rather than a trust is the presence of an express gift over in default of appointment. The argument is that the transferor (to use a neutral word) cannot intend that the property must be distributed to the beneficiaries in any event (i.e. a trust) since if this were his intention there would be no possibility of the property not being distributed, and so there could be no property remaining over which the gift over in default could operate. In other words, the existence in the transferor's mind of the possibility that property may not be distributed (evidenced by the transferor's desire to determine the destination of such property by means of a gift over in default) can only indicate that a power and not a trust was intended. A gift over in default is needed only if it is envisaged that the property may not be distributed, for example, in the context of a power of appointment, the exercise of which is always optional not compulsory. It must be stressed, however, that the absence of a gift over in default of appointment does not mean that there is a trust but only that as a matter of construction there may be a trust. But the presence of a gift over does mean that there cannot be a trust.

Burrough v Philcox (1840) 5 My& Cr 72

The settlor, S, gave his surviving child power to distribute S's estate among S's nephews and nieces 'either all to one of them, or to as many of them as my surviving child shall think proper'. The child died without making the choice. In accordance with general principles the power itself could not, of course, be exercised since the discretion lay with the child, who was dead. The court concluded that the words of the settlor indicated an intention that the class, i.e. the nephews and nieces, should as a whole benefit in any event and so the court in effect implied a trust for equal distribution in default of appointment. In other words, it was as if the settlor had made a gift over to them equally in default of the power to select being exercised.

In this case, Lord Cottenham found that a trust and a power both existed. He decided that property was initially subject to a power of appointment but that when the power was not exercised, the intention was that the property should be distributed and that the class as a whole should benefit in any event. In other words, the court found a trust for equal division in default of the power being exercised. In the case, the testator gave a life interest in property contained in a trust fund to his two children with remainders to their issue. The testator stated that if each of the children should die without leaving lawful issue, then the survivor of the two children should have the power to dispose of the property by will among the testator's nephews and nieces, or their children 'as my surviving child shall think proper'. There was no gift over in default of appointment. The testator's two children did both die without leaving lawful issue. Lord Cottenham said, after reviewing a number of cases, that the courts would carry out the general intention in favour of a class where there has been a failure to exercise a power of appointment and to select individuals from within that class.

Lord Cottenham said:

> . . . when there appears a general intention in favour of the class and a particular intention in favour of particular individuals of the class, to be selected by another person, and the particular intention fails from the selection not being made, the court will carry into effect the general intention.

Lord Cottenham said that the intention will be implemented by fastening a trust on to the property. In this particular case, Lord Cottenham felt that equal division would reflect the intention of the testator. This was, of course, a family trust.

In **Re Weeke's Settlement** [1897] 1 Ch 289, the court found that a power had been created in a case where there was no express gift over in default. Mrs Slade gave her husband a life interest in some property and went on to state 'and I give him the power to dispose of all such property by will amongst our children'. No appointment was made by the husband. If a trust had been imposed on the husband the children would have been entitled to take, but, as a power had been created, the property resulted back to the estate of Mrs Slade. Romer J said:

> If in this case the testatrix really intended to give a life interest to her husband and a mere power to appoint if he chose, and intended if he did not think fit to appoint that the property should go on default of appointment according to the settlement, why should she be bound to say anything more than she has said in this will?

Romer J then asked if there was any authority which prevented him from concluding that a power was intended:

> The authorities do not shew, in my opinion, that there is a hard and fast rule that a gift to A for life with a power to A to appoint among a class and nothing more must, if there is no gift over in the will, be held a gift by implication to the class in default of the power being exercised. In my opinion the cases shew . . . that you must find in the will an indication that the

testatrix did intend the class or some of the class to take – intended that the power be regarded in the nature of a trust – only a power of selection being given, as for example a gift to A for life with gift over to such of a class as A shall appoint.

Having failed to find an intention that the class should benefit in any event, Romer J held that a power had been created. (See also p. 136.)

There is more room for confusion when it is appreciated that powers of appointment exist within trusts and it may be that it is the trustee who is given the ability to decide on the destination of property. His being a trustee does not mean that his responsibility with regard to the property is a trust rather than a power. The issue is: is he under an obligation to distribute the property (a trust), or is the allocation of property by him permissive (a power)? If the trustee is given a power, it will be deemed a fiduciary power and the trustee is under the duty to consider from time to time whether or not to exercise the power, and must consider whether any particular appointment is appropriate. If he should fail to undertake this periodic consideration, the assistance of the courts may be sought to direct the trustee to act correctly. Also, the objects of the power may ask the court to intervene if the trustee exercises the power in a capricious manner. This imposes a greater burden on a trustee-donee than in the case of a power given to a non-trustee (a personal power) who, as has been seen, need not do anything at all. The holder of a personal power need never think about the power and whether he should exercise it. The donee of a personal power is able to exercise the power in a capricious manner without the courts being able to intervene.

Failed trusts

In some Commonwealth jurisdictions the courts have the ability to classify an attempt to create a purpose trust – which will generally be invalid – as a power and so to give some effect to the intentions of the transferor. The English courts have consistently refused to take this approach, saying that if as a matter of construction a trust is intended there is no way that the intention can be reclassified as an intention to create a power.

Taxation of trusts

Objective 10

Many trusts are created (or created in a particular form) to try to avoid or reduce tax for the settlor, the beneficiaries or both. Recent tax changes may well have reduced the attractiveness of trusts as a tax-saving vehicle.

The three taxes that are of main concern are income tax, capital gains tax and inheritance tax (although stamp duty and VAT are sometimes relevant). Unless otherwise stated all figures used for tax rates, personal allowances, etc. are those for tax year 2015/16 insofar as they are known at the time of writing. It is beyond the scope of this text to deal with these taxes other than in outline.

Income tax

Income tax is levied on income. The law is contained in the Income Act 2007, as amended by subsequent Finance Acts.

Individuals are entitled to personal allowances which in effect mean that the first slice of income is not liable to income tax. The personal allowance for individuals for income up to £100,000 is £10,600 for 2015/16. The personal allowance reduces where the income is above £100,000 – by £1 for every £2 of income above the £100,000 limit.

From 2015/16, basic rate taxpayers will be able to transfer up to £1,060 of their income personal allowance to their spouse or civil partner if neither party is liable to higher or additional rate income tax. This will help families where only one spouse/civil partner has taxable income. There are higher personal allowances for some categories of taxpayers including blind taxpayers. Until recently a higher personal allowance was available for taxpayers over the age of 65 but from April 2013 this higher personal allowance is being phased out. The allowance is frozen until it comes into line with the 'normal' personal allowance. For 2015/16 the allowance is £10,660 for those born before 6 April 1948. In any case the age-related allowance is means tested and for 2015/16 once income exceeds £27,700 it is reduced by £2 for every £1 of additional income.

For individuals, in 2015/16 the basic rate of income tax is 20 per cent. The higher rate, charged on taxable income between £31,785 and £150,000, is 40 per cent. Any taxable income above £150,000 is taxed at 45 per cent. Any dividend income that falls into the basic rate band is taxed at 10 per cent. Any savings income that falls into the first £5,000 of taxable income is taxed at 0 per cent. But the fact that non-savings income is taxed as the first slice of income, then savings income and then dividends means that for many taxpayers these lower tax rates will not be applicable.

Taxing trusts

The income generated by trust property is liable to income tax and the income is, in general, treated at this stage as belonging to the trustees and not to the beneficiaries. (The exceptions to this are where there is a bare trust in which case the beneficiary is directly liable to tax – **Baker v Archer-Shee** [1927] AC 844 – and where the income accrues directly to the beneficiary – **Williams v Singer** [1921] 1 AC 65.)

The income is not treated as a part of the trustees' personal income; they are taxed separately from their own income and the tax charged does not relate at all to the personal circumstances or income of the trustees. They are not entitled to a personal allowance to set against the income. Personal allowances are available only to 'individuals' and trustees are not classified as individuals. Also, the higher rates of income tax (currently 40 and 45 per cent) are payable only by individuals and so the trustees are not liable to it.

Levying tax on the trustees has at least one advantage to HMRC in that if the income under a trust is to be accumulated (and so turned to capital) it will never be distributed to the beneficiaries as income. If the initial charge was on the beneficiaries, rather than on the trustees, this income would escape income tax.

The rate of tax applicable to trust income depends on the nature of the income and the type of trust. For interest in possession trusts, where the beneficiary has the right to receive the income, dividend income is liable to tax at 10 per cent and all other income (for example, profit from a trade, rental income) is taxed at 20 per cent. For completeness, there are some items of that are treated by trust law as capital but as income for tax purposes. These items are liable to tax either at 45 per cent (the trust rate) or 37.5 per cent (the dividend rate) depending on the type of receipt.

If the trust is a discretionary trust or if the trustees have the power to accumulate the income, the trustees are liable to 'the rate applicable to trusts'. For 2015/16 this rate is 45 per cent. Dividend income is taxable at the special dividend rate applicable to trusts of 37.5 per cent. However, these rates are not payable on the first £1,000 of income. This band is liable to tax at the same rates as interest in possession trusts (see above).

Beneficiaries are liable to income tax on any income distributed to them or to which they are entitled. A beneficiary entitled under a discretionary trust is only liable to tax on income actually paid to him. All trust income paid over to beneficiaries by trustees will have been taxed in the hands of the trustees and is grossed up at the relevant rate to take account of tax paid by the trustees. (Grossing up involves a calculation. One must compute the sum which would, after deducting tax at the relevant rate, leave the amount actually received by the beneficiary. It is that grossed up sum that the beneficiary must declare as income.) For example, if a beneficiary receives £80 rental income under a fixed trust (taxed in the trustees' hands at 20 per cent), he must show an income of £100 in his income tax return. This is because a gross sum of £100 after the deduction of income tax at the relevant rate (here 20 per cent) will leave £80. Whether any tax is payable on the trust income by the beneficiary depends entirely on his tax position. If, like most people, his marginal rate of tax (the rate payable on any additional income) is the basic rate, there will be no more tax to pay. The tax credit will exactly match his liability to tax. If his marginal rate of tax is 40 per cent (the higher rate), then he will have an additional tax liability amounting to the difference between his tax credit and liability at the higher rate. At the moment this would amount to an extra charge of 20 per cent. If the marginal rate of the beneficiary is the lower rate, then a tax rebate may be claimed which will equal the amount of credit minus the rate that should have been paid. If the beneficiary should not have paid any income tax on this income at all, then he will be entitled to reclaim £20 (the amount equal to the tax credit) from HMRC. Examples of beneficiaries who are not liable to pay income tax are individuals whose income is below the level of the personal allowance and charities which are generally exempt from liability to income tax by statute. If the income is from dividends, the beneficiary cannot reclaim any tax credit whatever his income tax position.

It is possible to exploit the trust concept to save tax.

Example

Ivor Lott, a higher rate (40 per cent) taxpayer, takes money from his taxed income to make a series of gifts to his aunt, Mona Lott. The gifts come from his net income, so for each £2,000 which he gives to his aunt he has to earn £3,333, which, after bearing tax at 40 per cent, will produce the £2,000. He may decide to transfer a block of assets to trustees to hold on trust for his aunt. Ivor calculates the assets will produce £2,000 p.a. net after bearing Mona's, lower, rate of tax. (The transfer may, of course, have inheritance and capital gains tax implications.) The net effect will be that Mona continues to receive an increase in spending power of £2,000 (less any tax liability she may have) but Ivor sacrifices less of his income.

The alienation of income to a lower rate taxpayer is a very simple way to reduce the income tax payable, but as would be expected the opportunities to exploit it are restricted by statute. For example, the alienation of income through a trust will not reduce tax if the settlor or spouse has some interest in the trust property. A very simple example of this would be if, under the trust created by Ivor, he or his spouse was entitled to the remainder after Mona has died.

Capital gains tax

Capital gains tax is governed by the Taxation of Chargeable Gains Tax Act 1992, as amended by subsequent Finance Acts.

Capital gains tax is charged annually on the chargeable gains flowing from the disposal of capital assets. A disposal includes a sale. Also, if the owner of property gives an asset away, a capital gains tax liability will attach to the profit which could have been made had the property been sold for its market value. This deemed sale for market value takes place whenever there is a disposal which is not a bargain at arm's length. A disposal to a connected person is always treated as not being a bargain at arm's length and so the market value rule always applies to such a disposal. Among those connected to a disposer are his spouse and her relatives and the spouses of her relatives. Relatives include siblings, direct ancestors (parents, grandparents), lineal descendants (children, grandchildren, etc.) but not lateral relatives (aunts, uncles, nieces, nephews, etc.). Other connected people are the trustees of settlements created by the disposer.

The gain is calculated by deducting any allowable expenditure from the consideration received (or deemed to be received in the case of a gift). The most important item of deductible expenditure is the cost incurred in acquiring the asset, usually the purchase price. If the allowable expenditure exceeds the consideration received (or deemed to be received), a loss will result which can be set against a capital gain on another disposal and so reduce the tax on that other disposal.

There are a number of important exemptions from capital gains tax including disposals of motor cars, chattels for less than £6,000, tangible movable wasting assets (an asset is a wasting asset if it has a predicted useful life of 50 years or less). Perhaps the most valuable exemption covers the gain made on the disposal of an individual's only or main residence.

Capital gains tax is only levied on lifetime disposals. On death all assets vest in the deceased's personal representatives at the market value at the time of death. Any gain accumulated during the lifetime of the owner is ignored for the purposes of this tax and so is free of capital gains tax.

For 2015/16 capital gains made by individuals are taxed at either 18 per cent for basic rate income tax payers or 28 per cent for higher or additional rate income tax payers.

There is a 'concession' aimed *inter alia* at business owners who sell all or part of their business. Any gains up to a lifetime limit of £10m will be taxed at 10 per cent. This relief is popularly known as 'entrepreneurs' relief'.

Capital gains tax is an annual tax, and at the end of each tax year the taxpayer must calculate all his gains for the year and take away any losses made and tax will be due to the extent that the annual total exceeds the annual exemption. For 2015/16 the exemption is £11,100.

Taxing settlements

Capital gains tax has a number of special provisions governing 'settlements'. A settlement includes all trusts except those where property is held by trustees merely as nominees, or for a person who would be absolutely entitled were he not a minor or a person under some other disability, or for persons who are jointly entitled. The phrase 'jointly entitled' applies to both joint tenants and tenants in common. Thus, the definition of settlement excludes trusts where the trust may be thought of as a mere technical device. In such cases the trust property is regarded as belonging to the beneficiaries for capital gains tax purposes and so any disposal by the trustees will bring with it the same tax liability as if the beneficiary had himself disposed of the property.

If a settlement is created it will give rise to disposal of the settled property to the trustee. As the trustees and the settlor are connected people, the disposal will be treated as having been made at market value.

Once the settlement has been set up, capital gains tax may be payable if the trustees make actual disposals of trust property. For example, if part of the trust property is sold capital gains tax may become due. For 2015/16 the 28 per cent rate (above) applies to capital gains of trustees. The 2015/16 annual exemption for the trustees of most trusts is £5,550.

Tax may also become payable in the event of a deemed disposal of trust assets. The legislation states that on the happening of certain events the trustees are deemed to dispose of the trust assets.

One example of a deemed disposal is when a beneficiary becomes absolutely entitled to trust property. For example, if property is settled on Arthur, contingent upon his attaining the age of 30, he will become absolutely entitled when he is 30. At this point the property will cease to be settled property, the trustees will be deemed to dispose of the property at market value and any gain shown will be taxable. The trustees are also deemed to reacquire the property immediately for the same market value. If, however, the event giving rise to a beneficiary becoming absolutely entitled is a death, then although there will be the same deemed disposal and reacquisition at market value, there will be no capital gains tax liability. This reflects the general position that capital gains tax is not payable on death.

If a **tenant for life** dies but the settlement continues, there will be a deemed disposal and reacquisition at market value but no tax will be payable. Again, this is an example of the general rule that capital gains tax is not payable on death. The effect of this deemed disposal and reacquisition is to give a tax-free uplift to the trust property. This, in effect, wipes out any accrued gain.

If a beneficiary disposes of his interest under a settlement, there is no liability to capital gains tax unless he acquired the interest for money or money's worth.

Inheritance tax

Taxes on transfers of capital, particularly on gifts, are a feature of many legal systems. In most systems the tax is primarily aimed at taxing property transferred on the death of its owner. The United Kingdom has inheritance tax.

Inheritance tax is a relatively new tax, having been introduced in 1986. It is based on estate duty and capital transfer tax. Estate duty was introduced in 1894 and was replaced by capital transfer tax in 1974 and then by inheritance tax in 1986. Inheritance tax is governed by the Inheritance Tax Act 1984 as amended.

Inheritance tax was devised to be a tax primarily payable on death and any threat to *inter vivos* transfers was virtually removed. The tax was imposed on 'transfers of value' which were not exempted from the tax by the legislation. In general terms, a transfer of value is a disposition which has the effect of reducing the value of the transferor's estate. A gift and a transfer at an undervalue will be transfers of value but a sale at the market price will not. Under inheritance tax most *inter vivos* transfers made by individuals are Potentially Exempt Transfers (PETs) and will not be taxed unless the donor dies within seven years. If the donor dies more than three years but less than seven years from the date of the PET, the inheritance tax bill may be reduced by taper relief. This relief operates by reducing the rate of tax that would otherwise be charged. The reduction is:

- transfers more than three years but not more than four years before death: 20 per cent reduction;
- transfers more than four years but not more than five years before death: 40 per cent reduction;
- transfers more than five years but not more than six years before death: 60 per cent reduction;
- transfers more than six years but not more than seven years before death: 80 per cent reduction.

The only important example of an *inter vivos* transfer which is not a PET, and which may be immediately liable to tax, is a transfer into a discretionary trust. In addition, there is a wide range of exemptions from the tax, including transfers to spouses, charities and political parties and transfers which are made with no gratuitous intent.

For inheritance tax the tax threshold is £325,000 for 2015/16, and tax is only payable once the threshold is exceeded. It is currently intended that the threshold will remain unchanged until at least 2017/18. It is only necessary to include chargeable transfers of value made in the previous seven years in order to see if the threshold has been exceeded. Inheritance tax has one rate for lifetime transfers (20 per cent) and one rate for death transfers (40 per cent). But for deaths on or after 6 April 2012, an Inheritance tax rate of 36 per cent will apply where 10 per cent or more of the deceased person's net estate is left to charity.

The inheritance tax rules mean that it is possible to 'shift' large amounts of capital which otherwise would be liable to tax provided at all times the 'seven-year total' does not exceed the threshold.

The wide range of exemptions coupled with the possibility of making PETs means that it is feasible for a well-advised and forward-thinking individual to arrange the disposition of his property so that little if any inheritance tax is paid. The main planning strategies involve early *inter vivos* transfers, to take advantage of lower lifetime rates, PETS and the seven-year cumulation period.

On death all chargeable transfers made within the previous seven years, together with the value of any PETS made within the previous seven years, are added to the value of the deceased's property. This valuation is made on the basis of market value immediately prior to death, thus including a valuation for jointly owned property. Also included in the valuation is any property transferred *inter vivos* in which the transferee reserved a benefit operative within the seven years leading up to the death. Tax is payable at 40 per cent to the extent that the value of the property held on death exceeds the tax threshold.

The inheritance tax legislation contains a number of exemptions under which transfers are not liable for inheritance tax. Perhaps the most important example is the inter-spousal transfer exemption under which *inter vivos* transfers and transfers on death from one spouse to the other are not liable to tax. The exemption also applies to transfers between civil partners. On the death of a widow/widower or the survivor of a civil partnership, any inheritance tax-free allowance not used on the death of the first spouse/civil partner will increase the tax-free amount on the second death. The tax-free allowance has not been increased, but for married couples/people in a civil partnership the impact of the change on the second death may be important, particularly if no inheritance tax planning has been undertaken before the first death. The maximum tax-free amount available on the second death is twice the threshold at the date of the second death.

A further example may help to understand how inheritance tax works.

Example

On his death the property which a deceased owns and leaves by will is valued at £147,000. He leaves £59,000 to his wife. This is covered by an exemption and is not liable to tax and is left out of account when calculating liability. The value of chargeable transfers made in the seven years prior to his death is £247,000. What liability is there to inheritance tax at the 40 per cent death rate? As already discussed, the £59,000 left to his wife is not relevant, being covered within an exemption. The remaining £88,000 is added to the £247,000 of chargeable transfers made within seven years of his death and is treated as the 'top slice' of the total (£335,000). Tax is payable on that part of the £88,000 that exceeds the tax threshold (£325,000). In this case tax will be payable on £10,000 at 40 per cent (death rate).

As the entire tax-free amount is used on the first death, there will be no increase in the tax-free amount on the second death.

Taxing settlements

Inheritance tax has special and rather complex rules covering settlements and basically the legislation identifies three types of settlements:

- first, settlements with an interest in possession;
- second, settlements without an interest in possession (discretionary trusts); and
- third, accumulation and maintenance trusts. There are three main occasions when inheritance tax may become payable:
  - gift by the settlor to set up the trust or into a trust;
  - periodic charge;
  - exit charge.

The Finance Act 2006 made a number of very important changes to the impact of inheritance tax on trusts. The most important changes were to interest in possession trusts and to accumulation and maintenance trusts.

The broad effect of the changes was to drag many interest in possession trusts and accumulation and maintenance trusts into the inheritance tax charges regime that previously only affected discretionary trusts.

These provisions impact on trusts set up after 22 March 2006. The general effect is that the only lifetime gifts after 22 March 2006 which will not fall into the discretionary trust inheritance tax regime will be outright gifts to individuals or gifts to trusts for the disabled.

Currently, measures to simplify the administration of inheritance tax are in the course of being introduced. In the main the changes would take effect from 6 April 2015, and will only apply to trusts set up on or after 6 June 2014. There are proposals to change how a taxpayer's threshold is shared between trusts. Under the current system an individual can create a number of trusts each up to the £325,000 nil rate band and, as long as they are set up at least seven years apart, they will each be within the nil rate band. Under the proposed changes those using multiple trusts will be able to divide the nil rate band between them as they choose. So all the trusts that a taxpayer sets up will have to 'share' the nil rate band.

Interest in possession settlements

A settlement is an interest in possession settlement if there are beneficiaries who have an immediate entitlement to income produced by the trust property. It is now accepted that if there is a power to accumulate income this prevents there being an interest in possession settlement as there can be no entitlement to income: *Pearson* v *IRC* [1980] 2 All ER 479. The beneficiaries who are entitled to the income were regarded as the owners of the capital of the trust fund for inheritance tax purposes and the remaindermen were deemed to own nothing. The Finance Act 2006 has made important changes to the inheritance tax treatment of these trusts.

Interest in possession trusts created after 22 March 2006

Lifetime transfers into new or existing interest in possession trusts will potentially suffer an immediate inheritance tax entry charge at 20 per cent if the value exceeds the transferor's available inheritance tax nil rate band. This will be followed by periodic and exit charges.

Certain new interest in possession trusts will fall outside the new inheritance trust regime. For example, if a trust is set up under a will and the interest in possession trust arises immediately on the death of the testator and the beneficiary is the surviving spouse or civil partner, the transfer by the deceased will be exempt from inheritance tax.

Interest in possession trusts existing at 22 March 2006

There are transitional rules for trusts in existence on 22 March 2006. Such trusts are in the main outside the new inheritance tax regime. The pre-22 March 2006 rules will continue to apply until the interest in possession trust comes to an end. If at that point property remains in the trust, the discretionary trust regime will apply.

Non-interest in possession trusts

In the non-interest in possession type of settlement, the discretionary trust is the most important type. Unlike the case of the interest in possession trust, with a discretionary trust it is the trust itself that is regarded as taxable. Tax will be charged on the creation of the trust, on every tenth anniversary of its creation and when property passes out of the discretionary trust.

The creation of a discretionary trust will not be a PET and will normally be a chargeable transfer. In order to calculate what, if any, inheritance tax is payable, it is necessary to calculate the settlor's seven-year total and tax is levied according to whether or not the transfer is above the tax threshold.

On every tenth anniversary of the creation of the trust a periodic or automatic charge to tax will arise. The charge is levied on the relevant property, i.e. the property within the settlement immediately before the anniversary. The method of calculating the rate of tax payable is complex but once found the rate is used to find the amount of tax which would be due on the hypothetical transfer of the relevant property. The tax payable is 30 per cent of the tax payable on the hypothetical transfer of the relevant property. (As the highest rate that can be charged on the hypothetical transfer is 20 per cent, the highest rate that can be charged is 30 per cent of 20 per cent, i.e. 6 per cent. In some cases the rate will be less than 6 per cent.)

The Finance Act 2014 contains a new s 64(1A) of the Inheritance Tax Act 1984. This changes and simplifies the way that accumulated income is treated for the 10 year or exit charge. Instead of having to make detailed calculations involving when income was accumulated (often no formal decision to accumulate is made by trustees) income that has remained undistributed for more than five years at the date of the ten year anniversary will be treated as if it was part of the trust capital for the purposes of the ten year anniversary charge. Tax will be charged at the full rate (6 per cent) on any such undistributed income. The trustees will not be required to calculate how long the income has been accumulated and so at what rate tax is charged. This new rule applies to tax charges arising on or after 6 April 2014.

When capital leaves the discretionary trust, inheritance tax will be payable – the exit charge – and the tax will be levied on the reduction in the value of the trust fund. This would occur if capital was distributed to one of the beneficiaries. Again, the tax calculations are rather complicated but in essence the property leaving the trust is taxed at the appropriate fraction of the rate charged at the last ten-year anniversary. The appropriate fraction is the number of completed three-month periods since the last ten-year anniversary divided by 40 (the number of three-month periods in ten years). So if £10,000 of property is taken out of a trust eleven months after the last ten-year anniversary and the rate of tax charged at that anniversary was 6 per cent, the exit charge tax will be £10,000 × 6 per cent × 3 ÷ 40.

Accumulation and maintenance trusts

It is very common for a parent to wish to provide for his child through a trust but it is often considered unwise to give the child an absolute interest. It is, however, desirable that any income generated by the trust should be available to support and maintain the child. The answer is often the creation of an accumulation and maintenance trust, which is commonly set up for minors. Under such a trust there will be no one with an interest in possession. Under such a trust the beneficiaries will become entitled to the property or an interest in it on attaining a specified age, and in the meantime the income generated by the trust will be accumulated to the extent that it is not needed to maintain the beneficiaries.

Accumulation and maintenance trusts created after 21 March 2006

For trusts created on or after 22 March 2006, the regime for discretionary trusts will apply for lifetime transfers. If the value transferred is greater than the available nil rate band, there will be an 'entry' charge of 20 per cent on the value of transferred assets. There will also be a 'periodic' charge on the value of the assets every ten years from the commencement of the trust at up to 6 per cent. Additionally, there will be an exit charge on the value of assets leaving the trust at up to 6 per cent.

However, these new rules will be modified in some cases. For example, where there is a trust set up for a child under the will of at least one parent, provided that entitlement to the trust assets is outright at 18 there will be no periodic or exit charges. This is sometimes called a 'trust for bereaved minors'.

Where a trust is set up under the will of at least one parent, and the beneficiary will become entitled to the trust assets outright by age 25, no inheritance tax charges will apply while the beneficiary is under age 18. Restricted inheritance tax charges will, however, apply on the beneficiary becoming entitled to the trust assets between the ages of 18 and 25. In this situation the maximum rate of inheritance tax on acquiring the assets at age 25 would be 4.2 per cent. These trusts are called 'trusts for those age 18–25'.

Accumulation and maintenance trusts that were in existence on 22 March 2006

There are transitional provisions for accumulation and maintenance trusts existing at 22 March 2006. The previous (more favourable) inheritance tax treatment continues to apply if the terms of the trust provide (or are varied by 6 April 2008 so as to provide) that the beneficiary will become entitled to the trust assets outright by age 18. There will be inheritance tax periodic and exit charges from 6 April 2008 if the trust terms are not varied by then to give beneficiaries absolute entitlement by age 18 at the latest.

Summary

- This chapter deals with the main stages in the growth of equity and the development of the trusts concept, a flexible and evolving concept. The courts have the jurisdiction to supervise the administration of trusts.
- The origins of equity lie in a body of rules created by the Court of Chancery, initially presided over by the Lord Chancellor. The origins of the rules of trusts and equity lay in overcoming shortcomings of the common law.

- Initially equity was flexible – resulting in uncertainty and unpredictability. This uncertainty was followed, in the late seventeenth and eighteenth centuries, by the development of a body of precedent used in deciding cases, while the discretionary nature of equity was preserved.

- Cases of conflict between equity and the common law were addressed by (*inter alia*) the Judicature Acts 1873–75.

- The most important creation of equity was the trust.

- A definition of a trust (as opposed to description) is elusive, but the key elements of express private trusts are: a settlor who provides the trust property; trustees who hold the trust property subject to a range of duties and powers; and beneficiaries for whose benefit the trust exists and for whom the trustees hold and administer the trust property.

- As trust law developed it was recognised that beneficiaries have (at least very nearly) a proprietary interest, giving them the power to enforce the trust and rights against trust property.

- The principle of the *bona fide* purchaser for value without notice of an equitable interest was very important in protecting third parties against the rights under a trust but the principle is now of less importance as under the 1925 property legislation in many cases notice has been replaced by registration.

- There are several types of trusts: express, statutory, resulting and constructive trusts. Although many trusts are fixed (in that the extent of the beneficiaries' interests are expressly set out), some trusts are discretionary trusts under which the trustees exercise their discretion as to the extent particular beneficiaries (as opposed to other beneficiaries) are to benefit. Although many trusts are private (in that they exist to benefit an individual or a group of individuals), charitable trusts exist to benefit the public (or a section of it).

- The trust must be distinguished from other apparently similar concepts. The trust concept is a powerful one and may be used for a wide variety of purposes, including some purposes which some argue amount to exploitation of the concept. For example **Barclays Bank v Quistclose Investments Ltd** (1968) has been seen by some as providing an 'unfair' advantage to some creditors and thus is an application of the trust that some say is unjustifiable.

- Tax avoidance or reduction is a reason for the creation of many trusts (or the form that the trust takes). The main taxes that are relevant are income tax, capital gains tax and inheritance tax.

Further reading

General

D Bailey, 'Can we trust trusts?' TEL & TJ (2012) 140, October, 12–14.
Discusses the public perceptions of trusts including the impression that they are veiled in secrecy, are artificial devices, and are only used by the wealthy to achieve tax avoidance or evasion.

R Bartlett, 'When is a trust not a trust? The National Health Service' [1996] Conv 186.
Discusses the nature of trusts and argues that NHS trusts are not trusts in the sense that the word is used in this text nor are they trusts in the higher sense.

A Byrne, 'Trusts: the commercial applications' PLC (2014) 25(4) 35–40.
Wide-ranging discussion of the uses of trusts in a commercial context, including pensions and Quistclose trusts.

W Goodhart, 'Trust law for the twenty-first century' (1996) 10(2) Tru LI 38.
Includes a brief history of the trust and covers some modern uses. Concentrates on the need (in 1996) to reform the powers of trustees.

D Hayton, 'The development of equity and the "good person" philosophy in common law systems' (2012) 4 Conv 263–73.
Covers the emergence of equity. Discusses the development of equity and trusts. Covers the range of equitable interventions and the conflicts between common law courts and the Court of Chancery. Discusses developments since the Second World War.

P Millett, 'Equity – the road ahead' (1995) 9(2) Tru LI 35.
Forecasts a resurgence of equity and a re-evaluation of some of the basic principles. Deals with the evolution of equity, moving from its original domestic setting to the 'market place'. Also discusses the nature of fiduciary duties.

Development of equity

D Hayton, 'The development of equity and the "good person" philosophy in common law systems' (2012) Conv 4, 263–73.
Covers the emergence of equity. Discusses the development of equity and trusts. Covers the range of equitable interventions and the conflicts between common law courts and the Court of Chancery. Discusses developments since the Second World War.

Quistclose trusts

J Glister, '*Twinsectra v Yardley*: trusts, powers and contractual obligations' (2002) 16(4) Tru LI 223.
Discusses the House of Lords classification of *Quistclose* trusts. Discusses *Twinsectra Ltd v Yardley*. Was a *Quistclose* trust created?

S Love, 'A question of trust' NLJ (2013) 163(7561) 16–17, 24 May 2013.
Discusses *Challinor v Juliet Bellis & Co* and whether or not funds were held on a *Quistclose* trust.

L Oakdene and C Dalzell, 'Clear segregation' TEL & TJ (2013) 149, September, 20–2.
Discusses the principles governing the creation and effect of a *Quistclose* trust.

J-P Wood, 'Beware of importing principles of equity into commercial law' TEL & TJ (2013) 145, April, 17–20.
Discusses *Bieber v Teathers Ltd (In Liquidation)* and whether there was a *Quistclose* trust or a resulting trust.

The maxims of equity

Objectives

After reading this chapter you should:

1. Have an awareness of the nature of equitable maxims and their role.

2. Have a knowledge of a range of the equitable maxims and understand the way in which individual maxims have influenced the law in particular areas.

3. Understand the rule in Strong v Bird, by which beneficial ownership can pass to an executor or administrator in some circumstances.

4. Understand that in some cases donationes mortis causa provide an exception to the maxim that equity will not assist a volunteer and be aware of the key requirements of a valid donatio mortis causa.

5. Understand in outline the principle of estoppel.

Introduction

Objective 1

The maxims of equity may fairly be described as a set of general principles which are said to govern the way in which equity operates. They tend to illustrate the qualities of equity, in contrast to the common law, as more flexible, responsive to the needs of the individual and more inclined to take account of the parties' conduct and worthiness. It cannot be said that there is a definitive list of the maxims: different sources give different examples and some works prefer to avoid the term altogether in favour of a broader discussion of the character of equity. Above all, the maxims are applied only when the court feels it appropriate: none of the maxims is in the nature of a binding rule and for each maxim it is possible to find as many instances of its not having been applied as instances where it has been.

Tinsley v Milligan [1993] 3 All ER 65 is considered in detail in Chapter 11 (pp. 281–2).

The role of the maxims was discussed in the case of *Tinsley v Milligan* [1993] 3 All ER 65.

In the Court of Appeal a flexible approach was taken to the application of the maxim, 'he who comes to equity must come with clean hands', but in the House of Lords this was rejected. Such a flexible approach, depending upon such an 'imponderable factor' as public conscience, would lead to great uncertainty.

It is submitted that this cannot be taken as evidence that every maxim is binding in every situation which would appear to lie within its wording. The true answer may lie in the fact that the maxims are very broadly worded and cannot, as is stated above, be treated without more as binding rules. Rather they are the principles underlying various specific rules, instances of which are given below in the context of each maxim. The case of *Barrett v Barrett* [2008] EWHC 1061, [2008] 2 P& CR 17 (discussed at p. 56) may indicate the re-assertion of a more flexible, conscience based approach.

The following is a list of maxims, together with some of the instances of their application. It is not intended to be exhaustive. It will also become apparent that there is much overlap and in some cases contradiction between the maxims.

Equity follows the law

Objective 2

This is an attempt to indicate the relationship between common law and equity, which is a complex one. The traditional role of equity, as stated in 'Doctor and Student' 1523 by Christopher St German, was 'to temper and mitigate the rigour of the law', which implies that equity would intervene and overrule the common law if justice required it. It was stressed, even at that time, however, that it did not attempt to overrule common law judgments, but rather to act *in personam* on the parties to prevent injustice (as explained below, it is also a maxim of equity that it acts *in personam*). This maxim indicates that, where possible, equity will ensure that its own rules are in line with the common law ones. Examples of equity overcoming the effect of the common law are frequent enough, but it should be noted that in most cases the principle is that equity supplements but does not contradict the common law. Thus, in the case of the trust, the interests of the beneficiary are recognised, but so too, of course, is the status of the trustee as legal owner. The trust exists, as it were, behind the legal ownership.

For more on personal remedies see Chapter 17 (pp. 517–18).

Equally, the courts will in appropriate cases allow the common law effects to stand. For instance, in the case of *Re Diplock* [1948] 2 All ER 318 it was argued that, where money had been distributed to charities under the provision of a will which subsequently turned out to be invalid, the charities should be allowed to retain it. The Court of Appeal stated:

> It is in our opinion impossible to contend that a disposition which according to the general law of the land is held to be entirely invalid can yet confer upon those who, *ex hypothesi*, have improperly participated under the disposition, some moral or equitable right to retain what they have received against those whom the law declares to be properly entitled.

(On Re Diplock see further at p. 517.)

Where the equities are equal, the law prevails. Where the equities are equal, the first in time prevails

These two maxims are concerned with priorities, that is to say which of various interests prevails in the event of a conflict. The general rule, as one might expect, is that interests take effect in order of their creation, but, as regards equitable interests, these may be defeated if a *bona fide* purchaser acquires a subsequent legal estate without notice of the equitable one. This in turn raises the issue of notice, and to that extent the maxims have been affected by legislation on the question of what constitutes notice. For the purchaser of the legal estate to gain priority, however, it will be necessary for him to show that he is *bona fide*. If there is fraud, then the equities (of the legal owner and the equitable one) will not be equal and the equitable one will prevail. In **Pilcher v Rawlins** (1872) LR 7 Ch App 250, James LJ explained the position of the *bona fide* purchaser of a legal estate thus:

> such a purchaser's [i.e. the purchaser of a legal estate's] plea of a purchase for valuable consideration without notice is an absolute, unqualified, unanswerable defence, and an unanswerable plea to the jurisdiction of this Court [the Court of Appeal in Chancery]. Such a purchaser, when he has once put in such a plea, may be interrogated and tested to any extent as to the valuable consideration which he has given in order to show *bona fides* or *mala fides* of his purchase, and also the presence or the absence of notice; but when once he has gone through that ordeal, and has satisfied the terms of the plea of purchase for valuable consideration without notice, then . . . this Court has no jurisdiction whatever to do anything more than to let him depart in possession of that legal estate.

Again, if there is a conflict between a number of equitable interests, they will have priority in order of their creation, again subject to the 'equities being equal' (i.e. both parties not being at fault or guilty of fraud, etc.).

The sort of conduct by which a person might lose his priority, i.e. making the equities unequal, was characterised by the Privy Council in **Abigail v Lapin** [1934] AC 491 at 502 thus:

> In the case of a contest between two equitable claimants the first in time, all other things being equal, is entitled to priority. But all other things must be equal, and the claimant who is first in time may lose his priority by any act or omission which has, or might have had, the effect of inducing a claimant later in time to act to his prejudice.

Ranking after equitable interests in the matter of priorities are mere equities, so that the *bona fide* purchaser of an equitable estate without notice of the equity will take free of it. Mere equities are difficult to define and some writers have said that they cannot bind subsequent purchasers in any event. It is submitted that there are certain defined equities which do bind, subject to the above rule regarding the *bona fide* purchaser. Such defined equities are proprietary interests, including, for example, the right to have a conveyance set aside for fraud, the right to have a contract rectified and a right arising out of estoppel.

It is clear that the question of notice will be crucial in determining priorities, especially where both legal and equitable interests are in conflict. The general principle is that a purchaser is taken to have notice unless he can show he took all reasonable care and made inquiries and did not thereby acquire notice, whether actual, constructive or imputed. Actual knowledge means that he was actually aware of the interest; constructive knowledge that he would have acquired it had he taken all reasonable steps, and imputed knowledge is that which was possessed or should have been possessed by his agent acting on his behalf in the transaction. The detailed rules as to what is considered reasonable inquiry need not be examined here, but it should be remembered that in relation to real property the position is substantially affected by land charges legislation. Under this legislation many charges on land, both legal and equitable, will be void against a purchaser for value unless registered, and registration is deemed to be actual notice to all persons of the charge registered. Also important is the principle of 'overreaching' which has the effect of enabling a purchaser of land held on trust to take free of the beneficial interests even if he has notice of them. This occurs because the trust, and therefore the beneficial interests, attach to the purchase moneys rather than to the land in the case of land held on trust of land under the provisions of the Trusts of Land and Appointment of Trustees Act 1996.

Equity looks to the substance rather than the form

Courts of Equity make a distinction in all cases between that which is matter of substance and that which is matter of form; and if it finds that by insisting on the form, the substance will be defeated, it holds it inequitable to allow a person to insist on such form, and thereby defeat the substance.

Lord Romilly MR thus expressed this maxim in *Parkin* v *Thorold* (1852) 16 Beav 59. It should not be thought that this implies that formalities are never required, however. Equity will not enforce or recognise equitable interests where, for example, formalities are required by statute. Once again, this maxim is in the nature of a general principle only, which implies that equity is generally less concerned with precise forms than the common law. It is not necessary, for example, for the word 'trust' to be used before a trust can be created: the court looks not at the words of the settlor, but rather the result he was attempting to achieve.

For more on formalities see Chapter 4 (p. 113).

Equity will not permit a statute to be used as an instrument of fraud

This principle may be taken as a more specific example of the previous maxim regarding formality. It should be stressed that equity will not ignore statutory requirements normally, but only, as the maxim implies, where it would be unconscionable to allow a party to rely on a statutory requirement to another's detriment. This problem has commonly arisen in situations where contracts are only enforceable if in writing, as required by the Law of Property Act 1925 s 53(1)(b).

Bannister v *Bannister* [1948] 2 All ER 133

> In this case, A conveyed a house to B and B orally agreed to allow A to live in it rent free as long as she wished. This agreement was unenforceable as it was not in writing and B attempted to evict A. The Court of Appeal held that the agreement was enforceable, notwithstanding the requirement of writing and accordingly A was tenant for life.

For more on secret trusts and Rochefoucauld see Chapter 4 (p. 121).

This case is not without difficulty, because by holding A to be tenant for life the court gave her much wider powers, including the power to sell the land, than can have been intended. A further problem, that of the nature of the trust that equity imposes to prevent fraud, is discussed in the context of the similar case of *Rochefoucauld* v *Boustead* (1897).

One of the theoretical justifications for secret trusts is that not to enforce them would allow a statute, in this case the Wills Act 1837, to be used as an instrument of fraud. This is not, however, the only argument in their favour and accordingly they will be discussed separately later (in Chapter 4 at p. 122 et seq.).

Equity imputes an intention to fulfil an obligation

For performance and satisfaction see Chapter 18 (p. 535).

This is the basis of the equitable doctrines of performance and satisfaction, which are discussed in detail later (in Chapter 18, pp. 535–42) and simply means that where a person has undertaken an obligation his later conduct will, if possible, be interpreted as fulfilment of that obligation.

Equity regards as done that which ought to be done

This relates most obviously to specific performance. If vendor and purchaser have entered into a specifically enforceable contract (for example, for the sale of land), in equity the purchaser acquires a beneficial interest and the vendor holds the land on constructive trust for the purchaser. However, it should be noted that the duty of the constructive trustee is simply to convey the land to the purchaser in accordance with the terms of the contract. The trustee does not take on all the other duties normal to trusteeship, nor, for example, is the purchaser entitled to rents from the property until sale. As Cotton LJ stated in *Rayner v Preston* (1881) 18 Ch D 1:

For more on vendors as constructive trustees see Chapter 12 (p. 336).

For more on breaches of fiduciary duties see Chapter 12 (p. 300).

> An unpaid vendor is a trustee in a qualified sense only, and is so only because he has made a contract which a Court of Equity will give effect to by transferring the property sold to the purchaser, and in so far as he is a trustee he is so only in respect of the property contracted to be sold.

The purchaser was not therefore able, as the law then stood, to recover insurance money obtained by the vendor for a fire which occurred after he had contracted to sell the house (see further at page 332).

The maxim was also applied to a bribe received by a fiduciary in *A-G for Hong Kong v Reid* [1994] 1 All ER 1 (see further at p. 301).

Equity acts *in personam*

It is in the nature of equitable remedies that they generally operate against the person of the defendant, being enforceable by imprisonment for contempt. It is in this way that, as discussed above, equity could claim not to be interfering with the common law. The judgment at law in effect was binding on the whole world and equity intervened only against the individual defendant, who was prevented from enforcing his legal rights. Another feature of this principle is that equitable rights were not enforceable against everybody but could be defeated by the interest of the *bona fide* purchaser.

The *in personam* nature of the operation of equity also has specific relevance in relation to property and interests abroad. As a general rule, English courts will not entertain actions concerning title to foreign land. As Lord Campbell LC stated in *Norris v Chambres* (1861) 3 De GF& J 583:

> An English Court ought not to pronounce a decree, even *in personam*, which can have no specific operation without the intervention of a foreign Court, and which in the country where the lands to be charged by it lie would probably be treated as *brutum fulmen* [an empty threat].

The position is otherwise if the intended decree acts *in personam*, as equitable ones do, and also the defendant is within the reach of the English courts. As Lord Cottenham observed in *ex parte Pollard* (1840) Mont & Ch 239:

> contracts respecting lands in countries not within the jurisdiction of these courts . . . can only be enforced by proceedings *in personam* which courts of equity here are constantly in the habit of doing: not thereby in any respect interfering with the *lex loci rei sitae*. If indeed the law of the country where the land is situated should not permit or not enable the defendant to do what the court might otherwise think it right to decree, it would be useless and unjust

to direct him to do the act; but when there is no such impediment the courts of this country, in the exercise of their jurisdiction over contracts made here, or in administering equities between parties residing here, act upon their own rules, and are not influenced by any consideration of what the effect of such contracts might be in the country where the lands are situated.

For more on search orders and freezing injunctions see Chapter 19 (p. 557).

The *in personam* nature of remedies has also been discussed in relation to search orders and freezing injunctions. It should be noted that such orders are not effective against third parties abroad without the cooperation of the courts for the jurisidiction where these parties are situated.

Equity will not suffer a wrong to be without a remedy

This maxim indicates that equity will not allow the technical defects of the common law to prevent worthy plaintiffs from obtaining redress. It could be seen, therefore, as the opposite of the maxim that equity follows the law. There are numerous examples of the development of equitable doctrines and remedies intended to override the unjust result arising from the enforcement of legal rights. Perhaps the most obvious is the trust itself: the enforcement of the rights of the legal owner as against the person for whose benefit he had agreed to hold the property would clearly lead to injustice and so equity recognised the rights of that beneficial owner. Other examples include the use of specific performance to enforce contracts not enforceable at law and the use of injunctions to restrain threatened wrongs or to protect the plaintiff's interests pending trial.

He who seeks equity must do equity

Though the previous maxim indicates equity's willingness to intervene where the common law will not, it should not be thought that equity will automatically intervene whenever a certain situation arises. In general, one can say that wherever certain facts are found and a common law right or interest has been established, common law remedies will be available whether that produces a fair result or not. By contrast, equitable remedies are discretionary and the court will not grant them if it feels that the plaintiff is unworthy, notwithstanding that *prima facie* he has established an equitable right or interest. The maxim that he who seeks equity must do equity, together with the next two maxims, concerning 'clean hands' and delay, are aspects of this discretionary quality. It should not be supposed that the discretion is entirely unfettered. As Lord Romilly MR explained in *Haywood* v *Cope* (1858) 25 Beav 140:

> the discretion of the Court must be exercised according to fixed and settled rules; you cannot exercise a discretion by merely considering what, as between the parties, would be fair to be done; what one person may consider fair, another person may consider very unfair; you must have some settled rule and principle upon which to determine how that discretion is to be exercised.

So the person who seeks an equitable remedy must be prepared to act equitably, and the court may oblige him to do so. In the field of contract, the court will not grant an injunction to prevent breach for the benefit of a party who is not prepared to perform his side of the bargain (see *Chappell* v *Times Newspapers* [1975] 2 All ER 233). Where a contract is rescinded the party seeking rescission must be prepared to return all benefits received under it. A creditor may not be able to recover the full amount of a debt if the debtor can set off money owed to him by the creditor. The maxim is also behind the principle of mutuality of remedies (if specific performance is available to one party then it will be available to the other, even though damages would be adequate for that party) and the doctrine of election (see pp. 530–5).

For more on the doctrine of election see Chapter 18 (pp. 530–5).

This maxim refers to the plaintiff's future conduct, whereas the next refers to his past behaviour.

He who comes to equity must come with clean hands

The rather picturesque language of this maxim means that a party seeking an equitable remedy must not himself be guilty of unconscionable conduct. The court may therefore consider the past conduct of the claimant. Most cases concern illegal or fraudulent behaviour on the part of the claimant, and it is not clear to what extent the maxim is applicable outside such behaviour. Certainly, in the context of the granting of injunctions, which, like all equitable remedies, are discretionary, the principle has been broadly stated; for example, Wood J stated in *Cross* v *Cross* (1983) 4 FLR 235:

> He who comes to equity must come with a clean hand and any conduct of the plaintiff which would make a grant of specific performance inequitable can prove a bar.

It appears, however, that the 'uncleanness' must relate directly to the matter in hand, otherwise anyone might be denied a remedy simply because he was of bad character.

Dering v *Earl of Winchelsea* (1787) 1 Cox 318

This is illustrated in the case of ***Dering* v *Earl of Winchelsea***, where Sir Edward Dering, the Earl and another had acted as surety for Dering's brother, Thomas, for the due performance by Thomas of the office of Collector of Customs. Thomas defaulted and the Crown obtained judgment from Sir Edward for the amount lost. Sir Edward then sought to obtain a contribution from the other sureties. The Earl claimed that Sir Edward could not claim the share because of his own misconduct. Eyre LCB (having itemised some of Sir Edward's misconduct, including encouraging his brother to gamble, knowing his brother was using government money for this) did not accept that argument and stated that:

> . . . such a representation of Sir Edward's conduct certainly places him in a bad point of view; and perhaps it is not a very decorous proceeding in Sir Edward to come into this Court under these circumstances: . . . A man must come into a Court of Equity with clean hands; but when this is said, it does not mean a general depravity: it must have an immediate and necessary relation to the equity sued for, it must be a depravity in a legal as well as a moral sense.

He concluded that though Sir Edward might morally be the author of his own loss he could not be said to be so legally, so his conduct did not prevent him from recovering the contribution. A similar point was made more recently in *Argyll* v *Argyll* [1965] 1 All ER 611: the Duchess's immoral attitude towards her marriage did not prevent her obtaining an injunction to stop the Duke publishing an account of it.

The application of this maxim to situations where a claimant seeks the recognition of an equitable proprietary right was considered in the case of *Tinsley* v *Milligan*, referred to in the introduction to this chapter.

Tinsley v *Milligan* [1993] 3 All ER 65

The facts of this case were that the plaintiff and defendant each contributed to the purchase price of a house, on the mutual understanding that it was owned jointly between them. However, the conveyance was made into the sole name of the plaintiff only in order to enable the defendant to make fraudulent claims to housing benefit. After an argument, the plaintiff Tinsley moved out, claimed possession and asserted her legal title. Milligan, who admitted making the fraudulent claims, now sought a declaration that Tinsley held the house on trust for both of them. Tinsley contended that, since Milligan could not make her claim without admitting the evidence of her fraud, the court would automatically refuse to enforce a trust in her favour.

For more on resulting trusts and co-owners see Chapter 11 (pp. 271–94).

The Court of Appeal adopted a flexible approach and held that the fraudulent purpose was not relevant.

This approach was rejected by the House of Lords. The decision was, however, by a bare majority, and subject to strong dissent by Lord Goff.

It was clear that, according to ordinary resulting trust principles, Milligan would have had an equitable proprietary right to half the house on the basis of her contribution to the purchase price and the mutual understanding between herself and Tinsley that the house was jointly owned.

What difference did the fact of the illegal purpose make? The House clearly rejected the idea of assessing the quality of the illegality and of exercising a discretion to ignore it, as the Court of Appeal had done.

The majority in the House reached the conclusion that a party could assert an equitable title provided they could do so without relying on their own illegality. On the facts here Milligan could prove the existence of a resulting trust in her favour by virtue of her contributions and the mutual understanding: she did not have to rely on the illegality as it was not relevant why she had come to this arrangement with Tinsley. The case was thus distinguishable from cases such as *Tinker* v *Tinker* and *Gascoigne* v *Gascoigne*, where ordinary equitable principles presumed an outright gift to the legal title holder which could be rebutted only by evidence of the donor's purpose: if that purpose were an illegal one, the donor would not be allowed to use it to establish a trust in his favour.

In his dissenting judgment, however, Lord Goff argued powerfully against this approach and in favour of the broad principle, laid down by Lord Eldon in *Muckleston* v *Brown* (1801) 6 Ves Jr 52, to the effect that any plaintiff guilty of illegal or unconscionable conduct should be refused relief in equity. Accordingly, as Lord Eldon put it: 'Let the estate lie where it falls.' On these facts, Tinsley, as the legal owner, would have sole title. In Lord Goff's view, this should apply notwithstanding the unfair gain that Tinsley would thereby make, and that the consequences of the illegality, which they had both connived at, would fall solely on Milligan. His Lordship expressed some sympathy for Milligan, but, as he said:

> This is not a principle of justice; it is a principle of policy, whose application is indiscriminate.

Lord Goff did nevertheless acknowledge that there were exceptions to the general rule, one of which, upheld in *Tribe* v *Tribe* [1995] 4 All ER 236, is that a man may rely on evidence of his illegal purpose where that purpose has not, in fact, been carried out.

The recognition of an equitable right under a resulting trust despite an illegal purpose in *Tinsley* v *Milligan*, can be contrasted with the approach to the recognition of a constructive trust based upon an alleged agreement in support of an illegal purpose in *Barrett v Barrett* [2008] EWHC 1061 (Ch) [2008] 2 P& CR 17. In this case Thomas was declared bankrupt, so his brother John purchased Thomas's house from the trustee in bankruptcy, so that Thomas could go on living in it. John was thus the legal owner, and later John sold the house and purported to transfer some of the sale proceeds to his sister. Thomas claimed a constructive trust based on an agreement with his brother and his paying the house expenses. He did not allege a contribution to the purchase price (thus distinguishing the case from *Tinsley v Milligan*). Any attempt to rely on an agreement inevitably meant that Thomas revealed the purpose of the agreement, which was to defeat his creditors and was thus illegal, so Thomas was not allowed to plead the agreement. The maxim was thus reasserted, and with it the broader concept of conscionability.

For more on trusts to defeat creditors, see Chapter 6 (p. 147).

Delay defeats equity

Two matters must be noted here. First, the time in which an action for equitable relief may be sought may be governed by the Limitation Act 1980 and, second, even where there is no statutory limitation, it will be governed by the equitable principle of laches.

The Limitation Act 1980 lays down limitation periods in connection with the enforcement of trust matters. For example, s 21(3) provides, as a general rule, that an action by a beneficiary to recover trust property or in respect of any breach of trust shall not be brought after the expiration of six years from the date the right of action accrued. However, the section also provides, for example, that no time limit shall apply to an action by a beneficiary in respect of fraud by a trustee or an action by a beneficiary to recover trust property or its proceeds from a trustee. The other main types of equitable claims regulated by the Act are claims to the personal estate of deceased persons, claims to redeem mortgaged land and claims to foreclose mortgages of real or personal property. Equity may in very limited cases apply the same limitation to situations analogous to the express statutory ones. No statutory limitations apply to actions for breach of a fiduciary duty, or to setting aside for undue influence or to actions for rescission. In addition, the Limitation Act 1980 s 36 provides that nothing in the Act shall affect any equitable jurisdiction to refuse relief on the grounds of acquiescence or otherwise.

Time limits are considered further in Chapter 17 (p. 500).

Delay may be evidence of acquiescence, so the two issues cannot be separated. A failure to bring an action may tend to confirm other slight evidence that the innocent party has accepted or agreed to the breach of contract or other ground for seeking relief, thus preventing him from enforcing his right to remedies for that breach.

Whether the court will regard the claim as barred will be a matter to be determined on the facts. As with all equitable principles, flexibility is important. As the Privy Council stated in *Lindsay Petroleum v Hurd* (1874) LR 5 PC 221:

> The doctrine of laches in the Courts of Equity is not an arbitrary or a technical doctrine. Where it would be practically unjust to give a remedy, either because the party has, by his conduct, done that which might fairly be regarded as waiver of it, or where by his conduct and neglect he has, though perhaps not waived that remedy, yet put the other party in a situation in which it would not be reasonable to place him if the remedy were afterwards to be asserted, in either of these cases, lapse of time and delay are most material. But in every case, if an argument against relief, which otherwise would be just, is founded upon mere delay, . . . the validity of the defence must be tried upon principles substantially equitable. Two circumstances, always important in such cases, are the length of the delay and the nature of the acts done during the interval, which might affect either party and cause

the balance of justice or injustice in taking the one course or the other, so far as it relates to the remedy.

Delay in seeking an injunction, where the defendant was thereby encouraged to proceed with building work, thus making a subsequent injunction oppressive, was a ground for refusing an injunction to enforce a restrictive covenant in *Jaggard* v *Sawyer* [1995] 2 All ER 189.

This is discussed in Chapter 19 (p. 569).

Equity will not allow a trust to fail for want of a trustee

For more on appointment of trustees, see Chapter 14 (pp. 411–16).

For more on testamentary trusts see Chapter 14 (p. 392).

It would clearly be absurd if an otherwise valid trust could not take effect because no one had been appointed to act as trustee. The rules as to who has the power to appoint trustees are dealt with in detail later (see Chapter 14, pp. 411–16), but it should be remembered that the court has a residuary inherent jurisdiction to appoint trustees in circumstances where the settlor has failed to appoint, or has appointed persons who are now dead and has not given anyone else the power to appoint. It will thus ensure that the trust does not fail. It should also be noted that in practice the court will normally appoint under its statutory powers under the Trustee Act 1925, so the inherent jurisdiction will not normally need to be invoked. (The application of the maxim in relation to testamentary trusts is dealt with in Chapter 14 at p. 392.)

Equality is equity

In the absence of any evidence to the contrary, equity will tend towards the adoption of equal division of any fund to which several persons are entitled. One example of this, and one which it will be seen has wide-reaching implications, is to be found in *Burrough* v *Philcox* (discussed in Chapter 5 at p. 136). The testator having left his estate to certain relatives or such of them as his child should nominate, and the child having failed to nominate, the court held that the funds were held on trust for all the relatives in equal shares. There is even some authority for the proposition that, upon failure of an express trust for uncertainty of beneficial share, the property is to be held on trust for all the beneficiaries equally. Another instance is the division of a joint bank account upon divorce where it is impractical to make an accurate division of the fund between husband and wife: the court will order equal division. The same applies, as a prima facie assumption, where co-habitees are joint tenants of land; the joint tenant wishing to claim a greater than equal share would have to prove it. The adoption of equal division is, however, subject to any evidence to the contrary; so, for example, the court in *McPhail* v *Doulton* (discussed in Chapter 5 at p. 137) would not order equal division, which in any event would have been impossible, because it was clearly not what the settlor intended.

For more on trust powers see Chapter 5 (p. 137).

Equity will not assist a volunteer

For more on consideration see Chapter 4 (pp. 104–11).

A volunteer in this context is a person who has not given consideration for a bargain. We shall see (in Chapter 4 at pp. 104–11) in the context of constitution of trusts that equity will not enforce a covenant to create a trust in favour of a volunteer. This is also an instance of the next maxim.

Equity will not perfect an imperfect gift

For more on imperfect gifts see Chapter 4 (pp. 104–7).

Unless consideration is given, an undertaking to give something is unenforceable, being a mere gratuitous promise. Therefore, unless property in the thing promised has been transferred, the intended donee can do nothing to enforce. Likewise, where there is a gratuitous promise to create a trust, the property must have been vested in the trustees for the trust to be enforceable.

There are, however, certain recognised exceptions to the rule that equity will not perfect an imperfect gift, which will now be considered in detail. If one of these exceptions can be applied, it will mean that the various formal rules as to the transfer of different types of property, do not apply.

The rule in *Strong* v *Bird*

Objective
3

Where a donor intends to transfer ownership in personal property to another and maintains that intention until his death but fails to make an effective transfer during his lifetime, if, on the death of the donor, the property becomes vested in the intended donee as the donor's executor, that vesting is treated as completing the gift. This is the effect of a line of cases beginning with **Strong v Bird**.

Strong v *Bird* (1874) LR 18 Eq 315

B borrowed money from his stepmother and it was agreed that repayment was to be made by reducing by £100 per month the amount that she had previously paid B in rent. For six months she paid at the reduced rate, but thereafter went back to paying the full rent for a further three-and-a-half years until her death. The stepmother appointed B as her executor.

This was sufficient evidence of her intention to release him from the debt, but her right to sue was never formally surrendered. However, the court took the evidence as sufficient, since the stepmother was by her actions voluntarily surrendering her right to sue. B was not therefore obliged at common law to account for the debt and, under the subsequent case of **Re Stewart** [1908] 2 Ch 251, equity treated the gift as perfected. The reasoning in that case was given by Neville J:

> first that the vesting of the property in the executor at the testator's death completes the imperfect gift made in the lifetime and secondly that the intention of the testator to give the beneficial interest to the executor is sufficient to countervail the equity of beneficiaries under the will, the testator having vested the legal estate in the executor.

The executor holds the legal estate but, normally, subject to the equitable rights of the beneficiaries. Here there is sufficient evidence that those equitable rights are overturned.

It must be remembered that the donor's intention must be, and be evidenced to be, to give some specific immediate benefit to the donee: it is not sufficient that he intends to benefit him in some vague, general sense, or that he intends a benefit to take place only at the time of the donor's death.

Thus, in **Re Gonin** [1977] 2 All ER 720, where a mother expressed the intention to transfer her house to her daughter but, believing that she was unable to do this, wrote out a cheque in her daughter's favour instead, the necessary specific intent in respect of the house was lacking. Similarly, in **Re Wale** [1956] 3 All ER 280, a mother entered into a covenant to settle the benefit of certain shares on her children but never actually made the transfer. She could not be said to have a continuing intent to benefit the children under the settlement because later, apparently forgetting about the existence of the settlement deed, she treated the shares as her own and took the dividends for herself or gave them to her children as presents.

Where the supposed intended donor appoints the intended donee as his executor, it can be said that by a voluntary act he has completed the transfer of the property. Can the same be said where the intended donee is appointed administrator, since this appointment is not made by the donor himself? This was doubted, obiter, in **Re Gonin**, but the rule was applied to administrators in **Re Stewart** and it is submitted that this is the better view, in the light of Neville J's second ground, that the equity of the beneficiaries should countervail.

The rule has also been applied to trustees of an incompletely constituted trust.

Re Ralli's Will Trusts [1963] 3 All ER 940

In 1924 Helen had covenanted in her marriage settlement to assign all after-acquired property to the trusts of that settlement for the benefit ultimately of her nephews and nieces (who were volunteers). Under her father's will she was entitled to half the remainder of his estate after her mother's life interest. This remainder interest never came into her hands during her lifetime, since Helen died in 1956 and her mother in 1961. P was the sole surviving trustee of Helen's marriage settlement. So it was to P that Helen had covenanted to transfer the remainder but she never did this. It happened, however, that P was also the sole surviving trustee of Helen's father's estate. In other words, he held half the legal estate on trust, after Helen's mother's death, for Helen. The question was whether he was obliged to hold that interest for Helen's estate or on trust for the marriage settlement. It was held that he must hold it for the marriage settlement. P had acquired the legal estate, which is what Helen had covenanted to transfer to him. It was not relevant that he had acquired it by a different route. The marriage settlement was thus fully constituted and so enforceable by the beneficiaries.

Buckley J explained the situation thus:

In my judgment the circumstance that the plaintiff holds the fund because he was appointed a trustee of the will is irrelevant. He is at law the owner of the fund and the means by which he became so have no effect on the quality of his legal ownership. The question is: for whom, if any one, does he hold it in equity? In other words, who can successfully assert an equity against him disentitling him to stand on his legal right? It seems to me indisputable that Helen, were she alive, could not do so, for she has solemnly covenanted under seal to assign the fund to the plaintiff and the defendants can stand in no better position. It is of course true that the object of the covenant was not that the plaintiff should retain the property for his own benefit, but that he should hold it on the trusts of the settlement. It is also true that, were it necessary to enforce performance of the covenant, equity would not assist the beneficiaries under the settlement, because they are mere volunteers; and that for the same reason the plaintiff, as trustee of the settlement, would not be bound to enforce the covenant and would not be constrained by the court to do so, and indeed, it seems, might be constrained not to do so. As matters stand, however, there is no occasion to invoke the assistance of equity to enforce the performance of the covenant.

His Lordship concluded that the plaintiff could not withhold the benefit of the marriage settlement from the beneficiaries of that settlement, because it would be unconscientious to do so.

Again, it will be noted that it was not the settlor (Helen) who did an act which gave the trustee the legal estate: this happened because the terms of Helen's father's will provided for it. Once again, however, it appears that the equity of the beneficiaries of the marriage settlement prevails over the equity of the next of kin.

Donationes mortis causa

Objective 4

Some instances of *donationes mortis causa* provide an exception to the rule that equity will not assist a volunteer.

Donationes mortis causa are gifts made in contemplation of death. If the donor does not make an effective transfer of property to the donee during his lifetime, equity will step in to ensure that the personal representatives perfect the title.

Donationes mortis causa are often referred to as hybrid gifts, being midway between an *inter vivos* gift and a gift by will. In *Re Beaumont* [1902] 1 Ch 889, Buckley J said of a *donatio mortis causa* that it is

> a singular form of gift. It may be said to be of an amphibious nature, being a gift which is neither entirely inter vivos nor testamentary.

As stated *above, donationes mortis causa* are hybrid gifts, being somewhere between an *inter vivos* gift and a gift by will. They have some similarities with gifts by will. A *donatio mortis causa* resembles a testamentary gift in that it is revocable until death and takes effect only on death.

But a *donatio mortis causa* is not revoked by a later will – by the time the will becomes operative (the date of death) the *donatio mortis causa* has become absolute. However, it can be revoked by the express revocation of the donor during his lifetime or by the donor resuming dominion over the subject matter of the *donatio*. Additionally, the *donatio mortis causa* will be revoked if the danger or cause of the feared death ends before the donor dies.

Unlike a testamentary gift, however, which passes under the will and through the personal executors, under a *donatio mortis causa* property passes to the donee outside the will and not through the personal representatives.

In many cases, after the death of the donor, the co-operation of his executors is not needed to make the gift perfect, e.g. a gift of a chattel which has been delivered to the donee will be perfect on the death without any further action. However, in some cases it will be necessary for the executors to act to perfect the gift. For example, if the subject matter of the *donatio mortis causa* is land, the executors will be required to effect whatever transfer or conveyance is needed to perfect the gift. If necessary the courts will compel the executors to act. This is an example of an exception to the general rule that equity will not perfect an imperfect gift.

Requirements

In *Sen v Headley* [1991] 2 All ER 636, Nourse LJ said:

> [T]he three general requirements for such a gift may be stated very much as they are stated in Snell's Equity. First the gift must be in contemplation, although not necessarily in expectation, of impending death. Secondly, the gift must be made upon condition that it is to be absolute and perfected only on the donor's death, being revocable until that event occurs and ineffective if it does not. Thirdly, there must be a delivery of the subject matter of the gift, or of the essential indicia of title thereto, which amounts to a parting with dominion and not merely physical possession over the subject matter of the gift.

Again in *Re Craven* [1937] Ch. 423 Farwell J said:

> Generally speaking, it is not permissible by the law of this country for a person to dispose of his or her property after his or her death except by an instrument executed in accordance with the provisions of the Wills Act 1837. One exception to the general rule is the case of a *donatio mortis causa* but in order that it may be valid certain conditions must be exactly complied with; otherwise the attempted *donatio* is not effected and the property remains part of the property of the testatrix at her death passing under her will. The conditions which are essential to a *donatio mortis causa* are, firstly, a clear intention to give, but to give only if the donor dies, whereas if the donor does not die then the gift is not to take effect and the donor is to have back the subject-matter of the gift. Secondly the gift must be made in contemplation of death, by which is meant not the possibility of death at some time or other, but death within the near future, what may be called death for some reason believed to be impending. Thirdly the donor must part with dominion over the subject-matter of the *donatio*.

A gift made in contemplation of death

There is a requirement that the gift shall be in contemplation of death. This means that the donor must have some specific cause in anticipation. It is not necessary to think that dying from the contemplated cause is inevitable. It is widely thought that contemplation would be equally satisfied if the donor was, for instance, undertaking a dangerous journey and foresaw, not that death was inevitable, but that it was a strong possibility.

But in *Thompson* v *Mechan* [1958] OR 357, the risk of normal air travel does not satisfy the requirement of contemplation of death. It is also not sufficient merely to recognise that death will occur sometime: there must be some specific illness, cause or hazard in view, but it does not then matter if the death occurs in a way other than that contemplated, as in *Wilkes* v *Allington* [1931] 2 Ch 104, where the donor was suffering from an incurable disease (cancer), his contemplated cause of death, but in fact died of something else (pneumonia).

It is probable that the test is subjective. Although this point has not been expressly decided in an English case, some support can be found in *Re Miller* (1961) 105 Sol Jo 207. (See p. 61.)

The subjective nature of the contemplation was emphasised in the first instance case of *Vallee* v *Birchwood* [2013] EWHC 1449 (Ch), [2014] 2 WLR 543 in which Jonathan Gaunt QC (sitting as a Deputy Judge of the Chancery Division) decided that there was a valid *donatio mortis causa*. The case covers several of the key requirements for a valid *donatio mortis causa*. In particular the court discussed the requirements of parting with dominion, contemplation of impending death and the possibility of a DMC over land. For a discussion of the issues of parting with dominion and the possibility of a donatio mortis causa over land see pp. 63 and YYY.

The claimant was the adopted daughter of the deceased. When the claimant, who lived in France, visited the deceased on 6 August 2003, she said she would visit again at Christmas. The deceased said he was not expecting to live much longer and that when he died he wanted her to have the house in which he was living. He handed over the title deeds to the house and a key. He also gave the claimant his war medals and a photograph album. In mid-December 2003, the claimant was told that her father had died. She claimed that she was entitled to the house under a *donatio mortis causa*.

Jonathan Gaunt QC said that 'contemplation' was subjective and as the deceased was anticipating dying within about five months the gift was made in contemplation of impending death. The court rejected the argument that a gift must be made in contemplation of death 'within the near future'. The gap of four months did not prevent the gift being in contemplation of death.

Although *King* v *Dubrey* [2014] EWHC 2083 (Ch), [2014] All ER (D) 24 (Jul) is a first instance case which may go to appeal, it is possible that it signals a relaxation in the requirement of contemplation of death. K claimed that he was entitled to D's house under a valid *donatio mortis causa*. This was challenged by a number of animal charities which were named as beneficiaries under the last valid will that D made.

K moved in with his aunt D in 2007 and acted as her carer for about four years up to her death. In the period shortly before her death, D signed three documents to the effect that she wanted K to have the property in which she lived after her death, but none of those documents was a valid will. D handed him the title deeds to the property and said 'this will be yours when I go' or words to that effect. K put the deeds in a wardrobe in his own room. The documents were stored in a part of the house that in practice only K used. D died four to six months after handing over the title documents.

Mr Charles Hollander QC (sitting as a deputy judge) said that it is clear from *Sen* v *Hedley* that unregistered land can be the subject of a *donatio mortis causa* (see p. 67). He also considered that the handing over of the title deeds which K put in a cupboard in his own room satisfied the requirement of parting with dominion.

The strongest argument against there being a valid *donatio mortis causa* was that the gift was not made in contemplation of death.

There was no evidence that at the time D was seriously ill although her general health was failing. She had not visited the doctor for some time although she did have high blood pressure. She was not about to go on a dangerous journey or undergo an operation. Nor did she express a date by which she thought she would be dead or say that she thought that she would die shortly.

The charities argued that D had not contemplated her impending death when it was made. The charities argued that it was necessary for there to be some identifiable event that might cause the death of the donor or some identifiable, if not precisely defined, period in which the donor expects their death to occur.

Mr Charles Hollander said that in *Vallee* v *Birchwood*, in which the donor (who was unwell at the time) said that he did not expect to live much longer and that he might not be alive at Christmas (about five months away), the requirement of contemplation of impending death was satisfied. On the facts it was clear (the judge said) that D was becoming increasingly preoccupied with her death. In particular the contemplation was evidenced, he said, by a series of wills that D had tried but failed to make and the handing over of the title deeds, saying that when she died the property would be K's. This, the judge said, was enough to satisfy the requirement of contemplation of death.

It is not clear if the decision will be appealed. But in the meantime the decision appears to relax the requirement of contemplation of death; certainly both *Vallee* and *King* show that there is no need for the death to occur within a matter of days. Perhaps the case also shows a greater willingness to find a valid *donatio mortis causa* and in doing so implement the wishes of the deceased. If this is the case it means that potential challenges to *donationes mortis causa* will need to be made with more caution and also those drawing up wills will need to be aware that their terms may now more easily be overridden by a subsequent *donatio mortis causa*.

Conditional on death

The gift must be intended to take effect only on death. If the donor recovers, the gift cannot take effect. Any attempt to make an immediately effective gift cannot be *donatio mortis causa*. It must be clear that the donor expects that if he survives, then no transfer will occur. It is not necessary that this is expressed as it may be inferred if the gift is made in contemplation of death. In *Gardner* v *Parker* (1818) 3 Madd 184 Sir John Leach V-C said: 'If a gift is made in expectation of death, there is an implied condition that it is to be held only in the event of death.' This seems to be the case even if the donor knows he is going to die when it could be argued that as the donor does not expect to recover, an intention that the gift is conditional on death on the donor's part would be odd.

Parting with dominion

The donor must either hand over the thing to be given, or the documents which constitute the essential evidence of title, with the intention of surrendering dominion over the thing and not, for example, merely for safe keeping. Dominion is obviously not the same as ownership, since if the donor gave up ownership the gift would be immediately effective and not effective only on death. If the item is a chattel, delivery of the chattel itself will suffice, provided there is the right kind of evidence of intent to make a gift of it conditional on death.

Equally effective would be delivering the only means to obtain the chattel, such as the only key to a safety deposit box where a chattel was kept. The normally accepted view is that surrendering one of several keys will not be regarded as parting with dominion (see *Re Craven's Estate* [1937] 3 All ER 33 below). But in *Sen* v *Headley* and *Woodard* v *Woodard* (both below) the courts adopted a robust approach to this issue and did not regard the retention by the donor of a second set of keys to a house (*Sen* v *Headley*) or a car (*Woodard* v *Woodard*) as necessarily preventing there being an effective *donatio*. In both cases, as will be seen, the retention of physical dominion was merely theoretical rather than real. In both cases the donor was in hospital and dying. In both cases there was no evidence that the keys were kept with the intention of retaining dominion over the property. In reality the use of the retained keys to gain access to the property (thus asserting continued dominion) was so unlikely as to be ignored. Of course, had the donor retained the second set of keys with the intention of retaining dominion, there could have been no effective *donationes mortis causa* in these cases.

The requirement of parting with dominion was considered by Farwell J in *Re Craven's Estate* [1937] 3 All ER 33. A testatrix was about to enter hospital for a serious operation. In her will she had given her son a power of attorney over some shares and money in a bank account. She told her son to get the property transferred into his name as she wanted him to have it if anything should happen to her. The son, using the power of attorney, had the shares and the money transferred into his name. His mother died a few days later. Farwell J decided that when his mother instructed him to transfer the property into his name, having already given him a power of attorney, there was sufficient parting with dominion to satisfy the requirement for a valid *donatio mortis causa*. Farwell J said that the reason underlying the requirement to part with dominion was that the subject matter of the *donatio* must be some 'clear, ascertained and definable property'. It must not be open to the donor to alter the subject matter of the *donatio* or substitute other property between the date of the *donatio* and death. As long as the subject matter remains within the dominion of the donor such changes are possible. Farwell J said: 'However that may be, it seems to me that there must be such parting with dominion over the chattels or the property as to prevent the subject matter of the *donatio* being dealt with by the donor between the interval of the *donatio* and either his death or the return of the articles by the donee to the donor.' Farwell J said that, in the case, the mere granting of a power of attorney would not, itself, have been sufficient. An attorney simply acts as the agent of the donor and there is nothing to prevent the donor from dealing with the property, but in the instant case there was more. The evidence was that the mother had instructed her son to have the property transferred into his name which he did. 'By so doing and getting the shares transferred into the son's name, the testatrix did what was necessary to part with dominion.'

In the case of many assets (e.g. chattels), it is easy to deal with the requirement of parting with dominion simply by handing over the asset but how does the law deal with assets that are incorporeal such as bank accounts and accounts in building societies? In such cases the Court of Appeal in *Birch v Treasury Solicitor* [1951] Ch 298 decided that what has to be delivered is something which constitutes 'the essential indicia of title, possession of which entitles the possessor to the money or property purported to be given'. In the case of a building society account the pass book would satisfy the requirement. In *Re Weston* [1902] 1 Ch 680, handing over a Post Office savings bank book was sufficient.

Sen v Headley [1991] 2 All ER 636

This case covers a number of points, including the issue of delivery, parting with dominion and whether or not land could be the subject matter of a valid *donatio mortis causa*. The main issue on appeal was this last matter.

Mr Hewett had for many years had a close relationship with Mrs Sen. In 1986 he was taken terminally ill, was admitted to hospital and knew that he had not long to live. In response to Mrs Sen's enquiry as to what she should do with his house in the event of his death, he replied. 'The house is yours, Margaret. You have the keys. They are in your bag. The deeds are in the steel box.' The keys in question had been brought to Mr Hewett at his request by Mrs Sen. After his death she found them in her bag and assumed that he had put them there without her noticing. One of these keys was apparently the only key to a steel box at the house, in which the title deeds were kept. Mr Hewett had a set of keys to the house and Mrs Sen had another set. Mr Hewett knew that he did not have long to live and the 'contemplation of death' requirement was found to have been satisfied.

Nourse LJ said:

It cannot be doubted that title deeds are the essential indicia of title to unregistered land. Moreover, on the facts found by the judge, there was here a constructive delivery of the title deeds of 56 Gordon Road equivalent to an actual handing of them by Mr Hewett to Mrs Sen. And it could not be suggested that Mr Hewett did not part with dominion over the deeds. The two questions which remain to be decided are, first, whether Mr Hewett parted with dominion over the house; secondly, if he did, whether land is capable of passing by way of a *donatio mortis causa*. [Nourse LJ was unwilling to find that land was not capable of being the subject matter of a *donatio mortis causa*. This aspect of the case is dealt with below – see page 67.]

It is true that in the eyes of the law Mr Hewett, by keeping his own set of keys to the house, retained possession of it. But the benefits which thereby accrued to him were wholly theoretical. He uttered the words of gift, without reservation, two days after his readmission to hospital, when he knew that he did not have long to live and when there could have been no practical possibility of his ever returning home. He had parted with dominion over the title deeds. Mrs Sen had her own set of keys to the house and was in effective control of it. In all the circumstances of the case, we do not believe that the law requires us to hold that Mr Hewett did not part with dominion over the house. We hold that he did.

In *Woodard v Woodard* [1995] 3 All ER 980, one of the issues was that of delivery. A father was terminally ill in hospital. He had given his son the keys to his (the father's) car in order that the son could give his mother lifts to hospital. The father said several times that the son should keep the keys as he would not be driving the car any more. The father did not hand over the car registration document. The son later sold the car and the widow, who was the personal representative of the deceased, brought an action claiming the proceeds of sale for the estate. At first instance it was held that the father had made an *inter vivos* gift of the car to his son. The plaintiff appealed to the Court of Appeal where the son changed his defence to a plea of *donatio mortis causa*. The appeal was dismissed on the basis that there had been an effective *donatio mortis causa*, it being accepted that if there was an *inter vivos* gift it was conditional and made in contemplation of impending death. It was accepted that the words of the father were words of gift rather than, for example, an instruction to keep the car keys in order that the son would be able to use the car to visit hospital without there being an intention to give. It was, said the court, understood that if the father came out of the hospital he would have the car again. The main dispute was whether the deceased had parted with dominion over the car. One problem was whether a potential donor was able to make a gift when the object of the potential *donatio* was already in the possession of the donee as a bailee. It was argued that the only way that it was possible was if the potential donee handed the object back to the donor who then redelivered it to the donee. The court held that a gift was possible in such circumstances. The words operated to change the nature of possession from that of a bailee to that of a donee. This could result in an effective *donatio mortis causa*.

Another issue raised in **Woodard v Woodard** was whether a *donatio mortis causa* was possible given that there might have been another set of car keys. In **Re Craven's Estate** [1937] 3 All ER 33, the court had doubted if the parting with dominion requirement would be satisfied where a donor handed over a key to a locked box and retained a key for himself. In the instant case the court said that there was no evidence that there was another set and even if there was a second set it was probable that it was not with the deceased at hospital. If there had been another set of keys the court decided that whether or not dominion had been handed over would be a matter of deciding on the donor's intention. If the second set was retained to keep dominion over the car, then the requirements of a *donatio mortis causa* would not have been satisfied. In the instant case where the donor was in hospital suffering from a very grave illness, it would be unreal to conclude that there had not been a passing of dominion simply because there was or might have been a second set of keys in the donor's home which he was unable to use (and which he would remain unable to use unless circumstances changed dramatically).

The fact that the father had not handed over the registration document (or the certificate of insurance or service records) did not prevent there from being a *donatio mortis causa*. These documents were not essential indications of title: handing them over would simply go towards proving intention. (Megaw LJ doubted if the judge at first instance was correct in finding an intention to give the car either *inter vivos* or by way of a *donatio mortis causa*. However, he said that he did not feel sufficiently confident that the judge was wrong to lead him to dissent. He added that as to the other matters in the case he was fully in agreement with the rest of the court.) It was rather fortunate for the son that the court found that the car had passed to him as he had sold it and spent the £3,900 proceeds. While the case raises some interesting legal issues, it is, perhaps, an example of litigation which is rather difficult to justify. Dillon LJ thought it to be 'about the most sterile appeal that I have ever come across'. Both parties were on state benefits and legally aided and, had the son lost, there was no prospect of his satisfying the judgment.

The issue of parting with dominion was recently discussed by Jonathan Gaunt QC in **Vallee v Birchwood**. In the case the donor passed over the title deeds and a key to his house. Following **Sen v Hedley**, the court held that this was sufficient delivery for a valid *donatio mortis causa* and that, again following **Sen v Hedley**, it was possible for land to be the subject matter of a valid *donatio mortis causa*. (See below at p. 67.)

But one of the arguments put forward against there being a valid *donatio mortis causa* was that the donor had not parted with dominion over his house. He still lived there, the daughter did not in fact enter the house again until after the death of the donor and was not in any case, it was argued, at liberty to enter the house as and when she alone chose to. This state of affairs was contrasted with **Sen v *Hedley*** where the donor was in hospital and never returned to the house and in fact died only a few days after handing over the deeds and the key.

Jonathan Gaunt QC said:

> 37 . . . A gift by way of *donatio* does not become effective until the death of the donor, so the property remains both in law and in equity the property of the donor. There seems to be no reason why acts of continued enjoyment of his own property should be regarded as incompatible with his intention to make a gift effective on his death. Suppose, by way of example, that the subject matter of the gift was land already subject to a tenancy. Would the donor not be entitled to enjoy the rent while he lived? It seems to me that he would. He has not given it away. That would seem to be no different in principle from the donor continuing to enjoy his own house by living in it. The delivery of the deeds would have put it out of his power to transfer it and the handing over of the key as well would give the donee access to the house and diminish to some extent the donor's control.

> 41 It was also suggested to me that [the deceased] could have effected physical alterations to the house and, by retaining *de facto* possession and control, had not put it out of his power to do so. That is true in theory but in reality was never going to happen in the case of this elderly gentleman in failing health living in reduced circumstances in a dilapidated house in Reading – and *Sen* is authority that for this purpose the Court should look at the practical, and not the theoretical, possibilities.

> 42 There is no doubt that the concept of 'dominion' in this context is a slippery one. Its fundamental rationale appears to be that something must be done by way of delivery of the property or indicia of title sufficient to indicate that what is intended is a conditional gift and not something that falls short of that.

The judge took what he regarded as a practical and common sense approach to this issue in the case. But whether this is the correct approach is open to debate. It certainly is a rather liberal interpretation of what were previously understood to be the requirements for a valid *donatio mortis causa*. In fact in the context of *donationes mortis causa* of land the particular issue of dominion may well not be of very much long-term significance. It is probable that, as all land become registered land and that under the Land Registration Act 2012 land certificates are no longer issued, *donationes mortis causa* of land will no longer be possible. (See p. 67.)

Problem areas

A number of problems have arisen with respect to the *donatio mortis causa*.

Subject matter of a *donatio mortis causa*

A problem which arises is what kind of property can be the subject of a *donatio mortis causa*. This is closely linked with the requirement to part with dominion since one could not have a *donatio mortis causa* of property over which it is not possible to surrender dominion.

Cheques and shares

It seems therefore that the donor's own cheque made out to the donee cannot work as a *donatio mortis causa* since it always remains possible to cancel it, so the donor has not given up dominion over the money represented by the cheque. It is often said that there cannot be a *donatio mortis causa* of stocks and shares. This view is usually based on ***Ward v Turner*** (1872) 2 Ves Sen 431. In this case the court held that there was no effective *donatio mortis causa* over some South Sea annuities. It is possible that the decision was based on an inadequate delivery. In the case, only a symbol of title was delivered, not some essential indication of title or of the document needed to obtain possession. Here, only the receipts for the annuities were delivered. It may be that if the actual annuity documents had been handed over the decision would have been different. However, ***Ward v Turner*** has been followed in subsequent cases as being authority for railway stock not being subject to the doctrine (***Moore v Moore*** (1874) LR 18 Eq 474) and for building society shares not being subject to the doctrine (***Re Weston*** [1902] 1 Ch 680). But in ***Staniland v Willott*** (1852) 3 Mac & G 664, it was held that shares in a public company can be subject to a *donatio mortis causa*. There remains some doubt in this area. It may be, however, that the authority of ***Ward v Turner*** is not absolute and should be treated with caution. Additionally, as stated below, in ***Sen v Headley*** the court based its decision to include land within the classes of property that can be subject to a *donatio mortis causa*, at least in part, on the argument that to exclude land would be an anomaly. It may be that a similar argument could be used to support the case to include stocks and shares.

Land

For many years it was assumed, on the basis of nineteenth-century dicta, that land could not be the subject of a *donatio mortis causa*, and this was the main issue in ***Sen v Headley***, which finally concluded that it could. The problem arises because though the title deeds are good evidence of title, the owner is not prevented from acting as the owner, for example by declaring himself trustee for another, after he has surrendered them. This the Court of Appeal did not feel was crucial, though it will be remembered that they were also careful to point out that Mr Hewett had also in practice given up control of the house itself. The Court of Appeal decided that the doctrine of *donatio mortis causa* was anomalous and they were not willing to except land from it, as to do so would be itself anomalous.

In ***Vallee v Birchwood***, again the court allowed a DMC of land. In that case (see pp. 62 and 65), following ***Sen v Headley***, the court held that the delivery by the donor of the title deeds and a key to the house to the claimant accompanied by what he said, was a sufficient delivery of dominion over the property to constitute a valid *donatio mortis causa*.

But both ***Sen*** and ***Vallee*** were cases of unregistered land where title deeds were handed over by the donor. There has been no English case on *donationes mortis causa* of registered land. Since the Land Registration Act 2002, land certificates are no longer issued by the Land Registry. Unless a court held that handing over of the keys to a property alone constituted sufficient delivery for an effective *donatio* it is difficult to see how there can be an effective *donatio* of registered land. What essential indicia of title could be handed over by a would-be donor?

Digital property

Increasingly property only exists online, with no physical document of title which can be transferred as an 'essential indication of title'. For example, some bank accounts and savings accounts are only administered online and the account holder has no document which he could hand over to a donee. Perhaps if the account holder gave the donee the password and user name this would be held to suffice. But in such a case (and others involving digital property) the courts will need to decide whether or not a valid *donatio mortis causa* is possible over such property.

Contemplation of suicide

Is it possible to make a *donatio mortis causa* when contemplating suicide? The answer used to be 'probably not'. In the Irish case of ***Agnew v Belfast Banking Co*** [1896] 2 IR 204, the court held that a *donatio mortis causa* was not possible where the contemplation involved the then criminal offence of committing suicide as that would be against public policy. This view was adopted in ***Re Dudman*** [1925] 1 Ch 553. However, suicide is no longer a crime (Suicide Act 1961) and so, if the basis of ***Agnew v Belfast Banking Co*** and ***Re Dudman*** was that a gift cannot be given effect to by a criminal act, the law should now permit an effective *donatio mortis causa* in these circumstances. There may, of course, be public policy objections to such a gift. Additionally, it may be argued that since, presumably, one who attempts suicide rarely contemplates surviving, the requirement that the gift is intended to be conditional on death and that it will revert to the donor on recovery will be absent. It is to be assumed that in any case if death is contemplated from, for example, an illness and the donor later commits suicide, which was not contemplated when the gift was made, the gift would be good (see *Wilkes v Allington*, above).

Contemplation of death other than from a disease or illness

Can a *donatio mortis causa* only be made when the cause of death contemplated is disease or illness as opposed, for example, to a hazardous journey? Most of the cases do involve deaths from illness or disease. In ***Agnew v Belfast Banking Co*** [1896] 2 IR 204, it was said that the death must be from natural causes or incurred in the course of discharging some duty, possibly including self-sacrifice. This suggests that *donationes mortis causa* are possible in cases other than illness or disease.

In ***Re Miller*** (1961) 105 Sol Jo 207, a woman who was about to fly to Italy bought a policy of life assurance from a machine at the airport and then posted the insurance document to her sister. The plane crashed over Italy and she was killed. It was argued that she had made a *donatio mortis causa* of the policy. The executors asked the court to determine if there had been an effective *donatio mortis causa* or if the proceeds belonged to the estate. This argument that it was a valid *donatio mortis causa* was not upheld, Ploughman J deciding that she had not intended a *donatio mortis causa* (or indeed any gift at all) but that she had posted the insurance documents to her sister for safe keeping only. Additionally, Ploughman J doubted whether there was sufficient delivery as the letter was not delivered to the sister until after the woman was dead. The judge said there was no reason to apply the post rule and treat posting as the equivalent of delivery. But it is interesting to note that the court did not deny that a *donatio mortis causa* could have been made in these circumstances.

In ***Thompson v Mechan*** [1958] OR 357, the dangers of a normal air journey did not satisfy the requirements for a *donatio mortis causa*. Presumably, the contrary could be argued if the flight was unusually hazardous, perhaps using a light aircraft to fly over mountains or using an airline with a very poor safety record. Possibly the contemplation of a dangerous military mission could found a *donatio mortis causa*: ***Agnew v Belfast Banking Co*** [1896] 2 IR 204.

Can there be a *donatio mortis causa* if death is certain?

It has been argued that a *donatio mortis causa* is not possible if death is certain on the basis that if death is certain how, in any meaningful way, can the requirement of the gift being

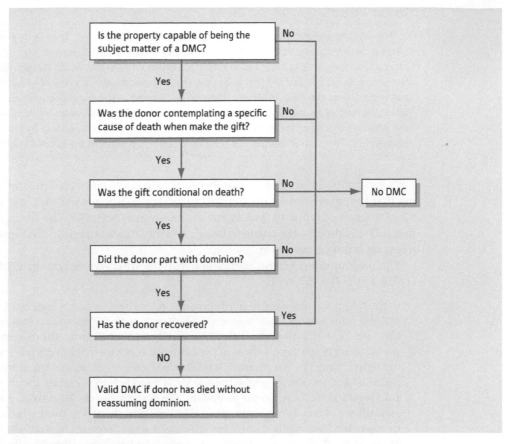

Figure 2.1 *Donatio mortis causa* (DMC)

conditional on death be met? The argument is that in such cases the only possibilities are an immediate *inter vivos* gift or an attempted testamentary gift (which would fail for non-compliance with s 9 of the Wills Act 1837).

Proprietary estoppel

Objective 5

Where a person spends money on property or otherwise acts to his detriment in reliance on a misrepresentation, the owner may be prevented from asserting his own rights against the person so relying. It may thus sometimes be an example of equity perfecting an imperfect gift, as the court may convey the property to the victim of the misrepresentation. However, it should be noted that the court has a wide discretion to take whatever steps are appropriate in the case to 'satisfy the equity' created by the estoppel. It should also be noted that proprietary estoppel of this nature is a cause of action in itself, rather than being a mere shield to liability, as is the case with other forms of estoppel such as promissory or common law estoppel.

For more on proprietary estoppel see Chapter 12 (p. 342).

An example of this principle, and its relationship to constructive trusts, is *Yaxley* v *Gotts* [2000] 1 All ER 711.

Yaxley v Gotts [2000] 1 All ER 711

In this case the plaintiff entered into an agreement with Gotts senior, that Gotts senior would purchase a certain house in need of refurbishment, and that the plaintiff would carry out the repair work and convert the property into flats, in return for which Gotts senior would transfer the ground floor flat to the plaintiff. In fact the house was purchased by Gotts senior's son, Alan, but the plaintiff did not know this at the time. However, when he discovered it, the plaintiff continued the renovation work that he had already begun and, when the flats were let, acted as agent in collecting the rents etc. After an argument, the plaintiff was excluded from the property and told by Alan that he had no interest in it. The plaintiff sought the granting of a 99-year lease of the ground floor flat.

The main issue was whether a proprietary right could be created in land, notwithstanding that the agreement for the plaintiff to receive an interest was oral, and so in breach of s 2 of the Law of Property (Miscellaneous Provisions) Act 1989. The Court of Appeal held that such a right could be created, though whether this was a result of estoppel or constructive trust is not entirely clear.

The preconditions for the operation of this doctrine were set out in **Willmott v Barber** (1880) 15 Ch D 96 by Fry J:

In the first place the plaintiff must have made a mistake as to his legal rights. Secondly, the plaintiff must have expended some money or must have done some act (not necessarily upon the defendant's land) on the faith of his mistaken belief. Thirdly, the defendant, the possessor of the legal right, must know of the existence of his own right which is inconsistent with the right claimed by the plaintiff. If he does not know of it he is in the same position as the plaintiff, and the doctrine of acquiescence is founded upon conduct with a knowledge of your legal rights. Fourthly, the defendant, the possessor of the legal right, must know of the plaintiff's mistaken belief of his rights. If he does not, there is nothing which calls upon him to assert his own rights. Lastly, the defendant must have encouraged the plaintiff in his expenditure of money or in the other acts which he has done, either directly or by abstaining from asserting his legal right . . . Nothing short of this will do.

What constitutes a sufficient act of detrimental reliance depends on the nature of the case, and a wide range of different types of act have been accepted.

Dillwyn v Llewelyn (1862) 4 De GF & J 517

In this classic case a father allowed his son into possession of land and purported to convey the land to the son, though the conveyance was in fact ineffective as it was not contained in a deed. In reliance on the mistaken belief that the land was his, the son spent £14,000 on building a house on the land, which the father encouraged him to do. The father then left the property to someone else by will. The reliance here was quite clear and the son was entitled to have the land conveyed to him.

It appears that once it has been shown that the guilty party gave an assurance to the innocent one leading the innocent party to believe they had an interest in the property, acts which could have been done in reliance on this will readily be presumed to be done in reliance, and the onus is on the person who gave the assurance to prove that the acts were not done in reliance on it. As Browne-Wilkinson V-C stated, *obiter*, in **Grant v Edwards** [1986] 2 All ER 426:

In many cases it is impossible to say whether or not the claimant would have done the act relied on as a detriment even if she thought she had no interest in the house . . . Once it has been shown that there was a common intention that the claimant should have an interest in the house, any act done by her to her detriment relating to the joint lives of the parties is sufficient detriment to qualify. The acts do not have to be inherently referable to the house. The holding out to the claimant that she had a beneficial interest in the house is an act of such a nature as to be part of the inducement to her to do the acts relied on. Accordingly, in the absence of evidence to the contrary, the right inference is that the claimant acted in reliance on such holding out and the burden lies on the legal owner to show that she did not do so.

The courts will clearly have to be careful to consider the exact nature of the claimant's belief if such a generous attitude to reliance is to be taken.

The recent trend has been away from strict adherence to the *Willmott* v *Barber* approach towards a more flexible approach, as indicated by Oliver J in *Taylor Fashions Ltd* v *Liverpool Victoria Trustees Co Ltd* [1981] 1 All ER 897 at 915:

> The application of the principle requires a very much broader approach which is directed to ascertaining whether, in particular individual circumstances, it would be unconscionable for a party to be permitted to deny that which, knowingly or unknowingly, he has allowed or encouraged another to assume to his detriment.

This unconscionability is established by the fact of the plaintiff's acting to his detriment in reliance on the assurance of the legal owner. This encouragement by the legal owner may be active, as in an assurance that the mistaken party has or will be granted an interest, or it may be passive, as in looking on while the mistaken party acts to his detriment. The acts done by the mistaken party must then be shown to have been done in reliance on that assurance. This is a matter of causation: it may be readily assumed, as in *Grant* v *Edwards* (above), but equally, depending upon the facts, it may be clear that causation has not been established, particularly where there are other plausible explanations for why the claimant behaved in the way he did. In *Wayling* v *Jones* [1993] EGCS 153, a particularly generous approach to the establishment of detrimental reliance was applied. W had remained living with J, and working for him for low wages, for many years. He had also been assured by J that J would leave him some property in his will, which he did not in fact do. It seemed clear from W's evidence that he would have remained with J even if the promise about the property had not been made. Balcombe LJ stated that there must be a sufficient link between the promises and the detriment, but that the promises did not have to be the sole inducement for the detriment. Given W's statement above, what degree of inducement was present here? A sufficient link was held to be established by the fact that W also stated that if J, having made the promises, had then stated that they would not be kept, W would have left. It is respectfully submitted that it is hard to see this as establishing 'but for' causation as it is usually understood.

The question of estoppel and its relationship to constructive trusts in the context of shared property is considered further in later chapters (see Chapters 12 at pp. 342 and 13 at p. 383).

Summary

- The equitable maxims provide a set of general principles which can be said to have influenced the development of equity. The maxims are examined in varying amounts of detail, identifying many of the particular areas of the law which have been affected, and which are dealt with later in the text.

See also Chapter 1 (p. 11).

- The maxim 'where the equities are equal the first in time prevails' establishes the basic rule of priorities, that is to say that where there are apparently overlapping or conflicting interests, a legal interest in property will take priority over an equitable one, and interests take priority in the order in which they were created, so an earlier interest will take priority over one created later.

- The maxim 'equity acts *in personam*' means that an equitable decree can bind an individual and hold him in contempt if he does not obey the decree, even in some cases where the individual is based abroad.

- The maxims 'equity will not perfect an imperfect gift' and 'equity will not assist a volunteer' mean that equity will not generally enforce an agreement in favour of someone who has not given consideration for it (has not 'paid' for the bargain), but there are exceptions.

- Under the rule in **Strong v Bird**, where the owner of property intends to give it to another but never completes the transfer, the gift may be completed if the intended donee is appointed the executor or administrator of the donor's estate on his death.

- The key requirements for a valid *donatio mortis causa* are a gift made in contemplation of death which is conditional on death and a parting with dominion over the subject matter of the gift.

- In some cases *donationes mortis causa* provide an exception to the maxim that equity will not assist a volunteer. In many cases simply handing over property will give the donee good title but in other cases (bank accounts and land for example) it will require the personal representatives to act in order to transfer title to the donee.

- Not all property can be the subject be matter of a valid *donatio mortis causa*. For example one's own cheque cannot be the subject matter of a *donatio mortis causa*. In the past there was doubt as to whether or not land could be the subject matter of a *donatio mortis causa* but it is now clear that certainly unregistered land can successfully be transferred by way of a *donatio mortis causa*. But doubts remain regarding registered land, particularly since the Land Registry has ceased issuing paper-based certificates of title.

- Under the principle of estoppel, a person who has relied on another's promise that certain property is his (the promisee's) or will be his in the future, may be able to enforce that promise and have the property transferred to him. This will only be possible if the court is satisfied that the promisee has acted to his detriment and that it would be unconscionable not to enforce the promise in his favour.

Further reading

The relationship between common law and equity

J E Martin, 'Fusion, fallacy and confusion' [1994] Conv 13.
Discusses the fact that equity and common law have not fused in the UK and compares the UK situation with that in New Zealand.

The equitable maxims

S Gardner, 'Two maxims of equity' [1995] CLJ 60.
Examines the application of the maxims 'equity regards as done that which ought to be done' and 'equity follows the law'.

M Halliwell, 'Equitable proprietary claims and dishonest claimants: a resolution?' [1994] Conv 62.
Considers the impact of dishonesty in the light of *Tinsley* v *Milligan*.

M Halliwell, 'Equitable property rights, discretionary remedies and clean hands' [2004] Conv 438–52.
Reflects on the 'clean hands' principle and its relationship to unconscionability. Focuses on the impact of the decision in *Tinsley* v *Milligan*.

P H Pettit, 'He who comes into equity must come with clean hands' [1990] Conv 416.
Considers whether the 'clean hands' principle has declined in importance.

The exceptions to the maxim that equity will not assist a volunteer: the rule in *Strong* v *Bird*

J Jaconelli, 'Problems in the rule in *Strong* v *Bird*' [2006] Conv 432.
Explains the development of the rule and its rationale and highlights key factors in its operation.

G Kodilinye, 'A fresh look at the rule in *Strong* v *Bird*' [1982] Conv 14.
A general analysis of the rule.

Donationes mortis causa

P V Baker, 'Land as a *donatio mortis causa*' (1993) 109 LQR 19.
Deals with *Sen* v *Headley* in which, contrary to earlier opinion, land was held to be capable of being the subject matter of a valid DMC.

Barlow A C H, 'Gifts *inter vivos* of a chose in possession by delivery of a key' (1956) 19 MLR 394.
A wide-ranging article that includes a discussion of the 'delivery' requirement with DMCs and, in particular, delivery where the subject matter is a chose in action and the effectiveness, in some situations, of the handing over of a key which is the means of accessing the subject matter of a DMC.

J Brook, '*King* v *Dubrey* – a *donatio mortis causa* too far?' Conv (2014) 6, 525–34.
Discusses *King* v *Dubrey* and whether or not a valid *donatio mortis causa* was created. Reviews the requirements for a valid *donatio mortis causa*. Also discusses if the case has endangered the formalities requirements under s 9 of the Wills Act 1837 for there to be valid testamentary disposition.

S Panesar, 'Title deeds to land and *donatio mortis causa*' (2014) Conv 1, 69–75.
Discusses *Vallee* v *Birchwood* and if there is a valid *donatio mortis causa* of land where the title deeds are transferred to the donee but the donor remains in control of the property for some months before death. Is it necessary for a donor to be terminally ill for a gift to be in 'contemplation' of death?

N Roberts, '*Donationes mortis causa* in a dematerialised world' Conv (2013) 2, 113–28.
Discusses if the abolition of the land certificate under the Land Registration Act 2002 makes it impossible to make a valid *donatio mortis causa* of registered land.

A Samuels, '*Donatio mortis causa* of a share certificate' [1966] 30 Conv 189.
Discusses the contentious point as to whether a DMC of shares is possible and if so what documents have to be delivered.

Proprietary estoppel

C Davis, 'Proprietary estoppel: future interests and future property' [1996] Conv 193G.
Considers how estopppel principles apply where the reliance has been on a promise of future property.

3

Trusts today

Objectives

After reading this chapter you should:

1. Understand and be able to explain that although the trust was initially created to be used in a domestic setting, the concept has been developed and is now often used for achieving business/commercial purposes. You should also understand that it is the flexibility of the trust that has facilitated the ever increasing range of applications.

2. Understand and be able to explain the main modern applications of the trust. Important applications of the trust concept include: pension provision, to avoid or at least minimise the impact of tax; unit trusts; to provide security for lenders and sellers of property; charitable trusts; to hold property on behalf of minors; to set up mechanisms for providing for one's family.

3. Understand that today trusts impact on individuals in a wide variety of contexts, often in situations where the layperson would not expect a trust to exist. One example is where a house is 'owned' by more than one person.

4. Understand that in some situations (for example, where the trust concept is used to provide a solution to disputes between cohabiting couples over the ownership of property) the solutions that trust laws provide sometimes seem at odds with what might be anticipated or expected, giving rise to claims that the law needs to be reformed. In fact there are proposals for reform in this area.

5. Understand that the trust (as recognised in England and Wales) is principally to be found in countries whose laws are based on the English common law (cf. civil law jurisdictions).

The trust concept in context

Objective 1

In the previous chapters the development of trusts was seen to have taken place in the context of solving private, family, problems. The reason why the law of trusts is still studied and is regarded as an important, perhaps vital, area of law is because the basic concept has been moulded, adapted and modified to deal with an enormous range of situations. The trust has moved out of the restricted area of the family into the commercial world. The concept which began as a way that a knight could protect his family while he was away, perhaps on a crusade, is now used in a wide variety of, sometimes complex, commercial and financial contexts.

The longevity of the trust is due to the fact that it is flexible, adaptable and versatile, and although of considerable antiquity the concept is still being developed and refined in exciting and creative ways.

Far from being a dry, remote subject, the law of trusts is a living, breathing, developing area of law. Trusts are used in a bewildering number of situations and a number of modern uses will be discussed in order to give a flavour of the versatility of the concept and to enable the relevance of trusts to everyday life to be appreciated. It is hoped that this discussion will serve to whet your appetite and fire your enthusiasm.

One key theme which runs through all the examples is that, unlike many other branches of the law, trust law can be used actively, creatively, inventively and imaginatively to solve a problem or to prevent a problem from arising, whereas in many areas the law is used in a reactive manner or is concerned to provide a framework to regulate activities.

However, there are problems for which the trust does not provide a solution. For example, it is generally not possible to provide benefits to purposes, as opposed to people, through the medium of a trust. Also there are some problems where the trust has been used to provide a solution but the results are far from satisfactory. An example of this is to be found in the area of the settlement of property disputes, particularly those involving the ownership of the family home.

This will be discussed in detail in Chapter 13.

There is currently a threat which *could* reduce the use and usefulness of trusts. One key characteristic of the trust is that the existence of a trust and its details can be kept away from public gaze. This can be very important where privacy and confidentiality are important. On 11 March 2014 the European Parliament voted in favour of revisions to the European Anti-Money Laundering Directive. There was general support from the Council of Ministers. There will be further negotiations within the European Commission and European Parliament.

One important feature of the proposals is the suggestion to establish a register for all trusts held in the EU. There are proposals that the register would be public. But at the time of writing it seems that each state will decide if the register should be public.

In a House of Lords debate, Treasury spokesman Lord Newby said that the government opposes a public central register of trusts and that the government considers registration of trusts to be a disproportionate approach and, in particular, one which undermines the common-law basis of trusts in the UK.

At the time of writing it is unclear the extent to which this proposal will be implemented and what level of detail will appear on the register. It seems that the register would have to record details that include the beneficiary with an interest in the trust's capital. Names and dates of birth would have to be disclosed. Under a discretionary trust, it seems that the beneficiaries must be disclosed as a class. Details of the subject of the trust would not be available.

The reason for the plans is to counteract tax avoidance. The UK is one of very few countries in the EU that uses trusts. Although trusts are widely used in the UK, they are little understood abroad. It seems that the rest of the EU views trusts with suspicion, believing them to be used for tax avoidance and money laundering. In fact this is rarely the case. It is thought that perhaps this 'ignorance' of the uses of trusts in the UK, often in a domestic context, has resulted in this proposal.

But whatever information that appears on the register, if it should become public, it would clearly threaten the future use of the trust. At the very least the increase in administration, gathering and registering the required details, would cause inconvenience and added expense to trusts. The effect could well result in either trusts being set up outside the EU or fewer trusts being set up.

Modern uses of the trust

Occupational pension funds

Objective
2

It is becoming commonplace for an employer to arrange a pension scheme for employees. Many employers find it almost essential to offer such a facility if they are to attract and retain employees. In many schemes both the employer and employee make pension contributions but in some cases the employer will make all the contributions. On retirement the employee will be entitled to an income and also will often be able to elect to take part of the entitlement in the form of a lump sum. Some pension schemes relate the entitlement of the employee to his salary at retirement. These are known as 'final salary schemes' or 'defined benefit schemes'. Under such schemes the size of the fund at any time needed to cover the current and potential pension payments is a matter for actuarial estimation. Because of the contribution levels or estimations about future investment returns, it may be that the estimates indicate that the fund is too large (or too small) to cover the liabilities both current and future. In the case of an actuarial surplus the vexed question arises as to whom the surplus belongs. This is discussed below. In other pension schemes the contributions will be invested to build up a fund which, on retirement, will be invested with an insurance company to buy an annuity and so the scale of the benefits depends on the size of the fund built up. Such schemes are known as money purchase schemes. Of late many companies have announced proposals to cease final salary schemes and replace them with money purchase schemes. This is very largely due to what companies regarded as the unacceptably high costs of providing final salary pensions.

The government is becoming increasingly concerned about how our ageing population will be financially supported in the future. Clearly the greater the percentage of people who retire with private pensions and who are not solely reliant on state support, the less will be the burden on the taxpayer. The problem is that many employees have not been within an occupational pension scheme and not all employers offered a pension scheme. The government has introduced a new law to make it easier for people to save for retirement. Under the Pensions Act 2008 most employees will be automatically enrolled into a pension scheme if they are not already in one. This provision, which is being phased in, will result in a far higher percentage of retired people having a private pension.

Why use a trust for pension schemes?

In most cases the pension scheme will be set up as a trust, with the contributions (from employees and usually from the employer as well) being paid to the trustees and being invested for the benefit of the employees/beneficiaries.

Underlying any pension scheme will be a contract between the employer and the employee under which obligations to contribute and benefits are set out. There is no requirement that a trust is established – for example, a pension scheme could be based purely on a contract between the employer and employee. But if a scheme operated purely contractually, there is no way that the employer could make a contribution – to whom would the contribution be paid?

In *Air Jamaica Ltd* v *Charlton* [1999] 1 WLR 1399 Lord Millett said:

> A pension scheme can, in theory at least, be established by contract between the employer and each employee and without using the machinery of a trust. Such a scheme would have to be very simple. It would look very like a self-employed pension policy. There would be no trust fund and no trustees. The employer would simply contract with each of his employees that, if the employee made weekly payments to the employer, the employer would pay the employee a pension on retirement or a lump sum on death. The employer would not make any contributions itself, since there would be no one to receive them.

There are a number of advantages to using a trust. First, this will separate the pension funds from other funds of the employer, which will be particularly important should the employer encounter financial difficulties. The beneficiaries will have a proprietary interest in the trust fund enabling them to assert a claim to the fund should the employer become insolvent. The trustees, who typically include representatives of the employer and of the employees, will be subject to strict fiduciary duties.

Another reason why pension schemes are often set up as trusts is because the tax/pension legislation requires an irrevocable trust to be used if important and generous tax advantages are to be obtained. As it is these tax advantages which allow the employer to offer such attractive pension plans to employees, it is almost inevitable that a trust will be used.

The employer who sets up the scheme can determine its structure, and unlike most trusts where the settlor's role ends once the trust has been created, with a pension trust the settlor (the employer) often has continued involvement.

But the protection outlined above can sometimes be more apparent than real if the employer has some control over the trustees (the employer may nominate trustees of the pension fund).

A very real problem with pension funds is potential fraud and the misappropriation or misuse of the pension funds. It was, partly, the ability of the employer to wield continued power that facilitated the fraud leading to millions of pounds of the Daily Mirror Group's employees' pension fund to go missing. The fraud came to light in 1991. Robert Maxwell was the head of a large number of enterprises including the *Daily Mirror* newspaper. After his mysterious death it was discovered that large sums of money had been misappropriated from the Daily Mirror pension fund.

One of the questions that the Daily Mirror pension fund affair raised was whether the trust was the appropriate vehicle for pension funds. It was thought by some that it was the unsuitability of the trust which caused or facilitated the syphoning of the Daily Mirror pension funds. Some argued, quite wrongly it is suggested, that the trust is inappropriate as it is a mediaeval concept unsuited to the modern device of the pension fund. This argument ignores the fact that trust law has developed and is at the heart of many modern commercial schemes. This is not to say that trust law may not need to be 'strengthened' in its application to pension funds. However, it may be argued that it would be impossible to devise any mechanism that was safe against the skilled and determined thief and that the disappearance of the Daily Mirror funds was a direct consequence of determined fraudulent behaviour rather than the result of any weakness of trust law.

In the aftermath of the Daily Mirror pension fund affair, the House of Commons Select Committee on Social Security Report on the operation of pension funds (1991–2) criticised 'mediaeval trust law' as an unsuitable basis for pension law and recommended, *inter alia*, that there should be a Pension Act to regulate pension funds. The Report also suggested the setting up of a committee of inquiry. The suggestion of the Select Committee was accepted and the government set up a Pension Law Review Committee to investigate the operation of pension funds under the chairmanship of Professor Goode (the Goode Committee) which resulted in the production of the Pension Law Reform Report (Cm 2342, 1993).

The Committee's main recommendation was that trust law should remain as the basis of pension schemes but that there should be a Pensions Act which would provide a regulatory framework for pension funds. It was also recommended that a Pension Regulator should be appointed with the power to monitor and enforce proper standards. The Regulator should have wide powers, and trustees should be required to submit annual reports to him. It was recommended that a compensation scheme should be set up to cover losses through fraud or theft. The Report also recommended that in the case of schemes with over 50 members, the members should have the right to appoint a proportion of the trustees.

The Committee made a number of other recommendations aimed at safeguarding pension funds, a detailed discussion of which is beyond the scope of this text. The Report was followed by the issue of a Pensions White Paper in June 1994, which endorsed many of the views of the Goode Committee. In particular, it was proposed that the law of trusts would remain as the basis for pension funds (see below). The White Paper proposed a number of important changes which would, it was intended, increase confidence in the security of pension funds and reduce the chances of another Daily Mirror type of scandal. Following on the White Paper, the Pensions Act 1995 was passed.

Exercise of powers by employers

In *Imperial Group Pension Trust Ltd* v *Imperial Tobacco Ltd* [1991] 2 All ER 597, the issue of the duties of employers when exercising powers contained in a pension scheme was considered. It was held that the fact that there was a contractual relationship of employer/ employee was important and that, in exercising any power under the scheme, the employer was bound by his obligation of good faith towards his employees. Browne-Wilkinson V-C, after having said that in traditional private trusts there would be no question of an 'outsider' being under a fiduciary duty, stated that pension scheme trusts were different in nature to traditional trusts under which the settlor, by way of bounty, transferred property to trustees to hold for the beneficiaries as objects of his bounty. In most traditional trusts, there would be no legal relationship between the parties apart from the trust, and the beneficiaries would be in the position of volunteers having provided no consideration for their benefits. Browne-Wilkinson V-C thought that a pension scheme was different. There was an element of consideration provided by the beneficiaries in that the benefits were part of the consideration which an employee received from the employer in return for the provision of his services. The employer had a fiduciary power in the 'full sense'. It was the duty of the employer to act in a way that did not offend 'the implied obligation of good faith' which was present in every contract of employment. The employer could exercise a power only in a way that was to his financial interest if to do so would not be a breach of this obligation of good faith.

Is there a separate law of trust for pensions?

It has to be admitted that the position is not clear and the attitude of the judges is not consistent. The uncertainty and lack of clarity is evidence of the problems that still exist when rules that originally developed in the context of family, often small-scale, trusts are extended to the commercial arena, where the trusts are often very large and often involve contractual relationships.

Although pension trusts are, in principle, simply another application of the trust concept, they do have some particular characteristics and problems. For example, as was stated by Browne-Wilkinson V-C in *Imperial Group Pension Trust Ltd* v *Imperial Tobacco Ltd*, unlike many trusts, pension trusts are intimately involved in the contractual arrangements between employer and employee. The provision of the pension scheme is part of the consideration that an employee receives from the employer in return for the services rendered under the contract of employment. The beneficiaries, unlike those in most trusts, provide consideration for the benefits received. There are other, practical, differences between pension trusts and most other trusts. They are often very large both in terms of the size of the trust funds and the number of beneficiaries. In *Imperial Group Pension Trust Ltd* v *Imperial Tobacco Ltd*, Browne-Wilkinson V-C considered that pension trusts 'are of quite a different nature to traditional trusts'.

But in *Cowan* v *Scargill* [1984] 2 All ER 750, Megarry V-C said that 'the trusts of pension funds are subject to the same rules as other trusts', and in the context of investment policy Megarry V-C said that there is 'no reason for holding that different principles apply to pension fund trusts from those which apply to other trusts'.

It does seem, however, that commercial reality is prevailing over dogged determination to view all trusts as being bound by the same rules, and there are a number of examples when the courts appear to be willing to consider pension trusts as different from non-commercial trusts. Additionally, there is evidence that the existence of commercial trusts in general, and pension trusts in particular, has influenced (and perhaps will continue to influence) the development of the law. For example, in order for a trust to be validly created the beneficiaries must be defined with certainty. The certainty tests were reviewed by the House of Lords in *McPhail* v *Doulton* [1970] 2 All ER 228. This case concerned a pension trust. Without the changes to the certainty test made in the case, the pension scheme would have failed and many, if not most, other pension schemes along with it. Another example of the courts acting in an innovative way in relation to pension trusts is *Mettoy Pension Trustees Ltd* v *Evans* [1991] 2 All ER 513. Here the court considered that the power of the employer to appoint a pension fund surplus was a fiduciary power. As there was nobody who could exercise the power, the court exercised it. This pension fund case is the only example of the court's exercising a fiduciary power.

This will be discussed in Chapters 4 and 5.

See Chapter 16 (p. 464) for a discussion of the rights of beneficiaries to information relating to the reasons for exercising a discretion by trustees.

The issue of the extent to which pension trusts were governed by general, as opposed to specific, trust rules arose again in a series of cases in the mid-1990s. In *Wilson* v *Law Debenture Trust Corp plc* [1995] 2 All ER 337, Rattee J was very positive in stating that:

> it would in my judgment be wrong in principle to hold that the long-established principles of trust law as to the exercise by trustees of discretions conferred on them by their trust instruments . . . no longer apply to them and that the trustees are under more onerous obligations to account to their beneficiaries than they could have appreciated when appointed on the basis of the relevant trust law as it has stood for so long.

This case, which involved an attempt by beneficiaries to force the trustees to disclose the reasons for the exercise of a discretion, is discussed later (see p. 465).

A further series of cases has similarly focused on the issue of whether and to what extent the basic trust rule of 'no conflict' applies to pension trusts. This rule of trusts states that a trustee must not place himself in a position where personal interest and his duty towards the beneficiaries come into conflict. The normal effect of the trustee acting in a situation where the conflict exists or may exist is that any transaction, purchase, transfer, etc. is void. It has to be admitted that the cases do not leave the position entirely clear.

In *Re William Makin& Sons Ltd* [1993] OPLR 171, Vinelott J thought that the rule did apply to prevent a liquidator as sole trustee exercising a discretion over the destination of a pension fund surplus. The liquidator wished that the discretion be exercised to allocate the surplus to the company, thus making it available to the creditors rather than using all or some of the surplus to increase benefits. In *British Coal Corporation* v *British Coal Staff Superannuation Scheme Trustees Ltd* [1993] PLR 303, Vinelott J (commenting on criticism of his decision in *Re William Makin& Sons Ltd*) said he considered it outrageous that a person who has the power to distribute a fund among a class which includes himself should be able to apply the fund, or any part of it, to himself.

In *Re Drexel Burnham Lambert UK Pension Plan* [1995] 1 WLR 32, Lindsay J adopted a more flexible, and some would say a more appropriate, approach. He thought that there was no reason to apply special rules to pension trusts and cited Sir Robert Megarry's decision in *Cowan* v *Scargill* in support of this approach but nevertheless was able to find in the case justification for not applying one of the most basic trust rules. In the case the trustees, who were also beneficiaries, sought the direction of the court regarding their exercise of a discretion regarding the distribution of a pension fund surplus on the winding up of the scheme. Under the terms of the scheme the trustees, after providing for stipulated liabilities, had absolute discretion to apply the surplus to secure further benefits and remaining amounts were to be apportioned among the employers. The court was asked whether the rule against entering engagements where personal interest and fiduciary duty conflict applied here. Clearly, to the extent that the trustees were beneficiaries, there might be a danger that in exercising their discretions they would be influenced by the effect of their decisions on their personal interests as beneficiaries.

The court held that the 'no conflict' rule was a positive rule and did not necessarily require issues of immorality or wrongdoing to be considered. However, the rules of equity, the court said, were adaptable and examples of existing exceptions to the general rule had been presented to the court. It was within the jurisdiction of the court to give directions permitting the implementation of the proposed scheme despite the position of conflict. The court decided that in this case the rule did not prevent the trustees from exercising their discretion. On the facts, they had taken a great deal of independent advice from professionals representing each class of interested beneficiary. There had been 'fine-tuning' to meet the argument of the interested parties. No one opposed the proposed scheme. There was no evidence that the trustees had unfairly attempted to take advantage of their position to enhance the benefits to the class to which they belonged.

The case involved a pension trust but it is arguable that the case shows a more 'realistic' approach to trusts in the commercial arena. The decision may of course be more general and not specifically commercially focussed, i.e. that the non-conflict rule does not apply where on the evidence there has not been an abuse of the trustees' position. In the particular case the trustees had not placed themselves in a position of conflict by 'pushing themselves forward to be trustees but rather were selected as persons able and willing to serve their colleagues in such a way'. He did not deal with an issue raised in other cases as to whether the general 'no conflict' rule can be ousted by an express provision in the trust deed.

Lindsay J said, in the context of pension trusts, that:

> [M]any laymen would see the fact that a man is both trustee and, as employee, a beneficiary as not only not a bar but a downright advantage to a man or woman in undertaking his or her important duties.

He, further, quoted the Goode Report – Pension Law Reform – published in 1993, which stated that:

In modern times conflicts of interests cannot be avoided. They have to be managed. As long as trustees are aware of the potential for conflict and know what is required of them as trustees, they will be able to carry out their duties to the best of their abilities.

In approving the proposal Lindsay J subjected it to 'jealous and scrupulous examination'.

In some cases the courts have used the contractual basis of pension schemes as a method of giving the courts powers of supervision and control.

Surpluses

A particular problem arises in relation to pension funds which contain surplus funds.

It was not uncommon for companies, deliberately or accidentally, to build up a larger pension fund than is needed to fund the potential liabilities (i.e. the pensions that must be paid out). During periods when the stock markets perform badly, surpluses are much more rare, indeed many funds may fall into deficit. There are three ways to reduce a surplus: first, by the employer ceasing to make any more contributions until the surplus has gone; second, by enhancing the benefits of present and future pensioners; and third, by transfer to the employer.

Employers and employees may both assert a right to a surplus under a resulting trust. Unlike 'normal' voluntary trusts, the provisions of the trust are a product of the agreement between the employer and the employees and in most cases the destination of a surplus will depend on an interpretation of the trust deed. Normally any clear statement in the trust deed will be conclusive. In some cases the trust deed may make no provision for the distribution of a surplus. But there appears to be a presumption that the trust deed does not exclude a resulting trust.

In *Davis v Richards and Wallington Industries Ltd* [1991] 2 All ER 563 Scott J said that a resulting trust could be excluded either by an express provision or by implication. In this case part of the surplus arose because the employer had made overpayments and the court decided that the part of the surplus relating to these overpayments should be returned to the employer as, in essence, the court decided that the overpayments were made as the result of inaccurate actuarial assumptions. The repayment was not due under a resulting trust and the court said that the part which related to the contributions of the employees was *bona vacantia*, there being no resulting trust under which the employees could claim. It can be argued that the employees did not intend to give out-and-out and that they should be entitled to recover a share of the surplus under a resulting trust.

In *Air Jamaica Ltd v Charlton* [1999] 1 WLR 1399 Lord Millett, giving the opinion of the Privy Council, said that *prima facie* a pension surplus was held on a resulting trust for those who contributed to the fund. As the fund was made up by equal contributions by the company and the employees, it should be held on a resulting trust, half for the company and half for the employees.

Employee ownership trusts

These trusts are attractive in some situations, giving commercial benefits in terms of employee commitment, loyalty and reduced staff turnover, all helping to make the business more successful. Also they can be an effective way of ensuring the succession of a business where, for example, the owner of a business has no family who wish to take over running of the company but the owner wants to retire.

Many schemes are set up as indirect employee benefit schemes whereby the shares in the company are held on an employee trust for the benefit of the staff.

From 1 October 2014 there can be income tax benefits and up to £3,600 of bonuses awarded to employees can be exempt from income tax.

In the 2013 budget the Chancellor announced capital gains and inheritance tax incentives where shares are transferred into an employee trust. These are contained in the Finance Act 2014.

As would be expected there are (complicated) rules that have to be met to qualify for the tax incentives but a detailed discussion is beyond the scope of this text.

Employee benefit trusts

These trusts are used by high-earning employees. The aim is to minimise income tax and national insurance contributions on earnings.

In essence the trust is a discretionary trust with 'offshore' trustees. It is designed as a repository for any earning that the employee does not need immediate access to. The idea is that the trustees can distribute the trust fund when it is tax advantageous to do so. This could be after the employee has retired or has become a non-UK resident. Ideally there is no employee tax charge until the trustees distribute benefits. This may be years after those benefits have been earned.

The tax regime relating to these trusts is very complex and the rules are tightening. As a result the trusts are normally set up and administered by specialist providers.

Personal injury trusts

By the use of appropriate trusts it is possible to ensure, for example, that damages received as the result of personal injury give the person awarded the damages the maximum benefits from the invested damages, while preserving, as far as possible, any entitlement to means-tested state benefits.

Trusts for disabled people

There can be significant tax advantages for trusts set up for qualifying disabled people. The Finance Act 2013 significantly simplified the taxation of these trusts. It is of course important, when setting up such a trust, to be careful that the trust will have as little effect as possible on the rights of the disabled person to receive state benefits.

Trading trusts

It is possible to set up a trust under which the trustees carry on a trade or profession. One of the main attractions of such a vehicle used to be as a tax shelter. Profits generated by a trading trust would bear tax at rates that compared very favourably with the rate of corporation tax or the high rates of income tax paid by individuals. At times when the rates of corporation tax and personal income tax have been reduced, much of the attractiveness of the trading trust will be removed.

Property held by nominees

There may be a number of reasons why the prospective purchaser of property would wish to keep his identity a secret. This may be particularly important in the area of commerce when a holding of property or shares is being built up and where, if the identity of the purchaser was known, opposition might grow or the price asked for future parcels of the property might be raised. In such a case it might well be prudent to arrange for the property to be transferred into the name of a nominee who will hold on trust for the 'real' owner. To the outside world the property will be owned by the nominee. If the property consists of shares, it will be the nominee who is registered as the owner of the shares.

The registration of shares in a nominal owner can also be of advantage to a purchaser who is able to negotiate a purchase without being concerned as to the identity of any 'real' or beneficial owner. This form of ownership may also be a sensible option if the owner plans to delegate to the nominee the power to manage the investments.

The government is currently planning to introduce legislation to improve the transparency of company ownership. The changes will affect anyone who directly or indirectly owns, is entitled to or controls more than 25 per cent of shares in a UK company. In such cases the identity of the beneficial owner will be recorded on a publicly available register. This will severely curtail the usefulness of nominee holdings in many commercial situations.

Blind trusts

These are trusts where the beneficiaries have no control over the trust assets, do not know how the trustees are dealing with trust assets and do not know what trust assets have been bought or sold.

These trusts are used, for example, by government ministers and are supposed to inspire confidence that any decisions made by the minister will not involve a conflict of interest if they make decisions that could affect the value of the trust assets.

The beneficiaries can take profits or income out of the trust, and of course when they retire from office the beneficiary can regain full control over the trust assets.

Investment trusts

Investment trusts are included in the discussion in order to make the point that they are not trusts at all. The term 'investment trust' is used to describe a company that has been set up to buy and hold shares of other companies. An investor in an investment trust company simply buys shares in that company in the usual way. The price or value of the shares depends on the value of the shares held by the company and its future prospects.

Unit trusts

Investing in unit trusts seems, superficially, to be very similar to investing in an 'investment trust'. But in fact unit trusts present a true example of the trust in operation. Unit trusts have provided a very valuable means for many people to invest their money in the stock exchange without attracting all of the usual risks. As a result of this opening up of the stock market, the trust has fulfilled a vital commercial function, both for the investors and for the companies seeking to use the stock exchange to raise finance.

A unit trust will be set up and will buy shares in companies. The establishment and running of unit trusts is very closely regulated by statute. The fund is valued and 'split' into units of equal value. Each contributor will be allocated a number of units reflecting his contribution. The public will be invited to buy units in the fund. Their purchase money will be deposited with the trustees until it is needed to buy more investments. The investments are vested in the trustees for the benefit of those holding units. The investment decisions will be made by the fund manager and clearly his skills are vital if the trust is to prosper. It is this delegation of the investment decisions to the manager that has removed some of the risk in stock market investment for the general public. Also the size of the underlying funds means that there can be a much wider spread of investments, again tending to reduce the risk. The unit trust industry has been very creative in offering a range of different funds in which the public can buy units. Some unit trusts are set up with the purpose of investing either for capital growth or for maximum income or for a balance between the two. Some unit trusts have been set up with a narrow investment focus. For example, there are unit trusts on offer which concentrate only on investing in Japanese companies.

The holders of units will receive income on their units, unless the unit trust is one set up only to achieve capital growth. The income is liable to income tax. Holders of units may sell their units. The value of a unit at any given time depends on the value of the underlying investments.

To provide security for lenders of money

See Chapter 1.

The distinction between trusts and contract was discussed earlier and particular attention was drawn to the issue of loans. It was decided in cases such as *Barclays Bank* v *Quistclose Investments Ltd* [1968] 3 All ER 651 that it is possible to have a loan and a trust existing side by side. The effect of this is that a well-advised lender can ensure security for his loan by attaching a trust to it. He then becomes a beneficiary under the trust, which, as was seen, provides very useful protection, particularly if the borrower becomes bankrupt.

(See also pp. 20–30, 99 and 266 for further discussion of Quistclose trusts.)

To provide security for buyers where goods are paid for in advance

The trust device can be used to provide security for a person who is paying for goods before they are ready for delivery. *Re Kayford* [1975] 1 All ER 604 is an example of this use (see p. 27). As noted, Megarry J said that the case concerned claims to deposits made by 'domestic' customers and that 'Different considerations may perhaps arise in relation to trade creditors'.

Retaining legal title

Where a supplier of materials fears for the financial future of the one he is supplying, he may use a 'Romalpa' clause or a reservation of title clause in the contract under which the materials are supplied (*Aluminium Industrie Vaassen B* v *Romalpa Aluminium Ltd* [1976] 2 All ER 552). The plaintiffs supplied aluminium foil. Under the terms of the contract title was not to pass until the defendants had paid all debts owed to the plaintiff. The defendants were required to store the foil in such a way that the foil supplied by the plaintiff could be identified. (The defendants bought foils from a number of suppliers.) When the defendants became insolvent, it was held that the plaintiffs were entitled to the foil held by the defendants that could be identified as having been supplied by the plaintiffs, the title to which remained with the plaintiffs under the terms of the contract of supply. However, the defendants had also sold on some of the unmixed foil and the proceeds were placed in a separate bank account. The court held that the defendants had sold the foil as the agent of the plaintiffs and so a fiduciary relationship existed between them. Thus, the court said, the plaintiffs were able to trace into the proceeds of sale. The court, it seems, considered that the retention of ownership satisfied the equitable tracing requirement of an equitable proprietary interest. (See p. 504 for further discussion of tracing.)

This particular device does not depend on or indeed involve a trust *per se* but may involve equitable tracing.

Voluntary arrangements with creditors

When a debtor enters into a voluntary arrangement with the requisite majority of creditors, assets are vested in the supervisor of the arrangement. An arrangement can be made by an individual or by a company. It has been held that these assets are held by the supervisor on trust for the creditors who are party to the agreement and the assets are not available to creditors generally on the liquidation of the company (*Re Leisure Study Group Ltd* [1994] 2 BCLC 65) or bankruptcy of the individual (*Re Bradley-Hole, ex p Knight* [1995] BCCC 418).

Land which is shared

Objective
3

The law relating to land which is held by more than one person was changed by the Trusts of Land and Appointment of Trustees Act 1996 as from 1 January 1997.

The property may be held on trust for the beneficiaries either as tenants in common or as joint tenants, but the legal estate must either be vested in one person or if there is more than one person the legal estate must be vested in them as joint tenants. A very common example of this type of trust is where a husband and wife buy a matrimonial home together.

Before 1997

If land was held by more than one person, a trust for sale, with a power to postpone sale, was imposed by the Law of Property Act 1925 ss 31–36 if there was not an express trust for sale. Section 25(1) of the Law of Property Act 1925 provided that a power to postpone sale should be implied into every trust for sale.

After 1996

The Trusts of Land and Appointment of Trustees Act 1996 made important changes which became operational from 1 January 1997. All trusts where the trust property includes land or any interest in land will be trusts of land. All such trusts, whether created before or after 1 January 1997, fall into this category with the exception of Settled Land Act settlements that were created before that date. Under a trust of land the trustees hold the legal estate on trust with a power to sell and a power to retain. The interests of beneficiaries are interests in land. The appropriate provisions contained in ss 31–36 of the Law of Property Act 1925 have been amended to impose trusts of land. The principle of overreaching remains and applies to sales under trusts of land. Any disposition of the legal estate in land will overreach the trusts, provided the proceeds are paid to two or more trustees or a trust corporation. (Overreaching describes the situation where land held on trust is sold. The interests of the beneficiaries are transferred from the land into the proceeds of sale.)

Under s 14 of the Trusts of Land and Appointment of Trustees Act 1996, any person who is a trustee of land or who has an interest in property subject to a trust of land may apply for a court order for sale. Unlike under s 30 of the Law of Property Act which s 14 modified, the powers of the court are not restricted to cases where the trustees refuse to exercise powers of disposition or where their consents cannot be obtained. The court can make any order relating to the exercise by the trustees of any of their functions. This can include relieving trustees from the need to obtain consent to the exercise of any function. The court can, under s 14, intervene to stop any dealing with land. Section 14 provides a list of factors that the court should take into account when exercising its powers under the section. These include the intentions of those who created the trust, the purposes for which the property is held, the welfare of any minor who occupies (or may reasonably be expected to occupy) the land as his home, and the interests of any secured creditor of a beneficiary. The court must also take account of the views of the beneficiaries when considering an application arising from the refusal or restriction of a beneficiary's right of occupation. It is open to doubt as to whether the existence of creditors means that their rights should prevail and lead to a sale.

Dear v *Robinson* [2001] All ER (D) 351 (Oct) is a case which is an example of the Court, of Appeal, taking into account changes in circumstances that occurred between the initial hearing and the appeal. At first instance, the court made an order for the sale of property but there then occurred a significant change of circumstances, which justified reversing the order, and postponing the sale. The property was held in the joint names of D and K. In 1988 D and K granted T a right of pre-emption to purchase the property at open market value. Later disputes arose between D and K (and R the second respondent) about their respective beneficial interests in the property and K applied for an order that the property should be sold.

D argued that the property should not be sold as he wanted to live in the property. Nevertheless an order for sale was ordered. After this order, D wanted to appeal and commenced to seek permission to appeal. He then acquired the benefit of the right of pre-emption from T's trustee in bankruptcy. D realised that he would now be able to buy the property at an advantageous price if the order for sale remained in force and he then sought to abandon his application for leave to appeal. On the other hand, R, who was supported by K, now wished the sale of the property to be postponed until after the right of pre-emption expired in 2008. The court held that D would be allowed to discontinue his application for permission to appeal. The significant change in circumstances since the judge's order (D's acquisition of the right of pre-emption, and the fact that the majority of the beneficiaries now opposed an immediate sale) meant that it was appropriate to reverse the judge's order for an immediate sale and to order that the sale be postponed until 2008. The court stated that D could not complain that such an order deprived him of the benefit of the right of pre-emption since it was clearly arguable that he had acquired that right as trustee on behalf of himself and his fellow beneficiaries. The appeal was allowed.

Settling property disputes

Objective 4

Traditionally, one of the most significant applications of the trust is in the area of settling disputes over the ownership of property. Often, two or more people claim to own a single piece of property, or claim that they are entitled to a share in a single piece of property. Disputes of this kind are particularly common in the context of the ownership of a 'family home'. Two people who may or may not be married to one another are involved in the acquisition of a house in which they will live. There are a large number of possible arrangements that may exist. One of the simplest cases is where the conveyance of the house is taken in the name of only one of them although both parties contribute to the purchase price. The law of trusts may well determine that the party in whose name the conveyance was taken holds the property on a resulting trust for them both, their shares in the beneficial interest being proportionate to their contributions. Other more difficult situations will often occur, for example, where one party makes no contribution to the purchase price but does make significant contributions to the family in other ways, perhaps by looking after the house and children, or by paying some of the family expenses or by doing work on the house. The law of trusts will determine what, if any, interest this partner will be entitled to as a result of this type of 'contribution'. The law may use the device of the resulting or the constructive trust to settle property disputes. (See pp. 14–18 for an outline of these types of trust and Chapters 11,12 and 13 for a full discussion.) Many of the cases deal with settling disputes over real property, often the family home, but trust law is also relevant to disputes relating to personal property.

See Chapter 11 (p. 261) for a detailed discussion of resulting trusts.

The House of Lords decision of **Stack v Dowden** [2007] 2 All ER 929 marked the start of a new approach and in most, if not all cases, the courts will use the constructive, and not the resulting, trust when deciding on the ownership of the beneficial interest in the family home. The case concerned a dispute over the ownership of a family home and in that context the court (and Baroness Hale, in particular) said that in such cases the starting point is to look at how the legal estate in the property is owned by the registered owner(s). If the legal title is held by a husband and wife as joint tenants, the presumption is that the beneficial ownership will be held as joint, equal owners. The burden is on the person who claims that the ownership should be different to produce evidence that the parties intended this to be different, so as to prove a 'constructive trust'. Similarly if the legal estate is vested in the sole name of one of the parties, the starting point when determining the beneficial ownership is that person in whose name the property is registered owns the entire beneficial interest. Again, the burden lies on the other party if they claim that they have a share or own the entire beneficial interest.

See Chapter 12 (pp. 261, 297) for a detailed discussion of constructive trusts.

If there is an express declaration of how the beneficial interest is held in most cases this will be conclusive. The above approach is only relevant where there is no such declaration.

The solutions provided by trust law to settling property disputes between home-sharers are often less than satisfactory. The Law Commission has looked into the issues involved in what has been described as an unfair and illogical area of law and on 31 July 2007 it published its report 'Cohabitation: the financial consequences of relationship breakdown' (Law Com. No. 307).

See Chapter 13 (p. 350) for a detailed discussion of shared homes.

It should be noted that if the dispute relates to the property of a married couple on divorce or, since the Civil Partnership Act 2004, the property of a same-sex couple whose formally registered partnership has been formally dissolved, the courts have a wide discretion when determining the property settlement and the normal trust principles referred to above do not apply.

Bodies not able to hold property

There are many bodies or entities that cannot hold property, and in many cases a transfer of property to be held on trust for the body or entity will provide a method for property to be held and used for their advantage.

See Chapter 9 (p. 199) for a discussion on unincorporated associations.

The issue of the property of clubs has been referred to above. The inability to hold property is a problem with any unincorporated association, including many charities. Transfer to trustees to hold for the association will in some cases be an appropriate course to adopt.

There are occasions when there are legal impediments to the holding of property such as the case of the inability of minors to hold the legal estate in land, discussed above.

A very old use of the trust concept involves the inability of a community of Franciscan friars to hold property because of their vow of poverty. If someone wished to benefit such a community, the transfer of property on trust for the monks was an obvious possibility.

Clubs and unincorporated associations

Unless a club has been incorporated it is not a legal person and cannot hold property, yet in the vast majority of cases there will be 'club' property. This may be money and in some cases land (perhaps the club house). It is common for the property of an **unincorporated association** to be vested in trustees for the benefit of the club members. They will normally hold the property for the members, to be dealt with according to the rules of the club. The trustees will usually be members of the committee of the club, and if the property is land the legal estate will be vested in (up to four) trustees as joint tenants on a trust for sale as the beneficial ownership is shared.

This will be discussed further in Chapter 9.

Trade union funds

Under the Trade Union and Labour Relations (Consolidation) Act 1992 s 12, provision is made for trustees to hold the union funds on trust for the union (not for the members). Individual members are able to seek the assistance of the courts if the trustees act improperly and the court may, if appropriate, order the removal of the trustees.

Minors

It is often not possible or desirable for property to be owned outright by minors. The Law of Property Act 1925 s 1(6) provided that a minor could not own the legal estate in land, but of course the legal estate could be vested in adults to hold on trust for the minor. The Law of Property Act 1925 did not prevent a minor from owning the equitable interest in land. A purported conveyance of a legal estate to a minor operated, under s 27 of the Settled Land Act 1925, as an agreement for valuable consideration to execute a settlement in favour of the minor and in the meantime to hold the land in trust for him. If a minor became entitled to a fee simple absolute in possession, the land became settled land (s 1(1)(ii)(d) of the Settled Land Act 1925).

Under the Trusts of Land and Appointment of Trustees Act 1996, which has been operative since 1 January 1997, the situation has changed. Schedule 1 contains a number of important provisions. Where, after 1996, a person purports to convey a legal estate in land to a minor or minors alone, it operates as a declaration that the land is held in trust for the minor(s), or, if he purports to convey it to the minor(s) in trust for any persons, it will operate as a declaration that the land is held in trust for those persons. If a person purports to convey a legal estate in land to the minor(s) and another person or persons of full age, the conveyance vests the land in the other person(s) in trust for the minor(s) and the other person(s). If a person purports to convey the legal estate in land to minor(s) and other person(s) of full age in trust for any persons, then this operates to vest the legal estate in the person(s) of full age on trust for the third parties.

As far as items of personalty are concerned there is no legal reason why a minor should not be the legal owner but, of course, there may well be practical reasons why minors, especially young minors, should not be the legal owners. This will often be the case if the property is very valuable or if it can be easily alienated or turned into cash which might be wasted away. In such cases the obvious answer is to arrange for the property to be held on trust for the minor. The terms of the trust may well state that the minor will be entitled to the property once he attains the age of majority.

Charities

See Chapter 10 (p. 216) for a detailed discussion of charitable trusts.

One of the earliest uses of the trust was to enable property to be given for a charitable purpose specified by the donor. The property would be transferred to trustees to hold on trust for the charitable purposes described by the transferor. This still remains a much-used application of the trust. Charitable trusts are an exception to the general rule that trusts must have human beneficiaries – trusts for such purposes being generally not possible.

Non-charitable purpose trusts

As a general rule it is only possible to create trusts with human beneficiaries and, in the main, trusts for non-charitable purposes are invalid. There are, however, a number of exceptions to this general rule.

It is possible to create a trust by will for the maintenance of particular animals or for the erection or maintenance of a specified tomb. Additionally, a trust for the saying of masses for the dead is valid. Perhaps the strangest of all these exceptional cases is *Re Thompson* [1934] Ch 342, where a trust to promote fox-hunting was held to be valid.

These trusts, while of comfort to the testator, are of limited application and although valid are not enforceable. The result of this is that if the trustees carry out the trust there is no problem, but if they will not there is no mechanism for enforcing the trust. These trusts are generally regarded as anomalous and the categories will not be extended.

See Chapter 9, p. 199, for a more detailed discussion of purpose trusts.

There are other situations where the courts have found a trust for purposes to be valid. One example is *Re Denley* [1968] 3 All ER 65, where land was conveyed to trustees to maintain the land as a sports ground, primarily for the benefit of the employees of a specified company. Goff J held the trust to be valid, distinguishing those purpose trusts where the benefit to individuals is indirect or intangible from those where the benefit to individuals is so direct that the persons benefited have a *locus standi* to apply to the courts to enforce the trust. Assuming that the trust that was found to exist was a true purpose trust and not a trust for individuals, the decision is very important and opens up the possibility of creating valid trusts which, although expressed to be aimed at achieving a purpose, provide a sufficiently direct and tangible benefit to a group of people.

Provision for family or dependants

The traditional application of the trust is in the context of family provision and this remains a very common use of the express trust.

The motive behind the trust could be simply to provide for the family. The settlor may try to make provision over a long period of time and may give a life interest in the property to his wife with the remainder to his children, perhaps on discretionary trust. This may be seen as a dynastic use of the trust, whereby the settlor seeks to control his wealth (and through his wealth his family) for a long period. However, equally the main object of the settlor could be to try to ensure that the family's financial affairs were managed and overseen by a group of selected trustees. The settlor may feel that the family cannot be relied upon to manage their own financial affairs or that the family might make decisions of which the settlor would not approve. In this context the settlor would be acting in a rather paternalistic manner.

When a settlor creates a trust for the benefit of his family, and to that end transfers property to the trustee, it may be that he is concerned not only to provide for the family but also to ensure, as far as he can, that the trust property is not sold and remains within the family. This might particularly be the case with a family home or heirlooms. A settlor may well decide to create his trust during his lifetime rather than by will as a will becomes a public document after death and the settlor may regard any provision that he makes for his family or others as a private matter. The device of the secret trust can be used by a testator to avoid this problem (see pp. 122–8).

If the trust is professionally drafted it will almost certainly be constructed to minimise the amounts of taxation payable. It may be that the only reason for the trust is to avoid or minimise tax.

Protective trusts

A parent may be considering setting up a trust for the benefit of an adult, but financially inexperienced, son who is married and has a family. The prospective settlor is aware that once a trust is set up the son will have a saleable or mortgageable interest. The father fears that the son will not act responsibly and may sell the interest or raise money on it, with the possible result that the benefit will be wasted away. This would affect not only the son but also his wife and children, about whom the settlor is also concerned. The settlor could decide to create a discretionary trust with the trustees having the discretion to make such payments to the son as they, the trustees, think fit. This would protect the trust funds and prevent the son from having the control over his interest that he would have under a fixed trust. This type of trust may not be what the settlor wants. Perhaps he would want to allow the son to take responsibility for his finances but protect him and his family from unwise decisions. Also, a discretionary trust requires regular and active administration.

The solution to the settlor's wishes may be a protective trust which will allow the son control and yet protect him and the family should he attempt any 'unsuitable' actions with the trust funds.

The settlor could draft his own protective trust or incorporate the provisions of the Trustee Act 1925 s 33. Under section 33 the son will be the principal beneficiary. The property will be held for the period of his life or for any lesser specified period, and, during that period the income will, without prejudice to any prior interest, be held on trust for the principal beneficiary, or until he does or attempts to do or allows any act or thing, or until any event happens, other than an advance under any statutory or express power, whereby, if the said income were payable to the principal beneficiary absolutely during that period, he would be deprived of the right to receive the income or any part of it, in any of which cases, as well as on the termination of the trust period, whichever first happens, this trust of the said income shall fail or determine.

Thus the interest would determine, for example, on the bankruptcy of the son or if the son attempted to alienate his interest. On the interest being determined, a discretionary trust will spring up under which the beneficiaries will be the son, his wife and children. The trustees will be able to use the trust property directly or indirectly to benefit the son. They could decide to apply the income from the trust property in maintaining or supporting the wife and children of the son. This would be of indirect benefit to him as it would discharge the son's moral or legal obligations towards his family. The trustees may decide to pay over income to the son but if he is bankrupt, or becomes bankrupt, this income will pass to the trustee in bankruptcy. It is far more probable that the trustees would decide to apply the income for the benefit of the son. They might, for example, pay some of the son's bills. This would benefit the son but nothing he could waste away would pass into his hands or would pass to the trustee in bankruptcy if he was bankrupt.

A protective trust is a very useful method of guarding against the consequences of bankruptcy or unwise behaviour, but it may be thought to be rather unfair as regards the son's creditors who, in effect, will be deprived of funds out of which their claims could have been met.

But a poorly drafted protective trust can have the often unwanted effect that one act of indiscretion (perhaps when the principal beneficiary is young) will cause the interest of the principal beneficiary to determine thus depriving the principal beneficiary of the right to income for the rest of his life.

Re Richardson's Will Trusts [1958] Ch 504 shows that it is possible to avoid this situation. What can happen is that a succession of protective trusts are set up. Perhaps one protective trust covers the principal beneficiary until he is 21, the next from 21 to 30, the next from 30 to 40 and so on. This would mean that if the principal beneficiary's interest determined when he was 20, the discretionary trust would spring up but continue only until he was 21 and then the next protective trust would come into play under which the principal beneficiary would have the right to income unless and until his interest determined and so on.

Secret trusts

When a testator dies his will becomes a public document and can be read by anyone. This might cause the testator difficulties if there is someone towards whom he owes a moral obligation but whose identity or existence he wishes to keep secret. Traditionally, the examples always given of such situations involve illegitimate children or mistresses.

The solution to the problem could be a secret trust. The testator would leave property to a legatee or devisee who agrees to hold the property on trust for the 'secret beneficiary'. The identity of the real beneficiary would not be revealed from the words of the will. Equity will prevent the legatee or devisee from breaking the promise and will enforce the secret trust.

The testator might create a fully secret trust where the legatee or devisee takes, on the face of the will, beneficially. In such a case the fact that there is a trust as well as the identity of the beneficiary is a secret. On the other hand, the testator might decide to set up a half-secret trust under which the legatee or devisee is named as a trustee but the identity of the beneficiary is not revealed (see pp. 122–8).

To preserve or control wealth

Many would say that it is natural for one who has built up wealth to want to retain control over it for as long as possible, even after death. Also, the wealth creator would wish to ensure that the wealth is preserved and not lost or wasted. The trust may be the means by which the achievement of these ambitions is sought. This use of the trust is common and was even more common in the past.

Traditionally, members of the settlor's family were appointed to act as trustees but it is becoming increasingly accepted that it is better to appoint professional trustees. Such trustees may be the family solicitor or the local bank. In all cases the professional will charge for his services but a higher level of efficiency should be brought to the administration.

The perpetuity rules (discussed at p. 161) restrict the period of time that the settlor can exercise control.

Tax saving

One of the very first applications of the trust in its original form, the use, was to avoid feudal dues, which was a form of taxation. In its modern guise, the trust is often used to avoid or minimise present-day taxes, especially income tax, capital gains tax and inheritance tax. However, recent legislative changes have reduced the opportunities for tax saving. Unfortunately, it is not possible to deal at length with the many uses of trusts in the field of tax planning, nor is it possible to cover, in depth, the way in which trusts are taxed. (Taxation is discussed in more detail at p. 37.)

National Health Service trusts

These 'trusts' have their origins in the National Health Service and Community Care Act 1990. The legislation states they must be set up in the form of corporate bodies and have the responsibility of providing and managing hospitals and other establishments or facilities. Although the 'trusts' do have fiduciary obligations towards the users of their services, it would appear that they are not trusts in the sense that the word is used in this text. It seems that the term 'trust' was adopted in an attempt to make the new regime for the provision of health services acceptable. People would, it was hoped, feel comfortable with and comforted by something called a 'trust'.

Trusts in the international arena

Objective 5

Many trusts that are created are designed to be non-resident trusts or are UK trusts that are later exported overseas. This is a very complicated and complex area of law. In most cases a trust is created as a non-resident trust or is exported to save tax.

The trust is a creature of the common law and of jurisdictions based on the common law. So there are few problems in trusts being recognised in other legal systems that are based on the common law. But the trust was not developed in any civil law jurisdiction, although concepts do exist with some of the features or characteristics of the trust. These have been developed from the Roman law idea of the *fiducia* under which property was transferred and the transferee, called the fiduciary, promised to deal with the property in a particular way. The fiduciary then promised to transfer the property back to the original owner or to another person as agreed with the transferor. This gave rise to enforceable rights and obligations but the remedies were only personal. Under a trust proprietary rights are created.

Additionally, the civil law of contract is wider than that of the common law and it is possible to create valid and enforceable third-party rights. Under the common law, the law of privity of contract prevents the creation of such rights. One of the great advantages of the trust is that third parties, the beneficiaries, do have enforceable rights. So it may be seen that the civil law did not need to develop trusts to enable these rights to exist.

In the past, while the trust was being evolved, the differences between the development of civil law systems and the common law were almost irrelevant as contact between different countries was very rare. Each system was able to develop in isolation. The position today is very different and international contacts are becoming more and more commonplace. How should a civil law jurisdiction react when confronted with a case involving a trust set up in England? One easy solution would be for civil law states to import and accept the concept of the trust into their own law. This, of course, was never a possibility, as this would involve backtracking over the development of civil law. The problem was addressed in the 1985 Hague Convention on the Law Applicable to Trusts and on Their Recognition, which covered expressly created trusts only. Any civil law state which signs the Convention will recognise the trust as a valid concept. The Convention outlines the main features of the trust and the consequences flowing from the creation of a trust. What the Convention does not require is that signatories adopt trusts into their legal system. The Recognition of Trusts Act 1987 brings the Convention into force as far as the United Kingdom is concerned.

This makes no difference to the English law of trusts and does not import the trust concept into civil law jurisdictions. It simply provides a framework for civil law courts to use when settling disputes that relate to trusts.

Article 2 of the Convention states that for the purposes of the Convention the term 'trust' refers to the legal relationship created *inter vivos* or on death by a person (the settlor) when assets have been placed under the control of a trustee for the benefit of a beneficiary or for a specified purpose. The characteristics of the trust are listed as:

(a) the assets do not form part of the trustee's own estate;

(b) the title to the assets stands in the name of the trustee (or another on the trustee's behalf);

(c) the trustee has the power and duty to manage the trust assets in accordance with the terms of the trust and any duty imposed on him by law.

Clearly, the English trust falls squarely within this description.

Summary

- Originally the trust developed to deal with domestic/family issues and problems, but the versatility of the concept led to the development of business/commercial applications. On the one hand this is a testament to the versatility of the trust concept, but on the other hand it has given rise to problems, in that rules etc. developed to cover domestic trusts do not always fit comfortably in a commercial setting.

- There is a very wide range of situations where trusts are used today. Important applications of the trust concept include: pension provision, to avoid or at least minimise the impact of tax; unit trusts; to provide security for lenders and sellers of property; charitable trusts; to hold property on behalf of minors; to set up mechanisms for providing for one's family.

- Today trusts impact on individuals in a wide variety of contexts, often in situations where the layperson would not expect a trust to exist. One example is where a house is 'owned' by more than one person.

- In some situations (for example, where the trust concept is used to provide a solution to disputes between cohabiting couples over the ownership of property) the solutions that trust laws provide sometimes seem at odds with what might be anticipated or expected, giving rise to claims that the law needs to be reformed. In fact there are proposals for reform in this area.

- The trust (as recognised in England and Wales) is principally to be found in countries whose laws are based on the English common law (cf. civil law jurisdictions).

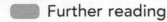 Further reading

Definition

R Bartlett, 'When is a "trust" not a trust? The National Health Service trust' [1996] Conv 186 Pensions.
Discusses the nature of trusts and argues that NHS trusts are not trusts in the sense that the word is used in this text nor are they trusts in the higher sense.

D Hayton, 'Trust law and occupational pension schemes' [1993] Conv 283.
The author argues that the trust which has been developed over centuries with refined rules to prevent the trustees from exploiting their position requires less supplementation than other legal structures. Trust law provides a sound edifice upon which to build pension schemes.

D Hayton, 'Pension trusts and traditional trusts: dramatically different species of trusts' [2006] Conv 229.
Provides an in-depth analysis of the practical workings of a pension trust in contrast to ordinary trusts and suggests areas for reform.

Lord Millett, 'Pension schemes and the law of trusts: the tail wagging the dog' (2000) 14(2) Tru LI 2.
Covers the respects in which contract law displaces trust law in relation to pension funds.

Commercial uses

P J Millett, 'Equity's place in the law of commerce' (1998) 114 LQR 214.
Explores the role of equity in the commercial world and looks at the use of breach of trust or breach of fiduciary duties as a remedy in a commercial setting.

Personal injury trusts

A Sands, 'Learning to trust' (2006) 150 SJ 758.
Discusses trusts in personal injury cases and highlights the need to take into account the impact on social security benefits.

Employee trusts

G Nuttall, 'Securing the succession' Tax (2014) 173 (4461) 14–17.
Discusses what such trusts are, their uses and tax implications.

The requirements of an express trust

Objectives

After reading this chapter you should:

1. Be aware that the settlor must have the capacity to declare a trust, that is, he must be mentally competent to do so.

2. Understand that the terms of the trust must be sufficiently certain, in that the settlor must have been clear in his intentions, and in identifying the trust property, the beneficial shares, and the beneficiaries.

3. Understand that the trust must be fully constituted, requiring the settlor, where necessary, to validly transfer the trust property to trustees.

4. Be aware that the settlor must, where necessary, have complied with any requirements as to formality.

5. Be aware of the differences between fully secret and half-secret trusts, know when they might be used and understand the requirements for each.

6. Have an understanding of secret trusts, as an exception to the requirement of formality for the disposition of property on death, and an appreciation of the arguments as to the basis for their validity.

The definition of the express trust

The express trust is, as its name implies, a trust which has been expressly and intentionally declared by its creator, known as the settlor (or, in the case of a trust created by will, known as the testator).

There are a number of requirements for the valid creation of an express trust, but the underlying objective of these requirements is that the settlor should have acted in such a way as to enable the courts, if necessary, to intervene to enforce the settlor's wishes. The settlor must, of course, be legally capable of declaring a trust and the people he intends to benefit must be capable of being beneficiaries. The settlor must show his intention to create a trust (even if he does not use the word 'trust'); he must make clear that he intends the legal owner of the property (which may be himself or someone to whom he is transferring it) to be subject to a binding obligation to the intended beneficiary. He must make clear who is to benefit under the trust in order that the court may know who has a sufficient interest to be able to sue. He must identify the property which is to be subject to the trust, and if he wishes persons other than himself to be trustees he must effectively transfer the property to them. Finally, in certain cases, he must do this in the form required by statute. These requirements are known respectively as capacity, certainty and constitution of trusts, and formality, and each of these aspects will be considered in the following sections of this chapter.

Capacity

Settlor

Objective 1

In general, any person who has the capacity to own any particular form of property has the capacity to create a trust of it and also to hold such property on trust. Four special situations should be noted.

Minors

Minors cannot be the legal owners of land and therefore cannot create a trust of a legal estate in land. Minors also cannot, unless they are either soldiers on active service or mariners at sea, make a valid will. Therefore they cannot normally create a valid trust by will. In relation to any other declaration of trust by a minor, the position is the same as for the validity of contracts by minors. It will be voidable, that is binding upon the minor unless he repudiates it on reaching his majority or shortly thereafter. Where, however, the settlement is obviously prejudicial to the minor's interest the court may decide that it is wholly void, and where the child is too young to appreciate the nature of the act he may plead *non est factum*, so that not even a voidable settlement is created. In such a case, any property transferred under the settlement must be held on resulting trust for the minor settlor.

Mentally disordered persons

Where the mentally disordered person is a 'person who lacks capacity' within the Mental Capacity Act 2005, and a deputy has been appointed for the management of their affairs, any purported disposition, including any declaration of trust, will be void because the person has ceased to have any legal control over their property. In such circumstances the Court of Protection has wide powers to direct the settlement of the person's property on trust, or indeed to make a will for the person in terms which the court believes the person would have made had they had the requisite mental capacity. Thus in *Re TB* [1966] 3 All ER 509, the court authorised a revocable settlement of the patient's property in favour of the patient's illegitimate son and his family. The patient being intestate, the law as it then stood would have meant that the son would receive nothing from his father's estate and the court was satisfied that the patient would have made provision for his son had he been mentally able.

Where no receiver has been appointed, any settlement will again be void unless the patient made it during a lucid interval when he could understand the nature of his actions. It will be for the person seeking to set the settlement aside to prove the mental incapacity. Much will depend upon the nature of the transaction involved and the sum of money involved compared to the settlor's total assets.

Re Beaney [1978] 2 All ER 595

In this case a mother, suffering from senile dementia, purported to transfer her house to an unmarried daughter who had looked after her for many years. Since this was the mother's only substantial asset this virtually disinherited her other children. The court held the transfer void.

As Judge Nourse QC stated:

> . . . if the effect (of the transaction) is to dispose of the donor's only asset of value and thus for practical purposes to pre-empt the devolution of his estate under his will or on his intestacy, then the degree of understanding required is as high as that required for a will and the donor must understand the claims of all potential donees and the extent of the property to be disposed of.

This is to be contrasted with the trivial gift of minor value. Also relevant will be the donor's previous record of mental health: if there is a long history of mental illness, then it will be much easier to prove incapacity at the time of the transaction in question. It should also be noted that transfers by the mentally incapable will not be set aside as against persons who have given valuable consideration and were unaware of the incapacity at the time of the transaction.

Corporations

Corporations only have those powers which are granted to them in their memoranda of association or which are reasonably incidental to the carrying on of their business. A declaration of trust by a corporation may thus be *ultra vires*. Under the Companies Acts, trading companies have powers, which are frequently exercised, to execute trust deeds in connection with the raising of money by the issue of debentures. It should also be noted that a person dealing with a company in good faith is not obliged to inquire into the company's capacity to enter into the transaction.

Statutory bodies

Bodies created by statute as corporations are in a similar position: the capacity will depend upon the provisions of the enabling statute. So, for example, the National Health Service Act 2006 s 51 provides that: 'Trustees may be appointed to hold property for the purposes of NHS Foundation Trusts or for any purposes related to the health service.' Regional and district health authorities frequently hold property on trust for charitable purposes to do with health care.

Beneficiary

Again, the general rule is that anyone who can be the legal owner of property can also be the beneficiary under a trust.

Minors

Minors cannot hold the legal estate in land, but they can be the beneficiary of a trust of land.

Aliens

Aliens can be the beneficiaries of trust of any property, with the exception of British ships and aircraft (of which they cannot be legal owners either).

Trustees

For more on capacity to be a trustee see Chapter 14 (p. 409).

It is perfectly possible for an individual to be both trustee and beneficiary of the same trust, but no trust exists where one person is the sole owner in law and equity of the property in question. Therefore, a sole beneficiary lacks the capacity to be sole trustee of the trust of which he is also the sole beneficiary. If the legal estate is transferred to him, the trust will disappear.

Certainty

Objective 2

It is obvious that the settlor must make his intentions clear in order to create a binding trust. He must express himself in terms which are sufficiently certain in order that the trustees may know what they are obliged to do, and to enable the court, if need be, to identify the obligations which it must enforce against the trustee. This requirement of certainty has long been regarded as falling into three parts. First, the settlor must make it clear that his intended trustees are under an obligation to carry out his wishes. Second, the settlor must make clear what property is to be subject to the trust. Third, the settlor must identify who is to be the beneficiary of the trust.

It should be stressed at the outset, however, that all these matters are ultimately a matter of construction. Much may turn on the precise words used or the circumstances in which they are used, but at the same time the courts are willing to accept any form of words provided it conveys the necessary information and intention.

It will also soon emerge that the 'three certainties' are often closely interrelated. Once the court has determined, as a matter of construction, what kind of gift the settlor intends to make (for example, whether it is a trust or merely a power), it will then be possible to see whether he has identified the property and beneficiaries with sufficient certainty for that particular kind of gift. As we shall see in the discussion of discretionary trusts, there is a wide range of possibilities as to how the court may interpret a particular gift, and its validity or otherwise may turn on quite narrow points of construction.

Intention

As was said by Lord Eldon in **Wright v Atkyns** (1823) Turn & R 143: 'the words must be imperative'. In other words, they must make it clear that the person holding the property is obliged to hold it for the benefit of others. Provided this is the case, however, there is no requirement to use any particular form of words to create the obligation. In Megarry J's words from **Re Kayford** [1975] 1 All ER 604: 'It is well settled that a trust can be created without using the word "trust" or "confidence" or the like; the question is whether in substance a sufficient intention to create a trust has been manifested.'

Paul v Constance [1977] 1 All ER 195

In this case, Mr Constance held a bank deposit account in his sole name but said to Mrs Paul, when referring to the account: 'The money is as much yours as it is mine.' This was accepted by the court as sufficient evidence that he regarded himself as holding the account as trustee for himself and Mrs Paul and accordingly she was entitled to claim a half share from Mr Constance's estate.

If, however, the words are indicative of some other kind of intention, such as an intention to make a gift, then this will not be construed as a trust.

Jones v Lock (1865) LR 1 Ch App 25

The facts of this case demonstrate the above point. Jones had placed a cheque, payable to himself, in the hands of his baby son, saying: 'I give this to baby; it is for himself, and I am going to put it away for him.' He then placed the cheque in a safe. Jones died six days later. The question then arose as to whether the cheque belonged to the baby or formed part of Jones's estate. This turned on whether, by his statement and actions, he had intended to make a gift of the cheque to the child or whether he intended to declare himself trustee of it for the child. Lord Cranworth concluded that Jones's intention could only have been to make a gift of the cheque. Such a gift was invalid as the law required the cheque to be endorsed, which Jones had not done. It could not be construed as a declaration of trust. An invalid gift cannot be construed as a valid declaration of trust.

The issue of intention, and of the general approach which indicates that the intention to make one kind of transaction precludes the intention to create another, arose in a rather unusual context in *Duggan* v *Governor of Full Sutton Prison* [2004] 2 All ER 966 which involved an interpretation of the prison rules with regard to prisoners' money. The rules state that money (cash) held by prisoners on their admission to prison is paid into an account under the control of the governor. The Court of Appeal held that this implied the relationship of banker and creditor between the governor and the prisoner, and that this precluded a relationship of trustee and beneficiary. Cash deposited with another as banker was neither the subject of a bailment at law nor of a trust in equity. There was no clear intention to create a trust expressed in the words of the rules themselves and no reason to construe the rule as imposing a trust which had not been expressed. The prisoner's claim that the governor was trustee of the money and that the money should therefore have been paid into a separate interest-bearing account was rejected.

Cases such as *Re Kayford*, together with *Barclays Bank* v *Quistclose* [1986] 3 All ER 651 and *Carreras Rothmans Ltd* v *Freeman Mathews Ltd* [1985] 1 All ER 155, appear to be an exceptional category of cases where, notwithstanding the apparent nature of the transaction, the courts were able to infer an intention on the part of the parties to create a trust. The Privy Council could make no such inference in *Re Goldcorp Exchange Ltd* [1994] 2 All ER 806. Further discussion of *Quistclose* trusts are found in other chapters in this text.

For more on *Quistclose* trusts see Chapter 1, p. 21, Chapter 3, p. 84, and Chapter 11, p. 266.

Re Goldcorp Exchange Ltd [1994] 2 All ER 806

In this case, the plaintiffs had purchased quantities of gold from a New Zealand company and had received a certificate of ownership. The crucial point, as the contract of sale made clear, was that no specific gold had been allocated to any specific purchaser: all the company had agreed to do was to make physical delivery to any purchaser upon seven days' notice. Neither was the gold to be drawn from a specific bulk; although the company undertook to keep a quantity of gold sufficient to meet all claims, it did not in any way give up its rights to buy and sell any gold or to deal with it as its own. The case was primarily concerned with whether legal title to the gold had passed to the purchasers: the Privy Council concluded that legal title had not passed. It based this view, which is the accepted law of the sale of goods, on the fact that in the case of a sale by description of non-ascertained goods, the parties cannot have intended that property in the goods would pass until they had been specifically allocated, or identified. For the same reason, the company could not be regarded as having declared a trust of any gold for the benefit of the purchasers, either of specific gold for specific purchasers or, since there was no agreed bulk from which the shares were to be drawn, of all the gold for all the purchasers jointly. The issue of certainty of subject matter is also relevant to this case and is discussed further below.

Note should also be taken of ***Don King Productions Inc v Warren*** [1998] 2 All ER 608. In this case K and W entered into partnership agreements in which W purported to assign the benefit of certain contracts to the partnership. In fact, several of the contracts contained express prohibition of assignment, so the assignment was ineffective. Lightman J held that this did not, however, prevent W from holding the benefit of the contracts on trust for the partnership, as it had also been agreed that the partners should hold all such contracts for the benefit of the partnership absolutely. Indeed the only way to give effect to the intentions of the partners, as expressed in the agreement, was that the benefits should be held on trust, since assignment in law was not possible. Since the court would not lightly infer a restriction on the freedom of parties to the contract, a clause restricting assignment at law *prima facie* does not prevent a declaration of trust of the benefit. This has subsequently been upheld by the Court of Appeal ([1999] 2 All ER 218).

A further difficulty arises where the settlor uses 'precatory' words, that is expressions of hope or desire that the donee of the property will use it in a certain way. Historically, such words were regarded as sufficient to create a trust obligation, but since ***Lambe v Eames*** (1871) 6 Ch App 597, the courts have taken a stricter approach. In that case the testator left his estate to his widow for her to dispose of 'in any way she may think best, for the benefit of herself and the family'. This was held to be ineffective to create a trust: the widow took absolutely. Thereafter, such expressions of hope or confidence may or may not impose a trust: it is as always a matter of construction, taking all the circumstances into account. There is no special magic in the use of any particular phrase. Rather, in the words of Cotton LJ in ***Re Adams and the Kensington Vestry*** (1884) 27 Ch D 394, the court must find out what 'upon a true construction, was the meaning of the testator'. Therefore, 'what we have to look at is the whole of the will which we have to construe'. In this case the testator's 'full confidence that (his widow) would do what is right as to the disposal thereof' did not impose a trust.

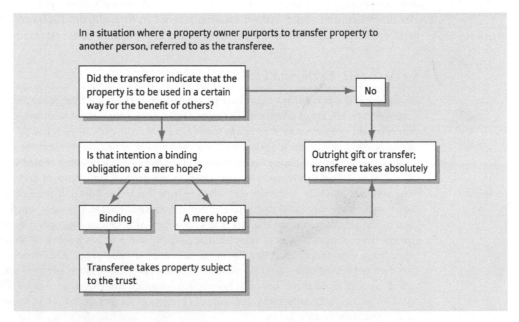

In a situation where a property owner purports to transfer property to another person, referred to as the transferee.

Did the transferor indicate that the property is to be used in a certain way for the benefit of others? → No

Is that intention a binding obligation or a mere hope?

Binding / A mere hope

Outright gift or transfer; transferee takes absolutely

Transferee takes property subject to the trust

Figure 4.1 Certainty of intention

As is clear from the above cases, where the words used are ineffective to impose a trust, the donee of the property takes it absolutely, in accordance with the rule in *Lassence* v *Tierney* (1849) 1 Mac& G 551. See also *Hancock* v *Watson* [1902] AC 14.

Subject matter

The settlor must identify the property which he intends to be the subject matter of the trust. Once again, the words must have a clear meaning that the trustees, and if necessary the court, can interpret. Thus, a phrase such as 'the bulk of my estate', used in *Palmer* v *Simmonds* (1854) 2 Drew 221, will not identify the subject matter clearly since it may mean different things to different people.

In *Re Goldcorp Exchange Ltd*, discussed above in the context of certainty of intention, the Privy Council clearly regarded the fact that specific property had not been identified in the contract as fatal both to the argument that property in the goods had passed in law, and to the argument that the vendor was holding such property on trust. As the Privy Council stated, common sense dictates that the buyer cannot acquire title until it is known to what goods the title relates. For the same reason, under a simple contract of sale of unascertained goods no equitable title can pass merely by virtue of the contract.

The Privy Council recognised, however, that the vendor could declare himself trustee of an undivided bulk of goods from which the purchasers' share was to be drawn: *Re Wait* [1927] 1 Ch 606. Thus, had Goldcorp agreed that the gold was to come from a specific stock owned by them, they might have become trustees of the whole of that stock. On the facts, this was clearly not the intention of the contract, however.

Re Goldcorp Exchange Ltd may cast some doubt on the decision in *Hunter* v *Moss* [1994] 3 All ER 215. In this case Moss, who owned 950 shares in a private company, orally declared himself trustee of 50 of them for the benefit of Hunter, but took no other steps to identify or separate the 50 shares. The difficulty of certainty of subject matter immediately presents itself: which 50 shares were held on trust for Hunter? The reasoning in *Re Goldcorp Exchange* was not available to the Court of Appeal, but the similar case of *Re London Wine Co (Shippers) Ltd* [1986] PCC 121 was considered, and distinguished on the ground that it concerned, as did *Re Goldcorp Exchange*, the passing of legal title. The conclusion in *Hunter* v *Moss* was that, since all the shares were identical, a declaration of a trust of 50 of them did not lack the necessary certainty. While it is true that in one sense one share was as good as another, and the court could order the transfer of any 50 of them to Hunter, it remains impossible to tell in the meantime which shares are, in equity, Hunter's, and therefore which he has the right to control or, for example, to trace into if Moss should dispose of any of the 950. *Hunter* v *Moss* has, however, been followed in *Holland* v *Newbury* [1997] 2 BCLC 369, in which the view was taken that *Re Goldcorp* could be distinguished on the grounds that shares were a special case.

One solution to such a problem, though one which could not be applied in *Hunter* v *Moss* as it was clearly not Moss's intention, would be to regard Moss as being trustee for himself and Hunter as tenants in common in the proportions 18:1. Hunter would then be the beneficiary of one-nineteenth of every share, and the problem of identifying particular shares as his in equity would not arise. This solution was applied in *Re Stapylton Fletcher Ltd* [1995] 1 All ER 192, again a case concerning legal title, to certain wines forming a bulk, separated from general stock of the vendors, but not yet specifically divided among the purchasers.

In so far as these cases concern transfers of legal title, they may also be relevant to the issue of constitution of trusts, discussed below.

In *Sprange* v *Barnard* (1789) 29 ER 320, a particular problem arose in that the testatrix gave certain stock to her husband, directing that 'the remaining part of what is left that he does not want for his own wants' he should bequeath in his will in certain specified ways. It was held that the husband took the stock absolutely. It was unclear what was bound by the trust because the 'remaining part', if any, would only be identifiable at his death. It is uncertain at the time when he received the money and a conventional trust would have come into existence at that time. It has been suggested, however, that in exceptional cases a gift in this form may be construed as giving to the donee a life interest only with remainder to those to whom the testator directed the donee to leave the property at the donee's death. There is also the possibility suggested in *Ottaway* v *Norman* [1971] 3 All ER 1325 by Brightman J that a 'floating' trust might be imposed, which is to say a trust suspended during the donee's lifetime and only attaching to the remaining property on the donee's death. It is submitted, however, that such a trust would pose considerable difficulties in that it would be unclear what rights of disposal the donee had during his lifetime: to what extent could he act to defeat the trust? Nevertheless, the concept has been adopted in *Re Goodchild* [1997] 3 All ER 63 in the context of mutual wills. It will be noted that this could never be a solution in a case like *Palmer* v *Simmonds*, because in that case the trust property can never be known as the definition is uncertain.

For more on mutual wills see Chapter 12 (p. 318).

It will be apparent, as an example of the close links that exist between the different aspects of certainty, that *Sprange* v *Barnard* is equally a problem of certainty of intention. Aside from the problem of the certainty of subject matter, the testatrix could be said to have been ambiguous as to whether she intended an outright gift or a trust, since she appeared, on the one hand, to have given the money outright to her husband, and on the other to have imposed a trust of part of it. It is submitted that these two are incompatible and that the notion of a floating trust must inevitably run up against that incompatibility: a person cannot be both the absolute owner and the trustee of the property.

In addition to identifying the property which is to be subject to the trust, the settlor must also identify what interest each beneficiary is to receive. No case, perhaps, demonstrates more clearly that the words used must have a definite and clear meaning than *Re Golay* [1965] 2 All ER 660, in which the testator stated that one 'Tossy', identified in the will as a Mrs F Bridgewater, was to receive 'a reasonable income from my other properties'. The point here was that 'reasonable' might have meant different things to different people. In particular it might have meant something different to the testator from the meaning applied to it by the trustees or the court. Ungoed-Thomas J, however, rejected this argument and the direction was upheld by the court as sufficiently certain. The term 'reasonable' was an objective yardstick and it would be drawing too fine a distinction to conclude that it might be uncertain because different people might have to apply it. The trustees were therefore obliged to pay T a reasonable income, and if necessary T could go to court for a declaration that the income she was receiving was not reasonable and seek to have it reviewed.

See Chapter 5 on discretionary trusts.

It will be observed that the trustees had no discretion in this matter. They were obliged to pay T a reasonable income, which the court held had a definite meaning. It is otherwise where the trustees are given a discretion as to the beneficial interest. The issue of discretions given to trustees and the extent of the court's power to interfere will be discussed in greater depth later.

Essentially, the courts can only control the trustees' exercise of discretionary powers to the extent of ensuring that they are not exceeded or exercised in bad faith. In *Re Golay*, the trustees were also instructed to allow Tossy 'to enjoy one of my flats during her lifetime'. This in effect gave the trustees the discretion as to which flat Tossy was to have. The court could, if necessary, intervene to oblige the trustees to do this but could not interfere with the trustees' choice of flat.

As *Golay* indicates, what is required of the settlor is not necessarily identification of the property and the interests, but rather that a means of identification be provided. In *Golay* the means was through the discretion of the trustees. Where the division of property, and hence the identification of beneficial interests, is left to some individual who is no longer able to make the choice, then the court cannot exercise that choice since it has no way of knowing how the choice would have been exercised.

Boyce v Boyce (1849) 16 Sim 476

This is the reason behind the failure of the gift in **Boyce v Boyce**, where two houses were left to two sisters, Maria and Charlotte. Maria was given the power to choose which of the houses she wanted and Charlotte was to receive the other. Maria died without making the choice. Charlotte's interest failed for lack of certainty as it was not clear which house she was to take. The only person who could make it certain, by choosing a house, was Maria; the court could not exercise her choice for her. Now that Maria was dead, no one could say what choice she would have made, since the matter was one for her entire discretion.

The result in *Boyce v Boyce* seems regrettable and, if possible, the courts try to avoid it. Thus, where no method of determining distribution is provided for in the will, the courts will attempt to find one.

Re Knapton [1941] 2 All ER 573

In this case, the testatrix provided for a number of houses that she owned to be distributed among several relatives and friends, but did not specify either who was to receive which house or how any choice was to be exercised. The court held that the beneficiaries had the right to choose a house in the order in which they were listed in the will. Among the beneficiaries were 'my nephews and nieces', not listed in any particular order. Here Simonds J adopted a civil law principle and held that the order of choosing was to be determined by lot, if the nephews and nieces could not themselves agree on an order.

This approach would not, of course, save a case like *Boyce v Boyce* because the testator had there specified a method of choice, which had become impossible.

Objects

See Chapter 5 on discretionary trusts.

The final element of the requirement of certainty is that the settlor shall have identified the persons who are to benefit under the trust. This will be discussed in much greater detail later, where it will be seen that a number of different tests may apply depending upon the nature of the trustees' powers and duties. Here it will be sufficient to consider the rule in relation to 'fixed' trusts, i.e. trusts where the trustees are under an obligation to distribute to named persons or to all members of a specified group. To carry out this obligation, trustees must clearly know who all the beneficiaries are. Where the beneficiaries are named in the trust this will present no problem. If they are identified as members of a class (for example, 'to all my children in equal shares'), then the class must be clearly defined so that the trustees know who each and every member is. This is frequently referred to as the 'list' principle: the trustees must be able to draw up a list of all the beneficiaries. Thus, in *Re Endacott* [1959] 3 All ER 562, Lord Evershed MR stated: 'no principle perhaps has greater sanction or authority behind it than the general proposition that trust by English law . . . in order to be effective, must have ascertained or ascertainable beneficiaries'. However, *Re Eden* [1957] 2 All ER 430 makes clear that the question is not whether all potential beneficiaries have been ascertained, but whether the evidence demonstrates beyond peradventure that it is impossible to ascertain the range of objects at that date. In other words, the crucial word is *ascertainable*. It is also clear that the fact that a large portion of the fund might have to be expended in tracing them is not of itself a ground for saying that ascertainment is impossible, though it would be unfortunate if the fund had to be spent in this way.

For more on certainty of objects see Chapter 5 (p. 140).

At the same time, injustice might arise in the case of a fixed trust if the principle of ascertainability were too strictly adhered to. For example, if the trustees, after making all reasonable inquiry, were unable to ascertain whether a particular beneficiary was still extant, would it be fair on the other beneficiaries to hold that no distribution could be made? Such a situation may be dealt with by the court making a 'Benjamin' order (*Re Benjamin* [1902] 1 Ch 723). This authorises the trustees to distribute to the known beneficiaries, reserving the right of the missing beneficiary, should he subsequently appear, to obtain his share by proceeding against the other beneficiaries or the trust property. It should be stressed that this kind of order cannot save a gift where the class is not identified with sufficient precision, but only benefits a class which is precisely defined but where members cannot be found.

Constitution

Objective 3

Where a settlor creates a trust by declaring himself to be the trustee of property then, provided that the requirements of formality and certainty are satisfied, the trust is complete and the beneficiaries acquire rights under it. This is because the property is already vested in the intended trustee, in this case the settlor. This is even true where the settlor declares the trust, intending the property to be held on trust by himself and others as trustees. Even though the other trustees have not yet received the legal title, provided that the settlor has shown an intention to make an irrevocable transfer to himself and the others as trustees, he is bound and can be required to carry out the terms of the trust by transferring the property to the trustees as a whole. This was held by the Privy Council in *T Choithram International SA* v *Pagarani* [2001] 2 All ER 492, where the settlor had shown an intention to make an immediate irrevocable transfer of property he owned to a charitable foundation of which he was one of the trustees.

If, however, it is the intention of the settlor to create a trust by transferring property to others (i.e. not including himself) to act as trustees, then the trust is incomplete until the transfer is made, and until that time it cannot be enforced by the beneficiaries. The settlor, whatever other legal obligations he may have acquired by his declaration, which will be considered below, is not trustee of the property he holds and the beneficiaries cannot act against him on the trust. The trustees hold no property on trust for the beneficiaries though they may be subject to trust obligations towards them (which is debatable).

Transfer formalities

The first issue to consider, then, is the necessary formalities for the settlor to transfer the legal estate in the trust property to the trustees. This will depend upon the nature of the property involved. In the words of Turner LJ in *Milroy* v *Lord* (1862) 4 De GF & J 264:

to render a voluntary settlement effectual, the settlor must have done everything which, according to the nature of the property comprised in the settlement, was necessary in order to transfer the property and render the settlement binding on him.

These formalities and methods will be essentially the same, whether it is intended to make an outright gift to the donee, or to transfer the legal property to the donee with the intention that he should hold the property on trust.

For chattels, mere delivery, provided that it is accompanied by the necessary intent to transfer property in the goods, is sufficient. This is amply demonstrated by the case of *Day v Royal College of Music* [2013] EWCA Civ 191, [2014] Ch 211, concerning property of Sir Malcolm Arnold, the composer. In 1976 he sent a box containing a variety of his property, including paintings, manuscripts, wine and many other things, to his daughter Katherine, and at the same time sent a postcard to his son Robert saying: 'All the books, pictures, sculptures etc. are for you and Katherine to share and keep or sell if you like! Dad.' There was a dispute about whether this statement included the manuscripts, but the Court of Appeal concluded from the facts that Sir Malcolm had intended a gift of the whole contents of the box. Nor was it relevant that Katherine and Robert had not acted as if they owned the manuscripts during their father's lifetime: the only intention which was relevant to the making of the gift was the donor's, i.e. Sir Malcolm's and, in the words of Lloyd LJ:

> There is nothing in the circumstances of the delivery . . . to suggest that Sir Malcolm drew a distinction between different parts of the contents of the boxes . . . Undoubtedly the message referred to the contents of the boxes, and showed that a gift was intended, not a mere temporary deposit for safe-keeping, and that the gift was to both children . . . In my judgment the only reasonable reading of the word 'etc' in the postcard is that it referred to everything else in the boxes.

Alternatively, a more formal method, and one more suited to the creation of a trust, is the deed of gift. This will avoid the need for actual physical delivery, which may be inconvenient: it is more likely to be the beneficiary rather than the trustee who requires physical possession. In appropriate circumstances a mere oral transfer of ownership without physical delivery may be sufficient, provided the means of acquiring physical possession is given. In *Thomas v Times Books* [1966] 2 All ER 241, Dylan Thomas's statement to a friend that he could have the original manuscript of *Under Milk Wood* if he could find it in one of a number of pubs where Thomas said he might have left it, was sufficient to give the friend ownership of the manuscript. In relation to the constitution of a trust of chattels, *Jaffa v Taylor* (1990) *The Times*, 21 March, makes it clear that physical delivery of the chattel to the trustees is not necessary, provided the trustees have all agreed to act as such and have received notice of the document declaring the trust. Such a transfer of chattels, be it outright or on trust, will, however, if they are part of a larger bulk of goods, require that they be identified. Cases such as *Re Goldcorp Exchange*, discussed above in the context of certainty, have stressed the need for goods to be specifically identified before legal title can pass: no property passes under a mere contract of sale by description for the supply of generic goods.

Unregistered land must be transferred by conveyance by deed (Law of Property Act 1925 s 52) and transfers of registered land must be by completion of the appropriate transfer form and registration in the Land Register (Land Registration Rules 2003). Equitable interests can only be transferred in writing (Law of Property Act 1925 s 53(1)(c)).

In the case of shares, these must be transferred by entry on the company's books following the completion of a proper instrument of transfer. Thus, in *Milroy v Lord*, a voluntary deed was executed by the settlor transferring shares to Lord on trust for Milroy. To complete the transfer, however, registration on the company's books was required. Lord, through a power of attorney, could have completed this further stage, but failed to do so. The transfer was held to be ineffective and thus the trust not properly constituted. This case is also a further authority that an invalid transfer is not to be construed as a valid trust. The settlor was not treated as having become trustee of the shares which he was purporting to transfer on trust, since clearly this was not his intention.

It is nevertheless possible in certain circumstances for the equitable or beneficial title to pass, even if the legal title has not. In *Re Rose* [1952] 1 All ER 1217, the Court of Appeal was prepared to hold that for tax purposes the settlor had disposed of his beneficial interest when he had done all that he personally could to divest himself of the shares. From then on he was therefore the trustee of the interest for the intended donee, even though the legal title did not pass until the transfer was entered on the company's books. This has been confirmed in the case of *Hunter v Moss* [1994] 3 All ER 215, referred to above in the discussion of certainty of subject matter. The case concerned whether the owner of shares had effectively declared himself to be trustee, but, on the question of when transfer to donee or trustee was effective, Dillon LJ stated:

> It seems to me, that if a person holds, say, 200 ordinary shares in ICI and he executes a transfer of 50 ordinary shares in ICI either to an individual donee or trustee, and hands over the certificate for his 200 shares and the transfer to the transferee or to a broker to give effect to the transfer, there is a valid gift to the individual or trustee of the 50 shares without further identification of their numbers. It would be a completed gift without waiting for registration of the transfer.

If this is true when a transfer of only some of the shares is intended, which was the particular problem in the case, then it must surely be true if all the shares are to be transferred. The principle in *Re Rose* has also been applied to registered land in *Mascall v Mascall* (1985) 50 P& CR 119, where a transfer was held to be complete on the completion of the documents of transfer but before registration of title.

Ordinarily one might expect equity to follow the law, and for the equitable interest to transfer when the legal title did. However, in *Pennington v Waine* [2002] 4 All ER 215, Arden LJ identified three exceptions to that principle. Firstly, where the donor had done all he could to transfer and the donee is in a position to complete the transfer himself, without further assistance from the donor; the scenario in *Re Rose*. Secondly, where there is detrimental reliance by the donee that may bind the conscience of the donor to justify the imposition of a constructive trust. This was the scenario in *Pennington* itself. In this case the donor had completed a transfer document but had never given it either to the donee or the company (and so had not done 'all he could' to complete the gift, unlike *Re Rose*). The donor, C, had also told the intended donee, H, that she wished him to act as a director, which he could only do if he became a shareholder, and H agreed to do so. He was also advised that there was no need for him to take any further action about the shares. Nevertheless, given H's agreement to act as a director, it would have been unconscionable for C to change her mind about the shares. Arden LJ's third scenario is where the court is able to construe a purported gift (or intended transfer to trustees) as a declaration by the donor (or settlor) of himself as trustee. These three alternatives were considered, and distinguished, by the Chancery Division in *Curtis v Pulbrook* [2011] EWHC 167 (Ch); [2011] 1 BCLC 638. In this case beneficiaries under certain family trusts obtained judgment against the trustee for breach of trust and sought a charging order against certain shares which they believed were held and beneficially owned by the trustee, P. P alleged that he had transferred the beneficial interest in the shares to his wife, A. Briggs J held the facts did not fall within either *Pennington* (which his lordship categorised as a case of estoppel), since A had not acted to her detriment in reliance on the promised transfer of the shares. Nor was it a case within *Re Rose*, since P had not done all that he could as he had not handed over the share transfer forms to allow A to have them transferred to herself. It was also clear that P had not intended to declare himself trustee; all his actions pointed to an intention to transfer the shares, though he did not complete the process. The shares were thus still his both legally and beneficially.

Enforcement of undertaking to settle

It can therefore be seen that, provided that all the other requirements of the valid declaration of a trust are present, once the property which is to be the subject matter of the trust has been properly transferred to the trustees, the trust is fully constituted and enforceable by the beneficiaries. It is equally true, obviously, that until this is done the beneficiaries have no rights to enforce under the trust. The question then arises as to whether the beneficiaries can ever oblige the settlor to make the necessary transfer. The trust of the property will not help them as it is as yet not in operation. There may, however, be some alternative legal or equitable rights which may help.

Where the settlor has merely made some gratuitous oral statement that he intends to create a trust, this clearly has no legal force; it is a mere gratuitous promise which as a general rule neither law nor equity will recognise, whatever moral obligation it may create. It may be, however, that the nature of the settlor's undertaking is more formalised. For example, the settlor may have entered into a written covenant with the trustees that he will transfer certain property to them on trust for the beneficiaries. Is there any way that such an undertaking can be enforced in equity?

It should be said immediately that equity has no special regard for the form of the undertaking. It may well be in the form of a covenant under seal but this in itself will have no special significance. Equity will intervene to enforce any promise to settle only on behalf of beneficiaries who have given consideration but not on behalf of any other beneficiary. Consideration means, in this context, valuable consideration, and also, in certain situations described below, marriage consideration. This is an application of the maxim that 'equity will not assist a volunteer', a volunteer being someone who has not given consideration.

This is referred to in Chapter 2 (p. 57).

Equity's intervention is through the application of another equitable maxim, that 'equity regards as done that which ought to be done'. In other words, once the undertaking to settle the property by transferring it to trustees has been given, equity treats the property as if it had already been transferred and will grant whatever order is necessary to give effect to the state of affairs.

Pullan v *Koe* [1913] 1 Ch 9

In this case, in a marriage settlement a wife had undertaken to settle any after-acquired property; that is, she had undertaken to add to the marriage trust any property which she might acquire later in life. She received a gift from her mother which was not added to the trust but simply placed in her husband's bank account, upon which the wife had a right to draw. After the husband's death the question arose as to whether the covenant to settle could be enforced and the money added to the trust.

In the words of Swinfen Eady J: 'In my opinion as soon as the £285 was paid to the wife it became equity bound by and subject to the trusts of the settlement. The trustees could have claimed that particular sum.' Equity would therefore be prepared to grant specific performance.

It is worth noting that, although it is customary to speak of enforcing the covenant, the effect of the maxim is rather greater than that. This is not merely a question of requiring the covenanting party to carry out his covenant, a personal obligation which would have been barred by limitation on the facts of *Pullan v Koe*. Rather, by holding that the property itself is bound as soon as it falls into the hands of the covenanting party, a right *in rem* is created, attaching to the property. It means, for example, that had the money been invested, any profit would also have been part of the trust. It also means that the trustees would have the right to trace the money had it been transferred elsewhere improperly.

As was stated in *Smith v Lucas* (1881) 18 Ch D 531 at 543, which was quoted with approval in *Pullan v Koe*:

> What is the effect of such a covenant in equity? It has been said that the effect in equity of the covenant of the wife, as far as she is concerned, is that it does not affect her personally, but that it binds the property: that is to say, it binds the property under the doctrine that that is to be considered done which ought to be done. That is the nature of specific performance no doubt. If, therefore, this is a covenant to settle future-acquired property of the wife and nothing more is done by her, the covenant will bind the property.

Finally, it should be noted that the definition of consideration in equity is wider than at common law. It includes all the things covered by the common law definition but also, in the case of marriage settlements like *Pullan v Koe*, 'marriage consideration'. The spouses and issue of the marriage are said to be within the consideration of the marriage and are treated as having given consideration. Issue includes children of the marriage and more remote issue. It probably includes stepchildren if treated as children of the family, but it does not include the next of kin as such nor any other relations; these are therefore 'volunteers' and cannot obtain equitable assistance.

That next of kin are volunteers and cannot obtain equitable relief is clearly demonstrated in *Re Plumptre's Marriage Settlement* [1910] 1 Ch 609. The facts were very similar to those of *Pullan v Koe*, except that it was the next of kin who were trying to enforce the covenant. Eve J stressed that the covenant was between husband and wife, and the next of kin were not parties to it, neither were they within the marriage consideration. In theory the trustees, who were parties, could have taken action at law for damages, but this was statute barred, as in *Pullan*. (As we shall see, it may well be that the court would direct them not to take such action for the benefit of the volunteers who might thereby gain indirectly what they could not obtain directly.) In any event, equity would not assist them.

It is perhaps a little difficult to understand why if, in *Pullan v Koe*, the covenant bound the property, it makes any difference who is trying to enforce it: what should matter is the property, not the beneficiary. The answer to this is that, as was said in *Pullan v Koe*, the covenant only binds the property to the extent that equity will grant specific performance to have the property added to the settlement. This remedy, and the maxim behind it, that equity regards as done that which ought to be done, will only be granted to a person whom equity regards as entitled, i.e. not a volunteer: a somewhat circular argument. Referring to the maxim, Lindley LJ, in *Re Anstis* (1886) 31 Ch D 596 at 605, stated:

> But this rule, though usually expressed in general terms, is by no means universally true. Where the obligation as to what ought to be done is not an absolute duty, but only an obligation arising from contract, that which ought to be done is only treated as done in favour of some person entitled to enforce the contract as against that person liable to perform it.

We should perhaps not be surprised to see what is, after all, an application of the doctrine of privity of contract, adapted by equity, applied to these cases which are essentially ones of contract or covenant.

Finally, since the maxim depends upon the remedy of specific performance, presumably the subject matter, the property which is sought, must be of a kind to which specific performance can be applied. In *Pullan v Koe* and in *Re Plumptre* it was specific property, which was still in the hands of the settlor and which in *Pullan* was accepted to be the product of the original property which should have been settled. What if the husband in *Pullan* had merely added the money his wife had received to his bank account, rather than buying specific bonds with it? Here specific performance could not have applied and the wife, though not a volunteer, would have been left with only the remedies at law, which were statute barred.

While equity requires consideration and gives no special importance to the formality or otherwise of the promise to settle, common law has always given particular status to covenants under seal, or deeds, and will enforce them even where no consideration is given. If a promise is contained in a deed, it should therefore be possible for anyone who is a party to that deed, whether volunteer or not, to obtain a remedy at law for breach of covenant. This is essentially what happened in *Cannon v Hartley* [1949] 1 All ER 50. In a separation agreement under seal, to which husband, wife and daughter were parties, the husband agreed to settle on the daughter anything which he might inherit from his parents. In due course he did in fact inherit from his parents but he did not settle the property. The daughter could not obtain specific performance in equity as she was a volunteer (this not being a marriage settlement). She was, however, a party to a covenant under seal and could therefore obtain the common law remedy of damages in compensation for the amount of her lost expectation.

It would seem to follow from *Cannon v Hartley* that anyone who is a party to a covenant should be able to sue on it at common law. The fact of their being a volunteer would appear to be irrelevant as far as the common law is concerned. In many cases, the promise to settle is contained in a covenant under seal made with the intended trustees, who are therefore parties to it. The logical conclusion would appear to be that trustees could sue for damages at common law for breach of the covenant to which they are parties. However, the courts have refused to allow this in a number of cases where the beneficiaries are volunteers.

Re Pryce [1917] 1 Ch 234

In this case, the trustees sought directions as to whether they should take proceedings to enforce a covenant to settle after-acquired property. The answer of the court was no. Since the next of kin were volunteers and were not parties to the covenant they had no right to enforce it. To direct the trustee to act would be to allow the next of kin (who were not themselves pursuing the matter) to obtain by indirect means a benefit which they could not obtain directly themselves. *Re Pryce* was followed in *Re Kay* [1939] 1 All ER 245, where an action for damages was specifically referred to, and the court directed the trustees not to take any proceedings.

The reasoning behind this approach is clear enough, but it does represent a clear interference with common law rights of the trustees as parties. It has nevertheless been followed in *Re Cook's Settlement Trust* [1964] 3 All ER 898. Here, Francis covenanted with his father, Herbert, that if he sold certain property the proceeds would be added to the family settlement, of which F's children ultimately became the beneficiaries. He sold a painting which formed part of the relevant property but retained the proceeds. It was held that the children, who were volunteers, were not entitled to require the trustees to take proceedings to enforce the covenant.

A number of other points emerge from this important case. First, Buckley J rejected the argument that a volunteer might enforce a covenant if he is 'specially the object of the intended trust or is within the consideration of the deed'. In other words, a beneficiary who is the specifically intended or identified beneficiary of the trust is in no better position than, for example, the statutory next of kin who ultimately emerge as the beneficiaries. The cases on 'marriage consideration' are an exception, though an important one, applying only to spouses, children or remoter issue and perhaps 'a beneficiary who is not within the marriage consideration but whose interests are closely interwoven with the interests of others who are within that consideration'. This is as far as such cases go and no other volunteer, no matter whether he is specifically contemplated as a beneficiary or not, can sue or require the trustees to act to enforce the covenant on his behalf (unless, as a party to the covenant, he seeks damages).

Secondly, it may also be noted that Herbert, who was a party to the covenant, had given valuable consideration. It was argued that the covenant was therefore enforceable as it had been given for consideration. However, the court drew a strict distinction between beneficiaries who had given consideration and those who had not. As regards the children, the covenant must be regarded as having been given voluntarily. They should not be allowed to benefit from the chance fact that someone else had given consideration and could presumably have enforced the covenant. In *Re Cook*, Herbert was dead but one must wonder whether his estate could have acted. This is, after all, the effect of ***Beswick v Beswick*** [1967] 2 All ER 1197, where the administratrix of a contracting party was entitled to act on the estate's behalf to enforce the contract. In effect, it was as if the contracting party himself was suing. The fact that the administratrix was also a third party to the contract who thereby derived benefit from the enforcement seems to have been regarded as a purely fortuitous circumstance.

These cases indicate then that trustees will be directed not to enforce, or at least will not be directed to enforce, their rights as parties to the covenant for the benefit of volunteers. It is not clear, however, what would happen if trustees, rather than seeking directions, simply proceeded to sue for damages. Their right to do so could hardly be denied: to refuse to recognise their rights would be a very different thing from simply instructing them not to enforce them.

There remains, however, a further problem. If trustees were to sue for damages, what would the measure of the damages be? In ***Cannon v Hartley***, where the intended beneficiary was suing, it was assumed that the measure of damages would be compensatory, although it was conceded that there might be some difficulty on the facts of the case in assessing the loss since the trust property lost was a reversionary interest which was difficult to value. In contrast to the beneficiary, however, the trustees have lost nothing, which would suggest that compensatory damages would be nominal and therefore suing would be a pointless exercise.

Re Cavendish-Browne's Settlement Trusts [1916] WN 341

This case has, however, been cited as authority for the proposition that substantial damages could be obtained. In this case, C had covenanted to settle certain property on trust but at her death had failed to do so. It was held that the trustees could obtain substantial damages equivalent to the value of the property. There appears to have been no discussion of the issue of assisting volunteers. Here, the covenant related to specific property and thus a measurable loss. It would therefore appear to give rise to an action in debt for a certain sum, rather than for compensation for breach; it would not appear to be applicable to covenants to settle after-acquired property such as was the case in ***Re Pryce***, ***Re Kay*** and ***Re Cook***.

There remains a further line of argument which may be of assistance to volunteers. It is clear that until the property covenanted to be settled has been transferred to trustees there is no enforceable trust of it. Once the promise has been given to trustees, might this promise not itself be the subject matter of a trust which the trustees hold for the beneficiaries and which the beneficiaries may require them to enforce? This was the view taken in *Fletcher* v *Fletcher* (1844) 4 Hare 67. Ellis Fletcher covenanted with trustees to transfer to them £60,000 on trust for his son, Jacob. Sir James Wigram V-C accepted that if the property were not in the hands of the trustees there was nothing that the court would do to require its transfer for the benefit of volunteers:

> I cannot, I admit, do anything to perfect the liability of the author of the trust, if it is not already perfect. This covenant, however, is already perfect. The covenantor is liable in law, and the Court is not called upon to do any act to perfect it. One question made in argument has been, whether there can be a trust of a covenant the benefit of which shall belong to a third party; but I cannot think there is any difficulty in that.

So once a settlor has covenanted with trustees, the trustees hold their right to sue on trust for the beneficiaries and the beneficiaries can require them to enforce that right. Now this is certainly true in the case of non-volunteers, as was seen in *Pullan* v *Koe*. The trustees could call for the transfer of the property and could seek specific performance of the covenant. To admit the authority of *Fletcher* v *Fletcher* would, of course, extend that situation to volunteers and completely undermine the maxim that equity will not assist a volunteer. It is submitted, however, that the case should be more restricted in effect. It implies, for example, that the chose in action, the debt, was to be held on trust. The facts suggest, though, no intention to create a trust of the right of action; the intention was to create a trust of the money. Also, the covenant being to settle a specific sum, gave rise to an action in debt, a chose in action. It was distinguished on this ground in *Re Cook*, where the promise was a mere executory contract to settle money in the future should it arise, which gave no cause of action that could be the subject matter of a trust.

The effects of the Contracts (Rights of Third Parties) Act 1999

In relation to contracts entered into after 11 November 1999, the effects of this Act must be considered. The general effect is that, in the words of s 1(1) '. . . a person who is not party to a contract (a "third party") may in his own right enforce a term of a contract if –

(a) the contract expressly provides that he may, or

(b) . . . the term purports to confer a benefit on him.'

What impact may this have on promises to place property on trust for a third party?

First, one may note that the act applies to contract, so presumably will not arise where the 'promise' to create a trust is an informal statement of some kind. Much more likely, however, is that the promise to settle property will exist in a contract or covenant with trustees. The intended beneficiary may then be able to sue on the contract (which exists between the settlor and the trustees), even though the beneficiary is not a party to it.

Two restrictions on the third party's right are stated in subsections (2) and (3). First, the right does not apply where the terms of the contract make it clear that the parties do not intend that the third party should have a right to sue, and secondly the third party must be clearly identified in the contract, either by name or as a member of a class.

Subject to these restrictions, it appears that the beneficiary would now have considerably greater powers to enforce the covenant. However, there remains the matter of the remedies available. The Act states (s 1(5)): '. . . the third party shall have available to him any remedy that would have been available to him in an action for breach of contract if he had been a party to the contract (and the rules relating to damages, injunctions, specific performance and other remedies shall apply accordingly)'. It is important here to recognise the distinction between being a party to a contract and having given consideration for it, and also the distinction between simple contracts and specialty (contracts by deed). In **Cannon v Hartley** (above) the daughter was able to obtain damages because she was a party to the covenant, even though she had not given consideration because the common law does not require consideration in a case where a contract is by deed. It is assumed that under the Act, the daughter could have obtained damages even if she had not been a party to the covenant, because she was clearly named as the intended beneficiary in it. It is argued, however, that she could not have obtained specific performance as she had not given consideration; she could not obtain specific performance as a party to the covenant, and it is hard to see why she should be able to do so as a third party. The statement in s 1(5) that the rules relating to remedies apply suggests that specific performance will still only be available for those who have given consideration. Thus in the typical case where A covenants with B that he will transfer property to B to hold on trust for C, C will only obtain specific performance of that covenant if he has given consideration; the situation in this respect is unchanged, though he may be able to obtain damages (even though not a party), if the requirements of the Act are fulfilled.

Summary

To summarise, then, a covenant to settle is enforceable only by those who have given consideration for it or, in the case of marriage settlements, who are within the consideration of the marriage. Those who have not given consideration, volunteers, cannot enforce the covenant in equity; neither can the trustees enforce it on their behalf. Volunteers cannot seek common law damages for breach of a covenant to which they are not parties; neither can trustees be directed to assist volunteers by exercising any common law rights they may have as parties. Volunteers can, however, sue for damages for breach of a covenant to which they are parties. If a fully constituted trust of a chose in action, such as an action in debt for a sum certain, can be construed, then the beneficiaries can require trustees to exercise that chose and hold the resulting property on trust for them. (See Figure 4.2.)

Equity will not assist a volunteer

There are certain other recognised exceptions to the rule that equity will not assist a volunteer. These are:

(a) where the intended donee has gained title to the property by being appointed administrator of the donor's estate (the rule in **Strong v Bird**);

For more on exceptions to the principle that equity will not assist a volunteer see Chapter 2 (p. 57).

(b) where the intended gift is imperfect but was given conditionally in contemplation of death (*donatio mortis causa*); and

(c) where, because of the donee's injurious reliance on the donor's promise, it would be unconscionable to allow the donor to refuse to carry out his promise (estoppel).

(As these do not relate exclusively, or in some cases at all, to the enforcement of covenants to settle on trust these have been dealt with at pp. 57–71 in the more general context of the maxim itself.)

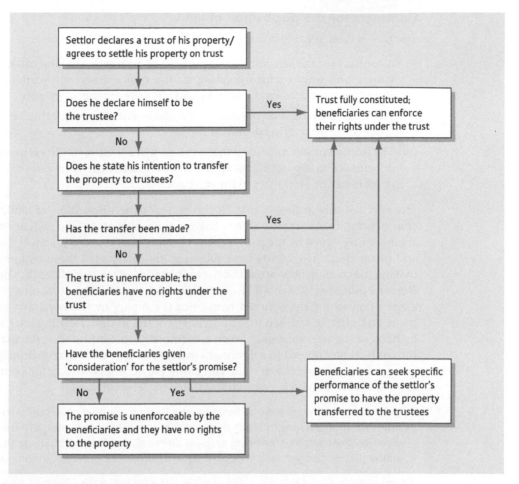

Figure 4.2 Constitution of trusts

Formality

Objective
4

As a general rule, there are no requirements that a trust be created in any specific form. Equity, looking to the substance rather than the form, merely requires that the settlor makes clear an intention to create a trust. As has been explained above, there may well be problems if the settlor has not made his intentions clear, but provided he has done so the law has little to say about the way he has done it.

To this general rule, there are a number of exceptions where statute requires a particular form to be adopted. These are declarations of trusts of land, declarations of trust by will and 'dispositions' (broadly meaning transfers) of existing equitable interests.

Land

It is indicative of the special nature and historical importance of land that there should be certain special formalities attaching to dealings in it. Students of real property law will be aware that transfers of a legal estate in land require a conveyance expressed to be by deed. In relation to trusts of land two provisions are significant.

Contracts for the disposition of land

The Law of Property (Miscellaneous Provisions) Act 1989 s 2 provides:

(i) A contract for the sale or other disposition of an interest in land can only be made in writing and only by incorporating all the terms which the parties have expressly agreed in one document or, where contracts are exchanged, in each.

(ii) The terms may be incorporated in the document either by being set out in it or by reference to some other document.

(iii) The document incorporating the terms or, where contracts are exchanged, one of the documents incorporating them (but not necessarily the same one) must be signed by or on behalf of each party to the contract.

The effect of this section is that all contracts for the disposition of land, which will of course include contracts to create or transfer trust interests in land, will be void unless they are in writing signed by the parties to the contract. Any oral contract will therefore be void and of no effect. The courts have subsequently interpreted these requirements strictly, making the creation of contracts by the exchange of letters very difficult. Thus, in **Firstpost Homes v Johnson** [1995] 4 All ER 355, neither the vendor's signature on a plan attached to a letter containing the contract terms, nor the typing by the purchaser of the vendor's name on the letter, satisfied the requirements of the section. Nothing less than the writing by hand of the relevant signature on a document constituting the principal document of the contract (as opposed to a document merely incorporated into the principal document, such as the plan in this case) could constitute the necessary writing for a binding contract. The reason for this strict approach was stated by Peter Gibson LJ:

> [s 2 was] intended to make radical changes to such contracts (i.e. contracts for the sale or disposition of interests in land) in a way that was intended to simplify the law and avoid disputes, the contract now being a simple document containing all the terms and signed by all the parties. [Subject, of course, to the provision in s 2 (iii) for the exchange of contracts.]

A further example of this strict approach may be found in the Court of Appeal's confirmation, in **United Bank of Kuwait v Sahib** [1996] 3 All ER 215, that the requirement of writing under s 2 has abolished the possibility of creation of a mortgage or charge by mere desposit of title deeds.

Two further points should be noted. First, the section does not apply to the creation or operation of implied, resulting or constructive trusts. Secondly, the section states that the word 'disposition' is to have the same meaning as in the Law of Property Act 1925. It would therefore seem that the cases discussing the meaning of the word 'disposition' in the Law of Property Act 1925 will apply equally here.

Trusts of land

The Law of Property Act 1925 s 53(1)(b) provides:

> A declaration of trust respecting any land or any interest therein must be manifested and proved by some writing signed by the person who is able to declare such trust or by his will.

Two distinctions between this section and s 2 should be noted. First, the requirement here is simply that the trust should be evidenced, rather than actually be, in writing. This appears, for example, to mean that the evidence need not be in existence at the time that the trust was declared, but merely that it should be available at the time when anyone seeks to enforce the trust. Secondly, and following from the first point, absence of writing will merely render the trust unenforceable rather than void and of no effect.

Dispositions of existing equitable interests

The Law of Property Act 1925 s 53(1)(c) provides:

> A disposition of an equitable interest or trust subsisting at the time of the disposition, must be in writing signed by the person disposing of the same, or his agent thereunto lawfully authorised in writing or by will.

Failure to comply with this requirement will render the purported disposition void. In other words, an oral disposition will have no effect and the equitable interest will remain with the person trying to dispose of it. If, however, the transaction does not fall within the meaning of 'disposition' then it can be effective, even though it is oral.

The reason for requiring dispositions to be in writing was summed up by Lord Upjohn in *Vandervell v IRC* [1967] 1 All ER 1. The subsection was, he said, 'to prevent hidden oral transactions in fraud of those truly entitled, and making it difficult, if not impossible, for the trustees to ascertain who are in truth the beneficiaries'.

Meaning of the term 'disposition'

Most of the case law on the section has centred around the meaning of the term 'disposition'. It should also be borne in mind that most of the cases also concerned various attempts to avoid or reduce tax liability, and it is perhaps not surprising therefore that the courts were reluctant to give effect to such attempts. Some of the arguments in these cases are therefore difficult to regard as logical, but should be seen in this tax context.

Section 53(1)(c) is the successor to a section of the Statute of Frauds 1677 where the equivalent phrase was 'grants and assignments', and clearly any direct transfer of an equitable interest will fall within the section. However, in *Grey v IRC* [1959] 3 All ER 603, the House of Lords rejected the argument that the meaning of 'disposition' should be limited to grants and assignments, preferring instead to give the word its natural meaning.

Grey v IRC [1959] 3 All ER 603

Mr Hunter, having established settlements for the benefit of his grandchildren, transferred to the trustees of those settlements 18,000 shares which he owned, directing the trustees to hold them on trust for himself. He then orally instructed the trustees to hold these shares for the benefit of his grandchildren. Later the trustees executed trust deeds which recited Hunter's previous oral instructions and declared that the shares had, since the date of the instructions, been held on trust for the grandchildren.

It must be understood that if the instructions were not a disposition within the meaning of the Act, then even though they were oral they would be effective to transfer Hunter's interest to his grandchildren. If, however, the instructions were a disposition, then that disposition would be void for want of writing: Hunter would remain the beneficiary of the shares. The subsequent deeds would then be the actual and effective disposition in writing of the value of the shares. At that time a document transferring the value of property in this way was subject to stamp duty *ad valorem* at a percentage of the value of the property transferred. By attempting to get rid of his interest orally, Hunter was hoping to avoid stamp duty. The Inland Revenue challenged this. The House of Lords concluded that the instructions were indeed a disposition within the ordinary meaning of the word since the beneficial interest in the shares previously vested in Hunter became vested in another. The instructions were thus of no effect because there was no writing. The subsequent deeds were the effective disposition, being in writing, and therefore attracted stamp duty.

As a result of *Grey* v *IRC*, then, disposition is to be given its natural meaning: a transaction whereby a beneficiary who has a beneficial interest at the beginning of the transaction no longer has it at the end of the transaction. This must presuppose, however, that the beneficial interest exists as a separate entity throughout. Whenever a sole owner, both legally and beneficially entitled, disposes of, for example, shares, it could be said that he is disposing of a beneficial interest. However, it is clear, and indeed was accepted by the parties in *Vandervell* v *IRC*, that s 53(1)(c) would not apply to such a case. The sole legal and equitable owner need only comply with the formalities, if any, required for transferring the legal estate. As we have seen, this may well be relevant in a discussion as to whether a trust has been properly constituted, but it is outside our concern here.

For more on variation see Chapter 8.

Vandervell v *IRC* [1967] 1 All ER 1 itself decided that where the sole beneficial owner absolutely entitled disposes of his interest by instructing his trustees to transfer the legal estate, he is in effect in the same position as the sole legal owner. It is in the nature of a bare trust such as this that the trustees, referred to as nominees, act under the orders of the sole beneficial owner, who could at any time call for the legal estate to be transferred to him (more will be said of this when the rule in *Saunders* v *Vautier* is discussed in relation to variation of trusts (see Chapter 6 at p. 157). It follows, therefore, that the beneficial owner may call upon the trustees to transfer the legal estate to others. This might simply be to change the trustees, the beneficiary retaining his beneficial interest. If, however, in Lord Upjohn's words, 'the intention of the beneficial owner in directing the trustee to transfer the legal estate to X is that X should be the beneficial owner, I can see no reason for any further document . . . expressly transferring the beneficial estate'. Put simply, s 53(1)(c) does not apply in such a situation and an oral transfer will be effective, providing any formalities for transferring the legal estate have been complied with.

Vandervell v *IRC* [1967] 1 All ER 1

The facts of *Vandervell* v *IRC* were that Mr Vandervell wished to endow a chair of pharmacology and to that end wished to give £150,000 to the Royal College of Surgeons. In an attempt to do this in a tax-efficient way he took the following steps. A bank held shares as nominees on a trust of which Vandervell was the sole beneficial owner. Vandervell instructed the bank to transfer the shares to the College, and instructed the College to grant to Vandervell's trust company an option to repurchase the shares for £5,000. Once the shares were transferred to the College, dividends were declared to the amount of £145,000. The question then arose as to whether Vandervell had effectively disposed of the shares: if he had not, he would be liable to surtax on the dividends. The Revenue argued that the transfer to the College was ineffective as not complying with s 53(1)(c). As stated above, this argument was rejected by the House of Lords. However, the obtaining of an option to repurchase proved fatal to Vandervell's case.

It will be recalled that Vandervell had instructed the trustees to obtain an option to repurchase the shares from the College for £5,000, and this had duly been done. For whose benefit did the trust company hold this option? The option itself gave no indication on this point and the majority of the House of Lords, following the Court of Appeal, concluded, as an inference from the primary facts, that the trustees were to hold on such trusts as might be declared. As no express trust of the option had been declared, in the meantime the trustees held on resulting trust for Vandervell.

This decision was reached in 1966. Meanwhile, in 1961 the trustees had exercised the option to repurchase the shares using £5,000 from trusts for the benefit of Vandervell's children and the shares were duly transferred to the trustees. With Vandervell's consent the shares were stated to be held for the children's settlement and the Revenue was informed of this. It should be remembered that at this time no one was aware of the subtleties regarding the beneficial ownership of the option. Between 1961 and 1965 dividends were declared on the shares and these were added to the funds in the children's settlement. The Revenue argued, however, that Vandervell had still not divested himself of his interest in the shares, so, in 1965 he executed a formal deed transferring to the trustees to hold for the children's settlement any interest that he might have in the option or the shares. Mr Vandervell died in 1967.

These events became the subject of litigation in *Re Vandervell's Trusts (No. 2)* [1974] 3 All ER 205, in which the executors of Vandervell's estate claimed the dividends. The nature of the 1961 transaction was crucial. The main issue was whether Vandervell still had an interest in the shares between 1961 and 1965. If he did, two things followed. First, the dividends which had been declared in those years would be his and he, or his estate, would have to pay surtax on them. Secondly, the dividends would form part of his estate and would be distributed under his will, which did not make provision for his children, rather than forming part of the children's settlement. (Clearly, Vandervell had made no provision in his will for his children as he imagined that he had already done so through the settlement.)

What, then, was the nature of the transaction in 1961 when the shares were repurchased? If as part of that transaction there was a disposition by Vandervell of his interest under the resulting trust, within s 53(1)(c), then it would be void for lack of writing, Vandervell's agreement being expressed orally. This would mean that Vandervell was still the beneficial owner of the shares with the consequences described above. If it were not a disposition, then the shares would be held by the trustees for the benefit of the children. The Court of Appeal held that it was not a disposition. Since it protected the interests of the children, this was a result to which Stephenson LJ, though he had his doubts, was 'happy to agree as it seems to me to be in accordance with the justice and reality of the case'.

The reasoning is nonetheless, it is submitted, open to question. As a result of the decision in *Vandervell v IRC*, Vandervell was the beneficiary of the option before 1961, though he may not have known it. After 1961, as a result of the decision in *Re Vandervell's Trusts (No. 2)*, he had no interest in the option or the shares. It is difficult to see why this is not a disposition or how it may be effectively distinguished from *Grey v IRC*.

For a disposition under s 53(1)(c) to arise there had to be some form of equitable property subsisting throughout the period from 1958 to 1967, and the main reasoning of the Court of Appeal was to deny this and to hold that the repurchase of the shares was a declaration of a new trust for which, of course, no writing was necessary as the property (shares) was personalty. The necessary intention to create the trust was manifested by the actions of the trustees and the approval of Vandervell. That the shares were purchased with money from the children's settlement showed that the intention was that the benefit of the shares should be held for the children. In the words of Lawton LJ, 'there is, in my judgment, ample evidence to infer, and I do infer, that a declaration of trust was made by the trustee company with the knowledge and approval of [Vandervell]'.

What, then, happened to the option held on resulting trust for Vandervell? This, it was held, disappeared. First, because the option was exercised and produced the shares. This was said to be a change from one kind of property into another and hence, by inference, one trust into another. This is difficult to follow as the conversion of the trust property into something else would not generally affect the continued existence of the trust. Secondly, and more convincingly, because the option was held on resulting trust. Resulting trusts exist simply to fill the gap where no express trust has been declared. Therefore, as soon as the express trust was declared (by buying the shares and the other evidence of declaration of trust) the resulting trust simply terminated, the gap having now been filled.

Two further arguments were put forward to support the decision in the case. One was that money from the settlement had been used to buy the shares and it would be a breach of trust if the shares were not then held on the same trusts as the money which had produced them. However, the same view could be taken of the option which had also produced them. Finally, Vandervell's actions in agreeing to the purchase meant that he was estopped subsequently from denying the children's interest.

Stephenson LJ, while supporting the result of the case, cast doubt on this reasoning. It was difficult to use Vandervell's conduct in 1961 as the basis of an estoppel, or indeed to support the 'declaration of trust' theory, since at the time neither Vandervell nor anyone else knew that he had an interest. In Stephenson LJ's words:

> The operation of law or equity kept for [Vandervell] an interest which he did not want and would have thought he had disposed of had he ever known it had existed. It is therefore difficult to infer that he intended to dispose or ever did dispose of something he did not know he had.

It remains to be seen whether, given its rather specific facts, *Re Vandervell's Trusts (No. 2)* will have any general importance. It may be, however, that it may serve to protect settlors who are unwilling to name the beneficiaries of trusts at the outset, preferring to do so at a later date. It is arguable, following *Vandervell*, that any resulting trust thereby accidentally created can silently disappear without falling foul of s 53(1)(c).

Disclaimer of beneficial interest

A disclaimer of beneficial interest on the authority of *Re Paradise Motor Co* [1968] 2 All ER 625 is not a disposition within s 53(1)(c). The Court of Appeal held this on the 'short ground' that 'a disclaimer operates by way of avoidance, and not by way of disposition'. In other words, the stepson in the case, when disclaiming shares which his stepfather had purportedly given him, was refusing a gift before he ever had it, rather than getting rid of the gift after receiving it.

Nomination by a member of an employees' pension fund

Employees' pension funds allow the potential pensioner to nominate a person who shall receive any benefits should the pensioner die before receiving the benefit himself. In *Re Danish Bacon Co Ltd Staff Pension Fund* [1971] 1 All ER 486, Megarry J doubted whether such a nomination could be regarded as a disposition. The pensioner was making a revocable gift of a possible future interest, rather than of one 'subsisting at the time of the disposition'. It was therefore doubtful if it fell within the wording of the section, though it was not necessary to decide the point since there was in any case sufficient writing to satisfy the section if need be. The same applies to the nomination of a beneficiary under a life insurance policy: *Gold* v *Hill* [1998] All ER (D) 355.

Declarations of trusts of beneficial interests

Where a beneficiary declares that he is holding his beneficial interest on trust for another this would appear not to be a disposition, but rather a declaration of a sub-trust, only requiring writing if it is of land. Following *Grainge* v *Wilberforce* (1889) 5 TLR 436, however, this would appear to be the case only where the sub-trust is different in terms from the head trust and the trustee-beneficiary has some active duties to perform (for example, if the beneficiary of the sub-trust were a minor and the income of the fund were to be accumulated). Where the sub-trust is on the same terms as the head trust it appears that the trustee-beneficiary may drop out of the picture and the trustees of the head trust then hold on trust for the sub-beneficiary. This would then constitute a disposition falling within s 53(1)(c).

Paul Matthews has, however, produced a very strong argument that all such declarations are in fact dispositions (Matthews 2005). The beneficiary who declares himself a trustee of that interest is disposing of his interest to the sub-beneficiary and should therefore comply with s 53(1)(c).

Creation of equitable charge by deposit of title deeds

In *United Bank of Kuwait* v *Sahib* [1995] 2 All ER 973, Chadwick J stated, *obiter*, that even if otherwise valid, the creation of an equitable charge (in this case a mortgage), by the deposit of the title deeds to the property mortgaged, was a dispositive act and thus bound by s 53(1)(c) and required writing. There are significant objections to this view. The creation of this lesser interest out of the greater (i.e. the mortgage out of the freehold) may, by analogy with the declaration of a sub-trust (above), be seen as the creation of a new equitable interest, rather than the disposition of a subsisting one, and would, since the subject matter is land, seem to be covered by s 53(1)(b) rather than s 53(1)(c). Secondly, given the long-standing practice of creating mortgages by deposit of title deeds, the effect of Chadwick J's view would be to invalidate every such mortgage since 1926: a serious practical consequence. The Court of Appeal has confirmed ([1996] 3 All ER 215) that, in any event, such mortgages are no longer possible without writing because of the requirements of s 2 of the Law of Property (Miscellaneous Provisions) Act 1989, and accordingly the Court of Appeal did not consider the issue of s 53(1)(c) in this context.

Specifically enforceable contracts

Where a purchaser has entered into a specifically enforceable contract of sale he may, of course, enforce the contract by decree of specific performance. It might therefore be thought arguable that, from the time that the contract is entered into, or at least at the point when it becomes specifically enforceable, the vendor is holding the property on constructive trust for the purchaser. If the contract were oral, and the subject matter of the contract was an existing equitable interest, this might be a way of disposing of such an interest without writing, so avoiding s 53(1)(c).

In *Oughtred* v *IRC* [1959] 3 All ER 623, the House of Lords arguably rejected such a view, at least to the extent of preventing such a contract from allowing the parties to avoid stamp duty. The subject matter in question in this case was the beneficial remainder interest in some shares. After the oral contract to transfer the beneficial interest, the transferor completed certain formal written transfers, reciting that the interest in the shares had been transferred by the contract. If effective, this would have meant that the formal documents would only have been declaratory and would have transferred nothing of value, so attracting only nominal stamp duty.

The House of Lords rejected the argument, and held that the formal documents were liable to stamp duty on the value of the shares. In the words of Lord Jenkins:

> If the subject matter of the sale is such that the full title to it can only be transferred by an instrument, then any instrument they execute by way of transfer of the property sold ranks for stamp duty purposes as the conveyance of sale, notwithstanding the constructive trust in favour of the purchaser which arose on the conclusion of the contract.

To some extent this raises the question of the nature of the purchaser's interest under the constructive trust, and what is left to be conveyed, but the case can be regarded as specific to its context: the courts' desire to prevent the avoidance of stamp duty. Certainly, this was the view of the Court of Appeal in *Neville* v *Wilson* (below), which is discussed in the next section, in the context of s 53(2). It seems fairly safe to conclude, therefore, that neither *Oughtred* v *IRC* nor, for reasons discussed below, *Neville* v *Wilson*, makes any authoritative statement as to whether entry into an oral, specifically enforceable contract, is a disposition within the meaning of s 53(1)(c).

Law of Property Act 1925 and implied, resulting and constructive trusts

Both s 2 of the Law of Property (Miscellaneous Provisions) Act 1989 and s 53 of the Law of Property Act 1925 state that 'nothing in this section shall affect the creation or operation of resulting, implied or constructive trusts' (s 2(5) and s 53(2) respectively). Clearly, any suggestion that such trusts could only be created in writing would defeat their very nature, since the one is implied from the parties' conduct while the other is imposed by the court.

In *Oughtred* v *IRC* (above), Lord Denning commented, *obiter*, that s 53(2) did not do away with the requirement of writing under s 53(1)(c) in that case. This view appears to have been decisively rejected by the Court of Appeal in *Neville* v *Wilson* [1996] 3 All ER 171.

Neville v *Wilson* [1996] 3 All ER 171

In *Neville*, certain shares in company A were held by two directors of that company on trust for company B. The Court of Appeal held that in 1969 the shareholders of company B had agreed orally to liquidate company B and distribute its assets. The beneficial interest in the shares in company A was, of course, part of those assets. The effect of the liquidation agreement was that each shareholder in company B agreed to give up his interest in the whole of the assets (including the beneficial interest in the shares), in exchange for all the other shareholders similarly giving up their interests, preparatory to those assets being divided among the shareholders in proportion to their shareholding. To the extent that these agreements related to the dispositions of existing equitable interests in the shares, the court had then to consider the impact of s 53(1)(c), and of *Oughtred* v *IRC*.

Nourse LJ, who gave the judgment of the court, regarded the two cases as directly parallel with regard to the effect of the transactions. Just as in *Oughtred* v *IRC* the son's oral agreement created a constructive trust in favour of the mother, so here each shareholder's oral or implied agreement created an implied or constructive trust in favour of the other shareholders. What then was the effect on this of s 53(1)(c)? In Nourse LJ's opinion, *Oughtred* did not prevent the Court of Appeal from applying s 53(2), since the decision of the majority in that case had not turned on the effect of s 53(1)(c) but rather on the nature of the subsequent written transfers. He stated categorically that s 53(1)(c) does not apply to the creation or operation of implied or constructive trusts. This is what s 53(2) literally says. Therefore, the Court of Appeal could see no convincing reason why s 53(2) should not apply to the type of agreement in this case. Not to apply it here would be to draw unnecessarily fine distinctions.

While this is undoubtedly a reasonable result, according with the opinion of Lord Radcliffe in *Oughtred*, as well as the literal words of the section, it might still be asked whether such cases are necessarily within the meaning of s 53(1)(c) in the first place. As Nourse LJ states in his judgment, the effect of the transaction is to *create* a constructive trust. How then is this the disposal of an existing equitable interest? Though there is no doubt that the vendor has such an interest, the effect of the agreement could arguably be that that interest is now held under a new trust by the vendor for the purchaser.

Trusts declared or disposed of by will

The Wills Act 1837 s 9, as amended by the Administration of Justice Act 1982 s 17, provides:

> No will shall be valid unless:
>
> (a) it is in writing, and signed by the testator, or by some other person in his presence and by his direction; and
> (b) it appears that the testator intended by his signature to give effect to the will; and
> (c) the signature is made or acknowledged by the testator in the presence of two or more witnesses present at the same time; and
> (d) each witness either –
>   (i) attests and signs the will; or
>   (ii) acknowledges his signature,
>
> in the presence of the testator (but not necessarily in the presence of the other witness), but no other form of attestation shall be necessary.

It is not proposed to discuss further the detailed requirements of valid wills beyond stating that this is a general provision relating to all forms of disposition by will, including trusts declared and equitable interests disposed of by will. Its provisions must therefore be adhered to when a testator declares a trust by will.

These provisions are, arguably, avoided by secret trusts, considered below.

Formality and fraud

These, then, are the statutory requirements in relation to the creation of and dealing in trust interests. Why should such provisions be necessary, particularly when in general equity avoids formal requirements? It should be remembered that these provisions are in general the successors to the requirements of the Statute of Frauds 1677. They are imposed therefore because of a fear that fraud may arise if oral evidence, with its attendant risk of perjury, is relied on. This is exemplified by Lord Upjohn's statement in *Vandervell* v *IRC*, quoted above.

Paradoxically, a statutory requirement can itself be used fraudulently. It is a maxim of equity that it will not allow a statute to be used as a cloak for fraud (referred to at p. 51), and it therefore follows that these statutory requirements will be set aside if they are being used in this way in individual cases.

Rochefoucauld v *Boustead* [1897] 1 Ch 196

In the leading case of **Rochefoucauld** v **Boustead**, the plaintiff mortgaged land to a third party who sold it to the defendant who agreed orally to hold it on trust for the plaintiff. The defendant then acted in breach of trust by selling the land and pocketing the proceeds, claiming that he was not bound by the trust of the land, which had not been declared in writing. The Court of Appeal upheld the trust saying that the formal requirements of the Statute of Frauds (the predecessor to s 53(1)(b)) did not prevent the proof of a fraud and it was clearly fraud for anyone who knows that land has been conveyed to them on trust to deny the trust and claim the land for themselves. So the plaintiff was entitled to produce oral evidence of the trust and the fact that the defendant was aware of the circumstances.

There is thus an obvious conflict here between the clear words of the statute and equity's jurisdiction to prevent fraud. Strictly speaking, equity's right to act *in personam* should only go so far as to prevent the fraudster from profiting from his fraud. In *Rochefoucauld* this could have been achieved simply by holding that the defendant held on constructive trust for the vendor (i.e. the third party). The court went further than this, however, and upheld the terms of the oral trust itself (i.e. for the plaintiff). On the basis of this case, then, it seems to be possible to say that the requirements of writing may be set aside and oral trusts upheld wherever the court feels it is necessary to prevent fraud, and perhaps in wider circumstances than that.

Despite this, however, more recent cases, such as **Bannister v Bannister** [1948] 2 All ER 133, have treated **Rochefoucauld v Boustead** as an example of a constructive trust imposed for unconscionability. Such an interpretation would, of course, avoid the requirement of writing anyway, in view of s 53(2), referred to above.

It further appears that the word 'fraud' must be viewed with some circumspection, particularly in the context of statutes requiring property interests to be registered. In such cases, the courts will, it seems, be reluctant to apply the maxim to protect those who have not registered their interests.

In **Midland Bank Trust Co Ltd v Green** [1981] 1 All ER 153, a father granted to his son an option to purchase the family farm. Under the Land Charges Act 1972 this interest should have been registered, but was not. The father subsequently sold the farm to his wife, with the apparent intention of defeating his son's interest. The House of Lords declined to apply the maxim to give the son the right to purchase. Referring to the earlier case of **Re Monolithic Building** [1915] 1 Ch 643, a case on similar registration requirements under the Companies Acts, Lord Wilberforce stated:

> It makes it clear that it is not fraud to rely on legal rights conferred by Act of Parliament; it confirms the validity of interpreting clear enactments as to registration and priority according to their terms.

Such enactments would, it therefore appears, be circumvented by the application of the maxim, which Lord Wilberforce indicated should not be applied to 'modern' registration statutes.

The avoidance of fraud is also traditionally given as a reason for upholding secret trusts, which are considered below.

Secret and half-secret trusts

Objective 5

The origin of secret trusts lies in the maxim that equity will not allow a statute to be used as an engine of fraud. The Wills Act 1837 section 9 sets out formalities that must be complied with if a valid will is to be made which effectively disposes of the testator's property. *Inter vivos* dispositions of equitable interests must comply with s 53 of the Law of Property Act 1925.

After the death of the testator her/his will becomes a public document and anyone can obtain a copy and inspect it provisions. It is probable that members of the deceased's family and/or those who believed that they should benefit under the will would be most likely to want to get sight of the will.

One can imagine circumstances where a testator would want to benefit X but would not wish members of his family to know about the benefit. A typical example might be where a man wishes to leave money to a mistress or illegitimate child that he does not want his family or the world to know about.

Putting a bequest to X in the will is not an option if secrecy is to be maintained.

A way round this is by using a secret trust.

There are two types of secret trusts – fully secret and half-secret. A fully secret trust arises where a testator leaves money to a beneficiary who, on the face of the will, appears to take absolutely, but who has in fact agreed to hold the property as a trustee for someone else.

A secret trust can also arise if a person decides to die intestate, relying on a beneficiary under the intestacy rules who has agreed to hold the property received under the intestacy rules as a trustee for someone else.

If the three requirements below (at pp. 124–5) are met, there will be a valid secret trust. (See **Stickland** v **Aldridge** (1804) Ves 516 and **Re Gardner** [1923] 2 Ch 230.)

A half-secret trust arises where the testator leaves property to a person who is expressed in the will to be a trustee but the terms of the trust are not set out in the will. So it is clear from the will that the person to whom the property passes cannot take the property absolutely. The terms of the trust are still secret, however, in that they have been communicated to the trustee separately and do not appear on the face of the will and so may still remain private.

Example

A secret trust arises where a testatrix (Donna) says to Ivor that she is leaving property in her will to him to hold on trust for Benny. There is nothing on the face of the will to indicate that Ivor is to take as a trustee. Ivor agrees to so hold the property and the will is executed in compliance with s 9 of the Wills Act 1837. Donna dies. If Ivor were allowed to keep the legacy for himself, relying on the express terms of the will and arguing that the trust in favour of Benny was ineffective as the Wills Act 1837 requires that any disposition of property must comply with the terms of s 9 if it is to be effective on death, he would be using the provisions of the statute as an engine of fraud as his promise to Donna would make it fraudulent on his part to claim the property as his own. If he had not agreed Donna would have had the opportunity to change her will. As it was she died believing that Ivor would keep his promise and that Benny would benefit under the trust.

The doctrine of secret trusts should not be confused with incorporation of documents by reference. Under this doctrine, where a document is referred to in the will and it exists when the will is executed and it can be identified, it is then regarded as part of that will and operates as a testamentary document. As such it becomes a public document once the testator has died.

Rules governing fully secret trusts

In the Court of Appeal decision of **Margulies** v **Margulies and Others** [2000] All ER (D) 344 Nourse LJ quoted with approval a statement of Peter Gibson LJ in **Kasperbauer** v **Griffith** (2000) 1 WTLR 333, which he (Nourse LJ) said was accepted by all sides as correctly stating the principles of secret trusts:

> [T]he authorities make plain that what is needed is: (i) an intention by the testator to create a trust, satisfying the traditional requirement of three certainties (that is to say certain language in imperative form, certain subject matter and certain objects or beneficiaries); (ii) the communication of the trust to the legatees, and (iii) acceptance of the trust by the legatee, which acceptance can take the form of silent acquiescence . . . It is an essential element that the testator must intend to subject the legatee to an obligation in favour of the intended beneficiary. That will be evidenced by appropriately imperative, as distinct from precatory language.

This neatly sets out the key requirements for there to be a valid secret trust and reinforces the fact that, before the death of the creator of the secret trust (the point at which the secret trust becomes effective), there are no legally binding obligations either on the part of the creator or the proposed secret trustee.

In the event, Nourse LJ was unable to find any relevant communication made by the proposed creator of the secret trust which was expressed in certain language and in imperative form. Additionally, there was a failure to establish any arguable case as to certainty of subject matter. Thus no valid secret trust was found to exist.

The three requirements set out in *Margulies v Margulies and Others* will now be dealt with in turn.

Evidence of intention to create a trust

Either written or oral evidence may be sufficient to prove the existence of the trust and contradict the express terms of the will. As with all trusts, however, the evidence must clearly show the intent to create a trust, to bind the beneficiary under the will to carry out the testator's wishes. There are several cases involving precatory words. For example, in *Re Snowden* [1979] 2 All ER 172, the evidence suggested that the testator had left property to her brother in the hope that he would do with it whatever he thought she would have wanted. This expression of hope, mere precatory words, was not sufficient to impose an obligation on her brother to deal with it in a particular way. Again in *McCormick v Grogan* (1869) LR 4 HL 82 the testator made a will leaving all his property to G. The testator told G about the will and said that a letter would be found with the will. The letter said: 'I do not wish you to act strictly to these instructions but leave it entirely to your own good judgement to do as you think I would if living and as the parties are deserving.' This, the House of Lords decided, did not create a secret trust as the letter did not seek to impose any legal obligation on G to act in any particular way.

And again in *Kasperbauer v Griffith* (2000) 1 WTLR 333, the court refused to find a valid secret trust in the absence of any proven intention to impose a binding obligation. The testator told his family how he wanted property to be dealt with after his death. He referred to his wife 'knowing what she had to do'. The evidence was that he was prepared to rely on his belief that his wishes would be carried out, imposing a moral and not a legal obligation. (See also *Margulies v Margulies* [2000] All ER (D) 344.)

Like any trust there must be certainty of beneficiaries and certainty of property as well as the certainty that a binding trust was intended.

Communication of the trust

If a beneficiary is left property by will that he is not to receive for his own benefit but is to hold it on secret trust for others, in order for the trust to be effective he must have been informed of the terms of the trust and have agreed to be bound by them, before the property is received by him, i.e. before the death of the testator. In the absence of this communication and acceptance (see below) the beneficiary is entitled to take the property beneficially. Similarly if a beneficiary under the intestacy rules has not been informed that he is to hold benefits obtained under the intestacy rules as a trustee and has not agreed to so hold the property (see below) he can take the property beneficially. In both situations if the beneficiary does not know he is intended to hold the property on trust, it is not unconscionable for him to take beneficially.

In *Wallgrave v Tebbs* (1855) 2 K& J 313, money and land was left to Mr Martin and Mr Tebbs as joint tenants. Neither had received any communication from the testator before his death, but afterwards it emerged that he had intended them to use the property for certain charitable works. It was held that Martin and Tebbs were not bound by this intention and so took the property absolutely.

It is not sufficient that the beneficiary be told simply that he is to be a trustee: he must be told the terms of the trust. In *Re Boyes* (1884) 26 Ch D 531, the beneficiary had previously been told that he was to be a trustee but no terms were communicated; it was held that the beneficiary held the property on resulting trust for the next of kin. He could not of course take beneficially as he knew he was to take the property as a trustee. It was only the terms of the trust that were not effectively communicated.

It is probably sufficient that the intended trustee be given the details in a sealed envelope 'to be opened in the event of my death'. As was said in *Re Keen* [1937] 1 All ER 452 by Lord Wright, this is equivalent to a ship sailing under sealed orders: the ship is sailing under orders even though the exact terms are not ascertained by the captain until later.

Acceptance of the trusteeship

The legatee will only be obliged to hold the property on trust if there has been a promise by the secret trustee that he will carry out the testator's intentions. The promise may be expressly made or tacit. Thus, in *Ottaway* v *Norman* [1971] 3 All ER 1325, a testator made a will in which he left his bungalow to his housekeeper absolutely. Some time later he told the housekeeper that he had left her the bungalow but that he intended that she would leave it to his son in her will. The son was present when this took place. Although the housekeeper said nothing she later made a will leaving the bungalow to the son. Later, after the son and the housekeeper had argued she made another will which left the bungalow to a friend. Brightman J found that a secret trust had been created. It was the duty of the housekeeper to expressly object if she did not wish to be bound by the secret trust obligations. Silence was taken to amount to acceptance.

Again in *Moss* v *Cooper* (1861) 1 J& H 352, the silence of the intended trustee was deemed to be sufficient. He will be bound unless he expresses his refusal to act.

It has been held that these same rules will apply to the nomination of a beneficiary under a life insurance policy: *Gold* v *Hill* (1998) *The Times*, 24 August. If such a beneficiary receives instructions, at any time before receiving the benefit, that he is to hold it on trust, he is bound by that trust. It would appear that the same could equally well arise upon a next of kin inheriting on intestacy.

Half-secret trusts

The rules governing these appear to be the same as those for fully secret trusts except in one important aspect. The trusts arising under a fully secret trust may be communicated to the trustees any time before the property vests in them, i.e. at any time before the death of the testator. However, in the case of a half-secret trust the communication must be before or at the same time as the will is made. It was said by Viscount Sumner in *Blackwell* v *Blackwell* [1929] AC 318 that:

> a testator cannot reserve to himself a power to make future unwitnessed dispositions by merely naming a trustee and leaving the purposes of the trust to be supplied afterwards . . . To hold otherwise would indeed be to enable the testator to 'give the go-by' to the requirements of the Wills Act because he did not choose to comply with them.

It is probable that the requirement of communication before or at the time that a will is made emanates from *Johnson* v *Ball* [1851] 5 De G& Sm 85. In *Blackwell* v *Blackwell*

	Communication to secret trustee					
	Before will made		Date will made		After will made	
	Half secret	Fully secret	Half secret	Fully secret	Half secret	Fully secret
General rule	✓	✓	✓	✓	✗	✓
Gift to secret trustees as joint tenants	✓	✓	✓	✓	✗	✓*
Gift to secret trustees as tenants in common	✓*	✓*	✓*	✓*	✗	✓*

*Only those to whom the trust has been communicated will be bound. Others will not be bound and can take beneficially (fully secret trust) or hold on trust for the residuary beneficiaries (half secret trusts).

Figure 4.3 Secret trusts – time of communication to secret trustees

Viscount Sumner having cited **Johnson v Ball** simply accepts that this is the correct rule without discussion.

It is difficult to understand this argument, since it appears to be the exact situation which is allowed by a fully secret trust. This difficulty is compounded by the fact that under a half-secret trust the beneficiary under the will or under the intestacy rules can never take the property beneficially. It should be noted, however, that the statement was *obiter* in **Blackwell v Blackwell** as the testator had communicated his purposes before the codicil was executed. In the subsequent case of **Re Keen**, where the statement was reiterated, the will referred to purposes to be communicated whereas in fact the purposes had already been communicated. There was thus an inconsistency which caused the trust to fail anyway. Nonetheless, in the absence of any further authority, there appears to be an inconsistency in the rules as to communication between half-secret and secret trusts.

Gift by will to co-owners

Where the testator leaves the property by will to co-owners, intending them to hold it on secret trust, the question arises as to how they must be informed of their trust obligations. The rules vary according to whether the trustees hold as joint tenants or tenants in common.

Where they hold as tenants in common, then only those trustees who are informed of the trust are bound by it. Where the trustees hold as joint tenants, then if some of them have been informed of the trust and have accepted it before the will is executed then all are bound. If none is informed or accepts before the execution of the will, but some accept afterwards, then only those who accept are bound. Note that this latter situation can arise only in the case of fully secret trusts because informing of the trust after the execution of the will is invalid anyway in the case of half-secret trusts. Authority for these rather illogical rules can be found in *Re Stead* [1900] 1 Ch 237, where the reason for them is stated to be the avoidance of fraud.

Amendments to the trusts

Where the testator makes any changes to the terms of the trust or to the property which is to be the subject of the trust, he must, of course, inform the intended trustees of those changes. If, for example, having left money in his will to certain persons and having informed them that they are to hold it on trust, the testator later adds to the gift, he must inform the trustees that they are to hold this on trust also, otherwise they will be entitled to that extra money themselves: *Re Colin Cooper* [1939] 3 All ER 586.

Theoretical basis for secret trusts

Objective
6

On the face of it there might seem to be nothing objectionable about a testator wishing to keep secret some of the dispositions he makes on death. However, it must be remembered that all dispositions on death should comply with the provisions of the Wills Act 1837 s 9, i.e. that they must be contained in a valid, signed and attested will (unless they fall within the rules relating to statutory intestacy or the testator is a privileged testator under section 11 of the Wills Act 1837 which provides that any soldier being in actual military service, or any mariner or seaman being at sea, may dispose of his property after death without formalities).

Clearly, the fully secret trust does not comply with the requirements of s 9 of the Wills Act 1837. On the face of the will the beneficiary takes the property for himself. The provision for the secret beneficiary is nowhere mentioned in the will. In the half-secret trust, though, the beneficiary is expressed in the will to be a trustee; the true beneficiary under the trust is again not identified in the will.

How then is this breach of the statute justified?

There are three main theories. The first theory is that secret trusts are an application of the maxim that equity will not allow a statute to be used as an engine of fraud. The second theory is that secret trusts are express trusts that arise independently and outside the will and are therefore not within the ambit of the Wills Act 1837 s 9. The third theory is that secret trusts operate as constructive trusts.

The traditional view is that secret trusts are an example of the maxim that equity will not permit a statute to be used as an engine of fraud. If the beneficiary under the will has accepted the obligation to hold the property on trust for others, it would clearly be fraudulent if he were later allowed to deny the trust on the ground that it was void in not complying with the statute.

The difficulty with the fraud argument is that it is less easy to apply to half-secret trusts. Here the beneficiary is stated in the will to be a trustee so even if he were to deny the trust he would still not be able to take the property beneficially if the trust were invalid for this or any other reason. It may be that the courts' reluctance to recognise half-secret trusts stemmed from this difficulty. It may also be remembered that other cases concerned with avoidance of fraud, such as *Rochefoucauld v Boustead*, have gone further than merely avoiding the fraud and have actually carried out the settlor's wishes.

A more modern view as to the basis for secret and half-secret trusts is that they arise entirely outside the will and thus do not need to comply with the Wills Act. This was stated in relation to half-secret trusts in *Blackwell v Blackwell* and was reiterated in the case of a potential secret trust in *Re Snowden*. Here, Sir Robert Megarry V-C acknowledged that fraud provided an historical explanation of the doctrine of secret trusts; the doctrine evolved as a means of preventing fraud. However, it was now clear, he said, that secret trusts may be established in cases where there is no possibility of fraud:

> The whole basis of secret trusts . . . is that they operate outside the will, changing nothing that is written in it, and allowing it to operate according to its tenor, but then fastening a trust on to the property in the hands of the recipient.

What practical effect might these theories have on the operation of such trusts? One effect can be seen in *Re Snowden* itself. If the trust is not one involving potential fraud, as most such trusts will not, then the special, high standard of proof appropriate to fraud cases will not have to be met. The standard of proof required to establish the existence of the secret trust is the ordinary civil standard.

Two further cases supporting the 'independent trust' theory are *Re Young* [1950] 2 All ER 1245 and *Re Gardner* [1923] 2 Ch 230. In *Re Young* one of the beneficiaries of a half-secret trust had actually witnessed the will. If the trust operated under the will this would render that legacy invalid. However, the beneficiary's interest was held valid: he did not take under the will but rather, by implication, under a separate trust. Similarly, in *Re Gardner* where a beneficiary under a half-secret trust had predeceased the testator, the interest of the beneficiary was held to have taken effect when the trust was created, which was before the beneficiary's death. The will merely had the effect of vesting the trust property in the trustee, who therefore held it on trust for the beneficiary's personal representatives.

Against this may be quoted the case of *Re Maddock* [1902] 2 Ch 220, where the trustee predeceased the testator. The secret trust was held to fail, which argues that the secret trust takes effect only at the time of the vesting of the property on the testator's death. Where the trustee is identified as such in the will (i.e. a half-secret trust), the trust may possibly be saved by the maxim that equity will not permit a trust to fail for want of a trustee.

It is widely accepted that the finding in *Re Gardner*, that a secret trust was constituted before the will took effect, may be wrong. However, it has been argued that where a testator revokes a will containing a secret trust, a claim on behalf of a would-be beneficiary may succeed, if based on estoppel. This claim would arise as soon as a testator goes back on a promise to the beneficiary and revokes or changes the will to affect the secret trust.

Secret trusts: express or constructive?

If secret trusts are permitted to circumvent the Wills Act 1837 s 9 to avoid fraud, then they should be regarded as constructive trusts. If, on the other hand, they exist entirely independently of the will, then they must be regarded as express trusts. The significance of this is whether the Law of Property Act 1925 s 53(1)(b) applies to them, or, in other words, is a secret trust of land required to be evidenced in writing? In *Ottaway* v *Norman* [1971] 3 All ER 1325, an oral fully secret trust of land was upheld. It is difficult, however, to uphold half-secret trusts as other than express and therefore writing would appear to be necessary, though no direct authority exists.

See Chapter 12 (p. 297) for a discussion of constructive trusts.

It is interesting to note that the High Court of New Zealand in *Brown* v *Pourau* [1995] 1 NZLR 352 upheld a secret trust as constructive, and therefore valid, even though the subject matter was land. The court did this, not on the 'fraud' argument, but rather on the more general principle of the 'remedial' constructive trust. The court conceded, however, that English and New Zealand views on the constructive trust differed, in that in England the constructive trust has not generally been regarded as a remedy.

This issue is discussed further in Chapter 12.

Summary

- An express trust is one expressly declared by a settlor or, where the trust is created by will, the testator.

- In order to be valid, an express trust must comply with certain requirements, which are set out in this chapter.

- The settlor must have the capacity, in the sense of mental ability, to declare a trust; the capacity of minors and the mentally incompetent is therefore curtailed.

- The terms of a trust must be certain, particularly in three ways. The settlor must intend to create a trust, as opposed to a gift or other relationship, and must impose a binding obligation on the trustees. The settlor must identify the trust property and the interest of each beneficiary. In the case of fixed trusts, the settler must identify all those beneficiaries or provide a means by which they can be identified.

- The trust property must be validly transferred to trustees, and the extent to which the beneficiaries may be able to enforce the settlor's promise to do so must also be considered.

- In the declaration of trusts of land and of trusts declared by will, the settlor or testator must comply with statutory requirements of writing. A beneficiary must also comply with the requirement of writing when transferring or disposing of existing beneficial interests.

- There is a basic difference between fully secret and half-secret trusts in that with a fully secret trust the fact that a beneficiary under a will holds the property on a trust is not revealed whereas with a half-secret trust, although the terms of the trust are not set out, the fact that the beneficiary takes as a trustee is stated in the will. The trusts are useful when a testator, knowing that once proved a will is a public document and its terms can be seen by any member of the public, wishes to keep the details of gifts/trusts off the face of the will.

- The basic requirements for fully secret trusts are an intention to create a trust, communication to the secret trustee and acceptance of the trust by the secret trustee.

- The basic requirements for half-secret trusts are the same as for fully secret trusts, except that communication has to be before or at the time that the will is made.

- Secret trusts are an exception to the requirement that in order to dispose of property on death the will has to comply with the formalities set out in the Wills Act 1937 s 9. There are several theories as to why secret trusts, which do not comply with these formalities, are nevertheless valid and effective. Also there is some dispute as to whether secret trusts are express or constructive trusts.

Reference

P Matthews, 'All about bare trusts' [2005] 5 PCB 266, 6 PCB 336.

Further reading

Certainty

J Martin, 'Certainty of subject matter: a defence of *Hunter* v *Moss*' [1996] Conv 223.

Constitution of trusts

J Garton, 'The role of the trust mechanism in the rule in *Re Rose*' [2003] Conv 364.
Argues that the rule in *Re Rose* has changed in the light of *Pennington v Waine*.

T Halliwell, 'Perfecting imperfect gifts and trusts: have we reached the end of the Chancellor's foot?' [2003] Conv 192.
Explains the rule in *Milroy v Lord* and the implications of *Pennington v Waine*.

S Haren, 'Gifting chattels: the available methods considered' [2014] 3 PCB 119.
Discusses *Day v Arnold* along with *Thomas v Times Books* and *Re Pennington*.

P Luxton 'In search of perfection: the *Re Rose* rule rationale' [2012] Conv 70.
Considers the principles in *Re Rose*, along with *Pennington v Waine* and *Curtis v Pulbrook*.

R P Meagher and J R F Lehane, 'Trusts of voluntary covenants' (1976) 92 LQR 425.

C Rickett, 'Completely constituting an *inter vivos* trust' [2001] Conv 515.
Critiques the decision in *Choithram v Pagarani*.

Formality requirements

G Battersby, 'Formalities for the disposition of equitable interests under a trust' (1979) 43 Conv 17.

B Green, '*Grey, Oughtred* and *Vandervell*, a contextual reappraisal' (1984) 47 MLR 385.

P Milne, '*Oughtred* revisited' (1997) 113 LQR 213.

Secret trusts

E Challinor, 'Debunking the myth of secret trusts' [2005] Conv 492.
Asserts that secret trusts are a covert device by which the courts avoid the statutory formalities for making a valid will. Discusses if there is a logical rationale for upholding secret trusts.

S Evans, 'Should professionally drafted half-secret trusts be extinct after *Larke v Nugus*?' (2014) Conv 3, 229.
Discusses if half-secret trusts when contained in wills drafted by solicitors can survive given that in *Larke v Nugus* (2000) WTLR 1033 the Court of Appeal stated that where a solicitor prepares a will for a client he should supply a statement of evidence where its validity is being contested. The statement should extend to all matters surrounding the making of the will which are relevant to the questions in the action and, in the view of Buckley LJ, this should extend to the circumstances leading up to the preparation and making of the will.
Suggests some of the reasons why a testator might wish to keep his dispositions secret, and outlines how secret and half-secret trusts can be used for this purpose.

J Glister, 'Disclaimer and secret trusts' (2014) Conv 1, 11–26.
Discusses if the disclaimer of a legacy by a fully secret trustee defeats the trust. Is the situation different (1) after the intended secret trustee accepted the obligation but before the testator died; and (2) between the testator's death and the secret trustee receiving the intended trust property? Is a secret trustee's duty to accept the trust property an equitable personal obligation?

D Kincaid, 'The tangled web: the relationship between a secret trust and the will' [2000] Conv 421.
Covers the essence of secret trusts and the relationship between a secret trust and a will. Discusses if a secret trust has an independent existence.

P Mathews, 'The true basis of the half secret trust' [1979] Conv 360.
Argues that the doctrine of incorporation by reference is the basis of half-secret trusts.

R Meagre, 'Secret trusts – do they have a future?' [2003] Conv 203.
Focuses on the extent to which secret trusts are used in practice.

M Pawlowski, 'Constituting a secret trust by estoppel' [2004] Conv 388.

D Wilde, 'Secret and semi-secret trusts: justifying distinctions between the two' [1995] Conv 366. Discussion of the justification for the differences between secret and half-secret trusts. Argues that the current situation represents the best balance between the state's insistence on formalities for a valid will and sympathy for the circumstances that commonly lead to the creation of a secret/half-secret trust.

5

Powers and discretionary trusts

Objectives

After reading this chapter you should:

1. Understand the difference between trusts and powers and the different obligations and discretions that may arise.

2. Understand the practical reasons for the use of discretionary trusts as opposed to fixed trusts.

3. Understand the role of the donee of a power of appointment in choosing who may benefit.

4. Be aware of the rights that the objects or beneficiaries may have to the trust property.

5. Appreciate the obligations imposed on the trustees of a discretionary trust with regard to the selection of objects (or 'beneficiaries').

6. Understand the effect that the obligation of selection has on the degree of certainty with which the beneficiaries or objects must be identified.

Trusts and powers, obligations and discretions

Objective 1

The chapter on express trusts assumed that such trusts were concerned purely with obligations imposed on trustees, and that trustees had no flexibility as to how their trust was to be implemented. Thus, where a trust requires distribution of income among the settlor's children, it was assumed that the trustee has merely to carry out that instruction. This chapter is concerned with situations where the trustee has choices and discretions to exercise and the effect that this may have on the rules as to the certainty with which the objects of the trust in particular must be identified.

Terminology

The language used to describe the various parties to powers and discretionary trusts is rather different to that usually used in the case of fixed trusts and it is important to be clear on this language at the outset. The person who has the power to select who will receive a benefit is referred to as the 'donee of the power' or the 'discretionary trustee'. The persons who may receive the benefit, if selected by the donee, are referred to as the 'objects' of the power, equivalent, in other words, to the beneficiaries of a fixed trust but, as we shall see, with very different, and much more limited, rights.

Trusts and powers distinguished

It is customary to distinguish between trusts and powers on the grounds that trusts are obligatory, whereas powers are discretionary. This is true but somewhat misleading, for it is possible and even normal for trustees to be given powers. In other words, they will be given discretion over matters to do with the carrying out of the trust. Thus, a trustee will normally have a duty to invest the trust fund, but will normally have a power to choose suitable investments from a defined range of choices.

Discretionary trusts

The term 'discretionary' trust implies a situation where the trustee has some form of power or discretion. Other terms have also been used, such as 'trust power' and 'power in the nature of a trust'. It is, it is submitted, unclear to what extent these situations need to be distinguished in practice. All are concerned, though, with situations where someone, who may be the trustee, has the power or discretion, i.e. the power to choose who, from a range of possible beneficiaries, shall actually receive benefits under the trust. If these terms are to cover all such situations, it will be apparent that there could be a wide variety of discretions involved. The possible gradations between unfettered discretion on the one hand and strict obligation on the other are considerable and so the rules of construction applicable to any of these devices will need to vary also. The fundamental requirement is that the court must be able to give effect to the settlor's wishes by requiring the trustees to carry out whatever obligations they may have in any given situation.

Role of the discretionary trust

Why then might a settlor choose to grant such a power to allow his trustees to decide who will receive the benefit, rather than identifying the beneficiary himself? Clearly, by doing this the settlor is giving up a measure of control over future distribution of the fund, but there may be a number of advantages in making that concession.

Protection of the trust fund

In the first place, the potential beneficiaries, or objects, of a discretionary trust do not have any property in the fund whereas the beneficiary under a fixed trust is equitable owner of his interest. The objects of a discretionary trust do not own anything until they are actually selected and receive their share. Formerly, this had certain tax advantages since what they received was not income and the capital did not belong to them either. This advantage has now been removed by the whole fund being subjected to periodic taxation instead. Since the discretionary objects do not own the fund or have an equitable interest in it, it cannot be subject to any control or disposition by them or be made liable for their debts. Thus, whereas a life tenant under a fixed trust may sell or mortgage his interest or use it as security for loans, the discretionary beneficiary owns nothing which he can sell or which his creditors can seize. The discretionary trust may therefore be a useful device for a settlor who wishes to protect family property against a spendthrift. Indeed, a particular form of trust, the protective trust, uses the discretionary trust in this way, turning a fixed trust subject to conditions into a discretionary trust if the beneficiary does anything which jeopardises the fund.

Adaptability to changing circumstances

The second advantage of the discretionary trust lies in its flexibility. The settlor is unlikely to be able to foresee all the changing circumstances which may in the future affect the needs of the beneficiaries. It is therefore sensible to give the trustees a discretion as to distribution of the funds in the light of those changing circumstances. In particular, it may be useful in the light of changing tax liability to ensure that income does not fall into the hands of higher-rate taxpayers.

The discretionary trust has thus been described as a popular mechanism for the fulfilment of estate planning aims. Administratively, it is uncomplicated. Income can be split at source among different taxpaying beneficiaries, and the inherent flexibility of the discretionary trust machinery allows vast numbers of objects to be named as eligible to benefit and concedes a power to trustees to determine needs and priorities among them from time to time. This, it is submitted, represents a fairly typical modern use of the discretionary trust: to adapt to changing personal and taxation circumstances among the potential beneficiaries.

Obligations in relation to powers of appointment

Objective
3

This section is concerned with the nature of the obligations which trustees and others in a fiduciary position generally have in relation to powers of appointment. The position of trustees and fiduciaries must be contrasted with that of non-fiduciaries. It has already been stated that trusts are obligatory whereas powers are discretionary. The trustee of a fixed trust must carry out the terms of the trust as set out by the settlor. Thus, if the trust requires the distribution of the trust income equally among the settlor's children, then that is what the trustee must do. The administrative problems which might arise, for example, if one of the children has disappeared, have been considered in connection with the question of certainty (see p. 98). If the settlor gives some named person the power to decide on the distribution instead of giving fixed instructions as to distribution, what obligations then arise? Such a power may be given to anyone, not necessarily the trustee. As has already been said, a power is discretionary: it does not have to be exercised. Where it is given to someone other than a trustee or other person in a fiduciary position, the donee of the power need do nothing: he is under no obligation to make a choice or to consider the candidates. Where, however, the power is given to a trustee or other fiduciary, though that trustee is not obliged to exercise the power, nonetheless, he must consider from time to time whether to exercise it. As Megarry V-C stated, in *Re Hay's Settlement Trust* [1981] 3 All ER 786:

> Normally the trustee is not bound to exercise a mere power and the court will not compel him to do so. That, however, does not mean that he can simply fold his arms and ignore it, for normally he must from time to time consider whether or not to exercise the power, and the court may direct him to do this.

When he exercises the power, he must of course (as in the case of all trusts and powers) confine himself to what is authorised, and not go beyond it. But this is not the only restriction.

Whereas a person who is not in a fiduciary position is free to exercise the power in any way he wishes unhampered by any fiduciary duties, a trustee to whom, as such, a power is given is bound by the duties of his office in exercising that power to do so in a responsible manner according to its purpose. In *Re Hay's Settlement Trust*, Megarry V-C went on to consider what this would entail in practice and suggested that the trustee in this position needs to be aware of the range of the class, 'the size of the problem' and whether, in relation to other possible claimants, a particular grant is appropriate. This formulation, however, may be too demanding. In *Re Gestetner* [1953] 1 All ER 1150, for example, Harman J indicated that the fiduciary donees of a power were under 'no obligation to do more than consider from time to time the merits of such persons of the specified class as are known to them and, if they think fit, give them something'. It seems clear, therefore, that the requirements of consideration and survey will depend very much on the size of the class involved, and that this in turn will affect the degree of certainty with which that class must be identified, an issue considered further below.

It was formerly believed to be the case that under the rule in *Re Hastings-Bass* (*Re Hastings-Bass* [1974] 2 All ER 193), the courts had the power to interfere with or overturn the trustees' exercise of their discretion where it is clear that the decision they had made was the result of a mistake as to the effect of that decision; this power has, however, been severely curtailed by recent decisions.

This is discussed in detail in Chapter 15 (p. 427).

Rights of the objects

Objective 4

The position of the objects of the power, i.e. the class of persons from whom the selection may be made, is in effect the mirror image of the position of the trustee. The objects have no beneficial interest because they cannot compel the trustee to exercise his power in their favour and give them a share. They have merely the hope, or *spes*, that they will be given a share. They do, however, have *locus standi* to go to court to enforce whatever obligations the trustee or donee does have. That is to say, they can require him to consider, where the donee is a fiduciary, and they can prevent him from exceeding his power or from acting fraudulently. In some types of discretionary trust, the trustee may be obliged to distribute even though he has a discretion as to whom he distributes to. In this 'exhaustive' type of discretionary trust it is arguable that, as a whole, the class of objects own the fund and therefore could all get together to require the trustees either to vary the trust or wind it up and distribute the fund to them: *Re Smith* [1928] Ch 915. This point will be considered further in relation to beneficiaries' powers.

See Chapter 6 (p. 157).

Whatever rights the class as a whole may have to call for distribution, it is clear that no individual has an interest in the fund, whether the discretionary trust is exhaustive or non-exhaustive: *Sainsbury v IRC* [1969] 3 All ER 919, *Gartside v IRC* [1968] 1 All ER 121.

There seems, therefore, to be a wide range of situations in which trustees might be given discretion as to the distribution of trust funds among a range of objects and a range of reasons why such a power would be given. However, all would appear to share the characteristic that a trustee, when given such a power, must periodically consider its exercise.

This would, however, appear to be the limit of the obligation: there would appear to be nothing that either the court or the potential beneficiaries can do to make the trustee exercise the power. The discretion lies entirely with the trustee, just as the power of choice lay with one of the sisters in *Boyce v Boyce* (see p. 103) and, the sister having died without making the choice, the court could not make it for her.

Further obligations: the discretionary trust

Objective 5

In a number of cases, however, the courts have considered whether any further obligations or rights exist. The cases fall into two categories, dealing with rather different factual situations.

Burrough v *Philcox*

Burrough v *Philcox* (1840) 5 My& Cr 72

The first line of cases starts with **Burrough v Philcox**. Here the settlor, S, gave his surviving child power to distribute S's estate among S's nephews and nieces 'either all to one of them, or to as many of them as my surviving child shall think proper'. The child died without making the choice. In accordance with general principles, the power itself could not, of course, be exercised since the discretion lay with the child, who was dead. The court concluded that the words of the settlor indicated an intention that the class, i.e. the nephews and nieces, should as a whole benefit in any event and so the court in effect implied a trust for equal distribution in default of appointment. In other words, it was as if the settlor had made a gift over to them equally in default of the power to select being exercised.

As Lord Cottenham said:

> [W]hen there appears a general intention in favour of the class and a particular intention in favour of particular individuals of the class, to be selected by another person, and the particular intention fails from the selection not being made, the court will carry into effect the general intention.

It should be noted that this does not affect the power itself. It does not suggest that the power is in some way obligatory. Rather, it merely concludes as a matter of construction that in addition to the power there is also a trust in default of the exercise of the power. The settlor could have expressly provided such a trust, or could have provided for a gift over to some third party, but did not do so. The court can, of course, give effect to the trust; it can carry out the obligation, which it does, in the absence of any formula for determining distribution, by adopting the maxim 'equality is equity' and distributing to the members of the class equally.

Application of the rule in *Burrough* v *Philcox*

First, this solution to the problem of the non-exercise of a power can arise only once the time or opportunity for the exercise has passed. If the donee is still alive but simply refuses to choose, then nothing can be done.

Secondly, it can apply only to a special power of appointment, i.e. a power to distribute within a limited class of objects. The reason for this is obvious: unless the class is a limited one, equal distribution is impossible. It cannot apply, therefore, either to a general power, which is one to appoint to anyone in the world, or to a hybrid power, to appoint to anyone except the members of a limited class.

Thirdly, as has already been indicated, this solution is possible only where the settlor has indicated that he wishes the class to benefit in any event. If the settlor were to provide for a gift over to some third party in the event of failure to exercise the power, he would clearly not be showing that he expects the class to get the money. In this case the money would go to the person entitled in default, not to the members of the class. (The absence of a gift over is not, however, conclusive either way: *Re Weeke's Settlement* [1897] 1 Ch 289.) As one would expect, this is a question to be determined on the facts of each case.

McPhail v Doulton

The particular form of power in *Burrough* v *Philcox* has been referred to as a trust power. Unfortunately, the same term has been used in the line of cases beginning with *McPhail* v *Doulton* [1970] 2 All ER 228. This concerned not a small family trust with a small group of potential beneficiaries, but a large benevolent fund for a wide range of people associated with a company. A large sum of money was set aside, out of the income from which the trustees were directed to make grants 'at their absolute discretion to any of the officers or employees or ex-officers or ex-employees of the company or any relatives or dependants of any such persons'.

In addition, the courts were faced with a different question. In *Burrough* v *Philcox* the power had not been exercised so the courts had to consider the consequences. In *McPhail* v *Doulton*, on the other hand, the courts had first to determine what kind of settlement the gift entailed. It was also different in that the power in *Burrough* envisaged a one-off decision on the distribution of future capital, whereas the discretion in *McPhail*, as is typical of discretionary trusts, entailed the continuing management and distribution of income. Was the settlement in *McPhail* a trust or a power? At first instance and by a majority in the Court of Appeal it was held to be a power, whereas the House of Lords held unanimously that it was a trust.

The courts having determined that this was a trust, the question must then be asked, what were the obligations of the trustees? As they were fiduciaries, there is no doubt that they must periodically consider distribution, but this, as we have seen, is true of any power held by a trustee. If the obligation is greater than that, one possible clue might be the way in which the court might enforce the trust if the trustees refused to act. One answer, as in *Burrough* v *Philcox*, is to 'give effect to the general intention' of the settlor by ordering equal distribution among the class. This would, however, be impractical in a case like *McPhail* v *Doulton* where the class of beneficiaries is so wide. As will shortly be seen, the view that the court took on the nature of the trustees' obligations in a *McPhail* v *Doulton* case and the measures that the court might take had major implications for the type of class which could be benefited by such a trust. Lord Wilberforce in *McPhail* v *Doulton* recognised that the trust had to be in such a form that the court could intervene. He said that it would do so

> in a manner best calculated to give effect to the settlor's or testator's intentions. It may do so by appointing new trustees, or by authorising or directing representative persons of the classes of beneficiaries to prepare a scheme for distribution, or even, should the proper basis for distribution appear, by itself directing the trustees so to distribute.

It may be that in some cases of the *Burrough* v *Philcox* type an equal distribution will be most appropriate, where the settlor might reasonably have contemplated an equal distribution as a reasonable way to deal with the property. This can hardly have been a sensible solution in a case like *McPhail* v *Doulton*, so some other kind of solution would have to be worked out. It is worth remembering, perhaps, that the court was not called upon to do this in *McPhail* v *Doulton* and so could perhaps allow itself the luxury of speculating in the abstract without having actually to face the problem.

This does not particularly help us to identify the precise nature of the trustees' obligations in such cases, however. The obligation to consider includes, it would appear, an obligation to survey the class in question. Such obligation to survey is apparently more demanding in the case of discretionary trusts. As Lord Wilberforce said in *McPhail* v *Doulton*: '[I]n each case the trustees ought to make such a survey as will enable them to carry out their fiduciary duty. A wider and more comprehensive range of enquiry is called for in the case of trust powers (i.e. discretionary trusts) than in the case of powers.'

Lord Wilberforce indicated that the mechanisms by which a trustee might carry this obligation out are very much a matter of degree. He said:

> He [the trustee] would examine the field, by class and category; might indeed make diligent and careful enquiries, depending on how much money he had to give away and the means at his disposal, as to the composition and needs of particular categories and of individuals within them; decide upon certain priorities or proportions, and then select individuals according to their needs or qualifications.

It is submitted, however, that it is difficult to recognise any clear difference between these obligations and those which Megarry V-C stated in *Re Hay* as applying to trustees exercising a power. It is clear that a difference is considered to exist, for example, by Megarry V-C in *Re Hay*: 'I consider that the duties under a discretionary trust are more stringent than those of trustees under a power of appointment.' It was not necessary in that case, however, to specify in what way they were more stringent. He did state, though, that the essence of the difference is that the beneficiaries under a trust (including discretionary trusts) have rights of enforcement which objects of a power lack. This is in line with Lord Wilberforce's statement in *McPhail* v *Doulton*: '[I]n the case of a trust power (i.e. discretionary trust), if the trustees do not exercise it, the court will.'

The distinction between powers and discretionary trusts appears, therefore, to be that the donee of a power does not have to exercise it – though if he is a fiduciary he must consider whether to exercise it – whereas the trustee of a discretionary trust must exercise that discretion. He must actually decide who of the class is to receive the money. This is true if the trust is exhaustive, since he is obliged to distribute the money, but, in the case of a non-exhaustive trust, it would appear that one exercise of his discretion would be to decide to accumulate and make no distribution. Presumably, however, he is only permitted to decide that after he has considered the class and made such survey as the particular class appears to demand. This can be illustrated by *McPhail* v *Doulton* itself. The settlor clearly envisaged some kind of benevolent fund for his employees. If his trustees had merely decided to accumulate the income without making the sort of survey that Lord Wilberforce envisaged, they would have been in breach of their trust. If *McPhail* v *Doulton* had been a power, on the other hand, it would appear that if the trustees had merely accumulated the income having decided not to make a survey at all, this decision could not be challenged. Obviously, the contrast between trusts and powers is greater if the discretionary trust is an exhaustive one, since here the money must be distributed. If the trust is non-exhaustive the money need not be distributed, but there must be good reasons, based on a survey of the class, why it has not been.

Pension fund surpluses: 'fiduciary powers in the full sense'

In *Mettoy Pension Trustees Ltd* v *Evans* [1991] 2 All ER 513, the above analysis was further complicated by the final recognition of a new sub-category of power, the 'fiduciary power in the full sense', which appears to have many similarities with the discretionary trust, but is apparently distinct from it.

The case concerned the ownership of surplus funds in a company pension fund. The pension fund was held by trustees, Mettoy Pension Trustees Ltd, under a deed which gave the parent company, Mettoy, a power of appointment of any surplus. Mettoy went into liquidation and the question arose as to whether Mettoy could release this power, thus permitting the surplus funds to go to Mettoy itself and hence to be used by the liquidators and distributed to Mettoy's creditors to meet Mettoy's debts. Was Mettoy, as donee of the power, entitled simply to abandon it without considering the class of potential objects, i.e. the pensioners?

As explained above, the donee of a power cannot be obliged to exercise it, and by implication may generally abandon it, thereby releasing the fund to those entitled in default. In this case, however, Warner J held that the donee could not release the power in this way. Mettoy had, apparently, a duty to consider the class of objects, though they could not be obliged to distribute to them. Warner J defined a power of this nature as fiduciary in the fullest sense.

This decision certainly appears to accord with the justice of the case. It was accepted that the surplus funds were probably in part made up of money that the pensioners themselves had put into the pension fund (they were not mere volunteers), and if Mettoy was under no obligation to consider them, giving Mettoy a power to do so would have been pointless: the money might as well have been held by Mettoy absolutely. To hold otherwise might also have made companies with large pension fund surpluses attractive to unscrupulous asset strippers, against whom the right of the pensioners ought certainly to prevail.

In reaching this conclusion, Warner J adopted an analysis of powers and discretions, classifying them into four categories:

> In this classification, category 1 comprises any power given to a person to determine the destination of trust property without that person being under any obligation to exercise the power or to preserve it. Typical of powers in this category is a special power of appointment where there is a trust in default of appointment. In such a case the donee of power owes a duty to the beneficiaries under that trust not to misuse the power, but he owes no duty to the objects of the power. He may therefore release the power but he may not enter into any transaction that would amount to a fraud on the power . . .
>
> Category 2 comprises any power conferred on the trustees of the property or on any other person as trustee of the power itself . . . I will call a power in this category 'a fiduciary power in the full sense'. A power in this category cannot be released: the donee of it owes a duty to the objects of the power to consider, as and when appropriate, whether he ought to exercise it; and he is to some extent subject to the control of the court in relation to its exercise.
>
> Category 3 comprises the discretion which is really a duty to form a judgment as to the existence or otherwise of particular circumstances giving rise to particular consequences.
>
> Category 4 comprises discretionary trusts, that is to say where someone, usually but not necessarily the trustee, is under a duty to select from among a class of beneficiaries those who are to receive, and the proportions in which they are to receive, income or capital of the trust property.

Several points may be made regarding this statement. First, it does not appear that the difference between categories 1 and 2 is merely between powers given to non-fiduciaries and powers given to fiduciaries. Warner J makes it clear that in certain circumstances, category 1 will be completely non-fiduciary, and hence, by implication, that on occasion it is fiduciary. It is clear that, in the context of this case, the important distinction between categories 1 and 2 is that category 1 powers can be released, whereas those of category 2 cannot. This does not provide in itself a test for which powers are in which category.

It will also be noted that the distinguishing feature of discretionary trusts is that the trustee has a duty to distribute among the class. This, as has already been explained, is only true for exhaustive discretionary trusts. It is clear that there are non-exhaustive discretionary trusts, such as *McPhail v Doulton* itself.

The other important implication of a power falling into category 2 concerns the remedies which are available for non-performance, or the extent and manner of the court's interference. His lordship concluded that the same range of possibilities was available as Lord Wilberforce suggested for discretionary trusts. In particular, just as Lord Wilberforce had spoken of the possibility of the court approving a scheme for distribution in the case of a discretionary trust, so Warner J felt that such a scheme could be applied to the power in the *Mettoy* case and he called upon counsel to formulate a proposal on this basis.

The advice of the Privy Council in *Schmidt v Rosewood Trust Ltd* [2003] 3 All ER 76, a case referred from the Isle of Man, also appears to erode the distinction between trusts and powers in certain contexts. Lord Wilberforce's comments in *McPhail v Doulton*, in which he pointed out the wide variety of different forms of settlement, and with them the interests created, between the rights of the beneficiary of a fixed trust on the one hand and those of the objects of a power on the other, is cited with approval. The case concerned the right to disclosure of trust documents. The trustees argued that this was a proprietary right, and that therefore the object of a power, who has no proprietary right in any part of the fund, could not claim disclosure. Lord Walker stated that a claim for disclosure did not depend upon a proprietary right, but was a matter of the court's discretion in the supervision of any trust. None had a right to disclosure, so in this respect the object and the beneficiary were in the same position, though in the exercise of its discretion, in this as in any other aspect of the court's intervention, the interest of the claimant would no doubt be significant. The object who, though he had no right to a share, had normally received payment under the trustees' discretion in the case of a small class, would be more likely to be able to obtain disclosure than one who was merely a member of a large class of remotely possible objects.

If the nature of the courts' role is to be blurred as between discretionary trusts and at least some powers, this will have important consequences for the test for certainty in such powers, as discussed below.

Certainty of objects

Objective 6

The nature of the trustees' obligations and the courts' powers to intervene will naturally have a serious effect in issues of certainty of objects, since clearly the objects or beneficiaries must be identified with sufficient certainty to enable the trustees and the courts to carry out their obligations, whatever they may be.

In the case of fixed trusts and powers

It is in the area of discretionary trusts that the issue of certainty of objects has presented most difficulties, particularly in the wake of *McPhail v Doulton*.

It has already been stated that the test for certainty of objects in the case of fixed trust is what is sometimes known as the 'list principle'. Since the fixed trust implies that the trustees have duties to each of the beneficiaries it is logical that they need to know who each and every one of the beneficiaries is. In the case of powers, however, the only obligation is to ensure that, if the power is exercised, it is exercised within the class of objects. Therefore, the donee of the power need only be able to ascertain that the individual he has chosen falls within the class. Thus, as was stated in *Re Gulbenkian* [1968] 3 All ER 785:

> The power is valid if it can be said with certainty whether any given individual is or is not a member of the class and does not fail simply because it is impossible to ascertain every member of the class.

Re Gulbenkian [1968] 3 All ER 785

In this case the settlement concerned included a special power for trustees to appoint in favour of Nubar Gulbenkian, and any wife and his children or remoter issue and any person in whose house or apartment or in whose company or under whose care or control or by or with whom he may from time to time be employed or residing. Clearly, a list of such people would have been impossible to draw up, but such was the nature of the power that such a list was irrelevant. The object of the power was to allow the trustees to make payments to individuals within certain categories whom they considered worthy of it. It follows therefore that it is perfectly possible to have a power to distribute to anyone in the world, or, as is often the case for tax purposes, to anyone except the settlor or his spouse.

The precise interpretation of the *Re Gulbenkian* or 'any given postulant' test has been carried on principally in the context of discretionary trusts, and it is in relation to such trusts that the discussion is continued below. As will be seen, the test for powers is the same as for discretionary trusts, with the probable exception that in the case of discretionary trusts there is the additional requirement of administrative workability.

The test of certainty in discretionary trusts

What test applies, then, to discretionary trusts? Prior to *McPhail v Doulton* the test was the same as for fixed trusts, that is that a list of all beneficiaries had to be capable of being drawn up: *IRC v Broadway Cottages Trust* [1955] Ch 20.

This was entirely suitable to a case like *Burrough v Philcox* but would, of course, have been fatal to *McPhail v Doulton* itself, since it would be impossible, and indeed hardly necessary to the settlor's intentions, to draw up a complete list of all the employees past and present, and their relations and dependants. *McPhail v Doulton* adopted the 'any given postulant' test similar to that for powers, and the validity of the *McPhail v Doulton* trust in the light of that test was further considered by the Court of Appeal in *Re Baden's Deed Trusts (No. 2)* [1972] 2 All ER 1304.

In analysing the 'any given postulant' test, the Court of Appeal drew a distinction between 'conceptual' and 'evidential' certainty, stating that the former is essential while the latter is not.

Conceptual certainty depends upon the precision of the words used by the settlor: do the words have a precise meaning, recognised by the trustees and the courts, to define the class the settlor intends to benefit?

Evidential certainty refers to the extent to which, as a matter of evidence in a particular case, specific persons can be identified as members of the class.

Thus, on the facts of *Re Baden* itself, the word in question was 'relative'. Two questions had to be considered. First, did the term 'relative' have a precise meaning that the trustees could understand and apply in defining the class? Secondly, was it possible to identify anybody who fell to be considered as being inside or outside that class? If the term 'relative' did not satisfy these tests, did this mean that the test for certainty had not been met and so the gift failed?

The court held that, to be valid, the class must be conceptually certain: the terms used must have a precise meaning. The court also held that the term 'relative' had such a precise meaning, though, ironically, the members of the court differed as to what that meaning was. The majority held that the term meant 'descendant of a common ancestor'. This inevitably meant that complete evidential certainty could not be obtained in this case. Though many people could no doubt show that they were relatives of company employees, most people in the world could not say either way. We may all be descendants of a common ancestor, but there is no way to prove it. The Court of Appeal held, however, that this is not fatal to the question of certainty. In the words of Megaw LJ:

> To my mind the test is satisfied if, as regards a substantial number of objects, it can be said with certainty that they fall within the trust; even though, as regards a substantial number of other persons, if they ever for some fanciful reason fell to be considered, the answer would have to be, not 'they are outside the trust' but 'it is not proven whether they are in or out'.

This statement identifies the problem clearly. There is no difficulty in having large numbers who are outside the class and who can be proved to be. Classifying people as outside the class helps to define it with more certainty. The problem arises where significant numbers cannot be classified. Numbers of people may definitely be in the class but there may be great uncertainty about many others. However, the majority in the Court of Appeal has indicated that this does not matter. Provided there is a 'substantial' number (whatever that means) who can definitely be identified as within the class, that is sufficient. Anyone who cannot be proved to be within the class is to be treated as if they are outside it. It is as if the class is not 'relatives' but 'anyone who can prove they are relatives'.

This approach may have the effect of excluding persons who are within the class but simply cannot prove it. Megaw LJ's words indicate, however, that in practice such persons are very unlikely to have to be considered anyway. Only close relatives, who should have no difficulty in proving the relationship, are likely to claim from the fund.

Why should it be necessary that a 'substantial' number of objects be identified in a discretionary trust? In principle, for a power to be exercised the money could be given to one member of the class, and therefore once one member has been identified, this should be enough. This appears to be the case at least where the power is given to a non-fiduciary and certainly a more relaxed attitude to the identification of the class is implicit in the decision in *Re Hay* in the situation where a power is given to a fiduciary.

In *Re Hay's Settlement Trust*, a hybrid power to distribute to anyone except the settlor and her spouse was followed by a discretionary trust on the same terms. Megarry V-C upheld the power. He identified the functions of the donees of the power in the terms outlined above. They were able to perform these functions for a class such as this. But the discretionary trust for the same class failed, partly on the ground of administrative unworkability, following Lord Wilberforce's view that the duty to survey here is stricter than for powers.

The decision, then, highlights the difference between powers and discretionary trusts. It seems clear that to fulfil their obligations the trustees must survey the class before deciding on distribution. It has been suggested that they must have at least some idea of the size of the class. It must be possible for the courts to carry out the trustees' obligations if the trustees themselves fail to do so. It thus becomes necessary to identify a number of people as members of the class so that the scale of the problem of consideration can be recognised.

It seems therefore to be perfectly possible to have a power of appointment among a very wide class, even of the whole world, or a hybrid power to distribute among a class of everybody except the settlor: *Re Manisty* [1973] 2 All ER 1203.

It is equally clear that a discretionary trust for such a class cannot be upheld. Such a class, though, appears to be both conceptually and evidentially certain within the tests laid down in *McPhail v Doulton* and *Re Baden*. It is presumably for this reason that a further restriction has been introduced in the case of discretionary trusts: the requirement that has come to be known as 'administrative workability'.

Lord Wilberforce introduced this concept when he suggested that a trust would fail if the class was so wide as not to constitute anything like a class, and thus to be administratively unworkable. Much debate followed as to the meaning of this concept and the reason for its introduction. It is assumed that the courts were wary of permitting the development of discretionary trusts for very large classes, partly because of the difficulty of controlling them, and partly because it was difficult to envisage how the reasonable trustee might carry out the settlor's intentions. It has also been suggested that a very wide class might be capricious on the settlor's part, implying a lack of serious intention, but it has been pointed out that the size of the class alone need not imply a lack of seriousness: Lord Wilberforce's example of a class too wide to be workable was 'the inhabitants of Greater London', but this could be perfectly serious, if the settlor happened to be a former chairman of the Greater London Council, for example. Such very wide trusts would inevitably be of a public nature, and, of course, public trusts have traditionally only been upheld, and enforceable, if they are charitable, since special rules would then apply. To allow non-charitable trusts for sections of the public would go against that principle.

Administrative workability, or the lack of it, was used to deny the validity of a trust in *R v District Auditor, ex p West Yorkshire Metropolitan County Council* (1985) 26 RVR 24.

In this case the council, anticipating its abolition, and having surplus funds which it had not sufficient time to expend before the deadline set by legislation, sought to create a trust 'for the benefit of any or all or some of the inhabitants of the County of West Yorkshire'. There was no doubt that this was a declaration of trust, and the court proceeded on the assumption that this class was conceptually certain, but it nonetheless was directly analogous with Lord Wilberforce's example of the inhabitants of Greater London. As Lloyd LJ succinctly put it:

> A trust with as many as two and a half million potential beneficiaries is, in my judgment, quite simply unworkable. The class is far too large.

He went on to cite the usual argument that the court might be called upon to enforce the trust, and that this was a valid reason for distinguishing between powers and trusts on this point.

It has been argued against this viewpoint that the ultimate purpose of all these discretions, be they trusts or powers, is to give effect to the settlor's wishes. It has been suggested therefore that the duty to survey, which seems to be a major stumbling block for discretionary trusts for large classes, must be seen in the light of that very size: in other words, that a settlor who creates a discretionary trust for a very large class cannot have intended to require his trustees to make such a rigorous or stringent survey of that class as if he had created a trust for a small class. Statements such as that of Megarry V-C in *Re Hay*, regarding knowing the size of the problem etc., should therefore be read in the context of the particular class involved. On the other hand, of course, it may be pointed out that this would mean that administrative workability would constantly retreat into the distance: the larger the class, the less the requirement to survey. Trusts for huge classes would have no duty to survey at all: would they still be trusts? Maybe the trustees would still be required to survey, but only a small proportion of the class: would such a survey have any real relevance to the exercise of their discretion? If the courts have policy reasons for restricting non-charitable public trusts, then such arguments are not likely to appeal to them.

Finally, we have seen, in the context of **Mettoy Pension Trustees Ltd v Evans**, that some powers at least have duties attached, though not so great as discretionary trusts, and that the court's intervention when such powers are not performed can be as great as for the non-performance of discretionary trusts. It must therefore be asked whether such powers also require to be limited to classes that are not administratively unworkable.

Re Barlow: a series of individual gifts

The requirements of the discretionary trust may be further compared to a case such as **Re Barlow**, where the will was held to contain a series of individual gifts.

Re Barlow [1979] 1 All ER 296

The testator had given her collection of paintings to the local authority with instructions to allow her family and friends each to purchase a painting at a fixed price. As a trust this gift would have failed for uncertainty because the term 'friend' had no one conceptually certain meaning. Browne-Wilkinson J held, however, that it was a series of individual gifts. Anyone who could come forward and show that, by even the strictest possible meaning of that word, he was a friend, was entitled to buy a picture. In respect of that individual the gift was effective.

Note the contrast with a typical trust case, however. Here there could be no question of surveying the class: there was no obligation to select who was to benefit. Anyone who was a friend could buy, so there was no 'class' as such involved. Each individual case had to be dealt with separately.

Summary

- Persons, called 'trustees', may be given obligations towards individuals, called 'beneficiaries', in respect of trust property.
- It is also possible for an individual, referred to as the 'donee', to be given a power to distribute property amongst a group of 'objects' and this may allow him the discretion as to who within the group should receive a share, and in what proportions.
- The usefulness of such arrangements is that they allow flexibility to changing future circumstances and protection of the fund against misuse by beneficiaries.
- This chapter explains that the relationship between the donee of a power and the objects of that power is very different from that between trustees and beneficiary. It also explains that the level of obligation can be almost infinitely variable. See Figure 5.1 below.
- The 'objects' of a power (or potential beneficiaries) can prevent its misuse, and may be able to compel the donee to make decisions, but they have no right to any part of the fund unless and until they are chosen.
- In the case of the discretionary trust it appears that the obligations of the trustee are greater than those imposed even on a fiduciary with a power of appointment.
- The exact extent of these obligations is not clear, but it involves a greater requirement to survey the class when considering distribution, together with the court's power to carry out the trust in the event of failure by the trustees.

	Fixed trusts	Discretionary trusts
Who determines the beneficial interests?	The settlor (in the terms of the trust settlement)	The trustee (by the exercise of his/her discretion)
What is the nature of the beneficiary's interest?	Fixed, vested interest (a specified share)	A mere *spes* (Hope), until selected (if selected)
What are the duties of the trustees in respect of distribution to beneficiaries?	To distribute to each beneficiary, according to his/her interest (as set out in the terms of the trust)	• To survey the class • To decide whether to distribute (or not, depending on terms of the trust) • To decide who, among the 'objects', shall benefit
What degree of certainty is required to identify the beneficiaries?	All beneficiaries must be ascertainable (i.e. identified or identifiable) (The 'list' principle)	• Class must be clearly defined (conceptual certainty) • It must be possible to say whether an individual is (or is not) a member of the class (subject to evidential limits) (The any given postulant test) • The trust must be administratively workable

Figure 5.1 Fixed and discretionary trusts compared

- The obligations on discretionary trustees have implications for the definition of the class to be benefited. As with all trusts and powers the class of objects of a discretionary trust must be identified with conceptual certainty; the words used must have a clear meaning that can be applied by the trustees and the court. Complete evidential certainty is not required. However, it is necessary that a substantial number of persons can be identified as falling within the class to be considered. Those who cannot be proved to be within the class are regarded as outside it.

- This may be contrasted with the 'list' principle required in the case of fixed trusts.

- In addition, the class of object in a discretionary trust must not be so wide as to be administratively unworkable, whereas even a class consisting of the whole world appears to be acceptable in the case of powers.

- The nature and practical effect of powers and discretionary trusts must be borne in mind. In the family settlement situation, no one seriously expects that the donee of a power to distribute to the whole world will actually do so or was ever intended to do so. Such powers are normally tax-reducing devices and distribution will take place, if at all, to the settlor's close relations.

- Discretionary trusts of the *McPhail v Doulton* type are by contrast quasi-charitable in nature and some consideration of the members of the class and their needs is expected by the settlor, who would nonetheless not expect remote members of the class to claim.

- This greater degree of control and consideration by the trustees is reflected, albeit vaguely, in the rules as to the settlements' construction.

Further reading

C T Emery, 'The most hallowed principle – certainty of beneficiaries in trusts and powers of appointment' (1982) 98 LQR 551.
Considers certainty of objects in different sorts of trust and power.

S Gardner, 'Fiduciary powers in Toytown' (1991) 107 LQR 214.
An analysis of *Mettoy Pensions* v *Evans* (1990).

I M Hardcastle, 'Administrative unworkability – a reassessment of an abiding problem' (1990) Conv 24.
Argues that objects must be sufficiently certain to be workable.

J W Harris, 'Trust, power and duty' (1971) 87 LQR 31.
Examines the beneficiary principle and tests for certainty of objects, focusing on *McPhail* v *Doulton* (1970).

L McKay, 'Re Baden and the third class of uncertainty' (1974) Conv 269.
Analyses *McPhail* v *Doulton* (1970), focusing on administrative workability.

Setting trusts aside

Objectives

After reading this chapter you should:

1. Understand (in outline only) when a trust may be set aside under the Insolvency Act 1986.

2. Understand (in outline only) the powers of the courts under the Matrimonial Causes Act 1973 s 37 to set trusts aside on divorce and the similar powers of the court when a formally registered civil partnership is formally ended.

3. Understand the powers of the court to set aside trusts under an application made under the Inheritance (Provision for Family and Dependants) Act 1975.

4. Understand when beneficiaries can end a trust under the rule in *Saunders* v *Vautier*.

5. Understand that the court has the power to set aside a trust if the settlor made a 'grave' mistake and it would be unconscionable for the court not to exercise its power to set aside the trust.

Trusts to preserve property from creditors

Objective
1

If the owner of property has total freedom of disposition of property, this will mean that he could transfer property into a trust and arrange its provisions to ensure that the property could not be taken to pay any debts which the owner/settlor may incur. He could, for example, transfer property to trustees for his wife for life. He assumes that he will benefit, at least indirectly, from the interest of his wife. He could transfer property on trust for his children when he is about to start a very risky business venture with the intention that if the business does badly and he incurs debts the trust property will be safe from the creditors and his children will continue to be provided for.

The problem that the law must address is should the owner's freedom of disposition and his ability to protect his property prevail over the rights of the creditors to be paid? Should the interest of the settlor to protect and provide for his family be given priority over the claims of creditors?

It is superficially attractive to argue that the right of the settlor to protect his property and provide for his family should prevail. However, the consequence of this would be that creditors would feel unsure as to whether or not a debt would be repaid and this would have a tendency to make banks, finance providers, suppliers, etc. much less willing to lend money or conduct business on the basis of credit. The result of this would be that businesses would find it very much more difficult to operate and potential businesspeople would find initial start-up finance much more of a problem to obtain.

The law has developed the concept of the protective trust as one method of protecting an individual from his creditors. (This type of trust is discussed in more detail on p. 90.) But it could be argued that it does place a debtor in an unreasonably advantageous position as compared with his creditors and may well put too great a value on protecting the debtor and his family at the expense of the creditors. However, it is not possible for a settlor to create a protective trust to guard against his own bankruptcy. Such a trust will be void as against the settlor's trustee in bankruptcy: *Re Burroughs-Fowler* [1916] 2 Ch 251.

The present position provides some sort of balance between the interests of property owners and creditors.

The Insolvency Act 1986 contains very significant provisions aimed at preventing a debtor from placing property beyond the reach of his creditors in two types of cases. First, the Act deals with transactions at an undervalue and renders activities within the Act void. Secondly, the Act addresses the case of an individual who enters into a transaction with the intention of defeating the claims of existing or future creditors.

The Insolvency Act 1986 repealed and replaced the previous statutory provisions, i.e. the Bankruptcy Act 1914 s 42 and the Law of Property Act 1925 s 172.

These provisions do remove an obvious method of protecting property from creditors but they should be read in conjunction with protective trusts and the protection afforded by the limited liability company, both of which may be useful in preserving assets.

Transactions at an undervalue

Bankruptcy Act 1914 s 42

This section provided that a trustee in bankruptcy could apply to the court to have a voluntary settlement set aside that had been made by the bankrupt within ten years of his bankruptcy. If the bankruptcy occurred within two years of the settlement it could be avoided without any qualification. But if the bankruptcy occurred more than two but less than ten years after the settlement, it could be avoided unless the parties claiming under it could show that at the time he made the settlement the settlor could pay all his debts without recourse to the settled property and that his interest in the settled property passed to the trustees.

The section did not apply to settlements made in favour of a purchaser in good faith for valuable consideration or to settlements made before and in consideration of marriage.

Any property recovered as a result of this section would be held by the trustee in bankruptcy for the benefit of the creditors generally.

Insolvency Act 1986

The Bankruptcy Act 1914 s 42 was repealed and replaced by what are now ss 339, 341 and 342 of the Insolvency Act 1986. The present law is in a number of respects different from the provision of the Bankruptcy Act but the underlying principle remains the same, i.e. to allow the trustee in bankruptcy to 'attack' certain transactions entered into at an undervalue by the bankrupt and to hold any property recovered for the creditors.

If an individual is adjudged bankrupt within five years of entering into a transaction at an undervalue, s 339 of the Insolvency Act 1986 gives the trustee in bankruptcy the power to apply to the court for an order restoring the position to what it would have been had the transaction not been entered into.

If the transfer takes place within two years of the bankruptcy, the transaction can be set aside without any further qualification. However, if the transaction takes place more than two but less than five years before the bankruptcy, it can only be set aside if the transferor was insolvent at the time of the transaction or becomes insolvent as a result of the transaction. There is a rebuttable presumption that the transaction renders the transferor insolvent if the transfer is made to one of the bankrupt's 'associates'. Thus unless the presumption is rebutted the transaction may be set aside. An associate is defined in s 435 and includes the transferor's spouse or relatives or the spouse of a relative. Also included are the transferor's spouse's relatives and their spouses.

The concept of transactions at an undervalue causes problems. The definition in s 339 includes a gift or a transaction on terms that provide that no consideration is received. It goes on to state that a transaction entered into in consideration of marriage or the formation of a civil partnership is at an undervalue.

Section 339(3)(c) states that a transaction under which the value of the consideration received by the bankrupt (in money or money's worth) is significantly less than the value (in money or money's worth) of the consideration provided by the bankrupt is a transaction at an undervalue. An example of this is if Peter sells a picture to Wendy for £10,000 at a time when it had a market value of £20,000. See *Agricultural Mortgage Corporation plc* v *Woodward* [1996] 1 FLR 226 for an example of a transaction at an undervalue under s 423 of the Insolvency Act 1986. (See p. 52.)

It will be for the courts to decide how much of an imbalance is necessary in order that the bankrupt receives 'significantly less' than he transfers.

Re Kumar [1993] 2 All ER 700

In this case, a husband and wife were the joint tenants of the matrimonial home worth about £140,000 which was subject to a mortgage. In June 1990 the husband agreed, with the consent of the mortgagee, to transfer his interest to his wife. The wife assumed full responsibility for the mortgage. Shortly afterwards it became clear that a number of the husband's debts could not be paid. The wife then presented a divorce petition and under a consent order she agreed that her claim for financial provision should be dismissed in consideration of the husband's (earlier) transfer of his share in the matrimonial home to her together with his agreement to make periodical payments to her. Three months later a bankruptcy order was made against the husband. The trustee in bankruptcy applied for an order under s 339 of the Insolvency Act 1986 to reverse the transfer of the husband's share in the home on the basis of its being a transaction at an undervalue. Ferris J held that the application should be granted. He said that in appropriate circumstances the consideration provided by the wife under the compromise could amount to consideration in money or money's worth. But the key factor was the value of the claim she was giving up. As the interest of the husband had already been transferred before the date of the consent order and there was no evidence that the wife had also agreed not to make any further capital claim (she knew he had no means to meet any such claim), the consideration that the wife provided did not amount to relevant consideration. Additionally, when the value of the equity of redemption was compared to the assumption of sole liability for the mortgage by the wife, it was clear that the consideration provided by him was significantly greater than the consideration provided by her. So there was nothing here to prevent the transaction from being at an undervalue.

Hill and another v *Haines* [2007] EWHC 1012 (Ch) is a more recent case concerning transfers at an undervalue in the context of a divorce settlement. After a divorce, and as part of the divorce settlement, an order was made under Matrimonial Causes Act 1973 ss 23 to 25 for the husband to transfer the matrimonial home to his wife. The husband was subsequently made bankrupt. The trustees in bankruptcy applied to have the transfer set aside under s 339 of the Insolvency Act 1986.

The court held that the applicant for ancillary relief under ss 23 to 25 of the Matrimonial Causes Act 1973 did not give consideration in 'money or money's worth' within the meaning of s 339(3)(c) of the Insolvency Act 1986 for relief obtained and that any transfer of property made by a bankrupt ex-spouse pursuant to either a court order made in the ancillary proceedings, or a settlement agreement, was a transaction at an undervalue and would be set aside on application by the trustees in bankruptcy.

The court may of course make an order against the original recipient of the bankrupt's property, but an order may not be made against a third party who acquired the property of the bankrupt in good faith for value and without notice of the relevant circumstances, i.e. in circumstances making s 339 applicable in the event of a bankruptcy within the following five years. This provision caused problems with unregistered land in that a purchaser within two years of bankruptcy would have notice of the undervalue and a purchaser within five years will be exposed if he had notice that the transferor was insolvent either before or as a consequence of the transfer. The main problem was with the sale of residential houses. Property would be caught which was contained in a marriage settlement, or which had been given away to another member of the family. Both the purchaser and any institution lending money for the purchase were at risk. It was very common for institutional lenders to insist on insurance against the risk. The Insolvency (No. 2) Act 1994 responded to this problem by providing additional protection from clawback to parties unconnected with the original transaction. The 1994 Act has eliminated the 'without notice' requirement and now a purchaser will be safe so long as he buys in good faith and for value. Section 2(2) provides that if an acquirer has notice of the relevant surrounding circumstances and of the relevant proceedings or was in some way connected to either party to the original transaction, then there is a rebuttable presumption that the acquisition was not in good faith. In effect, notice of relevant surrounding circumstances means knowledge that the transferor entered into the transaction at an undervalue. Notice of the relevant proceedings comprises notice of the fact that the bankruptcy petition has been presented or that the transferor has been adjudged bankrupt. The effect appears to be that the third party will be protected even if he knows there has been a transaction at an undervalue, so long as he does not actually know that the original transferor has gone bankrupt.

Transactions to defraud creditors

If a person was about to start a rather risky but potentially very profitable business enterprise, he would realise that if the business failed his property would be available to meet his debts. Alternatively, an individual might already have incurred so many debts that he fears that, before long, his debts will exceed his assets and put him at risk of being declared a bankrupt. How much better it would be if he could protect his property from any creditors who might have a claim against him in the future. The obvious solution would be to transfer his property to, perhaps, his wife with a view to it being her property and not his and so render it safe from his creditors. Alternatively, he might decide that a better course would be to transfer his property to trustees on trust for, perhaps, his wife and so again protect the property from his creditors. In either case his objective is the same: to safeguard his property while retaining the benefit for his wife and indirectly, through his wife, for himself.

Law of Property Act 1925 s 172

The law developed to restrict these opportunities. Section 172 of the Law of Property Act 1925, in broad terms, allowed transactions to be set aside if made with the intention to defraud creditors.

Under s 172 of the 1925 Act avoidance of a transaction was at the instance of anyone prejudiced by it, a phrase which clearly embraced those creditors whose claims were frustrated by the transaction. However, a transferee had a good defence if he could show that he had given good or valuable consideration and had taken the property in good faith without notice of the intention to defraud creditors. Under s 172 marriage consideration was regarded as sufficient to bring the transferee within this defence.

In *Re Butterworth* (1882) 19 Ch D 588 a successful baker made a voluntary settlement of most of his property on his son at a time when he was planning to enter a different business of which he had no experience. Three years later the bakery business became insolvent. The Court of Appeal decided that the creditors of the bakery business could upset the settlement and the settled property became available to pay them the money that they were owed. When the settlement was created the settlor had in mind possible creditors of the grocery business, but the court decided that an intention to delay or defeat any future creditors was sufficient to permit the settlement to be set aside. Sir George Jessel MR said that the principle was that 'a man is not entitled to go into a hazardous business, and immediately before doing so settle all his property voluntarily, the object being this: "If I succeed in business I make a fortune for myself. If I fail, I leave my creditors unpaid. They will bear the loss."'

In *Mackay* v *Douglas* (1872) LR 14 Eq 106 one about to enter a hazardous business settled property on his wife and children. At the time of the settlement, although the house was his major asset, he was solvent. Within a year the business ceased trading, with liabilities of over £300,000. The court decided that the settlement must be set aside and declared that it had long been the law that it was not necessary to show actual intention to defraud if the result of the settlement was to delay or defeat creditors. Malins V-C said it was not possible for an individual in the circumstances of the present case to settle the bulk of his property so that he took any profits from a hazardous operation but any losses to his creditors remained unmet.

It was not entirely clear what 'to defraud creditors' meant under s 172, although an intention to delay payment would be within the Act. Also *Re Butterworth* shows a settlement by a solvent settlor can be within the section. The case also demonstrates that the section could be invoked by creditors other than those against whom the settlor was seeking protection when he created the settlement. It also seemed that the intention would be inferred from the actions of the transferee. The intention to defraud creditors could be inferred if the necessary consequence of a transaction would be to defeat, hinder, delay or defraud creditors or to put assets belonging to the debtor beyond the reach of the creditors. There was a good deal of argument as to whether the fact that the defeat or delay of creditors was the inevitable result of a transaction meant that an irrebuttable presumption of intention to defraud arose. In *Freeman* v *Pope* (1870) LR 5 Ch App 538, Lord Hatherley said that if a person owing debts makes a settlement which takes away from his property an amount without which the debts cannot be paid, and therefore the inevitable consequence of a transaction is that some creditors will go unpaid, it is the duty of the judge to direct the jury that they must infer an intention to defraud creditors. However, in *Re Wise*

(1886) 17 QBD 290, Lord Esher said it was monstrous to say that a man intended to defraud creditors simply because that was the inevitable result of his actions.

Insolvency Act 1986

Section 172 gave rise to a number of uncertainties and problems. This rather unsatisfactory state of affairs no longer exists as s 172 has been repealed and replaced with what are now ss 423–425 of the Insolvency Act 1986.

Transactions affected

Section 423 applies to transactions at an undervalue where the court is satisfied that the transaction was entered into for the purpose of putting assets beyond the reach of a person who is making or who may make a claim against the disponer or for the purpose of otherwise prejudicing the interests of such a person in relation to a claim he is making or may make. Although there are clear differences between the new provision and s 172 of the Law of Property Act 1925, in general terms the new provision is aimed at the same types of transactions. The language of the section appears to apply to creditors existing at the time of the transaction and to subsequent creditors. It is thought that at least some of the cases on s 172 remain relevant when deciding if the transaction was entered into with the purpose of putting assets beyond the reach of a claimant or possible claimant.

But the use of the words 'for the purpose' of putting assets beyond the reach of claimants or otherwise prejudicing the interests of a person making, or who may make, a claim suggests that the courts may not assume that a man intends the necessary consequences of his actions and that it will be essential to prove that the settlor did have the intention to put assets beyond the reach of creditors.

The Insolvency Act can be invoked only if there is a transaction at an undervalue, whereas under s 172 of the 1925 Act a conveyance could be set aside even if full value had been provided if the transferor had not taken in good faith: *Lloyds Bank Ltd* v *Marcan* [1973] 3 All ER 754. The meaning of a transaction at an undervalue has been discussed above (see p. 148). To some extent, the defence available under s 172 to a purchaser who provided good or valuable consideration and who had taken the property in good faith without notice of the intention to defraud creditors has been preserved. But under the Insolvency Act, if the transaction was entered into in consideration of marriage or of entering into a civil partnership, it will be regarded as having been entered into at an undervalue. If a transaction is entered into at adequate or full consideration, it cannot be set aside under s 423 even if the transferee knew that the intention behind the transaction was to prejudice creditors.

Agricultural Mortgage Corporation plc v *Woodward* [1996] 1 FLR 226 illustrates s 423 in action. A farmer was indebted to the plaintiff under a mortgage for £700,000 and was threatened with an order for possession as he was in arrears with the mortgage payments. He was given a deadline to clear the arrears. Just before the deadline he granted a tenancy to his wife at an annual rental of £37,000, for the purpose of preventing execution of an order for possession as she would then be the occupant. The plaintiff claimed that this tenancy should be set aside as being at an undervalue and thus within s 423 of the Insolvency Act 1986. It was argued that taking the transaction as a whole, the rent was significantly below market value for the total benefits obtained. In addition to the tenancy *per se*, the wife was given a number of other benefits, namely safeguarding the family home and allowing her to keep the family farming going. The court took into account not only the actual rent paid but also the other benefits bestowed. It was held that the grant of the tenancy to his wife was one made for inadequate consideration and was caught by s 423 of the Insolvency Act 1986 and would be set aside.

Conditions for application and the need for intention

Perhaps the most important and potentially the most troublesome part of the provision is s 423(3), which imposes conditions that the court must be satisfied about before any order may be made. The transaction must have been entered into for the purpose either of (a) putting assets beyond the reach of a person who is making, or may at some time make, a claim against the transferor or (b) otherwise prejudicing the interests of such a person in relation to the claim which he is making or may make.

The legislation makes it clear that a transaction may be set aside even if at the time of the transaction there are no creditors, thus preserving the principle in *Mackay* v *Douglas* and illustrated in *Re Butterworth* (above).

Chohan v *Saggar* [1992] BCC 306 states that it is the dominant intention that is important and it matters not that there may be other motives underlying the transaction.

A different approach was taken in *IRC* v *Hashmi and Guauri* [2002] 2 BCLC 489 in which a trust was created. There were two motives for creating the trust (one to defeat creditors and the other to secure the family) and the deceased (who set up the challenged trust) would not, in the view of the court, have been able to say which was uppermost in his mind. The court decided that under s 423 the purpose of defeating creditors does not have to be the dominant purpose. But it has to be a real or substantial purpose of the transaction and not just a by-product of the transaction. The trust was accordingly set aside under s 423.

In an attempt to explain the substantial/dominant/by-product distinctions Arden LJ said:

> [S]uppose that I need to post a letter and also need to take the dog for a walk, and combine both operations in the same outing. [. . .] It is a meaningless inquiry to ask whether I regard one of those objects as superior to the other [. . .] [I]f I go to take the dog for a walk and going past the post-box find an unposted letter in my pocket and take the opportunity of posting a letter at the same time, it will not be correct to say that I had two objects in that walk. I had only the one object, that of walking with the dog, and the posting of the letter was but a consequence of it. On the other hand, if I decide to take the dog for a walk but take the view that I will use the opportunity to post the letter at the same time, it can be said that I had two objects in that outing even if I would not have posted the letter until another day but for the need to take the dog for a walk.

The 'substantial purpose' approach was also taken in *Beckenham MC Ltd* v *Centralex Ltd* [2004] EWHC 1287 (Ch), a first-instance decision where transfers were set aside under the Insolvency Act 1986 s 423. The court was satisfied that transfers were 'substantially motivated' by an intention to prevent the payment of a service charge being enforced by a management company.

The case concerned two business units in a business centre, the management and upkeep of which was covered by service charges paid by unit owners. There were covenants which required the owners to pay the service charges. Additionally, there were covenants that prevented the owners from transferring the units without obtaining an identical covenant to pay the service charge from the transferee. In fact units were transferred without the covenant being obtained.

C owned both units and transferred them to K which then transferred one to G and one to M. The management company, B, had obtained county court judgments against C and K. It was discovered that the transfers from K, G and M had been made for no consideration.

There was no evidence that C or K could cover the judgment debt without recourse to the value of the units. Thus, it was argued the effect of the transfers was to prejudice B. It was held that the evidence pointed to the transfers to G and M being substantially motivated by the desire to prevent B from seeking to enforce its judgment against the units.

Rubin v *Dweck* (2012) LTL 25/4/2012 Ch D (Bankruptcy Ct) is another case on s 423 and the purpose of a transfer. A property had been bought in 1982 after four years of marriage, with money given by D's mother to D and W equally. It had been registered in D's sole name. In 1995 D made a voluntary transfer of his interest in the property into the sole name of W.

The D's trustee in bankruptcy (R) argued that when the transfer took place D was starting a business and he had made the transfer in order to protect the property from future creditors. D argued, supported by W, that he had made the transfer in order to recompense W for sacrifices she had made during the marriage, and in order to ward off a divorce.

D said that from 1988 onwards the burden of the family's expenditure had fallen entirely on W. He had had a heart attack and had begun a new business venture which was not bringing in any income. W had worked long hours and sold a property that she had owned before the marriage.

D said that he had promised W that if his business failed he would give her his share of the matrimonial home as compensation for her efforts. By 1995, D claimed, the business was not succeeding and family finances were strained. W felt insecure and that she had not been treated fairly. W said that if he did not transfer the property to her she would divorce him. The court held that the transfer was not a transaction defrauding creditors to which s 423 applied as the court was not satisfied that D had transferred the property to W for the purpose of prejudicing the interests, or putting assets beyond the reach, of somebody who was making, or who might make, a claim against him. The evidence supported the finding that D had transferred the property to prevent a divorce and not to defraud creditors. At the time of the transfer the court said that there was no reason for D to put assets out of reach and no reason for him to foresee potential personal liabilities.

The court said (*obiter*) that it was not necessary to decide whether the transaction had been at an undervalue. Had it been necessary to decide that issue the court would have decided that there was an immeasurable consideration, but not consideration that could be said to be less in value than the value of the beneficial interest at the time.

Who can make an application under s 423?

As to the question of who may apply to the court, the answer to this is to be found in s 424, which states that only certain applicants are within the provisions of the legislation.

If the debtor has been adjudged bankrupt, application may be made to the court by the trustee in bankruptcy or with the leave of the court by the victim of the transaction. In other cases the application may be made by the victim of the transaction. The victim is anyone who is or is capable of being prejudiced by the transaction.

Orders of the court

By virtue of s 423(2) the court may make an order to restore the position to what it would have been had the transaction not been entered into and to protect those who have been victims of the transaction. The court cannot make an order against a third party who has acquired an interest in good faith, for value and without notice of the circumstances which make s 423 applicable.

The court may make a wide range of orders under s 425, including vesting the transferred property in or for the benefit of the persons on whose behalf the application is made.

It may require any property acquired with the proceeds of sale of the property involved in the transaction being attacked to be similarly transferred. Additionally, the court may order the payment of money in respect of benefits received from the debtor.

However, no order may prejudice property of a third party which was acquired in good faith, for value and without notice of the circumstances by virtue of which the provisions of s 423 may be applicable. (Under the new law, marriage or entering into a civil partnership is not regarded as valuable consideration, and so a transaction where the only consideration given is marriage consideration or the entry into a civil partnership may be attacked.)

These provisions do remove an obvious method of protecting property from creditors, but they should be read in conjunction with protective trusts and the protection afforded by the limited liability company, both of which may be useful in preserving assets.

Matrimonial Causes Act 1973 s 37

Objective 2

This allows a spouse (usually a wife) or civil partner who is bringing proceedings against their partner for financial relief to ask the court to set aside any disposition (including a disposition of property on trust) which was made with the intention of defeating a claim for financial provision.

If the disposition is about to be made the court can make an order to protect the interest of the applicant (s 37(2)(a)). Where the disposition has already been made the court can order that it be set aside. Dispositions, defined by s 37(6), include trusts (but not provisions in a will). Such dispositions are called 'reviewable dispositions' (s 37(4)).

The test of intention to defeat an application is subjective. If an application is made to set aside a disposition made within the three years prior to the application, the intention to defeat the application is presumed if the effect is to defeat a claim. This presumption can be rebutted (s 37(5)). In other cases intention must be proved.

A disposition cannot be set aside if made for valuable consideration (other than marriage consideration) to one who acted in good faith and who had no notice of the intention to defeat an application (s 37(4)). In *Sherry* v *Sherry* [1991] 1 FLR 307, the Court of Appeal found the necessary notice on the basis of constructive notice of the intention to defeat creditors. The concept of constructive notice makes it easier to challenge transactions than if actual knowledge has to be proved.

The Civil Partnership Act 2004 Schedule 5 Part 14 sets out similar provisions to those contained in the Matrimonial Causes Act 1973 s 37.

Inheritance (Provision for Family and Dependants) Act 1975 ss 10–13

Objective 3

The Act is aimed at allowing specified individuals to apply to the court for a provision from the estate of a deceased person who died domiciled in England or Wales, on the basis that the will or the intestacy provisions (or a combination of both) failed to make reasonable financial provision for the applicant. Those able to apply include the spouse or former spouse (unless remarried). This now includes parties to a same sex marriage.

Under the terms of the Civil Partnership Act 2004 the provisions of the Inheritance (Provision for Family and Dependants) Act 1975 applies in relation to a civil partnership in the same way as to a marriage. (See p. 356 for more discussion of the Civil Partnership Act 2004.)

Had the private member's Cohabitation Rights Bill 2013–14 been passed into law, those able to apply under the 1975 Act would have been extended to include surviving 'qualifying cohabitants' who would be able to claim on the same footing as a surviving spouse. But the bill will make no more progress as the 2013–14 session of parliament was prorogued before the bill had passed through all the necessary stages to become law.

A child of the deceased or a person whom the deceased treated as a child of the family in relation to a marriage to which the deceased had at some time been a party may apply. Applications may also be made by a person who was being maintained by the deceased immediately before the death of the deceased. In this last case the applicant can succeed only if it is shown that the deceased was making a substantial contribution towards his reasonable needs and that the deceased did not receive full valuable consideration in return.

The Law Reform (Succession) Act 1995 made an important change to the 1975 Act. The change introduces an additional class of applicant. A person who was living with the deceased as husband or wife for the two years ending with the death but who was not actually married to them may make a claim on the deceased's estate. This applies only if the deceased died on or after 1 January 1996. Except in the case of the spouse (and in limited situations a former spouse) the court is limited to making an award for maintenance (although this is not limited to mere subsistence). A spouse (and in limited situations a former spouse) may be made an award which is not limited to maintenance but is such provision as is reasonable in all the circumstances.

The 1975 Act provides a number of 'guidelines' that the courts must use when assessing a claim and deciding what, if any, award to make. The courts have the power to make a wide range of orders, including orders for periodic payments, the payment of a lump sum, transfer of property, the settlement of property and the variation of an existing settlement made on the parties to a marriage for the benefit of the surviving spouse or a child of the marriage or anyone treated as a child of that marriage.

It may prove tempting for an individual to adopt a plan in an attempt to prevent a successful application against their estate by reducing or eliminating the 'net estate' out of which any award must be funded. Under the predecessor to this Act, if property was given away before death it was not available to an applicant. The 1975 Act contains a number of 'anti-avoidance' provisions in an attempt to prevent such activities.

Section 10 is aimed at dispositions of property. The court may make an order against property in the hands of a transferee if the deceased made the transfer within six years of death and with the intention of defeating an application under the Act, provided that the transferee has not given full valuable consideration.

Section 11 of the Act is aimed at contracts to leave property by will which again could be used under the predecessor to the 1975 Act to defeat applications. Section 11 allows the court to modify the effect of the contract if it was made with the intention of defeating an application under the Act unless the transferee gave or promised for valuable consideration at the time that the contract was made.

The changes made to the intestacy rules under the Inheritance and Trustees' Powers Act 2014 may well reduce the number of claims under the Act by spouses as their entitlement has been 'improved' where the intestate leaves no issue. The Act also simplifies the way that the estate is divided where the intestate leaves a spouse and issue. Additionally the Act broadens the definition of a child of the family, which may well increase the number of applications.

The rule in *Saunders* v *Vautier*

Objective
4

Under the rule in ***Saunders* v *Vautier*** if all the beneficiaries are *sui juris* (aged 18 or over and of sound mind) and are between them entitled to the entire beneficial interest, they may all agree to instruct the trustee to transfer the trust property to them, or to someone else. In other words, the rule enables a trust to be set aside.

The rule in ***Saunders* v *Vautier*** sublimates the intention of the settlor to the wishes of the beneficiaries and is based on the concept of the equitable gift and the possession by the beneficiary of the equitable ownership of the trust property. It clearly recognises that in this context the interests of the beneficiary take precedence over the wishes of the settlor.

Saunders v *Vautier* (1841) 4 Beav 115

A testator created a trust under which the income of the trust property was to be accumulated until the beneficiary attained the age of 25, at which time both the capital and the accumulated income were to be transferred to the beneficiary. When the beneficiary attained the age of 21 (then the age of majority), he demanded that the trustees transfer the whole trust fund to him. He argued that he had a vested interest in the property and a direction by the testator which merely affected how he was to enjoy the property did not prevent him from instructing the trustees to transfer the trust property to him. If his interest had been contingent on attaining 25, he would not have been in a position to demand the property until he was 25 and had satisfied the contingency.

Lord Langdale said:

I think that principle has been repeatedly acted upon; and where a legacy is directed to accumulate for a certain period, or where the payment is postponed, the legatee, if he has an absolute indefeasible interest in the legacy, is not bound to wait until the expiration of that period, but may require payment the moment he is competent to give a valid discharge.

The ability to give the valid discharge referred to by Lord Langdale arises on attaining the age of majority, assuming that there is no lack of mental capacity.

The rule in ***Saunders* v *Vautier*** was originally developed in the context of trusts created under wills but was gradually extended to cover interests under *inter vivos* trusts as well. The rule has evolved to be applicable to trusts with two or more beneficiaries all of whom are *sui juris* and who between them are entitled to the whole beneficial interest, and to trusts where there are beneficiaries (all *sui juris*) entitled to successive interests. In each of these situations, if a unanimous agreement is made between the beneficiaries, the trustees must comply with the instructions of the beneficiaries as to the transfer of the trust property.

Thorpe* v *Revenue & Customs Commissioners [2009] EWHC 611 (Ch) illustrates the need for those seeking to use the rule to be entitled to the entire beneficial interest. T was the sole director of a company and a trustee of its pension scheme. T and his wife were the only employees of the company and the only members of the scheme. After the death of his wife, T became the only member. On the basis that he was the sole beneficiary of the scheme, T directed the trustees to transfer the scheme funds to him, relying on the rule in ***Saunders* v *Vautier***. The Court held that the rule in ***Saunders* v *Vautier*** did not apply where there were potential beneficiaries not yet in existence, however remote their interests might be or however unlikely it might be that those beneficiaries should come into existence. There remained the possibility that persons other than T might become entitled to an interest under the trusts of the scheme so it could not be said that T was necessarily entitled to the entire beneficial interest. This decision was upheld by the Court of Appeal ([2010] EWCA Civ 339.)

The rule has even been applied to discretionary trusts. In *Re Smith* [1928] Ch 915, an exhaustive discretionary trust was set up. The income and the capital were payable, at the trustees' discretion, to Mrs Aspinall, and any capital or income not so paid was to go to her children. Therefore, between them, Mrs Aspinall and her children were entitled to the whole of the trust fund and any income generated by it. They were all of full age.

Romer J said:

> It appears to me, that notwithstanding the discretion reposed in the trustees, under which discretion they could select one or more of the people I have mentioned as recipients of the income, and might apply part of the capital for the benefit of Mrs Aspinall and so take it away from the children, that the four of them, if they were all living, could come to the Court and say to the trustees, 'Hand the fund over to us'.

It is not possible to use the rule in *Saunders v Vautier* in the case of a non-exhaustive discretionary trust where the trustees had a discretion not only as to whom to select to be the recipients of the trust property but also to decide how much of the trust property, if any, to distribute. It would not be possible for the beneficiaries to claim that together they were absolutely entitled to the trust property as their individual or collective rights would depend on the exercise of the discretion by the trustee.

It is also not possible to use the rule in *Saunders v Vautier* if the body of beneficiaries consists of a fluctuating class, as again it would not be possible to say that any agreement was made by beneficiaries who between them were absolutely entitled because the agreement would not involve those who might later become within the class of beneficiaries.

What is the position if just one of several beneficiaries decides he wants to withdraw his 'share' of the trust property? In *Stephenson v Barclays Bank Trust Co Ltd* [1975] 1 All ER 625, Walton J said:

> Where the situation is that a single person who is *sui juris* has an absolutely vested beneficial interest in a share of the trust fund, his rights are not, I think, quite as extensive as those of the beneficial interest holders as a body. In general, he is entitled to have transferred to him . . . an aliquot share of each and every asset of the trust fund which presents no difficulty so far as division is concerned. This will apply to such items as cash, money at the bank or an unsecured loan, Stock Exchange securities and the like. However, as regards land, certainly, in all cases, as regards shares in a private company in very special circumstances . . . and possibly . . . mortgage debts the situation is not so simple, and every person with a vested interest in possession in an aliquot share of the trust fund may have to wait until the land is sold, and so forth, before being able to call upon the trustees as of right to account to him for his share of the assets.

There are examples of 'purpose' trusts where the rule in *Saunders v Vautier* has been used. For example in *Re Bowes* [1896] 1 Ch 507, a testator left money and directed that it was to be used to plant trees on a settled estate. The court held that the money was payable whether or not it was used to plant trees. The direction of the testator was ignored in favour of the wishes of the beneficiary.

Limitations of the rule

The rule does have its limits and the wishes of the beneficiaries are not always supreme. It is possible to use the rule to end a trust but it is not possible for beneficiaries to use it to control the way that trustees administer the trust or exercise their discretions. If the beneficiaries do not like how the trustees are acting, they can agree to end the trust and arrange to resettle the property, perhaps with new trustees with different powers and discretions. In *Re Brockbank* [1948] 1 All ER 287, Vaisey J said:

> It seems to me that the beneficiaries must choose between two alternatives: either they must keep the trusts of the will on foot, in which case those trusts must continue to be executed by the trustees . . . not . . . arbitrarily selected by themselves: or they must, by mutual agreement, extinguish and put an end to the trusts.

In *Re Brockbank* the dispute arose over the appointment of a trustee to replace a trustee who wished to retire. There was no one nominated in the trust instrument to appoint replacement trustees and so, under the provisions of s 36 of the Trustee Act 1925, the power to appoint was with the trustee who was to continue. The beneficiaries, who were all of full age and capacity and who were together absolutely entitled to the trust property, sought to impose their choice of trustee on the continuing trustee. The court refused to allow the beneficiaries to interfere with the exercise of a discretionary power to appoint.

Vaisey J stated:

> It is said that where all the beneficiaries concur, they may force a trustee to retire, compel his removal and direct the trustees, having the power to nominate their successors, to appoint as such successors such persons or person or corporation as may be indicated by the beneficiaries, and it is suggested that the trustees have no option but to comply. I do not follow this. The power of nominating a new trustee is a discretionary power, and in my opinion is no longer exercisable and indeed can no longer exist if it has become one of which the exercise can be dictated by others.

Section 19 of the Trusts of Land and Appointment of Trustees Act 1996 has altered the balance of control in such a situation from 1 January 1997. Beneficiaries may be able both

See Chapter 14.

to force a trustee to retire and/or nominate his successor.

The statement by Vaisey J (above) was made in the context of an application to appoint new trustees under s 36 of the Trustee Act 1925 but the comments are of relevance to beneficiaries attempting to use *Saunders* v *Vautier*. Again, in *Stephenson* v *Barclays Bank Trust Co Ltd* [1975] 1 All ER 625, Walton J stated:

> It appears to me that once the beneficial interest holders have determined to end the trust they are not entitled, unless by agreement, to further services of the trustees. Those trustees can of course be compelled to hand over the entire trust assets to any person or persons selected by the beneficiaries against a proper discharge, but they cannot be compelled, unless they are in fact willing to comply with the directions, to do anything with the trust fund which they are not in fact willing to do.

Beneficiaries can, of course, use *Saunders* v *Vautier* to end the trust and then to resettle the property on new trusts with trustees of their choice and on terms which they (the beneficiaries) determine. One of the reasons for the attitude of the courts, as stated in *Stephenson* v *Barclays Bank Co Ltd* (above), is that it prevents the trustees being forced to carry out duties very different from those which they originally accepted.

It is unclear whether the rule can apply to a trust of the *Re Denley* [1968] 3 All ER 65 type. Could all the 'beneficiaries' agree to end the trust and claim the property for themselves? (See pp. 202–3.)

Mistake

Objective 5

See Chapter 15 (p. 426) for discussion of mistake.

The courts have the discretionary power to set aside a trust if the settlor made a 'grave' mistake in creating it. The law has recently been reviewed by the Supreme Court in *Futter v HMRC, Pitt v HMRC* [2013] UKSC 26, [2013] 3 All ER 429. Lord Walker made it clear that the mistake must be 'grave' and one that would make it unconscionable for it not to be corrected. See Chapter 15, p. 435, for discussion of mistake and also see *Wright, Wright v (1) National Westminster Bank Plc and ors* (2014) Ch D, LTL 22/7/2014 (p. 437) in which a trust was set aside on the basis of a 'grave' mistake.

Summary

- Trusts may be liable to be set aside under a number of provisions, mainly statutory.

- Under the Insolvency Act 1986, a trust may be set aside under a variety of circumstances: for example, if the settlor transfers property at an undervalue or into a trust and the effect of the transfer into the trust is to defeat his creditors or potential creditors. Another example of a trust that can be set aside under this Act is a trust of property which is set up with the intention of preventing creditors (or potential creditors) from making a claim against it.

- The courts have very wide powers under the Matrimonial Causes Act 1973 s 37 and the Civil Partnership Act 2004 Schedule 5 Part 14. On a divorce or when a formally registered civil partnership is formally ended, the courts have the power to set aside trusts created to defeat a claim for financial provision.

- Under the Inheritance (Provision for Family and Dependants) Act 1975 the courts have wide powers to vary the distribution of property on a death (either under will or as a result of the intestacy rule). One of the powers is to set aside a trust of the deceased's estate.

- Beneficiaries, if all *sui juris* and together entitled to the entire beneficial interest, can bring a trust to an end under the rule in *Saunders v Vautier*.

- The court has the power to set aside a trust if the settlor made a 'grave' mistake and it would be unconscionable for the court not to exercise its power to set aside the trust.

Further reading

Insolvency

N Furey, 'Bankruptcy and the family – the effect of the Insolvency Act 1986' (1987) 17 Fam Law 316. Part of the article deals with the revision of the Bankruptcy Act 1914 s 42 and the Law of Property Act 1925 s 172. Discusses transactions at an undervalue.

R Potterton and S Cullen, 'Transactions at an undervalue' (1994) 138 Sol J 710. Discusses transactions at an undervalue and the effect of the Insolvency (No. 2) Act 1994.

7

Unlawful trusts

Objectives

After reading this chapter you should:

1. Be able to explain that trusts may fail for offending one of three perpetuity rules.
2. Understand the main changes made by the Perpetuities and Accumulations Act 2009.
3. Understand that capricious trusts applying property in 'useless' ways will not be enforced by the courts and that trusts which encourage a breach of the law are not lawful.
4. Understand that trusts may be liable to be set aside by the courts if they offend public policy by tending to weaken the family unit.

This chapter deals with a range of situations where a trust may be set aside or declared to have failed. In some cases the trust will contravene the provisions of statute and in others it will break judge-created rules. In some of the situations the trust is rendered void, in others merely voidable.

Trusts which offend the perpetuity rules

Objective
1

One of the key principles of English law is freedom of disposition. The law imposes very few restrictions on this freedom. Total freedom should, in theory at least, include the power to control how the property is to be used by those to whom the property is given, and to determine when and if it can be alienated by donees. However, this freedom for the donor would impose a restriction on the donees. Their ability to transfer could be limited by the conditions imposed by the donor. One man's freedom would be another man's restriction. The three rules to be discussed attempt to provide some balance between the freedom of the donor and the donee.

First, the rule against perpetuities, which is aimed at provisions that render property inalienable by specifying a long period of time before an interest becomes vested. The settlor may create a contingent interest under which the eventual identity of the beneficiary may not become certain for many years. For example, a settlor may create a trust under which property is held for the 'first of my descendents to play cricket for England'. It may be many years before a descendent plays cricket for England. Indeed it may be that no descendent ever plays cricket for England.

Until the identity of the beneficiary becomes certain the interest remains contingent rather than vested. Until an interest becomes vested there is no one who can alienate it; it is unsaleable. If it is many years (perhaps hundreds) before the interest becomes vested, the interest in the property is, in effect, rendered inalienable for that period of time. The perpetuity rule is aimed at preventing the postponement of vesting for what the law regards as an unacceptably long period of time. The delay which the law will allow is called the perpetuity period. Interests must vest within that period of time. The length of the perpetuity period will be discussed below.

Secondly, the rule against perpetual trusts will be examined. This rule again is directed towards attempts to tie up property and prevents the settlor from rendering the capital or income inalienable for long periods of time.

The third rule prevents a settlor from directing that income arising under a trust must be added to capital and not distributed for a period longer than the law regards as acceptable.

In each of these situations the settlor is attempting to impose a restriction on the freedom of the beneficiaries to exploit or alienate interests in property and the rules which will be discussed allow settlors to impose such restrictions only within strict limits.

The rules were originally in the main common law creations. The Perpetuities and Accumulations Act 1964 made significant changes to the rules and applies to settlements created after 16 July 1964.

The Law Commission Report – The Rules against Perpetuities and Excessive Accumulations (Law Com 251) – was published in 1998 and its recommendations are reflected in the Perpetuities and Accumulations Act 2009 which came into force on 6 April 2010. It applies to instruments taking effect after 5 April 2010. But it does not apply to wills executed before but taking effect after 5 April 2010.

One effect of introducing new legislation is, as was recognised by the Law Commission, to create the situation where there are three possible sets of perpetuity rules applicable to a trust. Which one is relevant depends on the date of creation of the trust.

- The pre-1964, rules apply to instruments created on or before 15 July 1964.

- The Perpetuities and Accumulations Act 1964 applies to instruments created between 16 July 1964 and 5 April 2010.

- The Perpetuities and Accumulations Act 2009 applies to instruments created on or after 6 April 2010.

The following discussion of the perpetuity provisions is not intended to be comprehensive and a full discussion will be found in a land law text.

The rule against perpetuities

Taking the example above again, a settlor may decide to transfer property on trust for 'my first descendant who plays cricket for England'. It may well be many years before it becomes clear who, if anyone, the beneficiary is to be. Until a descendant does play cricket for England, the interest will not become vested and the property will effectively be inalienable.

The perpetuity rule is aimed at contingent interests; an interest is contingent if it is subject to a condition which may not be met. The example above contains a contingent interest as the condition may never be met because it is not certain that one of the settlor's descendants will ever play cricket for England. The perpetuity rule prevents the creation of contingent interests in property which may vest only after what the law regards as an unreasonable time delay. The object is to prevent interests in property from being rendered sterile for what the law regards as an unacceptably long period of time.

The rule states that an interest in property must vest, if it vests at all, within the perpetuity period. It should be noted that the rule does not state that the interest must vest but only that if and when it vests it is within the perpetuity period.

The common law rule

Under the common law the perpetuity period ended 21 years after the death of a life in being at the time the interest was created. A period of gestation may be added to this. In theory anyone in the world who is alive when the interest was created could be a life in being although this could cause enormous practical difficulties. Often the creator of the interest will specify the lives in being for the purposes of the rule. Lives in being cannot be the lives of animals – only the lives of humans may be used. The settlor may specify the period within which the interest must vest using as the measurement the life of the person specified plus 21 years. For example, a settlor could state that the life to be used for the purposes of the perpetuity rule is to be that of the last surviving member of the England football team which won the World Cup in 1966. Sometimes a 'royal lives' clause was used. For example, the settlor could state that the life in being by which the perpetuity period is measured should be 'the life the last to die of the lineal descendents now living of Queen Victoria and twenty one years thereafter'. But in some situations it proved difficult if not impossible to identify all the 'lineal descendents now living' so an element of uncertainty existed. In both of these cases the settlor has ensured that the interest must vest within 21 years of the death of someone who is living at the date of the settlement. If there is no life in being, the period is 21 years. An interest is void if it might vest outside the perpetuity period. It does not matter that it will probably vest within the period or that the chances of it vesting outside the period are extremely remote. The rule is clear: the interest will be void if there is any possibility that it will vest outside the period. The result of the common law rule is that many trusts fail from the outset just because there is a remote possibility that the interest might vest outside the perpetuity period. The fact that it was highly likely that the interest would vest within the perpetuity period was not enough to save the trust. In the example given above, if property was left on trust for the settlor's first descendant to play cricket for England, the trust would offend the common law perpetuity rule, as the first descendant to play cricket might be selected more than 21 years from the death of anyone alive when the trust was created.

The Perpetuities and Accumulations Act 1964

The Perpetuities and Accumulations Act 1964 made very important changes to the common law rules for dispositions in instruments, changes which apply to trusts coming into effect on or after 16 July 1964.

If a disposition would fail under an application of the common law rule, it is possible to use s 3(1) of the 1964 Act. This introduced a 'wait and see' provision under which, if it is uncertain whether or not the interest will vest within the common law perpetuity period, it is possible to wait and see what in fact happens. If the interest does vest within the period, then all is well and good and the interest takes effect. If, however, the interest does not so vest, then it will be declared to be void. In the example above it is possible to wait to see if the first descendant to play cricket for England is determined within 21 years of the death of one living at the date the trust was created.

Section 3(5) of the statute defines the period that may be used when applying the 'wait and see' provision. Rather confusingly, the perpetuity period that is used when applying the 'wait and see' rule differs from that used under common law. The Act states that the period to be used is 'the perpetuity period prescribed by the Act'. The period specified by the Act, as at common law, permits the 'lives' to be either actually living or *en ventre sa mère*. However, there is an important difference between the common law period and that used when applying the Act. At common law there is no restriction on whose lives may be the lives in being. In contrast, s 3(5) of the Act provides a list of persons whose lives must be the lives in being for the purposes of what may be described as the statutory perpetuity period. The listed lives in s 3(5) are:

(a) the person by whom the disposition was made;

(b) a person to whom or in whose favour the disposition was made, that is to say –
  (i) in the case of a disposition to a class of persons, any member or potential member of the class;
  (ii) in the case of an individual disposition to a person taking only on certain conditions being satisfied, any person as to whom some of the conditions are satisfied and the remainder may in time be satisfied;
  (iii) in the case of a special power of appointment exercisable in favour of members of a class, any member or potential member of the class;
  (iv) in the case of a special power of appointment exercisable in favour of one person only, that person, or where the object of the power is ascertainable only on certain conditions being satisfied, any person as to whom some of the conditions are satisfied and the remainder may in time be satisfied;
  (v) in the case of any power, option or other right, the person on whom the right is conferred;

(c) a person having a child or grandchild within sub-paragraphs (i) to (iv) above, or any of whose children or grandchildren, if subsequently born, would by virtue of his or her descent fall within those sub-paragraphs;

(d) any person on the failure or determination of whose prior interest the disposition is limited to take effect.

In the case of a donor his life can only be used where the gift is made *inter vivos*. Where the disposition is made by will, the testator is dead when the disposition becomes operative and so his life cannot be used. In the case of donees there is an obvious problem. It should be noted that the restrictions on whose life may be used does not permit the use of a 'royal lives' clause. The Act deals with the position where there is no 'statutory' life in being: for example, a gift by will to the first man to land on Mars. In such a case the Act provides that the period shall be 21 years (s 3(4)(b)).

Section 1 of the 1964 Act permits disponers to expressly specify a perpetuity period of up to 80 years. This allows the disponer to avoid using lives in being to determine the vesting period. But of course lives in being could still be used and 'royal lives' clauses could still be specified.

Section 3(4)(a) states that, except where the disponer expressly chooses a period of time not exceeding 80 years as the perpetuity period under s 1, the perpetuity period shall be determined using the following principles. Where any persons falling within sub-section (5) (above) are individuals in being and ascertainable at the commencement of the perpetuity period, the duration of the period shall be determined by reference to their lives and no others, but the lives of any description of persons falling within paragraph (b) or (c) or subsection (5) shall be disregarded if the number of persons of that description is such as to render it impracticable to ascertain the date of death of the survivor.

It is rather strange that the 1964 Act did not simply abolish the common law rule. However, it is clear that the common law rule remains and that the 'wait and see' provision only applies to situations which would be void under the common law rule. So, with any provision it is necessary first to apply the common law rule and decide if there is any possibility that the interest might vest outside the perpetuity period. If the test is satisfied, i.e. there is no possibility that the interest will vest outside the perpetuity, then the provision is valid. If the common law test is failed and thus the provision would be void, then one uses 'wait and see'. If, in fact, the interest vests within the statutory perpetuity period, it is valid; if not, it is void.

The Perpetuities and Accumulations Act 2009

Objective 2

The 1993 Law Commission consultation paper – 'The Law of Trusts. The Rule Against Perpetuities and Excessive Accumulations' (Law Com. No. 133) – found that there were a number of problems with the then current law. The rules were complex, particularly in the area of the interface between the common law and the statutory provisions.

The Law Commission consultation paper made a number of points on the unsatisfactory state of the law. Uncertainty existed in the statutory list of lives in being under s 3(5) of the Perpetuities and Accumulations Act 1964. There was an inconsistency as to the identification of lives in being under the common law and statute. In a commercial context, where there may be no life in being, the period would be 21 years, which may be less than the parties would wish. The paper suggested that the perpetuity rules, which developed in the context of family trusts, fitted uncomfortably in a commercial context where contracts are being made by parties with equal bargaining powers. The rules were considered to operate harshly in some cases. For example, if a provision in a will offended the rule, it would be void and the property would then devolve as if the disposition had never been made. This may well result in the property passing to someone whom the testator had not planned to benefit. The rules were felt to be at odds with the modern attitude of the owners of property who were much less likely to wish to render property inalienable than were settlors in the eighteenth and nineteenth centuries. Additionally, the authors of the paper thought that the rule increased the costs of drafting settlements.

On 31 March 1998, the Law Commission issued a report – 'The Rules Against Perpetuities and Excessive Accumulations' (Law Com. No. 251) – which again examined the problems of the then current law, suggested modifications and put forward a draft bill. Its recommendations did not reflect the initial Consultation Paper. The overriding aims of the Law Commission were to simplify the rule and to set out the circumstances when the rule would apply. This, it was hoped, would make it easier for practitioners to advise on the applicability of the rule. It should, it was also hoped, facilitate dealings with land and give greater flexibility in dealing with property and drafting. Another result should be simpler and shorter legal documents and, perhaps, reduced costs.

The recommendations were reflected in the Perpetuities and Accumulations Act 2009.

The Act applies to instruments taking effect after 5 April 2010. But it does not apply to wills executed before but taking effect after 5 April 2010. The rule against perpetuities, under the then existing common law and statutory perpetuity periods is replaced in most cases with a single statutory perpetuity period of 125 years. The settlor can, of course, prescribe a shorter period of years. One consequence of this change is that the concept of lives in being will not be relevant to trusts governed by the 2009 Act and there will be no more 'royal lives' clauses. The 'wait and see' rule is preserved (s 7) as are the class closing provisions (s 8).

Why 125 years was selected is not clear but in most cases it will exceed the perpetuity period under the pre-existing law, where the period was a life in being plus 21 years or 80 years under the Perpetuities and Accumulations Act 1964. The life in being would have had to live at least to the age of 105 years to give a perpetuity period of over 125 years.

Section 1 sets out the situations covered by the rule against perpetuities. The estates, interests, rights and powers which the Act states to be within the application of the rule include:

- successive estates or interests, e.g. on trust for A then B then C. The rule is applied to each of the interests separately.

- an estate or interest subject to a condition precedent;

- where an estate or interest is subject to a condition subsequent, any right of re-entry in respect of land (or equivalent right for property other than land) if the condition is broken;

- successive interests under the doctrine of executory bequests;

- powers of appointment. These are void unless they become exercisable within the perpetuity period.

But the Act does not apply to most future easements, rights of pre-emption and options. All but one of these estates, interests, rights and powers exist under a trust. The exceptional category comprises successive interests under the doctrine of executory bequests.

The new rules do not apply to 'relevant' pension schemes, which are occupational pension schemes, personal pension schemes and public service pension schemes (ss 2(4) and 20(4)).

Among the exceptions s 2 states that the rule does not apply to an estate or interest created so as to vest in a charity on the occurrence of an event if immediately before the occurrence an estate or interest in the property concerned is vested in another charity (s 2(2)). This addresses and seems to preserve the *Re Tyler* [1891] 3 Ch 252 situation where a gift over from one charity to another may be outside the perpetuity rule. (See p. 203 for more on Re Tyler.) But it has been argued that this statutory provision might be narrower than was previously the case as it applies where the property becomes vested in 'another charity', and this could mean that it only applies where the gift over is to a charitable body but not if the gift over is to a charitable purpose.

The rule against perpetual trusts

This rule is aimed at preventing property from being tied up for long periods of time within a trust. While it is tied up it is inalienable and English law generally favours and encourages the free alienability and circulation of property.

It is generally agreed that the alternative perpetuity period contained in the Perpetuities and Accumulations Act 1964 s 1 (the 80-year provision) does not apply in this situation and the perpetuity period is always the common law period, i.e. a life in being plus 21 years.

If the settlor directs that the trust property must be kept and must not be alienated for a period which exceeds the perpetuity period, the trust will be void.

This rule does not apply to charitable trusts, which may last indefinitely, but is relevant in the case of non-charitable purpose trusts where the possibility of failure on the basis of offending this rule must always be borne in mind. If, for example, a settlor attempted to create a trust to maintain his tomb and a capital sum was placed on trust with the instruction to the trustees to invest the money and to use the interest only to maintain the tomb, the trust would be void. The settlor would, in effect, be directing the trustees to keep the capital indefinitely and so would offend the rule against perpetual trusts.

The Law Commission consultation paper 'The Law of Trusts. The Rule Against Perpetuities and Excessive Accumulations' (Law Com. No. 133) and the Law Commission report 'The Rules Against Perpetuities and Excessive Accumulations' (Law Com. No. 251) did not extend to any detailed discussion of this rule. The Law Commission said that the rule against inalienability was, in reality, just one of the devices that is employed to keep the development of non-charitable purpose trusts in check and that any consideration of the rule against inalienability belongs more properly in a review of the law governing non-charitable purpose trusts and unincorporated associations.

The Perpetuities and Accumulations Act 2009 s 18 states that the Act does not affect the rule of law which limits the duration of non-charitable purpose trusts. The section was included to ensure that the provisions of the Act did not change the existing law in an area on which the Law Commission had not consulted and which was regarded as outside the scope of their deliberations. Two comments may be made. First, can it be argued that this gives statutory seal of approval to such trusts which are generally regarded as anomalous at best and based on judicial error at worst? Secondly, there are some differences in what the perpetuity period is in such cases. For example, in *Re Hooper* [1932] 1 Ch 38 the period was 21 years and this is widely thought to be the appropriate period. But in *Re Denley* [1969] 1 Ch 373, where on one analysis there was a non-charitable purpose trust, the period was 21 years plus lives in being. The difference between the two cases was that in *Re Denley* there were lives in being but in *Re Hooper* there were not. Perhaps the opportunity should have been taken to prescribe a 'standard' perpetuity period for non-charitable purpose trusts.

See Chapter 9 (p. 199) for more on non-charitable purpose trusts.

The rule against accumulations

This rule is aimed at preventing the income from a trust from being accumulated (added to capital) for periods exceeding the perpetuity period. The rule is aimed at preventing property (the income) from being unavailable for a period considered by the law to be too long, by being added to capital rather than being distributed.

Before 6 April 2010

The rule was entirely the creation of statute. It was first created as a reaction to *Thellusson v Woodford* (1799) 4 Ves 227 in which a settlor's direction that income from his estate should be accumulated meant that none of his descendants who were alive at his death could enjoy any income.

The periods authorised by statute were contained in the Law of Property Act 1925 and the Perpetuities and Accumulations Act 1964.

Law of Property Act 1925 s 164

(a) the life of the settlor;

(b) 21 years from the death of the settlor;

(c) the minority(ies) of person(s) living (or *en ventre sa mère*) at the date of the settlor's or testator's death;

(d) the minority(ies) of a person(s) who, under the limitations of the instrument directing the accumulation, would for the time being, if of full age, be entitled to the income directed to be accumulated.

The Perpetuities and Accumulations Act 1964 s 13

(a) the period of 21 years from the date of the disposition;

(b) the duration of the minority(ies) of any person(s) in being at the date of the disposition.

After 5 April 2010

After examining the history and the current state of the law, the Law Commission consultation paper – 'The Law of Trusts. The Rule against Perpetuities and Excessive Accumulations' (Law Com. No. 133) – found the rule to be open to a number of criticisms. Complexity and uncertainty were found to exist. There could be inconsistency in the case of how long accumulations could last under a flexible trust. The rule could operate to frustrate the wishes of settlors and testators. For example, it was not possible to order an accumulation until the age of 25 years if the beneficiaries are under the age of four.

The Law Commission mooted three possibilities: (a) doing nothing; (b) abolishing the rule; (c) reforming it. The Commission recommended that some change is needed but felt that the choice lay between abolition and retention coupled with reform.

The recommendations made in the subsequent Law Commission Report – 'The Rules Against Perpetuities and Excessive Accumulations' (Law Com. 251) – were reflected in the Perpetuities and Accumulations Act 2009.

Section 13 of the 2009 Act abolishes the restriction on the period during which income can be accumulated, although in the case of charities s 14 imposes a restriction to 21 years (unless the provision to accumulate is made by the court or by the Charity Commissioners).

This does not mean that income can be accumulated indefinitely as interest must vest within the 125-year perpetuity period. The Act applies to instruments taking effect after 5 April 2010. But it does not apply to wills executed before but taking effect after 5 April 2010.

Trusts which offend public policy

Objective 3

Certain trusts will not be enforced by the law as being unlawful or against public policy. The law is not static and it may be that in the future the law declares other trusts to be unenforceable on the ground of public policy.

Capricious trusts

The courts take the view that they have some role to play in ensuring that property is used in a productive and 'useful' way. This has led to the courts striking down trusts on the basis that they are 'capricious', wasteful or useless.

In *Brown* v *Burdett* (1882) 21 Ch D 667, the court considered a trust under which a testatrix had directed that a house was to be unused (except for four rooms for her housekeeper) for a 20-year period was void. The testatrix directed that the rooms were to be closed off and the windows were to be blocked up. The trust was found to be a nullity. Bacon V-C said: 'I think I must "unseal" this useless, undisposed-of property. There will be a declaration that the house and premises were undisposed of by the will, for a term of 20 years from the testatrix's death.'

Again, in *M'Caig* v *University of Glasgow* (1907) 44 SLR 198, John Stuart M'Caig stated in his will that the income from his estate was to be used for the purpose of erecting 'artistic towers' and building statues of himself. Lord Kyllachy, on the issue of public policy, stated:

I consider that if it is not unlawful, it ought to be unlawful, to dedicate by testamentary disposition, for all time, or for a length of time, the whole income of a large estate – real and personal – to objects of no utility, private or public, objects which benefit nobody, and which have no other purpose or use than that of perpetuating at great cost, and in an absurd manner, the idiosyncrasies of an eccentric testator.

The same family also featured in *M'Caig's Trustees* v *The Kirk-Session of the United Free Church of Lismore* (1915) 52 SLR 347. In this case Catherine, the sister of the testator in the case above, provided in her will that 11 bronze statues of her parents and their nine children were to be erected, each to cost no less than £1,000. This again failed. Lord Salvesen said: 'In the first place, I think it is a sheer waste of money . . .'.

He went on to say that he thought it would be a dangerous thing to support a bequest of this kind, which can only gratify the vanity of testators, who have no claim to be immortalised, but who possess the means by which they can provide for a more substantial monument to themselves than many that are erected to famous persons by public subscription. A man may, of course, do with his money what he pleases while he is alive, but he is generally restrained from wasteful expenditure by a desire to enjoy his property, or to accumulate it, during his lifetime.

Lord Salvesen then pointed out that the M'Caigs had been thinking about erecting statues during their lives but could not bring themselves to part with the money.

Two points may be made. First, these decisions involve judicial value judgments that arguably should be left to the testator. Secondly, it appears that judicial interference will be restricted to dispositions by will, leaving open the opportunity for the owner of property to put it to 'wasteful' uses during his lifetime.

Trusts to encourage a breach of the law

In *Thrupp* v *Collett* (1858) 26 Beav 125, a trust to pay the fines of poachers was held to be void. It is clear that any trust which has as its object a breach of the criminal law will be void.

Trusts tending to weaken the family

Objective
4

Under this heading may be included trusts, or provisions in a trust, which tend to prevent a parent from carrying out their duties towards their children or which attempt to interfere with the way in which the duties are carried out. Also included are trusts which have a tendency to deter marriage or which may encourage a husband and wife to live apart. All of these types of trust will be perceived as leading to the weakening or breaking down of the family unit and as such the courts will not allow the trusts to be valid. In the last resort the court might find itself administering a trust and it would clearly be unthinkable that the court should be involved in the administration of a trust which strikes at the foundations of family life.

Conditions

In fact many, if not most, of the cases to be discussed involve not so much the validity of the trust *per se* but rather the validity of a condition under the trust. Conditions which tend towards weakening the family will be declared void. For example, property may be transferred to trustees to hold for the benefit of Peter 'on condition that if Peter should live with his mother the interest will be forfeited'. Or a benefit or interest may be expressed in such a way that it is intended only to take effect if a condition is satisfied. For example, the interest may be stated to be effective 'only if Wendy is not living with her husband'. The first example is an illustration of a condition subsequent, i.e. a condition which if satisfied will cause an interest to be forfeited. The second is an illustration of a condition precedent, i.e. a condition which must be satisfied before the interest can vest. It is arguable that both of the above examples should be regarded as trusts tending to weaken the family unit. Such conditions will be declared void if they are in fact found to have the effect of weakening the family unit.

Condition or determinable interest?

An element of confusion can arise with regard to deciding if a determinable interest or a condition has been created. An example of a determinable interest is where property is held for the benefit of a child 'until he shall live with his mother'. The effect is that the interest ends if and when the child goes and lives with its mother and it is beyond argument that the effect must be to tend towards separating the child from its mother as, if the two live together, the interest will end. It is, however, accepted that a provision of this kind is perfectly valid. The explanation is that the settlor has simply mapped out the precise interest given and the interest automatically and naturally comes to an end when the stated event occurs. The gift is never contemplated as absolute and it is always intended to last only up to the point that the condition is satisfied. By contrast a conditional gift is considered to be absolute from the outset, but when the condition is satisfied the gift is cut short. A gift to Austin 'unless he should buy a BMW motor car' is an example of a determinable gift which will be cut short if the BMW is purchased. It is often very difficult to decide whether a determinable interest or a condition subsequent has been created. This, of course, can make life very difficult for those trying to administer the property. In many cases the only safe course would be to ask the court to determine the nature of the provision but this can be expensive and create delay.

Effect of failure of a condition

If a condition subsequent is void, the interest takes effect as an absolute interest. If a condition precedent is void, the effect depends on whether the property involved is realty or personalty. In the case of realty the interest will fail totally. However, with personalty the result varies according to the reason for the failure. If the condition is *malum prohibitum* then the interest takes effect free from the condition, but if the condition is *malum in se* the interest fails. The difference between *malum prohibitum* and *malum in se* is rather difficult to define. An act which is *malum in se* includes activities which may seem to be 'wrong in themselves' as being contrary to morality. An obvious example would be a condition precedent involving murder: for example, a condition that an interest will vest only if Wendy has murdered Peter. *Malum prohibitum* covers acts which are not wrong in themselves but which have been made unlawful, for example by a statute. An example might be if an interest was subject to the condition precedent 'that Peter has been convicted of being drunk and disorderly in a public place'. Although being drunk may not be, of itself, morally wrong it may well involve a breach of the criminal law. This would be *malum prohibitum*.

Uncertainty of the terms of a condition

Many cases on conditional interests have been decided on the basis of uncertainty rather than on the basis of 'illegality'. In such situations the courts decided that the condition failed as its terms were not sufficiently clearly drafted to enable the court to oversee its operation, rather than that the condition was 'unlawful'.

Interference with parental duties

The courts will strike down trusts or conditions which have the object or effect of preventing a parent from carrying out their parental duties. Again, in this area many of the cases are concerned with the validity of conditions, particularly conditions subsequent.

In *Re Sandbrook* [1912] 2 Ch 471, for example, a testatrix gave her two grandchildren interests in a trust fund which were to last until 31 December 1927, when the capital was to be divided between them. The testatrix stipulated that their interests would be forfeited if the grandchildren should live with or be in the custody of or under the control of their father. The court held the condition to be void as contrary to public policy. The effect of the condition was to encourage the grandchildren to live apart from their father and to prevent him from exercising control or influence over them because the result of them living with, or being controlled by, their father was that their benefits under the trust would end. Such a condition will be void even if the parents are divorced: *Re Piper* [1946] 2 All ER 503.

The courts do, however, accept that some degree of 'interference' is not unacceptable. The attitude appears to be that while it is not acceptable to attempt to prevent a parent from exercising any of their duties it is permissible to attempt to influence the way those duties are carried out. For example, it may well be acceptable to impose a condition that the interest will be forfeited if the child is sent to a public school. The clear intention of the settlor would be to influence the decision of the parents as to what type of education the child should have, but it would not be aimed at removing the decision from the parents.

In *Blathwayt* v *Lord Cawley* [1975] 3 All ER 625, it was argued that a clause in a will which provided that the interest of a child should be forfeited if he became a Roman Catholic was void as it interfered with the decisions his parents might make as regards his upbringing. The House of Lords rejected the argument, Lord Wilberforce saying: 'to say that any condition which in any way might affect or influence the way in which a child is brought up, or in which parental duties are exercised, seems to me to state far too wide a rule'. In fact the House of Lords decided, by a majority of three to two, that, as a matter of construction, the clause did not apply.

In his judgment, Lord Wilberforce also discussed the validity of conditions which might be argued to discriminate on racial or religious grounds. Racial discrimination is covered by the Race Relations Act 1976 but there was at the time no statute that dealt with religious discrimination. Lord Wilberforce said that if the clause in the will was declared void this would lead to a substantial reduction in the firmly rooted freedom of testamentary disposition.

Lord Cross also addressed this issue, saying that while it is widely thought that it is wrong for a government to deal with some of its citizens less favourably than others because of differences of religious beliefs it does not follow that it is against public policy for an adherent of one religion to distinguish in the disposition of his property between adherents of his faith and others.

Trusts restraining marriage

The law draws a distinction between total and partial restraint of marriage (and presumably civil partnerships).

It is generally accepted that a trust or condition which acts in total restraint of marriage is void. A restraint is total if its object is to prevent any marriage taking place. Again, the distinction between a condition and a determinable interest must be remembered. It is possible to create an interest which determines on marriage, while it is not possible to impose a condition which causes an interest to be forfeited on any marriage. An example of a determinable interest is *Jones* v *Jones* (1876) 1 QBD 279, where the court found that the intention was to provide for a person until marriage rather than to deter marriage.

A partial restraint is one aimed at preventing a particular marriage or marriages. A partial restraint is *prima facie* valid.

Example

If an interest is given to Wendy 'unless she should marry' it would be a condition in total restraint on marriage. Whomsoever she marries, the interest will be forfeited. However, if the condition states that Wendy's interest will be forfeited if she marries Peter, or if she marries a merchant banker, it will operate as a partial restraint only and will be valid.

In *Jenner* v *Turner* (1880) 16 Ch D 188, a testatrix gave her residuary personalty to her brother, on trust, absolutely. However, if her brother married a domestic servant the interest would be forfeited. Later, the brother married a domestic servant and the court upheld the condition as being only a partial restraint on marriage. The brother could have chosen his wife from anyone in the world, except domestic servants.

However, there is an important difference between partial restraints in the case of realty and personalty. With personalty if there is no gift over on the marriage the restraint is merely *in terrorem* and void. In the case of the realty the partial restraint is never invalid. (See *Leong* v *Chye* [1955] 2 All ER 903, where a restraint against remarriage was held to be a partial restraint, and therefore *prima facie* valid.)

Trusts interfering between married couples or to deter a separated married couple from living together

If the object of a trust is to encourage or induce a married couple who are presently living together, with no plan to live apart, to separate, the trust will be void. Many of the cases are concerned with conditions which are aimed at inducing a separation.

In *Re Moore* (1888) 39 Ch D 116, a testator instructed his trustees to pay a weekly sum of money to his sister 'during such time as she may live apart from her husband'. When the sister separated from her husband, the Court of Appeal decided that this was a limited gift, the commencement and duration of which were fixed in a way which the law did not allow. The court decided that the gift tended to promote the separation of the sister from her husband.

A more modern example of a trust being set aside as tending towards the separation of a husband and wife is *Re Johnson's Will Trusts* [1967] 1 All ER 553, in which a father left his daughter £11,000 on trust but her interest was cut down to an income of £50 p.a. while she was living with her husband or so long as she remained married to him.

However, the cases must be read with care as in some situations the courts have upheld provisions which at first sight appear to encourage the separation of spouses. In these cases the courts have construed a condition as being intended to provide an income for a spouse while separated rather than as an attempt to promote the separation itself.

For example, in *Re Lovell* [1920] 1 Ch 122, a testator was living with a woman who had been deserted by her husband. In his will he gave her an annuity 'provided and so long as she shall not return to live with her husband and provided and so long as she shall not remarry'. If she returned to her husband or remarried the annuity was to be reduced by two-thirds. The court held that the purpose was not to encourage the woman to live apart from her husband, but simply to maintain her until she remarried or returned to her husband, and so the condition was valid.

Presumably the same principles apply in the case of civil partnerships.

Trusts for illegitimate children

Historically, trusts for unborn illegitimate children were void as offending public policy. It was thought that such trusts would encourage immorality by providing encouragement for the production of children by couples who were not married.

However, it was recognised that the effect of this was in fact to 'punish' the children and the attitude of the judiciary was changing when the Family Law Reform Act 1969 came into operation on 1 January 1970. This legislation radically altered the situation and meant that trusts for future illegitimate children were no longer void. The provision has now been replaced by the Family Law Reform Act 1987 – see sections 1 and 19.

It must be remembered that the situation remains unaltered with regard to dispositions made before 1 January 1970 and so many trusts may still be regulated by the 'old' law. As far as trusts created by will are concerned, the vital date is not when the testator died but rather when the will was executed. If a will was executed before 1 January 1970, any trust created by it will be governed by the old law.

Summary

- Under the perpetuity rules, trusts may fail for offending one of three perpetuity rules (the rule against remote vesting; the rule against perpetual trusts; and the rule against excessive accumulations of income).

- Recent changes in the law have been made under the Perpetuities and Accumulations Act 2009.

- The most significant change is the introduction of a 'standard' perpetuity period of 125 years.

- Capricious trusts applying property in 'useless' ways will not be enforced by the courts.

- Trusts which encourage a breach of the criminal law are not lawful.

- Trusts may be liable to be set aside by the courts if they offend public policy by tending to weaken the family unit. This includes trusts that tend to weaken the family: for example, trusts that interfere with the way that parents discharge their duties and responsibilities towards their children and trusts that restrain marriage or which interfere with the relationship of a married couple.

Further reading

Perpetuities

F Quin, 'The Perpetuities and Accumulations Bill: clarity or confusion?' (2009) 2 PCB 126.
The article analyses the provisions of the Perpetuities and Accumulations Bill (which became the Perpetuities and Accumulations Act 2009) and identifies some possible difficulties.

M Skinner, 'Matters of trust' (2009) 159 (7397), NLJ 1732.
Discusses the Perpetuities and Accumulations Act 2009 and its implications for testators making new wills.

Variation of trusts

Objectives

After reading this chapter you should:

1. Understand that proposals to vary trusts often reveal tensions between the original intention of the settlor and the interests of the beneficiaries and understand why, in some situations, the courts favour the interests of the beneficiaries.
2. Understand (in outline) the power of the courts to rectify trusts.
3. Understand that, although the courts have an inherent jurisdiction to make or agree to variations of trust, this is only possible in a limited set of circumstances.
4. Understand the main statutory provisions under which trusts can be varied, especially s 57 of the Trustee Act and the Variation of Trusts Act 1958.

Introduction

Objective 1

After a trust has been created, it may become apparent that it might be better if its original terms and provisions were altered. Perhaps the circumstances of the beneficiaries have changed or the impact of tax has altered following legislative amendments. It may be that the original, express, powers of investment are in need of review because of a changed economic or financial climate. In fact, the majority of occasions where it appears desirable to vary the terms of a trust involve tax avoidance or saving.

Often there will be a tension between the expressed wishes of the settlor and the interests of the beneficiaries. The problem is, which should prevail? Should the rule be that once a trust has been set up its provisions are set in stone and can never change whatever the circumstances? Or should the original expression of the settlor's wishes as contained in the trust be capable of being modified or even overridden in the interests of the beneficiaries?

The general approach of the courts has been that the original trust provisions must be obeyed and a breach of trust will be committed if a trustee deviates from those terms.

In *Re New* [1900–3] All ER Rep 763, Romer LJ said:

> As a rule the court has no jurisdiction to give, and will not give, its sanction to the performance by trustees of acts with reference to the trust estate which are not, on the face of the instrument creating the trust, authorised by its terms.

In some situations it may be possible for the beneficiaries to agree to changes being made but in other situations application to the courts will be necessary. However, in some cases, the courts have seemed rather reluctant to agree to any alterations to the original trusts.

But, as one of the key characteristics of the trust is flexibility, it will be no surprise to discover that a number of important exceptions to the *prima facie* rule of fidelity to the wishes of the settlor have been created. Some of these exceptions make it possible to change only provisions in the trust which relate to the management and/or administration of the trust but other exceptions make it possible to alter the beneficial interests.

It may be possible to argue that the resolution of the problem in favour of allowing variations has resulted in the wishes of the settlor being sacrificed in favour of the interests of the beneficiaries. However, in many cases it may well be that the changes made to the original trust terms reflect the wishes of the settlor, or at least what the settlor would have wanted had he known about the changed circumstances. The purpose behind many variations is ultimately to maximise the benefits flowing to the beneficiaries. This may follow from the modification of administrative provisions which will allow the trust to run in a more efficient and productive manner. Alternatively, the variation may alter the beneficial interests, but again such a change will usually be made in the best interests of the beneficiaries; perhaps the result of the change will be to save the trust, and therefore the beneficiaries, tax. It must be assumed that the settlor would wish the trust to run in an efficient way and to provide maximum benefits to those to whom he gave interests and so the changes may well reflect this overriding intention.

Historically, the courts exercised an inherent jurisdiction to approve of variations in trusts, but gradually trustees and beneficiaries have needed to invoke these powers less and less as various statutory provisions have been introduced.

See Chapter 6 (p. 157) for a discussion of the rule in *Saunders* v *Vautier*.

Under the rule in **Saunders v Vautier**, a trust can be ended if all the beneficiaries are *sui juris* and all agree. The trustees can be instructed to transfer the trust funds as the beneficiaries direct. It should be noted that this is not an example of variation of trust but rather is an example of ending a trust. However, the factors outlined above may play a part in deciding to end a trust.

Rectification

Objective 2

As part of its general jurisdiction to provide relief against the consequences of mistake, equity can rectify a trust instrument if it fails to express the true intention of the parties. Relief can be granted if the mistake relates to the 'meaning' or 'effect' of a document but not if the mistake relates to its 'consequences'.

Before the Administration of Justice Act 1982 rectification was not available if the trust was created by will. But under s 20(1) of the Administration of Justice Act 1982, the court has the power to rectify a will if it is satisfied that it fails to carry out the intentions of the testator as the result of a clerical error or a failure to understand his instructions.

Under the sub-section the court has the power to rectify the will so that it carries out the intentions of the testator. For example, rectification could be ordered if a testator wished to create a trust in his will but either his solicitor failed to understand the terms of the trust that the testator wanted or the will was drafted with a clerical error which had the effect of failing to reflect the testator's wishes as regards the terms of the trust.

It is not sufficient that subsequently it becomes clear that it would have been better if the trust created under a will contained different terms. In order to use s 20(1) the court must find either a clerical error or a failure to understand the testator's wishes. But it may be that in these circumstances a variation could be achieved under the provisions discussed elsewhere in this chapter.

The term clerical error was considered by Chadwick J in **Re Segleman** [1996] 2 WLR 173. The test of 'clerical error' was in the opinion of Chadwick J whether or not the solicitor had applied his mind to the significance and effect of the words used. If he had not the will could be rectified; if he had so applied his mind the will would have to stand in its original form.

Rectification is distinct from the process whereby the court corrects a mistake or error as a matter of construction of the words of an instrument where the courts can only act if the mistake and the real intentions of the parties are clear from the wording of the document, without any extrinsic evidence.

Inherent jurisdiction

Objective 3

As part of their role in supervising trusts, the courts claim a number of inherent powers to permit trustees to do acts not permitted by the terms of their trust. If those beneficiaries who are *sui juris* and of full age agree to the trustees acting beyond their powers, the courts could step in and agree (or, if appropriate, refuse to agree) to proposals on behalf of any beneficiary who lacks the legal capacity to participate in the agreement. However, the courts will allow deviation in a small number of cases.

Emergency

The courts have the power to allow the trustees to do some administrative act which is outside the terms of the trust if an emergency arises. The courts will use this power only if the act for which approval is sought relates to something that the settlor could not have foreseen at the time when the settlement was created. The power does not extend to changing beneficial interests.

Re New [1901] 2 Ch 534

In this case, the court approved of the trustees' participation in the reconstruction of a company in which the trust held shares. The shares were to be subdivided into shares with a lower value, which would be more marketable. The court empowered the trustees to agree to the reorganisation and to take up newly issued shares. Under the terms of the trust the trustees lacked the power to participate in such a reconstruction.

Romer LJ stated the extent and the limits of the court:

In the management of a trust . . . it not infrequently happens that some peculiar state of circumstances arises for which provision is not expressly made by the trust instrument, and which renders it most desirable, and it may even be essential, for the benefit of the estate and in the interests of all the *cestuis que* trusts, that certain acts should be done by the trustees which in ordinary circumstances they have no power to do. . . . In a case of this kind, which may reasonably be supposed to be one not foreseen or anticipated by the author of the trust, where the trustees are embarrassed by the emergency that has arisen and the duty cast on them to do what is best for the estate, and the consent of all the beneficiaries cannot be obtained by reason of some of them not being *sui juris* or in existence, then it may be right for the court, and the court in a proper case would have jurisdiction, to sanction on behalf of all concerned such acts on behalf of the trustees as we have referred to . . . The jurisdiction is one to be exercised with great caution, and the court will take care not to strain its powers . . . it need scarcely be said that the court will not be justified in sanctioning every act desired by trustees and beneficiaries merely because it may appear beneficial to the estate; and certainly the court will not be disposed to sanction transactions of a speculative or risky character.

Although Romer LJ said that a variation would not be approved *merely* because it benefited beneficiaries, he stressed that approval would not be given unless the proposal benefited the beneficiaries.

In *Re Tollemache* [1903] 1 Ch 955, *Re New* was described as the high water mark of the jurisdiction. In *Re Tollemache* the court refused to enlarge the investment powers of trustees as there was no 'emergency'.

Salvage

This inherent power will be exercised only in extreme situations. It may be used, for example, where a crisis occurs threatening the very existence of trust property. The court may sanction actions of the trustees to save the property where, under the terms of the trust, the power was lacking. In *Re Jackson* (1882) 21 Ch D 786, the court approved of the trustees taking steps to raise money to be used to avoid the collapse of buildings owned by the trust.

As with the power of emergency, the power of salvage only allows changes in the powers of management and administration of a trust. There is no power to sanction the alteration of beneficial interests. This power has been superseded by the Trustee Act 1925 s 57 (see p. 179).

Maintenance

If a settlement is created to provide for a minor but the enjoyment of the minor is postponed, perhaps because of a direction to accumulate, the court may disregard the terms of the trust and order that the minor is maintained from the income generated by the trust property.

Re Collins (1886) 32 Ch D 229 is an example of the court's use of this power. The testator directed that the income of his estate should be accumulated for 21 years and gave the accumulated property to his sister for life, remainder to her three sons and their children. The court ordered that an annual sum should be paid to the sister for the education and maintenance of her three sons. The court assumed that the testator would not have wished the beneficiaries to be unprovided for. It seems that jam tomorrow should not be a consolation for dry bread today. Farwell J said:

> Where a testator has made a provision for a family, using that word in the ordinary sense in which we take the word, that is the children's particular stirps in succession, but has postponed the enjoyment, either for a particular purpose or generally for the increase of the estate, it is assumed that he did not intend that these children should be left unprovided for or in a state of such moderate means that they should not be educated properly for the position and fortune which he designs them to have, and the court has accordingly found from the earliest times that where an heir-in-law is unprovided for, maintenance ought to be provided for him.

This is an example of the courts using their inherent jurisdiction to change the beneficial interests under a trust.

In fact, of course, in these instances the courts are 'ignoring' the expressed wish of the settlor in preference to their own assessment of the position.

This power is normally exercised in order to provide for a minor beneficiary but it is not limited to minors: *Revel v Watkinson* (1748) 1 Ves Sen 93. Nor is it limited, as with salvage or emergency, to situations which either were not foreseen or which unexpectedly arise: *Hayley v Bannister* (1820) 4 Madd 275.

Compromise

Under this inherent power the court can approve of compromises or agreements in cases where there is a dispute as to the precise meaning of the terms of a trust. The adult, *sui juris* beneficiaries may well be in agreement as to how the dispute should be resolved and the courts can agree to the compromise on behalf of beneficiaries who are minors or not *sui juris*. The dispute might relate to the administrative powers of the trustees or to the interests created under the trust. In the latter case some argue that when the court supplies consent it is participating in a variation or alteration of beneficial interests. However, it can be argued that a compromise is merely concerned to define, rather than alter, beneficial interests. ***Allen v Distillers Co (Biochemicals) Ltd*** [1974] 2 All ER 365 concerned the action to claim damages for deformities to children caused by the drug thalidomide taken by expectant mothers. A proposal was put to the court for approval of an alteration in the terms of the original settlement. It was proposed to postpone the infants' entitlement. Eveleigh J held that the court had no inherent jurisdiction as such to maintain control over a minor's property after he attained the age of majority. However, Eveleigh J also decided that it was possible to use the power of the court to approve of compromises to approve of the settlement which the parties had arrived at. The terms of the settlement of the action were sufficiently wide to authorise a postponement of entitlement and as such approval was granted. The case of ***Mason v Farbrother*** [1983] 2 All ER 1078 represents an attempt to use the power to approve of compromises. There was an uncertainty as to the exact meaning of an investment clause. However, the court was unwilling to approve of the particular change requested. It was accepted that the court had the power to approve of genuine compromises which fell somewhere between two opposing views of the meaning of a trust provision. What the court did not have the power to do was to approve of a new investment clause which did not so fall. To do so would be not to approve of a compromise (which simply 'defines' what the initial terms of the trust are) but to put in place an entirely different term. This would not be approving of a compromise but would be approving of a change. It was accepted that there was a genuine uncertainty, particularly as to how the express power of investment and the statutory powers of investment related to each other, but the proposed investment clause for which approval was sought represented a provision falling outside the differing views of the original clause. In fact, approval was given (see below) under s 57(1) of the Trustee Act 1925.

Despite the decision in ***Mason v Farbrother***, the power to approve of compromises was used by the courts in some cases to enable approval to be given to rearrangements of beneficial interests under settlements when in reality there was no dispute at all. In such cases the courts gave their consent on behalf of minors or other beneficiaries not able to consent for themselves. The power was being used to enable the courts to sanction variations where no other route was open. In ***Re Downshire Settled Estates*** [1953] 1 All ER 103, for example, the Court of Appeal gave its consent to the beneficial interests being restructured in order to save tax. The Court of Appeal in general, and Lord Denning in particular, accepted that the 'compromise' jurisdiction was of wide application and was not restricted to situations where there was a genuine dispute. However, the House of Lords in ***Chapman v Chapman*** [1954] 1 All ER 798 rejected this approach, deciding that the power was available only in cases of genuine disputes.

In the more recent case of ***D (a child) v O*** [2004] 3 All ER 780 the court was asked to approve of an arrangement to enable trustees to advance more than the 50 per cent limit imposed on the statutory power of advancement under s 32 of the Trustee Act 1925 in order to pay the school fees of an infant beneficiary. In the event the decision was made using the Variation of Trusts Act 1958 (see p. 184), but it was also argued that the court could give its approval using its inherent jurisdiction to approve of compromises. The court, having referred to *Chapman* v *Chapman* (1954) which set out the need for a genuine dispute as a prerequisite to the court being able to use the inherent jurisdiction, said that, although the inherent power could be used to authorise the expenditure of capital to which a minor was absolutely entitled for their maintenance (*Worthington* v *M'Craer* (1856) 23 Beav 81), in the instant case it was extremely doubtful whether there was a dispute between the beneficiaries as to their rights. Thus the case was outside the inherent jurisdiction.

See Chapter 8 (pp. 184–96) for a detailed discussion of the Variation of Trusts Act 1958.

Trustee Act 1925 s 57(1)

Objective 4

This provision has largely taken over from the court's inherent jurisdiction to approve of alterations to the management powers on the ground of emergency.

> Section 57(1) Where in the management or administration of any property vested in trustees, any sale, lease, mortgage, surrender, release, or other disposition, or any purchase, investment, acquisition, expenditure, or other transaction, is in the opinion of the court expedient, but the same cannot be effected by reason of the absence of any power for that purpose vested in the trustees by the trust instrument, if any, or by law, the court may by order confer upon the trustees, either generally or in any particular instance, the necessary power for the purpose, on such terms, and subject to such provisions and conditions, if any, as the court may think fit and may direct in what manner any money authorised to, be expended, and the costs of any transaction, are to be paid or borne as between capital and income.

The section requires only that the court is satisfied that the proposed alterations to the administrative powers are 'expedient'. This contrasts with the situation under the inherent jurisdiction, where the court must be satisfied that the settlor could not have anticipated the need for the power. Section 57(1) unlike the inherent power is not restricted to cases of emergency.

In *Re Downshire Settled Estates* [1953] 1 All ER 103, Lord Evershed set out what he saw as the object of s 57:

> . . . the object of s 57 was to secure that trust property should be managed as advantageously as possible in the interests of the beneficiaries, and, with that object in view, to authorise specific dealings with the property which the court might have felt itself unable to sanction under the inherent jurisdiction, either because no actual 'emergency' had arisen or because of inability to show that the position which called for intervention was one which the creator of the trust could not reasonably have foreseen, but it was no part of the legislative aim to disturb the rule that the court will not re-write a trust or to add to such exceptions to that rule as had already found their way into the inherent jurisdiction.

There are two key phrases in the sub-section.

First the sub-section states that it is concerned with powers of 'management or administration' and secondly that the sub-section can only be used if the court decides that it would be 'expedient' for a power to be conferred on the trustees.

It is clear that any variation agreed by the court must relate to powers of management or administration. There is no power under the section to alter beneficial interests. But, as will be seen later, the fact that the effect of a variation is to vary beneficial interests is not necessarily of itself fatal to an application if the variation of the beneficial interest is considered to be merely incidental to the variation of the powers of management. What the courts cannot do under s 57 is to simply re-write the trusts.

According to Farwell J in *Re Mair* [1935] All ER Rep 736, the section operates as if it had been inserted into the trust instrument as an overriding power.

One of its most common uses in the past has been to extend trustees' powers of investment (e.g. *Mason* v *Farbrother* (see p. 488)). But as the statutory powers of investment have been broadened under the Trustee Act 2000 the need for powers of investment to be enlarged will arise less often. (See p. 482.)

Under s 57, the courts have agreed to the sale of settled chattels (*Re Hope's Will Trust* [1929] 2 Ch 136) and to the purchase of a home for a beneficiary (*Re Power* [1947] 2 All ER 282). However, although the section applies to land, it cannot be used in relation to settled land (but see the Settled Land Act 1925 s 64 (p. 182)).

Expediency

The case of *Re Craven* [1937] 3 All ER 33 is an example of the section in operation and the court's search for 'expediency'. In her will the testatrix had left her residuary estate on trust for a number of beneficiaries (including her son Gilbert) with an ultimate trust in favour of a charity. She had given her trustees an express power of advancement *inter alia* 'for the purchase of a business or a share in a business'. The court was asked to decide if the trustees had the power to advance money to the son to enable him to become a member of Lloyd's. If they had no such power, the court was asked to approve of a variation of the power under s 57(1). In order to become a member the son was required to deposit a sum of money with Lloyd's. The money would be used as a fund out of which to meet his liabilities. Farwell J decided as a matter of construction that using money for such a purpose did not amount to the purchase of a business or of a share in a business, but rather was the means of enabling the son to carry on a profession which would not otherwise be open to him and so was not an advancement. Farwell J opined that s 57(1) is framed in very wide terms and was undoubtedly intended to allow the courts to grant trustees powers which they have not been expressly given but which would allow them to carry out transactions which would be beneficial and expedient for the benefit of the trust.

> The word 'expedient' there quite clearly must mean, in my judgment, expedient for the trust as a whole. It cannot mean that, however expedient it might be for one beneficiary, if it were extremely inexpedient from the point of view of the other beneficiaries, the court could sanction such a transaction. That the matter should be one which is, in the opinion of the court, expedient it must, in my judgment, be expedient from the point of view of the trust as a whole.

The court does not have to examine the position of every single beneficiary and decide whether or not the proposed variation would benefit each of those beneficiaries. The court simply has to take an overall view of the trust and the beneficiaries and decide if the variation would be expedient or not.

In *Re Craven*, Farwell J said it would obviously benefit Gilbert to become a member of Lloyd's but thought that it would not be expedient for the ultimate beneficiaries to allow part of the trust fund to which they might ultimately become entitled to be risked in the way proposed. Consent was refused as the proposal was not expedient for the trust as a whole.

In *Mason* v *Farbrother* (p. 488) the court refused to approve of a new investment clause under its inherent power to approve of compromise but did sanction the change under s 57(1). It was accepted that it was expedient for the management or administration of the trust that the trustees should have a wider power of investment. Additionally, the court found that inflation that had occurred between the passing of the Trustee Investments Act in 1961 and the date of the action was a special reason why approval should be given to a clause granting powers beyond those contained in the Trustee Investments Act 1961 (see p. 488).

In *Anker-Petersen* v *Anker-Petersen* (1991) 88/16 LS Gaz 32, Judge Paul Baker QC said that, where proposals to extend the trustees' powers of investment did not affect the beneficial interests, applications should normally be brought under s 57 rather than under the Variation of Trusts Act 1958. He said that, while some had expressed doubts as to whether or not s 57 was available in cases of extending investment powers, he saw no reason to adopt a restrictive construction. It was more convenient to use s 57 as the trustees were the natural persons to make the application; the consent of every beneficiary of full age was not essential and the court was not required to give consent on behalf of every category of beneficiary separately but would consider their interests collectively. These advantages would also lead to shorter and less expensive hearings.

See Chapter 16 (p. 482) for a discussion of the powers of investment under the Trustee Act 2000.

As mentioned above, the Trustee Act 2000 (p. 488) has made very significant changes to trustees' powers of investment. In brief, the trustee has (unless restricted by the terms of the trust) the same powers of investment as if he were absolutely entitled to the trust assets (s 3(1)). This should reduce the occasions when an application is needed to extend powers of investment. However, it may still be that, if the express terms of the trust which relate to the powers of investment are considered unduly restrictive, an application to vary powers of investment will be needed.

Variations of powers of management or administration that alter beneficial interests

The general rule under s 57 is that the court can approve of changes to powers of management or administration and that the section does not permit the court to approve of changes to beneficial interests.

In Court of Appeal decision of *Southgate* v *Sutton* [2011] EWCA Civ 637 Mummery LJ set out the general position:

> The expressions 'other transaction' and 'expedient' in s 57(1) are very broad. However, they are confined by the context of the 'management or administration' of the trust property. Thus, it has been held that there is no jurisdiction under s 57(1) to confer a power to depart from the beneficial interests under the trusts by re-writing, remoulding or re-arranging them. Variations of the beneficial interests under the trusts are not, as such, matters of 'the management or administration' of the trust property and 'trust property' cannot be equated with beneficial interests in the trust property.
>
> Rulings to that effect in *Re Downshire* [1953] Ch 218 at 248 and *Chapman* v *Chapman* [1954] AC 429 led to the passing of the Variation of Trusts Act 1958 (the 1958 Act). That created a new jurisdiction under which the court may, if it thinks fit, approve proposed arrangements varying trusts, including the beneficial interests under them, on behalf of infants, unborn persons and others, if the carrying out of the arrangement would be for their benefit.

Southgate v *Sutton* deals with this issue which may affect many applications under the Trustee Act 1925 s 57. The case seems to fly in the face of *Anker-Petersen* (1991) 88/16 LS Gaz 32 (above) where it was said that s 57 was appropriate as in the case there the variation would not change beneficial interests, suggesting that if changes to beneficial interests were involved s 57 should not (could not?) be used. What *Southgate* v *Sutton* shows is that there is no absolute answer if a variation changes beneficial interests, and each case has to be decided on its own facts, but a s 57 application will not necessarily fail *just* because there is some change to the beneficial interests.

As long as the court decides that the changes to the beneficial interests are just incidental to the changes in the powers of administration and management, then the changes can be approved.

Mummery LJ said:

> It has been held, on the other hand, that an application under s 57(1) to confer powers for the purpose of a proposed transaction is within the jurisdiction of the court, if the exercise of the powers conferred by the court under s 57(1) might only incidentally affect the beneficial interests in the trust property: see *Downshire* at 248 *per* Lord Evershed MR.
>
> The court must decide, on the particular facts of each case, on which side of the line the application falls. That may be difficult, especially when, as is the case here, the application is not opposed. The court is nervous about the fundamental matter of jurisdiction if it is asked to act without the benefit of adversarial argument that normally disciplines its decision-making processes.

One factor that is relevant to the decision is: what is the *real* purpose behind the application? Is it, at root, application to change powers of management or to change the beneficial interests? It may be that the scale of the changes to beneficial interests could be relevant. Although his decision was reversed, Mann J's judgment in *Southgate* v *Sutton* may be helpful. He said he was not satisfied that it fell within the court's powers under s 57(1). He regarded the effect of the proposed transaction on the beneficial interests in the trust property as rendering them 'conceptually different' rather than a change in how the interests are in fact enjoyed. He said that changes sought 'would create a different set of beneficial interests, qualitatively speaking, to those which currently exist'. A question of degree?

Settled Land Act 1925 s 64(1)

This provision applies to settled land and to land held on trust for sale and allows the court to agree to any transaction which, in the view of the court, benefits the land (or part of it) or which would benefit the beneficiaries under the settlement and which is a transaction that an absolute owner could carry out. This section confers a wide jurisdiction on the courts and can be used to make changes in beneficial interests as well as alterations to management powers.

In *Re Scarisbrick Resettlement Estates* [1944] 1 All ER 404, under s 64 the court allowed the trustees to raise money to enable the tenant for life to continue to live in the family home. It was considered that it was essential that he continued to live in the house in order to preserve it. The money was raised by the sale of capital investments.

In *Raikes* v *Lygon* [1988] 1 All ER 884, the court permitted trust property to be transferred to a second settlement in order to create a maintenance fund for a Tudor mansion. The aim was to ensure that the second fund qualified for exemption from inheritance tax. Peter Gibson J held that the terms of s 64(1) were wide enough to permit the creation of the second settlement.

Peter Gibson J identified the requirements that have to be met in order for the section to be applicable. There needs to be a 'transaction' that affects or concerns settled land which is not otherwise authorised by the Act or by the terms of the settlement. Additionally, the court must be satisfied that the proposal would be for the benefit of the land or the persons interested in it under the settlement. Lastly, the transaction must be one which could have been carried out by an absolute owner.

In *Hambro* v *Duke of Marlborough* [1994] 3 All ER 332, the beneficiaries under the settlement were the Duke of Marlborough and his son, the Marquis of Blandford, who was the tenant in tail of the remainder. The Marquis would be entitled to exercise the powers of a life tenant on the death of his father. The Duke was concerned that his son was not a suitable person to control large amounts of property, having been convicted of various criminal offences and having shown himself, in the eyes of the Duke, not to be a competent businessman. The proposal was disadvantageous to the Marquis, an ascertained beneficiary of full age and capacity, and he would not consent to it. It was sought to create a new settlement under which the Duke would be paid the income for life and then the income would be held on protective trusts for the Marquis and subject thereto both the capital and the income would be held on the trusts of the existing parliamentary settlement. The court held that the proposal was within the scope of s 64(1).

The court decided that the proposal to create a new settlement was a 'transaction' within s 64 and that the section permitted the court to vary the beneficial interest of an adult beneficiary of full capacity who did not consent so long as the variation was for the benefit of the settled land or of all the beneficiaries.

Matrimonial Causes Act 1973 s 24(1)(c), Civil Partnership Act 2004 and Marriage (Same Sex Couples) Act 2013

The Matrimonial Causes Act 1973 s 24(1)(c) is a very useful provision, enabling the court to make 'property adjustment' orders in matrimonial proceedings. Schedule 5 para 2 of the Civil Partnership Act 2004 contains provisions that mirror those of s 24(1)(c) of the Matrimonial Causes Act 1973, providing for property adjustment orders when a registered civil partnership is formally ended. The Marriage (Same Sex Couples) Act 2013 came into force on 13 March 2014. It applies to England and Wales. The Act allows two people of the same sex to get married. Under the Act marriage has the same effect in relation to same sex couples as it has in relation to opposite sex couples. Thus the courts have the same powers to make property adjustment orders on the divorce of same sex married couples as on the divorce of opposite sex married couples.

Under such orders, the court can override the rules of trusts which often lead to unsatisfactory results in the context of deciding on the beneficial ownership of property as between spouses. The court can make a wide range of orders, including the creation of a settlement and the variation of an ante-nuptial or a post-nuptial settlement in order to benefit a spouse or issue. Obviously, existing beneficial interests may be varied as a consequence of such an order.

In **Brooks v Brooks** [1995] 3 All ER 257, the House of Lords held that the words 'ante-nuptial or post-nuptial settlement' in s 24(1)(c) were to be given a wide meaning in the context of a section giving the court jurisdiction to vary a settlement. So, as long as the pension fund involved constituted a settlement made by the husband, the court had the jurisdiction to vary it. In the particular case, the pension scheme was a sole-member scheme which the husband had entered into to provide financial support for his wife and himself during retirement, with benefits payable to the wife in the event of the death of the husband. If his wife was still alive at the date of retirement, the scheme's rules allowed the husband to give a part of his pension to provide, from the date of his death, a deferred pension for his wife. This amounted to a settlement and thus could be varied on the dissolution of the marriage. It was the presence of these benefits and potential benefits to the wife that were crucial factors in determining that there was a marriage settlement. If a scheme only provides for benefits to the member of the scheme, it would not constitute a marriage settlement.

Lord Nicholls, with whom the other Law Lords concurred, said:

> This decision should not be seen as a solution to the overall pension problem. Not every pension scheme constitutes a marriage settlement. And even when a scheme does fall within the court's jurisdiction to vary a marriage settlement, it would not be right for the court to vary one scheme member's rights to the prejudice of other scheme members . . . A feature of the instant case is that there is only one scheme member . . . If the court is to be able to split pension rights on divorce in the more usual multi-member scheme . . . legislation will still be needed.

The Welfare Reform and Pensions Act 1999 includes a provision for pension sharing on divorce or annulment. This is available where a petition for divorce or nullity has been filed on or after 1 December 2000, but it is not available on judicial separation and is effective only after a court order.

So, for the first time, the value of a pension scheme member's rights can be transferred to their spouse.

The new s 21A, introduced into the Matrimonial Causes Act 1973, states:

> A pension-sharing order is an order which provides that one party's shareable rights under a specified arrangement, or shareable state scheme rights, be subject to pension sharing for the benefit of the other party.

The pension sharing is to be viewed as part of the total picture when it comes to dividing the assets on divorce. Note that pension sharing provisions do not apply to cohabitees or to same-sex partners, unless their partnership has been registered under the Civil Partnership Act 2004 (Civil Partnership Act 2004 Schedule 5 para 4).

Trustee Act 1925 s 53

This is, apparently, a little-used provision under which the court has the power to make an order with a view to applying the trust property for the maintenance, education or benefit of a beneficiary who is a minor. As a consequence of such an order, beneficial interests may be altered. In *Re Meux* [1957] 2 All ER 630, the court ordered the sale of a minor's reversionary entailed interest to the life tenant with the proceeds being transferred on trust for the minor. The effect of the order was not only to save estate duty but also to vary the interest of the minor and the life tenant.

In *Re Gower's Settlement* [1934] All ER Rep 796, the court allowed an infant's entailed interest to be mortgaged in order to raise money. In *Re Hayworth's Contingent Reversionary Interest* [1956] 2 All ER 21, the court refused to sanction the sale of the reversionary interest of a minor, the result of which would be to end the settlement. This was considered not to be for the benefit of the minor. In *Re Meux*, however, the court allowed the sale of trust assets but, unlike *Re Hayworth*, the proceeds were to be settled.

Variation of Trusts Act 1958

This is the most important statutory provision in the area of variation. It came into being because of the narrowness of the court's inherent power to sanction a compromise (see p. 178). This power had been 'developed' by the courts and used to enable approval to be given to rearrangements of beneficial interests under settlements when in reality there was no dispute at all. In such cases the courts gave their consent on behalf of minors or other beneficiaries not able to consent for themselves. In other words, the power was being used to enable the courts to sanction variations where no other route was open. In *Re Downshire Settled Estates* [1953] 1 All ER 103, for example, the Court of Appeal gave its consent to the beneficial interests being restructured in order to save tax. The Court of Appeal in general, and Lord Denning in particular, accepted that the 'compromise' jurisdiction was of wide application and was not restricted to situations where there was a genuine dispute.

However, the House of Lords in *Chapman v Chapman* [1954] 1 All ER 798 rejected this approach, deciding that the power was available only in cases of genuine disputes.

Lord Simonds said, after having discussed the inherent powers of conversion, maintenance and salvage:

> This brings me to the question which alone presents any difficulty in this case. It is whether this fourth category, which I may call the compromise category, should be extended to cover cases in which there is no real dispute as to rights and, therefore, no compromise, but it is sought by way of bargain between the beneficiaries to re-arrange the beneficial interests under the trust instrument and to bind infants and unborn persons by order of the court . . . It is not the function of the courts to alter a trust because alteration is thought to be advantageous to an infant beneficiary.

Lord Morton, who concurred with Lord Simonds, said that if the courts were able to agree to variations in such cases it would give rise to an 'undignified game of chess between the Chancery Division and the legislature'. If a settlement was varied to avoid tax, that variation might be followed by scores of similar applications. The legislature would then react by imposing tax on the altered settlements which would be closely followed by the beneficiaries going back to court to ask for approval for another variation to avoid the new tax.

This decision caused a great deal of frustration and created unfairness among beneficiaries. Particularly unfortunate was the difference created between a trust where the beneficiaries were able to use the rule in *Saunders v Vautier* to effect a rearrangement of their beneficial interests and a trust where *Saunders v Vautier* could not be used because, for example, some of the beneficiaries were under the age of 18. (*Saunders v Vautier* is discussed at p. 157.) Also, the decision threw up a difference between beneficiaries under a trust which came within the Settled Land Act 1925 s 64(1) and trusts which did not. Under s 64(1) the court could give approval for alterations in beneficial interests. It was therefore a matter of chance whether beneficial interests could or could not be varied.

The problem was referred to the Law Reform Committee in 1954 and a report was produced in 1957 (the Law Reform Committee Report, 'The Courts' Power to Sanction Variation of Trusts' (Cmnd 310, 1957)). As well as referring to the anomalous cases discussed above, the Committee felt that the decision in *Chapman v Chapman* had resulted in trusts that had been set up some time ago being rather harshly treated. The Committee felt that while modern trusts were often drafted with wide investment powers and with a good deal of inbuilt flexibility to cope with changing circumstances, this was not the case with trusts created more than 20 years previously. The effect of *Chapman v Chapman* was to condemn these established trusts to operate on the basis of the original, and perhaps now, inappropriate terms.

The Committee recommended radical changes in the law, which would in effect return to the position before *Chapman v Chapman* and reintroduce the flexibility that existed previously. The result was the Variation of Trusts Act 1958.

General operation of the Act

The general effect of the Act is to give to the court the power to approve of 'arrangements' varying or revoking all or any of the trusts, or enlarging the powers of the trustees of managing or administering any of the property subject to the trusts on behalf of specified categories of people. However, in most situations the court can give its approval only if the arrangement would be for the 'benefit' of those on whose behalf approval is being sought (see p. 187).

The important point to re-emphasise is that, under the Variation of Trusts Act 1958, beneficial interest may be varied and alterations may be made in the powers of management or administration. The Act extends to trusts of real or personal property, whether created *inter vivos* or by will.

In most cases the application will be made by the beneficiary currently entitled to the income of the trust fund. The trustees may apply if no one else will and if they are 'satisfied that the proposals are beneficial to the persons interested and have a good chance of being approved by the courts': *per* Russell J in **Re Druce's Settlement Trusts** [1962] 1 All ER 563. In most cases the settlor and all the beneficiaries should be parties to the application. The interests of unborn beneficiaries should be represented, and in the case of a class of beneficiaries all members at the date of the application should be joined. Minors who are beneficiaries should be represented by a guardian *ad litem*. If a beneficiary is a mental patient, the Court of Protection should be informed.

Width of the Act

The powers of the court are very wide, and approval may be given to an arrangement which results in beneficial interests being altered or which results in trustees' powers of management or administration being enlarged. In **Re Steed's Will Trusts** (later) Lord Evershed MR said that the word 'arrangement' was 'deliberately used in the widest possible senses so as to cover any proposal which any person may put forward for varying or revoking the trusts'.

The courts have approved of a wide range of variations, including approving arrangements giving wider powers of investment (see p. 488). The court may, for example, be asked to approve of a variation under which a tenant for life has the power to appoint the remainder and it is desired to put into effect a scheme whereby the tenant for life will give up his life interest and exercise the power of appointment. The object of such exercises may well be part of a plan to avoid or minimise inheritance tax on the death of the life tenant. If the proposed variation is regarded by the courts as involving a fraud on the power, the courts will not consent to it. (In **Re Robertson's Will Trust** [1960] 3 All ER 146 and **Re Brook's Settlement** [1968] 3 All ER 416, the court refused consent, but cf. **Re Wallace's Settlement** [1968] 2 All ER 209.)

On whose behalf may the courts approve of arrangements? (s 1(1))

Section 1 (1) of the Act sets out the persons on whose behalf the court can provide approval to a proposed arrangement to vary trusts.

The court may approve of arrangements on behalf of the following:

(a) any person having an interest, whether vested or contingent, who by reason of infancy or other incapacity is incapable of assenting; or

(b) any person (whether ascertained or not) who may become entitled, directly or indirectly, to an interest under the trusts as being at a future date or on the happening of a future event a person of any specified description or a member of any specified class of persons, so however this does not include any person who would be of that description, or a member of that class, as the case may be, if the said date had fallen or the said event had happened at the date of the application to the court; or

(c) any person unborn; or

(d) any person in respect of any discretionary interest under a protective trust where the interest of the principal beneficiary has not failed or determined.

The benefit requirement under s 1(1)

Unless an application is made on behalf of beneficiaries within category (d) above, the court cannot approve of an arrangement unless it would be for the benefit of the person on whose behalf approval is sought. The courts have taken a broad view of what constitutes a benefit, and, although in most cases it is financial benefit which is examined, it is by no means the only factor which the courts have taken into consideration. In *Re Holt's Settlement* [1968] 1 All ER 470, Megarry J said: 'The word benefit . . . is . . . plainly not confined to financial benefit, but may extend to social or moral benefit.'

In *Re Van Gruisen's Will Trusts* [1964] 1 All ER 843, Ungoed Thomas J said:

The court is not merely concerned with the actuarial calculation . . . the court is also concerned whether the arrangement as a whole, in all the circumstances is such that it is proper to approve it. The court's concern involves, *inter alia*, a practical and business-like consideration of the arrangement, including the total amount of the advantages which the various parties obtain and their bargaining strength.

There are cases where approval has been given even though the arrangement operated to the financial disadvantage of the person on whose behalf approval was given. In *Re Towler's Settlement Trusts* [1963] 3 All ER 759, a beneficiary would soon become entitled to a capital fund. Wilberforce J agreed to an application to postpone the vesting of the capital on the ground that there was evidence that the beneficiary was likely to deal with the fund in an irresponsible manner. In *Cowan v Scargill* [1984] 2 All ER 750, Sir Robert Megarry V-C said:

'Benefit' is a word with a very wide meaning, and there are circumstances in which arrangements which work to the financial disadvantage of a beneficiary may yet be to his benefit . . . But I would emphasise that such cases are likely to be very rare.

Sir Robert went on to say that there would be a heavy burden of proof on the person arguing that there would be a 'benefit' if the result of the proposal would be financially to disadvantage the beneficiary. However, while it is true that there are examples of the courts considering non-financial matters, in the vast majority of cases brought under the Act it is financial benefit which is argued.

However, in *Re Tinker's Settlement* [1960] 3 All ER 85n, the court refused to agree to an arrangement that was clearly to the financial detriment of those on whose behalf the agreement of the court was sought. A trust was set up under which property was held for the settlor's son and daughter. The trust stated that if the son died under the age of 30 his share would pass to the daughter for life with remainder to her children. In fact, the settlor had intended that if the son died under the age of 30 the property would pass to his (the son's) children. The court was asked to approve of an arrangement under which this intention would be carried through. The court was asked to consent on behalf of any unborn children of the daughter. This would have been to their financial disadvantage and the court refused to agree.

In many cases the financial advantage to the beneficiary is that the proposed arrangement will result in less tax being payable, either by the trust or by a beneficiary. The Law Reform Committee saw no reason why trusts should not be varied with a view to reducing the impact of taxation, thus accepting the principle of tax avoidance as constituting a benefit. However, in *Re Weston's Settlements* [1968] 3 All ER 338, the Court of Appeal refused to give approval to an arrangement on behalf of minor beneficiaries which was designed to avoid tax. The arrangement involved transferring the trust fund to trustees resident in Jersey. A vital part of the scheme was that the infant beneficiaries, who up to a few months before the application had been living in England, became resident in Jersey. Lord Denning MR said:

> [T]he court should not consider merely the financial benefit to the infants or unborn children, but also their educational and social benefit. There are many things in life more worthwhile than money. One of these things is to be brought up in this our England which is still 'the envy of less happier lands'. I do not believe it is for the benefit of children to be uprooted from England and transported to another country simply to avoid tax . . . The avoidance of tax may be lawful, but it is not yet a virtue. The Court of Chancery should not encourage or support it – it should not give its approval to it – if by doing so it would imperil the true welfare of the children.

The real basis of the decision is problematical. At first instance Stamp J refused to approve of the 'cheap exercise in tax avoidance'. He contrasted this with a 'legitimate avoidance of liability to taxation'. In the Court of Appeal Harman LJ argued that the lack of experience of the courts of Jersey in dealing with trusts and the lack of a Trustee Act were reasons why the transfer would not be beneficial. Harman LJ said that before he would be prepared to sanction the removal of the trusts there must be good reasons connected with the trusts themselves. Lord Denning's decision is, perhaps, a manifestation of his aversion to tax avoidance schemes. The case has been criticised on the basis that the moral and social welfare issues to which Lord Denning refers should be decided by the parents rather than the court.

It must not be thought that *Re Weston* is an authority for the proposition that the courts will never sanction arrangements involving exporting trusts in the interests of saving tax. There have been a number of cases decided both before and after *Re Weston* in which the courts have approved of arrangements under which trusts have been exported.

In *Re Seale's Marriage Settlement* [1961] 3 All ER 136, children were the beneficiaries under an English trust. The children had been brought up in Canada by their parents and were living in Canada when an application was made to seek consent to appoint new trustees in Canada to whom the trust property would be transferred to be held on similar trusts to those under the original settlement. The court agreed to the arrangement, which did not involve the children being uprooted simply for financial advantage.

Again, in the unreported case of *Re Chamberlain* (1976) 126 NLJ 1034, the court approved of the transfer of trust funds to Guernsey. The main beneficiaries were resident and domiciled in France, and other beneficiaries were resident and domiciled in Indonesia. Unlike *Re Weston*, the arrangement did not involve the beneficiaries being moved merely for the financial advantages which would follow.

In *Re Windeatt's Will Trusts* [1969] 2 All ER 324, all the beneficiaries under a trust had been living in Jersey for 19 years when the court agreed to an application to transfer the trust property to Jersey residents on trusts similar to those of the English settlement.

D (a child) v *O* [2004] 3 All ER 780 is a more recent case on 'benefit' where the Variation of Trusts Act 1958 was used to enable trustees to advance more than the 50 per cent limit then imposed on the statutory power of advancement under s 32 of the Trustee Act 1925 in order to pay the school fees of an infant beneficiary. It was decided that such a variation would be for the benefit of the infant and that, if necessary, the whole of the capital could be used to pay the school fees. In this case the variation would be to the financial benefit of the infant beneficiary in that other sources of money would not need to be sought and also there would be long-term benefits of receiving a 'good' education.

Ridgwell and Ors v *Ridgwell and Ors* [2007] EWHC 2666 (Ch) is a more recent case on both 'benefit' and the meaning of 'arrangement' under the Act. Under a settlement X was the tenant for life. After X's death and in default of an appointment by him either during his lifetime or in his will, the trust fund would be held for such of his children as were living at his death and who achieved the age of 30. There was a *per stirpes* provision if any of his children predeceased him themselves leaving children. Under the trust the trustees had the power during X's lifetime to pay or apply all or any part of the capital of the trust fund for the maintenance, education or benefit of one or more of X's children or remoter issue.

An application was made to vary the terms of a trust under Variation of Trusts Act 1958 s 1. The terms of the variation would mean that on the death of X a life interest would be created in favour of any surviving spouse. At the time of the application the children of X were all minors.

The court said that the addition of a life interest did not fundamentally alter the entire basis of the original trusts and that, therefore, the proposed variation was an arrangement within the terms of the Act.

The proposed variation would result in both advantages and disadvantages to X's issue. Any extended period would give the trustees a longer period in which to make advances to the children to effect inheritance tax savings and possibly capital gains tax savings. The disadvantage would be the postponement of their interest in remainder. The court held that the benefits outweighed the possible disadvantage to the issue and agreed to the variation.

Taking a risk as to whether a benefit will ensue

When the court is presented with a proposed arrangement, it may not be absolutely clear that it will operate to the (usually) financial advantage of those on whose behalf the approval of the court is sought. It may be that in some unforeseeable circumstances a disadvantage might result. This will not necessarily prevent the court from agreeing to the arrangement as the court is sometimes willing to take the risk. In *Re Holt's Settlement* [1968] 1 All ER 470, Megarry J was confronted by an arrangement which would be disadvantageous for certain unborn children. He was prepared to take the risk of such children being born and approved of the arrangement. In *Re Cohen's Will Trusts* [1959] 3 All ER 523, an arrangement was proposed which would benefit all the minor and unborn beneficiaries except in the (unlikely) event of the testator's wife, aged 80, dying after the testator's children. Danckwerts J approved of the scheme saying '[I]f it is a risk that an adult would be prepared to take, the court is prepared to take it on behalf of an infant'. Two points may be made. First, any risk may be covered by appropriate insurance. Secondly, it has been argued that the court should base its decision as to whether or not the risk should be taken on what risks a prudent and well-advised adult would take. However, the limit to the courts' willingness to approve is illustrated by *Re Cohen's Settlement Trusts* [1965] 3 All ER 139 where Stamp J made it clear that if there is one member of a class on whose behalf the court is asked to consent, who cannot possibly benefit, the court must refuse to consent.

See also *Ridgwell and Ors* v *Ridgwell and Ors* above.

Relevance of the settlor's intention

It is somewhat debatable to what extent the court is obliged to take the wishes of the settlor into account when deciding whether or not to give approval to an arrangement. Should the fact that the proposed arrangement would conflict with the intention of the settlor influence, deter or even prevent the court from approving?

Re Steed's Will Trusts [1960] 1 All ER 487

The Court of Appeal was asked to approve of an arrangement under which trust property would be held absolutely for a woman who, under the original trust, was the principal beneficiary under a protective trust. The evidence was that the protective trust had been set up because the settlor was worried that the woman would fall victim to her 'sponging' brother. If the proposed arrangement took effect the interests of the woman would no longer be protected and she would be in a position to yield to the temptation to use her interest under the trust to satisfy the demands of her brother. The settlor clearly set up the original trust to avoid putting the woman into that position. Although the proposed arrangement could be said to be for the financial benefit of the woman in that she would become absolutely entitled under the trust, the court refused to give approval basing its decision, at least in part, on the wishes of the settlor.

Re Remnant's Settlement Trusts [1970] 2 All ER 554

In contrast to **Re Steed's WT**, Pennycuick J approved of an arrangement which clearly resulted in the wishes of the settlor being overridden. A trust was set up giving interests to the children of two sisters, but the interests were subject to forfeiture if any of the children practised Roman Catholicism or married a Roman Catholic. In the event of a forfeiture there was an accrual provision in favour of the other children. The children of one of the sisters were Roman Catholic while the children of the other sister were Protestant. Approval was sought to delete the forfeiture clause. This proposal would clearly be detrimental to the Protestant children but was argued for on the basis of three grounds: first, it was said that the clause prevented the children from exercising a free choice as to what religion they should practise; secondly, that it acted as a deterrent in the choice of husbands; thirdly, that it was a source of possible family dissension. Pennycuick J considered that the first point had very little weight but agreed to the arrangement, being satisfied that the second and third points meant that it would be beneficial if the clause was removed. This, of course, defeated the intentions of the settlor.

In **Goulding v James** [1996] 4 All ER 865, Mrs Froud made a will giving her residuary estate in trust for her daughter, June, for life remainder to June's son Marcus, provided he attained the age of 40 years. If Marcus did not attain that age or if he died before June (whether or not he had attained the age of 40), the children of Marcus living at his death were to take the capital absolutely. If June died before Marcus and Marcus was under the age of 40, the trustees of the will were to have the power to release the capital of the residuary estate to Marcus. This would defeat the interests of the children of Marcus.

Mrs Froud died and June and Marcus applied to the court for approval to an arrangement to vary the trusts. Under the arrangement the estate would devolve as if her will had provided for 45 per cent of the residuary estate to be held for June absolutely, 45 per cent for Marcus absolutely and the remaining 10 per cent for the children of Marcus absolutely. At the time of the application Marcus did not have any children. However, actuarial evidence showed that the proposed arrangement was financially advantageous to the unborn grandchildren. Under the original provisions the value of their contingent interests was only 1.85 per cent of the residuary estate; under the arrangement it was a 10 per cent share.

Laddie J refused to approve of the arrangement which as far as the adult beneficiaries were concerned was 'the complete opposite of what was provided under the will and the settled intention of Mrs Froud'. There was evidence that the testatrix did not want June to be able to touch the capital and that she wanted to postpone the interest of Marcus until he was 40 as she considered that he had not settled down and was a 'free spirit'. Laddie J went on to say (considering himself bound by *Re Steed*) that as he had a discretion to exercise he considered this to be a case where it would not be appropriate to give approval to the arrangement to exercise it.

However, on appeal ([1997] 2 All ER 239) the Court of Appeal (Civil Division) decided that Laddie J had taken a too restrictive approach to interpreting the Act and approved of the arrangement. Laddie J had followed what he understood to be the *ratio* of *Re Steed's Will Trusts* and treated the intention of the settlor towards the *sui juris* beneficiaries as relevant to the decision as to whether or not the court should supply consent on behalf of the unborn grandchildren. The Court of Appeal said that the court was not to be regarded as standing in for the settlor but as supplying consent for those unable to supply it themselves.

The Court of Appeal considered that the jurisdiction under the Act was an extension to the consent principle and was based on *Saunders* v *Vautier*. (See p. 157.)

The wishes of the testatrix, to the extent that they related to these *sui juris* beneficiaries, were irrelevant or at least carried little weight, when making the decision as to whether or not to supply consent on behalf of the unborn grandchildren. There was no relevant intention with regard to the grandchildren.

The judge at first instance had been wrong to allow the evidence of the settlor's intention towards the two *sui juris* beneficiaries to outweigh the financial advantages to the unborn grandchildren.

Problem areas

Categories (a), (c) and (d) seem relatively straightforward but the meaning of 'any person having an interest' under section 1(a) has not been absolutely clear. Some assistance has been supplied by *Bernstein* v *Jacobson* [2008] EWHC 3454 (Ch) in which Blackburne J made a number of significant points. He interpreted the phrase 'having an interest' quite widely. He decided that this could be applicable where the administration of an estate had not been completed despite the fact that beneficiaries have no equitable right in any particular piece of property and all they have is the right to compel the proper administration of the estate. Blackburne J decided that the beneficiaries had 'interest' as required under s 1(1)(a) not confining 'interest' to an equitable interest under a 'normal' trust, and that 'trust' in s 1(1) included the type of 'trust' outlined in *Commissioner of Stamp Duties (Queensland)* v *Livingston* [1965] AC 694.

Category (b) merits further examination. Two particular problems are apparent. First, the provision permits the court to supply approval to an arrangement on behalf of 'any person . . . who may become entitled . . . to an interest under the trusts'. It is therefore explicit that the court cannot give approval on behalf of anyone who does possess an interest. Even the possession of a contingent interest which is extremely unlikely to become vested will be enough to remove the court's powers to approve.

In *Knocker* v *Youle* [1969] 2 All ER 914, approval was sought to an arrangement on behalf of a large number of individuals whose interests under the trust were subject to a contingency (and in some cases a double contingency). Additionally, the interests were determinable by the exercise of a testamentary power of appointment. In fact, wills had already been executed which exercised this power to determine the interests. In the case, income from part of a trust fund was held on trust for the daughter of the settlor for life, the remainder going to those she appointed in her will. In the event of an appointment not being made there was a gift over to the son of the settlor, and if he was dead to the four married sisters of the settlor, and if they were dead to their issue who attained the age of 21 and who were living at the death of the son. (The settlor's sisters were all dead.) It was impracticable to obtain the consent of all these people. The court held that approval could not be given under category (b) as the individuals did in fact possess interests under the trust, albeit that the interests were contingent. It was irrelevant that there was only the remotest possibility that the interests would ever vest. The clear words of the section prevented approval being given: the provision expressly covered only those who *may* become entitled to an interest and thus excluded those who did have an interest of any kind.

The court contrasted the position of beneficiaries who had an interest, albeit remote, with individuals who had a mere *spes successionis*. Examples of individuals possessing a *spes successionis* would include the prospective next of kin of a living person (***Re Moncrieff's Settlement Trusts*** [1962] 3 All ER 838). However, they may be outside the jurisdiction if they fall within the 'proviso' discussed below. Such persons would fall within the description of those who may become entitled and so the court could supply approval on their behalf. Another example falling within the class of those who may become entitled to an interest is where the settlor names the spouse of an unmarried individual as a beneficiary. As there is no way of knowing who the future wife will be, there clearly can be no question of asking for their consent. The court could supply approval on behalf of that future wife, whoever she may be. It would have been possible to apply for an order under ***Re Benjamin*** [1902] 1 Ch 723 in order to distribute the property (see p. 475).

The second problem revolves round what is often called the proviso to category (b). The section empowers the court to supply approval on behalf of any person who may become entitled to an interest on the basis of being, at a future date or on the happening of a specified event, a person who is within a specified description or a member of a specified class. The section continues with this proviso:

> [S]o however this paragraph shall not include any person who would be of that description, or a member of that class, as the case may be, if the said date had fallen or the said event had happened at the date of the application to the court.

This rather complicated provision limits the power of the court. It obliges the court to examine the situation at the date of the application. The date of the application has been construed as meaning the date when the originating summons is issued rather than the date of the hearing (Warner J in ***Knocker* v *Youle*** [1969] 2 All ER 914). The court must ask itself this question: are potential beneficiaries to be identified on the basis that they fall within a specific description or class and is that identification to take place at a future date or when a future event occurs? If the answer is yes, the court must then ask itself who would be identified as the beneficiaries if the relevant date was the date of the application or if the relevant event took place at the date of the application. The effect of the proviso is that the court cannot supply consent on behalf of such people.

For example, in ***Re Suffert's Settlement*** [1960] 3 All ER 561, the court was asked to supply approval to an arrangement on behalf of two cousins of Miss Suffert. She was the principal beneficiary under a protective trust. After her death the property was to be held on trust for such of her issue as she should appoint, and in the event of default the property was to be held for those who would be her statutory next of kin. At the date of the application her nearest relatives were three adult cousins. A variation was sought and the court was asked to supply approval on behalf of two adult cousins; the other cousin was a party to the proceedings and consented to the arrangement. The court was unable to give consent to a proposed arrangement on behalf of the two adult cousins as they would have been entitled to the property of the life tenant had the life tenant died intestate at the date of the application. In other words, the two cousins were within the proviso and the court could not provide consent on their behalf.

Some further illustrations will make the operation of this provision clearer. In *Knocker v Youle* (see p. 191), the court found an additional reason for refusing consent. The court identified 17 cousins who, if the trust failed or determined at the date of the application, would have been members of the specified class of beneficiaries in that they were both living and over the age of 21. The 17 cousins fell within the proviso and so the court was unable to provide agreement to the arrangement on their behalf.

In *Re Moncrieff's Settlement Trusts* [1962] 3 All ER 838, the court was unable to supply consent on behalf of an adopted son who would have been entitled had the life tenant died at the date of the application. He was covered by the proviso. However, the court was able to supply consent on behalf of the other next of kin as they would only be entitled in the event of the death of the life tenant and the prior death of the adopted son. In other words, their entitlement was subject to a double contingency. If the life tenant died but the adopted son was still alive they would not be entitled. This illustrates why it is often said that in order for the court to be able to supply consent there has to be a double contingency.

The overall purpose of the Act is to enable the court to supply agreement on behalf of beneficiaries who are not able themselves to agree and so, except in relation to (d), approval cannot be supplied by the court for beneficiaries who are identified and *sui juris*.

What is the basis of the variation?

There is a good deal of discussion as to the exact process that takes place which results in the trust being varied. The key is the precise nature and role of the court's approval. Does the court order itself actually effect the variation or is the variation the result of an agreement between beneficiaries, with the court merely supplying consent on behalf of some of the beneficiaries? This is not just an academic point. It has a very practical aspect to it. If the variation is essentially the result of an agreement, then the provisions of the Law of Property Act 1925 s 53(1)(c) become relevant (see p. 115). This provision requires any disposition of an equitable interest to be in writing: otherwise it is void. It is clear that a variation will often involve the disposition of beneficial interests from the original owners to the new owners under the terms of the variation. So any variation ought to be in writing if it is to be effective.

See Chapter 4 (p. 115) for more on the Law of Property Act 1925 s 53(1)(c).

Additionally, an important stamp duty issue used to arise. If the variation was achieved by a written agreement then, until 1985, *ad valorem* stamp duty was payable, whereas if it was the court order which effected the variation no duty was payable.

Wynn Parry J in *Re Hambleden's Will Trusts* [1960] 1 All ER 353 was of the view that the order of the court itself varied the trust. He said: 'I hold that the effect of my approval is effective for all purposes to vary the trusts.' However, in *IRC v Holmden* [1968] 1 All ER 148, Lord Reid said:

> Under the Variation of Trusts Act 1958 the court does not itself amend or vary the trusts of the original settlement. The beneficiaries are not bound because a court has made the variation. Each beneficiary is bound because he has consented to the variation. If he was not of full age when the arrangement was made he is bound because the court was authorised by the Act to approve it on his behalf and did so by making an order . . . The arrangement must be regarded as an arrangement made by the beneficiaries themselves. The court merely acted

on behalf of or as representing those beneficiaries who were not in a position to give their own consent and approval.

This would appear to settle the issue. However, the problems involving the Law of Property Act 1925 s 53(1)(c) referred to above were not considered, thus leaving the problem unsolved.

This problem confronted Megarry J in **Re Holt's Settlement** [1968] 1 All ER 470. Megarry J was aware that many variations had been agreed in the past which had not been made in writing. If he decided that the court supplied consent to an agreement to vary and that this agreement must be in writing to satisfy s 53(1)(c), it would bring into doubt the status of these variations, which had been assumed to be valid and had been acted upon. Megarry J was also aware of **Re Hambleden's Will Trust** [1960] 1 All ER 353, in which Wynn-Parry J stated that his view was that it was the order of the court *ipso facto* which varied the trust.

Megarry J rather reluctantly decided that there was no requirement for writing. He based his decision on two arguments which were put to him.

First, he said the agreement could be regarded as giving rise to a constructive trust under which the original beneficiaries held their beneficial interests on trust for those entitled under the agreement. Beneficial interests would pass under the constructive trust as soon as the agreement was reached. Section 53(2) exempts constructive trusts from the requirement for writing. This explanation is applicable to agreements which are specifically enforceable, because only then would a constructive trust arise. Also, the explanation is rather difficult to justify in the light of **Oughtred v IRC** [1959] 3 All ER 623 (see p. 119).

Megarry J's second ground was that when the Variation of Trusts Act 1958 gave the courts the power to grant their consent, by necessity, an implied exception to s 53(1)(c) was created.

As stated above, Megarry J was rather reluctant to accept the arguments put to him but he did so, saying:

> But I find it tempting; and I yield to it. It is not a construction which I think the most natural. But it is not an impossible construction; it accords with the long title; it accords with the practice which has been relied on for many years in some thousands of cases; and it accords with the consideration of convenience.

Resettlement or variation?

The Variation of Trusts Act 1958 gives the court the power to approve of an arrangement 'varying or revoking all or any of the trusts'. The court is not given the power to participate in a resettlement. It is often very difficult to draw the line where variation ends and resettlement begins.

This was the issue confronting Megarry J in **Re Ball's Settlement** [1968] 2 All ER 438. He said:

> If an arrangement changes the whole substratum of the trust, then it may well be that it cannot be regarded merely as varying that trust. But if an arrangement, while leaving the substratum, effectuates the purpose of the original trust by other means, it may still be possible to regard that arrangement as merely varying the original trusts, even though the means employed are wholly different and even though the form is completely changed.

In **Re Ball**, Megarry J was asked to approve of an arrangement varying a settlement under which a life interest was given to the settlor with remainder to his sons and grandchildren, subject to a power of an appointment. In default of any appointment, the fund was to be divided between the two sons of the settlor, or if either or both of the sons died before their father the share they would have received would be divided among their issue (i.e. the issue of the deceased son) *per stirpes*. The proposed scheme involved the fund being split into two equal portions, each being held on trust for one of the sons for life and then for each of the sons' children equally who were born before 1 October 1977.

Megarry J approved the arrangement, saying:

> In this case, it seems to me that the substratum of the original trust remains. True, the settlor's life interest disappears; but the remaining trusts are still in essence trusts of half the fund for each of the two named sons and their families . . . The differences between the old and new provisions lie in detail rather than substance.

So Megarry J suggests that one should identify the general aims and objectives of the original trust, and if these will continue to be achieved after the proposed alterations then the court may well decide that there is a variation rather than a resettlement. This may still be the court's decision even though the mechanisms employed to achieve the aims and objectives of the original trust have been totally changed.

However, in *Re Towler's Settlement Trusts* [1963] 3 All ER 759, Wilberforce J refused to sanction an arrangement. Under the trust a minor would become entitled to a quarter of the trust property when she attained her majority. The court was asked to approve of an arrangement under which her share of the trust fund was to be transferred to new trustees who would hold on a protective trust for the child with remainder to her issue. The arrangement was proposed because the child was considered to be immature and irresponsible. Wilberforce J, having said that it was difficult to define with precision where jurisdiction under the Act stops and having stated that he had no wish to cut down a useful jurisdiction, said:

> But I am satisfied that the proposal as originally made to me falls outside it. Though presented as a 'variation' it is in truth a complete new resettlement. The former trust funds were to be got in from the former trustees and held upon wholly new trusts . . . I do not think that the court can approve this.

In *Allen v Distillers Co (Biochemicals) Ltd* [1974] 2 All ER 365, Eveleigh J refused to sanction a proposed variation on the basis that it would in fact be a new trust. He said:

> In any event, I do not think the so-called variation would be a variation at all. It would be a new trust made on behalf of an absolute owner.
>
> If the court were to attempt to participate in the device suggested it would be making use of the Variation of Trusts Act 1958 to give it a jurisdiction not previously possessed and for a purpose not contemplated by the Act.

See also *Ridgwell and others* v *Ridgwell and others* (see p. 189) where the court said that the addition of a life interest did not fundamentally alter the entire basis of the original trusts and that, therefore, the proposed variation was an arrangement within the terms of the Act.

In *Roome* v *Edwards* [1982] AC 279 Lord Wilberforce gave some very helpful guidance on where the boundry lies between variation and resettlement.

> There are a number of obvious indicia which may help to show whether a settlement, or a settlement separate from another settlement, exists. One might expect to find separate and defined property; separate trusts; and separate trustees. One might also expect to find a separate disposition bringing the separate settlement into existence. These indicia may be helpful, but they are not decisive. For example, a single disposition, e.g., a will with a single set of trustees, may create what are clearly separate settlements, relating to different properties, in favour of different beneficiaries, and conversely separate trusts may arise in what is clearly a single

settlement, e.g. when the settled property is divided into shares. There are so many possible combinations of fact that even where these indicia or some of them are present, the answer may be doubtful, and may depend upon an appreciation of them as a whole.

Since 'settlement' and 'trusts' are legal terms, which are also used by business men or laymen in a business or practical sense, I think that the question whether a particular set of facts amounts to a settlement should be approached by asking what a person, with knowledge of the legal context of the word under established doctrine and applying this knowledge in a practical and common-sense manner to the facts under examination, would conclude. To take two fairly typical cases. Many settlements contain powers to appoint a part or a proportion of the trust property to beneficiaries: some may also confer power to appoint separate trustees of the property so appointed, or such power may be conferred by law: see Trustee Act 1925, section 37. It is established doctrine that the trusts declared by a document exercising a special power of appointment are to be read into the original settlement: see *Muir (or Williams) v Muir* [1943] AC 468. If such a power is exercised, whether or not separate trustees are appointed, I do not think that it would be natural for such a person as I have presupposed to say that a separate settlement had been created: still less so if it were found that provisions of the original settlement continued to apply to the appointed fund, or that the appointed fund were liable, in certain events, to fall back into the rest of the settled property. On the other hand, there may be a power to appoint and appropriate a part or portion of the trust property to beneficiaries and to settle it for their benefit. If such a power is exercised, the natural conclusion might be that a separate settlement was created, all the more so if a complete new set of trusts were declared as to the appropriated property, and if it could be said that the trusts of the original settlement ceased to apply to it. There can be many variations on these cases each of which will have to be judged on its facts.

This guidance was used by Blackburne J in *Egremont v Wyndham* [2009] EWHC 2076 (Ch) to decide that the proposed change to a trust was a variation and not a resettlement. Trusts involving two baronies were contained in several documents ending with a document dated 18 July 2008. The only living beneficiary was George who had a life interest but who would become absolutely entitled if he was alive on the vesting day. It was likely that he would be alive at this date. If George became absolutely entitled, not only would any future issue not benefit but also a large capital gains tax charge would be triggered.

The court was asked to approve of an arrangement under which the vesting date would be postponed which would benefit any unborn potential beneficiaries (on whose behalf the court was asked to supply agreement) but would clearly disadvantage George. One issue was whether the courts had the power to approve of the arrangement as a variation or whether it was a resettlement.

With that guidance in mind I have no doubt that the alterations to the pre-arrangement trusts contained in the arrangement which I have approved constitute a variation of those trusts and not a resettlement. The trustees remain the same, the subsisting trusts remain largely unaltered and the administrative provisions affecting them are wholly unchanged. The only significant changes are (1) to the trusts in the remainder, although the ultimate trust in favour of George and his personal representatives remains the same, and (2) the introduction of the new and extended perpetuity period . . . The concern here is whether, on the ground that they give rise to a resettlement, the variations to the trust, principally the extension of the trust period, might be said to give rise to a 'deemed disposal' under section 71(1) of the Taxation of Chargeable Gains Act 1992 or might lead to adverse consequences for inheritance tax or stamp duty land tax purposes. I propose to take this very shortly because, in my view, the approach of Lord Wilberforce in *Roome v Edwards* (cited earlier) is in point. I do not consider, for the reasons already summarised, that the arrangement does give rise to a resettlement . . .

Cy-près

See Chapter 10 for a detailed discussion of cy-près.

This is fully discussed in the section on charitable trusts (Chapter 10).

Summary

- As part of its general jurisdiction to provide relief against the consequences of mistake, equity can rectify a trust instrument if it fails to express the true intention of the parties. Relief can be granted if the mistake relates to the 'meaning' or 'effect' of a document but not if the mistake relates to its 'consequences'. Under s 20(1) of the Administration of Justice Act 1982, the court has the power to rectify a will if it is satisfied that it fails to carry out the intentions of the testator as the result of a clerical error or a failure to understand his instructions.

- In many cases trusts operate over a period of many years and circumstances and the law may well change. What may have been appropriate at the time the trust was set up may, over a period of time, become inappropriate (and sometimes expensive if tax laws change). Proposals to vary trusts may reveal tensions between the original intention of the settlor and the current interests of the beneficiaries. The courts, in some situations, tend to favour the interests of the beneficiaries.

- The courts have an inherent jurisdiction to make, or agree to, certain variations of trusts but this is only possible in a limited set of circumstances.

- The inherent powers of the courts to vary trusts have been largely overtaken by the (usually) wider statutory provisions, the chief of which are s 57 of the Trustee Act 1925 and the Variation of Trusts Act 1958.

Further reading

General

M Hayes, 'Breaking and varying trusts painlessly' (1998) 4 MLR 17.
Discusses the termination or variation of terms of trusts both with and without court assistance, statutory powers involved and tax implications.

Section 57 Trustee Act 1925

S Panesar, 'The extent of expediency' TEL & TJ (2014) 153, January/February, 5–7.
Discusses *Re English & American Insurance Co Ltd* (2013) EWHC 3360 (Ch) as to whether or not the court has power under the Trustee Act 1925 s 57 to apportion a trust fund between beneficiaries with an immediate interest and potential beneficiaries whose interests might come into existence in the future. The objective was to allow the trustee to make an early distribution to the current beneficiaries.

Section 53 Trustee Act 1925

O R Marshall, 'The scope of section 53 of the Trustee Act 1925' [1957] Conv 448.
Discusses *Re Meux* and *Re Gower's Settlement* and proposes a tentative analysis of the application of s 53.

Variation of Trusts Act 1958

R B M Cotterrell, 'The requirement of "benefit" under the Variation of Trusts Act' (1971) 34 MLR 96.
Survey of the requirement for 'benefit' before the courts can (in most cases) approve a proposed arrangement, with a particular focus on *Re Remnant*.

D M E Evans, 'Variation of trusts in practice' [1963] Conv 6.
Offers a wide-ranging discussion of the use of the Variation of Trusts Act 1958 and the form and effect of a court order.

S Evans, 'Variation clarification' [2011] 151–6.
Discusses *Bernstein* v *Jacobson* on whether a will could be varied under the Variation of Trusts Act 1958 to make better use of the spouse exemption for inheritance tax. Also a more general discussion of the Act.

P Luxton, 'An unascertainable problem in variation of trusts' (1986) 136 (6279) NLJ 1057.
Focuses on *Knocker* v *Youle* and the issues arising under s 1(1)(b) and the proviso to s 1(1)(b).

P Luxton, Variation of trusts: settlors' intentions and the consent principle in *Saunders* v *Vautier*' (1997) 60 MLR 719.
The article focuses on *Goulding* v *James*. The author argues that if a variation of trust under the Variation of Trusts Act 1958 is similar to an application of the rule in *Saunders* v *Vautier*, in that the court is providing consent for the beneficiary, the court should only consider questions of relevance to that beneficiary.

W Massey, 'Extending trust periods' (2010) 1013 Tax J 12.
Discusses the use of the Variation of Trusts Act 1958 to extend the trust period and the possible tax benefits.

J G Riddall, 'Does it or doesn't it? Contingent interests and the Variation of Trusts Act 1958' [1987] Conv 144.
A case note on *Knocker* v *Youle* and the issues arising under s 1(1)(b) and the proviso to s 1(1)(b).

9

Purpose trusts

Objectives

After reading this chapter you should:

1. Understand the meaning of the term 'purpose trust' and the difference between private and charitable trusts.

2. Be aware of the objections to purpose trusts and the principles behind those objections.

3. Be aware of the rule against perpetual trusts as it applies to purpose trusts.

4. Understand that these objections can be evaded and that trusts expressed to be for purposes may in some cases be recognised as ordinary private trusts for the benefit of persons.

5. Be aware of the exceptional cases where purpose trusts are recognised.

6. Be familiar with the concept of the unincorporated association, its legal structure and the different ways in which it may receive gifts and hold property.

7. Understand the different principles upon which assets may be held on the winding up of an unincorporated association.

The meaning of 'purpose trust'

Objective
1

Purpose trusts are trusts expressed to be for the fulfilment of purposes, rather than for the benefit of persons. So, for example, in *Re Astor* [1952] 1 All ER 1067, money was to be held on trust for 'the maintenance of good relations between nations [and] the preservation of the independence of newspapers'.

There are a number of grounds for objection to trusts expressed in this form, but first it is necessary to draw a distinction between private and charitable trusts. Charitable trusts are expressed to be for purposes, such as the relief of poverty. Indeed, they cannot be expressed to be for particular individuals or they would lack the element of public benefit essential to a valid charity. Provided that the expressed purpose is exclusively charitable, however, none of the difficulties arising with other purpose trusts will apply. Charitable trusts will be considered separately.

See Chapter 10 on charitable trusts.

In other cases, the principle set out in *Leahy v A-G for New South Wales* [1959] 2 All ER 300 by Lord Simonds applies:

A gift can be made to persons (including a corporation) but it cannot be made to a purpose or to an object: so, also a trust may be created for the benefit of persons as *cestui que* trust but not for a purpose or object unless the purpose or object be charitable. For a purpose or object cannot sue, but, if it be charitable, the Attorney General can sue to enforce it.

Objections to purpose trusts

Objective 2

There are four objections to non-charitable purpose trusts: certainty; the requirement of ascertainable beneficiaries (the 'beneficiary principle'); limitation to the perpetuity period; and public policy. It is frequently the case that several of these objections may arise on the same facts, although the courts may choose to rely on one or other of them separately.

Certainty

Just as it is necessary for the beneficiaries of a private trust to be 'certain', that is identifiable, or ascertained or ascertainable, so it is necessary for a trust for purposes to identify those purposes clearly. Therefore, vague and general purposes such as those referred to in *Re Astor* will be insufficiently certain. In the words of Roxburgh J in that case:

> If an enumeration of purposes outside the realm of charities can take the place of an enumeration of beneficiaries, the purpose must . . . be stated in phrases which embody definite concepts and the means by which the trustees are to try to attain them must also be prescribed with a sufficient degree of certainty.

Thus, trusts referring to 'constructive policies', 'benevolent schemes' and the like will fail at this first hurdle.

It should not be thought that a sufficiently precise purpose will succeed, for most will fail on other grounds. The certainty principle has, however, been important in denying validity to purposes which, though vague, seem to be analogous to the small group of valid purpose trusts. For example, in *Re Endacott* [1959] 3 All ER 562, the term 'some useful memorial to myself' was held to fail as too vague, even though it was argued to be similar to the anomalous category of trusts for tombs and monuments, which are valid.

The beneficiary principle

A much more general difficulty with purpose trusts is the requirement that a trust must have ascertained or ascertainable beneficiaries. This is in general because a trust is unenforceable unless there is a human beneficiary who can enforce his or her rights under the trust. Many purpose trusts may indirectly benefit individuals but unless these beneficiaries can be ascertained the trust will fail for lack of beneficiaries. *Re Denley*, which will be considered shortly, represents a significant exception to this principle and serves, perhaps, to emphasise the reason for the rule, which is, as pointed out in *Leahy*, that there must be beneficiaries to enforce, or on whose behalf the court can enforce. In the words of Sir William Grant MR in *Morice v The Bishop of Durham* (1804) 9 Ves Jr 399: 'Every trust (other than a charitable one) must have a definite object. There must be somebody, in whose favour the court can decree performance.'

It is clearly inconsistent with the obligatory nature of the trust that there should be no beneficiary to enforce it. And yet there are such trusts. Such trusts will be considered in more detail below. It is clear, however, that they are to be regarded as anomalous. Attempts to use them in support of a general proposition that purpose trusts might be valid were firmly rejected in *Re Astor*. They were there described as 'concessions to human weakness or sentiment' and elsewhere as 'occasions where Homer has nodded'. They now represent a limited and closed category and are strictly regarded as exceptions to the general principle already described, namely that a valid trust must have beneficiaries to enforce it.

Perpetuity: the problem of perpetual trusts

Objective 3

For more on perpetuities, see Chapter 7 (pp. 161–7).

A further objection to purpose trusts, and one which applies even to the anomalous cases, is that they offend the perpetuity rules. This issue is considered in more detail in a separate chapter, but applies in particular ways to purpose trusts.

There are two perpetuity rules. One, which is of general application to trusts, is that no trust must be drafted so that any interest under it can possibly vest outside the perpetuity period. At common law this period was a life or lives in being plus 21 years, a 'life in being' being a life by reference to which the trust or interest was created. However, under the Perpetuities and Accumulations Act 2009, which applies to instruments taking effect after 6 April 2010, this period is replaced with a statutory period of 125 years. So trusts cannot be drafted so as to provide successive interests for future generations for ever, because at some point in the future an interest will take effect (under the common law) more than 21 years after the death of any beneficiary alive now or, under the 2009 Act, more than 125 years after the trust came into effect. This aspect of the rule will apply to purpose trusts but it is unlikely to cause problems because the gift for the purpose will normally be made to take effect immediately.

The second aspect of the rule is what is normally referred to as the rule against perpetual trusts. As its name implies, this rule forbids an interest to last longer than the perpetuity period. No interest expressed to be for a human beneficiary can breach this rule since the individual interest can last only as long as the individual, which obviously cannot be longer than a life in being. An interest under a trust expressed to be for a purpose, on the other hand, clearly can exceed this period unless the trust specifically limits it to the perpetuity period. Thus, even where it is valid to set aside money for the maintenance of a tomb, this can only be for 'as long as the law allows', i.e. for the perpetuity period of 21 years. Therefore, a trust for a purpose must expressly state that the purpose is only to be carried out for the perpetuity period, or for some lesser period. The Perpetuities and Accumulations Act 2009 specifically states (in s 18) that it does not affect the limitation period for non-charitable purpose trusts which therefore remains a life in being plus 21 years or, where no life in being is referred to, 21 years.

Public policy

Considered in Chapter 7 in greater detail under the heading 'Capricious trusts' (p. 168).

A fourth ground upon which a purpose trust may be held to be invalid is that of public policy. The courts may conclude that the purpose is one which it regards as an inappropriate use of money. This argument has been used mostly in cases where the purpose is eccentric or capricious and the court regards it as useless. Thus, in **Brown v Burdett** (1882) 21 Ch D 667, the court concluded that the testatrix's instructions to seal up a house for 20 years would serve no useful purpose and so was void. Similarly, in **M'Caig's Trustees v The Kirk Session of the United Free Church of Lismore** (1915) 52 SLR 347, large sums were allocated to the building of monuments to family members. Lord Salvesen concluded that such expenditure would be 'a sheer waste of money' and so was void on grounds of public policy.

Evasion of the rules: cases where 'purpose trusts' may have private beneficiaries

Objective 4

It seems, however, that these principles can be avoided by the use of a number of alternative devices.

Re Denley [1968] 3 All ER 65 may be regarded as an evasion of the rule, but may perhaps be treated instead as an instance of construction. In this case land was given for the purpose of providing a sports ground 'primarily for the benefit of the employees of [a certain] company and secondarily for the benefit of such other persons as the trustees shall allow to use the same'. The terms of the gift therefore, though expressed to be for a purpose, nonetheless identified a class of beneficiaries with sufficient certainty as to give them *locus standi* to enforce the trust. These were the employees: the use of the facilities by others was regarded as an instance of a power granted to trustees, which did not require the same certainty. This was held by Goff J to validate the trust as a trust for persons and the beneficiary principle was fulfilled. He distinguished the instant facts from those of trusts for more general purposes:

> There may be a purpose or object trust, the carrying out of which would benefit an individual or individuals, where that benefit is so indirect or intangible or which is otherwise framed as not to give those persons any *locus standi* to apply to the court to enforce the trust, in which case the beneficiary principle would apply to invalidate the trust . . . The present is not, in my judgment, of that character . . . Where, then, the trust, though expressed as a purpose, is directly or indirectly for the benefit of an individual or individuals, it seems to me that it is in general outside the mischief of the beneficiary principle.

According to **Re Denley**, therefore, one device for avoiding the problems associated with purpose trusts is to draft a trust for the benefit of persons but to confine that benefit to the fulfilment of certain purposes. This is not without its problems. If the purpose is fulfilled and money remains (which could not have arisen in **Re Denley**), the issue of the ownership of that money must be addressed. This will be considered in the context of resulting trusts. Second, the beneficiaries in **Re Denley** could have been regarded as uncertain: the employees could change, and might have offended the perpetuity rule if the gift had not been specifically limited to the perpetuity period. Despite such questions, however, **Re Denley** clearly provides a solution, at least where the purpose is a specific one.

See Chapter 5 (p. 143).

The limits on the use of **Re Denley** to avoid the problem of lack of beneficiaries may have been indicated by the case of **R v District Auditor, ex p West Yorkshire Metropolitan County Council**.

This case, it will be recalled, concerned a discretionary trust for a very large group of objects, the inhabitants of West Yorkshire. The trust failed on the ground that the class was administratively unworkable. It would appear that this was a discretionary trust for persons not purposes, and failed under the certainty rules for that kind of trust. However, in his judgment Lloyd LJ referred to it as a non-charitable purpose trust, which is void:

For more on certainty of objects see Chapters 4 and 5.

> Nor can it be brought within the scope of such recent decisions as **Re Denley** . . . since there are, for the reasons I have given, no ascertained or ascertainable beneficiaries.

It would appear, therefore, that the test of certainty for a **Re Denley** type trust is the same as for a discretionary trust, the 'any given postulant' test. This seems logical, since presumably the trustees of the sports ground have only to know whether a person is or is not a member of the class, and is also subject to the administrative workability requirement, since the lack of this in the *West Yorkshire* case appears to be the reason for its not being saved by *Re Denley*. It is respectfully submitted that Lloyd LJ's use of the term 'ascertainable' in this context is incorrect. Given what has been said about ascertainability in the context of fixed trusts, it is difficult to see that ascertainability in its usually accepted sense is not present here. Indeed, it is unclear what role it might play in discretionary trusts, since there appears to be no right of every object to be considered, and therefore no need to know if they all exist.

See Chapter 4 (p. 103).

It has also been pointed out that in this respect the certainty test for a *Re Denley* case, which simply allowed use of the sports ground, would be different from a case like *Re Lipinski* [1977] 1 All ER 33, or any of the unincorporated association cases considered below: if the interpretation of the gift is that all members have an interest, and the constitution permits them to wind up the association and distribute the property, then a full list of members will be needed to make that distribution. Presumably, this should not normally be a problem with associations, since membership lists will be kept.

A further problem with *Re Denley* is whether, given that the rights of the employees are apparently restricted to the purpose of the gift, the employees are collectively the equitable owners of the sports field and could, under the rule in *Saunders v Vautier* (see p. 157), call for the winding up of the trust, the sale of the field and distribution of the sale proceeds, which was clearly not what the settlor intended. This is also an issue in cases of gifts to unincorporated associations (see below), where such rights are generally assumed to be circumscribed by the club rules.

A second possible method of providing money for a purpose is through the conveyancing device developed in *Re Tyler*.

Re Tyler [1891] 3 Ch 252

In this case money was donated to a charity, the London Missionary Society, with a request that the society should maintain the testator's family vault. If this request was not fulfilled, the money was to go to another charity, the Bluecoat School. The Missionary Society was encouraged to fulfil the request by the fact that it would thereby retain the gift. Potentially, therefore, the non-charitable purpose could go on being fulfilled, at least as long as there was sufficient money to make it worth the society's while to do so. It should be noted that the society was not obliged to carry out the purpose; it could choose instead to forfeit the money. The gift and the purpose were held valid, but any gift couched in terms obliging the charity to carry out the purpose will be void.

Third, a gift coupled with a power to use it to carry out a purpose will be valid. Since there is no obligation in such a case, there is no need for beneficiaries to enforce that obligation, so powers are not bound by the same requirements of identifiable beneficiaries, as has already been discussed with respect to express trusts.

Finally, other devices, such as incorporation, may be employed to carry out purposes. This puts the matter outside trust law altogether.

The exceptional cases

Objective 5

Despite the objections to purpose trusts, discussed above, there are nevertheless certain situations where they are recognised as valid though they are unenforceable without beneficiaries. This group is commonly referred to as trusts of imperfect obligation. It has been made clear in cases such as *Re Astor* that they are to be regarded as anomalous and will not be extended.

Tombs and monuments

It is valid for a settlor to give money on trust for the erection and maintenance of a tomb or monument. For example, in **Musset v Bingle** [1876] WN 170, the testator gave £300 for the erection of a monument to his wife's first husband. A further gift for its maintenance was invalid, however, as offending the perpetuity rule. It is clear, therefore, that any such gift must be specifically limited to the perpetuity period. This point was considered above. Secondly, it is clear that this exception extends only to fairly modest memorials such as tombstones, though the precise figure allowable is, naturally, not capable of definition. *M'Caig*, described above, shows that expensive statues do not fall within this group and are regarded as capricious and wasteful. Neither was the court willing to extend this category to cover *Re Endacott* where £20,000 was given to North Tawton parish council for the building of 'some useful memorial to myself'. This failed as being too uncertain, but a further objection was the large sum involved. It should further be noted that a monument within the church may be valid as charitable since it constitutes part of the fabric of the church and may be regarded as a satellite purpose to that of advancing religion.

Trusts for the maintenance of animals

A trust for animals generally may be charitable but a trust for the maintenance of individual animals, such as family pets, may be valid as a purpose trust. For example, in **Pettingall v Pettingall** (1842) 11 LJ Ch 176, a gift of £50 p.a. to maintain the testator's favourite black mare was held valid. Once again, the issue of perpetuity must be addressed, and it is usually assumed that such a gift will be limited to a period of 21 years. There is, for these purposes, no 'life or lives in being', since the animal's own lifetime cannot be used as the measure. While it would seem logical that the gift should be allowed to maintain the animal for the rest of its life, however long that proves to be, the courts have set their faces against such a solution as creating too uncertain a perpetuity period. If testators were permitted to define perpetuity periods by reference to the lives of long-lived animals such as tortoises, this would create considerable uncertainty as well as tying up property for too long. Lives in being must therefore mean human lives, as Meredith J held in **Re Kelly** [1932] Ir R 255. A longer period (50 years) was permitted in **Re Dean** (1889) 41 Ch D 552, but the perpetuity issue was not addressed in the case and it is generally considered to be wrong on this point. It would appear to be possible to lengthen the period by reference to human lives by using a 'royal lives' clause: in other words by stating, for example, that the gift will last no longer than 21 years after the death of the last survivor of the grandchildren of the present Queen, alive at the time of the coming into effect of the trust. The Perpetuities and Accumulations Act 2009 s 18 would appear to allow this.

Trusts for masses

This category may have been largely superseded by the case of **Re Hetherington** [1989] 2 All ER 129, which recognised that money given for the saying of masses, will be a valid charitable gift provided that the ceremonies are open to the public. In such a case it is not therefore necessary to consider their validity as non-charitable purposes. **Re Le Cren Clarke** [1996] 1 All ER 715 also confirmed that purely private religious ceremonies are not charitable, but the possibility of masses said in private being regarded as valid non-charitable purposes presumably still exists: see **Bourne v Keane** [1919] AC 815.

Re Thompson [1934] Ch 342

This case, which appears to be anomalous, recognised as valid a gift of money for the promotion of fox-hunting. It must be seen in its context, however, for the litigation was by the residuary legatee, Trinity Hall, Cambridge. Trinity Hall, being a charity, was bound to enforce its legal rights and thus was obliged to litigate to see if the gift was valid. It was, though, content to see the gift put into effect. Clauson J regarded the gift as valid, holding that a sufficient degree of enforceability was provided and that the beneficiary problem was avoided by the fact that the residuary legatee could demand the money if the purpose was not carried out. This is the case with nearly all purpose trusts since there will nearly always be a residuary legatee (though it is perhaps significant that in *Re Astor* the residuary legatee could not be ascertained at the time). To say that the residuary legatee can call for the money is not the same, it is submitted, as true enforceability by the beneficiary of the trust itself. The case is therefore to be regarded as of limited authority and does not appear to have been followed.

Unincorporated associations

Objective 6

Unincorporated associations are considered here because one might think that a gift to such an organisation would be a purpose gift and subject to the general objections discussed above. As will be seen, however, alternative interpretations of such gifts have allowed them to take effect. The linked issues of how an incorporated association holds property and how it should be dealt with on dissolution are also considered here for the sake of convenience.

An unincorporated association is what its name suggests: an association or grouping together of a number of persons for some common purpose without the formal creation of a corporation. Such associations have no legal personality; indeed, they do not have any legal existence other than through the agreement, often interpreted as contractual, between the members. In *Conservative and Unionist Central Office* v *Burrell* [1982] 2 All ER 1, Lawton LJ defined an unincorporated association as:

> two or more persons bound together for one or more common purposes . . . by mutual undertakings, each having mutual duties and obligations, in an organisation which has rules which identify in whom control of it and its funds rests and on what terms and which may be joined or left at will.

Typical associations are sports and social clubs, cultural groups and some charitable organisations. As it does not have a legal personality, an association cannot itself own anything or have property. And yet in the ordinary sense clubs and associations do exist, people subscribe to them as members, people give them money, so the law has to find some other way in which to give legal effect to that existence, particularly with respect to their property. As was stated by Viscount Simonds in *Leahy* v *A-G for New South Wales* [1959] 2 All ER 300:

> [The difficulty] arises out of the artificial and anomalous conception of an unincorporated society which, though it is not a separate entity in law, is yet regarded as a continuing entity and, however inaccurately, as something other than an aggregate of its members.

Three basic problems arise in connection with the property of unincorporated associations:

1. How are gifts of money to associations to be construed?
2. In what ways may an association hold its property?
3. What is to be done with the property of an association if it is wound up?

Clearly, these three questions are closely linked, particularly in how the court decides to distribute surplus funds on dissolution, which will depend very much on how it decides the property was given or held in the first place.

Gifts to unincorporated associations

For more on charitable associations see Chapter 10 (p. 252).

Here the effect of the courts' interpretation will depend very much on whether the association is charitable or not. If the gift is ostensibly for the association's purposes, and those purposes are charitable, then the *prima facie* assumption is that the gift is a purpose gift for charitable purposes. Indeed, this interpretation is favoured by the court since it will often enable a gift to survive even if the association has ceased to exist and the difficulties of application of cy-près are avoided. This is further considered in relation to *Re Finger* [1971] 3 All ER 1050.

If the association is not charitable, then the gift cannot take effect as a purpose trust since such trusts are invalid unless they fall within a very narrow group of exceptions. So whereas, in the context of charities, Buckley J stated in *Re Vernon* [1971] 3 All ER 1061n that '[e]very bequest to an unincorporated charity by name without more must take effect as a gift for a charitable purpose', in the context of non-charitable associations, Viscount Simonds stated in *Leahy v A-G for New South Wales* that 'a gift can be made to persons but it cannot be made to a purpose or to an object'. These contrasting approaches are essential if gifts are to be held valid and effective.

It being clear that a gift to an unincorporated association cannot take effect as a gift on trust for the association's purposes, the question must be asked: how do such gifts take effect? In *Neville Estates v Madden* [1961] 3 All ER 769, Cross J explained:

> Such a gift may take effect in one or other of three quite different ways. In the first place, it may, on its true construction, be a gift to the members of the association at the relevant date as joint tenants, so that any member can sever his share and claim it whether or not he continues to be a member of the association. Secondly, it may be a gift to the existing members, not as joint tenants, but subject to their respective contractual rights and liabilities towards one another as members of the association. In such a case a member cannot sever his share. It will accrue to the other members on his death or resignation, even though such members include persons who became members after the gift took effect. If this is the effect of the gift, it will not be open to objection on the score of perpetuity, unless there is something in its terms or in the rules of the association which precludes the members at any given time from dividing the subject of the gift between them on the footing that they are solely entitled to it in equity. Thirdly, the terms or circumstances of the gift or the rules of the association may show that the property in question is not to be at the disposal of the members for the time being, but is to be held in trust so that it or its income may be enjoyed by the association or its members from time to time. In this case, if the duration is not limited to the perpetuity period, the gift will fail unless the association is a charitable body.

The three possibilities are, therefore, an absolute gift to the present members, a gift to the members subject to their contractual rights and liabilities as members, or a gift on trust for the present and future members. As Cross J clearly indicates, which of them will apply depends on the construction of each gift.

Where the donor says only that the gift is to the association, then it is *prima facie* a gift to the present members, as Viscount Simonds said in *Leahy v A-G for New South Wales*:

> In law, a gift to such a society simpliciter (i.e. where, to use the words of Lord Parker of Waddington in *Bowman v Secular Society* [1917] AC 406 neither the circumstances of the

gift nor the directions given nor the objects expressed impose on the donee the character of a trustee) is nothing else than a gift to its members at the date of the gift as joint tenants or tenants in common.

It must be apparent, however, that such a simple solution, though it may preserve the gift, may tend in many cases to defeat the intention of the donor. Particularly in the case of philanthropic organisations, it is unlikely that the donor imagined the association members would simply take the money for themselves, or even that they had the power to do so.

The *prima facie* assumption can, of course, be rebutted by the circumstances or terms of the gift.

Leahy v A-G for New South Wales [1959] 2 All ER 300

In this case, the Privy Council considered the position where the donor had made his gift to an association's purposes. In this case the testator had left certain land to such order of Catholic nuns or Christian brothers as his executors should select and the residue of his estate on trust to use both capital and income 'in the provision of amenities in such convents as my executors shall select'. These gifts were not confined to charitable organisations and therefore the gift failed as a charitable gift (though it was in fact saved by legislation validating it as charitable).

Could these bequests take effect as gifts to non-charitable religious organisations?

The Privy Council found it difficult to interpret as an absolute gift to the members a gift stated to be for the benefit of the association (or, in this case, for the benefit of the religious order). It was recognised that such a gift could sometimes take effect as an absolute gift: this had been stated by Lord Parker of Waddington in **Bowman v Secular Society**. However:

> Greater difficulties must be felt when the gift is in such terms that, though it is clearly not contemplated that the individual members shall divide it among themselves, yet it is, *prima facie*, a gift to the individuals and, there being nothing in the constitution of the society to prohibit it, they can dispose of it as they think fit.

The Privy Council concluded that the gift in this case could not be construed as an immediate gift to the members absolutely for several reasons. The testator had expressed the gift in terms of a trust for a religious order and, although that could in law be interpreted as a gift to the members, it was doubtful whether that was the testator's intention. Secondly, at the time of his death the number of members might be very numerous and spread all over the world, depending on what order the executors chose, and it was not easy to believe that the testator intended an immediate gift to all of them. Finally, the nature of the property donated, freehold land, was not such that the testator could have imagined hundreds of monks or nuns owning as joint tenants. Accordingly:

> It seems reasonably clear that, however little the testator understood the effect in law of a gift to an unincorporated body of persons by their society name, his intention was to create a trust not merely for the benefit of the existing members of the selected order but for its benefit as a continuing society and for the furtherance of its work.

What, then, were the consequences of this conclusion? As a gift to a non-charitable association, the gift failed (though, as previously stated, legislation preserved it as a charitable gift). Whether a gift is made to individuals in their own names or in the name of their society, and the conclusion is reached that they are not to take beneficially, then they must take as trustees. If there is a trust, who are the beneficiaries? If they are ascertained at the date of the testator's death, then the trust can be effective. If, as in this case, the interpretation is that it is a trust for present and future members and the organisation potentially lasts for ever, then the beneficiaries are unascertained and not ascertainable within the perpetuity period. The trust is void for perpetuity. If it appears that the trust is for the purposes of the society, then of course such a trust is unenforceable and an imperfect exercise of the testator's power, and must fail.

Of the possible solutions, the contractual one, that the gift is to the members of the association subject to their contractual rights and liabilities, is the most attractive and poses the fewest problems. It was considered at length by Brightman J in *Re Recher's Will Trust* [1971] 3 All ER 401. In this case the testator left residuary estate to an antivivisection society. The gift failed because the society had ceased to exist before the testator's death, but if the society had not been wound up the court held that the gift would have been effective.

Brightman J considered the different possible interpretations, as described above and concluded in favour of the contractual one:

> It has been urged upon me that if the gift is not a purpose one, there is no half-way house between, on the one hand, a legacy to the members . . . as joint tenants beneficially, or as tenants in common beneficially, and, on the other hand, a trust for members which is void for perpetuity because no individual member acting by himself can ever obtain his share of the legacy. I do not see why the choice should be limited to these two extremes. If the argument were correct it would be difficult, if not impossible, for a person to make a straightforward donation, whether *inter vivos* or by will, to a club or other non-charitable association which the donor desires to benefit. This conclusion seems to me contrary to common sense.

He considered the nature of associations and the variety of their functions, some of which provide benefits to members and some of which do not. He rejected the idea that societies could be classified as inward looking, that is for the benefit of their members only, and outward looking, that is for philanthropic or other external purposes, or that the 'absolute gift' interpretation was appropriate to the first and the 'purpose trust' interpretation was appropriate to the second. Societies existed for a variety of reasons and purposes:

> [I]t is not essential that the members should only intend to secure direct personal advantage to themselves. The association may be one in which personal advantages to the members are combined with the pursuit of some outside purpose. Or the association may be one which offers no personal benefit at all to members, the funds of the association being applied exclusively to the pursuit of some outside purpose.

Nonetheless, in the case of an association such as the present one, it would be absurd to suppose that the testatrix intended the members to be entitled to an immediate share of the gift:

> In the case of a donation which is not accompanied by any words which purport to impose a trust, it seems to me that the gift takes effect in favour of the existing members of the association as an accretion to the funds which are the subject matter of the contract which such members have made *inter se*, and falls to be dealt with in precisely the same way as the funds which the members themselves have subscribed. So, in the case of a legacy, in the absence of words which purport to impose a trust, the legacy is a gift to the members beneficially, not as joint tenants or as tenants in common so as to entitle each member to an immediate beneficial share, but as an accretion to the funds which are the subject matter of the contract which the members have made *inter se*.

Brightman J explained the nature of the members' contract, based upon the constitution of the society, which lays down members' rights and liabilities. Any action contrary to the society's rules would entitle members to sue for breach of contract. He also noted that, though the society in question had a clause in its constitution vesting the society's property in trustees, these trustees would be bound to apply the money in accordance with the society's constitution. Nor does the contractual solution prevent the gift being distributed to the members if that is agreed upon:

> Just as two parties to a bipartite agreement can vary or terminate their contract by mutual assent, so it must follow that the . . . members of the . . . society could, at any moment of time, by unanimous agreement (or by majority vote if the rules so prescribe), vary or terminate their multi-partite contract. There would be no limit to the type of variation or termination to which all might agree. There is no private trust or trust for charitable purposes to hinder the process. It follows that if all the members agreed, they could wind up the . . . society and divide the net assets among themselves beneficially.

This power to wind up and distribute is important as it prevents the property being inalienable and thus offending the perpetuity rules.

The significance of this requirement emerged in *Re Grant's Wills Trust* [1979] 3 All ER 359, where Vinelott J explained it thus:

> It must as I see it, be a necessary characteristic of any gift in the second category [the second of Cross J's categories in *Neville Estates*], that the members of the association can . . . alter their rules so as to provide that the funds . . . shall be applied for some new purpose, or even distributed amongst the members for their own benefit. For the validity of a gift within this category rests essentially on the fact that the testator has set out to further a purpose by making a gift to the members of an association formed for the furtherance of that purpose, in the expectation that, although the members at that date when the gift takes effect will be free to dispose of the fund in any way they may think fit, they and the future members of the association will not in fact do so but will employ the property in the furtherance of the purpose of the association and will honour any special condition attached to the gift.

In other words, one can only interpret the gift as being to the members if the donor intends that they be free to use it, but merely hopes that they will spend it on the purpose. How can one imagine such a gift if the members are not in fact free to treat the gift as their own because the rules of the association prevent it and cannot be changed?

Thus, on the facts of *Re Grant*, the gift was to a local Labour party, and such a party did not have control over its assets since it was bound to adhere to decisions on such matters taken by the national Labour party at its annual conference. A further reason for holding that this was not a gift to the members was that the gift was conditional upon the local party headquarters remaining in the area, with a gift over to the national Labour party if they ceased so to remain.

Although the purpose trust argument will inevitably fail, for the reasons discussed above, there is no reason in principle why a gift should not take effect as a trust for members, provided the perpetuity problem and the requirement of ascertainability are solved. A gift which is interpreted as a trust for present and future members must fail because future interests may not take effect within the perpetuity period, subject perhaps to the 'wait and see' principle under the Perpetuities and Accumulations Act 2009. If the gift is limited to the perpetuity period, then the gift can be valid: this was stated in *Leahy* and is implicit in subsequent cases. Furthermore, the courts are willing, in appropriate cases, to interpret gifts which are ostensibly for purposes as gifts to the indirect beneficiaries. This, it will be recalled, was the solution adopted by Goff J in *Re Denley*, discussed above. The gift for the provision of a sports field was interpreted as a trust for the employees, who had *locus standi* to enforce. As Goff J stated:

> Where . . . the trust, though expressed as a purpose, is directly or indirectly for the benefit of an individual or individuals, it seems to me that it is in general outside the mischief of the beneficiary principle.

It will be recalled that *Re Denley* did not concern a gift to an association, but it did identify clearly the group who were to use and have the benefit of the facility: the employees for the time being. There was no problem of perpetuity because the gift was specifically limited to the perpetuity period.

Re Denley was considered in the context of a gift to an association in *Re Lipinski* [1977] 1 All ER 33, where a residuary gift was given to the Hull Judeans Association 'to be used solely in the work of constructing the new buildings for the Association'. This last stipulation clearly made it impossible to interpret the gift as an absolute one to the present members. In holding the gift valid, Oliver J addressed the matter in terms of a trust for the members, their interests being determined by the contract between them:

> If a valid gift may be made to an unincorporated body as a simple accretion to the funds which are the subject matter of the contract which the members have made *inter se* . . . I do not really see why such a gift, which specifies a purpose which is within the powers of the unincorporated body and of which the members of that body are the beneficiaries, should fail. Why are not the beneficiaries able to enforce the trust or, indeed, in the exercise of their contractual rights, to terminate the trust for their own benefit?

Referring to *Re Denley* as authority for the proposition that a trust expressed as being for a purpose can be a valid trust for the beneficiaries who indirectly benefit, provided they are ascertainable, Oliver J concluded:

> [T]he case appears to me to be one of the specification of a particular purpose for the benefit of ascertained beneficiaries, the members of the association for the time being . . . The beneficiaries, the members of the association for the time being, are the persons who could enforce the purpose and they must, as it seems to me, be entitled to enforce it or, indeed, to vary it.

It is recognised that whether the gift is dealt with as a trust or as a gift subject to contract, the result is the same on these facts, but it is submitted that the trust argument can only work where the purpose is for the benefit of the members. For a philanthropic society its purposes could not, perhaps, be held to be of direct or indirect benefit to a sufficiently defined class, just as some purpose trusts are too vague and their benefits too indirect for them to be valid. In such situations it would appear that the contractual approach is safer.

To summarise, there are a number of ways that gifts to unincorporated associations can be interpreted. They may be gifts to the present members, though this appears to be uncommon and is not likely where the association does not confer direct benefits on its members and exists for external purposes such as philanthropy. Gifts may sometimes take effect as trusts for the members, though again this would not be appropriate where it is clear that the members are not meant to benefit. The most satisfactory solution is for the gift to be interpreted as a gift to members, but subject to the constitutional rules of the association as to members' rights and liabilities, expressed as a contract between them. In such cases one such rule must permit the members to agree to wind up the association and distribute assets, otherwise the gift will fail as inalienable.

It has been pointed out, however, that the 'contractual' solution has the drawback, from the donor's point of view, that his gift to the association must be an absolute one: to make it for a purpose will mean that it must fail, unless the purpose is charitable, as explained above in the context of *Leahy* v *A-G for New South Wales*. If the gift is absolute, the donor is at the mercy of the members of the association. Whether they are free to sever individual shares, or to agree to distribute the money, thus defeating the donor's intent, is a matter of the society's rules, and not the terms of the donor's gift. In practice there is no method, therefore, by which the donor can ensure that his purpose is carried out. He can only hope that the members will fulfil his wishes.

Re Horley Town Football Club [2006] EWHC 2386, [2006] All ER (D) 34 provides a further instance of the application of the 'contractual' approach to property holding by clubs and societies. The second possibility referred to in *Neville Estates* v *Madden* was argued for by all parties, and the judge held that 'member' in this instance meant the full member for the time being, and not temporary and associate members, who had only been added to the club to allow them to use the club bar. The fact that the original gift was expressed in terms of a trust (bearing in mind that the gift pre-dated later analyses in *Leahy* v *AG for New South Wales* and *Neville Estates* (above)) did not prevent application of the contractual approach.

Funds held by unincorporated associations

The problems associated with how a society can 'own' property or hold funds are essentially the same as some of those discussed in relation to gifts above. Aside from the problem of the interpretation of the donor's wishes, the question of how money can be given to societies is the same as how they are able to hold it.

It will be recalled that the 'contractual' solution to the problem of gifts treated them as 'accretions to the funds which are the subject matter of the contract which the members have made *inter se*' (*Re Recher*). In other words, the ordinary funds of an association are held subject to the contract between the members. Apart from gifts, the other main source of such funds may well be members' subscriptions. In *Re Recher* it was explained: 'As and when a member paid his subscription to the association, he would be subjecting his money to the disposition and expenditure thereof laid down by the rules (of the association).'

Each member would therefore have contractual rights to prevent its misapplication. The committee members who have responsibility for its expenditure are thus also bound by those rules which may be enforced by action for breach of contract. It is clear, however, that some associations do not hold property and are not empowered to do so, as in the case of *Re Grant*, considered above.

Alternative solutions based on trusts pose the problems already considered. Clearly property cannot be held on trust for a purpose, unless charitable, and even if the trust is for the members of the association, avoiding the mischief of the beneficiary principle, those members will have to be certain or ascertainable. Such an answer was possible in *Re Denley*, where, obviously, a contractual solution was not possible, there being no association. In *Re Lipinski*, where, arguably, a trust solution was applied to the gift, such a solution was clearly not envisaged in respect of the association's general funds.

Even if the 'contractual' approach is adopted, there may still be some difficulties. A committee may have control of funds, but if the association has land, they will presumably be the legal owners of it. Whoever the legal owners are, it must be assumed that someone, perhaps the members, are the equitable owners. If this is the case, the usual trust problems arise: can the beneficiaries enforce their individual rights? Presumably not, as they have agreed to be bound by the constitution. The problem of members leaving and thereby surrendering their beneficial interest in the land would seem to involve the application of the Law of Property Act 1925 s 53(1)(c) since it is a disposition.

See Chapter 4 (p. 115).

Despite these difficulties, it is submitted that association assets are owned by the members but subject to the constitution which they have contracted to accept. The officers of the association, who may have control of the assets and also may be legal owners of the real property of the association, are similarly bound and individual members can enforce the arrangement by action for breach of contract.

Of course, the 'contractual' approach to asset holding cannot be adopted if the 'association' is not in fact an association in that it does not consist of a group of members bound together by a common interest. In *Conservative and Unionist Central Office* v *Burrell* [1982] 2 All ER 1, it was held that the Conservative party was not an association. The question arose regarding the basis upon which the treasurer of the party held party funds. Brightman LJ said that payments were held on the basis of a mandate or agency:

> If a contributor pays money to that treasurer, the treasurer has clear authority to add the contribution to the mixed fund that he holds. At that stage I think the mandate is irrevocable. That is to say, the contributor has no right to demand his contribution back, once it has been mixed with other money under the authority of the contributor.

Brightman LJ goes on to state, however, that the contributor retains the right to enforce his mandate, to the extent of preventing the funds being misapplied, though this mandate would expire when the contributor's money was used up.

This case offers an alternative method of holding money in this kind of situation, though not one which, it is submitted, could apply to bequests in wills (the donor, being dead, would not be able to create the agency). It also makes clear that the existence of a fund does not necessarily imply or require the existence of an association. Whether such a solution will be used in the case of gifts to unincorporated associations remains to be seen. Brightman LJ also noted that this right might expire if there was a change of treasurer, and that a former treasurer, to whom the mandate was given, might be liable for his successor's malpractices.

Winding up unincorporated associations: distribution of funds

Objective
7

The other problem that arises in connection with unincorporated associations is what to do with surplus funds when an association is wound up. The decisions on this issue are to some extent in conflict with the analysis above, and that would appear to be due to the fact that the courts have merely been concerned to provide a workable answer to the problem of distribution and have not addressed themselves to the question of how associations hold funds in the first place. To the extent that surplus funds are regarded as being held on resulting trust, they are an example of that concept whose general principles are to be found in Chapter 11. As will be seen, however, once again the trust concept has tended to be superseded by an approach based on contract.

One preliminary issue is when an association can be said to have been dissolved. In *Re GKN Sports Club* [1982] 2 All ER 855, Sir Robert Megarry V-C listed four methods of dissolution: (1) in accordance with the rules; (2) by agreement of all persons interested; (3) by order of the court in the exercise of its inherent jurisdiction; and (4) when the substratum on which the society was founded has gone, so that the society no longer had any effective purpose. So, on the facts of the case, Sir Robert was able to hold that the fourth method applied to a sports club which had ceased for some months to function and where, furthermore, deliberate steps had been taken to dismantle it (its stock of drinks had been sold, its club steward had been dismissed and its registration for VAT had been ended). This may be contrasted with the case of *Keene and Phillips* v *Wellcom London Ltd and others* [2014] EWHC 134 (Ch), [2014] All ER (D) 241 (Jan), in which *Re GKN* was considered. In 1987 it had been resolved to dissolve the association and distribute its assets, but in this case no action had ever been taken, though the association had ceased all activity. The Court held that mere inactivity did not bring the association to an end, but that it was now open to the trustees to dissolve it. (This association was, in fact, a charity, so the issue of application of the funds cy-près might have arisen.)

See further
Chapter 10 (p. 250).

It is also clear that an association ceases to exist if its membership falls below two (one 'member' cannot 'associate' with himself), at which point, according to **Hanchett-Stamford v A–G** [2009] Ch 173, the surviving member becomes the sole owner of the association's property and may dispose of it as he wishes.

Earlier cases tended to adopt the approach that surplus funds were held on resulting trust for the members. Thus, in **Re Printers' and Transferrers' Amalgamated Trades Protection Society** [1899] 2 Ch 184, it was held, there being no rule in the society's constitution on how to distribute surplus funds, that they were held on resulting trust for the existing members in proportion to their contributions. As the funds came only from members' contributions, this offered a sensible solution, but, it must be submitted, not a very logical one. No account was taken of the contributions of past members, nor of any payments which might have been made to individual members under the society's rules. If a resulting trust solution is to be applied, then it should take account of all contributors, which, of course, may present serious difficulties if these contributors cannot be found.

The underlying difficulty of a resulting trust approach is that it presupposes that the donors have not surrendered all title to the money. It will be remembered that the favoured solution, as far as both gifts and fees to associations are concerned, is that they are outright gifts to the members, subject to the contract in the constitution of the society. Logically, there should then be no place for a resulting trust back to the donors. Conversely, if the surplus is held on resulting trust, then the original donor must have given the money on trust, which is likely to create difficulties, though perhaps not in the case of mutual benefit

See Chapter 11
for a discussion of
Re Gillingham.

societies as in **Re Printers' and Transferrers'**. This is also a problem in cases such as **Re Gillingham Bus Disaster Fund**.

In the more recent case of **Re The Sick and Funeral Society of St John's Sunday School, Golcar** [1972] 2 All ER 439, the earlier resulting trust cases were not followed by Megarry J, who regarded the resulting trust as inappropriate:

> [M]embership of a club or association is primarily a matter of contract. The members make their payments, and in return they become entitled to the benefits of membership in accordance with the rules. The sums they pay cease to be their individual property, and so cease to be subject to any concept of resulting trust. Instead they become the property, through the trustees of the club or association, of all the members for the time being, including themselves. A member who, by death or otherwise, ceases to be a member thereby ceases to be the part owner of any of the club's property: those who remain continue owners. If, then, a dissolution ensues, there must be a division of the property of the club or association among those alone who are owners of that property, to the exclusion of former members. In that division, I cannot see what relevance there can be in the respective amounts of the contributions.

Accordingly, on the facts, four members who had ceased to pay membership subscriptions some years before were excluded from claiming, and the funds were distributed equally among members subsisting at the date of dissolution (subject to a provision for half shares for minor members, which was provided for in the constitution).

Two points may here be made. First, it may be thought that this answer would be more difficult to apply to gifts to the society as opposed to membership fees, though this should not be a problem if gifts are accepted as an accretion to the general funds of the society. Secondly, it may of course be that the rules of the society expressly or impliedly exclude distribution of the surplus among members. These two issues arose in **Re West Sussex Constabulary's**

Widows, Children and Benevolent Society 1930 Fund Trusts [1970] 1 All ER 544. Goff J, applying a contract solution, held that the surviving members received nothing since they had already received all they had contracted for, so the funds went *bona vacantia* to the Crown. As regards gifts from outside sources, the judge chose to distinguish between gifts in collecting boxes and similar things, which he regarded as outright gifts, and specific donations and legacies which were to be held on resulting trust for the donors. This solution obliges the court to distinguish between different kinds of gifts and leaves open the question of how these gifts had previously been held by the association, though perhaps a trust for the indirect benefit of persons *à la Denley* was possible here. A more completely contractual approach was taken in *Re Bucks Constabulary Fund (No. 2)* [1979] 1 All ER 623, where Walton J ordered equal distribution among surviving members in the same way as was done in the *Golcar* case, applying this principle to friendly societies as it already appears to be applied to other kinds of unincorporated associations. It is clear that Walton J was unable to accept the distinction drawn by Goff J between organisations for the exclusive benefit of members and those (such as benevolent funds) that provided benefits to third parties.

Summary

- Purpose trusts are those expressed to be for the carrying out of purposes, rather than for human beneficiaries.

- There are a number of conceptual difficulties with trusts which are expressed to be for abstract purposes.

- The most important of these difficulties is that there are no beneficiaries to enforce the trust.

- No trust can last forever (unless it is charitable), so purpose trusts may also be invalid because they potentially exceed the perpetuity period.

- In some cases, depending on the nature of the purpose, and the intended beneficiaries, it may, as in *Re Denley*, be possible to uphold such trusts as private trusts for individuals, but such cases are subject to the usual questions of certainty; the class of beneficiaries; and the purposes must be clearly defined and capable of enforcement by the courts.

- There are rare exceptional cases where purpose trusts are recognised but they are regarded as anomalous and no new types will be recognised.

- An unincorporated association, such as a club or society, is an association of individuals which has no separate legal personality of its own. Property 'of the society', received in the form of membership subscriptions or gifts or in other ways, may therefore be treated as gifts to or property of the members, subject to various restraints laid down in the club rules.

- When an association ceases to exist, as when it is wound up by a decision of its members, the association's property may be distributed in accordance with the principles of resulting trust, or in accordance with the club rules, as a contract between the members.

See Chapter 11.

Further reading

Purpose trusts

J Brown, 'What are we to do with testamentary trusts of imperfect obligation?' [2007] Conv 148. Discusses the exceptional cases, presents evidence as to the frequency of their use, and suggests statutory reform.

S Evans, 'Only people and horses' (2010) 154 (22) Sol J 16.
Advocates the expansion of the beneficiary principle to non-charitable benevolent funds.

M Pawlowski and J Summers: 'Private purpose trusts – a reform proposal' [2007] Conv 440.
Considers purpose trusts and the beneficiary principle, and suggests statutory reform to validate such trusts.

Unincorporated associations

S Baughen, 'Performing animals and the dissolution of unincorporated associations: the "contract-holding theory" vindicated' [2010] Conv 216.
Analyses three methods of asset distribution, following Hanchett-Stamford v A–G (2008).

S Gardner, 'New angles on unincorporated associations' [1992] Conv 41.
Considers distribution of funds on the winding up of a pension scheme, following *Re Buckinghamshire Constabulary* (1979).

P Luxton, 'Gifts to clubs: contract-holding is trumps' [2007] Conv 274.
Discusses *Re Horley Town Football Club* (2006).

P Matthews, 'A problem in the construction of gifts to unincorporated associations' [1995] Conv 302.
Considers cases where a gift is to members who may take their share, and cases where the gift is an accretion to the club funds.

C E F Rickett, 'Unincorporated associations and their dissolution' (1980) 39 CLJ 88.
Focuses on *Re Buckinghamshire Constabulary No. 2* (1979).

P St J Smart, 'Holding property for non-charitable purposes: mandates, conditions and estoppels' [1987] Conv 415.
Property holding by clubs, focusing on *Conservative Central Office* v *Burrell* (1982).

J Warburton, 'The holding of property by unincorporated associations' [1985] Conv 318.
Methods of clubs holding property, discussing *Denley*, *Grant* and *Neville Estates* v *Madden* (1961).

10

Charitable trusts

Objectives

After reading the chapter you will:

1. Understand what is meant in law by the terms 'charity' and 'charitable purpose'.

2. Understand the position of charities as exceptions to the rules on perpetuity, and to the requirements of human beneficiaries and certainty.

3. Appreciate the significance of the requirement of public benefit for charitable status and the changes brought in by recent statutory provisions and case law.

4. Have a detailed critical knowledge of a range of charitable purposes and the recent developments in this area.

5. Be aware of the limitation on political activities by charities.

6. Understand the extent to which charities must limit themselves to exclusively charitable activity.

7. Have a knowledge in outline of the various bodies and agencies which administer and supervise charities, and be aware of the role of the Charity Commission.

8. Understand the mechanisms by which money dedicated to particular charitable purposes may be allocated to alternative charitable purposes.

Introduction

Objective 1

This area of the law, particularly the meaning of 'charity' and 'charitable purposes', has for centuries been a matter of case law, and of a process of 'reasoning by analogy', dependent ultimately on the interpretation of the Preamble to the Charitable Uses Act 1601, the so-called 'Statute of Elizabeth'. The definition of charity was put on a statutory basis with the passage of the Charities Act 2006, while the administration of charities, already subject to statutory intervention, underwent a further overhaul under the 2006 Act. This legislation has now been consolidated into the Charities Act 2011 and references are to that Act unless otherwise indicated.

We shall see, however, that the legal meaning of charity has not in fact been changed significantly, but rather that the new statutory definition seeks to preserve the previous meaning whilst clarifying those areas which did not sit easily within the previous definitions but which were in practice recognised as charitable.

Note that a good deal of guidance on the definition, recognition and supervision of charities can be obtained from the Charity Commission website, **www.charitycommission. gov.uk**.

Charitable organisations

It is traditional to consider the law of charities as part of the law of trusts, since many charities are organised as trusts, but in fact charitable organisations may take a number of forms. They may be organised as companies, incorporated and having legal personality. They may be unincorporated and organised as trusts. They may also, since 2012, be run as Charitable Incorporated Organisations, or CIOs, a new form of corporate body, available only to charities, introduced by the Charities Act 2006. The relevant legislation is now to be found in Part 11 of the Charities Act 2011.

These different forms of organisation each offer advantages and disadvantages. If a charity is organised as a conventional company, it must register not only with the Charity Commission, but also on the Companies Register, and submit two sets of annual accounts to comply with charity and company legislation. Against this, a company, having a corporate personality, can hold assets itself, whereas trust property must usually be held by the trustees, which creates complexity when trustees change. A company may also enter into contracts in its own right and also provides its directors with limited personal liability, which is not available to the trustees of a charitable trust. The CIO is intended to provide the advantages of both types of organisation without the disadvantages; corporate personality and the capacity, for example, to enter contracts, and limited liability, without the additional burdens of having to be registered with Companies House, since a CIO need only be registered with the Charity Commission. It is likely to be an attractive structure particularly for small and medium sized charities, and it is relatively easy to convert existing trusts and companies into CIOs.

In each case the organisation will have purposes which comply with the definition of charity, as will any gift expressed to be for charitable purposes. Those who manage charities may be trustees or they may be directors of a charitable company, but in either case their role and duties are substantially the same, and are subject to the supervision of the Charity Commission, as described below. The Charities Act 2011, s 177 states:

'charity trustees' means the persons having the general control and management of the administration of a charity.

While s 353 of that Act provides:

'trusts' –

(a) in relation to a charity, means the provisions establishing it as a charity and regulating its purposes and administration, whether those provisions take effect by way of trust or not, and

(b) in relation to other institutions has a corresponding meaning.

Use of the terms 'trust' and 'trustees' in this chapter must be read in the light of these definitions.

Definition of charity and charitable purpose

To be recognised as a charity, however, the trust must have purposes which fall exclusively within the definition of charity. The Charities Act 2011 states in subsection 1(1):

> For the purposes of the law of England and Wales, 'charity' means an institution which
>
> (a) is established for charitable purposes only, and
> (b) falls to be subject to the control of the High Court in the exercise of its jurisdiction with respect to charities.

It has also been held, in *Gaudiya Mission* v *Brahmachary* [1997] 4 All ER 957, that the definition does not include institutions and organisations constituted under foreign jurisdictions, but applies only to charities established in England and Wales.

What, then is a 'charitable purpose'?

The Charities Act 2011 provides a list of specific purposes which are charitable:

> 3(1) A purpose falls within this subsection (i.e is a charitable purpose) if it falls within any of the following descriptions of purposes –
>
> (a) the prevention or relief of poverty;
> (b) the advancement of education;
> (c) the advancement of religion;
> (d) the advancement of health or the saving of lives;
> (e) the advancement of citizenship or community development;
> (f) the advancement of the arts, culture, heritage or science;
> (g) the advancement of amateur sport;
> (h) the advancement of human rights, conflict resolution or reconciliation or the promotion of religious or racial harmony or equality and diversity;
> (i) the advancement of environmental protection or improvement;
> (j) the relief of those in need by reason of youth, age, ill-health, disability, financial hardship or other disadvantage;
> (k) the advancement of animal welfare;
> (l) the promotion of the efficiency of the armed forces of the Crown or the efficiency of the police, fire, rescue or ambulance services;
> (m) any other purposes –
>   (i) that are not within paragraphs (a) to (l) but are recognised as charitable purposes by virtue of section 5 (recreational and similar trusts, etc.) or under the old law,
>   (ii) that may reasonably be regarded as analogous to, or within the spirit of, any purposes falling within any of paragraphs (a) to (l) or sub-paragraph (i), or
>   (iii) that may reasonably be regarded as analogous to, or within the spirit of, any purposes which have been recognised, under the law relating to charities in England and Wales, as falling within sub-paragraph (ii) or this sub-paragraph.

As well as including a long list of specific charitable purposes, the Act, in paragraph (m) above, preserves existing charities, referring to any other purpose recognised as charitable under the old law.

In other words, anything which is not specifically listed but which is already recognised under existing law as charitable continues to be charitable; nothing which was a charitable purpose under existing law will cease to be so under the 2011 Act. The Act further preserves the existing law in Schedule 7, part 1, paragraph 1, which states:

A reference in any enactment or document to a charity within the meaning of the Charitable Uses Act 1601 or the preamble to it is to continue to be construed as a reference to a charity as defined by section 1(1).

Secondly, reasoning by analogy. Paragraph (m) refers, in (ii) and (iii), to anything being charitable which is regarded as analogous to or within the spirit of the specific purposes listed in s 3(1) or to any existing charity, and to anything which is analogous to that analogy.

This means that the process of reasoning by analogy, which was regarded as one of the main benefits of the case law approach, and a major barrier to the introduction of a statutory definition which might prove inflexible, is preserved. It means that something which is not currently recognised, in that it is not, for example, on the s 3(1) list, may nonetheless be upheld as charitable if it can be argued that it is similar to and fulfils a comparable purpose to something which is already recognised. A classic example given under the previous law was that the promotion of cremation and establishment of crematoria was analogous to the establishment and upkeep of graveyards and would thus be charitable; both these activities fulfil a similar purpose: the disposal of the dead. As the section is worded the process can be infinite, with analogy upon analogy upon analogy, to allow continuous development of the law. Several of the specific purposes referred to above will be considered in more detail later.

Motive of the donor

It is clear that the reason why the donor has chosen to give money to charity is irrelevant to the charitable status of the gift. As was stated in *Re Delany* [1902] 2 Ch 642:

> The care of the aged, poor and the like is a charity . . . whether the persons who devote their lives to it are actuated by the love of God, a desire for their own salvation, or mere pique, or disgust with the world.

The same would seem to apply to those who donate money for those, or any other, charitable purposes. The converse is also true. The fact that a donor is motivated by charity or considers his purpose to be charitable will not make the gift charitable. As has already been stated, charity is a matter of legal definition and the donor's opinion is irrelevant.

Charities and the Human Rights Act 1998

It should be noted that the Human Rights Act 1998, which came into force in October 2000, may have an impact in this area. The Act makes it unlawful for 'public authorities, including private bodies that carry out public functions', to act in a manner which is incompatible with the European Convention on Human Rights.

Charities are not 'public bodies' for these purposes merely because they are charities, but if they carry out public functions, particularly if they do so in conjunction with, for example, local authorities, they may be caught by the Act. Thus, for example, the provision of care homes could be subject to Article 3, the right not to be subjected to torture or inhuman treatment, and Article 8, the right to respect for private and family life. It seems unlikely that the Act will have any dramatic effect in this area, but time, and case law, will tell.

The Court of Appeal, in *Heather v Leonard Cheshire Foundation* [2002] 2 All ER 936, has held that a charity providing residential care in the private sector does not perform a public function within the meaning of s 6 of the Human Rights Act 1998.

Advantages of charitable status

Certainty

Objective
2

It has already been stated that purpose trusts will fail if the purpose is not stated with sufficient certainty. This rule does not apply to charities. Provided the wording of the gift allows it only to be spent on charity, it does not matter that the charitable purpose is only vaguely stated, or that no purpose is stated at all. Thus, a gift simply 'for charitable purposes' or, as in *Moggridge* v *Thackwell* (1792) 1 Ves Jr 464, a gift to A 'to dispose of to such charities as he shall think fit' will be valid.

Beneficiary principle

For more on
the beneficiary
principle, see
Chapters 5 and 9.

As has already been stated, the Attorney-General, representing the Crown, appears on behalf of the objects or 'beneficiaries' of charities, thus removing the problem of enforceability which lies behind the requirement of ascertainable beneficiaries in other trusts. Those bodies with responsibility for management and supervision of charities are considered below in the section 'Administration of charities'.

Perpetuity

See Chapter 9
(p. 220).

Since purposes may last for ever, so might a trust for a purpose, thus offending the rule against perpetual trusts unless a limitation is expressly stated in the gift.

Charities are not bound by this rule and may therefore last for ever. There are many charities of considerable age which continue to operate. Thus, where a gift is made of the income from a particular fund to a charity in perpetuity, it will never be possible to release the capital from the fund: *Re Levy* [1960] Ch 346 (subject to the power to authorise a 'scheme' – see further below).

For more on
perpetuities, see
Chapter 7 (p. 161).

Charities are, though, bound by the rule against perpetuities proper, which is to say the rule is that a gift must vest within the perpetuity period. Thus, in *Re Lord Stratheden and Campbell* [1894] 3 Ch 265, money was bequeathed to the Central London Rangers, a charity. The gift was to take effect 'on the appointment of their next lieutenant colonel'. Since this might not occur within the perpetuity period, the gift was void. This situation would now be covered by the 'wait and see' provisions of the Perpetuities and Accumulations Act 1964 s 3 or in the case of trusts or gifts coming into effect after 6 April 2010, s 7 of the Perpetuities and Accumulations Act 2009.

There is, however, an exception to this. If the gift takes effect as a gift over from one charity to another, then the gift to the second charity does not have to take effect within the perpetuity period, on the principle, stated by Shadwell V-C in *Christ's Hospital* v *Grainger* (1849) 60 ER 804, that there is no more perpetuity created by giving to two charities rather than one. In other words, once the money has been given to one charity it may remain there for ever. If it is subsequently transferred to another charity, it is no more tied up than it would have been if it remained with the first. This principle is preserved by the Perpetuities and Accumulations Act 2009, s 2.

Taxation and related advantages

Charities enjoy considerable tax advantages and this is often a significant motive in seeking charitable status: many cases on charitable status arise because that status is challenged by the Revenue. Additionally there can be significant tax incentives to make donations to charities.

The principal advantages are:

(a) *Income tax*. Charities are not liable to income tax on any trading profits they make, provided these are spent exclusively on the purposes of the charity and arise either from a trade carried on in pursuit of the primary purpose of the charity, or from work done by the beneficiaries of the charity, for example sale of work by the residents of a home for the elderly. A similar exemption applies in respect of corporation tax.

In many cases the trade of a charity became mixed with a non-exempt trade so that the tax exemption would become 'tainted' and leave the charity potentially exposed to tax on the trade as a whole. The Finance Act 2006 addressed this problem and introduced a provision which allows a trade to be split and the profits apportioned between the exempt and taxable activities. A similar exemption applies in respect of corporation tax.

Additionally, gifts to charities are sometimes within the Gift Aid scheme which gives significant income tax advantages where the gift is made by an individual who pays UK tax. Under the scheme, gifts are regarded as having been made with basic rate tax deducted by the donor. The charity can reclaim the basic rate tax from HM Revenue & Customs (HMRC) on the gross equivalent, i.e. the amount before basic rate was deducted.

At the moment the basic rate of income tax is 20 per cent. If a donor gives a charity £1,000, the charity can claim £250 from HMRC meaning that the charity benefits by £1,250 for an outlay of £1,000 by the taxpayer.

If the donor pays tax at the higher rate (40 per cent) or the additional rate (45 per cent) he can claim from HMRC the difference between the higher/additional rate of tax 40 per cent or 45 per cent and the basic rate of tax 20 per cent on the total 'gross' value of the donation to the charity. For example, if a higher rate (40 per cent) taxpayer donates £1,000 to a charity he is treated as giving the grossed up amount, i.e. £1,250. The charity can claim the £250 from HMRC and the donor can claim a £250 rebate from HMRC. This means that the charity can benefit by £1,250 while costing the taxpayer only £750.

The Small Charitable Donations Act 2012 gives effect to the Gift Aid Small Donations Scheme which was announced in the 2011 budget. Under the scheme, from 6 April 2013, charities will be able to claim a top-up payment from HMRC on cash donations up to £20 made by individuals via street collections etc. without needing to prove that the donors were taxpayers. This will also apply to collections made in churches etc. or to money collected in the collecting boxes that many charities place in various locations. In most cases the maximum that can be claimed under this provision will be on an income of £5,000 p.a. which will result in a top-up payment of £1,250. In any tax year the maximum that a charity is entitled to claim top-up payments on is ten times the amount donated to the charity under gift aid. Charities will only qualify for top-up payments on cash donations if they have been in existence for at least two years, and have made a successful gift aid claim in at least two of the previous four tax years without a period between claims of two or more consecutive years.

Some organisations run 'payroll giving schemes' under which employees can decide to donate a part of their salary to a chosen charity. The donation is taken from the employees' salary before income tax is deducted. The employee pays over the donation to an approved Payroll Giving Agency. This encourages charitable giving by providing a tax-effective way for employees to make charitable donations. For example, for a basic rate (20 per cent) taxpayer a donation of £100 will cost him only £80 in lost income. A £100 donation will cost a 40 per cent taxpayer £60 and a 45 per cent taxpayer £55.

If qualifying shares or a qualifying interest in land is given to a charity, the donor can claim tax relief on the value. If the property has a value of £1,000 this provision will save a basic rate taxpayer £200, a higher rate taxpayer £400 and an additional rate taxpayer £450.

(b) *Inheritance tax.* Transfers to charities are not liable to inheritance tax. In the 2011 budget the Chancellor announced that as from April 2012, the rate of inheritance tax will be reduced to 36 per cent on those estates where 10 per cent or more is left to charity.

(c) *Capital gains tax.* Charities are not liable to tax on any capital gain made by them, provided it is applied solely to charitable purposes. Additionally, donors of property to charities are not liable to pay capital gains tax on their donations.

(d) *Rates.* Charities are entitled to an 80 per cent reduction in non-domestic rates on premises they occupy. This may be increased to 100 per cent by the charging authority. Certain religious buildings are wholly exempt.

(e) *VAT.* Charities are generally subject to value added tax but there are, however, some VAT reliefs on certain goods and services which are purchased and on income from qualifying fund-raising events.

Requirement of public benefit

Objective 3

As a general rule, a gift, to be charitable, must be for the benefit of the public or a section of the public, as opposed to a private or closed group. The question must be considered in relation to each of the heads of charity in turn, but some general observations may be made.

The 2011 Act, s 2(1)(b) states that, to be charitable, a purpose must be for the public benefit, but it does not provide a definition; s 4(3) merely states:

> In this Chapter any reference to the public benefit is a reference to the public benefit as that term is understood for the purposes of the law relating to charities in England and Wales.

We must therefore look initially to the previous case law on this issue.

The requirement of public benefit excludes all organisations where private individuals take profits or dividends. Thus, education is generally charitable, so that even public schools where fees are paid may be charitable, but only so long as they are not run for private profit, as in *Re Girls' Public Day School Trust* [1951] Ch 400.

Similarly, this requirement will exclude anything in the nature of a mutual benefit ociety, where benefits are limited to those who have contributed to the funds. Thus, in *Re Holborn Air Raid Distress Fund* [1946] Ch 194, a fund collected by employees of a certain firm to provide money for the relief of distress suffered by any employees as a result of air raids could not be charitable. The benefits were limited to the employees of a company which, as we shall see, is too limited a class anyway, but the deciding factor for Lord Greene MR was the self-help nature of the fund:

> The point, to my mind, which really puts this case beyond doubt is the fact that a number of employees of this company, actuated by motives of self-help, agreed to a deduction from their wages to constitute a fund to be applied for their own benefit without any question of

poverty coming into it. Such an arrangement seems to me to stamp the whole transaction as one having a personal character, money put up by a number of people, not for the general benefit, but for their own individual benefit.

A question of some difficulty arises, however, when attempting to define public benefit. Charities must in general be for the benefit of the public or of a section of the public, and the meaning of these terms was considered at length in **Oppenheim v Tobacco Securities Trust** [1951] AC 297. In this case, a fund was created to provide education for the children of the employees and former employees of British American Tobacco Ltd. This constituted a substantial number of people: it was estimated that the total number of employees was over 110,000. Size was not, though, the crucial factor. The House of Lords concluded that this group did not constitute a section of the public because there existed between them a 'personal nexus', which is to say they were defined by a common relationship, in this case that of employment by one particular company. Lord Simonds said in his judgment that to constitute a section of the community the group eligible to benefit must not be numerically negligible and:

> that the quality which distinguishes them from members of the community . . . must be a quality which does not depend on their relationship to a particular individual . . . A group of persons may be numerous but, if the nexus between them is their personal relationship to a single *propositus* or to several *propositi*, they are neither the community nor a section of the community for charitable purposes.

This means that a group which is defined by being, for example, descendants of a named individual or employees of the same firm or members of the same club cannot be a section of the public and so a gift limited to their benefit cannot be charitable.

Lord Simonds himself described this as a difficult, artificial and even illogical branch of the law and others have criticised this 'personal nexus test'. It takes little account of the number of potential beneficiaries involved except to recognise that the number must not be negligible. Valid trusts exist where the number of beneficiaries is very much smaller than was the case in **Oppenheim**. It is also rather absurd that the same group may be defined in a different way so as to avoid offending the rule. An educational trust for the benefit of children of tobacco workers, for example, would be valid. It appears that certain 'common denominators' are acceptable where others are not. It is valid to limit a charitable trust's benefit to the inhabitants of a particular town or village or to the members of a profession, or even to the pupils of a particular school, as in the case of closed scholarships to certain university colleges. By contrast, it is not valid to limit such benefits to employees of the same firm or descendants of the same ancestor, as has been shown.

While a trust cannot be charitable if it is exclusively for such a restricted group, it is apparently acceptable to give preference to a restricted group, as in **Re Koettgen** [1954] 1 All ER 581. In that case a trust had the stated object of commercial education among the public, but directed that preference be given to the employees of a particular company for the expenditure of up to 75 per cent of the fund. This appears to be the maximum percentage that would be acceptable and it should be noted that only preference is given: the restricted group has no exclusive right to any part of the fund.

It should also perhaps be remembered that it is not necessary that the public at large actually takes advantage of the charity, but merely that it should be available to them. Indeed, the terms of the charity may be restricted to the poor, or to children requiring education or to the members of a particular faith and in that sense not all the public are eligible. The important feature, however, is that no restriction other than that defining the purpose of the charity should be imposed. It has been pointed out that a bridge is open to all, even though not everyone will have occasion to use it.

Though the Charities Act 2011 does not alter the meaning of public benefit, s 4(2) removes the supposed former presumption of benefit which applied to the poverty, education and religious charities:

> In determining whether that requirement (of public benefit) is satisfied in relation to any such purpose, it is not to be presumed that a purpose of a particular description is for the public benefit.

This has proved to be an ambiguous and controversial provision, particularly in the context of charities which charge fees, which are discussed in the section below.

First, some clarification is needed: in what sense has it ever been assumed or presumed that a poverty, educational or religious charity was for the public benefit? The case of *The Independent Schools Council* v *Charity Commission* [2011] UKUT 421 (TCC); [2012] 1 All ER 127, discussed further below, explained that public benefit has two meanings. The first is whether the purpose is itself beneficial to the community, which in other contexts we might refer to as a 'charitable purpose'. It is true that under previous law, it was customary to refer to poverty, education and religion 'and other purposes beneficial to the community' as a shorthand definition of charity, but poverty, education and religion had no particular status or privilege; education in the conventional sense would be a charitable object because education per se was recognised as beneficial, but equally a specific educational purpose might not be charitable, for example, the training of pickpockets, because that is clearly not beneficial to the community.

The second meaning, with which we are concerned here, is whether or not a sufficiently large number of people can benefit, and whether the group that can benefit are defined in such a way as to be a section of the community (following the rules in *Oppenheim*, etc.). This is referred to as the 'public' element or aspect. Given the analysis in *The Independent Schools Council* v *Charity Commission*, it is not clear that the section has added very much to the interpretation of what is or is not charitable. In that case the Upper Tribunal held that there was no presumption of benefit in either sense and that, even in the case of educational trust, each case had to be decided on a case-by-case basis.

This case has emphasised that it is the task of the trustees to determine whether they are fulfilling the 'public' element requirements. This point is considered further below with regard to charities which charge fees (see p. 225). Nonetheless, it is the job of the Charity Commission to provide guidance on this point. Section 17 states that the Charity Commission should issue guidelines in pursuance of its public benefit objective, which is to promote awareness and understanding of the operation of the public benefit requirement. Such guidelines are not legally binding and function as advice.

Guidelines issued in 2013, amended after taking into account the decision in *The Independent Schools Council* v *Charity Commission*, state:

> To satisfy the 'public aspect' of public benefit, the purpose must:
>
> ● Benefit the public in general, or a sufficient section of the public.
> ● Not give rise to more than incidental personal benefit.

The Commission also provides more detailed guidance in relation to particular types of charitable purpose, which confirms the application of the principles set out in *Oppenheim* v *Tobacco Securities Trust* [1951] AC 297 and elsewhere as to what may constitute a section of the public. This can be found at the Commission's website: **www.charitycommission. gov.uk**. It is also a requirement that the trustees report annually on how they have achieved their objectives and fulfilled the public benefit requirement, so it is possible for the Commission to scrutinise a charity's activities in practice and intervene where appropriate.

Charities which charge fees

A specific concern with regard to public benefit has been the position of charities which charge fees for their services, such as public schools and 'private' hospitals, since the very act of charging suggests exclusion of the public at large.

The Commissioners (as they then were) indicated that they would follow the guidelines indicated in *Re Resch* [1969] 1 AC 514 (which concerned a fee-charging hospital). Subsequently the Commission issued the guidelines set out above (including the reference to unreasonable exclusion by inability to pay fees). This was challenged by an organisation representing a large number of fee-paying schools in *The Independent Schools Council* v *Charity Commission* (above). Having concluded that whether a charity is for the public benefit is essentially a matter to be determined on a case-by-case basis, the Upper Tribunal held that the Charity Commission had erred in assuming that public benefit could only be satisfied if the poor are not 'unreasonably' (i.e. in the Commission's view) excluded. It is required that provision be made for the 'poor' which is more than *de minimis* or merely token, but beyond that it is for the trustees themselves to determine what provision is required. It may also be added that 'poor' in this context means 'unable to pay the full fees or full cost'. The level of provision for the poor – taken with benefits to the not so poor who would otherwise be unable to pay the fees – must be at a level which equal or exceeds the minimum which any reasonable trustee could be expected to provide. The current Commission guidance, cited above, reflects that decision.

Charitable purposes: specific examples

Objective 4

Given that the Act provides for the preservation of previous law, it is appropriate to look at some of the purposes listed in the Act and look at the previous case law to see how these purposes may be interpreted.

Trusts for the prevention or relief of poverty

This is analogous to the previous category, trusts for the relief of poverty, though with the extension to prevention.

Poverty: absolute or relative?

Poverty may mean different things to different people. Those who have been wealthy but are no longer so may regard themselves as poor even though still comparatively well off. Support for the relative approach is to be found in the words of Sir Raymond Evershed in *Re Coulthurst* [1951] Ch 661:

> Poverty, of course, does not mean destitution. It is a word of wide and somewhat indefinite import, and, perhaps, it is not unfairly paraphrased for present purposes as meaning persons who have to 'go short' in the ordinary acceptation of that term, due regard being had to their status in life and so forth.

Two points may be elucidated from this statement. First, a person may in legal terms be poor without being entirely without means. The term is wide enough to embrace anyone who does not have enough for what may be regarded as their normal condition of life. Thus, in *Re de Carteret* [1933] Ch 103, the term was taken to cover women with an income of between £80 and £130 per annum. Though in straitened circumstances such a level of income would not have put them among the poorest in 1933. Secondly, the reference in Sir Raymond Evershed's statement to 'regard being had to their status in life' seems to imply that poverty is different for different people and dependent on the level of wealth to which they are accustomed. Does a millionaire become poor when he loses half his millions? It would appear from *Re de Carteret* that one may be legally poor even though others are poorer, but there must surely be some limit on the extent to which accustomed lifestyle can affect a person's individual definition of poverty. Such a limit appears to have been identified by Lord Simonds in *IRC* v *Baddeley* [1955] 1 All ER 525:

> There may be a good charity for the relief of persons who are not in grinding need or utter destitution . . . but relief connotes need of some sort, either need for a home, or for the means to provide for some necessity or quasi-necessity, and not merely for an amusement, however healthy.

It is submitted that the reference to necessity or quasi-necessity implies an objective, absolute standard, rather than one relative to the station in life of the claimant.

Restriction to those who are poor

It is clear that, whatever the definition of poverty is to be, the gift must be in terms that exclude those who are not poor. The gift in *Re Gwyon* [1930] 1 Ch 255 failed on this ground. The purpose of the somewhat eccentric gift in this case was to provide 'knickers', a variety of short trousers, for boys in Farnham. It may be that the provision of trousers could be regarded as a necessity, but the gift did not restrict the claimants to poor boys in Farnham. It could thus not be for the relief of poverty and so failed as a charity. Nor have the courts been very ready to assume that poverty is implied by other terms used to identify the class, except in exceptional circumstances. Such an exceptional case is *Re Niyazi* [1978] 3 All ER 785. A relatively small sum (£15,000) was left to build a working men's hostel in Famagusta, Cyprus. The size of the gift, the use of the term 'hostel' and the chronic housing shortage in Famagusta were all regarded as evidence that the hostel would only be used by those too poor to afford anything better. This case has been and should be regarded as borderline, if only because it fails to interpret the gift on its face, normally a basic principle of charity law, and seeks to go behind the actual wording and take account of extrinsic facts.

Public benefit requirement in poverty cases

Trusts for the relief of poverty form a major exception to the usual rule as laid down in *Re Oppenheim*. The courts have long accepted the so-called 'poor relation' exception, whereby a valid trust can be established for the relief of poverty among the settlor's poor relations. This is valid so long as the class of beneficiaries is not further restricted, for example, to a group of named relations. The question was reviewed in *Dingle* v *Turner* [1972] 1 All ER 878. In this case, a trust was established for the benefit of poor employees of Dingle & Co. The class was therefore identified by a personal nexus, that is they were all employees of the same firm, such as had been held invalid in *Re Oppenheim*. On the authority of the 'poor relations' cases, the court held that poverty was an exception: a trust for poor persons who are also identified by a common ancestor, employment by the same firm or some other personal nexus, does not lack the necessary public benefit.

The essential difference between charitable and private trusts in this area is between gifts for the relief of poverty among poor people of a particular description (which is charitable), and gifts to particular persons, the relief of poverty being the motive of the gift (which is not charitable). A gift for the relief of poverty in a particular class of relations could therefore be charitable: in *Re Scarisbrick's Will Trust* [1951] 1 All ER 822, the class named was 'the relations of my son and daughter'. It appears that even a selected group of relations may qualify, in the light of *Re Segelman* [1995] 1 All ER 676. In that case the testator listed some, but not all, of his siblings, and stated that they, together with their issue, formed the class to be benefited.

The Commission accepts that traditionally poverty cases have been viewed more generously, in that the benefits may be limited to a more closely knit group than is possible under other heads of charity. The Commission recognises as a general principle that what is acceptable as a restriction will depend upon the purpose of the charity, so public benefit will vary. Accordingly, where the charity is for the relief of poverty, the Commission accepts that the class to benefit may be defined by a 'personal connection' (equivalent to the 'personal nexus', referred to in *Oppenheim*). The Commission's guidelines refer to restrictions to family connections, employer connections, participation in the same trade or profession or membership of the same club or society as having, on occasion, been recognised as valid groups in the past, but the Commission also qualifies this with the statement:

> Although these restrictions have been held to be capable of being accepted as a sufficient section of the public where the charitable aim is relieving poverty, that does not mean that every restriction of the beneficial class will now be acceptable. Even where all the beneficiaries have to be poor, there may be circumstances in which the restrictions on who can benefit are either so limited or irrational as to outweigh the normal public character of the relief of poverty.

The case of *A-G v Charity Commission* [2012] WTLR 977 has confirmed that s 4(2) (abolishing the 'presumption' of public benefit) has had no impact on poverty charities. The relief of poverty must be carried out in such a way as to be for public benefit in the 'first' sense (see public benefit, above) but, providing that it is, poverty charities may be limited to the narrower classes which have formerly been recognised in cases like *Dingle* v *Turner* (above). The case has also emphasised that there is no distinction to be drawn here between the 'relief' and the 'prevention' of poverty, as referred to in s 3(1) of the Act.

Trust for the advancement of education

This is specifically referred to in the list in s 3(1) of the 2011 Act, and, once again, the previous case law is instructive.

Lord Hailsham, in *IRC* v *McMullen* [1980] 1 All ER 884, said of education:

> when applied to the young [it] is complex and varied . . . It is a balanced and systematic process of instruction, training and practice containing both spiritual, moral, mental and physical elements.

It may be assumed therefore that anything which forms part of the normal educational process and which can be said to fall within that definition will be regarded as education, and that any trust for the advancement of such things will be charitable, subject to the requirements of public benefit. Certainly, physical education and sports, together with games of a more cerebral nature and other extra-curricular activities such as field trips, have all been held to fall within the ambit of education, provided they are for the young, who it is assumed are still undergoing a process of education and development. The courts will reserve to themselves the right to exclude things which they regard as harmful: Harman J in *Re Shaw* [1957] 1 All ER 748 stated that schools for prostitutes or pickpockets would not be regarded as charitable. Subject to such value judgements, however, those things which are normally associated with education both mental and physical, together with ancillary activities, will ordinarily be recognised as valid objectives to be promoted through charity.

Education and politics

Attempts to disseminate political propaganda under the guise of education have been consistently rebuffed by the courts. Similarly, educational charities will be restrained from using their resources for political purposes. Thus, in *Baldry* v *Feintuck* [1972] 2 All ER 81, Sussex University Students' Union, a registered charity, was restrained from spending money on a campaign to restore free school milk. Since this was an attempt to challenge government policy, it was regarded by the courts as political and not charitable. This has been confirmed in the case of *Re Webb* v *O'Doherty* (1991) *The Times*, 11 February, where an injunction was granted to restrain a students' union from spending money in support of a campaign against the Gulf War. Hoffmann J drew a clear distinction between the discussion of political issues, which could be a legitimate educational activity and so charitable (see *A-G* v *Ross* [1985] 3 All ER 334), and campaigning in the sense of seeking to influence public opinion on political matters, which cannot be charitable. The whole issue of political activity by charities is a difficult one and will be considered further at a later stage.

That the line between education and political propaganda is a fine one is indicated in the Charity Commission's own policy on the issue, as stated in its guidelines. Where the charity's objects include the advancement of education, care should be taken not to overstep the boundary between that and political propaganda. If the avowed objects of the organisation are ambiguous, the Commission is entitled to look at the surrounding circumstances to determine the true purpose of the organisation before deciding whether or not to register it as a charity. Thus, in *Southwood* v *A-G* [2000] All ER (D) 886, the express objects of PRODEM were 'the advancement of the education of the public in the subject of militarism and disarmament'. In practice this went beyond educating the public in peaceful means of dispute resolution, and identified 'militarism' with current policies of western governments with the intention of challenging those policies. This 'clear and dominant message' was political, and, accordingly, Carnwath J upheld the Commissioners' decision to refuse registration. The decision was subsequently confirmed by the Court of Appeal ((2000) *The Times*, 18 July).

In the conduct of research, a charity must aim at objectivity and balance in the method of conducting research projects; and in publishing research the aim must be to inform and educate the public rather than to influence political attitudes. (One is tempted here to observe that research which is not balanced and objective is hardly good research and would surely be of little educational value anyway.)

Educational charities: public benefit

The test for public benefit in educational charities, which states that, to be charitable, an educational trust must be for the benefit of the public or a section of the public, and not be limited to a group identified by some personal nexus, has already been discussed above. The specific issue of fee-paying schools under the 2011 Act is referred to above. It may also be noted that the Upper Tribunal in *The Independent Schools Council* v *Charity Commission* [2011] UKUT 421 (TCC); [2012] 1 All ER 127, rejected any suggestion that fee-paying schools were socially divisive or that the education they provided was not for the public benefit (in the sense of not being for a charitable purpose).

Advancement of the arts, culture, heritage or science

This new heading would appear to cover in part those things which were formerly, rather uncomfortably, placed under the head of education.

Research

Research could come under a number of headings, depending on the topic of the research, but it is clear that the subject of the research must itself be useful, a value judgement, and that the gift must make some provision for the information gained to be disseminated and made available for study. The essential characteristic here is that gifts, to be charitable, must be for the advancement of the subject researched, not merely the acquisition of knowledge in a vacuum.

Thus, in *Re Hopkins* [1964] 3 All ER 46, money was given to the Francis Bacon Society to search for the Bacon–Shakespeare manuscripts. In other words, money was provided to discover documentary proof that Shakespeare's plays were written by Francis Bacon and to discover the original manuscript of these plays. This gift was held to be a charitable one. In the words of Wilberforce J:

> A search for the original manuscript of England's greatest dramatist (whoever he was) would be well within the law's conception of charitable purposes. The discovery would be of the highest value to history and to literature.

The broader requirements of research, if it is to be charitable, were also identified by Wilberforce J:

> [T]he requirement is that, in order to be charitable, research must either be of educational value to the researcher or must be so directed as to lead to something which will pass into the store of educational material, or so as to improve the sum of communicable knowledge in an area which education may cover – education in this last context extending to the formation of literary taste and appreciation.

In *Re Shaw* [1957] 1 All ER 748, in which George Bernard Shaw left money for the development of a 40-letter alphabet and the translation of one of his plays into this new alphabet, Harman J indicated that the mere acquisition of knowledge would not *per se* be a charitable object. *Re Hopkins*, on the other hand, indicated that it would, provided it was of educational value to the researcher. The whole issue of the position of research as a charitable object has been further considered and clarified in *McGovern v A-G* [1981] 3 All ER 493 by Slade J, who stated:

> (1) A trust for research will ordinarily qualify as a charitable trust if, but only if (a) the subject matter of the proposed research is a useful object of study; and (b) it is contemplated that the knowledge acquired as a result of the research will be disseminated to others; and (c) the trust is for the benefit of the public, or a sufficiently important section of the public. (2) In the absence of a contrary context, however, the court will be readily inclined to construe a trust for research as importing subsequent dissemination of the results thereof. (3) Furthermore, if a trust for research is to constitute a valid trust for the advancement of education, it is not necessary either (a) that the teacher/pupil relationship should be in contemplation, or (b) that the persons to benefit from the knowledge to be acquired should be persons who are already in the course of receiving 'education' in the conventional sense.

Artistic pursuits

A gift for the promotion of artistic pursuits *per se* is not charitable, if for no other reason than that it is too vague. Trusts for specific artistic purposes, on the other hand, may be charitable. As Lord Greene said in *Royal Choral Society v IRC* [1943] 2 All ER 101: 'In my opinion, a body of persons established for the purpose of raising the artistic state of the country is established for charitable purposes.'

So it has been held that a trust for the promotion of the works of a famous composer is charitable: *Re Delius* [1957] 1 All ER 854. Artistic purposes may also include social graces, as was shown in *Re Shaw's Wills Trust* [1952] 1 All ER 49, where the wife of George Bernard Shaw left money for what was described as a sort of finishing school for the Irish people, where 'self control, oratory, deportment and the arts of personal contact' were to be taught. Vaisey J concluded that the gift was charitable, stating that education included 'the promotion and encouragement of those arts and graces of life which are, after all, perhaps the finest and best part of the human character'.

To hold such a gift to be charitable, the court has to be convinced that the thing to be advanced is of artistic merit. The work of an established composer or social graces have been held to be meritorious, as the two cases previously mentioned indicate. Where there is any doubt as to the merit, however, the court may take the evidence of expert opinion. Once again, it does not matter whether the donor himself considers the matter of merit.

This was made very clear in the case of *Re Pinion* [1964] 1 All ER 890. Here, the testator left his studio and contents to be used as a museum to display his collection of art. Experts were of the opinion that the collection was virtually worthless and of no artistic merit whatever. One expert even expressed surprise that the testator had not managed to acquire even one item of value, if only by accident. The display of this collection could not be regarded as of any educational value and, accordingly, the gift failed as a charity. In the words of Harman LJ, 'I can conceive of no useful object to be served by foisting on the public this mass of junk.'

These purposes, which fitted rather awkwardly under the general educational heading, are now specifically articulated in the 2011 Act, which refers in s 3(1)(e) to 'the advancement of citizenship or community development'; and in (f) to 'the advancement of the arts, culture, heritage or science'. Science is thus formally added to the arts as a legitimate topic for promotion.

Trusts for the advancement of religion

Under previous law the term 'religion' was held, by Lord Parker in *Bowman v Secular Society* [1917] AC 406, to include any monotheistic theism or belief in one God. The Charities Act 2011, while preserving, in s 3(1)(c), the advancement of religion as a charitable purpose, formally recognises the wider scope of religion, by stating, in s 3(2)(a), that religion 'includes (i) a religion which involves belief in more than one god, and (ii) a religion which does not involve belief in a god'.

It should be noted that also included under this heading are satellite religious purposes, such as the maintenance of religious buildings. This extends even to tombs and monuments if they are part of the fabric of the church. Other satellite purposes include the support of sick and aged clergy: see *Re Forster* [1938] 3 All ER 767.

Despite the obvious implications for the issue of public benefit, it does not apparently matter that the members of the religious group are few or that, at least in the context of Christian sects, their theology is doubtful. In *Thornton v Howe* (1862) 54 ER 1042, a trust was established for the publication of the writings of Joanna Southcott, a religious mystic who believed herself to be with child by the Holy Ghost. This was held to be charitable. More recently, in *Re Watson* [1973] 3 All ER 678, a similar trust was established to publish books and tracts by Hobbs, the leader of a very small non-denominational Christian group. Though expert theologians considered the works to have no merit, the group were sincere in their beliefs.

Public benefit in religious charities

The public benefit requirement of religious trusts is met not from the numbers of persons who participate in the religious group or activity but rather that the community as a whole benefits from the presence of religious people in it. The law assumes that some religion is better than none and that religious people are an asset and an example to everyone. As Cross J said in *Neville Estates v Madden* [1961] 3 All ER 769: 'The court is entitled to assume that some benefit accrues to the public from attendance at places of worship of persons who live in this world and mix with their fellow citizens.'

In the guidelines on public benefit and the advancement of religion, the Commission expresses this in terms of a range of social benefits, the broadest of which are 'the promotion of social cohesion' and 'the inspiration religion can provide for others'.

The principle that public benefit derives from the presence of religious people in the community inevitably implies that religious people who are isolated from the community cannot benefit it. This was held to be so in *Gilmour v Coats* [1949] 1 All ER 848. A gift was given to a small contemplative order of nuns. This community was cloistered and had no contact with the outside world. The House of Lords held that the gift was not charitable. The necessary public benefit was not to be found in the prayers and intercession which the nuns made on behalf of members of the public who requested it; this was held to be 'manifestly not susceptible of proof in a court of law'. Nor was benefit to be found in the edifying example set by the nuns' spiritual life, nor in the fact that that religious life was open to any Catholic woman who might choose it.

In short, then, the public benefit derived from religious charities is not the direct one of membership of a religious group nor the spiritual benefit which believers presumably believe they derive from living a religious life. For a religious gift to be charitable, the public must be able to derive a benefit from the presence of religious people in the community.

The public accessibility argument seems also to have held sway in *Re Hetherington* [1989] 2 All ER 129, a case concerning the saying of masses for the soul of the testator. There had previously been doubts over the charitable status of such gifts since, as in *Gilmour*, the primary intended benefit, to the soul of the deceased, was not quantifiable in the courtroom. However, in *Hetherington*, Browne-Wilkinson V-C held, first, that the saying of masses for the dead was *prima facie* charitable as a religious purpose and, secondly, that the public benefit was provided by the fact of the masses being said in public. Once again, it was not that individuals might participate in the ceremonies, but rather that their public nature provided an edifying example of religious observance.

That purely private religious services are not charitable has been confirmed in *Re Le Cren Clarke* [1996] 1 All ER 715. The contrast between this case and *Re Hetherington* was that in *Re Hetherington* the services could be conducted either in public or in private, and the judge was entitled to take a benignant view of the gift and assume that they would be held in public. In *Re Le Cren Clarke*, on the other hand, evidence clearly indicated that the services were conducted in private, so there was no room for a benignant assumption where the facts were clear (though it was also held on the facts that the services were merely ancillary, so the gift as a whole was upheld as charitable). The case appears also to recognise faith healing as charitable within this heading of charity.

On the 'access' point, the Commission states that it would generally expect the religion to be open to anyone interested and that if some form of tithing (i.e. the members of the group paying some of their income for the church's support) were applied, there would be a need to ensure that the poor were not excluded. As in all public benefit, any exclusion could not be arbitrary and should relate to the fulfilment of the charities' purposes.

The advancement of health or the saving of lives

This will include, among other things, trusts formerly recognised under the heading of trusts for the sick and aged. Examples of valid charitable trusts for the aged or sick are numerous: *Re Robinson* [1950] 2 All ER 1148 provided for gifts to persons over 60 years of age; *Re Lewis* [1954] 3 All ER 257 provided for a gift of £100 each to ten blind girls and ten blind boys in Tottenham. Neither of these, it should be noted, contained an additional requirement of poverty. The absence of a poverty requirement means that the poor can even be excluded, by, for example, charging for the facilities provided. In *Re Resch's Will Trusts* [1969] 1 AC 514, a private hospital charging fees to patients was held to be charitable. (Note, however, that no private profit was made.) In *Joseph Rowntree Housing Association* v *A-G* [1983] 1 All ER 288, the question arose of whether such associations had to limit themselves to poor tenants in order to retain their charitable status. The court held not. However, this must be seen in light of the discussion about public benefit in fee-charging charities above.

Relief of the sick and aged includes ancillary purposes such as providing nurses' accommodation or facilities for the relatives of the critically ill.

Section 3(2)(b) states that this heading includes the prevention or relief of sickness, disease or human suffering. The Act also identifies as a charitable purpose the relief of those in need by reason of youth, age, ill health, disability, financial hardship or other disadvantage (section 3(1)(j)), which would cover this heading as well as poverty cases.

The advancement of animal welfare

This purpose had been identified as charitable prior to the 2006 Act and is now specifically referred to (in section 3(1)(k) of the 2011 Act, 'the advancement of animal welfare'). The benefit involved here is not that which animals may derive from being protected or cared for, but rather the indirect moral benefit to mankind. As Swinfen-Eady LJ observed in *Re Wedgewood* [1915] 1 Ch 113:

> A gift for the benefit and protection of animals tends to promote and encourage kindness towards them, to discourage cruelty, and to ameliorate the condition of brute creation, and thus to stimulate humane and generous sentiments in man towards the lower animals; and by these means promote feelings of humanity and morality generally, repress brutality, and thus elevate the human race.

Once again, it is the indirect benefit to the community as a whole which counts and so, as with religion, it is necessary that the example of kindly behaviour is a public one. An attempt to protect animals in isolation from humans thus lacks the necessary benefit, as emerged in *Re Grove-Grady* [1929] 1 Ch 557. In this case, the testator left money to provide 'a refuge or refuges for the preservation of all animals, birds or other creatures not human . . . so that they shall be safe from molestation and destruction by man'. Since man was entirely excluded, he had no opportunity to be elevated and so there was no public benefit. Valid animal charities have often been concerned with organisations such as animal hospitals and homes: it is submitted that organisations involved in wildlife preservation and nature reserves satisfy the benefit requirements because humanity, though controlled, is not excluded. There is also commonly a strong educational element. That the animals' own benefit is irrelevant is further stressed by the fact that human benefit outweighs animal welfare in matters such as vivisection and organisations opposed to vivisection are not charitable.

Sporting and recreational trusts

The 2011 Act refers specifically to the advancement of amateur sport as a charitable purpose (s 3(1)(g)), and expands on this in s 3(2)(d) by explaining that 'sport' means sports or games which promote health by involving physical or mental skill or exertion.

Purely recreational pastimes were not recognised as charitable purposes, and many trusts have failed to achieve charitable status because they have included the promotion of sports and recreation. Thus, in *IRC* v *City of Glasgow Police Athletic Association* [1953] 1 All ER 747, the Association had as its object 'to encourage and promote all forms of athletic sport and general pastimes'. Although it existed to improve the police force's efficiency, the inclusion of a merely recreational element was fatal to its charitable status. Advancement of amateur sport under the 2011 Act would not save it either since the purposes included 'pastimes' outside sport.

Fears for the charitable status of a number of organisations having a partly recreational purpose led to the passing of the Recreational Charities Act 1958, the amended provisions of which are now to be found in s 5 of the 2011 Act:

(1) It is charitable (and is to be treated as always having been charitable) to provide, or assist in the provision of, facilities for –
   (a) recreation, or
   (b) other leisure-time occupation,
   if the facilities are provided in the interests of social welfare.
(2) The requirement that the facilities are provided in the interests of social welfare cannot be satisfied if the basic conditions are not met.
(3) The basic conditions are –
   (a) that the facilities are provided with the object of improving the conditions of life for the persons for whom the facilities are primarily intended, and
   (b) that –
     (i) those persons have need of the facilities because of their youth, age, infirmity or disability, poverty, or social and economic circumstances, or
     (ii) the facilities are to be available to members of the public at large or to male, or to female, members of the public at large.
(5) Nothing in this section is to be treated as derogating from the public benefit requirement.

Subsection (4) then states that the section refers in particular to certain specific facilities such as village halls and women's institutes.

The purpose of the statute was therefore, in effect, to add to the categories of valid charity the provision of certain recreational facilities. It is to be noted that the general requirement of public benefit is not removed. This would presumably mean that recreational facilities for the disabled, while perhaps satisfying the requirement of social benefit, would not be for public benefit if the benefit were restricted to the employees of a particular firm. This would even be so if the intended beneficiaries were poor, despite *Dingle* v *Turner*, because a recreational facility would not be for the relief of poverty.

The section only validates those recreational facilities which are for 'social welfare'. Subsections (2) and (3) then state the minimum requirements for 'social welfare'. Clearly, the courts could decide that social welfare is lacking even where subsection (2) is satisfied: for example, if the court felt that the leisure activity were harmful, despite being intended to improve the conditions of life of the primary beneficiaries. These minimum requirements are intended to exclude facilities run for profit, which would not be provided with the object of improving conditions of life, but rather with the object of making money. Facilities open to the public generally must still be there for the object of improving the conditions of life of the primary beneficiaries. These beneficiaries may be the public at large or perhaps some more restricted group who it is anticipated will make most use of the facilities. Thus, a public bath-house will, as its name implies, be open to the public, but it is presumably intended primarily to improve the lives of those too poor to have their own baths. Whoever the primary beneficiaries are, it is clear that their condition of life can be improved even if they do not fall into one of the specified deprived categories identified in the Act. As Bridge LJ stated in *IRC* v *McMullen*: 'Hyde Park improves the condition of life of residents in Mayfair as much as for those in Pimlico or the Portobello Road.' This view was approved by the House of Lords in *Guild* v *IRC*.

Guild v IRC [1992] 2 All ER 10

In this case the testator left the residue of his estate to the Town Council of North Berwick 'for use in connection with the Sports Centre in North Berwick or some similar purpose in connection with sport'. At the time of his death the Town Council of North Berwick had ceased to exist, so the question arose whether the money could be applied cy-près (the principles of which are explained below). However, it was first necessary to decide whether the bequest was charitable. Was a sports centre provided in the interests of social welfare in accordance with the Act? Applying Bridge LJ's view, Lord Keith stated:

> The fact is that persons from all walks of life and all kinds of social circumstances may have their conditions of life improved by the provision of recreational facilities of a suitable nature.

Accordingly, the facilities here were so provided and the gift was charitable. It appears to follow that, where facilities are available to the general public, they will only fail for lack of social welfare if they are for private profit, or the facilities are 'unsuitable'. The House of Lords was satisfied that the facilities of a sports centre were 'suitable'. Only if access is restricted, it seems, must the class benefited, or at least the group primarily benefited, be within the deprived categories.

It should also be noted that the testator did not restrict the gift solely to the sports centre, but allowed it to be spent, in the alternative, on 'some similar purpose in connection with sport'. It was argued that this was too uncertain and might allow the money to be spent on purposes outside the Recreational Charities Act and hence not charitable. The House of Lords adopted the 'benignant' approach which is traditionally adopted by the English courts to the interpretation of charitable gifts. (Though this was a Scottish case, concerned with tax, the same approach must be adopted for England and Wales.) As a matter of construction of the gift, the testator must have intended something similar to the sports centre, and since the sports centre satisfied the requirements of the Act, then so would the 'similar' purpose. This will clearly be significant to the broader issue of certainty in charities, considered above, and also to the requirement of exclusive charitability.

Though this case could, presumably, now fall within the specific heading of the advancement of amateur sport, the general approach to interpretation is still valid.

Trusts for the benefit of localities

It has already been noted, in discussing public benefit, that the inhabitants of an area such as a town or parish can constitute a section of the public and thus satisfy the requirement of public benefit. This is subject to the Commission's guideline that if the benefit is to a section of the public, the opportunity to benefit must not be unreasonably limited either by geographical or other restrictions.

There is in addition a long-established rule of construction that if a trust is created for the benefit of a particular area, town, village, etc., it is treated as being for charitable purposes within that area, even though no specific purposes are stated. The most extreme example of this is probably *Re Smith* [1932] 1 Ch 153, where the gift was simply 'to my country, England'. This was treated as being limited exclusively to charitable purposes in England. It should be noted that this rule will not apply if the testator identifies specific purposes. If these are charitable then the gift will be charitable, but if the money is to be spent, or could be spent, on non-charitable purposes the gift will fail and the fact that it is for a particular place will not save it. Thus, in *Houston v Burns* [1918] AC 337, money was left for public, beneficial or charitable purposes in a particular parish. As will shortly be seen, public and beneficial purposes are not necessarily charitable and so the gift could not be a valid charitable one. The idea of locality has been contrasted with other attempts to restrict to racial or ethnic groups: such restrictions are not taken as implying charitable intent.

It appears, however, that the locality argument can apply to uphold a gift as charitable even where the class to be benefited is some defined group within the locality, rather than merely for the benefit of the locality as a whole, again subject to the Commission's guidelines. Thus, in *Goodman v Saltash Corporation* (1882) 7 App Cas 633, the House of Lords interpreted rights held by the corporation for the benefit of the freemen of the borough as being held on charitable trust. As Lord Selborne stated (at 643): 'A gift subject to a condition or trust for the benefit of the inhabitants of a parish or town, or of a particular class of such inhabitants, is (as I understand the law) a charitable trust.'

Whether the limitation is merely to a locality, or to a class within that locality, it must be stressed that, though no specific purpose is stated in the gift, the trustees can only apply it to charitable purposes within the class.

This point was brought out clearly in the case of *Peggs v Lamb* [1994] 2 All ER 15.

Peggs v Lamb [1994] 2 All ER 15

Since time immemorial the freemen of the Borough of Huntingdon had enjoyed grazing rights on certain common lands. In the course of time these rights had been commuted to money payments, and some of the lands had been sold off and the money reinvested, so that there was now a substantial money income available for distribution. At the same time the number of freemen (originally the voters of the borough, but since 1835 for most purposes an obsolete category of residents in the borough) had declined, so that by 1991 there were only 15 members of the class.

The issue before the court was the nature of the freemen's rights, and the possibility of amendment of the terms of the trust, which was registered as a charity.

After a lengthy discussion of the nature of the right, Morritt J, following *Goodman* v *Saltash*, concluded that the property was held on charitable trust. It followed, therefore, that the trustees must apply the funds to charitable purposes. The trustees had been in the habit of distributing the income equally among the freemen, so that, with the rise in income and the fall in the number of freemen, each freeman was now receiving about £30,000 per annum. In Morritt J's view this was clearly not a proper application of the funds. The vital point here was that, however the money was applied, it must be in fulfilment of the purpose of the gift. Morritt J recognised that in some cases an equal distribution might be a proper fulfilment of the purpose, but it was not so here:

> I do not think that the usage since time immemorial justifies the presumption that the trust existed for the purpose of benefiting the freemen individually, though the provision of such benefits might in suitable circumstances be the way in which the purpose is achieved. There is a difference between the purposes of the trust and the means by which the purpose may be achieved.

A trust whose purpose was equal distribution could not be charitable, because such a purpose could not come within the spirit and intendment of the preamble. Neither could the trust in this case be interpreted as a private trust, because it would have been void for perpetuity.

The purpose of the charitable trust must be fulfilled in some way other than by equal distribution, and yet the rights were clearly restricted to the class of freemen, which by 1991 was very small. The terms of the trust were therefore amended (see below, under 'Cy-près'). It seems rather unlikely that the anomalous and anachronistic class of freemen would constitute a section of the public under present guidelines, but the issue of equal distribution is still valid and would apply even if the class were, for example, the inhabitants of Huntingdon.

Charities, political purposes and activities

Objective
5

A political trust is one which has as its purpose the changing of the law. Thus, in *National Anti-Vivisection Society* v *IRC* [1947] 2 All ER 217, one of the purposes of the society being to change the law regarding vivisection, the court held that it could not be a charity. One former reason for not holding political trusts to be charitable, as indicated by Russell LJ in *Incorporated Council for Law Reporting for England and Wales* v *A-G* [1971] 3 All ER 1029, is that such a purpose could not have been contemplated when the Statute of 1601 was passed. The more conventional reasoning, applied in the *National Anti-Vivisection Society* case, is that given by Lord Parker in *Bowman* v *Secular Society* [1917] AC 406:

> [A] trust for the attainment of political objects has always been held invalid, not because it is illegal . . . but because the court has no means of judging whether a proposed change in the law will or will not be for the public benefit.

It was assumed, by Lord Wright in the *National Anti-Vivisection Society* case, that the courts must not usurp the role of the legislature; the courts cannot decide whether a change in the law is beneficial, and so must start from the assumption that the law as it stands is correct. The term 'political', therefore, 'was not limited to party political measures but would cover activities directed to influence the legislature to change the law in order to promote or effect the views advocated by the society.'

The line between seeking to treat society's ills and seeking to cure them through legislation is a difficult one to draw, but the Charity Commission has indicated that charities who indulge in political activity which is more than merely ancillary to their main purposes risk loss of charitable status. It is also clear that political activity includes activity in relation to foreign governments, as in the case of Amnesty International, which seeks to influence foreign government policy: for example, by seeking the release of political prisoners and banning torture. It was held, in *McGovern v A-G* [1981] 3 All ER 493, not to be charitable.

In its report, 'Private Action, Public Benefit', which led to the passing of the Charities Act 2006, the Government Strategy Unit recognised the important potential role of charities as advocates of social change, and suggested the current law was unclear as to what activities are permitted.

The current guidelines from the Commission state that a charity cannot exist for a political purpose, which is any purpose directed at furthering the interests of any political party, or securing or opposing a change in the law, policy or decisions either in this country or abroad. Nevertheless, campaigning and political activity can be legitimate and valuable activities for charities to undertake, but only in the context of supporting the delivery of their charitable purposes. Thus charities can campaign for a change in the law, policy or decisions where such change would support the charity's purposes. An example would be campaigning for an increase in social security benefits, if this would further the charity's objective of relief of poverty. Further guidance can be found on this on the Commission's website: **www.charitycommission.gov.uk.**

The crucial distinction is between having political aims, which could not be charitable, and having charitable aims, which one might seek to promote through political activities, which could be within a charity's function.

A further potential issue for charities is that, should a charity mount a campaign, let us suppose, for a change in the law in pursuit of its charitable objectives, and if that legal change becomes a 'political issue' forming part of a political party's agenda, the charity may be regarded as a 'third party campaigner' under the Transparency of Lobbying, Non-Party Campaigning and Trade Union Administration Act 2014. This will mean that the charity must register with the Electoral Commission and will be subject to limitations on its expenditure on its campaign. This will impose an additional layer of bureaucracy on charities.

Exclusively charitable requirement

The general rule

Objective
6

Since, to achieve charitable status, a gift's purposes must fall within the definition of charity, it follows that a gift cannot be charitable if some of its purposes are not charitable. It has already been seen, for example, that the inclusion of political purposes will prevent an organisation from being charitable (*McGovern v A-G*), even though the organisation may have other purposes which by themselves would be charitable. Settlors who identify a number of purposes for their gifts must therefore be particularly careful to ensure that all these purposes are charitable, otherwise the whole gift may fail: if a trust is created for several purposes, it will not usually be possible to save the charitable ones and reject the others. It is therefore customary to include some saving clause to the effect that the gift is to take effect only in so far as the purposes are recognised as charitable. Even where no specific purposes are stated, the settlor must ensure that the money can be spent only on charity. A direction that money be spent on 'charitable purposes' is, of course, perfectly valid since there is no need to identify purposes with the certainty required for other trusts, but, if some other general adjective such as 'benevolent' is used, this will normally fail as a charity: benevolence is not synonymous with charity. Thus the Privy Council, in *A-G of the Cayman Islands* v *Wahr-Hansen* [2000] 3 All ER 642, has held that gifts to 'organisations or institutions operating for the public good' and acting 'for the good or for the benefit of mankind' were not exclusively charitable purposes; the words used were wider than charity. It is also a general rule that a limitation to, for example, 'charitable and deserving' is effective whereas a gift to 'charitable or public' is not, for in the first case the money must go to charitable purposes whereas in the second it can go to public purposes which are not necessarily charitable. (Indeed, the phrase seems to recognise that the two words are not the same.) See *Re Sutton* (1884) 28 Ch D 464 and *Blair* v *Duncan* [1902] AC 37 respectively. Another example is the benignant approach adopted in *Guild* v *IRC*, where the phrase 'or some similar purpose' was held to imply 'some similar *charitable* purpose', since the primary purpose was charitable (see further under 'Sporting and recreational trusts', above). Such cases must be seen as matters of construction on the words of each case, however.

To this exclusivity rule there are, however, several exceptions.

Ancillary purposes

A trust will not fail as a charity if the non-charitable purpose is merely ancillary to the main, charitable one. This is inevitably a matter of degree. It is also a matter of the function of the non-charitable purpose. It appears from *McGovern* v *A-G* (above), in the words of Slade J, that:

> [T]he distinction is between (a) those non-charitable activities authorised by the trust instrument which are merely incidental or subsidiary to a charitable purpose and (b) those non-charitable activities so authorised which themselves form part of the trust purpose. In the latter but not the former case the reference to non-charitable activities will deprive the trust of its charitable status.

Thus, the political activities of Amnesty International discussed above fell into the second category and so the organisation could not be charitable.

Whether a purpose is merely ancillary is very much a matter of considering the underlying purposes of the gift, viewing the gift as a whole. Thus, in *Re Le Cren Clarke* [1996] 1 All ER 715, the testatrix left her estate 'for the furtherance of the Spiritual Work now carried on by us'. The context made it clear that the testatrix was thinking of the faith healing which she and a small group of friends participated in: this was the essence of the work referred to, and the religious services she and her friends held which, being private, were not in themselves charitable, were merely ancillary to that essence.

Severance

Depending upon the wording used by the settlor, it is sometimes possible to separate charitable and non-charitable purposes and divide the fund between them, or in other words to sever the charitable part from the non-charitable. This will allow the charitable part to take effect validly, provided it does not fail on some other ground. The validity of the non-charitable part will then be determined by the application of the rules relating to non-charitable trusts or may possibly take effect as some other form of transfer. Severance is only possible, however, where it is clear from the wording of the gift that the donor intended some form of division of the fund; it cannot apply where the donor simply lists a number of purposes or beneficiaries to which a single fund is to be applied or where the trustees are allowed to choose from a range of purposes. Thus, a common form may be to state that such of the fund as is needed may be applied to a charitable purpose and the residue be applied to something else. The question arises of how the fund is to be divided between the charity and the non-charitable gift. The *prima facie* rule is for an equal division based on the maxim that equality is equity. Thus, in **Salusbury v Denton** (1857) 3 K & J 529, money was left for the founding of a charity school and for the testator's relatives. No indication was given as to the division of the fund, so the court ordered equal division. Often, however, such a division is impractical and indeed is clearly not the donor's intention, as in the example given above where only the residue is to be spent on the non-charitable purpose. The court still has to make a division and must find sufficient evidence upon which to make that division.

Re Coxon [1948] Ch 747

In this case, the testator left £200,000 to the City of London for charitable purposes but also provided that out of this fund the members of the board of trustees were to be paid an attendance fee of £1 at meetings and that £100 be spent on an annual banquet for the trustees. The court held that equal division was not appropriate and decided that the maximum amount needed to meet these non-charitable costs be set aside and that the rest of the fund was applied exclusively to charity.

Where the amount to be spent on charity cannot be quantified the whole gift will fail as a charity, though, as a matter of construction, where the gift is for a charitable and a non-charitable purpose, if the non-charitable purpose fails the whole fund can then be applied to charity. It is also the case that where money is given to a charity with the understanding that the charity will maintain the donor's tomb the gift is regarded as exclusively charitable even though part of the fund will be spent on that non-charitable purpose. (Note that there must not be an obligation on the charity to maintain the tomb, though the continuance of the gift may be dependent on their doing so.)

Charitable Trusts (Validation) Act 1954

The function of this legislation is to protect certain charitable trusts whose validity had been brought into question by the decision in the following case.

Chichester Diocesan Fund v Simpson [1944] 2 All ER 60

In this case the testator had left his residuary estate for 'such charitable institutions or other charitable or benevolent object or objects as his executors might in their absolute discretion select'. The use of the term 'charitable' or 'benevolent' was fatal since it permitted the trustees to select benevolent purposes which might not be charitable within the meaning of that term. The House of Lords stressed that 'charity' had a technical, legal meaning and that 'benevolent', besides being uncertain, did not have the same meaning. The testator's use of the term benevolent may indicate that he intended the money to go to purposes that were charitable 'in the popular sense', but that sense was not necessarily the same as the legal meaning. Thus, the gift failed as it was not exclusively charitable.

This decision called into question the validity of a large number of trusts previously assumed to be valid charities and so the Charitable Trusts (Validation) Act 1954 was passed to protect them. It is of declining importance since it applies only to trusts taking effect before 16 December 1952. It therefore preserves existing trusts but not later ones, presumably on the grounds that the drafters of later trusts and gifts should be aware of the problem and take account of it.

The Act applies where the terms of the gift are such that the money can be applied exclusively to charitable objects but can be applied to other, non-charitable objects as well. Such a provision is referred to in the Act as an 'imperfect trust provision'. The Act further states:

> any imperfect trust provision contained in an instrument taking effect before the sixteenth day of December 1952, shall have, and be deemed to have had, effect in relation to any disposition or covenant to which this Act applies –
>
> (a) as respects the period before the commencement of the Act, as if the whole of the declared objects were charitable; and
> (b) as respects the period after that commencement, as if the provision had required the property to be held or applied for the declared objects in so far only as they authorise use for charitable objects.

In other words, whatever these charities were spending their money on before the date of commencement is deemed in retrospect to be charitable. After the date of commencement they are allowed to spend it only on charitable purposes, whatever the terms of the trust say.

The Act does not apply where the terms of the trust divide the fund between charitable and non-charitable purposes (though severance might apply here). It applies only where there is an undivided fund which by its terms can be applied exclusively to charity. This will be clear if the settlor refers to charity specifically or lists purposes including charitable ones. A problem arises where charity is not specifically mentioned. It is submitted that provided there is reference, express or implied, to charitable and non-charitable purposes, this will be sufficient to bring the trust under the Act. Charity may be inferred from phrases such as 'charitable or benevolent' or even 'benevolent or welfare purposes', as in *Re Wykes* [1961] Ch 229. It should be added, however, that in *Re Gillingham Bus Disaster Fund* [1958] 2 All ER 749, the Court of Appeal was divided on whether the reference to charity needed to be express rather than implied.

The Act was considered in *Ulrich v Treasury Solicitor* [2005] 1 All ER 1059. This case concerned a trust deed of 1927 established for the benefit of a class of beneficiaries: the employees of a company and their families. The trust was not specifically limited to the relief of poverty, and it was therefore argued that it was not a charitable trust and that it did not have a sufficient flavour of charity to be an 'imperfect trust provision' under the Act. Hart J applied a broad construction to the wording of the Act and held that it was not confined to trusts where charitable purposes were expressly stated, but included cases where the purposes could be construed as including charitable ones. It was possible within the broad wording of this trust to apply the money to a charitable purpose, the relief of poverty, and the money had so been applied. Accordingly it fell within the Act and so would be construed as for charitable purposes only.

Discrimination

The effects of anti-discrimination legislation on charity should be noted.

The Equality Act 2010 identifies certain 'protected characteristics' and states that it is illegal to discriminate against people on the grounds of these characteristics. The characteristics are: age, disability, gender reassignment, marriage and civil partnership, pregnancy and maternity, race, religion or belief, sex and sexual orientation. Broadly speaking, therefore, it is illegal to treat people less favourably, or more favourably, because of these characteristics. Under s 193 of the Act, however, charities can sometimes provide exceptions to this principle. A charity limiting its benefits to people of a particular race would be in breach of the principle and s 193 provides that where the class to be benefited is defined with reference to colour that reference is to be disregarded, and the charity is to be available to benefit the class which results when the reference to colour is ignored (see below for the application cy-près of charities previously restricted to certain races). The Act does allow a charity's benefits to be limited to persons with other protected characteristics. It is thus possible to have a charity whose benefits are limited to a single-sex group or persons of a particular sexual orientation, or to limit its membership to those professing certain religious beliefs (as long as, in that case, this requirement existed before 2005). This limitation, under s 193(2), must be a proportionate means of achieving a legitimate aim of the charity, or must be imposed for the purpose of preventing or compensating for a disadvantage linked to the protected characteristic. Other forms of limitation may be approved by the appropriate minister of state.

Administration of charities

Objective 7

For more on trusteeship generally see Chapters 15 and 16.

The general rules as to the administration of trusts and the nature of trusteeship, its powers and duties, will be considered later. Many of these rules apply to charitable trusts as to private ones. It is the purpose of this section to consider those rules which are particular to charities and the bodies which have special functions in relation to charities. Regulations regarding the administration of charities, particularly relating to the Charity Commission, are now to be found in the Charities Act 2011. It is not intended to deal with administration in detail, but to outline the main agencies of charitable administration.

The principal authorities having a role in the functioning of charities are: (1) the Attorney-General; (2) the trustees; (3) the Charity Commission; and (4) the Official Custodian for Charities.

The Attorney-General

The Attorney-General represents the Crown as *parens patriae*, which means that he appears in any proceedings on behalf of the charitable objects or potential beneficiaries. He will be joined as a party to any action concerning charities, he may act against charity trustees in any dispute as to the existence of a valid charity and he has the power to act to recover charity property from third parties. The nature of his role as representative of the objects of charity was discussed in **Brooks v Richardson** [1986] 1 All ER 952, where the court quoted with approval *Tudor on Charities*:

> By reason of his duty as the Sovereign's representative protecting all the persons interested in the charity funds, the Attorney-General is as a general rule a necessary party to charity proceedings. He represents the beneficial interest; it follows that in all proceedings in which the beneficial interest has to be before the court, he must be a party. He represents all the objects of the charity, who are in effect parties through him.

Trustees

Charity trustees, as has already been stated in the introduction, are defined in s 177 of the Charities Act 2011 as persons having the general control and management of the administration of the charity. In general, they are in the same position as trustees of private trusts, except that they do not have to act unanimously, but may act by majority. There are significant restrictions upon who may be a charity trustee. Section 178 provides a long list of those who are excluded, including those convicted of offences of dishonesty or deception, bankrupts and those who have made a composition with creditors, those who have been removed from charity trusteeship by the Commission or the court and those who are disqualified from company directorship. To assist them in enforcing such ineligibility, the Commission keeps a register of those removed from office, and it is also empowered to waive the disqualification upon application from the person disqualified. The Act also makes it a criminal offence to act as a trustee while disqualified.

In addition to the general powers and duties of trustees, charity trustees have specific duties which include seeking registration, informing the Commission of any changes in the charity, and informing it if the charity ceases to exist. Their powers include the right to seek the advice of the Commission on any matter to do with the charity. They may be removed by the Commission for misconduct or mismanagement.

Charity trustees must, of course, comply with charity law but, in reaching decisions and exercising discretions, it has recently been emphasised that trustees must show self-reliance, rather than depending upon the Charity Commission, which now appears to be taking more of a back seat and was, in any case, never directly responsible for the running of charities. Thus the Upper Tribunal in *The Independent Schools Council* v *Charity Commission* [2011] UKUT 421 (TCC); [2012] 1 All ER 127 (discussed above at p. 224) emphasised that it was for the trustees to determine whether their charity was complying with the requirements of public benefit. The Charity Commission itself has stated that 'an effective charity is run by a clearly identifiable board or trustee body that has the right balance of skills and experience, acts in the best interests of the charity and its beneficiaries, understands its responsibilities and has systems in place to exercise them properly' (*Hallmarks of an Effective Charity*).

Charity accounts, reports and returns

Part 8 of the 2011 Act requires trustees to keep accounts in prescribed form, to prepare an annual statement of accounts, to have these audited in the case of large charities, and to prepare and send to the Commission an annual report detailing the charity's activities for the year and an annual return for each financial year. The annual report will be available for public inspection. Failure to file an annual report or return is a summary offence. The Commission has power in some circumstances to dispense with these requirements. For unincorporated charities with an annual income of less than £250,000 there is a simplified accounting procedure.

The Charity Commission

The office of Charity Commissioner was abolished in 2006 and replaced by a body corporate called the Charity Commission, to which all of the Commissioners' functions were transferred. The Charities Act 2011 s 14 sets out the Commission's five general objectives, which are:

(a) the public confidence objective,

(b) the public benefit objective,

(c) the compliance objective,

(d) the charitable resources objective, and

(e) the accountability objective.

These objectives are defined as follows:

1. The public confidence objective is to increase public trust and confidence in charities.
2. The public benefit objective is to promote awareness and understanding of the operation of the public benefit requirement.
3. The compliance objective is to promote compliance by charity trustees with their legal obligations in exercising control and management of the administration of their charities.
4. The charitable resources objective is to promote the effective use of charitable resources.
5. The accountability objective is to enhance the accountability of charities to donors, beneficiaries and the general public.

The general functions of the Commission, as set out in s 15 of the 2011 Act, mirror the objectives and include the following:

1. Determining whether institutions are or are not charities.
2. Encouraging and facilitating the better administration of charities.
3. Identifying and investigating apparent misconduct or mismanagement in the administration of charities and taking remedial or protective action in connection with misconduct or mismanagement therein.
4. Determining whether public collections certificates should be issued, and remain in force, in respect of public charitable collections.
5. Obtaining, evaluating and disseminating information in connection with the performance of any of the Commission's functions or meeting any of its objectives.
6. Giving information or advice, or making proposals, to any Minister of the Crown on matters relating to any of the Commission's functions or meeting any of its objectives.

These also include the maintenance of a register of charities and the production of the annual report.

Annual report

Under Schedule 1, paragraph 11 of the 2011 Act, the Commission must produce a report annually on its activities, to be placed before Parliament. This has proved to be a useful source of information on the current thinking of the Commission, which is very important to those bodies seeking recognition as charities.

Institution of inquiries

Section 46 permits the Commission to institute inquiries from time to time into particular charities or groups of charities. Such inquiries may be made by the Commission itself or by a person appointed by it. Such inquiries can take many forms: they may be public or private, and may consist of anything from an exchange of letters to a formal inquiry under oath. In carrying out this inquiry the powers of the Commission to obtain information are very wide. It may direct any person to furnish accounts and written statements and answers to questions and to verify these by statutory declaration. It may require such persons to furnish copies of any relevant documents and if necessary to attend in person to give evidence. Evidence may be taken on oath. The Commission also has wide discretion to publish the report of the inquiry, or its results, in such form as it thinks fit.

Apart from the powers in connection with inquiries, s 52 also gives the Commission wide powers to require documents to be produced, and to take copies of them, and to have furnished to it any information relating to any charity relevant to the discharge of its functions.

Powers to act for the protection of charities

If, having made an inquiry under s 46, the Commission is satisfied that there has been misconduct or mismanagement in the administration of a charity, or that it is necessary to act to protect charity property, it has wide powers under sections 76 to 85 to act for the protection of charities. Among other things, it may suspend (for up to 12 months) any trustee or officer of the charity, may order the appointment of additional trustees, may vest charity property in the Official Custodian, may order anyone holding charity property not to part with it without its approval, may order any debtor of the charity not to pay money to the charity without its approval, may restrict the transactions which may be entered into on the charity's behalf without its approval, and may appoint a receiver and manager in respect of the property and affairs of the charity. In addition, if it is satisfied both that there has been mismanagement etc. and that it is necessary to protect charity property, the Commission may, by its own motion, remove trustees, officers or employees, or establish a scheme for the charity's administration. The Commission has indicated that any decision to intervene will depend upon its perception of the extent of the risk to charitable assets, to vulnerable beneficiaries or to public trust and confidence in the sector. If there is a sufficient risk, the Commission will take proportionate action.

Removal of trustees

Section 80 also allows the Charity Commission to remove trustees on the grounds of bankruptcy, mental incapacity, failure on the trustee's part to act or declare his willingness or unwillingness to act, or on the ground of the trustee's absence from the country, when such absence impedes the proper administration of the charity. Trustees removed under this section are thus ineligible and liable to prosecution (see 'Trustees', above). The Commission may also appoint trustees either to replace ones removed or, where there are no or insufficient trustees or where the Commission deems it necessary, to increase the number of trustees.

Concurrent jurisdiction with the court

Under s 69, the Commission has concurrent jurisdiction with the High Court to make orders appointing or removing trustees and employees of charities and vesting and transferring property, as well as powers to establish schemes for charity administration (the term 'scheme' is discussed further below). It may only exercise its powers under this section upon the application of the charity or the Attorney-General or, in the case of schemes, on an order of the court. In the case of very small charities (with an income of less than £500 p.a.) it may act upon the application of the charity trustees, or of any person interested in the charity, or, where the charity is local, of any two or more inhabitants of the local area. It may proceed as if it had received an application from the charity itself in cases where the trusteeship is vacant or the trustees absent or incapable, or where a sufficient number of the trustees apply. (Ordinarily, a majority of trustees would have to agree to the charity's applying.) It may also act to establish a scheme in the case of a charity where the Commission is satisfied that the trustees should have applied for such a scheme and have not, and then only if 40 years have elapsed since the date of the charity's foundation: this is a way in which very old and useless charities can be changed and their funds reallocated, even if the trustees refuse to act.

The Commission is also required to give notice to the trustees before exercising any jurisdiction under this section.

Registration

Section 29 of the Charities Act 2011, provides:

(1) There continues to be a register of charities, to be kept by the Commission in such manner as it thinks fit.

(2) The register must contain –

(a) the name of every charity registered in accordance with section 30, and

(b) such other particulars of, and such other information relating to, every such charity as the Commission thinks fit.

Section 35 further provides:

(1) If a charity required to be registered by virtue of section 30(1) is not registered, the charity trustees must –

(a) apply to the Commission for the charity to be registered, and

(b) supply the Commission with the required documents and information.

(2) The required documents and information are –

(a) copies of the charity's trusts or (if they are not set out in any extant document) particulars of them,

(b) such other documents or information as may be prescribed by regulations made by the Minister, and

(c) such other documents or information as the Commission may require for the purposes of the application.

(3) If an institution is for the time being registered, the charity trustees (or the last charity trustees) must –

(a) notify the Commission if the institution ceases to exist, or if there is any change in its trusts or in the particulars of it entered in the register, and

(b) so far as appropriate, supply the Commission with particulars of any such change and copies of any new trusts or alterations of the trusts.

Thus, it is the duty of the Commission to maintain the register and of the charity trustees to apply for registration and to inform the Commission if the charity is wound up. Certain excepted charities are permitted, but not required, to register.

The effect of registration and non-registration is set out in s 37(1):

An institution is, for all purposes other than rectification of the register, conclusively presumed to be or to have been a charity at any time when it is or was on the register.

The Act also provides for mechanisms for interested parties to object to registration or to apply for deregistration, indicating that the decision whether to grant registration is the Commission's, subject to appeal to the Tribunal. In practice, therefore, it is the presence of an organisation on the register which determines whether it is charitable, with all the advantages that that entails. The view of the Commission on what is charitable is therefore crucial.

There are certain charities which are not required to register. These fall into three categories. First, those referred to in the 2011 Act as exempt charities, which are listed in Schedule 3 to the Act, and include such bodies as universities, the British Museum, the Church Commissioners and Friendly Societies, among others. These bodies may not be registered and are not subject to the Commission's supervision, being expressly excluded from ss 46 and 18, for example, as they are accountable in other ways. Secondly, charities whose gross income does not exceed £100,000 and which are excepted by the Commission or by ministerial regulation are not required to register, but are otherwise subject to the Act. Thirdly, very small charities, whose total annual income does not exceed £5,000, are similarly not required to register, but are otherwise subject to the Act.

Advice to charity trustees

Section 110 provides that the Commission may, on written application of any charity trustee, give its opinion or advice on any matter affecting the performance of the trustee's duties as such. It also states that a trustee acting in accordance with the opinion or advice of the Commission shall be deemed, as regards his responsibility for so acting, to have acted in accordance with his trust. The trustee will therefore not be in breach of trust if he follows the advice, unless he knew or had reasonable grounds to suspect that the advice was given in ignorance of material facts or that a decision of the court had been obtained or was pending on the issue.

The Official Custodian for Charities

This officer of the Commission, designated by it to act as such, acts as trustee for charities in accordance with directions from the Commission. Charitable property may therefore be vested in him, but he has no powers of management which may be exercised by other trustees. His function is thus simply to provide greater security in respect of trust property. In particular, either the Commission, under s 76, or the court, under s 90, may order that charity property be vested in him.

Appeals

The Charities Act 2011 provides that decisions of the Commission are appealable to the 'Tribunal'. This body was created by the Tribunals, Courts and Enforcement Act 2007 to bring together the jurisdiction of a large number of tribunals previously created for specific purposes or under specific legislation (including the Charity Tribunal created under the Charities Act 2006). It consists of two divisions, the First-tier Tribunal and the Upper Tribunal.

> (2) The Tribunal has jurisdiction to hear and determine –
> (a) such appeals and applications as may be made to the Tribunal in accordance with Chapter 2, or any other enactment, in respect of decisions, orders or directions of the Commission, and
> (b) such matters as may be referred to the Tribunal in accordance with Chapter 3 by the Commission or the Attorney General.

Decisions of the First-tier tribunal may be appealed to the Upper Tribunal, and from there to the Court of Appeal.

Details of those decisions of the Commission which may be appealed to the Tribunal are set out in Schedule 6 to the 2011 Act, and include decisions regarding registration of a charity, disapproval or removal of a charity trustee, decisions to institute inquiries and a wide range of other orders by the Commission. Those who may appeal include the charity involved, and those who are the trustees of the charity.

Schemes and cy-près

Schemes

The High Court and, under the Charities Act 2011 s 69, the Charity Commission, have a concurrent jurisdiction to establish schemes for the administration of charitable funds. Thus, it may be that money has been left by will for a charitable purpose without any arrangement being stipulated for the fund to be managed, or the testator may not have identified a specific charitable purpose. Thus, a scheme may be approved to appoint new trustees, unless the identity of the trustees is crucial to the testator's intentions (*Re Lysaght* [1965] 2 All ER 888), or to resolve administrative difficulties arising out of uncertainty (*Re Gott* [1944] 1 All ER 293). A scheme may even be ordered by the court where this would defeat a gift over, though the court declined to exercise this power in *Re Hanbey's Wills Trust* [1955] 3 All ER 874.

In all these cases some arrangement will need to be made if the money is to be used effectively and it will be necessary for the court or the Commission to approve an arrangement for this. Alternatively, the trustees may wish to extend their powers of investment to increase the yield of the fund or to consolidate different funds held separately; again, a scheme will need to be approved. It will be recognised that in this case a form of variation is taking place. In its most extreme form, the trustees may wish to change the purposes to which the fund is put: this will require application of the doctrine of cy-près, explained below, which will again be effected by a scheme. In general, the Commission cannot itself institute a scheme, but may act when the trustees apply to it, and occasionally even when the trustees do not so apply (see 'Concurrent jurisdiction with the court', above). The courts may direct a scheme as a result of proceedings, for example, for the determination of the validity of the charity, and will commonly then refer the matter to the Commission to draw up the details of the scheme.

A relatively straightforward example of a scheme can be seen in *Re Robinson* [1923] 2 Ch 332, where the terms of a religious charity required the preacher to wear a black gown during services. The 'scheme' was simply to remove that stipulation from the gift, and this was duly done.

The term 'scheme' can therefore cover any arrangement or amendment to the charity, from changing its name, up to a major reorganisation of its funds or even changing its purposes. This latter change is referred to as application cy-près and requires further consideration.

Cy-près doctrine

The meaning of application cy-près

Objective
8

To apply funds cy-près is to apply them to purposes as near as possible to the purposes originally specified. A number of preliminary points may be made before considering the details of this principle. First, the trustees of a charity, like the trustees of a private trust, have the duty to fulfil the donor's wishes: if, for example, a testator leaves property for a charitable purpose, it will be the duty of the trustees to apply it to that purpose. If a charitable organisation has certain specified charitable purposes, then those having control of its funds must apply them to those purposes. To apply funds cy-près is therefore a form of variation and will require the sanction of the courts or the Charity Commission. Secondly, the doctrine will apply only to funds devoted to charity, so it is a prerequisite that the original gift, or organisation, is charitable.

Where an express private trust fails, the money or other subject matter of the trust is held on resulting trust for the donor. Where a charitable trust fails at the outset, the property may either be held on resulting trust for the donor or in certain circumstances the property may be applied cy-près to another charitable purpose. Failure at the outset, or initial failure as it is usually known, arises where for some reason the gift can never take effect or, for reasons discussed below, it is felt inappropriate that it should. The cy-près doctrine applies also to subsequent failure where a valid charitable fund or organisation has existed but, on one of a number of possible grounds, is wound up and the funds applied to other charitable purposes.

Conditions for the application of funds cy-près

Until the passing of the Charities Act 1960, these rules could apply only where the original purpose had actually failed or at least was impracticable and it therefore could be realistically said to have 'failed'. The Charities Act 1960 extended the application of the rules to situations not of failure but rather of convenience, in effect giving trustees a discretion to seek to apply the money in other ways on the grounds of efficiency. While this should no doubt have led to the more effective use of charitable funds, it has created difficulty in the application of cy-près rules and it is submitted that it is necessary to consider the position before 1960 and then look at the effect of the statutory amendments.

Before the Charities Act 1960

Prior to the Charities Act 1960, the circumstances where charitable funds could be applied cy-près were extremely limited. Cy-près could arise only where the original purpose was impossible or impracticable.

A-G v *Ironmongers Company* (1834) 2 My & K 576

In this case, money had been devoted to 'the redemption of British slaves in Turkey and Barbary'. By 1833 there were no such slaves and it was felt that 'the altered circumstances of those countries left little or no demand for the bounty of the testator', and, accordingly, Lord Brougham ordered the money to be applied cy-près. It will be noted that the failure was subsequent. The fund had presumably been applied to the original purpose for many years (the gift was originally made in 1723) but now there was no longer any use for it. The same principle applied to initial failure, that is that the purpose had to be impossible or impracticable, but in this case that would be decided when the gift was originally made. Thus, to give money in a will to the redemption of slaves in 1833 would have failed at the outset.

The requirement of impossibility or impracticability clearly restricted the opportunity for application cy-près, though the courts interpreted the phrase quite widely. For instance, in **Re Dominion Students' Hall Trust** [1947] Ch 183, the object of the charity was to provide a community of citizenship, culture and tradition among members of the British Community of Nations and to that end it maintained a student hostel in Bloomsbury. The terms of the trust required, however, that the benefits be limited to students of European origin. Cy-près was ordered to remove the racial bar on the ground that to continue it would render the trust impracticable. Evershed J pointed out:

> It is not necessary to go to the length of saying that the original scheme is absolutely impracticable. Were it so, it would not be possible to establish in the present case that the charity could not be carried on at all if it continued to be so limited as to exclude coloured members of the Empire . . . it is said that to retain the condition [of excluding non-whites], so far from furthering the charity's main object, might defeat it and would be liable to antagonise those students, both white and coloured, whose support and goodwill it is the purpose of the charity to sustain.

Effect of the Charities Act 1960

The Charities Act 1960 substantially extended the situations in which charitable funds may be applied cy-près. It should be stressed, however, that it amended only the requirement of impossibility or impracticability: other conditions for application cy-près, which will be considered later, still apply as before the 1960 Act. The Charities Act 2011, s 62, now provides:

(1) Subject to subsection (3), the circumstances in which the original purposes of a charitable gift can be altered to allow the property given or part of it to be applied cy-près are –
   (a) where the original purposes, in whole or in part –
       (i) have been as far as may be fulfilled, or
       (ii) cannot be carried out, or not according to the directions given and to the spirit of the gift,
   (b) where the original purposes provide a use for part only of the property available by virtue of the gift,
   (c) where –
       (i) the property available by virtue of the gift, and
       (ii) other property applicable for similar purposes,
       can be more effectively used in conjunction, and to that end can suitably, regard being had to the appropriate considerations, be made applicable to common purposes,
   (d) where the original purposes were laid down by reference to –
       (i) an area which then was but has since ceased to be a unit for some other purpose, or
       (ii) a class of persons or an area which has for any reason since ceased to be suitable, regard being had to the appropriate considerations, or to be practical in administering the gift, or
   (e) where the original purposes, in whole or in part, have, since they were laid down –
       (i) been adequately provided for by other means,
       (ii) ceased, as being useless or harmful to the community or for other reasons, to be in law charitable, or
       (iii) ceased in any other way to provide a suitable and effective method of using the property available by virtue of the gift, regard being had to the appropriate considerations.
(2) In subsection (1) 'the appropriate considerations' means –
   (a) (on the one hand) the spirit of the gift concerned, and
   (b) (on the other) the social and economic circumstances prevailing at the time of the proposed alteration of the original purposes.
(3) Subsection (1) does not affect the conditions which must be satisfied in order that property given for charitable purposes may be applied cy-près except in so far as those conditions require a failure of the original purposes.

Subsequent failure

It was undoubtedly the principal objective of this section to allow reallocation of funds in useless charities to more effective purposes and to that end most of the instances provided for are cases of 'subsequent failure'. It enables trustees to apply for cy-près and avoids the necessity for continuing pointless charities which were not actually impossible. In cases where money had already been applied to charity, it would continue to be so applied and the court or the Charity Commission will approve a suitable scheme for the use of the money on new purposes. There is no question in such a case of the next of kin of the original donor recovering the money, for, as Romer LJ said in *Re Wright* [1954] 2 All ER 98: 'Once money has been effectually dedicated to charity, whether in pursuance of a general or a particular charitable intent, the testator's next of kin or residuary legatees are for ever excluded.' The issue that the court will be required to determine is whether the situation before it falls within the provisions of s 62. The approach to this has been to view s 62 in the light of the 'spirit of the gift', which is taken to mean the basic intention underlying the gift. Thus, in *Peggs v Lamb* (considered above under 'Trusts for the benefit of localities'), Morritt J, having concluded that the rights of the freemen were held on charitable trust, took the view that it would not be necessary to use s 13 of the 1993 Act (what is now s 62, quoted above) merely to declare the terms of the trust as they then were, i.e. general charitable purposes among the freemen. (He felt entitled to assume these purposes, even though the original grant of the common land was very ancient and any documentation had been lost.)

The class of freemen was now, however, very small (15 members), so that it was doubtful if it still constituted the public or a section of it. In any case, Morritt J considered the underlying purpose of the gift to be the benefit of the borough as a whole, though restricted directly to the freemen, who would at one time have constituted a significant proportion of the population. Accordingly, he felt able to apply s 13(1)(d) (now s 62(1)(d)), to conclude that the original gift was defined by a class which had ceased to be suitable for the achievement of the underlying purpose, and to direct a scheme for application cy-près for the benefit of the inhabitants of the borough as a whole.

In *Varsani v Jesani* [1998] 3 All ER 273, the Court of Appeal considered the meaning of s 13(1)(e)(iii) (what is now s 62(1)(e)(iii)). This case concerned a religious charity in which property (a temple) was used for the benefit of a Hindu sect. The sect had undergone a schism, splitting into two groups, both of which claimed to be the true successors to the original sect (and thus that the property could continue to be applied to the original purpose through them). The court held that the facts that the sect had split, and that the minority group could no longer use the facilities previously available, was sufficient to indicate that the original purpose, the promotion of the sect, was no longer a suitable or effective use of the property and a scheme was ordered. In further proceedings to determine the scheme ([2002] P & CR D11), Patten J held that in such a case the court must adopt an essentially agnostic role and could not enter into a debate as to the relative merits of the different religious groups. Articles 9 and 14 of the European Convention on Human Rights (freedom of conscience, thought and religion, and anti-discrimination, respectively) were described as a 'long stop' in the exercise of any scheme-making power, but were not directly relevant to the facts. The court should aim at a division of the assets which facilitated the carrying out of the two new charitable purposes (of the two divisions of the religious sect) and achieved a fair balance between the two groups. Accordingly, the minority group would be paid £250,000 out of the sect's assets to enable it to establish a new temple, while the majority group would retain the existing temple and the balance of the other assets.

Note that the current law, as set out in the 2011 Act, requires the court or the Commission to take into account not only the spirit of the gift but also the social and economic circumstances prevailing at the time of the proposed alteration.

It should also be noted that the section, and cy-près principles, will not apply in cases where the terms of the gift themselves make clear what is to happen in the event of the charity ceasing. This would be the case, for example, where there is provision for a gift over from one charity to another, should the first charity cease or a particular event happen (see above at p. 242), or in a case such as *Keene and Phillips v Wellcom London Ltd and others* [2014] EWHC 134 (Ch), [2014] All ER (D) 241 (Jan). Here the charity was organised as an unincorporated association, and the association's rules provided that, in the event of the charity being wound up, the assets were to be distributed to the association's members in proportion to their contributions. The Chancery Division held that there was no need to consider cy-près.

See further,
Chapter 9 (p. 212).

Initial failure

A rather different problem presents itself in cases of initial failure. Here it is not a question of taking the opportunity to reallocate money to new charitable purposes when the old ones fail but rather whether, the original purposes having failed, the money can be applied to charity at all. As we shall shortly see, if it is to be so applied further conditions must be met. In cases of alleged initial failure two questions must be asked: has the original charitable gift failed, and, if it has, can the money be applied cy-près or must it go on resulting trust to the settlor's estate? To rephrase, a gift may be saved in one of two ways: either the court may determine that the initial gift has not failed, in which case cy-près is not relevant, or the court may hold that the initial gift has failed but that the money may be applied cy-près. The first of these questions requires us to consider the wording of the gift and what constitutes failure, and the second requires us to consider the other requirement for application cy-près in cases of initial failure, that requirement being that the settlor or testator demonstrates general charitable intent.

Has the original gift failed?

It is submitted that for these purposes failure means literally that the gift cannot, or cannot practicably, be carried out. It cannot have been the purpose of s 13 (now s 62) to extend the situations where charitable gifts fail at the outset, even if the wording of the section can be taken to include situations of initial failure. Before deciding whether the original gift has failed, however, it will be necessary to consider the precise wording of the gift; it may be possible to interpret the gift in wider terms than appear literally, or it may be that a purpose which has apparently disappeared has not in fact done so. It must be stressed that this is not the same question as whether the donee had a general intention to benefit charity.

Turning first to the form of the original gift, as a general rule the terms of gifts must be taken literally. If a specific purpose or organisation is stated as the donee, then that is presumed to be what the settlor intended and his specific gift is no wider or narrower than that. Thus, in *Re Spence* [1978] 3 All ER 92, the testator left money to the Blind Home, Scott Street, Keighley. This home was run by an organisation that also ran other homes. It was held that the money must be applied only for the home referred to in the will and not for the general purposes of the organisation. In certain special situations, however, a more generous interpretation may be applied.

Re Faraker [1912] 2 Ch 488

In this case, the testatrix left money to a particular named charity. Some years earlier this charity and several others had been amalgamated under a scheme by the Charity Commissioners. At first instance it was held that the charity thereby ceased to exist and so the gift failed. The Court of Appeal, however, reversed this and held that the amalgamated charities were entitled to the legacy. In effect the named charity continued as part of the amalgamated charities.

In the words of Farwell LJ:

In all these cases one has to consider not so much the means to the end as the charitable end which is in view, and so long as that charitable end is well established the means are only machinery, and no alteration of the machinery can destroy the charitable trust for the benefit of which the machinery is provided.

It should be noted that this continuation was held to exist despite the fact that the new consolidated charity was not limited to the benefit of widows as had been the original one, and to that extent the gift was applied to slightly wider purposes than the testatrix had stated. The Court of Appeal seems to have regarded this change as a matter of drafting and not sufficiently substantial to destroy the original charity, which the Charity Commissioners in any event had no power to do.

In *Re Finger* [1971] 3 All ER 1050, Goff J was prepared to hold that the original gift had not failed, by virtue of the nature of the organisation to which it was given. He drew a distinction between gifts to corporate bodies and gifts to unincorporated associations. In the case of the latter Goff J applied the dictum of Buckley J in *Re Vernon's Will Trust* [1971] 3 All ER 1061n:

> Every bequest to an unincorporated charity by name without more must take effect as a gift for a charitable purpose . . . If the gift is to be permitted to take effect at all, it must be as a bequest for a purpose. A bequest which is in terms for a charitable purpose will not fail for lack of a trustee but will be carried into effect . . . by means of a scheme.

Commenting on this, Goff J went on:

> As I read the dictum . . . the view of Buckley J was that in the case of an unincorporated body the gift is *per se* a purpose trust, and provided that the work is still being carried on will have effect given to it by way of a scheme notwithstanding the disappearance of the donee in the lifetime of the testator.

In other words, where the gift is made to an unincorporated charity, it is to be regarded as a gift to the purpose of that organisation (it cannot be a gift to the organisation itself since that is not a legal entity and cannot hold property). It is not, therefore, relevant that the organisation has ceased to exist: provided the purpose itself continues, the gift has not failed. On the facts in *Re Finger*, a gift to the National Radium Commission, a defunct unincorporated charity, did take effect and the fund would be applied by a scheme. Of course, this will not always be the case: both Buckley J and Goff J stated that the gift would not take effect if the organisation had ceased to exist if the terms of the gift made it clear that the continuation of the organisation was an essential prerequisite of the gift.

This approach to gifts to unincorporated charities cannot, however, be applied to charitable corporations. Since they have legal personality, a gift to a corporation without any further qualification will *prima facie* be a gift to the organisation itself. Therefore, if that organisation has ceased to exist the gift will fail. As Buckley J said in *Re Vernon*:

> A bequest to a corporate body, on the other hand, takes effect simply as a gift to that body beneficially, unless there are circumstances which show that the recipient is to take the gift as trustee. There is no need in this case to infer a trust for any particular purpose.

Applying this to the facts of *Re Finger*, Goff J felt that there was no ground for inferring a purpose trust on the facts before him in the case of a gift to a charitable corporation and accordingly, the charitable corporation having ceased to exist, the gift failed.

Goff J compared the present case, where gifts were made to a number of different sorts of charity, to the case of *Re Meyers* [1951] 1 All ER 538, where it had been possible to infer a purpose gift in circumstances where a large number of bequests had been made, all of them to hospitals, both corporate and unincorporated. Whether a gift can be interpreted as one to the named organisation or one to its purposes must depend upon the facts in each case, but it is clear from *Re Finger* that a purpose gift will be readily inferred where the donee organisation is unincorporated, but will only exceptionally be inferred where the donee organisation is a corporation. It is also interesting to note in passing that the courts will readily infer a gift to a charitable purpose but they cannot do this if the purpose is not charitable: a gift to a non-charitable unincorporated association cannot take effect as a gift to its purposes; it must take effect, if at all, in other ways (see pp. 206–11).

The fact that a charitable corporation takes the gift outright (subject to evidence of a contrary intention) means that it may be applied to the corporation's activities generally, and not necessarily to the charitable purposes of the organisation. It can, for example, be available to meet the charity's debts (*Re ARMS Alleyne v A-G* [1997] 2 All ER 679), even where the charity was insolvent at the time of the gift taking effect.

General charitable intention

When charitable gifts fail *ab initio*, for example because the intended donee organisation has ceased to exist, the court must then consider whether the gift may be applied cy-près. As has already been stated, this may only happen in a case of initial failure if the donor has shown general charitable intention. This means that the terms of the gift and the surrounding circumstances indicate that the donor had more than merely the intention to give to a particular purpose or organisation but was motivated to give to charity in a broader, more general, sense. Parker J, in *Re Wilson* [1913] 1 Ch 314, highlighted the difference between two kinds of case:

> First of all, we have a class of cases where, in form, the gift is given for a particular charitable purpose, but it is possible, taking the will as a whole, to say that, notwithstanding the form of the gift, the paramount intention, according to the true construction of the will, is to give the property in the first instance for a general charitable purpose rather than a particular charitable purpose, and to graft on to the general gift a direction as to the desires or intentions of the testator as to the manner in which the general gift is to be carried into effect.

In such a case, though the particular purpose fails, the general purpose survives and must be put into effect by means of application cy-près. This is in contrast with the other type of case: 'where, on a true construction of the will, no such paramount general intention can be inferred, and where the gift, being in form a particular gift – a gift for a particular purpose – and it being impossible to carry out that particular purpose, the whole gift is held to fail'.

Therefore, the question is whether the true construction is that the settlor had in mind one particular charitable purpose and no other or whether he wished to benefit charity generally and merely identified the particular purpose or organisation as the means to achieve this.

Since the existence or otherwise of the necessary general charitable intention is a matter of construction to be decided on the facts of each individual case, it follows that it is very difficult to give any general rules. Some individual pointers may, however, be noted.

First, in the case of gifts to particular organisations, it appears that where the testator leaves money to a particular organisation, the *prima facie* assumption is that the testator intended the gift to go to that organisation alone and had no broader charitable intention (subject, of course, to the purpose gift argument in *Re Finger*). Where the testator leaves a gift to an organisation which never existed, the court may be able to find general charitable intention.

Re Harwood [1936] Ch 285

This approach was taken in this case. The testatrix left money to two organisations: the Wisbech Peace Society and the Peace Society of Belfast. The Wisbech Society had existed but had been wound up before the testatrix's death. Accordingly, the gift failed and Farwell J further found that the testatrix had no general charitable intention in respect of this gift.

He said:

> I do not propose to decide that it can never be possible for the Court to hold that there is a general charitable intent in a case where the charity named in the will once existed but ceased to exist before the death. Without deciding that, it is enough for me to say that, where the testator selects as the object of his bounty a particular charity and shows in the will itself some care to identify the particular charity which he desires to benefit, the difficulty of finding any general charitable intent in such a case if the named society once existed, but has ceased to exist before the death of the testator, is very great.

Such difficulty could not be overcome in the present case. Farwell J pointed to such matters as the precise way in which the testatrix had identified the organisation, and it may be taken that the more precise the reference to the organisation, the less likely is the possibility of finding general charitable intent.

The 'Peace Society of Belfast', on the other hand, had never existed. It could not be said, therefore, that the testatrix had any particular organisation in mind. As Farwell J stated:

> I doubt whether the lady herself knew exactly what society she did mean to benefit. I think she had a desire to benefit any society which was formed for the purpose of promoting peace and was connected with Belfast. Beyond that, I do not think that she had any very clear idea in her mind.

He concluded:

> [T]here being a clear intention on the part of the lady, as expressed in her will, to benefit societies whose object was the promotion of peace, and there being no such society as that named in her will, in this case there is a general charitable intent, and, accordingly, the doctrine of cy-près applies.

A number of further comments may be made on this case. First, it would appear that an alternative solution in respect of the Belfast society might have been that which was used in *Re Finger*, to the effect that the testatrix intended to promote a charitable purpose which had presumably not ceased, and, accordingly, the gift need not have failed in the first place. Secondly, it is clear from Farwell J's words that his finding of general charitable intention was not based solely on the fact that the Belfast society had never existed; although it did tend to show that the testatrix had wider intentions, this was apparently supported also by the whole tenor of the will. Thirdly, it seems, with respect, a little strange to have general charitable intent in respect of the one gift and not of the other. These last two points may be answered, perhaps, by remembering that this issue is always a question of construction: the existence or otherwise of the society intended to benefit is merely one factor in determining the presence of general charitable intent.

In *Re Finger*, Goff J felt able to distinguish *Re Harwood* on the matter of gifts to particular organisations which had ceased to exist. Faced with a gift to a corporate charity which had ceased to exist, though that gift could not be saved on the purpose trust argument discussed above, nevertheless Goff J felt able to find general charitable intent. He pointed out that Farwell J had not said that it would be impossible to find general charitable intent, merely that it would be difficult. He regarded the circumstances in *Re Finger* as very special in that the bulk of the estate was left to charity, that the organisation to which this bequest had been made was a coordinating body for various charitable purposes rather than having one purpose, and that, therefore, the testatrix cannot have had a particular purpose in mind, and finally there was external evidence that the testatrix regarded herself as having no relatives and, therefore, cannot have envisaged the money going other than to charity.

A second pointer to the finding of general charitable intent, or rather to not finding it, is the principle that the court is not entitled to assume that, because the testator has made several charitable gifts, he necessarily has charitable intent in relation to other money in the estate. As Buckley J rather memorably put it in *Re Jenkins's Will Trusts* [1966] 1 All ER 926:

> The principle of *noscitur a sociis* [a man is known by his associates] does not in my judgment entitle one to overlook self-evident facts. If you meet seven men with black hair and one with red hair you are not entitled to say that here are eight men with black hair. Finding one gift for a non-charitable purpose among a number of gifts for charitable purposes the court cannot infer that the testator or testatrix meant the non-charitable gift to take effect as a charitable gift when the terms are not charitable, even though the non-charitable gift may have a close relation to the purposes for which the charitable gifts are made.

It will be observed that the issue here was not of an organisation which had ceased to exist, but one of the interpretation of a purpose. If the interpretation was that it was non-charitable, as was *prima facie* the case here, then the gift must fail, since no trust can generally exist for a non-charitable purpose. Cy-près would have no relevance. External evidence was admissible to refute that *prima facie* interpretation in *Re Satterthwaite's Will Trusts*.

Re Satterthwaite's Will Trusts [1966] 1 All ER 919

> The testatrix left money to nine different organisations, seven of which were charities, one of which was not and one of which did not exist as a charity at the date of the will. The manner of the drafting was clearly important here. The testatrix had informed an official of the Midland Bank that she hated the human race and wished to leave her estate to animal charities. Nine were selected apparently at random from the telephone directory. Both these facts indicated that the testatrix really had no specific organisations in mind but had the necessary general intent. The gift to the London Animal Hospital was therefore treated as one to a non-existent charity rather than to a specific non-charitable organisation of the same name. The evidence of the circumstances of the drafting also outweighed the fact that one of the gifts was to a valid non-charity, since the testatrix probably did not know that it was not charitable.

It is clear that this approach must be viewed with caution. Commenting upon this principle of 'charity by association', as he called it, Megarry V-C said in *Re Spence* [1978] 3 All ER 92:

> If the will gives the residue among a number of charities with kindred objects, but one of the apparent charities does not in fact exist, the court will be ready to find a general charitable intention and so apply the share of the non-existent cy-près . . . [I]t seems to me that in such cases the court treats the testator as having shown the general intention of giving his residue to promote charities with that type of kindred objects, and then, when he comes to dividing the residue, as casting around for particular charities with that type of objects to name as donees. If one or more of these are non-existent, then the general intention will suffice for a cy-près application. It will be observed that, as stated, the doctrine depends, at least to some extent, upon the detection of 'kindred objects' in the charities to which the shares of residue are given; in this respect the charities must in some degree be *eiusdem generis*.

Having discussed cases such as *Re Satterthwaite*, he further pointed out that these cases were all cases of gifts to bodies which did not exist:

> The court is far less ready to find such an intention where the gift is to a body which existed at the date of the will but ceased to exist before the testator died, or . . . where the gift is for a purpose which, though possible and practicable at the date of the will, has ceased to be so before the testator's death.

In other words, the cases were at least assisted by the fact that they also fell within the principle in *Re Harwood*.

The case before Megarry V-C concerned a gift to a purpose which had become impossible since the date of the will and furthermore the 'association' could only be with one other gift, which he felt was insufficient to show a general intent (it will be remembered that there were some nine different gifts in *Re Satterthwaite*, all to animal welfare purposes). Accordingly, in *Re Spence*, the gift having failed, it could not be applied cy-près:

> I do not say that a general charitable intention or a genus cannot be extracted from a gift of residue equally between two: but I do say that larger numbers are likely to assist in conveying to the court a sufficient conviction both of the genus and of the generality of the charitable intention.

In conclusion, it may be repeated that each case is to be assessed on its own facts and the court will take account of all the evidence, including the circumstances in which the will was made, in determining whether the testator had the necessary general charitable intention. The cases discussed above indicate that among the relevant factors are whether the intended donee actually existed and whether the rest of the will shows general intent, as, for instance, by the presence of other charitable gifts.

In case of either initial or subsequent failure s 67 provides:

(2) Where any property given for charitable purposes is applicable cy-près, the court or the Commission may make a scheme providing for the property to be applied –
   (a) for such charitable purposes, and
   (b) (if the scheme provides for the property to be transferred to another charity) by or on trust for such other charity,
   as it considers appropriate, having regard to the matters set out in subsection (3).
(3) The matters are –
   (a) the spirit of the original gift,
   (b) the desirability of securing that the property is applied for charitable purposes which are close to the original purposes, and
   (c) the need for the relevant charity to have purposes which are suitable and effective in the light of current social and economic circumstances.

The 'relevant charity' means the charity by or on behalf of which the property is to be applied under the scheme.

Anonymous donations

The Charities Act 2011 provides for general charitable intent to be presumed, and hence application cy-près, in certain categories of charitable gift. Section 63 states:

(1) Property given for specific charitable purposes which fail shall be applicable cy-près as if given for charitable purposes generally where it belongs –
   (a) to a donor who after –
      (i) the prescribed advertisements and inquiries have been published and made, and
      (ii) the prescribed period beginning with the publication of those advertisements has expired, cannot be identified or cannot be found; or
   (b) to a donor who has executed a disclaimer in the prescribed form of his right to have the property returned.

The Commission is to prescribe the form of the advertisement and inquiries to be made. Section 64 states:

(1) For the purposes of section 63 property is conclusively presumed (without any advertisement or inquiry) to belong to donors who cannot be identified, in so far as it consists of –
   (a) the proceeds of cash collections made –
      (i) by means of collecting boxes, or
      (ii) by other means not adapted for distinguishing one gift from another, or
   (b) the proceeds of any lottery, competition, entertainment, sale or similar money-raising activity, after allowing for property given to provide prizes or articles for sale or otherwise to enable the activity to be undertaken.

(2) The court or the Commission may by order direct that property not falling within sub-section (1) is for the purposes of section 63 to be treated (without any advertisement or inquiry) as belonging to donors who cannot be identified if it appears to the court or the Commission –
   (a) that it would be unreasonable, having regard to the amounts likely to be returned to the donors, to incur expense with a view to returning the property, or
   (b) that it would be unreasonable, having regard to the nature, circumstances and amounts of the gifts, and to the lapse of time since the gifts were made, for the donors to expect the property to be returned.

There is also provision for a donor in certain circumstances to request the return of his donation.

Small, unincorporated charities; alteration of purposes, transfer and expenditure of capital

Sections 267 and 268 provide that where a charity has a gross income of less than £10,000, does not hold any land on charitable trusts, and is not a corporate body, the trustees, by a two-thirds majority, may resolve to transfer the charity's property to another charity, or divide it among other charities (provided they have received written confirmation from the trustees of the other charity or charities that they are willing to accept the property).

This power is exercisable only where the trustees are satisfied that the transfer is expedient in the furtherance of the transferor charity's purposes and are satisfied that the purposes of the transferee charity are substantially similar to those of the transferor charity.

Alternatively, s 275 provides that the trustees of such a charity may, by a two-thirds majority, resolve to modify the charity by replacing all or any of its purposes with other charitable purposes, provided again that the trustees are satisfied that it is expedient in the interests of the charity for the purposes to be replaced, and that as far as is practicable the new purposes consist of or include purposes that are similar in character to those that are to be replaced. The watchwords are, therefore, a lack of effective application of resources, and the requirement of new charities or purposes as close as possible to the old ones. In addition, under s 280, the trustees of any unincorporated charity may, by a two-thirds majority, amend their administrative powers and procedures.

Having made their resolution, the trustees must give public notice of it, and must also inform the Charity Commission, which may also demand further particulars and receive representations from interested persons. The resolution may then be implemented within 60 days, unless the Commission raises objections.

Sections 281–285 also provide that unincorporated charities may in certain circumstances spend their capital, where the trustees are satisfied that the charity's purpose could be carried out more effectively if capital as well as income were spent.

None of these provisions applies to exempt charities or to charitable companies.

Fund-raising and public collections

Part II of the Charities Act 1992, as amended by the Charities Act 2006, seeks to regulate various forms of fund-raising and collection by and on behalf of charities. Professional fund-raisers, which is to say those who are in the business of fund-raising or who solicit money for reward, in particular may only act on behalf of a charity if they do so in accordance with an agreement in a prescribed form. These Regulations also require such fund-raisers to make their books available to the charity, and to transmit any money collected to the charity in prescribed form (usually within 28 days of collection).

Acting without such an agreement or falsely representing that money is being raised under such an agreement is a summary offence and may be prevented by injunction. The professional fund-raiser must indicate the institutions on whose behalf the money is being raised, and any payment received of £100 or more is subject to a right to cancel within seven days.

Also regulated is anyone not a professional fund-raiser, but who runs a business which participates in a promotional scheme in which it is represented that money will thereby be applied to philanthropic purposes. In particular, such a person will be required to indicate what proportion of the profit made under the scheme will be donated to the purpose.

Regulations concerning public charitable collections under Part 3, Chapter 1 of the Charities Act 2006 which will require, *inter alia*, local authority permits and certificates from the Charity Commission, are not yet in force.

Summary

- The term 'charity' has a specific legal meaning, developed over many centuries in case law and now to be found in the Charities Act 2011 which preserves the previous case law principle of flexibility and the development of new purposes to meet changing circumstances.

- Status as a charity, however organised, has certain advantages in that a charitable trust has no individual beneficiaries and can last forever, as well as having significant tax exemptions.

- An essential feature of a charity is that it must be for 'public benefit', that is that its benefits are available to the public or a section of the public, as that is defined by case law. The nature of this public benefit can vary between different types of charity, and the rules for charities which are for the relief of poverty are less strict than those for other charitable purposes.

- The statutory definition of charitable purpose, which is built upon previous case law and practice, encompasses a wide range of different objectives, of which the classic examples are the relief of poverty, the advancement of education and the advancement of religion, but a wide range of cultural, recreational and scientific activities are also included.

- Charities must not have political purposes, though they may participate in political activities, such as lobbying, to promote their charitable objectives.

- Charities must confine themselves to charitable activities, except where the non-charitable activity is merely ancillary to the main charitable purpose.

- Charities are administered by trustees (or, where the charity is incorporated, by directors), whose role is in many ways similar to that of the trustees of private trusts, though there are additional responsibilities to do with registration and reporting. Charities are also subject to overall monitoring by the Charity Commission.

- It is possible in certain circumstances for funds which have been given for charitable purposes to be reallocated to different charitable purposes. This is most often where circumstances have changed and the funds can be more effectively used in other ways. This may involve the application of the funds cy-près or other mechanisms.

Further reading

Charities generally

A Dunn, 'Demanding service or servicing demand? Charities, regulation and the policy process' [2008] MLR 247–70.
Reviews the historical role of charities and the impact of the Human Rights Act.

A Dunn, 'The governance of philanthropy and the burden of regulating charitable foundations' (2012) Conv 114–28.
Offers a general criticism of the regulatory regime for charities.

'Trusted and Independent; Giving Charity back to Charities' (The Hodgson Report) https://www.gov.uk/government/uploads/system/uploads/attachment_data/file/79275/Charities-Act-Review-2006-report-Hodgson.pdf
A critical review of charity law and the operation of the 2006 Act; contains a range of recommendations about the administration of charities.

The recent reforms

R Cordon, 'Private action, public benefit: the implications for charities' (2002) 152 (7060) NLJ 10.

D G Cracknell, 'Legal developments' (2004) 148 (48) Sol J 8.

D G Cracknell, 'Charity's new look' (2006) 150 (21) Sol J 684.

J Edwardes, 'Twelve heads are better than four' (2004) 154 (7137) NLJ 1076.

A Lawton, 'Charity shake-up' (2004) 148 (24) Sol J 721.

J Warburton, 'Charity members: duties and responsibilities' [2006] Conv 330.
Considers the implications for charity members of the new charitable structures under the 2006 Act.

Public benefit

J Hackney, 'Charities and public benefit' (2008) 124 LQR 347.
Discusses the meaning of public benefit in the light of the 2006 Act, and *IRC v Pemsel* (1891).

N Hancox, 'An education in charity' (2008) 158 (7305) NLJ 113.

M Harding, 'Trusts for religious purposes and the question of public benefit' [2008] MLR 159–82.

A Holt, 'Reassessing "public benefit"' [2008] 152 (48) SJ 10.
Explains how the courts assess public benefit.

J Jaconelli, 'Adjudicating on charitable status – a reconsideration of the elements' [2013] Conv 2, 96–112.
Analyses the determination of an entity's charitable status, including the elements of the charitable purpose test and the challenge of showing that a benefit is conferred on a sufficient proportion of the public or class of the community. It refers in particular to *R (on the application of Independent Schools Council) v Charity Commission for England and Wales* (2011).

F Moss, 'New ingredient' [2011] 155 (40) SJ 10.
Analyses the decision in *The Independent Schools Council* v *Charity Commission*.

A Rahmatian, 'The continued relevance of the "poor relations" and the "poor employees" cases under the Charities Act 2006' [2009] Conv 12.

Charities and political activity

A Dunn, 'To foster or to temper? Regulating the political activities of the voluntary and community sector' (2006) LS 26(4), 500.

J Kilby, 'Playing by the rules' (2009) 153 (35) SJ 15.
Comments on the Charity Commission guidelines on political activity.

11

Resulting trusts

Objectives

After reading this chapter you should be able to:

1. Understand that a resulting trust is one where the beneficial interest in property returns to (or perhaps never leaves) the transferor.

2. Understand and explain the two classes of resulting trust as stated by Megarry J in *Re Vandervell Trusts (No. 2)* (1974) and the doubts about Megarry J's statement expressed by Lord Browne-Wilkinson in *Westdeutsche Landesbank* v *Islington London Borough Council* (1996).

3. Understand and explain situations where a resulting trust can arise, e.g. where an express trust fails, where there is a failure to dispose of the entire beneficial interest and where a trust is set up to benefit individuals but a surplus remains after the purpose has been achieved.

4. Understand and explain:

   - that where a purchase is made in the name of another person or where property is transferred into the name of another purpose a resulting trust may arise.

   - the presumption of advancement and what the effect of s 199 of the Equality Act 2010 will be.

   - the effect of the presence of an unlawful or illegal reason for a transfer into the name of another or purchase in the name of another.

Introduction

Objective
1

Under a resulting trust the settlor obtains or perhaps retains an equitable interest in the settled property. Although it may be suggested that a resulting trust can arise under an express trust where the settlor expressly retains an interest for himself, the term is more usually reserved to apply to those situations where the interest that accrues to the settlor does not arise as the result of an expressed decision on his part. In fact in some cases having an interest under a resulting trust is the last thing that the settlor/transferor would want.

> ### Example
>
> If Arthur transfers property to trustees and makes it clear that they are to hold the property on trust but does not in any way state what the trusts are or who the beneficiaries are to be, a resulting trust will arise and the trustees will hold the property on trust for Arthur. As discussed below, it is probable that instead of the beneficial interest leaving and then returning to Arthur it never leaves Arthur at all.

The origin of 'resulting' is the Latin word *'resultare'* meaning to spring back. This at first sight appears to be an appropriate way of describing the trusts because it might be thought that the equitable interest, having been disposed of by the settlor, results, or returns to the settlor. However, in fact it may be argued that the beneficial interest never leaves the settlor and so the idea of the interest returning to the settlor is misleading.

This argument is supported by Megarry V-C in *Re Sick and Funeral Society of St John's Sunday School, Golcar* [1972] 2 All ER 439, where Megarry V-C stated:

> A resulting trust is essentially a property concept; any property that a man does not effectually dispose of remains his own.

Support can also be found in *IRC v Vandervell*. At first instance Ploughman J said ([1966] Ch 261 at 275):

> As I see it, a man does not cease to own property simply by saying 'I don't want it.' If he tries to give it away the question must always be, has he succeeded in doing so or not?

On appeal to the House of Lords ([1967] 2 AC 291), Lord Upjohn quoted the statement of Ploughman J with approval.

Under a resulting trust the transferor/settlor retains the beneficial interest. This was dealt with in *Vandervell v Inland Revenue Commissioners* [1967] 2 AC 291 when the retention of a beneficial interest by the transferor destroyed the effectiveness of a tax avoidance scheme which the transferor was seeking to implement. The House of Lords affirmed the principle that a resulting trust is not defeated by evidence that the transferor *intended* to part with the beneficial interest if he has not in fact succeeded in doing so.

Resulting trusts differ in a number of important ways from express trusts and, in particular, the formalities for creation prescribed in the Law of Property Act 1925 s 53(1)(b) do not apply to resulting trusts (s 53(2)).

Implied or resulting trusts?

Definitions in the law of trusts are usually difficult, and resulting trusts are no exception. One particular problem is that in many cases resulting trusts are said to arise as a result of the implied intention of the settlor and are thus often referred to as implied trusts. While it can be argued that in many cases resulting trusts arise as the result of the implied or presumed intention of the settlor, this is not always the case. Thus, some but not all resulting trusts may without inaccuracy be described as implied trusts. For example, it is sometimes argued that the trusts arising under a mutual will (see p. 318) are implied but they are certainly not an example of resulting trusts.

See Chapter 12 (p. 318) for a discussion of mutual wills.

The example given above where Arthur transfers property to trustees and makes it clear that they hold as trustees but does not say who the beneficiaries of the trusts are to be is an example of a trust which is both implied and resulting. In such a case the trustees will hold the property on trust for Arthur. This can be described as an implied trust on the basis that if the settlor fails to name the beneficiaries then it can be presumed that he would want the property held by the trustees for himself. It can also be described as a resulting trust on the basis that the beneficial interest results, or returns, to the settlor.

The view that resulting trusts are based on the presumed intention of the settlor is difficult to support in some instances where the last thing that the individual would have wanted was a trust under which he had a beneficial interest. One example of this is *Vandervell v IRC* (see above on p. 116) when Vandervell was found not to have disposed of the entire equitable interest in property (shares) and as a consequence was beneficially entitled under a resulting trust. The effect of this was that Vandervell became liable to a large income tax bill. As part of the object of Vandervell's transfer was to avoid his liability to tax, it is rather difficult to imagine that he had any unexpressed intention to create a resulting trust which rendered him liable to pay the tax which he was planning to avoid!

In this chapter the description resulting trust, rather than implied trust, will be used.

Examples of resulting trusts

There are a number of situations where resulting trusts have been found to exist by the courts. There is no real link between them except, perhaps in some cases, the presumed intention of the settlor. A number of examples of resulting trusts may help to gain a flavour of the topic. A more detailed coverage of the various types of resulting trusts will be found later in the chapter. Resulting trusts come into being if a settlor intends to create a trust and transfers property to trustees but the trust fails to take effect as the settlor intends, perhaps because there is uncertainty as to who the beneficiaries are or as to what their interests should be. Again, resulting trusts come into being if the settlor has failed to dispose of the entire beneficial interest in the property.

Example

Donna transfers property to trustees to hold on trust for Ben for life but nothing is stated about what happens to the property after Ben dies. To the extent that the settlor has failed to dispose of the interest, it will be held on resulting trust for him. So the property will be held on trust for Ben for life, remainder on a resulting trust for Donna.

If property is bought but put in the name of someone else, a resulting trust may well come into being. In such cases there is, traditionally, a presumption of resulting trust. But if the parties stand in certain relationships, the presumption of resulting trust is replaced by the presumption of advancement. For example, if a husband purchases in the name of his wife or a father purchases in the name of his child, a presumption of advancement arises. More recent cases have tended to view the presumptions either as applicable only in the last resort, where there is no evidence of what the parties actually intended, or easily rebutted by evidence of intention.

The presumption of advancement will be abolished by s 199 of the Equality Act 2010. At the time of writing, the Government is considering when it will come into force. But this abolition will not apply to anything done before the commencement of the section or anything done pursuant to any obligation incurred before the commencement of the section. So the presumption of advancement will remain relevant in relation to any transfer made before the section comes into force.

Many cases of this type of resulting trust centre round the purchase of a family home either by spouses or by cohabitees. But recent cases have been decided on the basis of common intention constructive trusts, rather than on the basis of resulting trusts. In *Stack v Dowden* [2007] 2 All ER 929 Lady Hale based her arguments on the presumption that if the

For more on the
ownership of
shared homes
see Chapter 13.

legal estate in a property is in joint names the parties would share the beneficial interest equally. The burden of proof was on the party who was claiming that the beneficial interest was held in different proportions. Lady Hale argued that if a property was in the sole name of one of the parties, the burden of proof was on the other party if he claimed an interest in the beneficial ownership.

Also, if property which is already owned is transferred into the name of someone else, a resulting trust may arise.

A last example of where resulting trusts may arise is when property is set aside for a particular purpose, perhaps the education of a child, but there is money left after the purpose has been achieved. The surplus may be held on resulting trust for the providers of the fund. All of these situations will be discussed in this chapter.

Categorisation of resulting trusts and the role of intention

Objective
2

In *Re Vandervell's Trusts (No. 2)* [1974] 3 All ER 205 Megarry J divided resulting trusts into two categories: presumed and automatic resulting trusts. Presumed resulting trusts arise because of the presumed intention of the transferor of property. An example of this type of resulting trust is where there is a transfer of property into the names of others (see p. 271). In such situations it is presumed (in most cases) that the transferor would not want the transferee to benefit and so the transferee is presumed to hold the property on a resulting trust for the transferor. Automatic resulting trusts, Megarry J said, do not depend on any intention of the parties but arise where the transferor has not disposed of all the beneficial interest. Examples of this type of trust are to be found in the section, 'Failure to dispose of the entire beneficial interest', later in this chapter (p. 267).

In the following case Lord Browne-Wilkinson stated that there are two situations that may lead to a resulting trust. Lord Browne-Wilkinson's categorisation differed from that of Megarry J.

Westdeutsche Landesbank v *Islington London Borough Council* [1996] 2 All ER 961

See also Chapter 1.

Lord Browne-Wilkinson set out what he described as relevant principles of trust law
These included:

(i) Equity operates on the conscience of the owner of the legal interest. In the case of a trust, the conscience of the legal owner requires him to carry out the purposes for which the property was vested in him (express or implied trust) or which the law imposes on him by reason of his unconscionable conduct (constructive trust).

Under existing law a resulting trust arises in two sets of circumstances:

(A) where A makes a voluntary payment to B or pays (wholly or in part) for the purchase of property which is vested either in B alone or in the joint names of A and B, there is a presumption that A did not intend to make a gift to B: the money or property is held on trust for A (if he is the sole provider of the money) or in the case of a joint purchase by A and B in shares proportionate to their contributions. It is important to stress that this is only a presumption, which presumption is easily rebutted either by the counter-presumption of advancement or by direct evidence of A's intention to make an outright transfer: see *Underhill and Hayton* pp 317ff, *Vandervell v IRC* [1967] 1 All ER 1 at 8, [1967] 2 AC 291 at 312ff and *Re Vandervell's Trusts (No. 2), White v Vandervell Trustees Ltd* [1974] 1 All ER 47 at 63ff, [1974] Ch 269 at 288ff.

[Note the Equality Act 2010 s 199 will abolish the presumption of advancement in relation to transfers or purchase made after the section comes into force. The Government is considering when to implement the section.]

See also Chapters 1, 3, 4 and 12 for further discussion of *Quistclose* trusts.

(B) Where A transfers property to B on express trusts, but the trusts declared do not exhaust the whole beneficial interest: ibid and *Barclays Bank Ltd v Quistclose Investments Ltd* [1968] 3 All ER 651, [1970] AC 567.

Both types of resulting trust are traditionally regarded as examples of trusts giving effect to the common intention of the parties. A resulting trust is not imposed by law against the intentions of the trustee (as is a constructive trust) but gives effect to his presumed intention. Megarry J in *Re Vandervell's Trusts (No. 2)* suggests that a resulting trust of type (B) does not depend on intention but operates automatically. I am not convinced that this is right. If the settlor has expressly, or by necessary implication, abandoned any beneficial interest in the trust property, there is in my view no resulting trust: the undisposed-of equitable interest vests in the Crown as *bona vacantia*: see *Re West Sussex Constabulary's Widows, Children and Benevolent (1930) Fund Trusts* [1970] 1 All ER 544, [1971] Ch 1.

To the extent that Megarry J's class of automatically arising resulting trusts is thought not to depend on the intention of the 'trustee', there is an obvious conflict.

It should be noted that Lord Browne-Wilkinson's category A resulting trust appears only to apply where there is a voluntary payment. Megarry J would, it is assumed, extend his first category to include voluntary transfers of personality. It is open to argument whether or not this formed part of the *ratio* of *Westdeutsche* and/or if it accurately represents Lord Browne-Wilkinson's view.

On the issue of intention, Lord Browne-Wilkinson doubted if Megarry J was correct when he said that automatic resulting trusts did not depend on any intention of the parties, and Lord Browne-Wilkinson thought that both types of resulting trust involved evaluating intention.

In *Westdeutsche Landesbank* v *Islington London Borough Council* (1996), Lord Browne-Wilkinson said that in this second case of resulting trusts, regarded by Megarry J as automatically arising, it may be in fact that the courts do (or at least should) assess the intention of the transferor. In some cases, it seems, it may be that the evidence points towards the transferor abandoning any undisposed of beneficial interest should the trust fail. If this is the case then clearly there can be no resulting trust. In such cases the automatic resulting trust will be replaced by the transferor's intention to abandon any or all of the interest in the property. The property would, on the failure of the trust, become *bona vacantia*. This *may* be relevant to cases such as *Re Gillingham Bus Disaster Fund* [1958] 2 All ER 749. In that case a resulting trust was found to exist in respect of anonymous donations remaining after the purposes of the trust had been fulfilled. Harman J said the resulting trust arose automatically and did not rest on any assessment of intention on the part of the donors. To the extent that *Westdeutsche* states that intention is relevant, the reasoning in *Re Gillingham* cannot now be accepted (see also p. 270).

The basis of resulting trusts was further discussed (by the Privy Council) in *Air Jamaica Ltd v Charlton* [1999] 1 WLR 1399. Again, there was a discussion on intention as being fundamental to resulting trusts.

The case concerned pension fund surpluses. Clause 4 of the trust deed stated that no moneys which had been contributed by the company shall in any circumstances be repayable to the company. Under section 13 of the pension plan the company could end the plan at any time and the court stated that this had in fact happened. The provisions of the pension plan trust deed which covered what should happen to any surplus in this event were ineffective. The provisions infringed the rules against perpetuities and so were void.

In the case Lord Millett said that with resulting trusts the key was intention. In the case the intention highlighted was the absence of intention to pass a beneficial interest:

Like a constructive trust, a resulting trust arises by operation of law, though unlike a constructive trust it gives effect to intention. But it arises whether or not the transferor intended to retain a beneficial interest – he almost always does not – since it responds to the absence of any intention on his part to pass a beneficial interest to the recipient. It may arise even where the transferor positively wished to part with the beneficial interest, as in *Vandervell v Inland Revenue Commissioners* [1967] 2 AC 291.

In that case the retention of a beneficial interest by the transferor destroyed the effectiveness of a tax avoidance scheme which the transferor was seeking to implement. The House of Lords affirmed the principle that a resulting trust is not defeated by evidence that the transferor intended to part with the beneficial interest if he has not in fact succeeded in doing so. As Ploughman J had said in the same case at first instance ([1966] Ch 261 at 275):

'As I see it, a man does not cease to own property simply by saying "I don't want it." If he tries to give it away the question must always be, has he succeeded in doing so or not?'

Lord Upjohn expressly approved this [in *Vandervell v IRC*).

See Chapter 1 (p. 21) for more detail on *Barclays Bank Ltd v Quistclose Investments Ltd* [1968] 3 All ER 651.

Lord Millett said that in cases such as this one (*Air Jamaica Ltd v Charlton*) where there is a failure to give away – in this case because the provision failed under the rules against perpetuity – the law would fill in the gap left by the failure. In the vast majority of cases the transferor will not have provided for what should happen in the event of failure. The prospect of failure will not have occurred to most transferors. The law will make an *assumption* that the transferor would have intended to retain the beneficial interest. The alternative – *bona vacantia* – would not have been the intention. The law therefore responds to the *presumed intention* of the transferor.

It is possible to argue that there is another category of resulting trust, such as that in *Barclays Bank Ltd v Quistclose Investments Ltd* [1968] 3 All ER 651, where the resulting trust was created intentionally. In the case, some argue that a resulting trust arose under which the lender of money was the beneficiary when the only purpose for which the money was lent (paying a dividend) was not carried through. In fact, the issue of the type of trust which arose was not discussed in *Quistclose*, but in *Re EVTR* [1987] BCLR 646 it was stated that such trusts were in fact to be categorised as resulting trusts. However, it may well be that the *Quistclose* trust is simply an example of a resulting trust arising because (in this case) the lender has not given out and out and does not part with the entire beneficial interest in the money lent. This is argued as being the case above. (See p. 28, *Twinsectra v Yardley* [2002] 2 All ER 377 and the judgment of Lord Millett.)

This is discussed in more detail in Chapter 1 (p. 28).

Possible future roles for resulting trusts

There have been debates about a possible expanded and expanding role for resulting trusts and for their playing a part in the developing area of restitution. It has been argued that resulting trusts arise if a person either transfers property to another for no consideration or contributes value to the purchase of property for no consideration *and* has no intention to give the beneficial ownership of the property to its recipient. Here, a resulting trust will arise to prevent the unjust enrichment of the recipient of the property. The resulting trust is, it is argued, based on the intention not to make a gift. This would give rise to resulting trusts in many more situations than if a resulting trust arose only on the basis of an intention to create a trust and to retain the beneficial interest under it. Others have argued that this is incorrect and that a resulting trust can be replaced by any evidence that there was no intention to create such a trust. To the extent that the House of Lords accepted this latter view was correct in *Westdeutsche Landesbank v Islington London Borough Council* (1996), the argument seems, at the moment, to have been settled.

Examples of situations where resulting trusts have come into being

Failure of an express trust

If a settlor tries to create an express trust but the attempt fails, in some cases a resulting trust will arise. If, for example, it is clear that a trust is intended but the settlor fails to name the beneficiaries or fails to describe them with sufficient certainty or does not define the interest they are to take with enough certainty, the property will be held on resulting trust for the settlor. A resulting trust will arise if it is intended to create a charitable trust but it fails, perhaps because the purposes selected by the settlor are not exclusively charitable (**Re Diplock** [1944] 2 All ER 60). If a settlor attempts to create a charitable trust but there is initial impossibility (for example, because the body for which the property is to be held ceased to exist before the trust was set up), there will be a resulting trust for the settlor, unless there was a general charitable intention, in which case a cy-près application may be possible. Again, if a trust fails because it offends the perpetuity rules there will be a resulting trust. A trust may fail as a consequence of non-compliance with a formality necessary for successful creation and again a resulting trust will arise. If a trust offends public policy there will be a resulting trust.

The resulting trusts in this type of case are based on the equitable maxim 'equity abhors a vacuum'.

Re Ames' Settlement [1946] 1 All ER 689

> There was an attempt to create a marriage settlement in 1908. The father of the intended husband agreed to settle £10,000 on the usual trusts 'in case the marriage should be solemnised'. In 1926, the marriage was declared void *ab initio*. The legal effect of this declaration was that the parties were not married and never had been married and as a consequence the marriage settlement failed totally. Vaisey J decided that it was a simple case where the consideration (the marriage) had wholly failed and as a consequence a resulting trust arose. By this time the settlor was dead and so the property was held on resulting trust for the benefit of his estate.

In *Essery* v *Cowlard* (1884) 26 Ch D 191, a woman who was planning to marry transferred property to trustees to be held for herself, her intended husband and their issue. The marriage never took place although the couple lived together and they had some children. The court held that the trust failed and the woman was able to reclaim the property. Pearson J said that even if the couple married later the purposes of the trust could not be achieved as the children already born (who were among those intended to benefit) could not take as they were illegitimate. At the time when the case was decided, illegitimate children could not take under trusts and even if their parents married subsequently they would not be legitimated. So, the purposes for which the trust was intended (the benefit of the couple and their children) could not be carried out. The trustees held the property on resulting trust for the woman.

See also *Air Jamaica Ltd* v *Charlton* (1999) (see pp. 265–6).

Failure to dispose of the entire beneficial interest

The situation may arise, usually accidentally, where a trust has been created but the settlor has not effectively disposed of all, or in some cases any, of the beneficial interest. For example, the settlor might transfer property to trustees to hold for Arthur for life but make no mention as to what is to happen when Arthur dies. Another example would occur if the settlor transferred property to trustees to hold for Arthur for life and then to his children in equal shares and Arthur dies without children. In such cases the trustees will hold the property on resulting trust for the settlor when Arthur dies. In other cases, the settlor may clearly intend to create a trust but fails totally to declare who the beneficiaries are to be; again, a resulting trust will arise.

The explanation of such cases is that the settlor keeps that which he has not parted with. So, to the extent that he has failed to transfer the beneficial interest, the settlor will keep it. (See discussion at pp. 260–1.)

See Chapter 4 (p. 116) for more discussion of *Vandervell v IRC* (1967).

In some cases it may require the courts to decide that there has in fact been a failure to transfer all the beneficial interest that the settlor intends to pass and believes he has passed. This occurred in ***Vandervell v IRC*** (1967) (see also p. 116).

Vandervell v IRC [1967] 1 All ER 1

Vandervell intended to dispose of the entire beneficial interest in the shares from which he wished the Royal College of Surgeons to benefit. He was convinced that he had disposed of all of his interest in the shares but, as will be recalled, the House of Lords decided that as he had arranged for the reservation of an option to repurchase, and had not disposed of the benefit of the option, that benefit was held on resulting trust for him. Not only would this have come as a surprise and disappointment to Vandervell but the fact of the resulting trust only became apparent to Vandervell some years after the original share transfer, when the court decision was made.

See Chapter 1 (p. 10) for more on *Westdeutsche Landesbank v Islington London Borough Council* (1996).

In cases of failure to dispose of the entire beneficial interest, it is a question of construction as to whether a resulting trust arises or not. An attempt has to be made to assess the intention of the individual settlor.

Lord Browne-Wilkinson in ***Westdeutsche Landesbank v Islington London Borough Council*** [1996] 2 All ER 961 categorised *Quistclose* trusts (see p. 28) as trusts arising where there was a failure to exhaust the whole beneficial interest.

One situation where a resulting trust does not arise is where property is held on trust for a beneficiary absolutely who dies intestate, leaving no one entitled to his property under the provisions of the intestacy rules. In such a case the Crown takes the property as *bona vacantia* (see ss 45 and 46 of the Administration of Estates Act 1925).

Trusts for particular help for beneficiaries where there is a surplus after the purpose has been completed

Individuals may decide to establish a trust to help some named beneficiaries and they state the way that the trust funds are to be used. For example, a trust may be set up 'for the education of Peter's children' and contributions are made to the trust fund by a number of people. Once the children's education has been completed, who will be entitled to any remaining property if the trust does not specify its ownership? One solution is a resulting trust under which the surplus will be held for the donors who will be entitled to an interest proportionate to their contributions. However, it may be that as a matter of construction the remaining property should be held for the beneficiaries as the donors intended to give the property irrevocably. A third possibility is that the surplus belongs to no one and should pass to the Crown as *bona vacantia*. A fourth possibility is that the settlor intended that the trustee should take any surplus personally (see ***Re Foord*** [1922] 2 Ch 519).

A general rule is to be found in the judgment of Page-Wood V-C in *Re Sanderson's Trusts* (1857) 3 K&J 497:

> If a gross sum be given, or if the whole income of the property be given, and a special purpose be assigned for that gift, the court always regards the gift as absolute, and the purpose merely as the motive for the gift, and therefore holds that the gift takes effect as to the whole sum or the whole income, as the case may be.

In other words, the transfer is presumed to be out and out and so a resulting trust will be the exception rather than the rule.

The next case may be regarded as perhaps unusual and exceptional in the light of this statement of Page-Wood V-C.

Re the Trusts of the Abbott Fund [1900] 2 Ch 326

Funds were left in the will of Dr Abbott to support his two sisters who were deaf and dumb. His trustee died and it was found that the money had disappeared. An appeal was launched by a Mr Smith among others inviting subscriptions to enable the ladies to live in lodgings in Cambridge, and to provide for 'their very moderate wants'. Considerable sums were raised and a large surplus remained when the ladies died. There was no express provision for disposing of any surplus. The court was asked to determine who was entitled to these funds. Were they held on resulting trust for the subscribers or were the personal representatives of the ladies able to claim the funds? The court held that there was a resulting trust as there was no intention on the part of the subscribers to part with their money irrevocably and they did not intend that the fund should become the absolute property of the ladies, merely that the trustees should have the discretion as to whether to use the money for the benefit of the two ladies. Stirling J said that he could not accept that the donors would have intended the ladies to become the absolute owners of the property. He said it could not be imagined that the donors would have wished that, if one of the ladies had become bankrupt, the property would be available to pay her debts. That would be the result of the ladies being absolute owners of the property. Stirling J went on to say that the ladies would not be without some rights over the fund. If, for example, the trustees had not done their duty (perhaps because they failed to exercise their discretion properly), the ladies could apply to the court to have the fund administered properly.

This case should be compared with *Re Andrew's Trust* [1905] 2 Ch 48. The Rt Revd Joseph Barclay, the first Bishop of Jerusalem, died in 1881 leaving seven infant children. Friends raised £900, which they gave to trustees with the power to use the funds for the education of the children. By 1899 the children had completed their formal education and the trust was terminated, leaving surplus funds. The court decided that the intention of the subscribers was to create a trust for the benefit of the children and that education was just a method of benefiting them, which was appropriate at the time of setting up the fund. Therefore, the surplus was not held on resulting trust but belonged to the children absolutely. In other words, the court found that the subscribers intended to give irrevocably.

It may well be that the decision of the court in *Re Abbott* was influenced by the fact that all the beneficiaries were dead, whereas in *Re Andrew's Trust* they were alive. This meant that in *Re Abbott* there could be no question of the beneficiaries continuing to need help; in *Re Andrew's Trust*, as the beneficiaries were all alive, they could continue to be in need of help in a general way, if not in the particular way mentioned by the subscribers. This really ought not to have had any relevance to the decisions, as the court should have been attempting to establish the intention of the subscribers at the time when they made their contributions.

Re Osoba [1979] 2 All ER 393

A testator left money on trust for the maintenance of his daughter and for the training of her up to university grade. After the daughter finished university there were funds remaining. How should the trustees hold these funds? The Court of Appeal held that there was no resulting trust because the testator intended to make an absolute gift to his daughter, and the fact that the will specifically mentioned maintenance and education was merely an expression of the motive of the testator for making the gift rather than an indication that he had given the property for a specific and limited purpose only. So again, the court decided that the gift was an out and out one and so precluded the possibility of there being any resulting trust.

Buckley LJ said that if a testator gives the whole of a fund to trustees, then in the absence of any contraindication he will be regarded as having shown an intention to pass the full ownership of the property. The fact that the testator said the gift was made for a particular purpose will not affect this position.

The view of Buckley LJ is consistent with the statement of Page-Wood V-C in *Re Sanderson's Trusts* (see p. 269).

Re Gillingham Bus Disaster Fund [1958] 2 All ER 749

In this case, the court was again asked to decide on the ownership of surplus funds. A large amount of money was collected after a number of Royal Marine cadets were killed or injured when a bus ran into them. After various sums had been paid out, there remained a substantial amount of money. The court was asked to decide what the trustees should do with these surplus funds. One major problem was that a large number of people had subscribed to the fund and much of it had been raised by means of street collections. The two competing claims were that a resulting trust should exist and that the Crown was entitled as *bona vacantia*. The court decided that the surplus should be held on resulting trust for the contributors, despite the fact that it would obviously be difficult, if not impossible, to trace all the contributors, especially those who had given by way of street collection.

Harman J said:

The general principle must be that where money is held upon trust and the trusts do not exhaust the fund it will revert to the donor or settlor under what is called a resulting trust. The reasoning behind this is that the settlor or donor did not part with his money out and out but only *sub modo* to the intent that his wishes as declared by the declaration of trust should be carried into effect. When, therefore, this has been done any surplus belongs to him.

Harman J went on to say that in these cases a resulting trust arises where the expectations of the settlor have, for unforeseen reasons, not come to fruition.

If Harman J based his decision on a resulting trust arising automatically (without the intention of the transferors being relevant), this reasoning may need to be reconsidered in the light of the statement of Lord Browne-Wilkinson in *Westdeutsche Landesbank* v *Islington London Borough Council* [1996] 2 All ER 961 (see p. 264). This will be the case if the statement means that intention is relevant in cases of resulting trusts regarded by Megarry J as automatically arising, and that in some cases (and perhaps *Re Gillingham* is one of them) there may be evidence that points towards the transferor abandoning any undisposed of beneficial interest should the trust fail. If such intention is found to exist then there can be no resulting trust and the property should accrue to the Crown as *bona vacantia*.

Unincorporated associations: surplus funds

See Chapter 9 (p. 199) for more on unincorporated associations. The problem of the ownership of surplus funds often occurs if an unincorporated association ceases to exist.

Transfers into the names of others

Objective 4

If someone who is the owner of property decides to transfer it to another, what rights are created in the transferred property? One possibility is that the transferee is the outright owner of the property and the transferor no longer has any rights. Another possibility is that the transferee takes as trustee and holds the property on trust for the transferor. In attempting to decide on the ownership, it is necessary to deal with land and personalty separately.

In some instances the ownership of property is settled by applying either the presumption of resulting trust or the presumption of advancement (if the transfer was made before s 199 of the Equality Act 2010 comes into force). Where the presumption of resulting trust applies, the transferee will hold the property on trust for the transferor (or on trust for the transferor and the transferee). If the transfer took place before s 199 of the Equality Act 2010 comes into force, where the transferor was the father of the transferee or the husband of the transferee or stood *in loco parentis* to the transferee, the presumption of resulting trust was replaced by the presumption of advancement. (These two presumptions are discussed in more detail later in this chapter.)

In the past, these presumptions were used to decide ownership in many situations. However, it seems that increasingly the presumptions are being used as 'last resorts' to decide cases where there is little or no evidence of actual intention. In all cases the preference must be that the actual intentions should be the basis of any decision.

But in any case if, as it appears in many (perhaps most) cases of voluntary transfer, a gift rather than a resulting trust for the donor is intended, logically, if any presumption should be relevant it should be a presumption of gift (or advancement).

In *Kyriakides* v *Pippas* [2004] 2 FCR 434 (Ch) the court cited, with approval, the statement of Lord Phillips MR in *Lavelle* v *Lavelle* [2004] 2 FCR 418.

> The case law has developed in such a way that even 'comparatively slight evidence' will rebut the presumption and a 'less rigid approach should also be adopted to the admissibility of evidence to rebut the presumption of advancement'.

The judge in *Kyriakides* v *Pippas* went on to state that he suspected the 'position we have now reached is that the courts will always strive to work out the real intention of the purchaser and will only give effect to the presumptions of resulting trust and advancement where the intention cannot be fathomed and a "long-stop" or "default" solution is needed'. It is assumed that this will also apply to cases of transfer into the name of another (as opposed to purchase in the name of another).

 ## Presumption of resulting trust

Land

Before 1925, in order to prevent a resulting trust from arising, it was necessary to insert an express statement into a voluntary conveyance of land that the property was being transferred to the use of the transferee. Section 60(3) of the Law of Property Act 1925 provides some help if the property is land (including leaseholds) by providing that in a voluntary conveyance a resulting trust for the grantor shall not be implied merely by reason that the property is not expressed to be conveyed for the use or benefit of the grantee.

There is uncertainty as to the precise effect of the subsection. Before the section was enacted, it was necessary to insert into a conveyance a provision such as 'unto and to the use of' the transferee in order to ensure that the conveyance was effective and that there was no resulting trust in favour of the transferor. The current position has been said to be 'debatable' (e.g. the remarks of Russell LJ in **Hodgson v Marks** [1971] 2 All ER 682). In **Tinsley v Milligan** [1993] 3 All ER 65, Lord Browne-Wilkinson said that it was arguable that the position had been changed by the 1925 legislation. The effect of the subsection appears to be to create a general rule that there will not be a resulting trust and so the property will belong, outright, to the transferee. There will not be a resulting trust *merely* because the transferor fails to state that the transfer is made for the benefit of the transferee. Of course, there is nothing to prevent a resulting trust arising if this is found to be what the transferor intended, but the point of s 60(3) is that such a trust will not arise *just* from the fact that there is no statement that the transfer is for the benefit of the transferee. In other words, on this interpretation, the effect of the subsection is to reverse the burden of proof regarding the existence of a resulting trust.

Lohia v Lohia [2001] WTLR 101 appears to be the first English case in which the decision was dependent on an interpretation of s 60(3).

Lohia v Lohia [2001] WTLR 101

Property was purchased in equal shares by a son and his father in 1955 with the assistance of a mortgage. Subsequently, in 1965, the property was transferred into the sole name of the father. The father died intestate in 1971.

The son claimed he had a 50 per cent interest in the property. The claim was dependent upon the transfer of the property into the father's sole name in 1965. The son claimed that he had no knowledge of the transfer made in 1965. There was no evidence of the transfer, save for the Land Registry record, which stated that the property had been transferred to the father 'not for value'. It was on that basis that Nicholas Strauss QC found that there was a transfer to the father in 1965. He rejected the son's allegation of forgery. The judge decided that, on the evidence and on the balance of probabilities, the transfer was more probably as a result of a family arrangement. Nicholas Strauss QC, having considered a number of cases and academic literature cited to him, stated that the presumption of a resulting trust arising from a voluntary transfer of property had been abolished by s 60(3) Law of Property Act 1925.

The claim for the 50 per cent share was rejected.

Strauss QC did, however, make it clear that, in his view, a resulting trust could arise on the basis of evidence of intention to create a resulting trust rather than a gift. In the event, Strauss QC, having considered the evidence, decided that on the balance of probabilities a gift was intended. It is often suggested that, despite s 60(3), if the transferee is intended to take the property beneficially, this should be clearly expressed in the documentation. This would appear to be sensible to ensure, beyond any doubt, that the settlor's intention is implemented.

The son appealed to the Court of Appeal.

Lohia v Lohia [2001] EWCA Civ 1691

The son claimed that the judge was wrong in his conclusions as to the effect that s 60(3) had upon the application of the presumption of a resulting trust on a voluntary transfer. The son conceded that, if his appeal upon the judge's factual findings failed, his second ground on s 60(3) was also bound to fail. The Court held, dismissing the appeal, that on the basis of the available evidence the judge was entitled to have concluded that the transfer was made on the basis of a family arrangement. Thus, unfortunately, the Court of Appeal did not have to make a decision on whether or not the presumption of a resulting trust on a voluntary transfer survived s 60(3). But Mummery LJ said:

> It would certainly appear from the language and statutory context of Section 60(3) that (1) the provision rules out any possible argument that a resulting trust should be implied merely from the absence of the words 'unto and to the use of' in a conveyance which had hitherto been included in . . . ; and (2) there is nothing in the subsection which precludes the implication of a resulting trust in the case of a voluntary conveyance by reason of circumstances other than the omission of the words 'unto and to the use of' from the conveyance.
>
> On the point whether the effect of the 1925 Act is to abolish the presumption of a resulting trust arising from a voluntary conveyance, I would prefer to express no concluded view, as it is unnecessary to do so for the disposition of this appeal.

Thus, subject to the statement of Strauss QC and the view expressed by Mummery LJ, the issue is no nearer a solution.

An opportunity to discuss s 60(3) arose in **Hodgson v Marks** but was not taken up.

Hodgson v Marks [1971] 2 All ER 682

Mrs Hodgson owned a house in Edgware and took in Evans as a lodger. She liked and trusted Evans but her nephew did not. The nephew tried to persuade Mrs Hodgson to turn Evans out, and in an attempt to stop this she transferred the house into the name of Evans. It was orally agreed that the house would remain hers. Four years later Evans sold the house to Marks, who was unaware of the agreement made between Evans and Mrs Hodgson. What was the position of Mrs Hodgson? Was she protected against Marks?

The Court of Appeal held that, although her agreement with Evans was not evidenced in writing as required by s 53(1)(b) of the Law of Property Act 1925, Mrs Hodgson was entitled under a resulting trust. The court decided that if an attempt to create an express trust failed, that was the occasion for a resulting trust to come into being. The court listened to evidence of Mrs Hodgson's intention and this played a part in the finding of a resulting trust. The interesting aspect of this case is that s 60(3) was not discussed at all.

Pure personalty

If the property is pure personalty, s 60(3) does not apply and the general equitable principles govern the situation. So, if the effect of s 60(3) is to abolish the doctrine of resulting trusts applying to voluntary transfers of land, we are left with voluntary transfers of land being treated differently from voluntary transfers of personalty. While it is not unusual for different rules to apply it does seem a little strange that in the context of the intention of the donor, the type of property transferred should be so crucial in deciding whether or not a resulting trust exists. These principles provide that in cases of voluntary transfer into the name of another a resulting trust will be presumed to arise and the transferee will hold the property on trust for the transferor. This is called the presumption of resulting trust. This same presumption will apply if the property is transferred into the names of the transferor and another. The presumption will be that the property is held on trust for the transferor.

This presumption is supposed to be based on the presumed intention of transferors in that they would not wish to part with the beneficial ownership as the result of a voluntary transfer. This does seem debatable as it is hard to see why these voluntary transfers should not, normally, be intended as outright gifts. It could be argued that if one transfers property into the name of another, then an intention to make an outright gift should be assumed to be the norm, and that if this is not what is intended this should be made clear by an express provision or it should be apparent from the evidence of surrounding circumstances. It would be rather unusual for an individual who wished to create a trust not to say so expressly; most people, surely, would state that a trust was intended?

The current position seems to be that, while the presumption of a resulting trust still exists, it can be relatively readily rebutted and an intention to make a gift discovered. Or perhaps the presumption is only used if there is no satisfactory evidence of intention.

An example of the presumption of resulting trust may be seen in the case of *Re Vinogradoff*.

Re Vinogradoff [1935] WN 68

In 1926, Mrs Vinogradoff voluntarily transferred £800 of War Loan, which stood in her name, into the joint names of herself and her granddaughter Laura, aged four years. Mrs Vinogradoff continued to receive the income from the War Loan. When Mrs Vinogradoff died, the ownership of the War Loan had to be determined. Farwell J held that the presumption of resulting trust applied and that the granddaughter held the property for the benefit of the estate of Mrs Vinogradoff. (The fact that the granddaughter was under the age of majority did not prevent her from being the trustee under a resulting trust (see p. 409).)

Transfer into joint names

Before 1996, if Arthur transfered real property into the joint names of himself and Ben, the presumption of resulting trust led to the property being held on trust for the transferor, Arthur, alone. However, if there was no resulting trust, land was held by Arthur and Ben jointly on a trust for sale and the income was held for them until sale. Once the land was sold, the proceeds will be held for the two transferees.

Transfers of land on or after after 1 January 1996 are governed by the Trusts of Land and Appointment of Trustees Act 1996 s 5 and Schedule 2, and the property will be held on a trust of land with power of sale. However, if the property is personalty and no resulting trust arises, a number of possibilities exist. The first solution may be that Ben is to have the capital after Arthur dies, but in the meantime Arthur is to have the income. Secondly, as much of the capital as is left at Arthur's death is to belong to Ben. Thirdly, there may be a simple gift to Arthur and Ben as joint tenants.

Rebutting the presumption

The presumption of resulting trust can be rebutted by evidence that at the time of the transfer the intention of the transferor was not to create a trust, e.g. by evidence that the transferee should have the outright ownership of the property.

The burden of producing evidence to rebut the presumption of a resulting trust is an evidential burden. If the transferee succeeds in rebutting the presumption, then unless the transferor can bring evidence to discharge the legal burden and show that an express trust was created, the claim to ownership by the transferor will fail and the property will be held for the transferee.

Presumption of advancement

The presumption of advancement displaces the presumption of resulting trusts where certain relationships exist between the transferor and the transferee. For example, transfers from a husband to his wife give rise to the presumption of advancement. The presumption is based on the assumption that the transferor, where these relationships exist, intends the transfer to satisfy, at least in part, a moral obligation towards the transferee.

The presumption of advancement may itself be rebutted by evidence that the transferor intended that the transferee should take the property on trust for the transferor and that no gift was intended (see below).

The presumption has been under review for a number of years and has been subject to a number of criticisms and suggestions for reform.

In *Pettit* v *Pettit* [1969] 2 All ER 385, Lord Diplock opined that the presumption of advancement between husband and wife was outdated, being based on values of earlier generations. He thought that the presumption should play little part in deciding the allocation of interests in modern cases.

See Chapter 13 (pp. 365–82) for more on *Stack* v *Dowden*.

In 1999, the Law Commission issued a consultation paper, 'Illegal Transactions: the effect of illegality on contracts and trusts' (Law Com. No. 154), in which the abolition of the presumption was mooted. In 2002 the Law Commission published a discussion paper, 'Sharing Homes' (Law Com. No. 278), in which the presumption was said to be 'somewhat anachronistic'. But in the Report 'The Illegality Defence' (2010) Law Com. No. 320, the abolition was not recommended. This was in the main due to the uncertainty that *Stack* v *Dowden* [2007] 2 All ER 929 has created in this area.

However, the Government decided that legislation was needed to amend or abolish the presumption of advancement, which discriminates between men and women, before the Government could carry out its commitment to ratify Article 5 of Protocol 7 of the European Convention on Human Rights. In the event, the abolition of the presumption was included in the Equality Act 2010 s 199. The Government is considering when the section will come into force.

S 199 Abolition of presumption of advancement

(1) The presumption of advancement (by which, for example, a husband is presumed to be making a gift to his wife if he transfers property to her, or purchases property in her name) is abolished.
(2) The abolition by subsection (1) of the presumption of advancement does not have effect in relation to –
   (a) anything done before the commencement of this section, or
   (b) anything done pursuant to any obligation incurred before the commencement of this section.

Despite the section giving some examples of when the presumption applies, it is clear that the section will abolish the presumption in all situations. What is not absolutely clear is the meaning of 'obligation' in s 199(2)(b). Does it mean only legal obligations or will moral obligations be included?

Once the section is operative where there would have been a presumption of advancement, there will be a presumption of resulting trust, although in such cases it may well be that the presumption will be readily rebutted.

Although the section states that the abolition will not apply to anything done or to transfers made before the date the section comes into force, it remains possible, but probably unlikely, for the presumption to be abolished by the judiciary in such situations.

The discussions that follow reflect the current position and will also remain relevant in situations involving anything done before s 199 comes into force and anything done pursuant to any obligation incurred before s 199 comes into force. Additionally the discussions will be relevant in cases where a settlor has excluded the provisions of s 199. The presumption will continue to have relevance for some years to come.

Relationships that give rise to a presumption of advancement

The presumption of advancement (or gift) arises when certain relationships exist between the transferor and the transferee. The relevant relationships involve a moral obligation on the part of the transferor towards the transferee. The presumption is based on the assumption that the transfer was intended to satisfy, at least in part, that moral obligation.

In *Bennett* v *Bennett* (1879) 10 Ch D 474 Sir George Jessel MR explained the basis of the presumption:

> The doctrine of equity as regards presumption of gifts is this, that where one person stands in such a relation to another that there is an obligation on that person to make a provision for the other, and we find either a purchase or investment in the name of the other, or in the joint names of the person and the other, of an amount which would constitute a provision for the other, the presumption arises of an intention on the part of the person to discharge the obligation to the other; and therefore, in the absence of evidence to the contrary, that purchase or investment is held to be in itself evidence of a gift.
>
> In other words, the presumption of gift arises from the moral obligation to give.
>
> That reconciles all the cases upon the subject but one, because nothing is better established than this, that as regards a child, a person not the father of the child may put himself in the position of one *in loco parentis* to the child, and so incur the obligation to make a provision for the child . . .
>
> But the father is under that obligation from the mere fact of his being the father, and therefore no evidence is necessary to shew the obligation to provide for his child, because that is part of his duty. In the case of a father, you have only to prove the fact that he is the father, and when you have done that the obligation at once arises; but in the case of a person *in loco parentis* you must prove that he took upon himself the obligation.

The presumption applies to the transfers between:

- father and his legitimate child;
- husband and wife;
- a man and his fiancée whom he later marries;
- one who stands *in loco parentis* to another person and that person.

But the presumption does not apply to transfers between:

- father and illegitimate child or stepchild (unless the father stands *in loco parentis* to the child);
- wife and husband;
- mother and her child (unless the mother stands *in loco parentis* to the child);
- a man and his cohabitee.

The fact that the presumption does not arise where a wife transfers property to her husband seems to run counter to the European Convention on Human Rights. This is one of the reasons why the presumption will be abolished by s 199 of the Equality Act 2010 once the section comes into force.

The position between a father and his illegitimate child appears not to have been affected by the Family Law Reform Act 1987, and it remains the position that there is no presumption of advancement between a father and his illegitimate child unless the father stands *in loco parentis*.

As stated above, there is no presumption of advancement between mother and child. This seems extraordinary as the basis of the presumption is the moral responsibility of the transferor to the transferee. Certainly, in the second decade of the twenty-first century, it can be argued that both a father and a mother owe a moral responsibility to a child. The approach of the law, however, is rather different. While preserving the traditional view that there is no presumption of advancement, the current approach of the courts is to adopt the attitude of Sir George Jessel MR, which he expressed over a century ago in *Bennett* v *Bennett* (1879) 10 Ch D 474: 'In the case of a mother . . . it is easier to prove a gift than in the case of a stranger: in the case of a mother very little evidence beyond the relationship is wanted.'

For an example of the existence of the presumption of resulting trust rather than of advancement between mother and daughter, see *Sekhon* v *Alissa* [1989] 2 FLR 94 (see p. 280). The Australian case of *Nelson* v *Nelson* (1995) 312 ALR 133 will, perhaps, provide an example for the English courts, encouraging a review of the law in this area. In *Nelson* v *Nelson* the court ruled that a voluntary transfer from a mother to her child did give rise to a presumption of advancement.

Brown v *Brown* [1993] 31 NSWLR 582 is another Australian case in which the presumption of advancement *was* said to apply to fathers *and* mothers.

Re Cameron [1999] 3 WLR 394 at 409 suggested that the presumption *should* apply between mother and child.

In *Close Invoice Finance* v *Abaowa* [2010] EWHC 1920 (QB) Mr Picken QC, sitting as Deputy Judge, held that the distinction between a father and a mother, in the context of the presumption of advancement, cannot stand today. In many situations it makes no practical difference that the court starts from the position of a presumption of resulting trust, which can be very easily rebutted, rather than from the position of a presumption of advancement. But it may be very significant in some cases. See, for example, *Tinsley* v *Milligan* (p. 281). Also, a transfer from an individual to one to whom he stands *in loco parentis* will cause the presumption to come into play. (See next section for a discussion of *in loco parentis* relationships.)

In practice, in many situations the presumption is often weak and often is fairly easily rebutted. In *McGrath* v *Wallis* [1995] 2 FLR 114 Nourse LJ, having cited the House of Lords decision in *Pettitt* v *Pettitt* [1969] WLR 966, said that the presumption of advancement was a judicial instrument of last resort.

Some illustrations of the presumption will help to set the presumption into context and will illustrate some of the categories outlined above.

A relatively modern case involving the presumption of advancement and its rebuttal on a transfer from a father to a child is *Lavelle* v *Lavelle* [2004] EWCA Civ 223. G was the father of T. G bought a flat in 1997. The flat was transferred into the name of T. T argued that it had always been G's intention to convey the flat to her by way of gift and produced a disputed document, purported to be signed by G in support.

In the event the presumption was rebutted. The judge decided the evidence pointed towards the transfer of the flat to T not being intended to be by way of gift, but being made merely to try to avoid inheritance tax purposes.

The judge found that T held the flat on trust for G.

In *Beckford* v *Beckford* (1774) Lofft 490 it was held that the presumption of advancement did not arise between a father and his illegitimate or stepchild (although, of course, it may be that the father assumes an *in loco parentis* relationship (see below) and then the presumption of advancement would arise).

The presumption of advancement also applies as between a man and woman who plan to get married and the marriage takes place. In the case of an engagement ring, s 3(2) of the Law Reform (Miscellaneous Provisions) Act 1970 provides for a statutory presumption of advancement even if the marriage is not celebrated. There is, of course, no reason why the gift of the ring should not be made subject to an express condition for its return should the marriage not take place.

In *Cox* v *Jones* [2004] 3 FCR 693 (Ch) the couple disputed the ownership of the engagement ring. The situation was covered by the Law Reform (Miscellaneous Provisions) Act 1970 s 3(2). J's claim to the ring failed as he had not established that he had told C that he was giving her the ring on the basis that he would want it back if the engagement ended. So the presumption of advancement was not rebutted.

In **Re Gooch** (1890) 62 LT 384, the father of a director of a company bought some shares in the company in the name of his son (the director). The son handed over all dividends declared on these shares to his father. The reason for the purchase was to enable the son to satisfy the rules of the company which required a director to hold a specified number of shares. The court decided that the presumption of advancement was rebutted, finding that the evidence showed that the father bought the shares only in order that a technical rule of the company was met and not in order to pass the beneficial ownership in the shares to his son.

The presumption of advancement was rebutted in **Simpson** v **Simpson** [1992] 1 FLR 601, where a husband transferred his bank account into the joint names of himself and his wife. On the facts, the husband did not have the necessary mental capacity to make a gift and the property was held, after his death, by his wife on resulting trust for his estate.

Other relationships

Although, technically, there may be no presumption of advancement between mother and child or father and illegitimate child, it may be that in some such relationships the transferor is *in loco parentis* to the transferee and so the presumption applies for this reason.

In **Bennett** v **Bennett** (1879) 10 Ch D 474, Sir George Jessel MR said that the term *in loco parentis* describes the situation when a person takes upon himself (or herself) the duty of the father of a child to make provision for that child. It is important to realise that the relationship does not arise simply because some provision is made for a child; the essence of the concept is that the provider assumes the responsibility for providing for the child. The responsibility which has to be assumed is the moral obligation recognised by equity, and the presence or absence of a legal duty imposed by statute is irrelevant. The presumption of advancement (or gift) arises from this moral obligation and the court assumes that a transfer is intended to be in discharge of this obligation.

Sansom v **Gardner and McCarthy** [2009] EWHC 3369 (QB) is a first-instance decision which involves the presumption of resulting trust and the impact of illegal motives on a claim based on the ownership of property under a resulting trust. But here we deal with the requirements for there to be a *loco parentis* relationship giving rise to a presumption of advancement.

S provided the purchase price for a house which was conveyed into the name of G. G later sold the house and bought a second house with the proceeds. S put the property in the name of G as part of a plan to evade capital gains tax on the subsequent sale of the property.

The court held that there was no presumption of advancement although S and G had had a close relationship. The court considered that the closeness that existed between S and G, and any generosity extended by S to G, stemmed from the fact that he (G) had been working as S's right-hand man, and no doubt had intimate knowledge of his business affairs. There was no evidence that there was an *in loco parentis* relationship under which S intended to take upon himself the duty of a father.

Thus this was a case of purchase in the name of another, giving rise to a presumption of resulting trust. *Tinsley* v *Milligan* [1994] 1 AC 340 HL (see below) applied as the claim of S was based on the presumption of resulting trust and he did not have to rely on the evidence of his intention to evade tax.

In cases involving transfers to children by mothers where the presumption of resulting trust arises, the courts appear very ready to find that the evidence presented is enough to rebut the presumption and find that a gift was intended.

Evidence admissible to rebut a presumption

Both the presumption of resulting trust and the presumption of advancement can be rebutted by evidence. However, there are limitations on the evidence which is admissible.

One of the restrictions is illustrated by *Shephard* v *Cartwright* [1954] 3 All ER 649.

Shephard v *Cartwright* [1954] 3 All ER 649

In 1929, a father allotted shares in his company to three children. In 1934, they authorised the father to deal with the shares and dividends and later signed the necessary documents to enable the shares to be sold. At no time did they appreciate the legal consequences of what they were doing. The father sold the shares and paid the proceeds into the children's bank accounts. Later the children signed a document authorising the father to withdraw money from these accounts. The father exhausted the accounts through a series of withdrawals. When the father died in 1949 the question arose as to whether the shares had been given to the children, applying the presumption of advancement (in which case the father's estate would have to repay the children), or whether the presumption was rebutted and the shares were held on resulting trust. The House of Lords held that there was no evidence to rebut the presumption of advancement and so the children were entitled to seek repayment.

In the course of his judgment, Viscount Simonds discussed the evidence that is admissible in such cases. He said that acts and declarations of the parties before or at the time of the transfer (or so soon after the transfer that they could be regarded as contemporaneous) were admissible as evidence either for or against the party who performed the act or made the statement. However, later acts or declarations were admissible only against the party who made them and not in his favour. The effect of this is to prevent a person transferring property and then building up a case in his favour by making statements or performing acts.

But in *Lavelle* v *Lavelle* [2004] 2 FCR 418 Lord Phillips MR applied a different and more flexible approach to the admissibility of evidence which, if followed in subsequent cases, will permit the intentions of the parties to be ascertained in a wider range of cases:

[I]t is not satisfactory to apply rigid rules of law to the evidence that is admissible to rebut the presumption of advancement. Plainly, self-serving statements or conduct of a transferor, who may long after the transaction be regretting earlier generosity, carry little or no weight. But words or conduct more proximate to the transaction itself should be given the significance that they naturally bear as part of the overall picture.

Evidence of improper motives

Although recent decisions have developed the law in this area, initially the generally held view was that the courts would not allow an individual to use evidence of his own improper motives for a transfer to rebut a presumption. For example, using this approach, if Arthur transfers property to his wife, giving rise to the presumption of advancement, Arthur could not try to rebut the presumption and claim that there was a resulting trust by arguing that he did not intend to give the property to his wife as he only transferred the property for the (illegal) purpose of tax evasion, and that he always intended that the property would remain his. If this evidence was admitted, it would allow Arthur to set up his own unlawful act to rebut the presumption of advancement. This is an example of the application of the maxim 'he who comes to equity must come with clean hands'.

Lord Goff, in *Tinsley* v *Milligan*, pointed out that the strict indiscriminate application of the principle – which, as Lord Mansfield said in *Holman* v *Johnson* (1775) 1 Cowp 341, is a principle of policy rather than a principle of justice – could lead to unfair consequences. The courts are clearly unwilling to accept such a consequence and so have developed exceptions to the rule. See particularly the cases of *Tinsley* v *Milligan* and *Tribe* v *Tribe*, both of which are discussed below.

Gascoigne v *Gascoigne* [1918] 1 KB 223

In this case, a husband took a lease in his wife's name as he was trying to keep the property out of the hands of his creditors. He argued that the presumption of advancement should be rebutted as he did not intend to give the property to his wife. The court held that he was unable to use the evidence as it would involve setting up his own attempt to defraud creditors. It did not matter that his wife was aware of the scheme; she was still able to claim the property as the presumption of advancement remained unrebutted.

An apparently similar case was *Tinker* v *Tinker* [1970] 1 All ER 540, where a husband transferred the matrimonial home into the name of his wife in order to protect it from creditors of his business. The Court of Appeal held that the presumption of advancement stood unrebutted and the wife was entitled to the house. The court found that in this case the husband, unlike the husband in *Gascoigne* v *Gascoigne*, acted honestly and without any fraudulent motive. But, as Lord Denning MR said, the husband was on the horns of a dilemma when, later, the issue of ownership had to be decided. As against his creditors he wanted to argue that the house belonged to his wife, whereas against his wife he wanted to argue the house was his. The court held that the presumption of advancement which arose on the transfer to the wife remained and was not rebutted.

Sekhon v *Alissa* [1989] 2 FLR 94

In this case, a mother and her daughter both contributed to the purchase price of a house which was conveyed into the name of the daughter alone as part of a possible plan for the mother to evade capital gains tax when the house was sold. The mother already owned another house. Under capital gains tax a person is not liable for tax on the sale of their only or main residence. If the second house was part-owned by the mother, this exemption would not apply to her interest on the sale of that house as her other house would attract her exemption. So when the second house was sold the mother would be liable for tax on any gain attributable to her share of the property. If the second house was treated as owned by the daughter alone, not only would the mother escape tax but so would the daughter as she could claim it was her only or main residence and so it would fall within the exemption. Later, the mother alleged that the house should be held by the daughter on a resulting trust for herself and the daughter. The daughter argued that the usual presumption of resulting trust was rebutted as her mother had intended a gift. The daughter said there was a moral, but no legal, obligation to repay her mother. Alternatively, it was argued that the money that the mother had contributed was intended to be a loan giving her no beneficial interest in the property. The court held that there was not sufficient evidence, either of gift or loan, to displace the presumption of a resulting trust with the beneficial interest being proportionate to their contributions. Hoffmann J said that the fact that the parties may have decided to have the house conveyed into the name of the daughter with a view to a possible tax advantage did not necessarily bear any relation to what the beneficial interests were actually intended to be. The fact that the mother had a fraudulent intention (the evasion of tax) did not prevent her from relying on the presumption as the purpose had not been carried out. The mother, it was said, had not come anywhere near to an actual plan. She had been told by a friend that there would be a tax problem and that it might be a good idea if she was not named in the conveyance.

In *Sekhon* v *Alisa* Hoffmann J referred to *Chettiar* v *Chettiar* [1962] 1 All ER 494, in which the fraudulent scheme had been carried through and in which Lord Denning had said that if a purpose had not been carried through the mere plan would not necessarily prevent a party from relying on the true intention. There are decisions which suggest that, perhaps, Hoffmann J erred. Case law indicates that the courts have required 'genuine repentance'. (See, for example, *Bigos* v *Boustead* [1951] 1 All ER 92.) If the only reason a fraudulent scheme was not carried through was that there had been a delay or some other factor, rather than repentance on the part of the mother, then the presence of the fraudulent plan should have prevented her from asserting her interest in the property. (See *Tinsley* v *Milligan*, below; but also *Tribe* v *Tribe*, p. 285.) Additionally, it may be thought rather surprising that the presumption of resulting trust was not found to be rebutted. In *Bennett* v *Bennett* (1879) 10 Ch D 474 (p. 278), Sir George Jessel MR emphasised how little evidence was required, beyond the relationship, to rebut the presumption. In the instant case there was, in fact, additional evidence that the mother may have intended a gift to her daughter. In *Sekhon* v *Alissa*, the mother, rather than the father, was in reality financially responsible for her. The father was retired and the main financial burden for the family was on the mother. There was evidence that the mother was anxious that her daughter be provided for. Nevertheless, despite this evidence, the court found that the presumption had not been rebutted.

The cases discussed above may need to be reconsidered in the light of *Tinsley* v *Milligan* [1992] 2 All ER 391, in which the Court of Appeal reviewed the law regarding the admission of evidence involving the wrongful act of the party seeking to adduce the evidence.

Tinsley v *Milligan* [1992] 2 All ER 391

Two joint owners of a house, Tinsley and Milligan, agreed to transfer it into the sole name of Tinsley. The reason for this was to enable Milligan to defraud the DSS into paying her housing benefit. Tinsley was aware of the scheme and indeed perpetrated frauds of her own. Later Milligan confessed her fraud to the DSS. The Court of Appeal granted Milligan a declaration that Tinsley held the property on trust for both Tinsley and Milligan as equitable tenants in common. This was in spite of the fact that Milligan used the evidence of her intention to defraud in order to support her claim that she had not intended to give the property to Tinsley. It was argued on behalf of Tinsley that if there was any element of fraud that was the end of the matter and the court would not enforce the trust which Milligan claimed existed.

Nicholls LJ examined the position when the courts applied the common law doctrine *ex turpi causa non oritur actio* (no right of action arises from a base cause). The authorities seemed to establish that the court should apply a public conscience test. Under the test the court must balance the adverse consequences of granting relief against the adverse consequences of refusing relief. The court must determine if it would be an affront to the public conscience to grant the relief sought. His Lordship thought it would be a remarkable reversal of the traditional function of law and equity if the common law doctrine of *ex turpi* was applied in a more flexible way than its equitable counterpart and felt that the mere presence of fraud or illegality should not automatically mean that the relief sought should not be granted. In determining where the equitable balance lay, the court would take into account, *inter alia*, the nature and seriousness of the illegality, the extent to which the failure to enforce the claim would result in an unjust enrichment or unmerited windfall, the extent to which enforcement might act as an encouragement to others to behave in an illegal manner and the relative culpability of the parties. His Lordship thought that the authorities relied on by Tinsley, including **Tinker** v **Tinker** and **Gascoigne** v **Gascoigne**, should be regarded as instances where the court felt that to have granted relief would have been an affront to the public conscience and they were not to be regarded as laying down a fixed rule.

Rowan v *Dann* (1992) 64 P& CR 202

In this case, there was an improper motive (frustrating possible creditors to ensure that the land would be available for a proposed joint business venture) for a farmer granting tenancies of some land to his potential business partner. The tenancies were granted, it was claimed, as part of a proposed joint business venture which in fact never got off the ground. The tenant paid no rent on the basis that the farmer had retained shooting rights over the land. These rights were worth far less than the rent that could have been charged for the land. At first instance Millett J found that the intention was that an interest was created in trust to apply the property for the joint venture, and when it failed there was a resulting trust for the farmer despite the farmer's 'dirty hands'. The appeal, which was based on the argument that the resulting trust was unenforceable owing to the taint of the improper purpose, was dismissed.

The Court of Appeal held that there was an enforceable resulting trust, using the 'equitable balance' approach used by the Court of Appeal in **Tinsley v Milligan**. Scott LJ referred to **Gascoigne v Gascoigne** (p. 280), in which a husband was unable to rebut the presumption of advancement by using his own dishonest intention.

In **Rowan v Dann**, there was no question of the presumption of advancement being in issue; the relevant presumption was that of resulting trust. Additionally Scott LJ said that, unlike **Tinsley v Milligan**, in the instant case the improper purpose had not been carried through and there was no evidence that any creditor had been disadvantaged. Scott LJ also said that he wished to apply the flexible approach advocated by the Court of Appeal in **Tinsley v Milligan**, and he saw no reason why the 'equitable balance' should not come down firmly on the side of the farmer. The improper intention was common to both the farmer and the tenant. Woolf LJ agreed and stressed that the farmer did not need to call into evidence his improper purpose in order to support his claim based on the presumption of resulting trust. Unlike **Tinsley v Milligan**, where the intention was that the house was intended to be the long-term home for the two women, in the instant case the purpose of the tenancies was to provide 'temporary receptacles to keep assets out of the reach of Mr Rowan's creditors until they could be made available to the joint venture'. (But, when **Tinsley v Milligan** was heard by the House of Lords (below), the concept of the 'equitable balance' was not applied.)

After the decision in *Rowan v Dann* had been made, *Tinsley v Milligan* was heard by the House of Lords.

Tinsley v Milligan [1993] 3 All ER 65

By a majority of three to two, the House agreed with the Court of Appeal and upheld the claim of Milligan that the property was held on a resulting trust by Tinsley for both women as equitable joint tenants. The decision is based on a procedural matter rather than on public policy. The House rejected the balance of conscience/equitable balance approach of the Court of Appeal. This approach, under which the court has the task of assessing whether or not to apply the rule of public policy that the courts will not assist someone with unclean hands, was unanimously condemned. Lord Goff articulated the main reasons for the rejection, saying that it amounted to a revolutionary change in the law which should be instituted by Parliament rather than the judges and that it introduced uncertainty – relying as it did on the unpredictable assessment by the court in each case as to where the balance lay. There was, however, no unanimity as to what the correct approach should be. The majority, having rejected the approach of the Court of Appeal and that of the minority (see below), held that interests under illegal transactions can be enforced but only if the party can establish his title without relying on his own illegality. In the case of establishing an equitable interest in property, the key factor was whether there was a presumption of resulting trust or of advancement. In the instant case there was a presumption of resulting trust. Milligan could rely on the presumption and did not need to plead the illegal purpose to support her claim. Had the situation been one where there was a presumption of advancement (perhaps a father buying property in the name of his daughter) and the father sought to rebut the presumption by arguing there was no intention to give because the object of putting the property into the daughter's name was to achieve an illegal purpose, the position would be different. The father could not use the evidence of his illegal purpose, in his own favour, to rebut the presumption of advancement. (But see *Tribe v Tribe*, p. 285, for the position if the purpose has not been carried through.)

One particular issue that the majority approach of the House of Lords in *Tinsley v Milligan* raises is that the claim succeeded despite the illegal or fraudulent behaviour. The court appeared to regard defrauding the Department of Social Security as a rather minor matter. Would the decision have been different if the behaviour had involved more serious offences? Lord Goff mentions transfers of property by groups of terrorists or armed robbers into the name of a third party who is not directly involved with the criminal activity. Would the courts simply use the approach of the majority and say that if the interest can be claimed without pleading the illegal behaviour then the claim will be upheld? As the majority of the court failed to accept that there is any overriding principle of public policy which would permit the court to deny the claim, the answer would seem to be that the interests of the terrorists and the armed robbers would be enforceable in the courts. Lord Goff, in a dissenting judgment, rejected the view of the majority and said that in every case a court of equity would refuse to assist an applicant who came with unclean hands even though the applicant need not rely on the fraudulent or illegal purpose to establish his claim. He said that in the instant case the court would refuse to enforce the resulting trust in Milligan's favour as the property had been placed in the name of Tinsley for a fraudulent purpose. The property would lie where it fell. This allows for no discretion and applies whatever the 'merits'. The main object is to implement the policy of discouraging fraudulent or illegal behaviour. Lord Goff said the underlying public policy is the deterrence of illegality, and the force of this deterrent effect is based on the existence of a known rule and the strict enforcement of it.

Tinsley v *Milligan* was applied in the Court of Appeal case, *Lowson* v *Coombes* [1999] 2 WLR 720. The plaintiff and defendant never married but in 1980 they purchased a flat for £5,500. The plaintiff provided £3,000 towards the purchase price and the defendant the remaining £2,500. The flat was conveyed into the sole name of the defendant as they were concerned to try to ensure that the plaintiff's wife did not have a claim over the property. The flat was sold in 1981 and the couple moved to Spain where they bought a villa. In June 1983, they returned to England, having sold the villa, and bought another property from the proceeds of sale. The property was conveyed into the sole name of the defendant. This property was sold in 1989 and the couple purchased another, again conveyed into the sole name of the defendant. In December 1991 the couple separated. The judge had found that there was evidence of a common intention to buy the property in equal shares. The Court of Appeal decided that this was a case which was on all fours with *Tinsley* v *Milligan* (which had not been cited at first instance). In this case there could be an illegality, there being an attempt to prevent a claim to property by one party of a marriage by the other and to prevent her from seeking an order under s 37(2) of the Matrimonial Causes Act 1973. The couple were not married and so there was no presumption of advancement and, as in *Tinsley* v *Milligan*, the plaintiff could rely on the presumption of resulting trust to establish his claim. *Tinker* v *Tinker* (p. 280) was distinguished and an older case (*Cantor* v *Cox* (1976) 239 EG 121, in which the existence of dishonest motive was fatal to a claim to establish a beneficial interest by a cohabitant) was said not able to stand with *Tinsley* v *Milligan* and must be taken to have been disapproved of by the House of Lords in *Tinsley* v *Milligan*.

More applications of *Tinsley* v *Milligan* include the Court of Appeal decisions of *Mortgage Express* v *Sandra McDonnell* (2001) LTL 22/5/2001 and *Woodman* v *Tracey* (2002) LTL 13/6/2002.

This latter case was a decision on whether or not a contribution to the purchase price of a house had been made and whether or not a fraudulent element had any impact on the claim to establish a trust.

Woodman v Tracey (2002) LTL 13/6/2002

W and R were married and jointly owned a house. The marriage broke up and W and R were divorced. W met T and a plan was agreed under which T would stand in the shoes of W with respect to the mortgage. However, this was not acceptable to the mortgagor.

It was then agreed that W and R would sell the property to T, who would obtain a mortgage in his sole name. For the purposes of the mortgage the property was valued at £45,000. A mortgage of £38,000 was obtained. This was the amount needed to redeem the existing mortgage. The advance was made on the assurance that W would pay £7,000 towards the purchase price. The £7,000 represented W's share of the equity in the property. In fact the £7,000 was never paid. The mortgage had been acquired by a fiction. W and T moved into the house and after the relationship broke up T remained in occupation. W claimed that T held the property on trust for himself and W. T claimed that W had made no contribution to the purchase price.

It was decided that in fact W had made a contribution in the form of her equity that was in the house at the date of the transfer.

T had benefited from that equity because he had purchased the property for £38,000 when it was valued at £45,000.

On the argument that W was prevented from establishing her claim under the trust because of the fraud involved in obtaining the mortgage, it was decided that as W did not have to rely on fraud to succeed in her claim the fraud was no bar to her claim. W simply relied on the presumption of resulting trust arising from the purchase (to which she contributed) in the name of T. (On this point the court relied on *Tinsley v Milligan*.)

The issue of the use of evidence of an unlawful purpose was again at the heart of the argument in *Tribe* v *Tribe* [1995] 4 All ER 236. In this case, the court had the problem of a transfer intended for an unlawful purpose in circumstances where the presumption of advancement arose. In fact, the unlawful purpose was not carried through and the court allowed evidence of unlawful purpose to be brought in to rebut the presumption.

Tribe v *Tribe* [1995] 4 All ER 236

A father took his son into his business and gradually transferred shares into the name of his son after the landlord made a substantial claim for dilapidation. As this was a transfer from father to son the presumption of advancement arose. The father believed that the landlord's claim might threaten the continued viability of the business, thinking that he might have to sell the business to raise the money to meet it. The object of the transfers was to convince the landlord that he (the father) no longer owned shares in the company and so could not sell them and so would not be able to raise the money to pay the claim. In the event, the claim was settled and the landlord was never made aware of the share transfers. The father now claimed the shares back, saying it was always accepted that the son would transfer the shares back as and when the father demanded their return. The father argued that he had intended to retain a beneficial interest in the shares and conceal it from his creditors. The son refused to transfer the shares back to his father. The son argued that in such a case his father could not use the unlawful purpose as evidence in support of his claim. In order to try to rebut the presumption of advancement the father was adducing the evidence of the unlawful purpose. There was, it was argued, a general rule of public policy that prevented such evidence from being used to support the claim. (In cases such as *Tinsley* v *Milligan*, where there was a presumption of resulting trust, evidence of the unlawful purpose did not have to be relied upon; the claimant simply based her argument on the presumed resulting trust.) At first instance, the court allowed the father to bring in the evidence of the unlawful purpose – attempting to deceive his creditors – on the basis that the purpose had not been carried through. The claim of the father succeeded.

In other words, the court, having heard the evidence of the father including the unlawful purpose, found that the son held the shares on a resulting trust for his father. The appeal was unanimously dismissed by the Court of Appeal. The court agreed with the judge at first instance that, in a case where the presumption of advancement arose, evidence of the unlawful purpose would be heard and would not prevent the recovery of the property where the unlawful purpose had not been carried through. Both Nourse LJ and Millett LJ found support in the Australian decision of *Perpetual Executors and Trustees Association of Australia Ltd* v *Wright* (1917) 23 CLR 185, in which property had been put into the name of the plaintiff's wife to defeat possible creditors should his business fail. In the event no such creditors were defrauded. In that case Barton ACJ said:

> Had there been creditors to hoodwink or, at any rate, had there been any attempt at such an act, the case would probably have been different. But, so far as we know, there were no creditors to hoodwink, and the whole thing rested on what might happen but never did happen. That such a state of things, carried no further, is not a bar to the respondent's claim to what is beneficially his own is to me apparent . . .

Nourse LJ went on to state that the exception to the rule excluding evidence of unlawful purpose extends to the situation in the case he was deciding:

> On this state of the authorities I decline to hold that the exception does not apply to a case where the presumption of advancement arises but the illegal purpose has not been carried into effect in any way. **Wright**'s case, 23 CLR 185, supported by the observation of the Privy Council in *Palaniappa Chettiar* v *Arunasalam Chettiar* . . . is clear authority for its application and no decision to the contrary has been cited.

Millett LJ also discussed the possible need for repentance, which has been argued as being required in order to admit evidence of unlawful or improper purposes:

> But I would hold that genuine repentance is not required. Justice is not a reward for merit; restitution should not be confined to the penitent. I would also hold that voluntary withdrawal from an illegal transaction when it has ceased to be needed is sufficient.

Millett LJ also suggested that it was not unacceptable for a husband to place property in the name of his wife in order to protect it from possible future business debts. However, such a transfer would succeed only if the husband divested himself entirely. Evidence of the intention to protect the property from creditors would not, of itself, rebut a presumption of advancement. In fact, such evidence would support it.

Earlier in this chapter the modern approach to the two presumptions was discussed and it was pointed out that in some situations the courts seemed to adopt the policy of accepting that there was a presumption but allowing it to be readily rebutted. For example, in the case of mother and child it has been said that, despite the arguments that today there should be a presumption of advancement based on the moral responsibility that a mother has towards her child, there is in fact no such presumption. However, the courts readily accept that there is evidence to rebut the presumption of resulting trust in favour of a gift. In many cases whether there is a presumption of advancement or a readily rebuttable presumption of resulting trust is merely academic. However, in the light of the House of Lords decision in *Tinsley* v *Milligan* and the Court of Appeal decision in *Tribe* v *Tribe*, in situations where there is an illegal or improper purpose it may be vital whether or not a presumption of advancement arises. If a presumption of resulting trust arises, the claim of the transferor can succeed irrespective of the illegal or fraudulent purpose, as the claim can be established using the presumption and not by relying on evidence of the illegal or fraudulent purpose. It matters not in such a case if the purpose has been carried through or not. Where a presumption of advancement arises and there is an illegal or improper purpose that has been carried through, the presumption may not be rebutted using evidence of that illegal or improper purpose. In other cases where the presumption arises, where the illegal or fraudulent purpose has not been carried through, evidence of this purpose may be used to rebut the presumption. It does appear to be curious that the outcome of a case depends (at least in part) on which presumption happens to be applicable. In *Tribe* v *Tribe*, at first instance, Judge Weeks QC commenting on the implications of *Tinsley* v *Milligan* said:

> . . . it is not for me to criticise their Lordships' reasoning, but with the greatest respect I find it difficult to see why the outcome in cases such as the present one should depend to such a large extent on arbitrary factors, such as whether the claim is brought by a father against a son, or a mother against a son, or a grandfather against a grandson.

In *Tribe* v *Tribe*, in the Court of Appeal, Nourse LJ said that he found much force in this observation.

In *Tinsley* v *Milligan*, Lord Goff called for a review by the Law Commission.

The 1999 Law Commission Consultation Paper No. 154, 'Illegal Transactions: the effect of illegality on contracts and trusts', considered, amongst other issues, the situation where activities connected with a claim under a trust involved some type of illegal or fraudulent behaviour. In other words, it covered the *Tinsley* v *Milligan* area of law.

In 2010, the Law Commission published a report – 'The Illegality Defence' (Law Com. No. 320) – which made recommendations for a radical change in the law. In most cases a claimant beneficiary would be able to rely on their normal right to enforce the trust. But where a trust is created with the intention of concealing the true ownership of property and in connection with the commission of a criminal offence (whether or not an offence is actually committed), the courts should, the Report recommended, have a discretion as to whether or not a claimant could rely on his normal legal rights. An example of a transaction that would be affected by the recommendations might be where someone transferred property into the name of another with the intention of defrauding creditors.

However, in March 2012 the Ministry of Justice stated, in the Report on the implementation of Law Commission proposals, that it had been decided not to implement the recommendations of the Law Commission:

> The Government has decided not to implement this report because, overall, we are not satisfied that there is a sufficiently clear and pressing case for reform and we are not satisfied that if the draft Bill became law it would improve on the current situation sufficiently to make legislating worthwhile. The number of cases involving illegality in trusts which are taken to court each year is low, the case law in this area is highly controversial and it is not clear that there are significant numbers of cases that are being wrongly decided. In addition, section 199 of the Equality Act 2010 will, when commenced, abolish the presumption of advancement, which was a significant factor in why the Law Commission were concerned with the state of the current law. The application of the draft Bill is also very wide and there is some concern about the risk of unintended consequences and of a new statutory scheme introducing new uncertainties in the law. Therefore, on balance, and given that reform of this area of the law cannot be considered a pressing priority for the Government at present.

It seems from this statement that the Government is not closing the door to implementing the recommendations in the future.

To the extent that after *Stack* v *Dowden* the presumption of resulting trust has been abandoned (at least where the purchase or transfer is in a domestic setting and involves a property which is a home), the consequences of making a claim to a share or a greater share in the property may be affected where there is an illegal or immoral motive. In *Tinsley* v *Milligan*, where the presumption of resulting trust arose, the claimant based her claim on the presumption and did not have to use the evidence of the illegal or immoral motive to support her claim. But if *Tinsley* were decided today, under *Stack* v *Dowden* the presumption of resulting trust would not be applicable, the presumption raised would be that equity follows the law. In order to rebut the presumption, Milligan would need to ring into evidence her illegal or immoral motives. This is not allowed and so her claim would fail and the beneficial interest would follow the legal title and would vest in Tinsley alone. For the sake of completeness it should be noted that in *Stack* v *Dowden* Lord Neuberger agreed with the result that the rest of the court arrived at, but based his decision on the resulting trust.

See Chapter 13 (p. 350) for more on *Stack* v *Dowden*.

Similarities between resulting and constructive trusts were highlighted in *O'Kelly* v *Davies*[2014] EWCA Civ 1606 where the Court of Appeal held that there is no distinction between a resulting and a constructive trust that is sufficient to make a resulting trust enforceable in the face of an illegal purpose and a constructive trust unenforceable.

Purchases in the names of others

As mentioned earlier (at p. 271) under 'Transfers into the names of others', in some instances of purchases in the names of others, the ownership of property is settled by applying either the presumption of resulting trust or the presumption of advancement. Where the presumption of resulting trust applies, the transferee will hold the property on trust for the transferor (or on trust for the transferor and the transferee).

Again, as already stated (at p. 271), modern cases tend to show that the courts will always strive to work out the real intention of the purchaser and will only give effect to the presumptions of resulting trust and advancement where the intention cannot be fathomed and a 'long-stop' or 'default' solution is needed.

As discussed above in **Kyriakides v Pippas** [2004] 2 FCR 434 the court cited, with approval, the statement of Lord Phillips MR in **Lavelle v Lavelle** [2002] 2 FCR 418 in which he said that case law has developed in such a way that even 'comparatively slight evidence' will rebut the presumption, and a 'less rigid approach should also be adopted to the admissibility of evidence to rebut the presumption of advancement'. The judge in **Kyriakides v Pippas** went on to state that he suspected the 'position we have now reached is that the courts will always strive to work out the real intention of the purchaser and will only give effect to the presumptions of resulting trust and advancement where the intention cannot be fathomed and a "long-stop" or "default" solution is needed'.

Ahmad and another v *Gould* [2005] EWCA Civ 1829 is a Court of Appeal decision where G claimed, *inter alia*, that he was entitled to an interest in property purchased in the name of the Ahmads under a resulting trust as he had, he claimed, contributed to the purchase price. His claim failed. The case illustrates how difficult it is to override the provisions of an express agreement about ownership of property with, in this case, a claim based on a resulting trust.

In the case, the court found there was an agreement that a property would be bought by the Ahmads and that Gould could buy it from them at market value if and when he was financially able to do so. The agreement went on to say, the court found, that the purchase would provide Mr Gould with a home and that he would make the mortgage payments *in lieu* of rent.

This, the court held, was not an agreement giving Gould an interest in the property (under a resulting trust or otherwise) and was only an agreement to enter into a contract for the sale of the property in the future.

Gould appealed, claiming he had an interest under a resulting trust (a) because he had paid £37,000 into Mrs Ahmad's bank account and (b) because he had negotiated a £10,000

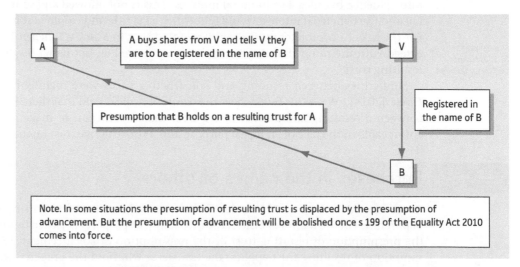

Figure 11.1 Purchase in the name of other(s)

reduction in the price of the property. The Ahmads claimed that they were not aware that the £37,000 was to be paid into the account and did not know for sure why it was being paid. Additionally, they claimed they were unaware of the price reduction.

The court found that, in the light of the agreement that the court of first instance had found, it was not possible to find that the payments were made in accord with any agreement under which Gould would obtain an interest in the property under a resulting trust or otherwise.

Figures 11.1–11.5 set out examples of purchase in the name of others.

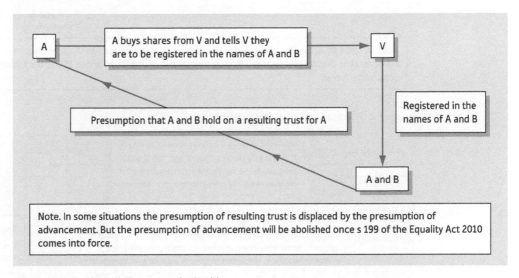

Figure 11.2 Purchase in the name of other(s)

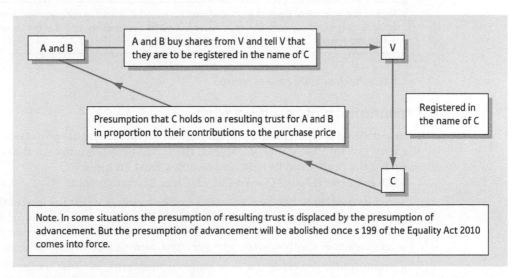

Figure 11.3 Purchase in the name of other(s)

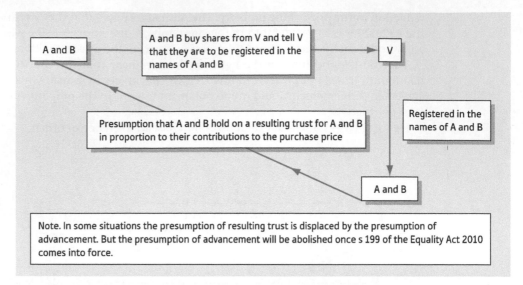

Figure 11.4 Purchase in the name of other(s)

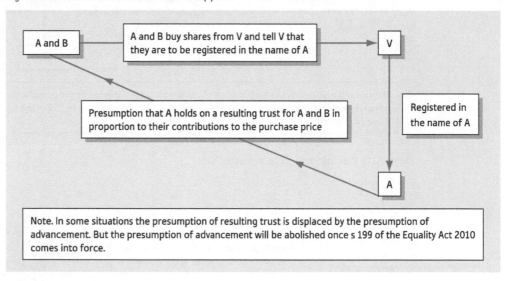

Figure 11.5 Purchase in the name of other(s)

Presumption of resulting trust

If the person who is purchasing property and who is providing the purchase money has the property put into the name of another, there will be a presumption that the purchaser intended the property to be held on a resulting trust for himself.

In **Dyer v Dyer** (1788) 2 Cox Eq Cas 92, Chief Baron Eyre said:

> The clear result of all the cases, without a single exception, is that the trust of the legal estate, whether freehold, copyhold or leasehold; whether taken in the name of the purchasers and others jointly, or in the names of others without the purchaser; whether in one name or several; whether jointly or successive, results to the man who advances the purchase-money.

The presumption can arise in a wide range of situations, as Chief Baron Eyre suggests. It arises in the simple case where Peter provides all the purchase price for a piece of land and has it conveyed into the name of his friend Wendy. If the property had been conveyed into the joint names of Peter and Wendy, the application of the presumption would result in the legal estate being held by Peter and Wendy on trust for Peter alone. The presumption will also be relevant if Peter and Wendy had both contributed to the purchase price of a piece of land which was conveyed into the name of Wendy only. Wendy would hold the legal estate as trustee for herself and Peter. The size of the interests of Peter and Wendy would be determined by comparing their respective contributions. If Peter contributed one-third of the purchase price and Wendy two-thirds, the beneficial interest would be owned one-third by Peter and two-thirds by Wendy.

The leading case is *Fowkes v Pascoe* (1875) 10 Ch App 343, in which the presumption was discussed at length and Mellish LJ emphasised how the weight of the presumption varied from case to case. He said that in a situation where the property was placed in the name of a stranger, perhaps the purchaser's solicitor, the presumption would apply and the inference that a trust was intended would be very strong indeed. However, if the property was placed in the name of someone who, though not his wife or child, was someone whose position made it probable that a gift was intended, the inference of trust would be weaker and the court would look to any available evidence in rebuttal. But if there was no evidence or if the evidence was too weak, the presumption of resulting trust would prevail, even if the court did not believe that this would reflect what the transferee would have wanted.

Fowkes v Pascoe (1875) 10 Ch App 343

In the case Mrs Baker bought some £7,000 worth of stock and had it placed in the joint names of herself and John Pascoe, the son of Mrs Baker's daughter-in-law. On her death the court was asked to decide on the ownership of the stock. The court held that there was sufficient evidence to rebut the presumption and the stock was owned by Pascoe. Two facts were considered particularly important in establishing that Mrs Baker intended to make a gift to Pascoe. First, Pascoe was living in Mrs Baker's house and she provided for him. Secondly, she already held stock in her own name. If she intended to retain the beneficial ownership of the stock bought in the name of Pascoe, it was odd that she did not buy it in her own name as she had done the other stock. The fact that Pascoe kept the transfer a secret and that Mrs Baker enjoyed the income from the stock during her life were not considered to be sufficiently important to stop the court from deciding that the presumption was rebutted.

The court decided in *Savage v Dunningham* [1973] 3 All ER 429 that an arrangement between people sharing a leased house under which, although the lease was in the name of one of them, all would contribute part of the rent, was not a situation of purchase in the name of another and so the presumption of resulting trust did not apply. Ploughman J held that, although there was no reported case, he considered, on general principles, that a resulting trust could apply to a lease, for example, where others contribute to a premium paid by the tenant. However, he held that there was no authority for the proposition that contributions to rent constituted a contribution to a 'purchase price'. Rent is paid for the use of the property rather than for the acquisition of a capital asset.

Vajpeyi v Yusaf [2003] All ER (D) 128 (Sep) is a first-instance decision which centres on the presumption of resulting trust and its rebuttal. In the case a property was conveyed into the sole name of Y. V and Y were in a relationship but were not married (V was already married to someone else). In 1980 a property was bought for £29,500 as an investment and to let out. Y was a student at the time of the purchase but was anxious to get a foot onto the property ladder.

Y raised a £20,000 mortgage. V provided the balance of the purchase price and paid for the legal fees, stamp duty, etc. This amounted to £10,000. V, who was some 12 years older than Y and already owned a property, borrowed the £10,000. The relationship between Y and V continued despite V entering an arranged marriage which subsequently ended in divorce.

Then, in 1994, the relationship broke down. In the instant case V claimed that the property was held by Y on a resulting trust for herself (V) and Y. On the basis of the alleged contribution (£10,000) a 33.98 per cent share was claimed by V.

It was held that there was a presumption that the property was bought by Y on trust for himself and V. This presumption, the courts said, was not a strong one in all the circumstances of the case and that it had been rebutted by Y. The £10,000 was a loan and not a contribution to the purchase entitling V to a share in the ownership. One factor that influenced the decision was the amount of time that elapsed before the alleged trust was asserted. V had not claimed the rents or a share of the property for 20 years. If V considered she had an interest in the house, surely she would have claimed a share of the rents?

The court considered that 'the common sense of the situation' pointed to there being a loan. Given the respective situations of Y and V, it could be thought probable that V used her position and good credit rating to raise the money to help Y to buy the property rather than intending to contribute to the purchase price and to obtain an interest in the property.

Curley v *Parkes* [2004] All ER (D) 344 (Oct) states that any resulting trust arising with respect to property bought in the name of another will arise (if at all) at the time of the purchase.

The claimant and defendant had been cohabiting in a house bought by the defendant and registered in her sole name. The claimant's employer subsequently required him to relocate. His employer offered financial help with the moving costs and with the purchase of a new property. As a result, the employer bought the property from the defendant. Then, in April 2001, another property was bought in the defendant's name alone. It was paid for by the proceeds of the old property, a mortgage in the defendant's sole name, and cash paid by the defendant. The claimant paid no part of the purchase price, despite receiving money under the relocation scheme. He also received a payment each month from his employer with respect to the higher mortgage payments.

Between May and November 2001, the claimant paid the defendant about £9,000 in six instalments. This was to compensate the defendant for the deposit on the new property and for legal and removal expenses. On the subsequent break-up of the relationship, the claimant argued that the property was held on a resulting trust by the defendant for the defendant and claimant. The claimant argued that he had contributed to the purchase price of the property by the payments he had made in 2001.

The court held that where property is bought in the name of another, a resulting trust would arise once and for all at the date the property was acquired. In this case, the court decided, there were no findings of fact to support the claimant's view that his payments of £9,000 (paid to compensate the defendant for the deposit, and in respect of legal expenses and removal costs) had contributed to the purchase price of the property. Therefore, the claimant had no beneficial interest in the property under a resulting trust.

As stated above, it may be argued that in recent cases the presumption is regarded as a long-stop, only to be applicable if there is no evidence of actual intention or is, if applicable, easily rebutted.

See also *Kyriakides* v *Pippas* [2004] 2 FCR 434 above (at p. 271).

Presumption of advancement

See Chapter 10 (p. 275) for more information on the abolition of the presumption of advancement.

This presumption will replace the presumption of resulting trust in the same situations as have been discussed above in the context of transfers into the names of others. (The presumption will be abolished by s 199 of the Equality Act for all transfers etc. made after the section comes into force. The section is not yet in force.)

Again, the presumption varies in weight from case to case and is weak in the case of a transfer by a husband into the name of his wife but stronger in the case of a transfer into the name of a child by its father.

The presumption can, of course always be rebutted by sufficiently strong evidence. As indicated above, in some cases slight evidence may suffice, whereas in other cases the evidence will have to be strong before the court will decide that the presumption has been rebutted. But the modern approach is illustrated by *McGrath v Wallis* in which Nourse LJ, having cited the House of Lords decision in *Pettitt v Pettitt* [1969] WLR 966, said that the presumption of advancement was a judicial instrument of last resort. It can be rebutted, Nourse LJ said, by comparatively slight evidence.

In *Warren v Gurney* [1944] 2 All ER 472, a house was bought by Gurney and conveyed into the name of his daughter who was about to marry Warren. The father retained the title deeds. Some years later Gurney signed a document which said that the house was to be divided between his three daughters. The Court of Appeal decided that the presumption of advancement was rebutted but that the document was not admissible evidence, having been produced after the conveyance to the daughter and it could therefore not be used to support the interest of the father. The court considered the retention of the title deeds by the father as very important and said that if the father had intended a gift it would have been expected that he would hand over the deeds to the daughter. It is arguable that if this was the only evidence it would be, by itself, insufficient. One of Gurney's children gave evidence that before the house was bought Gurney had discussed his intention to buy a house and asked advice as to which house to purchase, but had also said that Warren would be paying for the house as and when he could. This was clearly inconsistent with the view that the father was giving the house to the daughter.

McGrath v *Wallis* [1995] 2 FLR 114

In this case, a father and son lived in the family home, which was in the sole name of the father. The father decided to sell the house and use the proceeds to buy another. As he was unemployed, he was unable to obtain the mortgage necessary to provide the additional money needed to buy the new house. The mortgage offer was made to the son and the new house was conveyed into the sole name of the son. The father instructed his solicitor to draw up a declaration of trust under which the house would be held by the son on trust for himself and his father in unequal shares (20 per cent and 80 per cent). However, the solicitor did not send the deed to the father and it was never executed. When the father died intestate, the court was asked to decide how the property was owned. At first instance the court decided that, as the father had contributed to the purchase but the property was conveyed into the name of the son alone, the presumption of advancement arose and those arguing that the property was held on resulting trust for the father and the son had failed to discharge the burden of proof. The ensuing appeal was allowed. The court should, it was said, look at all the circumstances of the case to determine whether or not they did or did not support an inference that the intention of the transferor (the father) was that he should retain an interest in the property. In the circumstances, the court found that there were three decisive factors. First, it was only the son who was acceptable to the mortgagee. Secondly, the father never told the son that he had instructed the solicitor not to proceed with the deed of trust. Thirdly, no reason was suggested as to why the father should want to divest himself of all interest in the property. Nourse LJ, having cited the House of Lords decision in *Pettitt v Pettitt* [1969] WLR 966, said that the presumption of advancement was a judicial instrument of last resort. The presumption (together with the presumption of resulting trust) remained useful in deciding questions of title but they are rebutted by comparatively slight evidence. The court decided that, although *Pettitt v Pettitt* was a case involving a husband and wife, the same principles applied to the instant case where the parties were father and son. Nourse LJ thought that in the instant case the evidence available was markedly more than slight and found that the presumption of advancement was rebutted.

Admissible evidence to rebut a presumption

The principles discussed above in the context of transfers in the names of others also apply here. (See p. 279.)

Applicability of the presumptions after *Stack* v *Dowden* and *Jones* v *Kernott*

It may be that the **Stack v Dowden** [2007] 2 All ER 929 and **Jones v Kernott** [2011] UKSC 53 approach will (in many domestic situations) replace the application of the presumption of resulting trust and advancement. The court, rather than use the presumptions of resulting trust, decided the cases on the basis that unless there was strong evidence to the contrary, the equitable interest would follow the legal estate. If this approach is embraced by the courts, the presumption of resulting trust (and advancement) will have less relevance in deciding issues of ownership. It is not absolutely certain but it is generally thought that **Stack v Dowden/Jones v Kernott** apply to property bought as a family home (or other purchases of a home in a domestic context) but not to houses bought as an investment or for other commercial purposes nor to personal property. In these cases both the presumptions discussed above will still apply (until the Equality Act 2010 s 199, which abolishes the presumption of advancement, comes into force).

The family home

See Chapter 13 for a detailed discussion of shared homes.

One of the most important examples of purchases in the name of another occurs in the context of the acquisition of a family home.

Summary

- A resulting trust is one where the beneficial interest in property returns to (or perhaps never leaves) the transferor.

- The classic starting point to the understanding of resulting trusts is *Re Vandervell Trusts (No. 2)* (1974) where Megarry J stated that there were two classes of resulting trust: (a) presumed resulting trusts, where the trust is based on what the intention of a transferor is presumed to be; and (b) automatic resulting trusts where the intention of the transferor is irrelevant. But, in *Westdeutsche Landesbank v Islington London Borough Council* (1996) Lord Browne-Wilkinson doubted that intention was always irrelevant in category (b) resulting trust, as in some cases ignoring intention would lead to a result contrary to the wishes or expectations of the transferor.

- There are many situations where a resulting trust may arise. For example, a resulting trust may arise if an attempted express trust fails, or where a transfer into a trust fails to dispose of the entire beneficial interest, or where a trust is set up to to help individuals and after the purpose has been achieved a surplus remains.

- A resulting trusts may arise where there is a transfer of property into the name of another person or where property is purchased in the name of another.

- In most of these cases of transfer into the name of another or of purchase in the name of another, the presumption of resulting trust applies. In a narrow range of cases this presumption will be replaced by the presumption of advancement, which will be abolished when s 199 of the Equality Act 2010 comes into force. Even if these presumptions may be relatively easily rebutted, it may be argued that the presumptions are now out of date and need to be reviewed. The courts' traditional attitude towards the presumptions should be contrasted with the approach in some Commonwealth jurisdictions where, it may be said, a more enlightened and modern attitude is in evidence, particularly in relation to the presumption of advancement.

● In some situations the presence of an unlawful or illegal reason for the transfer may give rise to issues if the transferor claims to be entitled under a resulting trust.

Further reading

The role of resulting trusts

W Swadling, 'A new role for resulting trusts?' (1996) 16 LS 110.
Discusses, *inter alia*, the relationship between resulting trusts and restitution and the role, if any, that resulting trusts play in restitution, where the constructive trust is the normal vehicle.

The presumptions

G Andrews, 'The presumption of advancement: equity, equality and human rights' [2007] Conv July/August 340.
Deals with the presumption of advancement and the extent to which it offends fundamental human rights. Discusses contravention of the European Convention on Human Rights. Argues for the abolition of the presumption.

A Dowling, 'The presumption of advancement between mother and child' [1996] Conv 274.
Discusses the anomalous nature of the presumption of advancement.

J Glister, 'Section 199 of the Equality Act 2010.' How not to abolish the presumption of advancement [2010] 73 (5) MLR 807.
Deals with the Equality Act 2010 s 199 which abolishes the presumption of advancement and covers the consequences of s 199 lacking retrospective effect.

S Greer, 'A last resort' (2007) 157 (7273) NLJ 696.
Discusses when the presumption of advancement should apply and highlights the bias whereby the presumption operates for gifts given by husbands to wives, but not vice versa.

P Hewitt, P Fudakowska and A Cloherty, 'A new era of equality?' (2010) 160 (7437) NLJ 1417.
Deals with the decline in cases relying on the 'presumption of advancement' and discusses the abolition of the presumption by the Equality Act 2010 s 199.

J Mee, 'Resulting trusts and voluntary conveyances of land' [2012] Conv 307.
Discusses whether the Law of Property Act 1925 s 60(3) which prevents a resulting trust from arising on a voluntary conveyance of land, preferring the interpretation which abolishes the previous doctrine of presumption of resulting use.

Illegal/immoral motives

I Cotterill, 'Property and impropriety – the *Tinsley* v *Milligan* problem again' (1999) LMCLQ 465.
Deals with *Lowson* v *Coombes* and the reliance principle.

P Creighton, 'The recovery of property transferred for illegal purposes' (1997) 60 MLR 102.
Looks at Australian and English cases to demonstrate change in courts' approach to proprietary claims based on transaction with illegal purpose.

D Hertzell and C Lody, 'A sharper focus' (2010) 160 NLJ 495.
Comments on *Tinsley* v *Milligan* and discusses the recommendations of the Law Commission on reform.

P Pettit, 'Illegality and repentance' (1996) 10 Tru Ll 51.

Discusses *Tribe* which is an example of an exception to *Tinsley* where the illegal purpose has been withdrawn by the person putting the illegal purpose forward before the illegal purpose has been wholly or partly carried into effect.

F D Rose, 'Gratuitous transfers and illegal purposes' (1996) 112 LQR 386.

Wide-ranging article looking at the effect of illegal purposes and discusses in particular *Tinsley*, *Tribe* and *Nelson*.

Discusses the courts' approach to illegal purposes in the light of *Tinsley* v *Milligan*.

Joint bank accounts

M C Cullity, 'Joint bank accounts with volunteers' (1969) 84 LQR 530.

Analytical study of the problems associated with joint accounts.

C Paget, 'The presumption of advancement' (2011) 127 TEL & TJ 22.

Deals with the presumption of resulting trust and its rebuttal in the context of a joint bank account.

12

Constructive trusts

Introduction

Objective
1

A constructive trust arises by operation of law, rather than as a result of the parties' intention. As it is imposed by law two questions must be addressed: when will it be imposed and why?

It must also be noted that in a major area where constructive trusts may be imposed, cases of improper gains by those in a fiduciary position, there is an overlapping but separate issue of the personal liability of a fiduciary to account for any improper gains. Strictly speaking, a constructive trust should only be imposed where the court determines that certain property, perhaps the result of improper gain, is trust property, with all the consequences of trusteeship that this implies. However, there is also a tendency to refer to fiduciaries and others as 'accountable as trustees' in other situations even though strictly no trust property as such exists and the defendant is not a trustee. Therefore this chapter must concern itself not only with trusts, but also with personal liability, and attempt to distinguish the situations in which the different principles will apply.

Constructive trusts: institutional or remedial?

On the question of whether a constructive trust is an institution, coming into existence when certain prerequisites are fulfilled, like other trusts, or a remedy, imposed at the discretion of the courts, there appears to be a difference of approach between English practice on the one hand and American and Commonwealth practice on the other. The American view has been that the constructive trust is a remedy to be imposed whenever the defendant's conduct is unconscionable, for instance when he would be unjustly enriched. A similar approach has been taken in New Zealand where, for instance, in *Brown* v *Pourau* [1995] 1 NZLR 352, secret trusts have been upheld as an example of the remedial constructive trust.

The traditional view in England has been to view it as a substantive institution like any other trust, arising, therefore, only in certain situations. In the recent past, however, attempts were made to expand the constructive trust. The 'constructive trust of the new model' was championed by Lord Denning in *Hussey* v *Palmer* [1972] 3 All ER 744, where he allied constructive and resulting trusts and said: 'The two run together: it is a trust imposed whenever justice and good conscience require it.' Subsequently, in *Eves* v *Eves* [1975] 3 All ER 768, he described the new model constructive trust as the latest example of equity's continued capacity for childbearing, and applied it to allow a woman a share in a house in which she had cohabited. This particular application of the constructive trust is discussed at length in another chapter: suffice it to say here that the courts appear to have returned to a more traditional analysis in family home cases. In addition, the comments of the Court of Appeal in *Re Goldcorp Exchange*, referred to below, appear to indicate a reluctance to expand the situations in which constructive trusts will operate.

For constructive trusts and cohabitation, see Chapter 13.

The distinction between institutional and remedial constructive trusts was spelt out by Lord Browne-Wilkinson in *Westdeutsche Landesbank* v *Islington London Borough Council* [1996] 2 All ER 961 at 997:

> Under the institutional constructive trust, the trust arises by operation of law as from the date when the circumstances give rise to it: the function of the court is merely to declare that such trust has arisen in the past. The consequences which flow from such trust having arisen (including the possibly unfair consequences to third parties who in the interim receive trust property) are also determined by rules of law, not under discretion. A remedial constructive trust, as I understand it, is different. It is a judicial remedy giving rise to an enforceable equitable obligation; the extent to which it operates retrospectively to the prejudice of third parties lies in the discretion of the courts.

It is in part the courts' concern with prejudice to third parties, particularly creditors, which has made them reluctant to develop the remedial idea. This theme was taken up again in

Re Polly Peck (No. 4) [1998] BCLC 185, in which a remedial constructive trust was sought, as so often, to gain priority over unsecured creditors. Quoting Lord Browne-Wilkinson's statement above, Mummery LJ concluded that no subsequent cases had imposed such a trust, and the court would not do so here, particularly as the situation was governed by the statutory scheme for distribution of assets upon insolvency:

> Even the most enthusiastic student of the law of restitution would be forced to recognise that the scheme imposed by statute for a fair distribution of the assets of an insolvent company precludes the application of the equitable principles manifested in the remedial constructive trust.

A further note of caution about too great an extension of constructive trusts may be found in *Re Goldcorp Exchange Ltd* [1994] 2 All ER 806, where, it will be remembered, the respondents had entered into contracts with Goldcorp to purchase non-allocated shares in bullion, on terms which entitled them to take physical delivery of the bullion on seven days' notice, but which expressed the interest of the purchasers meanwhile to be in portions of an undivided bulk. The Privy Council found it impossible to recognise that the respondents had any equitable proprietary interest in the bullion, since such an interest could not arise until specific trust property had been identified. To recognise such an equitable interest would be to go against the terms of the contracts. On the possible use of the constructive trust as a remedy, the Privy Council commented:

See Chapter 4 for *Re Goldcorp Exchange Ltd.*

> Finally, it is argued that the court should declare in favour of the claimants a remedial constructive trust, or, to use another name, a restitutionary proprietary interest over the bullion in the company's vaults. Such a trust or interest would differ fundamentally from those so far discussed, in that it would not arise directly from the transaction between the individual claimants, the company and the bullion, but would be created by the court as a measure of justice after the event.

The court considered the various possible grounds upon which such a trust might be imposed, and concluded that it could not arise in this case. The company had not been unjustly enriched, nor, though in breach of contract, had it acted wrongfully with respect to the 'trust' subject matter.

> [T]he claimant's argument really comes to this, that because the company broke its contract in a way which had to do with bullion, the court should call into existence a proprietary interest in whatever bullion happened to be in the possession and ownership of the company at the time when the competition between the non-allocated claimants [i.e. the respondent purchasers] and the other secured and unsecured claimants first arose [i.e. when receivers were appointed by a bank that held a debenture from the company]. The company's stock of bullion had no connection with the claimant's purchases, and to enable the claimants to reach out and not only abstract it from the assets available to the body of creditors as a whole, but also to afford a priority over a secured creditor [i.e. the bank, by virtue of the debenture], would give them an adventitious benefit devoid of the foundation of logic and justice which underlies this important new branch of law.

It is clearly the effect on others, as well as the lack of any identifiable property to which it could attach, that led the court to refuse to impose such a trust in that case.

As to why the constructive trust is imposed, the answer must be to protect the interest of some innocent party, or to prevent some party who is less innocent from profiting. To this extent the constructive trust is a remedy rather than a substantive institution. It is a form of trust, but perhaps to call it by that name may have led some to see it as too much like other trusts. It is clear that the obligations of the constructive trustee are very different from the obligations of the trustee of an express trust and furthermore vary between different trust situations. Indeed, the limited nature of the trustee's obligations under a constructive trust has led to them reasonably being described by Paul Matthews (2005) as bare trusts; the function of the constructive trustee is to hand over the trust property when called upon to do so by the beneficiary. The usual purpose for which a constructive trust is imposed is to make the trustee liable to the various remedies for breach of trust. These remedies are considered further later, but here we must consider the prerequisites for their application as regards constructive trusts. As we shall see, the principal debate is whether proprietary remedies in particular are appropriate in all these situations. As well as the instances of constructive trusts discussed in this chapter, reference should also be made to Chapter 13, where the so-called 'common intention' constructive trust is analysed in the context of shared homes.

For equitable remedies for breach of trust, see Chapter 17.

Improper gains by persons in a fiduciary position

The fiduciary relationship

Objective
2

The essence of a fiduciary relationship is the fact that the fiduciary has undertaken to act for the other person in some matter, and the other's reasonable expectation that the fiduciary will act exclusively in his, the other's, interest. Some fiduciary relationships arise purely by virtue of the status of the parties to the relationship; such status-based relationships include trustee and beneficiary, agent and principal, director and company, partners and senior employees and company. Others arise as a matter of fact in particular circumstances, and factors which may tend to indicate such a relationship include the existence of an undertaking by the alleged fiduciary to the other party, reliance placed by the other on the alleged fiduciary, the other party's property being under the control of the alleged fiduciary, and the vulnerability of the other party, in that some power or discretion affecting the other's interest may lie with the alleged fiduciary.

The objective of equity

Where any person in a fiduciary position obtains a profit or gain by virtue of that position, he may not keep it for himself but will be liable for it to the person to whom he is in a fiduciary relationship. This principle was stated by Lord Herschell in **Bray v Ford** [1896] AC 44, thus:

> It is an inflexible rule of a Court of Equity that a person in a fiduciary position . . . is not, unless otherwise expressly provided, entitled to make a profit; he is not allowed to put himself in a position where his interest and his duty conflict. It does not appear to me that this rule is . . . founded upon principles of morality. I regard it rather as based on the consideration that, human nature being what it is, there is a danger, in such circumstances, of the person holding a fiduciary interest being swayed by interest rather than duty, and thus prejudicing those he is bound to protect. It has, therefore, been deemed expedient to lay down this positive rule.

This liability may arise without any fraud or misconduct by the fiduciary. In **Boardman v Phipps** [1966] 3 All ER 721, Lord Cohen said of the fiduciaries: 'They acted with complete honesty throughout and the respondent [i.e. the beneficiary] is a fortunate man in that the rigour of equity enables him to participate in the profits which have accrued as a result of the action taken by the appellants . . .'

Similarly, in *Regal (Hastings) Ltd* v *Gulliver* (below), Lord Russell of Killowen pointed out:

> The rule of equity which insists on those, who by use of a fiduciary position make a profit, being liable to account for that profit, in no way depends on fraud, or the absence of *bona fides*; or upon such questions or considerations as whether the profit would or should otherwise have gone to the plaintiff, or whether the profiteer was under a duty to obtain the source of the profit for the plaintiff, or whether he took a risk or acted as he did for the benefit of the plaintiff, or whether the plaintiff has in fact been damaged or benefited by his action. The liability arises from the mere fact of a profit having, in the stated circumstances, been made.

Only in one situation may fiduciaries keep the profit for themselves. They may do so if they have the informed consent of those to whom they stand as fiduciaries.

There are two basic kinds of remedy available to equity to prevent a fiduciary from profiting. The proprietary remedy is to make the unfair gain the subject matter of a trust. This mechanism and its effect were explained in *A-G for Hong Kong* v *Reid* [1994] 1 All ER 1, considered further below in the context of bribes:

> As soon as the bribe was received it should have been paid or transferred instanter to the person who suffered from the breach of duty. Equity considers as done that which ought to be done. As soon as the bribe was received, whether in cash or in kind, the false fiduciary held the bribe on constructive trust for the person injured.

This analysis is considered further below when the role of personal and proprietary remedies is reviewed, but the effect is that in equity the gain (in that case a bribe) is and always was, as soon as received by the fiduciary, trust property.

The other remedy by which the fiduciary may be deprived of his unfair gain is to make him personally accountable for it to the person for whom he is a fiduciary. This is a personal remedy: in other words, he must give up an amount equivalent to the gain; no specific property is made subject to a trust.

These two remedies can exist together in the same case. For example, it was stated in *Reid* that if the assets held by Reid on constructive trust were no longer worth as much as the bribe had been, Reid would be personally accountable for, and liable to make up, the shortfall.

Strictly speaking, a case should be regarded as one of constructive trust only where the proprietary remedy is imposed, but, in practice, the courts have tended to speak of trusteeship and accountability without making this distinction, and in many cases, indeed, it will make no practical difference which remedy is applied. If a full picture of this topic is to be gained, it is necessary to consider cases applying either or both remedies.

The property alleged to be held on constructive trust must, of course, come into the hands of the alleged fiduciary as a result of that fiduciary relationship. A constructive trust cannot therefore be applied to property acquired by operation of law, as, for example, in *French* v *Mason* (1998) *The Times*, [1998] All ER (D) 486, where an employer acquired intellectual property designed by his employee, by operation of s 39 of the Patents Act 1977.

Fiduciary situations

Before turning to the question of remedies, it is first necessary to consider when a fiduciary relationship will exist.

The 'classic' fiduciary relationship may be taken to be that of trustee and beneficiary: it is clear that a trustee must not put his personal interests in conflict with those of the trust. An example of this principle may be found in the leading case of *Keech* v *Sandford* (1726) Sel Cas Ch 61.

Keech v *Sandford* (1726) Sel Cas Ch 61

Here the lease of the profits of a market was held on trust for a minor. The trustee sought to renew the lease on behalf of the trust but, this being refused, then renewed the lease for his own benefit. The minor sought an assignment of the lease. It was held that the lease must be held on constructive trust for the infant and that he was entitled to an account of the profits received by the trustee.

A contrasting case, not dissimilar on its facts, is *Re Biss* [1903] Ch 40.

Re Biss [1903] Ch 40

In this case, the owner of certain premises refused to grant a renewal of the lease to the tenant or, after the tenant's death, to the widow and administratrix of the tenant's estate. He did, however, grant a renewal to the deceased's son, who was engaged with the widow, his mother, in carrying on the deceased's business on the premises. The widow sought to have the new lease treated as being held by the son for the benefit of the estate. The Court of Appeal held that the son held the lease for himself.

On the facts there was no fiduciary relationship, as Sir Richard Collins MR said:

> In the present case the appellant is simply one of the next of kin of the former tenant and had, as such, a possible interest in the term. He is not, as such, trustee for the others interested, nor is he in possession. The administratrix represented the estate and alone had the right to renew incident thereto, and unquestionably could renew only for the benefit of the estate.

The position of the son was quite different:

> [H]is position cannot be put higher than that of any other tenant in common against whom it would have to be established, not as a presumption of law but as an inference of fact, that he had abused his position.

As it was a question of fact, the son was entitled to show the circumstances in which he had acquired the lease, in order to show that no abuse of his position had taken place. Such facts could not be presented:

> where the party is by his position debarred from keeping a personal advantage derived directly or indirectly out of his fiduciary or quasi-fiduciary position; but when he is not so debarred I think it becomes a question of fact whether that which was received was in his hands an accretion of the interest of the deceased, or whether the connection between the estate and the renewal had not been wholly severed by the action of the lessor before the appellant accepted a new lease. This consideration seems to get rid of any difficulty that one of the next of kin was an infant. The right or hope of renewal incident to the estate was determined before the plaintiff intervened.

In the words of Romer LJ:

> Where the person renewing the lease does not clearly occupy a fiduciary position 'he' is only to be held to be a constructive trustee of the renewed lease if, in respect of the old lease, he occupied some special position and owed, by virtue of that position, a duty to other persons interested.

By contrast, in ***English v Dedham Vale Properties Ltd*** [1978] 1 All ER 382, it was held that a fiduciary relationship did exist. In this case, during negotiations for the purchase of land, the purchasers, purportedly acting for the vendors, sought and obtained planning permission for the land. The vendors were unaware of this and had they known it would presumably have influenced the purchase price. The purchasers were, in effect, 'self-appointed agents', in a fiduciary relationship with the vendors and liable to account to them for the profit resulting from the grant of planning permission.

It will not be possible to explore all the situations where a fiduciary relationship arises but the particular cases above may be taken as illustrative. One of the most extreme examples is, perhaps, *Reading* **v** *Attorney-General*.

Reading v *Attorney-General* [1951] 1 All ER 617

In this case an army sergeant stationed in Cairo was paid money to assist in smuggling. He did this by riding on lorries carrying contraband while wearing his army uniform, to enable them to pass unhindered through army checkpoints. Some £20,000 he received in this way was seized by British military authorities and Reading sought to recover it. He was held unable to do this because he was in a fiduciary position and accountable for any profit he made out of his position as a Crown servant. The Court of Appeal in that case stated that:

> a fiduciary relationship exists (a) whenever the plaintiff entrusts to the defendant property tangible or intangible and relies on the defendant to deal with such property for the benefit of the plaintiff or for purposes authorised by him and not otherwise; and (b) whenever the plaintiff entrusts to the defendant a job to be performed . . .

Directors as trustees

A particular issue has arisen as to whether directors of a company are in general to be regarded as trustees for the company and accountable for any misapplication of its assets.

In *Regal (Hastings) Ltd* **v** *Gulliver* [1942] 1 All ER 378, it was said of directors: 'Directors of a limited company are the creatures of statute. In some respects they resemble agents: in others they do not. In some respects they resemble managing partners: in others they do not.'

Regal (Hastings) Ltd v *Gulliver* [1942] 1 All ER 378

In this case directors of R had subscribed the majority of the shares in a subsidiary, A Ltd. When R came under new control, the directors made a profit from their holdings in A Ltd. They were held accountable to the new controllers of R for that profit. R itself had had insufficient funds to take up the shares in A and had agreed to the directors doing so. They had thus been enabled to acquire the shares solely because of their positions as directors of R. Despite the honesty of the directors, there was clearly a possibility of conflict of interest.

Belmont Finance v *Williams Furniture (No. 2)* [1980] 1 All ER 393

In this case, the plaintiff company was wholly owned by CIF Co, which was wholly owned by the defendants. It was agreed that the plaintiff company would buy a fourth company at an inflated price and that the chairman of the fourth company would buy all the shares in the plaintiff company (i.e. from CIF). This transaction was held to be unlawful under the Companies Acts. When Belmont became insolvent, the receiver claimed from CIF the money received for Belmont's shares. The Court of Appeal held that CIF were constructive trustees.

Buckley LJ explained the situation thus:

A limited company is of course not trustee of its own funds; but in consequence of the fiduciary character of their duties the directors of a limited company are treated as if they were trustees of those funds of the company which are in their hands or under their control, and if they misapply them they commit a breach of trust.

IDC v Cooley [1972] 2 All ER 162

In this case, the defendant was a director of the plaintiff company who, after attempting unsuccessfully to negotiate a development project with a public gas board on his employers' behalf, was offered the contract in his personal capacity. He accepted, securing his release from his employers by falsely claiming to be ill. He had thus deliberately put his personal interest in conflict with his pre-existing duty as a director and was held accountable for the benefits he had received from the contract. This was despite the argument that he had received the offer in his personal capacity and not as a director.

This can be contrasted with the Australian case of **Queensland Mines v Hudson** (1978) 18 ALR 1, where a company director, aware that his company was financially unable to exploit certain mining licences, resigned and, with the full knowledge of his former employers, developed the mines himself. The difference between this case and the last is perhaps that in Hudson the director acted openly and with consent, whereas in **IDC v Cooley** the director acted *mala fides*.

In **Guinness plc v Saunders** [1990] 1 All ER 652, the House of Lords, if not actually describing directors as trustees, made clear that directors are subject, as trustees are, to the rule that they may not profit from their fiduciary position. In the case of trustees, they may do so if the trust deed provides for it; in the case of directors, the right to remuneration is determined by the company's articles of association.

Guinness plc v Saunders [1990] 1 All ER 652

In this case the appellant, W, a director of Guinness, had received £5.2 million for his part in assisting in the takeover by Guinness of another company, Distillers. This money was received by W in good faith under a contract entered into between W and two other directors, who together were the members of a committee of the board of Guinness, set up to implement the takeover bid. The two directors purportedly entered into this contract on behalf of the company. The amount W was to receive was determined as a percentage of the total purchase price agreed for the takeover.

It was held that W was not entitled to retain the money, because the contract was void. The articles of association did not empower the committee of the board to authorise this payment on the board's behalf. In the words of Lord Templeman:

Equity forbids a trustee to make a profit out of his trust. The articles of association of Guinness relax the strict rule of equity to the extent of enabling a director to make a profit provided that the board of directors contracts on behalf of Guinness for the payment of special remuneration or decides to award special remuneration. Mr Ward did not obtain a contract or a grant from the board of directors. Equity has no power to relax its own strict rule further than and inconsistently with the express relaxation contained in the articles of association.

Furthermore, in agreeing a contingency fee, W was inevitably putting his interest and his duty in conflict, since the more Guinness paid for Distillers, the greater would be W's fee: his duty to negotiate a good price conflicted with his interest in enhancing his own fee. His honest belief that the contract was valid made no difference to this:

[T]he failure of Mr Ward to realise that he could not properly use his position as a director of Guinness to obtain a contingent negotiating fee of £5.2 million from Guinness does not excuse him or enable him to defeat the rules of equity which prohibit a trustee from putting himself in a position in which his interests and duty conflict and which insist that a trustee or any other fiduciary shall not make a profit out of his trust. (*Per* Lord Templeman.)

Accordingly, W was not entitled to retain the money, nor was he entitled to any payment *quantum meruit* for the work he had done under the contract. (On this last point see the section below on 'Remuneration', at p. 315.)

The personal remedy of liability to account for improper profits applied to the Court of Appeal's decision in *Gwembe Valley Development Co v Koshy (No. 3)* [2004] 1 BCLC 131. K was the managing director of GVDC and also a major investor, through another company, Lasco, of which he was the majority shareholder. K arranged for Lasco to lend a quantity of Zambian currency to GVDC, for which GVDC acknowledged a debt of $5.8 million, as the 'price' of the Zambian money. In fact Lasco had acquired the currency for only $1 million, so K was able to make a very large profit on the deal. As in *Guinness*, the issue arose of the extent to which the 'no profit' rule could be avoided by GVDC's articles of association. Here the articles permitted its directors to enter into contracts with the company on their own behalf, but this did not override the other requirement, which was to disclose all interests in such contracts at a meeting of directors. K had not done this, and the fact that some other directors were aware informally that K had an interest in the loan contract did not comply with this requirement of disclosure. The trial judge was entitled to conclude that K was guilty of dishonest concealment. The case was not therefore time-barred. Accordingly, K was bound to account to GVDC for the profit he had made.

See further under Chapter 17 'Time limits'.

The trust property

Objective 3

It is clear that improper profit by a fiduciary renders that fiduciary personally liable to account to his principal for that profit.

However, to make the fiduciary a trustee of property, with the proprietary rights that that implies for the principal, something further must be established. This point was made by Millett LJ in *Paragon v Thakerar* [1999] 1 All ER 400. The term 'constructive trust' has been applied in two separate situations which, he said, has led to confusion.

There is further discussion of this remedy in Chapter 17 (p. 502).

> The first covers those cases where the defendant, though not expressly appointed as trustee, has assumed the duties of trustee by a lawful transaction which was independent of and preceded the breach of trust and is not impeached by the plaintiff. The second covers those situations where the trust obligation arises as a direct consequence of the unlawful transaction which is impeached by the plaintiff.

It is only in the first case that a constructive trust can arise, for:

> [i]n the first class of case the constructive trustee really is a trustee. He does not receive the trust property in his own right but by a transaction by which both parties intend to create a trust at the outset and which is not impugned by the plaintiff. His possession of the property is coloured from the first by the trust and confidence by means of which he obtained it, and his subsequent appropriation of the property to his own use is a breach of trust.

Paragon v Thakerar itself concerned property allegedly acquired through fraud. In such cases it is misleading to describe the acquirer as a trustee of the property:

> Such person is not in fact a trustee at all, though he may be liable to account as if he were. He never assumes the position of trustee, and if he receives the trust property at all it is adversely to the plaintiff by an unlawful transaction which is impugned by the plaintiff.

In other words, property cannot be held on constructive trust unless the fiduciary acquired it legitimately in his fiduciary capacity (that is, on behalf of his principal) before the wrongful transaction complained of.

It is thus relatively straightforward to see that a trustee receives the trust property in his capacity as trustee and is bound to hold it for the beneficiary; he will be subject to a proprietary remedy; he will hold any gains that are made on the property on constructive trust. Equally other fiduciaries, such as agents or company directors, may come into possession of property on behalf of their principals or company as a result of their fiduciary role and again will hold that property on constructive trust.

Examples of such proprietary claims follow.

Harrison (JJ) (Properties) Ltd v Harrison [2002] 1 BCLC 162

In this case directors of a company who disposed of company property in breach of their fiduciary duty were to be treated as having committed a breach of trust and thus to be constructive trustees of any company property they thereby acquired. In this case H, a director, had acquired some land from the company, failing to disclose that planning permission had been granted, making it much more valuable. He was thus able to buy the land for £8,400 and sell it, having made considerable improvements, for £230,000.

The important distinction was that the director (obviously in a fiduciary position) transferred to himself property over which, as director, he had 'pre-existing trust-like responsibilities', and he thus held it on constructive trust.

This principle was again asserted in **Clark v Cutland** [2003] 4 All ER 733 in the Court of Appeal. One director, R, made unauthorised payments to himself from the company of £145,000, which he paid into his pension fund.

As in **Guinness v Saunders**, the payment to R by himself had clearly been made without the company's authority and in breach of the company's articles. This, the court held, made R the constructive trustee of the money and therefore liable to a proprietary remedy. In turn this allowed the money to be traced to the pension fund. It was accepted that the trustees of the pension fund did not have sufficient (or indeed any) knowledge of the breach of duty, and so could not be personally liable, but that did not prevent tracing to them as innocent volunteers. A charge on the pension fund for the £145,000 was the appropriate remedy.

For tracing see Chapter 17 (p. 504). In each of these cases the property involved clearly belonged to the company and had been under the control of the fiduciary who had then misused it.

If it is the case, as Millett LJ indicates, that the fiduciary must hold some property on the claimant's behalf, in advance of the alleged breach of duty, it must also be said that the term 'property' has been given a wide meaning.

Boardman v Phipps [1966] 3 All ER 721

In the leading case of **Boardman v Phipps** (above), the facts were that the appellants, Boardman and CW Phipps, were respectively the solicitor to and a beneficiary of a family trust. The respondent, JA Phipps, was another of the beneficiaries of the trust. The trust property included a minority shareholding in a private company, Lester & Harris Ltd. In 1956 Boardman and one of the trustees, an accountant called Fox, became dissatisfied with the way this company was performing and the appellants, Boardman and CW Phipps, attended the annual general meeting of the company as proxies for Fox and another of the trustees. They were thus enabled to attend the meeting and to obtain private information about the company by virtue of their positions *vis-à-vis* the trust. The trust had no power and would not have sought the power to purchase additional shares in the company but, with the knowledge of the two trustees for whom they held proxies, the appellants decided to try to acquire the remaining shares (those not held by the trust) for themselves. There then followed lengthy negotiations, throughout which Boardman purported to be acting for the trustees and during which he was enabled to obtain important information regarding the current value of the shares and of the company's assets. Eventually, the appellants were able to acquire all the shares of the company other than those owned by the trust.

Thereafter, the company was reorganised and substantial dividends were obtained.

The respondent had been asked if he objected to the appellants' acquisition of control of the company, but the appellants had not disclosed sufficient material facts to him to be able to claim his consent. He sought a declaration that the appellants held five-eighteenths (his interest in the trust) of their own shares on constructive trust for him, that they should render an account of the profits they had obtained and that they should transfer that portion of the shares and that share of the profits to him. At first instance, the respondent obtained the declaration of trust and the account of profits. The appellants appealed to the Court of Appeal and subsequently to the House of Lords which upheld, by a majority of three to two, the decision at first instance.

It must be remembered that the appellants were not the legal owners of the trust property, and one must consider what it was that belonged to the trust which the appellants misused for their own gain. The answer would appear to be the knowledge which they obtained by being able to attend board meetings and the opportunity to undertake negotiations for the purchase of shares which, it must be remembered, they did by representing themselves at all material times as acting for the trust. This being a private company, they could not have obtained this information in any other way. The acquisition of knowledge did not necessarily bar them from acting on their own account. In the words of Lord Cohen:

[T]he mere use of any knowledge or opportunity which comes to the trustee or agent in the course of his trusteeship or agency does not necessarily make him liable to account. In the present case had the company been a public company and had the appellants bought the shares in the market, they would not, I think, have been accountable. But the company is a private company and not only the information but the opportunity to purchase these shares came to them through the introduction which Mr Fox gave them to the board of the company and in the second phase . . . it was solely on behalf of the trustees that Mr Boardman was purporting to negotiate with the board of the company.

The majority in the House of Lords therefore concluded that the information was the property of the trust and furthermore had been misused by the appellants who were therefore accountable. It made no difference that the trust had lost nothing. Indeed, it had gained to the extent that its own shares had increased in value. Nor did it matter that the trust was unable and unwilling to take the action which the appellants had taken on their own behalf, though one might have thought there was a considerable difference between the present situation and taking for oneself that which one has the duty to obtain for the trust, a distinction argued unsuccessfully by the appellants. The appellants were therefore not only accountable for the profits that they had made, but also subject to a declaration by the court that they held a proportion of the shares they had purchased (which were the 'product' of the knowledge), on constructive trust for the respondent.

This view of information as the property of the trust has not been without its critics, not least Lord Upjohn, who gave a dissenting judgment in the case:

The real rule is, in my view, that knowledge learnt by a trustee in the course of his duties as such is not in the least property of the trust and in general may be used by him for his own benefit or for the benefit of other trusts unless it is confidential information which is given to him (1) in circumstances which, regardless of his position as a trustee, would make it a breach of confidence for him to communicate it to anyone for it has been given to him expressly or impliedly as confidential, or (2) in a fiduciary capacity, and its use would place him in a position where his duty and his interest might possibly conflict.

Greater difficulties arise where a profit or gain has been made, but it is difficult to make the connection between that gain and any property which belongs to, or is acquired on behalf of, the company for, despite Millet LJ's analysis in *Paragon* v *Thakerar* (above), it is clear that there are situations where the fiduciary has only acquired the gain as a result of his breach of duty, and yet the courts have come to recognise a proprietary remedy, a trusteeship, of that gain. The most obvious example of such a gain is a bribe or secret commission.

In *A-G for Hong Kong* v *Reid* [1994] 1 All ER 1 the Privy Council held that bribes received by a deputy public prosecutor in Hong Kong were to be treated as held on constructive trust for the Crown, which could therefore assert proprietary remedies against the bribes and the property in which the bribes had been invested. This led to the criticism that it was difficult to describe a bribe as the principal's property, or property that the fiduciary had a duty to acquire on behalf of his principal, since he clearly should not have acquired it at all.

This point was taken up by the Court of Appeal in the case of *Sinclair Investments (UK) Ltd* v *Versailles Trade Finance Ltd* [2011] EWCA Civ 347; [2011] 4 All ER 335.

Sinclair Investments (UK) Ltd v *Versailles Trade Finance Ltd* [2011] EWCA Civ 347, [2011] 4 All ER 335, [2011] 3 WLR 1153

This case concerned a 'ponzi' scheme, whereby funds received from investors, together with loans from banks, which were supposed to be used to finance the trading activities of the defendant's companies (the Versailles group), were in fact used to pay dividends to investors. The relevant defendant companies in fact carried on no, or almost no, trading activities at all. The prime mover of this scheme was Cushnie, a major shareholder in the defendant companies. Cushnie was a director of TPL (and hence a fiduciary towards TPL), the company which received the money from investors. Cushnie allowed this money to be paid to another company, Versailles, in which Cushnie held shares. The apparent success of the Versailles group had enabled Cushnie to secure a loan of £9.975 million from a bank to purchase a house and also to sell some of his shares in Versailles for £28.6 million. It was against the proceeds of these assets that Sinclair was making its claim. When the scheme collapsed, the winding up of the Versailles companies and of TPL was ordered, and the receivers reached several settlements with Cushnie (who was afterwards convicted of fraud), taking control of the assets and paying some of them to the banks in repayment of the loans.

TPL, which suffered considerable losses as a result of Versailles' activities, asserted a proprietary claim against the sale proceeds of Cushnie's shares in Versaiilles and against banks which had been reimbursed for loans made to Versailles. Sinclair was the assignee of TPL's claims. Cushnie's profit on the sale of his shares was a gain which he was enabled to make because of his breach of his fiduciary duty (in allowing the misapplication of TPL's funds by Versailles) but the share sale proceeds were not TPL's property, and they were not the product of TPL's property (i.e the shares had not been purchased by Cushnie with TPL's money, for example).

Accordingly, the money was not held on constructive trust and Sinclair could only assert a personal claim.

As the money which Sinclair sought to recover had been paid out by the receivers to the banks, as third parties, the difference between a proprietary claim based on constructive trust and a merely personal one was potentially crucial. As explained by Lewison J at first instance:

Before his sale of those shares he did not owe trustee-like duties in relation to that specific property. It follows, in my judgment, that the claim by TPL to the profit realised by Mr Cushnie on a sale of those shares is a claim based on the transaction which gave rise to those profits, and the circumstances in which it was made. It is, therefore, a case which falls into [Millett LJ's] second class (in **Paragon v Thakerer** [1999] 1 All ER 400); and gives rise to a personal remedy only. Since the claim gives rise to a personal remedy only, it is not open to TPL to trace those profits into the proceeds of sale of the Kensington property and to assert a proprietary claim to those proceeds. The settlement of personal claims between VTFL and Mr Cushnie cannot be undone by TPL in reliance on a personal claim.

Or as Lord Neuburger expressed it in the Court of Appeal:

> The difference is vital, because, if TPL is correct, it was the beneficial owner of those proceeds, and its beneficial ownership would override, subject to the question of notice, the payments made to the banks in so far as they were made out of the proceeds of sale. On the other hand, if the defendants' case is right, Mr Cushnie's duty is to account to TPL for the proceeds of sale, which is a personal remedy which would not override the payments already made to the banks.

His Lordship acknowledged that there was a clear commercial causal link between Cushnie's profits and his misuse of his fiduciary position and of the funds which he controlled on behalf of TPL. Nevertheless, his Lordship stressed that that in itself did not automatically suggest that TPL should be the owners of Cushnie's profits:

> Why, it may be asked, should the fact that a fiduciary is able to make a profit as a result of the breach of his duties to a beneficiary, without more, give the beneficiary a proprietary interest in the profit? After all a proprietary claim is based on property law, and it is not entirely easy to see conceptually how the proprietary rights of the beneficiary in the misused funds should follow into the profit made on the sale of the shares.

Thus, though the increase in the value of Mr Cushnie's shares, and his ability to borrow money for his house, may have arisen because of his breach of duty in the misuse of TPL's assets, it could not be said that the shares had been acquired with TPL's money, so his gains were not the product of TPL's money in a proprietary sense. TPL could therefore not assert a property right over these gains, but only a personal remedy for breach of fiduciary duty (which was, of course, of no use against a third party).

It will be noted, of course, that **Sinclair** is not a case of a bribe or secret commission in the sense of money being paid to the fiduciary for doing something which is almost certainly against his principal's interest, as in **Reid.** The Court of Appeal in **Sinclair**, nevertheless, cast doubt on the decision in **Reid** which, as a Privy Council decision, it was not, of course, bound to follow.

The issue of proprietary remedies over bribes and secret commissions arose again in **FHR European Ventures LLP v Cedar Capital Partners LLC** [2014] UKSC 45, which was a more straightforward 'commission' case.

FHR European Ventures LLP v Cedar Capital Partners [2014] UKSC 45

In this case C was acting as advisor to F in their negotiations for the acquisition of an hotel in Monte Carlo. At the same time C entered into an agreement with the vendors of the hotel that he would receive from them a fixed commission of £10 million for securing a purchaser for the hotel. He did not inform F of this. This commission was subsequently held to be a secret profit and, at first instance, it was held that F were entitled to an account of that profit (in other words a personal remedy, rather than the proprietary one based on a constructive trust). F appealed.

C was an agent and thus a fiduciary and so was not entitled to profit from a breach of his fiduciary duty; the issue was whether a personal or proprietary remedy was available. The Court of Appeal (*sub nom FHR European Ventures LLP and others* v *Mankarious and others* [2013] EWCA Civ 17, [2013] 3 All ER 29), considered the approach taken in *Sinclair* v *Versailles*. In the words of Sir Terence Etherington C:

> [The Sinclair case] divides into three broad categories the situations in which a fiduciary obtains a benefit in breach of fiduciary duty. The first category ('category 1') is where the benefit is or was an asset belonging beneficially to the principal (most obviously where the fiduciary has gained the benefit by misappropriating or misapplying the principal's property). The second category ('category 2') is where the benefit has been obtained by the fiduciary by taking an advantage of an opportunity which was properly that of the principal. The third category ('category 3') is all other cases. According to the analysis and conclusion of Lord Neuberger MR, the situations in categories 1 and 2 give rise to a constructive trust, but those in category 3 do not. The issue in the present case arises out of the difficulty of ascertaining the borderline between category 2 and category 3.

Applying these categories, the Court of Appeal decided that case fell within category two rather than category three, because F had been denied the opportunity of negotiating for a lower purchase price, because they did not know that C was to receive £10 million out of the purchase price. Had they known this they could perhaps have negotiated for a total purchase price £10 million less than they actually paid. C had thus taken 'advantage of an opportunity which was properly that of the principal (F)'.

In reaching this conclusion, the Court acknowledged the difficulty in distinguishing between categories two and three, and expressed the hope that the Supreme Court would overhaul the entire area of constructive trusts in order to provide a coherent and logical legal framework.

The Supreme Court, in its turn, concentrated on the specific issue of whether a bribe or secret commission should be subject to a constructive trust and concluded that it should. In the Court's judgment (ironically again delivered by Lord Neuberger):

> The notion that the Rule (of proprietary liability) should not apply to a bribe or secret commission received by an agent because it could not have been received by, or on behalf of, the principal seems unattractive. The whole reason that the agent should not have accepted the bribe or commission is that it puts him in conflict with his duty to his principal. Further, in terms of elementary economics, there must be a strong possibility that the bribe has disadvantaged the principal.

Acknowledging that the law is not always consistent, the Supreme Court concluded that for practical and policy reasons, bribes and commission should be subject to a proprietary remedy; the bribe was held on trust for the principal. The practical reason is one of simplicity, attempting to bring the proprietary remedy in line with the personal duty to account, and to avoid the perhaps artificial distinctions that had to be drawn in the Court of Appeal. The main policy is to do all that is possible to discourage bribery which, as Lord Templeman said in *Attorney General for Hong Kong* v *Reid* [1994] 1 AC 324, 330H, 'is an evil practice which threatens the foundations of any civilised society'. As the Supreme Court also said in *FHR*, 'Secret commissions are also objectionable as they inevitably tend to undermine trust in the commercial world'. In so far as the case resolves the issue with regard to bribes and commissions it is to be welcomed; to use the law as effectively as possible to prevent a fiduciary from making gains from these practices seems only right.

The remaining question is the extent to which it might be applied to all gains by a fiduciary, and what limiting factors may be applied. Is the decision in *Sinclair* wrong on its facts, given the much more tenuous connection between Cushnie's gains and his breach of duty to TPL? The Supreme Court in *FHR* rather cautiously stated that *Sinclair* should be treated as overruled 'at least in so far as they followed or relied on *Metropolitan Bank* v *Heiron* (1880) 5 Ex D 319 or *Lister & Co* v *Stubbs* (1890) 45 Ch D 1', which the court regarded as the two decisions going against the awards of proprietary remedies, and which the court also overruled. This, it is submitted, does not necessarily set aside the point made by Lord Neuburger in *Sinclair*, quoted above, that 'it is not entirely easy to see conceptually how the proprietary rights of the beneficiary in the misused funds should follow into the profit made on the sale of the shares'.

Whilst the Supreme Court in *FHR* stressed at the outset that its judgment was about bribes and secret commissions, the adoption of a general principle that the proprietary remedy should be available wherever the personal duty to account existed, may imply a wider ambit. If it is attempted to apply this case to all gains by fiduciaries, it seem likely that, as often happens with 'simple' rules, exceptional cases will arise which seem unfair, if convoluted distinctions are not made, and this may encourage a further debate on the relationship between the 'no conflict' rule and the 'no profit' rule which are said in *Bray* v *Ford* to underlie the liability of the fiduciary.

The relative merits and impact of personal and proprietary remedies are discussed below in the section 'Personal or proprietary remedies: denying the fiduciary his improper gains' (p. 312).

Gains made through breach of fiduciary duty: 'class two' constructive trusts

While it has been stressed above that a constructive trust properly so called can only be imposed on property which has been legitimately acquired in a fiduciary capacity and then misapplied or misappropriated by the fiduciary, the term 'constructive trust' has also been applied to cases where a fiduciary has acquired property by misuse of fiduciary powers where he had no previous interest in or duty in respect of that property.

Millet LJ in *Paragon* said of such a person: '(He) is not in fact a trustee at all, though he may be liable to account as if he were.' Subsequent cases have referred to such situations as 'class two' constructive trusts (being the second type referred to by Millet LJ in *Paragon*). This, it is submitted, is unfortunate and confusing, since it appears that the remedy in such a case is a personal one, to account for improper gains; there is no 'trust' in the sense of property being recoverable as trust property.

Sinclair v *Versailles* (discussed above at p. 308) was expressly stated by Lewison J to be an example of such a case. A further instance is *Halton* v *Guernroy* [2006] EWCA 801.

Halton v Guernroy [2006] EWCA Civ 801, [2006] All ER (D) 302

In this case the claimants and defendant were shareholders in an airline. To seek further finance, the parties entered into a voting agreement, vesting voting control in the defendant. The claimants alleged that D had used this power to vote itself extra shares, which had now increased in value. The claimants alleged that D had a fiduciary duty not to use its voting power to obtain profit for itself. The Court of Appeal held that the shares could not be held on constructive trust for the claimants. Whilst it may be that the voting rights were held in a fiduciary capacity and had been acquired by a lawful transaction (the voting agreement), thus falling within Millett LJ's first class of case, it was the shares that the claimants were alleging to be held on trust and which they were seeking to recover. The shares themselves were acquired by the breach of duty itself and so fell into Millet LJ's second category and are not therefore held on constructive trust. In the words of Carnwath LJ: 'the new shares came into existence "only by reason of the transaction impeached"'. Nor were they sufficiently the product of the voting rights, which were, in the Court's view, merely part of the means by which the defendant acquired the new shares. This was fatal to the claimants' case, as a personal claim was time-barred.

Another example is that of *Gwembe Valley Development Co* v *Koshy (No. 3)* [2004] 1 BCLC 131, considered above in the context of director's duties, and followed in *Halton*.

In that case a director of GVDC failed to disclose that he had an interest, as director and majority shareholder, in a second company, Lasco, which made a substantial profit from lending money to GVDC. Though a fiduciary to GVDC, the director did not owe that duty in respect of any property of GVDC: any liability for his undisclosed profit arose directly from the transaction (lending the money) which gave rise to the profit.

It remains to be seen what impact, if any, the decision in *FHR* v *Cedar*, discussed above, might have on such cases.

This distinction between 'class one' and 'class two' trusts has arisen in the context of the interpretation of s 21 of the Limitation Act 1980. The normal limitation period applies to a claim in equity, but s 21(1) provides that 'no period of limitation shall apply to an action by the beneficiary under a trust, being an action (a) in respect of any fraud or fraudulent breach of trust to which the trustee was party or privy; or (b) to recover from the trustee trust property or the proceeds of trust property in the possession of the trustee, or previously received by the trustee and converted to his own use'. The courts have consistently held that 'class one' trusts fall into the subheading (b) but that class two 'trusts' do not.

For time limits on actions, see Chapter 17 (p. 500).

 ## Personal or proprietary remedies: denying the fiduciary his improper gains

In *A-G for Hong Kong* v *Reid* [1994] 1 All ER 1 the Privy Council held that bribes received by a deputy public prosecutor in Hong Kong were to be treated as held on constructive trust for the Crown, which could therefore assert proprietary remedies against the bribes and the property in which the bribes had been invested. One motive for this decision is to prevent the fiduciary from keeping any of his gains, since this would not have been possible, without imposing a constructive trust, to deny Reid all the gains he made, not only from the amount of the initial bribes, but also that arising from the increase in value of the property in which the bribes had been invested. The Supreme Court on *FHR* v *Cedar*, discussed above, has confirmed that bribes and secret commissions received by fiduciaries are to be treated as held on constructive trust.

It is clear that where a trustee has taken property from the trust and invested it for his own profit, that property, and the profit derived from it, should be held on constructive trust for the beneficiary: the property is already the beneficiary's anyway, and the profit has been derived directly from it. It is not a very great extension of this principle to *Keech* v *Sandford*, where the property was the lease which, though not trust property, it was the trustee's duty to have renewed for the beneficiary's benefit. Similarly, it is possible to regard the confidential information in *Boardman* v *Phipps* as the property of the trust which the solicitor had used to his advantage.

The principles enunciated in *A-G for Hong Kong* v *Reid* were upheld by the High Court in *Daraydan Holdings Ltd* v *Solland International Ltd* [2005] 4 All ER 73, where Laurence Collins J stated that there were powerful policy reasons for preventing fiduciaries from retaining gains obtained by breach of fiduciary duty, even where that meant that a creditor of that fiduciary could not retain such gains for which he had not himself given consideration. The interests of the creditor are thus second to those of the person to whom the fiduciary duty is owed.

It is, therefore, a fundamental rule that a fiduciary should not be able to profit from misuse of this fiduciary position, because of the danger of conflict of interest. How then is this profit to be prevented? Whatever remedy is used, it is clear that, if the profit is to be removed from the fiduciary, it can only be given to the person for whom he is fiduciary. If the profit is in the form of gains from the use of trust property, then this is profit which should be the beneficiary's; but in a case of bribes or other illicit receipts not derived from the use of trust property, paying them to the beneficiary is to give that beneficiary a windfall which he would never receive other than as a result of the fiduciary's wrongdoing. The only reason the beneficiary, or the employer in *Reid*, receives the windfall is that he is the most innocent party, though there is perhaps the view that the principal always suffers, albeit indirectly, where a fiduciary acts wrongfully, and money represents a crude measure of compensation for that harm. In *Reid*, for example, it was assumed that the bribers, from whom the money ultimately derived, had no right to the return of the money, as they were themselves guilty of illegal conduct (even supposing that any had wished to come forward to claim it).

Secondly, if the object of imposing an equitable remedy, of whatever type, is to deny the fiduciary his unconscionable gain, does it make any difference whether the remedy used for this is personal or proprietary? Very often it is simply a question of recovering the unconscionable gain from the fiduciary: if he is solvent, either remedy will do. But a proprietary remedy has several important consequences. As mentioned above, if, as in *Reid*, the unconscionable gain has been invested at a profit, merely to make the fiduciary personally liable for the amount of the gain would leave him with the profits, and he would still be profiting from his breach of duty.

A further advantage of a proprietary remedy is that the property may be traced into the hands of third parties, other than the *bona fide* purchaser without notice: in *Reid* the houses bought with the bribes were in the name of Reid's wife and solicitor, but as neither was a *bona fide* purchaser, tracing was possible. If a merely personal remedy is imposed, it is unlikely that the third party can be made liable unless dishonesty is established (see further below under 'Liability of strangers'). In *Sinclair* the claim was against third parties, the banks, against whom a personal claim could not be made.

The third effect is that, if a trust is imposed on gains, they are not available to meet the fiduciary's debts. This was a point taken up by Lord Neuburger in *Sinclair*:

> But the difference (between personal and proprietary claims) very much matters to the other creditors of the defaulting fiduciary, if he is insolvent. A person with a proprietary claim to assets held in the name of an insolvent person is better off than a secured creditor, and all such assets are unavailable to other creditors. That is not to suggest that there is anything commercially objectionable about proprietary claims, whose existence is well established and appropriate, but it is, I think, a reason for not extending the reach of such claims beyond what is established by authority and accords with principle . . .

The Supreme Court in *FHR* v *Cedar* acknowledged that this had been an important reason in *Sinclair* and 'has considerable force in some contexts' but doubted its importance in the case of bribes and secret commissions (as in *FHR* itself), since the bribe should not be part of the fiduciary's estate at all (isn't that true of all 'improper' gains?) and the bribe probably resulted in a detriment to the principal, for which the receipt of the bribe will in some sense be compensation.

These considerations have led to a debate as to the circumstances in which a proprietary remedy should be imposed. The result of *Reid* appeared to impose one in all cases of profit by fiduciaries. This has been criticised as draconian and inflexible and may be unfair on creditors, and was rejected in *Sinclair* (where the dispute was in effect between the company owed the fiduciary duty and the creditor banks, and there was no question of Cushnie retaining improper profits). Lord Neuburger concluded:

(Counsel for the Claimants) suggested (with Lord Millett's extrajudicial support) that, essentially as a matter of equitable policy, a fiduciary should not be allowed to profit from his breach of duties, even to the extent of retaining any profit from such an asset after compensating a claimant in full. If that is indeed correct, then it seems to me that this should be dealt with by extending, or adjusting, the rules relating to equitable compensation rather than those relating to proprietary interests. Such a course, as I see it, would do less violence to the law as consistently laid down (where it has been specifically addressed) in a number of domestic cases of high authority, whereas it would involve little interference with established authority relating to equitable compensation. In addition, the law relating to proprietary interests, being within the law of property, is inherently rather less flexible than the law relating to equitable compensation. Furthermore, extending the law relating to equitable compensation in such a case would interfere far less with the legitimate interests of other creditors than extending the law relating to proprietary interests.

Given this statement, it is perhaps interesting that the Supreme Court should have reached the conclusion in *FHR* following the approach in *Reid*.

To make a fiduciary accountable not only for property misused, but also for the profits obtained by that misuse, denies the benefit to the fiduciary while leaving the gains available to meet the claims of general creditors. Yet other remedies may be available, as in **Lord Napier and Ettrick v Hunter** [1993] 1 All ER 385, concerning the right of an insurer who had met an insured's loss to recover money which the insured had recovered in damages representing the same loss. Lord Templeman considered that the imposition of a trust on the money would create 'fearsome' practical difficulties:

> Fortunately, equity is not so inflexible or powerless. In order to protect the rights of the insurers under the doctrine of subrogation equity considers that the damages payable by the wrongdoer to the insured person are subject to an equitable lien or charge in favour of the insurer.

(Note, though, that there was no issue here of a profit made on the money concerned.)

Trustees as directors

If trustees are appointed directors of companies in which the trust holds shares, are they accountable for the fees they receive as directors? As usual, the issue is whether the directorship was acquired as a result of the trusteeship. In **Re Macadam** [1945] 2 All ER 664, the articles of a company permitted trustees of a trust holding shares in the company to appoint directors. The trustees appointed themselves as directors. Cohen J held them accountable for their fees:

> [A]lthough the remuneration was remuneration for services as director of the company, the opportunity to receive the remuneration was gained as a result of the exercise of a discretion vested in the trustees, and they had put themselves in a position where their interest and duty conflicted. In those circumstances, I do not think this court can allow them to make a profit out of doing so, and I do not think the liability to account for a profit can be confined to cases where the profit is derived directly from the trust estate.

He contrasted the present situation with that in **Re Dover Coalfield Extension** [1907] 2 Ch 76, where a Mr Cousins had contracted to serve as a director of the company in return for remuneration. He was then issued with the shares necessary to qualify him as a director and held these shares on trust. As he had become a director before he became trustee of the shares, he could not have used his position as trustee to acquire the directors' fees and

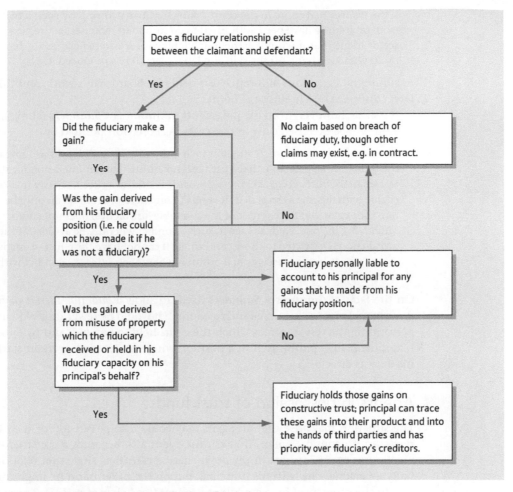

Figure 12.1 Reclaiming improper gains from fiduciaries

accordingly he was not accountable. As Cohen J pointed out: '[T]he root of the matter really is: Did he acquire the position in respect of which he drew the remuneration by virtue of his position as trustee?'

Remuneration for work done

The strict effects of imposing remedies to prevent a fiduciary from profiting from his position may be mitigated by the court awarding him payment for work he has done for the benefit of the trust or person to whom he is fiduciary, at least in cases where he has acted *bona fide*.

In **Boardman v Phipps**, referred to above, the judge at first instance, while recognising that the solicitor to the trust could not keep the profit he had made, held that he was nonetheless entitled to payment for his services, which had considerably enhanced the value of the trust property, apart from the gains he had made himself. Wilberforce J pointed out that, if Boardman had not undertaken the work, the trust would have had to pay an expert to do the job for them:

> If the trustees had come to the court asking for liberty to employ such a person, they would in all probability have been authorised to do so, and to remunerate the person in question. It seems to me that it would be inequitable now for the beneficiaries to step in and take the profit without paying for the skill and labour which has produced it.

Accordingly, a generous allowance was made for Boardman's work, and this decision was later confirmed by the House of Lords.

It is clear, however, from the judgments in *Guinness v Saunders* (above), that this jurisdiction is to be exercised only in rare cases. As Lord Goff pointed out:

> The decision [to make such an allowance in *Boardman v Phipps*] has to be reconciled with the fundamental principle that a trustee is not entitled to remuneration for services rendered by him to the trust except as expressly provided in the trust deed. Strictly speaking, it is irreconcilable with the rule as so stated. It seems to me therefore that it can only be reconciled with it to the extent that the exercise of the equitable jurisdiction does not conflict with the policy underlying the rule. And, as I see it, such a conflict will only be avoided if the exercise of the jurisdiction is restricted to those cases where it cannot have the effect of encouraging trustees in any way to put themselves in a position where their interests conflict with their duties as trustees.

On the facts of *Guinness v Saunders* itself, to allow a *quantum meruit* payment for work done would clearly encourage such a conflict: it would be rewarding W in another way for performing the very contract which the court held to be void, and by entering which W had most plainly put himself in a position where his interests were in stark conflict with his duty as director.

Agents in possession of trust funds

The situation may arise that an agent may come into possession of trust funds and it is necessary to consider when, if at all, the agent also becomes a constructive trustee. His position as agent does not imply *per se* that he is trustee, since that relationship is essentially a personal one with his principal, but on the other hand he might on occasion fall within the category of intermeddling stranger (see below at p. 335). The conflict between the two principles was succinctly stated by Bacon V-C in *Lee v Sankey* (1872) LR 15 Eq 204:

> [A] mere agent of trustees is answerable only to his principal and not to *cestuis que* trust in respect of trust moneys coming into his hands merely in his character of agent. But it is also not less clearly established that a person who receives into his hands trust moneys, and who deals with them in a manner inconsistent with the performance of the trusts of which he is cognisant, is personally liable for the consequences which may ensue upon his so dealing.

This would appear to indicate that a person who has possession of trust funds and deals with them innocently is not a trustee, whereas one who deals fraudulently or in a manner he knows is against the trust becomes a trustee. Clearly, merely having knowledge of the trust would not be sufficient; it is knowing that it is being misused that is crucial.

The actions of the agent must make him more than merely an agent. In the words of AL Smith LJ in *Mara v Browne* [1896] 1 Ch 199:

> If one, not being a trustee and not having the authority from a trustee, takes upon himself to intermeddle with trust matters or to do acts characteristic of the office of trustee he may therefore make himself a trustee of his own wrong, i.e. a trustee *de son tort* or, as it is also termed, a constructive trust.

That principle was applied in the following case.

Williams-Ashman v Price and Williams [1942] 1 All ER 310

Here the facts were that solicitors had received trust funds into the firm's account and had made unauthorised investments with the funds on the instructions of the trustee. Bennett J pointed to *Mara v Browne* as authority that an agent could be liable only if he took on the characteristics of a trustee. The beneficiaries had a remedy against the real trustees and therefore there was nothing inequitable in excusing the agent. On the present facts, the solicitor had acted honestly throughout and had acted on the instructions of the trustees. His failure to inquire, as he might have done, what were the trusts on which the property was held and hence what investment was authorised, did not render him a trustee. Acting honestly on the instructions of their principal is not acting as trustees and, accordingly, the solicitors were not liable as such. Bennett J contrasted this with the case of *Blyth v Fladgate* [1891] 1 Ch 337, where solicitors had made the unauthorised investments on their own initiative, after the death of the trustees.

The position of agents was summarised in *Carl Zeiss Stiftung v Herbert Smith (No. 2)* [1969] 2 All ER 367, by Edmund Davies LJ:

(A) A solicitor or other agent who receives money from his principal which belongs at law or in equity to a third party is not accountable as a constructive trustee to that third party unless he has been guilty of some wrongful act in relation to that money.

(B) To act 'wrongfully' he must be guilty of (i) knowingly participating in a breach by his principal; or (ii) intermeddling with the trust property otherwise merely than as an agent and thereby becoming a trustee *de son tort*; or (iii) receiving or dealing with the money knowing that his principal has no right to pay it over or to instruct him to deal with it in the manner indicated; or (iv) some dishonest act relating to the money. These are indeed but variants of that 'want of probity' to which I have earlier referred.

Liability of the partners of constructive trustees

The House of Lords, in *Dubai Aluminium v Salaam* [2003] 1 All ER 97, has confirmed the judgment of Rix J at first instance, on the question of when a partnership can be vicariously liable for the acts of one of the partners. The case arose out of the settlement out of court that the partnership, Amhursts, made with the claimant on the basis of the assumed dishonest assistance of one of its partners, A, in a complex fraud also involving the defendants, S and T, and others. The settlement assumed A's dishonest assistance, although this was strongly denied by A throughout. A had drawn up contracts and consultancy agreements, which formed part of the transactions constituting the fraud. Under s 10 of the Partnership Act 1890 the partnership could be vicariously liable for 'any wrongful act or omission of any partner done in the ordinary course of the business of the firm' which caused loss to the claimant.

The House of Lords confirmed that 'wrongful act' included an act which was wrongful in equity, such as dishonest assistance in a breach of trust or fiduciary duty, as in this case, and was not restricted to tortious wrongs. Their lordships also discussed at length the meaning of 'in the ordinary course of business' in the context of deliberate wrongs and concluded that doing acts which would, if honest, have been within the ordinary course of business, was still within the ordinary course even if done for dishonest purposes. Accordingly, as it was part of A's job, as a solicitor, to draw up contracts and consultancy agreements, his doing so in this case was still within the ordinary course of the firm's business, even though done for allegedly dishonest motives. It was also irrelevant that some of A's acts were not done in his capacity as a member of the firm, since some relevant acts were; in this respect the House of Lords reversed the Court of Appeal decision.

Mutual wills

 ### The problem

Objective
4

The mutual will is another example of where the trust concept is used to provide a solution to a problem, but here the solution creates so many problems that mutual wills are avoided in many cases by legal practitioners.

It must be very common for two people (often, but not necessarily, a married couple or civil partners) to discuss what they want to happen to their property when the first of them should die and who should receive the totality of their property when they are both dead. They may agree that, for example, whichever of them survives will enjoy the property of the first to die and that the survivor will make a will under which all their property, including that inherited from the other, is left to their son. In this way the son will ultimately receive all of the property of his father and mother. There are, obviously, many other forms that the agreement could take. For example, the survivor may be given a life interest in the property of the first to die rather than an absolute interest, or the agreement may not extend to all of the property of the parties or the survivor may not receive any interest in the property of the first to die which, under the terms of the agreement, passes directly to the ultimate beneficiary.

The parties may also agree that they will not revoke their wills made in pursuance of their agreement. This agreement will reflect their common intention that their plan should be carried through and that it should not be thwarted by one or other revoking their will, particularly after the death of the first to die.

Sometimes the parties intend that the agreement to make and then not to revoke wills should be binding in honour only. But it may be that the parties want the agreement to be legally binding and that if either party breaks the agreement legal consequences should follow.

One obvious difficulty with an agreement not to revoke wills is the rule that wills, despite any agreement to the contrary, are always revocable. Revocability is one of the fundamental characteristics of a will (see **Re Heys' Estate** [1914] P 192).

 ### The solution

In order to avoid the problem caused by the rule that wills are always revocable and to ensure that the terms of agreements are honoured, equity has developed the concept of mutual wills.

The origins of the doctrine are to be found in **Dufour v Pereira** (1769) 1 Dick 419. In brief, if mutual wills are found to have been made, a trust will arise on the death of the first to die which will cover all the property within the terms of the agreement. If the survivor subsequently revokes their will and makes a new will that does not reflect the terms of the agreement, equity does not prevent the survivor from revoking their will (thus preserving the revocability rule); but when the property passes to the personal representatives of the second to die, they take the property within the agreement subject to a trust in favour of the agreed ultimate beneficiary(ies).

In **Re Dale (deceased)** [1993] 4 All ER 129, Morritt J described mutual wills thus:

> The doctrine of mutual wills is to the effect that, where two individuals have agreed as to the disposal of their property and have executed mutual wills in pursuance of the agreement, on the death of the first (T1) the property of the survivor (T2), the subject matter of the agreement, is held on an implied trust for the beneficiary named in the wills. The survivor may

thereafter alter his will because a will is always inherently revocable, but if he does his personal representatives will take the property subject to the trust.

Three comments may be made on this quotation. First, as will be discussed later, although there is considerable discussion on the point, mutual wills are more usually considered to be constructive, rather than implied, trusts. Secondly, the trust that arises 'for the beneficiaries named in the wills' refers to the beneficiaries named in the original, mutual wills. Thirdly, the parties must have agreed not to revoke their mutual wills.

In *Re Goodchild* [1997] 3 All ER 63, Morritt LJ described mutual wills as anomalous. Perhaps this may explain the strictness of the approach of the Court of Appeal towards the doctrine of mutual wills.

A summation of the current law was set out by Mr Jonathan Gaunt QC sitting as a deputy judge of the Chancery Division in *Charles v Fraser* [2010] EWHC Civ 2124.

I take the law on mutual wills to be as follows:

(i) Mutual wills are wills made by two or more persons, usually in substantially the same terms and conferring reciprocal benefits, following an agreement between them to make such wills and not revoke them without the consent of the other.

(ii) For the doctrine to apply there has to be what amounts to a contract between the two testators that both wills will be irrevocable and remain unaltered. A common intention, expectation or desire is not enough.

(iii) The mere execution of mirror or reciprocal wills does not imply any agreement either as to revocation or non-revocation.

(iv) For the doctrine to apply it is not necessary that the second testator should have obtained a personal financial benefit under the will of the first testator . . .

(v) It is perfectly possible for there to have been an agreement preventing revocability as to part of the residuary estate only, in which case the doctrine only applies to that part.

(vi) The agreement may be incorporated in the will or proved by extraneous evidence. It may be oral or in writing.

(vii) The agreement must be established by clear and satisfactory evidence on the balance of probabilities.

(viii) The agreement is enforced in equity by the imposition of a constructive trust on the property which is the subject matter of the agreement. The beneficiaries under the will that was not to be revoked may apply to the Court for an order that the estate is held on trust to give effect to the provisions of the old will.

(ix) The action relates only to the dispositive part of the will. The new will is fully effective to deal with non-dispositive matters, such as the appointment of Executors. Accordingly where the doctrine applies the Executors appointed under the final will hold the assets of the estate on trust to give effect to the earlier will.

The key requirements in order for mutual wills to exist are the following:

- the parties must have entered into an agreement as to the disposition of their property;
- the parties must intend the agreement to be legally binding;
- the parties must agree that they will not revoke their wills, and
- the parties must execute wills that reflect the agreement.

Some issues relating to mutual wills

The execution of wills to reflect an agreement gives rise to a number of difficulties, some theoretical, others practical. For example:

- When do mutual wills, in the technical sense, 'exist'?
- What evidence is required to prove the existence of an agreement?
- If the agreement relates to land, does it satisfy the requirements of writing and signatures contained in the Law of Property (Miscellaneous Provisions) Act 1989?
- What remedies, if any, are available if one party does not execute the will in the terms agreed?
- What are the implications of one party making a will in furtherance of their agreement but then revoking it while the other party is still alive?
- What are the legal implications of the survivor revoking their will and making another leaving all or some of their property to someone other than the agreed, ultimate, beneficiary?
- What property is covered by the agreement?
- If property is impressed with a trust, what powers has the survivor to deal with the property?
- When does the trust come into being?
- What type of trust is it?

These and other problems will be discussed more fully below.

Such are the potential problems of mutual wills that in **Charles v Fraser** the judge said, 'I think it was the plain duty of any solicitor . . . faced with two [people] wishing to make reciprocal wills, to ascertain their intentions as to revocation, to advise as to the effect of making mutual wills . . .'

But, despite the problems relating to mutual wills, when the Law Reform Committee considered mutual wills in their Twenty-Second Report, 'The Making and Revocation of Wills' (Cmnd 7902, 1980), their recommendation, after having noted that mutual wills were extremely rare but that they did give rise to a number of problems, was that mutual wills should not be abolished and that the difficulties they create would be better clarified by judicial development than by legislation.

But notwithstanding that the use of mutual wills is thought to be unusual and is often not recommended by solicitors, the case law continues to expand. There have been at least two relatively recent cases in which the law on mutual wills has been central: **Fry v Densham-Smith** [2010] EWCA Civ 1410 and **Charles v Fraser** [2010] EWHC Civ 2124.

An area of possible confusion is the difference between mutual wills and 'mirror' wills. If two people make wills that are wholly or mainly identical and which both leave assets to the same beneficiaries but who do not agree that their agreement to make the wills is legally binding nor do they agree not to revoke their wills, they are making what are commonly called 'mirror' wills and not mutual wills. A legally binding agreement to make the wills and an agreement not to revoke are essential for there to be mutual wills. A testator is perfectly free to revoke a 'mirror' will at any time and the provisions of any later will will be totally effective.

Requirement for an agreement

The key requirement is that there must an agreement between the parties as to the destination of property on their respective deaths, that they will make wills to reflect the agreement and that neither will revoke their will without the acquiescence of the other party. Additionally the parties must intend that their agreement will be legally binding. Like any legally binding agreement it must be supported by consideration.

In *Re Dale* Morritt J said:

> There is no doubt that for the doctrine to apply there must be a contract at law. It is apparent from all the cases to which I shall refer later, but in particular from *Grey* v *Perpetual Trustee Co Ltd* [1928] AC 391, that it is necessary to establish an agreement to make and not revoke mutual wills, some understanding or arrangement being insufficient.

Morritt J then quoted Viscount Haldane in *Grey* v *Perpetual Trustee Co Ltd*, in which he said: 'without such a definite agreement there can no more be a trust in equity than a right to damages at law'.

While the agreement may be expected to be in writing, even recorded in the wills, oral evidence (as in *Re Cleaver* [1981] 2 All ER 1018) may be sufficient.

Consideration

The agreement must include promises to make wills to reflect the agreement and mutual promises not to revoke the wills so made (or at least an intention that their wills are intended to be mutually binding even if not expressed in the language of revocation: *per* Carnwath J in *Re Goodchild*). In other words, as Morritt J stressed in *Re Dale*, the parties must enter into a contract, supported on each side by consideration.

Initially it was thought that mutual wills could only come into being if the survivor took a benefit under the will of the first to die. This, it was argued, constituted the consideration necessary for a legally binding contract. However, in *Re Dale*, Morritt J held that merely to execute one's will in accordance with the agreement was a sufficient detriment to constitute consideration. The consideration to support the contract is the execution of the will and promising not to revoke it.

Morritt J said:

> It is to be assumed that the first testator and the second testator had agreed to make and not to revoke the mutual wills in question. The performance of that promise by the execution of the will by the first testator is in my judgment sufficient consideration by itself. But, in addition, to determine whether a promise can constitute consideration it is necessary to consider whether its performance would have been so regarded . . . Thus it is to be assumed that the first testator did not revoke the mutual will notwithstanding his legal right to do so. In my judgment, this too is sufficient detriment to the first testator to constitute consideration.

Proving the agreement

Existence of the agreement must be proved using the normal civil burden of proof – the balance of probabilities. If the legally binding agreement is not proved to exist, then there will be no mutual wills and, for example, the survivor can make a new will which can effectively leave the property to whomsoever they wish. The survivor may be subject to a moral obligation to ensure that property is left to particular beneficiaries, but there will be no legal obligation and property will not be subject to the trust referred to above.

In some instances the court has indicated that the starting point is that in most cases parties would not want to create mutual wills. For example, in *Re Goodchild* [1997] 3 All ER 63 the court said, 'The test must always be, suppose that during the lifetime of the surviving testator the intended beneficiary did something that the survivor regarded as unpardonable, would he or she not be free not to leave the combined estate to him?'

Again, in *Charles* v *Fraser* [2010] EWHC 2154 (Ch), Jonathan Gaunt QC said that, when assessing the evidence, the courts will have in mind the inherent improbability that a testator would be prepared to give up the possibility of changing their will in the future, whatever changes in circumstances may have occurred.

In other words, it is often considered that it is inherently unlikely that the parties would intend to restrict their freedom of testamentary disposition.

Although Lord Cottenham suggested in *Dufour v Pereira* that if testators executed identical wills it was possible to infer an agreement not to revoke, more recent cases state that this is not a correct statement. But it is accepted that the execution of identical wills may well be evidence of an agreement, while not by itself be sufficient to warrant a finding of mutual wills: *Grey v Perpetual Trustee Co Ltd* [1928] AC 391. This point was also made in *Re Oldham* [1925] Ch 75, where Astbury J added: 'They may have thought it quite safe to trust one another . . . But that is very different from saying that they bound themselves by a trust that should be operative in all circumstances and in all cases.' Astbury J opined that in the absence of any agreement, the fact that the parties had both given each other absolute, as opposed to life, interests in each other's property argued against a binding trust.

But in *Re Cleaver*, sufficient evidence of agreement was available. In this case, an elderly couple married. They kept their assets separate but made wills in similar terms, each leaving the other their residuary property absolutely, with a gift over to the husband's children. After the death of the husband, the widow amended her will several times, ultimately leaving her property on terms different from those agreed. It was held that she was bound by the agreement and accordingly held the property on trust. Evidence of the agreement arose from the fact that the wills were made on identical terms and at the same time, and that various identical amendments had been made by both during the husband's lifetime.

In *Re Goodchild* the court found that there was insufficient evidence of the agreement to create mutual wills. At first instance and on appeal the need for an agreement was restated. In the High Court ([1996] 1 All ER 670) Carnwath J said that: 'The plaintiff needs to show that there was some agreement, or representation intended to have legal effect, to which the court should give effect.'

On appeal ([1997] 3 All ER 63) it was argued that an agreement was not necessary. All that was needed was a common understanding between the two testators that the wills would be mutually binding. The argument then proceeded in terms that if neither has given notice of withdrawal from the understanding the obligation becomes a legal one on the death of the first to die. This argument was based on an analogy with secret trusts where equity does not allow property to be dealt with in a way that is inconsistent with an agreement or understanding. However, the analogy with secret trusts was not accepted, particularly as mutual wills (unlike secret trusts) relate to the property of two people and thus an agreement is needed. Morritt LJ said that he considered that the principles applicable to fully secret trusts do in substance require proof of a contract. He cited Brightman J in *Ottaway v Norman* [1971] 3 All ER 1325, who said in relation to secret trusts:

> The essential elements which must be proved to exist are: (i) the intention of the testator to subject the primary donee to an obligation in favour of the secondary donee; (ii) communication of that intention to the primary donee; and (iii) the acceptance of that obligation by the primary donee either expressly or by acquiescence.

Morritt LJ went on to say: 'But if those principles do not require exactly the same degree of agreement as does a contract at law there is no reason to import that lesser requirement into the doctrine of mutual wills.'

In any event, the court said that there was clear authority for the need for an agreement to create mutual wills. Leggatt LJ referred to Nourse J in *Re Cleaver*, who stated:

> It is therefore clear that there must be a definite agreement between the makers of the two wills; that that must be established by evidence; that the fact that there are mutual wills to

the same effect is a relevant circumstance to be taken into account, although not enough of itself; and that the whole of the evidence must be looked at.

Leggatt LJ then said: 'I am satisfied that for the doctrine to apply there must be a contract at law.'

Honourable engagements do not suffice. Leggatt LJ went on to say:

Two wills may be in the same form as each other. Each testator may leave his or her estate to the other with a view to the survivor leaving both estates to their heir. But there is no presumption that a present plan will be immutable in future. A key feature of the concept of mutual wills is the irrevocability of the mutual intentions. Not only must they be binding when made, but the testators must have undertaken, and so must be bound, not to change their intentions after the death of the first testator. The test must always be, suppose that during the lifetime of the surviving testator the intended beneficiary did something which the survivor regarded as unpardonable, would he or she be free not to leave the combined estate to him? The answer must be that the survivor is so entitled unless the testators agreed otherwise when they executed their wills. Hence the need for a clear agreement.

Morritt LJ agreed that an agreement is required.

The requirement for an agreement was again the issue in **Birch v Curtis** [2002] EWHC 1158 (Ch). This is a first-instance decision on mutual wills or rather on a situation where mutual wills were not found to exist.

The judge (Rimer J) explored both case law and academic articles and came to the (unsurprising) conclusion that an essential element of mutual wills is an agreement not to revoke. Rimer J said: '[T]he key question in every case, including this one, is still whether or not there is any evidence justifying the finding that the parties were each contractually committing themselves to a testamentary disposition which, so far as the survivor was concerned, was to be irrevocable.'

The case had one unusual aspect in that when the alleged mutual wills were executed (about ten days apart) it was anticipated that one of the testators (the wife) would die well before the other. Normally when wills are executed there is no particular expectation as to which will die first. In the light of this expectation, although the husband was a beneficiary under the will of the wife, she was given no benefit under the husband's will. In most cases wills which are, or which are alleged to be, mutual wills give reciprocal benefits.

It was argued that the expectation (that the wife would die first, which was what happened) *ought* to justify a finding that both testators must be taken to have agreed that the husband's will was to be irrevocable after the wife's impending death. The judge did not accept the argument.

In fact, the judge decided that there was no acceptable evidence of an agreement not to revoke, so, when the husband subsequently made new wills that were different from his initial will, this did not give rise to any claims by beneficiaries under his initial will, on the basis of mutual wills.

Olins v Walters [2009] Ch 212 is a Court of Appeal case in which the essentials of the agreement needed to create mutual wills were again in issue.

A husband and wife made wills in 1988 in similar terms. Later they executed codicils at which time there was evidence that the husband was worried about the survivor being put under pressure to change their will. The solicitor explained the concept of mutual wills to them. The codicils included the statement, 'This codicil is made pursuant to an agreement made between [my husband/wife] and me for the disposal of our property in a similar way by mutual testamentary dispositions.'

At first instance, the court held that, despite arguments that there was not sufficient evidence of the terms of the contract, there were valid mutual wills.

Norris J said that it 'was an irreducible core that there had to be a contract between the two testators and that in return for the first one agreeing to make a will in form X and not to revoke it without notice to the second one, the second one made a will in form Y and agreed not to revoke it without notice to the first one. If such an agreement was established, equity imposed a form of constructive trust.' In the instant case, the assertion that the agreement was not meant to be a binding agreement was rejected. Norris J stated that signing formal documents recording an agreement that had earlier been reached in principle, having received a written explanation of the effect of signing the documents, showed an intention that the agreement should have legal effect and that the absence of any express mention of revocation did not make the documents incapable of enforcement as mutual wills.

In the Court of Appeal the key issues related to whether or not there was an effective contract. The questions related to (1) the sufficiency of the evidence for the finding of a mutual wills contract between the husband and wife, and (2) the sufficiency in law of its terms.

It was argued that the terms of the contract were not sufficiently clear in that, for example, the contract failed to set out exactly what its scope was. Did it cover only inherited property or did it include the property of the survivor?

The only judgment was given by Mummery LJ – the other two judges simply said they agreed with him.

Mummery LJ drew a distinction between the type of agreement needed in the context of mutual wills and the requirements for a legally enforceable contract necessary in order to make a claim for, e.g. damages, specific performance, etc.

Mummery LJ said:

It is a legally *necessary* condition of mutual wills that there is clear and satisfactory evidence of a contract between two testators. However, the argument resting on the alleged insufficiency or uncertainty of the terms of this contract is misconceived. The case for the existence of mutual wills does not involve making a contractual claim for specific performance or other relief. The claimant in a mutual wills case is not even a party to the contract and does not have to establish that he was.

The obligation on the surviving testator is equitable. It is in the nature of a trust of the property affected, so the constructive trust label is attached to it. The equitable obligation is imposed for the benefit of third parties, who were intended by the parties to benefit from it. It arises by operation of law on the death of the first testator to die so as to bind the conscience of the surviving testator in relation to the property affected.

It is a legally *sufficient* condition to establish what the judge described as 'its irreducible core' which he analysed as a contract between two testators, T1 and T2:

. . . that in return for T1 agreeing to make a will in form X and not to revoke it without notice to T2, then T2 will make a will in form Y and agree not to revoke it without notice to T1. If such facts are established then upon the death of T1 equity will impose upon T2 a form of constructive trust (shaped by the exact terms of the contract that T1 and T2 have made). The constructive trust is imposed because T1 has made a disposition of property on the faith of T2's promise to make a will in form Y, and with the object of preventing T1 from being defrauded.

Mummery LJ said that:

The answer to the sufficiency point is, I think, summed up in a single sentence in Snell's *Principles of Equity* (31st ed) para 22–31, 'Mutual wills provide an instance of a trust arising by operation of law to give effect to the express intention of the two testators'.

He concluded that the intentions of the husband and wife were sufficiently expressed in order to bind the conscience of the survivor.

There have been two fairly recent cases on mutual wills in general and the need for an agreement in particular. If one considers the evidence of agreement in *Charles* v *Fraser* [2010] EWHC 2154 (Ch) to be less than convincing, then there seems even less evidence in *Fry* v *Densham-Smith* [2010] EWCA Civ 1410.

As stated above in *Charles* v *Fraser*, Jonathan Gaunt said that when assessing the evidence the courts will have in mind the inherent improbability that a testator would be prepared to give up the possibility of changing their will in the future, whatever changes in circumstances may have occurred. But despite this statement, which is widely accepted as being an accurate statement of the law, in *Fry* v *Densham-Smith* the Court of Appeal was prepared to find mutual wills where there was no direct evidence of the necessary agreement for mutual wills and there was no copy of the will in question. It may be that the court was willing to push the boundaries of mutual wills.

At first instance the court held that there were valid mutual wills, despite arguments that there was not sufficient evidence of the terms of the contract.

The law therefore appears to have moved on from *Birch* v *Curtis* in which Rimer J held that he could not find that a mutual wills agreement had been entered into in the absence of direct evidence of that agreement. However, this must be a positive shift in the law because the usual civil test of evidence ought to apply. If the court finds that on the balance of probabilities the testators entered into a mutual wills agreement this should suffice even if there is no direct evidence of such an agreement. Therefore in appropriate circumstances the court will infer that a contractually binding mutual wills agreement has been entered into by the testators.

In *Charles* v *Fraser* [2010] EWHC Civ 2154, Jonathan Gaunt QC sitting as a deputy High Court judge found that there were mutual wills despite the lack of any direct or written evidence of an agreement to make mutual wills. Nothing on the face of the wills suggested that they were mutual wills.

In 1991 two elderly sisters agreed on how their property should be left and wills were made reflecting that agreement. After the death of the first to die, the survivor revoked her will and made a new one which differed significantly from the first will. Subsequently she made another will which again differed significantly from the first will.

Jonathan Gaunt QC, sitting as a High Court judge, having said that the starting point was that it is unlikely a testator is prepared to give up the possibility of changing their will, decided that mutual wills had been made.

He placed considerable weight on the fact that the division of shares was detailed and clearly thought through by the sisters in 1991. But nothing in the wills suggested they were mutual wills.

Before either of them died, the sisters when speaking to beneficiaries referred to 'the will' in the singular. There was evidence that the sisters had told beneficiaries that they did not want the dispositions changed.

It was held that there was sufficient evidence to show that the sisters had entered into a binding contractual agreement in relation to the terms of their wills which (with respect to the survivor) was irrevocable.

The need for writing

The requirement for writing was raised in *Healey* v *Brown* [2002] 19 EG 147.

The case states that where the subject matter is land, s 2 of the Law of Property (Miscellaneous Provisions) Act 1989 applies to the contract that arises between testators who make mutual wills, the contract being a contract to dispose of land. (Section 2(1) of the Law of Property (Miscellaneous Provisions) Act 1989 states: 'A contract for the sale or other disposition of an interest in land can only be made in writing and only by incorporating all the terms which the parties have expressly agreed in one document or, where contracts are exchanged, in each.')

The result was that, in the absence of the required writing, the contract between Mr and Mrs Brown, upon which the mutual will would be based, in effect, did not exist.

Section 2(5) of the Law of Property (Miscellaneous Provisions) Act 1989, however, states that s 2 does not affect the creation or operation of resulting, implied or constructive trusts.

David Donaldson QC argued that it was possible for equity to impose a constructive trust on the property received by the survivor from the first to die for the benefit of the intended beneficiary under the mutual wills. In any case, this type of constructive trust did not, the judge stated, depend on a binding contract being shown to exist. In support, the judge cited **Lloyds Bank plc v Rosset** (see pp. 353 and 367). The constructive trust comes into existence to counter a situation where it would be unconscionable for a claimant's expectations to be defeated.

What property is subject to the trust?

Objective 5

Two issues are involved here. First, as a matter of construction, what property do the parties intend to be covered by their agreement? Secondly, having established the property covered by the agreement, on the death of the first to die does the trust that arises apply to just the inherited property or to both the inherited property and the property of the survivor?

In the case of **Re Green** [1950] 2 All ER 913, the wills provided for the survivor to divide the residue in half and treat half as his absolutely and to leave the other half to certain agreed beneficiaries. It was held that the trust only applied to half the residue and so a subsequent will that the survivor made could operate only with regard to the other half. It is submitted that the question of which property is bound by the trust is a matter of construction in each case, but it would seem logical that, subject to evidence to the contrary, the property of each of the testators should be bound by the trust, or at least the property that each held at the time of the death of the first to die.

The second issue which must be considered is the ambit of the trust: whose property is bound? There are a number of possibilities: the trust may apply only to the property that the survivor receives from the other (it must apply of course to at least that property) or it may apply to all the property of both parties, so the survivor may lose control over their own property as well.

In **Re Hagger** [1930] 2 Ch 190, the court held that the trust attaches at least to all of the survivor's property which was owned at the date of the death of the first to die. This view was also taken in **Re Cleaver** [1981] 2 All ER 1018. In **Re Dale (deceased)**, Morritt J said that the trusts attached to all of the property that the survivor owned at the date of his death.

In **Re Hagger**, a husband and wife made a joint will in which they left their property at the death of the first to die to be held on trust and, in relation to a specific piece of property, left it to the survivor to sell and divide the proceeds between certain beneficiaries, including Eleanor. This property was owned jointly by the parties to the will and would therefore normally pass to the survivor by right of survivorship. If, however, the whole of the property was fixed with the trust, the survivor would be trustee and the estate of Eleanor, who had survived the wife, but had predeceased the husband, would be entitled to her share. Clauson J stated that the earlier case of **Dufour v Pereira** (1769) 1 Dick 419 decided:

> that where there is a joint will such as this on the death of the first testator the position as regards that part of the property which belongs to the survivor is that the survivor will be treated in this court as holding the property on trust to apply it so as to carry out the effect of the joint will.

Thus, from the time of the wife's death, the husband held the property on a trust under which Eleanor had a beneficial interest. The result was, therefore, that Eleanor was beneficially entitled and the claim of her personal representatives to the property was successful.

Further aspects of this issue are discussed below under 'Position of the survivor'.

When does the trust arise?

An important and linked question is: when does the trust arise? The generally accepted approach is to hold that as soon as the first of the parties dies the survivor holds that property, and perhaps his own as well, on an implied or, more probably, a constructive trust. He cannot henceforth revoke his will and thereby interfere with the terms of the trust, effectively leaving the property otherwise than on the terms agreed.

It appears that the trust must arise at the time of the first death. Since until that time, if one party breaks the agreement, the other may change their will, it only becomes inequitable for the survivor to change his will when it is impossible for the other party to change theirs: in other words, after that person has died.

It has been argued that the trust arises only when the survivor takes the benefit of it. In **Re Hagger**, Clauson J expressed the view that **Dufour v Pereira** was authority for the view that the trust arose automatically:

> But in any case it is clear that Lord Camden has decided that if the survivor takes the benefit conferred on him by the joint will he will be treated as a trustee by this Court, and he will not be allowed to do anything inconsistent with the provisions of the joint will.

The existence of a benefit to the survivor is most significant to those who would argue that mutual wills are a form of constructive trust. **Re Cleaver** appears to treat mutual wills as one of a wider category of cases in which equity will intervene to impose a constructive trust where a benefit has been taken. However, this argument is no longer tenable since **Re Dale (deceased)**, in which Morritt J decided that mutual wills can arise irrespective of whether or not the survivor takes a benefit from the will of the first to die.

There does seem to be a potential problem with the argument that the trust arises on the death of the first to die because until then either party is able to revoke or alter their will in response to the actions of the other. It may be that while both parties are alive one of them loses the mental capacity to revoke or alter their will. On the argument rehearsed above, could it be said that at the point that testamentary capacity is lost, the trust should arise?

Position while both parties are alive

Objective 6

Prior to the death of the first of the parties, it appears that they may agree to revoke or alter their agreement. If one of them cancels the agreement unilaterally or does not make the agreed will or, having made the will, revokes it, the innocent party may have a contractual right to damages, though these would be difficult to quantify. Any action for breach of contract would have to be brought by the parties to the agreement. An action by the intended ultimate beneficiary would fail because of lack of privity of contract. It has been suggested that damages would only be available where the breach was intentional and not, for example, where it occurred automatically, as on remarriage: *Re Marsland* [1939] Ch 820.

A further use of contractual solutions has been suggested, based upon *Beswick v Beswick* [1967] 2 All ER 1197. It will be recalled that the administratrix of Peter Beswick's estate was able to obtain specific performance of the contract entered into by Peter and his nephew. It is argued that the estate of the first to die could obtain specific performance of the agreement contained in the mutual wills against the survivor. This would avoid having to rely upon a trust at all. However, this argument was rejected by Morritt J in *Re Dale*, although *Beswick v Beswick* was not cited.

In *Re Anne Hobley* (1997) unreported, mutual wills were made in 1975 by a husband and wife. The husband later executed a codicil, inconsistent with the agreement, leaving one property (to which the original agreement applied) to a different beneficiary. Having inherited on her husband's death, the wife made a will in 1992 which was substantially different from her 1975 will. The court decided that the codicil of the husband, unilaterally altering his will in a way that was inconsistent with the agreement, released the wife from the agreement and left her free to make the 1992 will, her property passing under the terms of this 1992 will. The fact that the codicil made only a minor (though not insignificant) change did not prevent the wife from being released.

Position of the survivor

Under some agreements the property of the first to die is left to the survivor absolutely who agrees to leave all the property within the agreement to the ultimate beneficiary. As has been seen above, as soon as the first death occurs a trust is imposed on the property covered by the agreement.

The question arises then as to whether the survivor is entitled to deal with his own property during his lifetime and whether any property that the survivor acquires after the death of the first to die is also bound by the trust. In *Re Hagger*, the court held that the trust attaches at least to all of the survivor's property which was owned at the date of the death of the first to die. In *Re Dale (deceased)*, Morritt J said that the trusts attached to all of the property that the survivor owned at the date of his death. There are apparently no authorities directly on the point under discussion. One possible solution to the first question, which was put forward in relation to secret trusts in *Ottaway v Norman* [1971] 3 All ER 1325, is that of the floating trust which, in Brightman J's words, 'is in suspense during the lifetime of the primary donee, but attaches to the estate of the primary donee at the moment of the latter's death'. This concept was discussed in the Australian case of *Birmingham v Renfrew* (1937) 57 CLR 666, from which the following passage was quoted by Nourse J in *Re Cleaver*:

> The purpose of an arrangement for corresponding wills must often be . . . to enable the survivor during his life to deal as absolute owner with the property passing under the will of the first party dying. That is to say, the object of the transaction is to put the survivor in a position to enjoy for his own benefit the full ownership so that, for instance, he may convert it and expend the proceeds if he choose. But when he dies he is to bequeath what is left in the manner agreed upon.

The 'floating trust' idea was taken up in *Re Goodchild* by Carnwath J, who, having referred to *Birmingham v Renfrew*, said of the trust imposed by equity: 'It is an unusual form of trust since it does not prevent the surviving spouse using the assets during his lifetime. It is a kind of floating trust which finally attaches to such property as he leaves on his death.' In *Re Goodchild* (on appeal) Leggatt LJ, having said there was no express agreement not to revoke the wills, stated that the existence of a mere expectation was not sufficient to impress the arrangement with a floating trust, binding in equity. One assumes from this that, had an agreement been found to exist, Leggatt LJ would have accepted the concept of the 'floating trust'.

One very obvious problem with a floating trust is that if the survivor is free to deal with the property during his lifetime he could, in effect, frustrate the agreement by, for example, giving all or most of the property away or by selling the property and gambling the proceeds away. In *Birmingham* v *Renfrew*, Dixon J said:

> No doubt gifts and settlements, *inter vivos*, if calculated to defeat the intention of the compact, could not be made by the survivor and his right of disposition, *inter vivos*, is, therefore, not unqualified.

See Chapter 4 (p. 102).
There are considerable difficulties with this idea, however, which are discussed in greater detail in Chapter 4.

Revocation by subsequent marriage: effect on mutual wills

In *Re Goodchild* [1996] 1 All ER 670, a husband and wife had discussed the disposition of their property and had executed simultaneous wills in the terms agreed. The wills were in identical form in favour of the survivor and then in favour of the plaintiff, their son. The wife died and then the husband remarried and subsequently made a will that was inconsistent with the agreement made with his first wife. The plaintiff claimed, *inter alia*, that there were mutual wills and that the property of his late father was held on trust for him. In the event the court was not able to discover sufficient evidence to enable the court to conclude that the parties intended to execute wills that were intended to be mutually binding and which were not to be revoked. There was not sufficient evidence to establish the necessary contract (referred to above). This was enough to decide the arguments based on mutual wills. However, it was further argued that, even if an agreement to make mutual wills that would not be revoked had been found to exist, that would not have been relevant as the husband's will was automatically revoked on his remarriage by the operation of s 18 of the Wills Act 1837. Counsel referred to *Re Marsland* [1939] 3 All ER 148. Carnwath J said that the decision was not conclusive authority in the instant case, as *Re Marsland* was not a case on mutual wills and in any event that case turned on the interpretation of 'revoke' in a deed.

In *Re Marsland* it was held that there was not a breach of a covenant in a deed 'not to revoke a will' where the will was revoked not by an act specifically designed to effect a revocation (e.g. execution of a later will) but by operation of law, i.e. by virtue of s 18 of the Wills Act 1837, which states that (in most situations) a will is automatically revoked by marriage of the testator. Carnwath J opined that irrespective of the continued existence of the will the enforceability of mutual wills depends on the existence of the trust imposed by equity. Presumably, this argument does not affect the position of revocation of a will by remarriage before either of the parties is dead, as until the first dies it is probable that there is no trust. In such a case it may well be that no action for damages could be brought.

On appeal, the *Marsland* issue was not discussed in any of the judgments. However, the court did (unanimously) uphold the decision at first instance that there was insufficient evidence of an agreement for mutual wills to exist.

The basis of mutual wills

Objective
7

In order to preserve the rule that a will may always be revoked and that a new will can be made leaving the testator's property to different beneficiaries, the concept of mutual wills must operate by assuming that the survivor holds the property on trust and so has already surrendered absolute ownership over it.

There has been some dispute as to the theoretical basis for mutual wills. Some argue that it is necessary for the survivor to take some benefit under the will of the first to die and it is this benefit which makes it unconscionable for the agreement not to be adhered to. On the other hand, it has been said that this element of benefit is not necessary and it is the promise itself which is important. In such a case, it would be unconscionable to allow the survivor to break the agreement having allowed the first to die in the belief that its terms will be carried through.

To the extent that it would be unconscionable to allow a party to receive the property and then break the agreement which enabled him to receive it, they would appear to be constructive and are so considered here. But some argue that the trust is implied, reflecting what the parties intended. The argument continues that the trust cannot be a constructive trust, as such trusts are imposed by the courts irrespective of the intentions of the parties.

In *Re Cleaver* [1981] 2 All ER 1018, the court considered that mutual wills were an example of constructive trusts.

In the case of *Re Dale (deceased)* [1993] 4 All ER 129, Morritt J, in an action on a preliminary issue of law, discussed the basis of the doctrine. The issue before Morritt J was whether the doctrine of mutual wills could operate if the survivor took no benefit under the will of the first to die. Morritt J decided that it was not necessary for the survivor to take a benefit.

In *Re Dale*, Morritt J discussed mutual wills in terms of their being imposed by the courts to prevent a fraud. This suggests support for the constructive trust analysis (see Figure 12.2). After stating the core requirements for mutual wills (a legally binding contract to make and not to revoke mutual wills), Morritt J said that the basis of the doctrine was fraud, or rather the prevention of fraud. The fraud that the court would seek to prevent is that of the survivor in refusing to adhere to the bargain which was intended to be binding.

Morritt J quoted Lord Camden LC in *Dufour v Pereira*:

> If the other then refuses, he is guilty of fraud, can never unbind himself, and becomes a trustee of course. For no man shall deceive another to his prejudice. By engaging to do something that is in his power, he is made a trustee for the performance, and transmits that trust to those who claim under him.

Morritt J opined that it is the promise itself which makes it unconscionable to go back on the agreement. He said that the doctrine applied to cases where the survivor took a benefit; there was no reason to restrict it to such cases. There was no reason why such a principle should not be applied in cases where no benefit was taken. To apply the doctrine in such cases was both consistent with all the authorities and supported by some of them. It was also in furtherance of equity's original jurisdiction to intervene in cases of fraud.

Conclusions on mutual wills

This is, arguably, a situation where the law of trusts can serve the parties badly.

It must be acknowledged that the form of trust contained in mutual wills is a strange and inconvenient one. The ultimate beneficiaries may be unaware of the existence of the trust and, even if they are, it will be difficult to enforce during the survivor's lifetime,

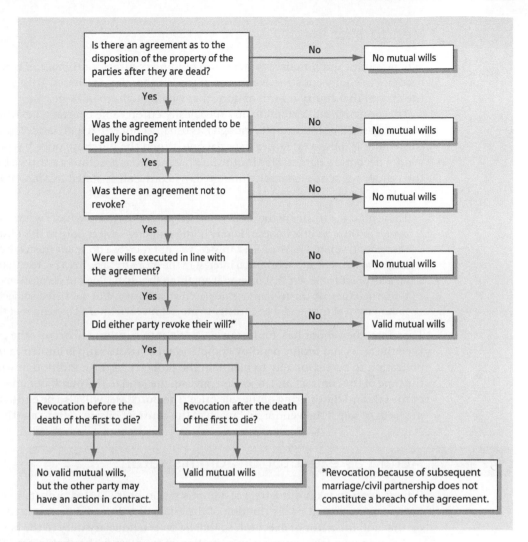

Figure 12.2 Mutual wills

especially if the trust is to be regarded as 'floating'. There may also be some difficulty with issues of certainty of trust property, particularly if the trust is a 'floating trust'. It may fairly be said that the problems and uncertainty of mutual wills outweigh any possible advantages. Additionally, the decision in *Re Goodchild* further muddies the waters. In that case, although it was perfectly clear what both of the parties wanted and expected, the failure of the court to discover the requisite 'formal' agreement resulted in these expectations being frustrated. In other areas where trusts are used to provide a solution the courts have more recently taken a more 'relaxed' approach. For example, in the context of the family home, trusts are found to exist, based on the concept of the 'common intention' of the parties even in the absence of a formal or formalised agreement. As stated above, it will be most unusual for a professional adviser to suggest mutual wills to his clients. In its Twelfth Programme of Law Reform (Law Com No 354) the Law Commission announced a review of mutual wills.

Vendors of land

Objective
8

See Chapter 2
(p. 52).

Where vendor and purchaser enter into a binding contract for the sale of land, the vendor becomes in equity constructive trustee of the land for the purchaser. This is an example of the maxim that equity regards as done that which ought to be done.

This principle will extend to any specifically enforceable contract, i.e. where an award of damages will be inadequate, though it is usually concerned with land. The nature of the trusteeship is, however, rather a special one. When the purchase price has been paid, the vendor becomes a bare trustee for the purchaser, who is absolutely entitled, but until then the vendor remains personally interested. As Lord Cairns stated in **Shaw v Foster** (1872) LR 5 HL 321:

> The vendor was trustee of the property for the purchaser; the purchaser was the real beneficial owner in the eyes of a Court of Equity of the property subject only to this observation, that the vendor, whom I have called a trustee, was not merely a dormant trustee, he was a trustee having a personal and substantial interest in the property, a right to protect that interest, and an active right to assert that interest if anything should be done in derogation of it. The relation, therefore, of trustee and *cestui que* trust subsisted, but subsisted subject to the paramount right of the vendor and trustee to protect his own interest as vendor of their property.

Therefore, the vendor has, for instance, the right to continue to occupy the property or to keep the rents and profits pending completion. His trusteeship is limited in practice to an obligation to act reasonably to maintain the property in the condition in which it was at the time of the contract and, of course, give up the land to the purchaser upon completion of the sale and the offering of the sale price. The purchaser will also be entitled to trace the proceeds of sale if the vendor, in breach of the contract of sale, sells to another.

Acting as executor or administrator

Where a person takes out letters of administration or is granted probate in order to carry out the management or distribution of the estate of a deceased person, a trust is imposed on that administrator or executor, so that he owes a fiduciary duty to the beneficiaries.

A person who takes on the administration of an estate without obtaining this authority does so improperly, and is referred to as executor, or administrator, *de son tort*. Is such a person then constructive trustee of the property of which he has improperly taken charge?

James v Williams [1999] 3 All ER 309

In this case a mother died intestate, which meant that her property should have passed to her three children (a son and two daughters) equally. In fact the son, without following the proper procedure and obtaining letters of administration, simply took possession of the mother's house, and continued to live in it, with his elder sister. When he died he left the house to his elder sister, who in turn left it to her daughter. When this happened the younger sister, the plaintiff in the case, sought the third share that she should have received under her mother's intestacy.

There was no doubt that the brother was administrator *de son tort* because he had acted improperly, had never administered the estate as he should have done, and had knowingly acted contrary to his sisters' rights. Was he also constructive trustee of the house, in which case his elder sister and her daughter would also be fixed with the trust since they had acquired their rights through him? In this case it was particularly important that he should be trustee because any personal claim against him would be time-barred; the mother had died in 1972 and the younger sister would have had 12 years from then to assert her claim, whereas no such time limit would apply to property held on trust.

The Court of Appeal held that the son did indeed hold the house on constructive trust and thus the younger sister could claim her third share. This decision was based, according to Aldous LJ, on the equitable maxim that 'Equity envisages that what should have been done has been done'. The son should have taken out letters of administration so the court would act as if he had done so. There are several problems with this, though it produced a fair result on the facts. The approach of the Court of Appeal appears to be remedial, whereas in other contexts the courts have shown a strong desire to avoid this approach. It is also clear, and the Court of Appeal acknowledged, that the administrator *de son tort* will not always be a constructive trustee, so the precise limits are unclear. It is perhaps significant that in this case, as well as acting improperly as administrator, the son had retained property which he knew was not his, which may be why the constructive trust is appropriate in this case. One can draw an analogy with other cases where property has been retained when it should have been handed over, for example, to an employer.

Acquisition of property by killing

It was held in *Re Crippen* [1911] P 108 that a person who murdered another should not be entitled to gain from the deceased's estate. Therefore, Dr Crippen, having been next of kin to his wife and having inherited her estate as a result of murdering her, was not beneficially entitled to it. If, as in this case, the property had actually come to the murderer, a constructive trust was imposed for the benefit of those next entitled under the deceased's will or intestacy. Dr Crippen could not therefore leave his wife's property to his mistress in his own will.

On an intestacy, property would normally be inherited 'upon the statutory trusts', that is to say, to the child of the deceased (if any), or, if the child is dead, to any issue of the child, and, failing such issue, to the deceased's siblings and their issue. Where the child was the murderer, clearly that child could not inherit from the murdered parent, as above, but, following *Re DWS* [2001] 1 All ER 97, neither could the issue of that child. This was the effect of s 47(1) of the Administration of Estates Act 1925, but this has now been amended by s 46A, inserted by the Estates of Deceased Persons (Forfeiture Rule and Law of Succession) Act 2011. Under this provision the forfeiting killer is treated for inheritance purposes as dying immediately before the intestate victim, thus allowing the killer's children, siblings, etc., as next in line under the statutory trusts, to inherit. This does not affect the courts' powers under the Forfeiture Act 1982.

It appears that the forfeiture rule applies to manslaughter but to what other forms of killing is not clear. It does also extend to other forms of gain such as receiving the benefit of an insurance policy on the deceased's life. The Forfeiture Act 1982 provides that this forfeiture rule may be modified by the courts. It further provides under s 2(2):

> The court shall not make an order under this section modifying the effect of the forfeiture rule in any case unless it is satisfied that, having regard to the conduct of the offender and of the deceased and to such other circumstances as appear to the court to be material, the justice of the case requires the effect of the rule to be so modified.

It also provides that applications must be made within three months of the killer's conviction. Section 5 states that the court has no power to modify the forfeiture rule in favour of a person convicted of murder.

In *Dunbar v Plant* [1997] 4 All ER 289, the Court of Appeal has clarified the position with regard to lesser forms of killing, stating that the forfeiture rule applies to murder, manslaughter and related offences including assisting suicide. In that case, the defendant was the survivor of a suicide pact, who might have been charged with the latter offence, though in fact she was not. In determining whether to exercise the power to modify under the Forfeiture Act 1982, the paramount consideration was the defendant's culpability. Accordingly, in this case, the rule would be modified, and the defendant would receive the benefit of all the property which she had inherited by right of survivorship. The survivors of suicide pacts would almost always be held entitled to inherit, since they were more deserving of sympathy than punishment.

Licences

This may be seen as an example of the new model constructive trust mentioned in the introduction. An early instance is the judgment of Lord Denning in *Binions v Evans* [1972] 2 All ER 70. In this case, a widow had a contractual licence to live in a house for life rent-free. The house was sold to another who then sought to evict the widow. It might have been assumed that the licence was purely contractual and hence binding only on the parties, not on the purchaser. Lord Denning held that the purchaser was bound by the licence:

> In these circumstances, this court will impose on the (purchaser) a constructive trust for her benefit: for the simple reason that it would be utterly inequitable for the (purchaser) to turn the widow out contrary to the stipulation subject to which he took the premises.

It should be noted, however, that the majority view was that the widow had a life tenancy of which the purchaser had notice. The important question, then, is whether a licence is merely contractual, and hence personal and binding only on the parties, or whether it can bind third parties by making them constructive trustees of the licensee's interest.

The situation was reviewed in *Ashburn Anstalt v Arnold* [1988] 2 All ER 147. On the facts, the court held that the plaintiff would not have been bound had the defendant been merely a contractual licensee. Fox LJ reviewed the situations involving contractual licences where constructive trusts had been considered. He concluded that *Binions v Evans* was 'a legitimate application of the doctrine of constructive trusts', the reasons being that the intention of vendors and purchasers at the time of sale was that the purchasers should give effect to the tenancy, and that the vendors took a lower price for the property on this understanding.

The general conclusion is that stating that someone purchases subject to the licence is not enough on its own: 'The court will not impose a constructive trust unless it is satisfied that the conscience of the estate owner is affected.' So the purchaser's conduct must be considered: is it sufficiently unconscionable to justify imposing a trust? Accordingly, the facts of *Ashburn Anstalt* were not such as to give rise to a constructive trust.

These principles were subsequently considered in *IDC Group v Clarke* [1992] 08 EG 108, where the issue was whether an agreement by deed to allow access to a flat as a fire escape was merely a licence, or whether it created an easement or constructive trust which would be binding on the sub-lessee of the flat, who was not party to the original agreement. In considering *Ashburn Anstalt*, the Vice-Chancellor summarised the court's conclusions as follows:

The Court of Appeal put what I hope is the quietus to the heresy that a mere licence creates an interest in land. They also put the quietus to the heresy that parties to a contractual licence necessarily become constructive trustees. They also held that the mere fact that property is sold subject to a contractual licence is not sufficient to create a constructive trust. They held that the mere fact that somebody has purchased with notice of claim does not give rise to a constructive trust.

The Vice-Chancellor stressed the need for certainty in questions of title to land and the dangers that might be posed by constructive trusts which would not be subject to the usual rules of conveyancing. Importance was also placed on the fact that the deed creating the agreement was professionally drafted and that the wording did not imply third-party obligations.

The Vice-Chancellor therefore concluded that, though a constructive trust might be construed from a licence, such a construction could not be made here:

> In my judgment, the decision in *Ashburn Anstalt* does not warrant the creation of a constructive trust unless there are very special circumstances showing that the transferee of the property undertook a new liability to give effect to provisions for the benefit of third parties. It is the conscience of the transferee which has to be affected and it has to be affected in a way which gives rise to an obligation to meet the legitimate expectations of the third parties.

There was no evidence of such an assumption of liability by the sub-lessee here.

Liability of strangers

Objective 9

Strangers to the trust are persons who are not themselves express trustees of it or in fiduciary positions *vis-à-vis* the trust. While the rule that a trustee or other fiduciary may not profit from that position, as considered above, is a strict one, the position of strangers is more complex. Only those strangers who intermeddle in the trust will become liable and much depends upon their state of mind when doing so.

We are primarily concerned here with the personal liability that may arise on strangers in certain situations. Just as it is not possible to consider constructive trusts imposed upon fiduciaries without also considering the personal liability, in the case of strangers, it is necessary to consider personal liability, since such strangers are frequently described as accountable as constructive trustees, even though there may be no 'trust property', or no property presently in the hands of the stranger. In *Novoship (UK) Ltd v Nikitin* [2014] EWCA Civ 908, Longmore LJ, delivering the judgment of the Court of Appeal, described the liability thus:

> The nature of the liability, as it seems to us, is that the knowing recipient or dishonest assistant has, in principle, the responsibility of an express trustee.

It is important to understand though, that this does not make the stranger a trustee or a fiduciary, but merely that he is subject to the same remedies that a trustee would be liable to.

A stranger may receive trust property into his hands and may then be subject to remedies based upon tracing that property into his hands. This is of course subject to the exception of the *bona fide* purchaser for value without notice: this is an application of general principles and the details of the proprietary remedies available are discussed further in Chapter 17.

In considering the personal liability of a stranger, the specific issue which must concern us here is the state of mind of the stranger necessary for such personal liability to arise.

There are two main ways in which a stranger may intermeddle with trust property. First, he may assist another in a breach of trust without ever coming into contact with the property itself: this may now be referred to as 'dishonest facilitation'. Secondly, he may receive the trust property or allow it to pass through his hands: what has traditionally been referred to as 'knowing receipt and dealing'. In either of these cases the term 'trust' can be taken to include a fiduciary relationship, and 'trust property' taken to include property obtained in breach of such fiduciary relationship and fixed with a constructive trust.

Accessory liability for dishonest facilitation

When may a stranger, or accessory, be personally liable for assisting or procuring another's breach of trust where he personally has never received any trust property? This particular species of accessory liability has in the past been referred to as 'knowing assistance', but it is now clear that this terminology is wrong. It appears now to be clear that to be liable in this situation the accessory must himself be dishonest in his intentions and, furthermore, it is irrelevant whether the trustee himself is dishonest. Such was the conclusion of the Privy Council in *Royal Brunei Airlines* v *Tan*.

Royal Brunei Airlines v *Tan* [1995] 3 All ER 97

In this case, a travel agency company, BLT, had a contract with the appellant airline as their agent and to act as trustee of money received from ticket and carriage sales. The respondent, Tan, who was managing director and majority shareholder, caused some of this money to be used for the company's general trading purposes, in breach of trust. BLT having become insolvent, the appellants wished to pursue their rights against Tan. On the assumption that he had not received any of the trust money, upon what basis could he be made liable?

Two main points of principle emerged. The first was that, to be liable, the accessory had himself to be acting dishonestly. Lord Nicholls, giving the judgment of the Board, defined dishonesty so as to give it its ordinary meaning.

He acknowledged that dishonesty normally carried a 'strong subjective element', and that for the most part dishonesty is to be equated with conscious impropriety. However, the standard is objective in that individuals cannot be permitted to set their own standards of honesty. 'If a person knowingly appropriates another's property, he will not escape a finding of dishonesty simply because he sees nothing wrong in such behaviour.'

For proprietary remedies, see Chapter 17 (p. 504).

This point has been further emphasised by the Privy Council in *Barlow Clowes International Ltd (in liquidation)* v *Eurotrust International Ltd* [2006] 1 All ER 333. In this case the Privy Council reasserted the objective test laid down by Lord Nicholls in *Royal Brunei Airlines* v *Tan* (1995), in which he stated: '[I]n the context of the accessory liability principle acting dishonestly, or with lack of probity, which is synonymous, means simply not acting as an honest person would in the circumstances. This is an objective standard.'

The honesty, or dishonesty, of a person who facilitates a breach of trust will be judged by ordinary standards. That the defendant himself adhered to different standards is irrelevant. The decisions of the Privy Council in *Tan* and *Barlow Clowes* were followed by the Court of Appeal in *Starglade Properties Ltd* v *Nash* [2010] All ER (D) 221 EWCA Civ 1314 [2010] in which it was again stressed that the standard was that of ordinary honesty, and the fact that some might regard that standard as too high was irrelevant. In this case N was the director of a company L. L agreed that, if any money was obtained as a result of proceedings against a third party, L would hold this money on trust for division between itself and S. By the time the money was obtained from the third party, L was insolvent, and N, as director of L, arranged for the money to be distributed to L's various creditors, to the exclusion of S. S brought an action against N alleging his dishonest assistance in L's breach of trust. There was evidence that N had wished to frustrate S's claim to the money as he felt that S had taken an unfair advantage of him. He had taken legal advice as to whether it would be lawful for L's creditors to be given priority over S's claim and it appeared that the position on this point was unclear. The Court of Appeal held that N was liable for dishonest assistance. Whether priority should be given to certain creditors was beside the point. N had intended to defeat S; he had not asked whether to do so would be dishonest. The deliberate removal of the assets of an insolvent company so as to entirely defeat the just claim of a creditor was not in accordance with the ordinary standards of honest commercial behaviour.

Furthermore, dishonesty is not the same thing as negligence, and an accessory will not be liable merely for being negligent, for, as Lord Nicholls stated in *Tan*: 'As a general proposition, beneficiaries cannot reasonably expect that all the world dealing with their trustees should owe them a duty of care lest the trustees are behaving dishonestly.'

The requirement of dishonesty in this situation had previously been put forward by Millett J in *Agip (Africa) Ltd* v *Jackson* [1992] 4 All ER 385, in which he also gave some examples of what might constitute dishonesty:

> The true distinction is between honesty and dishonesty. It is essentially a jury question. If a man does not draw the obvious inferences or make the obvious inquiries, the question is: why not? If it is because, however foolishly, he did not suspect wrongdoing or, having suspected it, had his suspicions allayed, however unreasonably, that is one thing. But if he did suspect wrongdoing yet failed to make inquiries because he 'did not want to know' or because he regarded it as 'none of his business' that is quite another. Such conduct is dishonest, and those who are guilty of it cannot complain if, for the purpose of civil liability, they are treated as if they had actual knowledge.

Dishonesty may thus be seen as having two forms. It may, as Lord Nicholls suggested, involve conscious wrongdoing or, as in Lord Millet's example, not asking questions despite having suspicions; what is referred to as 'Nelsonian knowledge'. Either of these will be sufficient to give rise to liability. So, for example, it was clear in *Barlow Clowes International Ltd (in liquidation)* v *Eurotrust International Ltd*, referred to above, that the director of the defendant company had strong suspicions as to the source of the money passing through the company's hands, but did not make inquiries.

Actual or 'Nelsonian' knowledge, giving rise to dishonesty, is to be contrasted, as Millet J implied, with naivety or ignorance, even if this seems unreasonable or is the result of incompetence. This point has been brought out clearly by the case of *A-G of Zambia* v *Meer Care & Desai & others* [2008] All ER (D) 406 (Jul). The facts were that money was allegedly being stolen from the government of Zambia and laundered by being passed through the client account of the defendant solicitors. One of the partners, M, in particular, was alleged to be dishonestly assisting in this process. The trial judge found M to be dishonest, but the Court of Appeal disagreed. M was much less knowledgeable or experienced than he believed himself to be in such matters and held views about the law relating to money laundering which the court described as 'incomprehensible'. It was thus possible to conclude that he honestly believed that there was nothing illegal going on and did not recognise that his firm was in effect receiving stolen money (even though, presumably, a competent solicitor would have realised these things).

In the words of Lloyd LJ:

> The question, was he dishonest or not, is to be answered in favour of honesty unless fraud is proved on the balance of probabilities, bearing in mind the need for cogent evidence for an allegation as serious as fraud. In our judgment, on the material that was before the judge, the more probable explanation for Mr Meer's conduct is that he was honest, albeit foolish, sometimes very foolish, and far from competent in his understanding, as well as in his application and observance, of relevant professional duties, above all the need to comply with the warnings about money-laundering.

Nevertheless, one may suppose that, the more outlandish the defendant's assertions of ignorance, the less likely the court is to believe that that is truly the state of his mind. It may be hard to believe that the defendant is really that stupid, but if the court decides that he is, he is not dishonest.

A second point is that it is the dishonesty of the accessory that matters, not the state of mind of the trustees. Thus, it will be possible to hold an accessory liable even though the trustees are themselves acting honestly. To hold the opposite would be absurd, for it would allow a dishonest intermeddler to escape liability merely because the trustees were honest, possibly because he himself had misled them. The possibility of a dishonest accessory being liable for misleading an honest trustee had been seen in *Eaves* v *Hickson* (1861) Beav 136, where a stranger forged a marriage certificate to induce trustees to distribute trust property to his illegitimate children. The trustees acted honestly, believing, because of the stranger's fraud, that the children were legitimate.

Thus, it is now clear that dishonesty on the part of the trustees is not a prerequisite of liability of the accessory:

> The trustee will be liable in any event for the breach of trust, even if he acted innocently . . . But *his* state of mind is essentially irrelevant to the question whether the *third party* should be liable to the beneficiaries of the trust. If the liability of the third party is fault based, what matters is the nature of his fault, not that of the trustee. (*Per* Lord Nicholls in *Royal Brunei Airlines* v *Tan*, above.)

Accessory liability in this situation is thus revealed as a substantive liability in its own right, based upon the wrong of the accessory in interfering with the trust, and standing separate from the liability which might also arise upon the trustees. Since this liability can only be personal, not proprietary, it is something of a misnomer to refer to it as constructive trusteeship: the Privy Council never referred to it as such in *Royal Brunei Airlines* v *Tan*.

On the facts of the case, the Privy Council concluded that there was liability on Tan: he was dishonest in using the money in the way that he did, even if he hoped to be able to repay it. It did not matter whether the company, as trustee, was dishonest (though on the facts, since Tan was in effect the company, the Privy Council was of the view that the company was also dishonest).

Novoship (UK) Ltd v *Nikitin* [2014] EWCA Civ 908 makes it clear that the remedies against a dishonest facilitator can extend not only to a liability for loss, but also to a liability to account for profits, provided that a sufficient causal link can be shown between the stranger's profit and the breach of duty. In that case a businessman, Y, and two companies controlled by him, were alleged to have assisted M, an employee of N, to commit breaches of his fiduciary duty to N (they had bribed him). M had granted charters on behalf of N to Y's company H, and H had made profits from the charters. In principle H could be accountable for the profits on the charters, but the Court of Appeal held that there was insufficient causal link between the bribe and the profits.

The account of profits is discussed further in Chapter 17 (p. 502).

Recipient liability: receipt and dealing

As stated above, if the intermeddling stranger actually receives the trust property into his hands, he should be subject to a proprietary remedy: the beneficiary should be able to recover the property itself from the stranger, unless the stranger is a *bona fide* purchaser without notice. If, however, the stranger no longer has the property or its product, or the property is no longer traceable in his hands, he cannot be subject to a proprietary remedy. What circumstances, and, in particular, what state of mind must be present in the stranger, before he can be personally liable to account for the value of the trust property?

The prevailing view, which tends to equate recipient liability with accessory liability, is that to be found in the judgment of Megarry V-C in *Re Montagu's Settlement Trusts* [1992] 4 All ER 308.

> [I]f the recipient of trust property still has the property or its traceable proceeds in his possession, he is liable to restore it unless he is a purchaser without notice. But liability as a constructive trustee is wider, and does not depend upon the recipient still having the property or its traceable proceeds. Does it suffice if the recipient had 'notice' that the property was trust property, or must he have not merely notice of this, but knowledge, or 'cognizance' as it has been put?
>
> In the books and the authorities the word 'notice' is often used in place of the word 'knowledge', usually without any real explanation of its meaning. This seems to me a fertile source of confusion; for whatever meaning the layman may attach to these words, centuries of equity jurisprudence have attached a detailed and technical meaning to the term 'notice' without doing the same for knowledge.

Megarry V-C further distinguished the proprietary and personal liabilities:

(1) The equitable doctrine of tracing and the imposition of a constructive trust by reason of knowing receipt of trust property are governed by different rules and must be kept distinct. Tracing is primarily a means of determining the rights of property, whereas the imposition of a constructive trust creates personal obligations that go beyond mere property rights.

(2) In considering whether a constructive trust has arisen in a case of the knowing receipt of trust property, the basic question is whether the conscience of the recipient is sufficiently affected to justify the imposition of such a trust.

(3) Whether a constructive trust arises in such a case primarily depends on the knowledge of the recipient and not on notice to him; and for clarity it is desirable to use the word 'knowledge' and avoid the word 'notice' in such cases.

These passages were quoted with approval, and Megarry V-C's judgment described as 'seminal . . . characteristically penetrative in its treatment of authority', by Nourse LJ in *BCCI v Akindele*.

BCCI v Akindele [2000] 4 All ER 221

The facts here were that the defendant, A, had entered into an agreement with one company (I) to buy shares in another company (BCCI Holdings). The agreement guaranteed a high rate of return, and had a number of other rather odd features. In fact, the arrangement was entered into by the officers of the holding company to conceal dummy loans by which the company was enabled fraudulently to buy its own shares. Under the agreement A received some $6.6m, and when I went into liquidation the liquidators sought to claim against A both for assisting in the fraud and as a knowing receiver.

The Court of Appeal applied the 'dishonesty' test from **Royal Brunei v Tan** and accepted the trial judge's finding that A was not dishonest and could not therefore be liable as a facilitator. Nourse LJ then considered the appropriate test for 'knowing receipt'. He considered a number of authorities, and in particular **Belmont Finance v Williams Furniture (No. 2)** [1980] 1 All ER 393, which he held to be clear authority that dishonesty was not a necessary ingredient of liability in knowing receipt.

If dishonesty is not required, then what is the necessary level of knowledge? Essentially, the division in the authorities was between the requirement of actual knowledge (as typified by Megarry V-C in **Re Montague**) and cases in which constructive knowledge was enough. Following Megarry V-C's point (2) above, Nourse LJ concluded:

> Just as there is now a single test of dishonesty for knowing assistance, so ought there to be a single test of knowledge for knowing receipt. The recipient's state of knowledge must be such as to make it unconscionable for him to retain the benefit of the receipt. A test in that form, though it cannot, any more than any other, avoid difficulties of application, ought to avoid those of definition and allocation to which previous categorisations have led.

On the facts of the case, A did not have sufficient knowledge to make him liable as a knowing receiver.

Nourse LJ also recognised the importance of adopting an approach adapted to the circumstances of commercial transactions: '[The test] should better enable the courts to give common sense decisions in a commercial context in which claims for knowing receipt are now frequently made.'

It is suggested that the assumption of a single test is deceptively simple; though, as Nourse LJ stated, this will allow 'common sense' decisions, it is nonetheless difficult to predict what those decisions might be. It has been argued by, for example, *Lewin on Trusts* and *Goff and Jones on Restitution*, that the five-fold categorisation given by Peter Gibson J in **Baden, Delvaux and Lecuit v Société Générale pour Favoriser le Développement du Commerce et de l'Industrie en France SA** [1983] BCLC 325, though primarily for the purposes of defining the *bona fide* purchaser without notice, might also provide guidance as to what level of knowledge would be 'unconscionable' in a commercial context. Stephen Morris QC in the Chancery Division in **Armstrong v Winnington Networks** [2012] EWHC 10 (Ch) held that the first three categories of notice; (i) actual knowledge (ii) wilfully shutting one's eyes to the obvious, and (iii) wilfully and recklessly failing to make such enquiries as an honest and reasonable man would make, would constitute unconscionable knowledge sufficient to make a receiver personally liable, but that the fourth and fifth categories – (iv) knowledge of circumstances that would indicate the facts to an honest man, and (v) knowledge which would put and honest and reasonable man on inquiry – would make the receipt 'unconscionable' only if, on the facts actually known to the defendant, a reasonable person would either have appreciated that the transaction was probably in breach of trust or would have made inquiries or sought advice which would have revealed the probability of breach of trust.

On the other hand, on the assumption that knowledge is required, the court may readily find evidence that knowledge was in fact present. Thus in **Cowan de Groot Properties v Eagle Trust** [1992] 4 All ER 700, Knox J concluded:

> In my judgment, it may well be that the underlying broad principle which runs through the authorities regarding commercial transactions is that the court will impute knowledge, on the basis of what a reasonable person would have learnt, to a person guilty of commercially unacceptable conduct in the particular context involved.

It has been suggested that the real issue here is whether the 'knowing receiver' has been unjustly enriched, applying, in other words, principles of restitution. In *Hillsdown Holdings* v *Pensions Ombudsman* [1997] 1 All ER 862, Knox J started from Megarry V-C's premise in *Re Montagu* (above) that the basic question is whether the recipient's conscience has been sufficiently affected to justify the imposition of a trust. To the extent that this approach would mean a strict liability subject to a defence of change of position, Nourse LJ in *BCCI* v *Akindele* doubted its suitability to commercial transactions, preferring the fault-based liability based on 'unconscionable knowledge', as adopted in that case.

The approach taken in *BCCI* v *Akindele* was endorsed by the Court of Appeal in *Charter plc* v *City Index and others* [2008] 3 All ER 126, which was principally concerned with the contribution that might be sought by one 'knowing receiver' against others. In the words of Carnwath LJ (with whom Mummery LJ agreed):

> City Index's liability to Charter does not depend solely on receipt of the money paid in breach of trust, but on their retaining it or paying it away in circumstances where it would be unconscionable to do so. Although the directors' legal duty arose at an earlier stage, it was only when City failed to return the money that Charter suffered any loss.

It is clear from this case that a claim against an intermeddling stranger may be either a claim for compensation for loss to the claimant, or a claim to profits made by the intermeddler, regardless of any loss to the claimant whose property has been intermeddled with, or, indeed, both. At the same time, since there may be both loss to the claimant and profit by the stranger, the two claims are not always clearly distinguished. In *Akindele* it was said that the issue was whether it was unconscionable to allow Mr Akindele to keep his profit, but of course the claimants had also suffered loss. In *Charter*, the claim was for loss and the Court of Appeal concluded that such claims were compensatory within the wide meaning of the Civil Liability (Contribution) Act 1978, and so one wrongdoer could claim contributions from other wrongdoers, to meet the claim of the victim. No claim for profits was argued in the case, and Hale LJ declined to say whether a claim for profits could fall within the compensatory definition under the 1978 Act (as indeed, logically, it would appear not to).

In *Williams* v *Central Bank of Nigeria* [2014] UKSC 10, [2014] All ER (D) 172, the Supreme Court considered the nature of the claim against a knowing receiver and stressed that such a person is not a trustee. In that case the claimant alleged he had been the victim of a fraud perpetrated by the Nigerian security services in 1986, and that the defendant bank had knowingly received trust moneys as a result; such a claim would be time-barred unless the bank fell within the meaning of the term 'trustee', which, the court concluded, it did not. In reaching their judgment, the Supreme Court considered, *inter alia*, *Paragon Finance plc* v *Thakerar & Co* [1999] 1 All ER 400, discussed above.

This case may now have clarified the difficult relationship between the constructive trust and the duty to account. In the words of Lord Sumption:

For the remedy of account, see Chapter 17 (p. 506).

For time limits on actions see Chapter 17 (p. 500).

> The essence of a liability to account on the footing of knowing receipt is that the defendant has accepted trust assets knowing that they were transferred to him in breach of trust and that he had no right to receive them. His possession is therefore at all times wrongful and adverse to the rights of both the true trustees and the beneficiaries. No trust has been reposed in him. He does not have the powers or duties of a trustee, for example with regard to investment or management. His sole obligation of any practical significance is to restore the assets immediately . . . It does not make him a trustee or bring him within the provisions of the Limitation Act relating to trustees.

The case was primarily concerned with the issue of limitation in Chapter 17 (p. 501).

Proprietary estoppel

Objective
10

For more on
proprietary
estoppel, see
Chapters 2 and 13
(pp. 69 and 383
respectively).

The general nature of the principles of proprietary estoppel is set out briefly in an earlier chapter. In practice, the argument is often raised in relation to the rights of cohabitees in shared accommodation.

The basic principle of a proprietary estoppel is that equity recognises the claimant as having an interest in land when he believes he has, where he acts to his detriment in reliance on that belief. Furthermore the belief must have been created by some kind of representation by the true owner of the property.

Traditionally, the belief has been that the property belongs to the claimant and the classic requirements as set out in *Willmott v Barber* (1880) 15 Ch D 96 fits most appropriately to such a belief. It is clear, however, that the belief may be not that the claimant already owns the property, but that he expects to be given it later, for example, in the true owner's will: 'One day all this will be yours, my boy.'

See Chapter 2
(p. 69).

It is now clear that such a belief can be the foundation for the establishment of an interest by estoppel but at the same time it creates many additional problems. How serious or specific does the representation by the true owner that he will one day give the claimant an interest have to be before it is reasonable for the claimant to rely on it? What property right should the claimant be granted to satisfy the estoppel? What would happen, for example, if, after making the 'promise', but before the expected transfer, the true owner disposes of the property elsewhere?

These issues were considered by the House of Lords in the cases of *Yeomans' Row* v *Cobbe* [2008] 4 All ER 713 and *Thorner* v *Major* [2009] 3 All ER 945. In the first of these the House of Lords appeared to have curtailed the scope of estoppel severely and even, perhaps, to have denied it altogether as the basis of a proprietary claim, while the second of these cases appears to have restored the balance.

Thorner v Major [2009] 3 All ER 945

The appellant (David) appealed against a decision of the Court of Appeal that proprietary estoppel could not operate in his favour so as to entitle him to inherit the estate of his deceased uncle (Peter). At the time of his death in 2005, Peter had owned a farm of substantial value and also had considerable savings. He had made a will in 1997 leaving the residue of his estate, including his farm, to David but had subsequently destroyed the will (because of a dispute with another legatee) and died intestate. David had worked at Peter's farm for no remuneration from 1976 onwards, and, by the 1980s, he had come to hope that he might inherit the farm. No express representation had ever been made, but David relied on various hints and remarks made by Peter over the years, which he claimed had led him to believe that he was to inherit the farm. In 1990, Peter had handed David a bonus notice relating to two policies on Peter's life, saying 'that's for my death duties'. It was David's case that at that point his hope had become an expectation.

The issues for the House of Lords were (i) the character or quality of the representation or assurance made to David; (ii) whether, if the other elements for proprietary estoppel were established, David must fail if the land to which the assurance related was inadequately identified or had undergone a change during the period between the giving of the assurance and its eventual repudiation. The House held that to establish a proprietary estoppel, the relevant assurance had to be clear enough. What amounted to sufficient clarity depended on context. The majority rejected the requirement that the representation should be 'clear and unequivocal'; nor was the actual intention of the representor crucial.

The important question was whether the representations made were reasonably under-stood by the representee to be ones he could rely on. It was enough that the assurance given by P's conduct would, in Lord Hoffmann's words 'reasonably have been understood as intended to be taken seriously as an assurance that could be relied on'. Again, it cannot be necessary that the claimant has to believe that the representor's statement indicates that the representor is legally bound, since David did not claim this. Such a requirement would be difficult to meet in cases where the representation is one about future inheritance since, as was pointed out in *Gillett v Holt* [1998] 3 All ER 917, even if the promise is con-tained in a valid will, that will can always be revoked (as indeed happened in this case, though not in any way which indicated a change of intention towards David). In this case the 1990 incident (the handing over of the insurance bonus) had marked the transition from hope to expectation, but it had not stood alone, and the evidence had demonstrated a continuing pattern of conduct by Peter for the remaining 15 years of his life. Acting on a mere hope of inheritance would be unreasonable, but it was reasonable for David to believe that Peter's behaviour was intended to be relied upon and reasonable for David to rely on it in the way that he did. It was acknowledged that Peter was a taciturn farmer, not given to overt expression, so his veiled hints and indirect suggestions that David was to inherit were enough in this context.

A further issue is as to the identification of the property to which David is entitled. In this case it consisted of the farm which David expected to inherit, but the farm could and did vary in size. That was not fatal to the claim, however, since it was assumed that the property was to consist of the farm, as it existed at Peter's death, even though that was not completely the same as the farm as it existed at the time of the representations. This may be a question of extent; if Peter had subsequently sold the farm and bought a different one, the representation would presumably no longer apply. A further related question, then, is: could Peter sell the farm after he made the representation? The assumption is that equity can be flexible. Though David's right to inherit can only crystalise when Peter dies, never-theless, in the meantime, David could prevent Peter acting in breach of his promise and bring an immediate claim for proprietary estoppel, at which point the court can make an order giving David such an interest as to prevent his suffering a detriment.

While this bolder application of the principles of estoppel is to be welcomed after the restrictions of *Yeoman's Rowe v Cobbe*, it must be recognised that there is a danger in allowing the creation of property rights without any of the normal formalities. (The issue of the conflict with s 2 of the Law of Property (Miscellaneous Provisions) Act 1989 is con-sidered in Chapter 2 (p. 69).) Similarly, in *Thorner v Major*, the effect is to circumvent the requirements of the Wills Act. Peter died intestate, but an interest has been created by inheritance without any formal documentation, and no will signed and witnessed.

It has been noted by various commentators that the relatively open and generous view of estoppel taken in *Thorner* is in marked contrast to *Yeomans' Row v Cobbe* [2008] 4 All ER 713, decided by the House of Lords less than a year earlier, where a claim by estoppel was rejected. Though in the latter case Lord Scott almost rejected the concept of estoppel as establishing property rights, his view was in the minority and the decisions in the two cases can be reconciled, however. One important distinction is the context of the represen-tations: in *Thorner* it was the informal conversations of two taciturn farmers, whereas in *Cobbe* it was the discussions taking place in a formal pre-contractual situation between two potential business partners. The claimant in *Cobbe* was well aware that the oral agreement 'subject to contract' to sell the land was unenforceable and yet he went ahead and under-took work obtaining planning permission and drawing up development plans, which he had not been encouraged to do by the defendants. Given the formality of the situation (unlike that in *Thorner*) if the same question had been applied, was the representation one which the claimant could reasonably rely on? The answer would have been no. Accordingly, the claimant could not have title to the land, though he was entitled to a payment *quantum meruit* for this work.

The similarity between this and the so-called 'common intention' constructive trust is obvious. In that case there is a common intention between the legal owner and the claimant that the claimant should have a share in the property, and the claimant relies on that intention. In his judgment in *Thorner* v *Major*, Lord Scott wished to separate the two and said that estoppel should be limited to cases of representations about present ownership, whereas any case involving a promise of future rights should be dealt with as constructive trusts. In so doing he referred to the 'remedial' constructive trusts which, as stated at the beginning of this chapter, has generally been rejected in England and Wales. None of the other judges in *Thorner* pursued this issue.

The relationship between constructive trusts and estoppel was discussed in *Banner Homes* v *Luff Developments*, which featured a *'Pallant* v *Morgan* equity' (*Pallant* v *Morgan* [1952] 2 All ER 951).

Banner Homes v Luff Developments [2000] 2 All ER 117

L reached an informal (and hence unenforceable) agreement with B to go into partnership for the purchase and development of certain land. In pursuance of this agreement, L bought an 'off the shelf' company, S Ltd, which was to purchase the land as a joint venture between L and B. L then had second thoughts about their arrangement with B, and started looking for an alternative partner. They did not inform B of this, however, because they feared that B might then become a rival for the purchase of the land in question. B, on their part, relied on the agreement in that they did not make any attempt to buy the land for themselves, as they might well have done, but for the agreement. S Ltd purchased the site, using funds from L Ltd, who then announced that they were withdrawing from the agreement. B sought the declaration of a constructive trust of the land for their benefit.

Echoing Lord Millett's comment in *Paragon* v *Thakerer* (above), that the fiduciary relationship must precede the wrongdoing, the Court of Appeal identified the relationship as arising out of the agreement for the joint enterprise:

> A *Pallant* v *Morgan* equity may arise where the arrangement or understanding precedes the acquisition of the relevant property by one of the parties to that agreement. It is the pre-acquisition arrangement which colours the subsequent acquisition by the defendant and leads to his being treated as a trustee if he seeks to act inconsistently with it.

The inconsistent act here was, of course, L's failure to inform B of their change of heart, and B's reliance on that, giving L the advantage that B did not seek to acquire the land on their own account. Accordingly, it was inequitable to allow L to retain the sole benefit of the land, via S Ltd, and a constructive trust of half of S Ltd's shares was declared for the benefit of B.

It remains to be seen whether there is significant difference between a situation of common intention between the parties, which is usually referred to as an example of remedial constructive trust, and one where there is a unilateral statement by one party which is relied on detrimentally by the other, an example of estoppel. In either case, the underlying role of the courts is to recognise that it would be unconscionable to allow the owner of the legal interest to assert his rights, and to prevent this by giving the innocent party an interest in equity. In the context of proprietary estoppel, the correct approach is the broad one advocated in *Taylor Fashions Ltd* v *Liverpool Victoria Trustees Co Ltd*. The interest the court grants should be the minimum equity necessary to do justice.

See Chapter 2 (p. 70).

It follows that such an interest can take effect only when the court recognises it, which may have implications as regards the rights of third parties. Furthermore, to satisfy the equity, the court may give the innocent party any of a range of different rights, varying from a share in the property to mere rights of occupation.

Hammersmith and Fulham LBC v Top Shop Centres [1989] 2 All ER 655

In this case, a lease was granted by trustees to a development company, with a term that they were entitled to re-enter the property if the company went into liquidation. In due time this occurred, and the trustees sought repossession and obtained an order for forfeiture of the lease from the Court of Appeal. However, the company had previously granted sub-leases to various tenants, including the borough council. These leases ceased to exist when the head lease to the development company was forfeited, but the trustees never informed the sub-lessees of the situation, and receivers appointed by the company's mortgagors continued to collect rents as if the sub-leases still existed. It was therefore argued that the trustees were estopped from obtaining repossession by their failure to inform the council. The council had acted to its detriment in not applying for a new sub-lease, or seeking relief from forfeiture under s 146(4) of the Law of Property Act 1925. Warner J held that the estoppel applied:

> In a nutshell, I think that, the London and Manchester companies (who held the mortgages on the property) having, with the co-operation of the trustees, encouraged the council to assume to its detriment its sublease subsisted, it would be unconscionable for the defendants now to be permitted to deny it.

It was not disputed that if an estoppel arose, it would bind successors in title. Accordingly, it bound the defendants, who had purchased the land from the trustees.

Similarly, in *JT Developments* v *Quinn* (1991) 62 P & CR 33, the appellants were estopped from going back on their assurance, given to the plaintiff, that he would be granted a new lease, because he had relied on this assurance and undertaken improvements on the building. In *Lim Teng Huan* v *Ang Swee Chuan* [1992] 1 WLR 113, where joint tenants entered into an unenforceable agreement that the plaintiff would give up his share in exchange for other land, which was relied on by the defendant in that he constructed a house on the land, the Privy Council held that the plaintiff was estopped from enforcing his right to the land, and the defendant was entitled to a declaration that he was the sole owner, subject to the payment of compensation. The Privy Council applied the *dicta* in *Taylor Fashions* (above), stressing that unconscionability is the key factor.

It is clear that the minimum equity may sometimes merely be an occupational right, a licence, rather than a lease or freehold right. In *Matharu* v *Matharu* (1994) 68 P & CR 93, a wife was granted such a licence for life. She had spent money on extensive repairs to the family home which her father-in-law, the true owner, had represented to her as belonging to his son, her husband (now deceased). Unlike the previous cases, reliance was not on an assurance that the house was hers or that she had any right of ownership, but merely that, since the house was her husband's, she, as his wife, would have a right of occupation.

Sledmere v *Dalby* (1996) 72 P & CR 196 has emphasised the importance of the unconscionability element in estoppel cases. Thus, though there has been detrimental reliance on a statement by the legal owner, that does not necessarily mean that it would be unconscionable for the owner or a successor in title to assert his legal rights. In this case, D had carried out repairs on the house in the belief that he and his family would have a licence to live there until the children left home. This undertaking had been given by the owner S (D's father-in-law), at a time when D was unemployed and his wife seriously ill. Subsequently, circumstances had changed. S had died and the property had passed to his widow, who was not well off. D, on the other hand, was now employed and his children were grown up and were also at work, though one still lived at home. Accordingly, in the light of the change in circumstances, the court felt that S's widow was entitled to assert her right to possession of the property which she wished to live in. This would not lead to an unconscionable result in relation to the widow. On the issue of injurious reliance, the case of **Powell v Benney** [2008] P & CR D31 is instructive.

Powell v Benney [2008] P & CR D31

H owned several properties, in one of which he lived. He became friendly with P and his wife who, when H became incapable of looking after himself, began to take care of him and manage his affairs. H told P and his wife several times that he was going to leave his properties to them and signed a document purporting to leave them the properties (though this was not a valid will). He also invited them to use the properties. P and his wife spent time tidying and improving the properties and adapting one for music lessons (P was the owner of music shops where he had formerly given lessons). H died intestate and the properties passed to his cousins, one of whom, B, was also the personal representative. P and his wife claimed the properties on the grounds of estoppel or constructive trust; both were rejected by the trial judge.

On appeal, the Court of Appeal referred to two kinds of estoppel, bargain and non-bargain. In the bargain variety it would have to be shown that there was some bargain or agreement about the properties. H had said he would leave the properties to P but he had not required them to undertake the improvements, which had been undertaken entirely at their own discretion, even though H may have known about them. Nor was a common intention constructive trust (the only one contended for) possible in the absence of such intention, which would equate to the bargain necessary to support the estoppel. The non-bargain estoppel required the judge to satisfy the equity which arose because of P's expenditure. The value of the properties was out of all proportion to that expenditure; the judge's order for a payment of £20,000 to meet P's expectations was a reasonable award.

Summary

- The constructive trust is one imposed by law. The situations in which a constructive trust may arise are many and varied and this chapter gives an overview of some of those situations.

- English law (in contrast to some Commonwealth and US jurisdictions), regards the constructive trust as a substantive institution, not a remedy at the discretion of the court, so it follows that the particular facts of a case must fall into one of those situations.

- It is a principle of equity that no one in a fiduciary position should profit unfairly from that position. Some fiduciary situations arise as a matter of course out of certain formal relationships, such as trustee and beneficiary, others are imposed as a matter of fact, often due to the relative power of the parties.

- Constructive trusts may be imposed to prevent such improper gains being made by persons in a fiduciary situation. There are, however, many situations where fiduciaries may be subject to personal liability to account for their gains. These can arise even if it is not possible to identify a misuse of trust property. The relative merits of personal and proprietary remedies in such cases should be assessed critically.

- Mutual wills are sometimes used where (usually) two people have identical (or perhaps similar) wishes as to what should happen to their property should they die first and then what should happen to property after they are both dead. Despite the fact that a will is always revocable, if there are valid mutual wills but one party (in breach of the agreement) revokes their will, the personal representatives of that party will hold property covered by the agreement on trust for those entitled under the agreement.

- The key requirements for valid mutual wills include an agreement to make mutual wills that is intended to be legally binding and a promise not to revoke.

- There are sometimes problems in deciding what property is covered by the agreement and by mutual wills. Ideally the wills will be carefully drafted but if there is uncertainty the courts may need to be involved to construe the agreement.

- Before either party has died it seems that either party may revoke their will. There may be a remedy in contract. After the death of the first to die there is sometimes a problem over what their powers are over both their own property and the property inherited from the other party.

- On the death of the first to die a trust springs up over property covered by the mutual will agreement. There is some uncertainty as to the legal basis of that trust but many favour it being a constructive trust.

- There are also various minor instances of constructive trusts, imposed for example on vendors of land, agents, and those who have acquired property by killing.

- In certain situations strangers who are not in a fiduciary position may have personal obligations imposed upon them for 'intermeddling', that is interfering dishonestly in another's breach of trust or fiduciary duty, or receiving trust property knowing it to be such. In these cases the state of mind of the defendant is crucial to establishing liability.

- The principle of estoppel may give proprietary or other rights to an individual who has relied to their detriment on the representations of others as to their present or future rights to property. This chapter examines proprietary estoppel and compares it to the constructive trust.

Reference

P Matthews, 'All about bare trusts' [2005] 5 PCB 266, 6 PCB 336.
Examines the powers and duties of trustees of bare trusts. Argues that constructive trusts are bare trusts.

Further reading

Liability imposed on fiduciaries

P Birks, 'The content of fiduciary obligations' (2002) 16 Tru LI 34.
Liability for breach of fiduciary obligations and the expanding role of negligence.

S S Churk, 'Avoidance of loss, *Regal Hastings* and the no conflict rule' (2013) Comp Law 34(3) 73.
A critique of Regal, in which the author suggests that the case is not founded on clear authority and is an unwarranted extension of the 'no conflict' rule.

T Dugdale, 'Partnership liability in relation to trust property' (2002) 18 PN 7.
Considers vicarious liability of law firms for dishonest partners.

A Hicks, 'The remedial principle of *Keech* v *Sandford* reconsidered' [2010] CLJ 287.
Considers whether *Keech* v *Sandford* provides a legitimate basis for the judgment in *A-G for Hong Kong* v *Reid*.

A Hicks, 'Proprietary relief and the order in *Boardman* v *Phipps*' [2013] Conv 232.
Basing his analysis on the printed case papers, the author questions why there has been confusion over the nature of the remedy in the case and assesses the factors which lead to the recognition of a constructive trust.

R Lee, 'Rethinking the content of the fiduciary obligation' [2009] Conv 236.
Analyses the fiduciary concepts of loyalty, good faith and care.

P J Millett, 'Equity's place in the law of commerce' (1998) 114 LQR 214.

P J Millett, 'Restitution and constructive trusts' (1998) 114 LQR 399.
Two articles considering the effect of equitable proprietary right on commercial cases and comparing them with restitutionary claims.

Arguing for and against the imposition of proprietary remedies on gains by fiduciaries

R Chambers, 'Constructive trusts and breach of fiduciary duty' [2013] Conv 241.
An analysis of *FHR* v *Cedar* in the Court of Appeal.

A D Hicks, 'Constructive trusts of fiduciary gain: *Lister* revived?' (2011) Conv 62.

D Hayton, 'Proprietary liability for secret profits' (2011) 127 LQR 487.

D Hayton, 'The extent of equitable remedies: Privy Council versus Court of Appeal' (2012) 33 Comp Law 161.

R Hughes, 'From Hong Kong to Versailles: proprietary remedies flowing from breach of fiduciary duty' (2012) 4 PCB 148.

R Goode, 'Proprietary liability for secret profits – a reply' (2011) 127 LQR 493.

W Swadling, 'Constructive trusts and breach of fiduciary duty' (2012) 18 Trusts and Trustees 985.

G Virgo, 'Profits obtained in breach of fiduciary duty: personal or proprietary claim?' (2011) 70 CLJ 502.

Mutual wills

M Ambrose, 'The feeling's mutual' (2003) 153 (7086) NLJ 979.
General survey of mutual wills including *Healey* v *Brown*. Discusses the Law of Property Miscellaneous Provisons Act 1989 s 2(1) – the requirements for a valid contract for the disposition of land and the possible relevance of the Contracts (Rights of Third Parties) Act 1999.

A Brierley, 'Mutual wills – Blackpool illuminations' (1995) 58 MLR 95.
Discusses *Re Dale*.

L Carkeek, 'Sister Act' NLJ (2010) 160 (7437) NLJ 1418.
Discusses *Charles* v *Fraser*, and the need for sufficient evidence to find mutual wills.

S Gratton, 'Mutual wills and remarriage' [1997] Conv 153.
Discusses the consequences of remarriage on mutual wills.

G Griffiths, 'At best inconvenient and at worst little short of disastrous? Recent considerations on mutual wills' (2011) 6 Conv 511.
Discusses *Charles* v *Fraser* and *Fry* v *Densham-Smith* and deals with the evidence needed to establish a contract not to revoke the wills. Covers the standard of proof required.

R Hughes, 'Mutual wills' (2011) 3 PCB 131.
Discusses *Fry* v *Densham-Smith* and *Charles* v *Fraser* and compares constructive trusts with proprietary estoppels.

P Luxton, '*Walters* v *Olin*: uncertainty of subject matter – an insoluble problem in mutual wills?' [2009] Conv 498.

Discusses *Walters* v *Olin*, focusing on whether there was sufficient evidence of a mutual wills contract, and, if so, whether the contract was invalid for uncertainty. Looks at other issues, including the requirement for intended irrevocability and the problems determining what property was subject to the trust and how the property was held by the survivor.

M Pawlowski, 'Kept in suspense' (2010) 245 PLJ 22.

Discusses the concept of a suspensory or 'floating' constructive trust in the context of ownership of the family home, proprietary estoppel, mutual wills and secret trusts.

N Richardson, 'Floating trusts and mutual wills' (1996) 10 Tru LI 88.

Discusses the concept of a 'floating' constructive trust in the context mutual wills.

Liability of strangers

G Andrews, 'The redundancy of dishonest assistance' [2003] Conv 398.

Argues for a tort-based liability.

S Elliott and C Mitchell, 'Remedies for dishonest assistance' (2004) 64 MLR 16.

Discusses dishonest assistance as a secondary liability, and the remedies available.

S Gardner, 'Moment of truth for knowing receipt?' (2009) 125 LQR 20.

An analysis of *Charter* v *City Index* (2007).

C Mitchell, 'Dishonest assistance, knowing receipt, and the law of limitation' [2008] Conv 226.

Discusses the meaning of third-party liability 'to account as a constructive trustee'.

D Ryan, '*Royal Brunei* dishonesty: clarity at last?' [2006] Conv 188.

Comments on *Barlow Clowes* v *Eurotrust* (2005).

Estoppel

M Balen and C Knowles, 'Failure to estop: rationalising proprietary estoppel using failure of basis' [2011] Conv 176.

Considers whether unconscionability or unjust enrichment are necessary for estoppel claims.

N Davda, 'The *Pallant* v *Morgan* equity' (2013) PLJ, no. 307 22.

A further analysis of the doctrine.

H Delany and D Ryan, 'Unconscionability: a unifying theme in equity' [2008] Conv 401.

Considers the role of unconscionability in estoppel, constructive trust and commercial fraud cases.

M J Dixon, 'Proprietary estoppel: a return to principle?' [2009] Conv 260.

An analysis of *Thorner* v *Major* (2009).

N Hopkins, 'The *Pallant* v *Morgan* equity?' [2002] Conv 35.

Presents *Banner Homes* v *Luff Development* as a new doctrine.

M Lower, 'The *Pallant* v *Morgan* equity' [2012] Conv 379.

The '*Pallant* v *Morgan*' equity is discussed, and its relationship to the constructive trust and to breach of fiduciary duty assessed.

B McFarlane and A Robertson, 'Apocalypse averted: proprietary estoppel in the House of Lords' (2009) 125 LQR 535.

Discusses *Thorner* v *Major* (2009) and *Cobbe* v *Yeoman's Row* (2008).

J Mee, 'Proprietary estoppel and inheritance: "enough is enough"?' [2013] Conv 280.

A critical analysis of the remedy and whether it is disproportionate to the detriment incurred, arguing for the courts to adopt a more restrained approach.

N Piska, 'Hopes, expectations and revocable promises in proprietary estoppel' (2009) 72 MLR 998.

Discusses the requirement of belief that promises were made and the reasonableness of reliance.

13

Shared homes

Objectives

After reading this chapter you should be able to:

1. Understand that if relationships break down there may be competing claims to the ownership or beneficial ownership of a shared home but that the issue of ownership may arise in a variety of other situations such as the death or bankruptcy of one of the parties.

2. Understand (in outline) the statutory powers that the courts have on granting a divorce, a decree of nullity or a decree of judicial separation (or when a civil partnership is formally ended) to decide how property should be owned by the parties.

3. Understand the consequences where a conveyance or transfer expressly deals with both the legal and the beneficial interests in the property.

4. Understand the impact of *Stack v Dowden* and *Jones v Kernott* and the role of the common intention constructive trust in settling property disputes, and appreciate the different approaches that flow from the cases where the legal title is in joint names as opposed to where the legal title is in a sole name.

5. Explain that despite the need for reforms and the various proposals for reform, the current government is not willing to introduce legislation to reform the law.

Introduction

Within a relationship between two people who live together, the most expensive asset is likely to be their home. This chapter deals with the very important situations when two (or more) people contest the ownership (usually the beneficial ownership) of a property in which they live.

After outlining the main issues the development of the law will be discussed, culminating with an analysis of the key cases of *Stack v Dowden* and *Kernott v Jones*.

Many argue that this is an area where the use of trust law often produces results that seem unfair to the parties and which do not seem appropriate, given the societal situation in the early twenty-first century.

Over the past years there have been frequent calls for reform, usually legislative reform, including proposals from the Law Commission, but the government has announced that it does not intend to introduce any reforms during the current parliament.

So, if the law is to be developed or even reformed, it will be achieved by judicial and not legislative reform. Many argue that this is the wrong approach and that reform should be legislative.

The main situations

Objective 1

Those involved in disputes of this kind may be a married couple, civil partners, a cohabiting couple (a male and a female or two males or two females), or two or more people who simply decide to buy a house together to share and in which to live. Under the Marriage (Same Sex Couples) Act 2013 a married couple can now include two people of the same sex.

Most cases under discussion involve a cohabiting, unmarried, couple or a couple in a civil partnership. The parties are usually a man and a woman who 'set up home' together. They may live in a house that one of them owned before the relationship started, or the house may be bought during the relationship. In the latter case the transfer/conveyance may or may not deal with the ownership of the beneficial interest, although modern transfers/conveyances almost always will. The legal title may be vested in one or both parties.

One or both parties may contribute towards the purchase price of the house; in other cases one of them may pay all or most of the purchase price and the other may pay other bills and/or look after the house and the family.

In many, if not most, cases the parties will not discuss how the property will be owned and so what the shares will be in the event of the relationship breaking down. Most couples do not plan for a breakdown. They assume that the relationship will last. Also it seems that many people still believe in the myth of the common law marriage and that unmarried but cohabiting couples have similar, if not identical, rights to married couples.

But sometimes, during a relationship, the parties discuss or even agree on the ownership of the beneficial interest in the property, however in most cases this does not happen.

The contest over beneficial ownership usually arises if the relationship breaks down. But issues of ownership may arise: for example, if one of the parties becomes bankrupt and the trustee in bankruptcy claims the house; or if the house was bought with the aid of a mortgage and the payments are not made and the mortgagor wishes to sell the house to cover the debt; or on the death of one of the parties where the issue may be to what extent the deceased owned the house and thus the extent to which the house falls into their estate.

In the case of married couples or parties in a civil partnership, the courts have wide statutory powers to decide how the property should be owned by the parties in the event of a divorce, decree of nullity, decree of judicial separation, or on the formal ending of a civil partnership. But, as with cohabiting couples discussed above, in other situations involving married couples or parties in a civil partnership, the law of trusts is used to settle disputes: for example, if one of the parties becomes bankrupt, or if the mortgagor wishes to sell the house to cover unpaid mortgage payments, or on the death of one of the parties.

Currently many people are living in rented accommodation either through choice or necessity. In these cases the parties will not have to rely on the law of trusts and the often less than satisfactory solutions to issues of ownership *inter se*. But there are still significant numbers who live in property owned by one or both parties and who will have to rely on the law of trusts to determine how ownership is split between them.

Solutions in outline

As this is a difficult and developing area of the law, an initial outline of what will be covered and many of the solutions that the courts have used will, it is hoped, make the topic more easily assimilated. The ownership of the shared home is a difficult area of the law of trusts for at least two reasons. First, it has sometimes been uncertain what the legal rules are and how they apply in particular cases and, secondly, there is often a tension between what appears to be 'fair' and the decision made after applying the legal principles.

Assistance in settling property disputes may be had from s 14 of the Trusts of Land and Appointment of Trustees Act 1996, which provides a method of resolving disputes over the ownership of land. The section allows an application to court for an order declaring the extent and location of the beneficial interests in land. In exercising this jurisdiction, the court is directed to have regard to a number of factors contained in s 15 (for further detail see p. 445).

A number of (mainly recent) cases shed some light on what rules are applicable but the situation still remains less than clear. Of these cases the most important are: *Lloyds Bank plc v Rosset* [1990] 1 All ER 1111, *Oxley v Hiscock* [2004] 3 All ER 703, *Stack v Dowden* [2007] 2 All ER 929, *Abbott v Abbott* [2008] 1 FLR 1451 and *Kernott v Jones* [2011] UKSC 53; [2011] 3 WLR 1121. But many questions remain to be answered.

If there is a valid *express declaration of the trusts*, then, in the absence of fraud or mistake, this will be conclusive.

If a *married couple divorce* (or the marriage is declared a nullity or if the parties obtain a decree of judicial separation) the Matrimonial Causes Act 1973 s 24 gives the courts the power to decide who should have ownership of the home. The decision is not based on an application of the laws of trust or on the parties' intentions or who in law owned the property. Section 25(1) states that the first consideration should be the welfare of any child of the family while they are a minor but, subject to that, the courts have wide powers to make property adjustment orders. The decision may result in a variation of the trusts on which the home had been held. A similar jurisdiction exists when a *civil partnership* is formally ended.

But in other situations affecting married couples or civil partnerships (e.g. death or bankruptcy) and in all disputes between cohabitees or property sharers, the laws of trust will be used to provide a (sometimes unsatisfactory) solution to any dispute over ownership.

In the main the courts have used two trust concepts to provide solutions to these disputes: *resulting trusts* and *common intention constructive trusts*. *Proprietary estoppel* has also been used in some cases. All three of these will be covered in this chapter.

See Chapter 11. The application of the presumptions of resulting trust and advancement were discussed in an earlier chapter. It is doubtful to what extent if at all these presumptions apply in the present context, particularly if the contesting parties are husband and wife. (For the situation where the property is the home, see *Stack v Dowden* below.) Where resulting trusts are used the division of the ownership of property is (in the main) based on a mathematical approach. Ownership reflects the money contributions to the purchase. When s 199 of the Equality Act 2010 comes into force, the presumption of advancement will be abolished. However, this abolition does not apply to anything done before the commencement of the section or anything done pursuant to any obligation incurred before the commencement of the section. So the presumption of advancement will remain relevant in relation to any transfer made before the commencement of the section.

In *Stack v Dowden* [2007] 2 All ER 929 the majority of the House of Lords based their decision on constructive trusts and said that constructive trusts rather than resulting trusts were the tool of choice in this area. (However, Lord Nueberger, while agreeing with the outcome of the majority, based his decision on the resulting trust.)

Baroness Hale based her decision in *Stack* v *Dowden* (in effect) on the maxim that equity follows the law, so that, for example, where the legal ownership is in joint names, the presumption is that the beneficial interest will also be jointly owned where the title documents do not deal with the beneficial interest. If one party wishes to claim that they own more than a joint beneficial interest, the onus is on that party to prove their claim. Unless the presumption is rebutted by evidence that the parties intended some other division of the beneficial interest (a common intention constructive trust), the parties will hold in equal shares.

In *Lloyds Bank plc* v *Rosset* [1990] 1 All ER 1111 Lord Bridge set out what he saw as the two ways in which a common intention constructive trust can come into existence: a trust which would, if established, rebut the presumption that equity follows the law. Once it has been established that a claimant has a share, the size of the share has to be quantified. The modern approach to quantification is to base the decision on a survey of the whole course of dealings between the parties and taking into account any and all conduct that throws light on what the parties intended. The key case here is *Oxley* v *Hiscock*. One particular aspect of this case (the power of the courts to come to a decision which is 'fair' as opposed to what the parties intended) was criticised in *Stack* v *Dowden* and some subsequent cases.

The most recent significant case is *Kernott* v *Jones* [2011] UKSC 53; [2011] 3 WLR 112. The Supreme Court said that resulting trusts to decide the ownership of a shared home were not appropriate in a domestic context. The constructive trust based on the common intention of the parties should be the concept of choice when deciding on the ownership of a shared home, particularly in the case of cohabiting couples.

But the current applicability of *Rosset*, the implications of *Stack Abbott* and *Kernott*, and the *possibility* of legislative intervention at some time in the future all mean that the situation is by no means clear.

A typical situation

Example

A typical situation might involve Walter Wall and Sophie Bed, who decide that they will live together. A house is chosen and it is conveyed into Walter's name. The house is bought with the help of a mortgage, which is taken out by Walter, who also pays the initial deposit. The couple agree that Walter will make the monthly payments to the bank in respect of the mortgage and that Sophie will take a low-paid part-time job so that she can devote much of her time to looking after the house and bringing up the children which they plan to have. They never discuss the beneficial ownership of the house. Before taking the part-time post, Sophie had a highly paid job and had excellent career prospects. Sophie gave up her rented flat in order to live with Walter in the new house. Sophie does not contribute directly to the mortgage payments but she does a good deal of work on the house, including painting and helping with the renovation of the house which was in a dilapidated state when it was bought. All the renovation materials are paid for by Walter.

After a number of years the couple separate and Walter moves out of the house. Soon afterwards Walter seeks to obtain possession and Sophie's defence is that she has a beneficial interest in the house. She argues that the house was conveyed to Walter to hold on a trust under which she is a beneficiary.

It might well be argued by Sophie that, as she has contributed so much to the family and, indirectly, to the purchase of the house, the fair result would be to find that Sophie has an interest under a trust, and this would not only provide her with a valuable piece of property but would also be a good defence to the claim of Walter.

However, as we shall see, unless Sophie can argue that her conduct (e.g. giving up the well-paid job and career prospects) amounts to conduct from which the court can infer a common intention to share the property beneficially, it is very probable that Sophie will not be entitled to any beneficial interest at all. If this is so, many would argue that the law needs to be changed as it fails to recognise the 'rights' of Sophie and does not reflect the expectations present in modern society. An additional factor is that often the parties have to engage in an expensive (and often bitter) legal 'battle' in order to establish their respective rights in the property.

Any easy way to avoid problems

In the light of the uncertainty, the moral is quite clear. The parties should always agree what their rights in the property will be in advance of a purchase and ensure that the conveyance or transfer reflects, in writing, the agreement.

In **Kernott v Jones** [2010] All ER (D) 244 (May) Wall LJ said:

> I described this case as a cautionary tale. So, in my judgment, it is. The purchase of residential accommodation is perhaps the single most important financial transaction which any individual transacts in a lifetime. It is therefore of the utmost importance, as it seems to me, that those who engage in these transactions, and those who advise them, should take the greatest care over such transactions, and must – particularly if they are unmarried or if their clients are unmarried – address their minds to the size and fate of the respective beneficial interests on acquisition, separation and thereafter. It is simply impossible for a court to analyse personal transactions over years between cohabitants, and the costs of so doing are likely to be disproportionate in any event. Cohabiting partners must, it seems to me, contemplate and address the unthinkable, namely that their relationship will break down and that they will fall out over what they do and do not own.

In other words, the parties should ensure either that their agreed shares in the beneficial ownership are properly reflected in the property registration/conveyance documents or that their intentions are recorded in a written agreement.

But in many if not most cases when a couple is involved in buying a house to live in, the last thing on their minds is the prospect of the relationship ending and it is understandable why, in practice, couples fail to agree or even discuss how the property is owned or what should happen if the relationship fails. And in some cases the parties are poorly advised or ignore the advice.

The Law Commission in its Eighth Programme of Law Reform (2001) Law Com. 274 said:

> It is widely accepted that the present law is unduly complex, arbitrary and uncertain in its application. It is ill-suited to determining property rights of those who, because of the informal nature of their relationship, may not have considered their respective entitlement.

Disadvantaged women

As will be discussed, under the current law, it is often the case that, when cohabitees split up, the woman (it is usually, but not always, the woman who is seeking to establish a right) will not be able to establish an interest in the home. It is often considered strange that the woman would have a far better chance of establishing a claim against the estate of her dead partner. This point is even more apparent after the amendments to the Inheritance (Provision for Family and Dependants) Act 1975 made by the Law Reform (Succession) Act 1995. Prior to the amendments, a cohabitee could only establish a claim against the estate of their dead partner on the ground that the distribution of the property was unreasonable if it could be shown that the claimant was financially dependent on the deceased. After the changes, financial dependence no longer needs to be established if the applicant and the deceased had been living together as husband and wife for the two years immediately leading up to the death. The legislation lists a number of guidelines that the court should use in assessing a claim. Among those relevant here are the contribution that the applicant made to the welfare of the family, including looking after the house and family. These are specifically factors that the courts will ignore when assessing a claim made during the lifetime of both parties.

The lack of legislative reform

Most people agree that reform is needed and many think that the reform should be legislative rather than judicial. There is less agreement on what the reform(s) should be.

On 31 July 2007 the Law Commission published its report, 'Cohabitation: The Financial Consequences of Relationship Breakdown' (Law Com. No. 307). The report and other Law Commission publications are discussed under 'Reform' below. (See pp. 385–90.)

The government has, however, announced that it does not intend to introduce reforms in the current parliament.

So there is still no immediate prospect of legislative reform of this difficult and complicated area of the law. Any development or reform has been left in the hands of the judiciary.

Currently pre-nuptial and post-nuptial agreements cannot be enforced as contracts and they cannot take away the powers of the courts to make property orders. The only option is to ask the court to make an order that reflects the terms of the agreement.

The Law Commission published its report, 'Matrimonial Property, Needs and Agreements' (Law Com. No. 343) on 26 February 2014 which recommends the introduction of enforceable 'qualifying nuptial agreements'.

The current position is that in *Radmacher* v *Granatino* [2010] UKSC 42 the Supreme Court recognised the potential legal effect of pre-nuptial agreements but each agreement will, under *Radmacher*, be considered on a case-by-case basis. (See pp. 389–90 for more on pre-nuptial and post-nuptial agreements.)

Married couples: divorce, decree of nullity or decree of judicial separation

Objective 2

As many cohabitees subsequently marry, their disputes may be settled under the Matrimonial Causes Act 1973 s 24 under which there is an adjustive jurisdiction which will avoid the need to rely on the law of trusts.

The Marriage (Same Sex Couples) Act 2013 came into force on 13 March 2014. Under the Act (which applies to England and Wales) marriage has the same effect in relation to same sex couples as it has in relation to opposite sex couples. Thus the courts have the same powers to make property adjustment orders on the divorce of same sex married couples as on the divorce of opposite sex married couples.

If the couple is in dispute in the course of matrimonial proceedings in relation to a divorce, or a decree of nullity or of judicial separation, the Act permits a judge to make an order, irrespective of how the property is held, according to the rules of trusts. The Act directs that the first consideration of the judge should be the welfare of any child of the family while a minor. Subject to that, the court has very wide powers. For example, the judge may order that one of the parties should transfer property to the other or order a settlement of property of one of the parties for the benefit of the other. Additionally, the court may order that the property is sold.

But the statutory provisions are relevant only if the parties are in the course of a divorce or are seeking a decree of nullity or of judicial separation. If the parties decide merely to separate, or if the dispute arises on the death or bankruptcy of one of the parties, the normal trust rules will apply in order to decide on the beneficial ownership of property.

Despite s 2(1) of the Law Reform (Miscellaneous Provisions) Act 1970, which provides that the rules which apply to settling property disputes between spouses also apply to formerly engaged couples, s 24 does not apply to engaged couples. In *Mossop* v *Mossop* [1988] 2 All ER 202, the court decided that s 24 could not apply to engaged couples who never marry as it is a prerequisite to the application of the section that there is a marriage.

Civil partnership: formal termination

The Civil Partnership Act 2004 s 72 and Schedule 5 contains similar provisions to those in s 24 of the Matrimonial Causes Act 1973. These provisions apply where a registered civil partnership is dissolved. In other words, the partners will be treated in a similar way to a married couple when it comes to the court allocating the ownership of their shared home. Thus, there can be property adjustment orders, and the application of the 'normal' trust rules will not be relevant.

But, in other cases, not involving the formal ending of the relationship, the trust rules will still be relevant. For example, on the death of one of the partners, the ownership of a shared home may be an issue in the context of the administration of the will of the deceased partner. The Civil Partnership Act is limited to those same-sex couples who register their partnership, and the problems discussed below both in terms of establishing and quantifying beneficial interests in 'shared' property (most importantly in the context of shared homes) will continue to be relevant to same-sex couples who choose either not to register their partnership or choose not to formally dissolve their registered partnership.

The provisions of the Act also leave many 'homesharers' exposed to the problems outlined above. For example, opposite-sex cohabiting couples and those who simply decide to share a home will still be exposed to the vagaries of the existing law.

All other situations not involving marriage or civil partnership: the key issues

In this area of law legislation has played a very small role. This seems likely to continue as the coalition government announced that it had no plans to legislate on this area of law and would not implement the recommendations of the Law Commission in 'Cohabitation: The Financial Consequences Of Relationship Breakdown' (Law Com. No. 307). It is not clear what a change of government would bring to this area of law. There have been at least two bills introduced by private members which sought to reform the law but to date nothing has been passed into law. So currently reform is in the hands of the judiciary and this is despite the many calls for statutory reform by members of the judiciary, academics and others.

It is not surprising therefore that the pace of reform has been fairly slow and, as is often the case with judge-led reforms, decisions have often left open questions that are then addressed (or partially addressed) in later cases.

Recently, though, the Supreme Court has heard several cases on this subject and the opportunity was taken (especially by Lady Hale) to set out some principles to be followed in disputes over the ownership of a shared home. The most recent key case is **Kernott v Jones** [2011] UKSC 53; [2011] 3 WLR 1121. In this case the court said that resulting trusts (which had been used as the basis of decisions on the ownership of a shared home) were not appropriate concepts in this domestic context. The constructive trust based on the common intention of the parties is now the concept of choice when deciding on the ownership of a shared home, particularly in the case of cohabiting couples.

Introduction

Lord Diplock, in **Gissing v Gissing** [1970] 2 All ER 780, stressed that:

> [t]he legal principles applicable to the claim are those of the English law of trusts and in particular, in the kind of dispute between spouses that comes before the courts, the law relating to the creation and operation of 'resulting, implied or constructive trusts'.

The initial task of any claimant is to establish that they have *some* interest in the property. In **Burns v Burns** [1984] 1 All ER 244, Fox LJ stated:

> If a plaintiff is to establish that she has a beneficial interest in the property, she must establish that the defendant holds the legal estate upon trust to give effect to that interest. That follows from **Gissing v Gissing** (1971). For present purposes I think that such a trust can only arise (a) by express declaration or agreement or (b) by way of a resulting trust where the claimant has directly provided part of the purchase price or (c) from the common intention of the parties.

Fox LJ was discussing the common situation where the legal title is in the name of one party only and his inclusion of resulting trusts must now be read in the light of **Stack v Dowden** in which it was said that the remedy of choice is the common intention constructive trust).

The second stage, once it is established that a party has an interest (under whatever type of trust), is quantifying the interest. The interest is valued at the time of the sale, rather than, as had been argued in some cases, at the date of separation. (See **Burns v Burns** [1984] 1 All ER 244.) Naturally, this is a more attractive proposition for claimants when property values have gone up since separation rather than, as may have been the case in the recent past, if values have gone down.

But the size of the respective interests can change as a relationship progresses. In **Stack v Dowden**, Baroness Hale said:

See p. 375 for more on ambulatory constructive trusts.

> The fact that the ownership of the beneficial interest in a home is determined at the date of acquisition does not mean that it cannot alter thereafter. My noble and learned friend Lord Hoffmann suggested during argument that the trust which arises at the date of acquisition, whether resulting or constructive, is of an ambulatory nature.

Loans

If there is evidence of an agreement that money contributed towards the purchase or improvement of a property was intended to be a loan, while the lender is able to claim the repayment of the loan, they will not thereby be entitled to an interest or a larger interest in the ownership of the property.

This was the basis of the Court of Appeal decision in *Chapman v Jaume* [2012] EWCA Civ 476.

Express declaration of trust

Objective
3

In most situations, if the transfer or conveyance expressly sets out how the beneficial interest is to be held, this will be regarded by the courts as conclusive. If there is an express declaration, there is no need to see if there is a constructive or common intention trust, indeed there is no possibility of inferring one because in the absence of one of the vitiating factors discussed below, the declaration of trust will be regarded as conclusive.

Does the transfer or conveyance deal effectively with the ownership of the beneficial interest?

Ideally the transfer document or conveyance will simply and unambiguously set out how the beneficial interest is owned by the parties.

Anything short of this clear unambiguous statement may cause problems as the courts have adopted a fairly strict approach here and it is always advisable to ensure that the title documents deal fully and unambiguously with the beneficial interest. In *Harwood* v *Harwood* [1991] 2 FLR 274, the transfer of the family home was taken in the joint names of the husband and wife. There was no declaration as to the beneficial ownership, but the transfer did state that the survivor of the transferees could give a valid receipt for capital money arising on the disposition of the property. Slade J held that this did not amount to a declaration that the beneficial interest should be held for the husband and wife as joint tenants.

In *Stack v Dowden* [2007] 2 All ER 929 a key issue was the effect of the inclusion in the transfer deed of a clause stating that the survivor of them was entitled to give a valid receipt for capital money arising from a disposition of the property. It was unclear whether the parties had discussed how they wished to own the property.

If it had been established that the parties understood the significance of the declaration in the transfer deed, the inference that they intended to hold the property as beneficial joint tenants, the court stated, would have been irresistible. But there had been no finding of fact that both parties had understood the significance of the declaration. Thus, the court found, an inference could not be drawn in respect of the parties' intention as to beneficial ownership and so there was not an express declaration of trust.

Subsequent agreement to vary the agreement and proprietary estoppel

In *Stack v Dowden* [2007] 2 All ER 929, Baroness Hale said:

> 49 In the olden days, before registration of title on certain events, including a conveyance on sale, became compulsory all over England and Wales, conveyances of unregistered land into joint names would in practice declare the purchasers' beneficial as well as their legal interests. No-one now doubts that such an express declaration of trust is conclusive unless varied by subsequent agreement or affected by proprietary estoppel: see *Goodman v Gallant* [1986] Fam 106.

Again in *Clarke v Meadus* [2010] EWHC 3117 (Ch) it is said that express declarations of trust could be overriden by proprietary estoppel resulting from promises and representations made after a deed was executed.

Fraud or mistake

It is clear that if a declaration is tainted by fraud or mistake on the part of the parties it will not be effective.

In *Pettitt* v *Pettitt* [1969] 2 All ER 385 Lord Upjohn said:

> . . . the beneficial ownership of the property in question must depend upon the agreement of the parties determined at the time of its acquisition . . . If [the] document declares not merely in whom the legal title is to vest but in whom the beneficial title is to vest that necessarily concludes the question of title as between the spouses for all time, and in the absence of fraud or mistake at the time of the transaction the parties cannot go behind it at any time thereafter even on death or the break-up of the marriage.

The declaration of trust is a sham

If the declaration of trust is found to be a sham it will be ignored. In *Pankhania* v *Chandegra* [2012] EWCA Civ 1438, [2012] All ER (D) 132 (Nov) Patten LJ:

> The question of what constitutes a sham trust has been the subject of considerable discussion in recent years, particularly in the context of attempts to shield assets from the claims of divorced spouses or creditors. But what is, I think, clear is that it must be shown both that the parties to the trust deed . . . never intended to create a trust and that they did intend to give that false impression to third parties or to the court.

In the case the Court of Appeal reconfirmed what was generally thought to be law, that an express declaration of trust is conclusive unless it is set aside, varied or rectified.

Declaration of trust using the Land Registry forms

Before 1 April 1998 the Land Registry form only contained an opportunity for transferees to declare that the survivor was able to give valid receipt for capital money received on a sale. This form was in use when the transfer was made in *Stack* v *Dowden* in which case both the Court of Appeal and the House of Lords (see below) found that making this declaration did not amount to an agreement to hold the beneficial interest as joint tenants. The form in use from 1 April 1998 has changed and is now much clearer and more informative to the layperson. There is now a box for transferees to tick indicating how the beneficial interest is to be held: for example, as joint tenants or tenants in common in equal shares or as tenants in common in unequal shares. So the lack of understanding and appreciation that was found to exist in *Stack* v *Dowden* should not be such an issue for transfers after 1 April 1998. However, it is not mandatory to use the tick boxes and so it is still possible for there to be transfers where there is no express declaration of how the beneficial interest is held.

In *Stack* v *Dowden* Baroness Hale said:

> Form TR1, in use from 1 April 1998, provides a box for the transferees to declare whether they are to hold the property on trust for themselves as joint tenants, or on trust for themselves as tenants in common in equal shares, or on some other trusts which are inserted on the form. If this is invariably complied with, the problem confronting us here will eventually disappear. Unfortunately, however, the transfer will be valid whether or not this part of the form is completed . . . However desirable such a declaration may be, it is unrealistic, in the consumer context, to expect that it will be executed independently of the forms required to acquire the legal estate. Not only do solicitors and licensed conveyancers compete on price, but more and more people are emboldened to do their own conveyancing. The Land Registry form which has been prescribed since 1998 is to be applauded. If its completion and execution

by or on behalf of all joint proprietors were mandatory, the problem we now face would disappear. However, the form might then include an option for those who deliberately preferred not to commit themselves as to the beneficial interests at the outset and to rely on the [the principles of law discussed in this chapter].

Judicial advice

In the light of the (normally) conclusive nature of an express declaration of trust, in *Carlton* v *Goodman* [2002] EWCA Civ 545 [2002] 2 FLR 259 Lord Ward said: 'Perhaps conveyancers do not read the law reports. I will try one more time: always try to agree on and then record how the beneficial interest is to be held. It is not very difficult to do.'

This is obviously wise advice but on the basis of past cases it is unlikely to be universally taken.

An agreement between the parties

If there is a written agreement between the parties as to how the beneficial interest is held, then in the absence of fraud or mistake, this will be conclusive.

Is there an agreement between the parties that is intended to be legally binding?

The initial question to be answered of course is if there was actually an agreement between the parties.

Unlike other agreements made in a social context, contracts regarding the ownership of land are presumed to have been made with the intention to create a legally binding contract. In *Pettitt* v *Pettitt* [1969] 2 All ER 385, Lord Diplock said that the normal presumption of no intention to create legal relations that applied to agreements in a domestic setting did not apply to the acquisition of property by husband and wife. It is to be assumed that the position as between a non-married couple is, if anything, more likely to tend towards an intention to create legal relations. Such an agreement must comply with the provisions of the Law of Property Act 1925 s 53(1)(b), as it amounts to a declaration of trust over an interest in land.

Similarly, if there is a written agreement as to how the beneficial interest is held this will be conclusive, provided that there was an intention to create legal relations.

If it had been established that the parties understood the significance of the declaration in the transfer deed, the inference that they intended to hold the property as beneficial joint tenants, the court stated, would have been irresistible. But, there had been no finding of fact that both parties had understood the significance of the declaration. Thus, the court found, an inference could not be drawn in respect of the parties' intention as to beneficial ownership and so there was not an express declaration of trust.

Judicial solutions
Resulting trust

A resulting trust will arise where the property is registered in the name of one party but the other makes a contribution to the purchase price. The contribution will show an intention to own a share of the property. When the court quantifies the extent of the beneficial interest, it applies a simple arithmetical calculation. The share is a direct reflection of the contribution. So if a house is bought and transferred into the name of one of the parties only but the other party contributes 30 per cent of the purchase price, the beneficial interest will be shared 70:30 between the parties.

Paying part of the purchase price, making mortgage repayments and (in **Springette v Defoe** [1992] 2 FLR 388) the discount available to a sitting tenant have all been regarded as contributions sufficient to give an interest under a resulting trust. But payments towards (or making) improvements or repairs will not be regarded as contributions to the purchase price. Neither will payments of general household bills.

Midland Bank v Cooke [1995] 4 All ER 562

In this case the matrimonial home was conveyed into the sole name of the husband, having been bought by means of a mortgage, his savings and a joint wedding gift of £1,100 from his family. Later, the house was charged with a second, much larger, mortgage in favour of the bank to secure repayment of his company's overdraft with the bank. The wife apparently consented to the charge having priority over any charge she might have over the property. As is becoming common, the 'fight' in the case was not between the couple but between the couple on one hand and the bank on the other. The County Court accepted that the wife's consent had been obtained by undue influence. She had made no contribution to the mortgage payments but had contributed to improvements. The judge decided that the only basis for the wife having an interest in the property was that the wedding gift used in the purchase was half owned by her. On this basis, contribution to the purchase price was 6.47 per cent (half of the wedding present (£550) as percentage of the total cost of acquisition (£8,500)) and thus her share, under the resulting trust, was calculated at 6.47 per cent. All other contributions, including the improvements, looking after the family, etc., were ignored.

But in the Court of Appeal, Waite LJ giving the only judgment, decided that her interest should be 50 per cent. Waite LJ inferred a common intention and based his decision that she should have a 50 per cent share on a common intention constructive trust.

The contrast with constructive trusts should be noted here. Under constructive trusts, the relative contributions are only one of the factors that the court will take into account when quantifying a beneficial interest. Discussing the constructive trusts solution, Baroness Hale, in **Stack v Dowden** [2007] 2 All ER 929, supported the view that the court should

[u]ndertak[e] a survey of the whole course of dealing between the parties and tak[e] account of all conduct which throws light on the question of what shares were intended.

In **Stack v Dowden** both Baroness Hale and Lord Walker said that in the context of settling domestic disputes the constructive and not the resulting trust is the tool of choice. Lord Walker said that 'in a case about beneficial ownership of a matrimonial or quasi-matrimonial home (whether registered in the names of one or two legal owners) the resulting trust should not in my opinion operate as a legal presumption, although it may (in an updated form which takes account of all significant contributions, direct or indirect, in cash or in kind) happen to be reflected in the parties' common intention'. In contrast, Lord Neuberger, while agreeing with the result, based his decision on resulting trusts. But in the light of the views of the majority, this cannot be thought to have any authority.

The decision of the House of Lords has not been reflected in some subsequent Court of Appeal cases where the size of the respective interests has been based largely, if not entirely, on the amounts of the respective contributions to the purchase price. For example, in **Laskar v Laskar** [2008] EWCA Civ 347, Lord Neuberger (sitting in the Court of Appeal and giving the unanimous judgment) said that as the purchase was as an investment it was not a case where the presumption that equity follows the law applies. But even if the presumption did apply, he thought that on the facts it was rebutted and went on to say:

I can see no reason not to fall back on the resulting trust analysis, namely that in the absence of any relevant discussion between the parties, their respective beneficial shares should reflect the size of their contributions to the purchase price, subject to any subsequent actions or discussions having the effect of varying those shares.

In *Stack* v *Dowden* itself, the outcome (albeit based on intention) actually reflected the parties' respective contributions to the purchase price shares.

New model constructive trusts

In a series of cases decided in the 1970s Lord Denning MR seized on Lord Diplock's statement in *Gissing* v *Gissing* that a constructive trust would arise 'whenever the trustee has so conducted himself that it would be inequitable to deny the *cestui que* trust a beneficial interest in the land acquired'. Lord Denning used this statement in a series of cases to bring flexibility and, in his view, fairness and justice into this area of law. In Lord Denning's view, all that was needed to invoke a constructive trust was that it would be inequitable for the defendant to deny that the claimant has a beneficial interest. It was not essential for the claimant to prove that she had made a financial contribution to the purchase of the house. It seems that the key feature was that the house had been acquired by their joint efforts.

In *Hussey* v *Palmer* [1972] 3 ALL ER 744, Lord Denning explained the concept:

[I]t is a trust imposed by law whenever justice and good conscience require it. It is a liberal process, founded on large principles of equity, to be applied in cases where the defendant cannot conscientiously keep the property for himself alone, but ought to allow another to have the property or a share in it. The trust may arise at the outset when the property is acquired, or later on, as circumstances may require.

Eves v *Eves* [1975] 3 All ER 768

A married man and a woman began to live together. Four years and two children later, the relationship ended and a dispute arose as to the ownership of the house in which they lived. When the house was bought the man said to the woman that the house would be conveyed into his sole name because she was under 21. The woman made no financial contribution to the purchase of the house but did a great deal of very heavy work on the property in order to improve it. The Court of Appeal held that the woman had a quarter share in the beneficial interest.

Lord Denning, after quoting Lord Diplock's statement (above) that the court could find a trust if it would be inequitable to deny that the claimant had a beneficial interest in the land, found that a constructive trust existed and that under the trust the woman had a one-quarter share. He stated that the woman would in the past have been in a most unfair position, having no claim on the property:

And a few years ago even equity would not have helped her. But things have altered now. Equity is not past the age of child bearing. One of her latest progeny is a constructive trust of a new model. Lord Diplock [in *Gissing* v *Gissing*, discussed above] brought it into the world and we have nourished it . . .

Lord Denning went on to say that the Court of Appeal had followed the advice of Lord Diplock in a number of cases, including *Binions* v *Evans* [1972] 2 All ER 70, *Cooke* v *Head* [1972] 2 All ER 38 and *Hussey* v *Palmer* [1972] 3 All ER 744, and continued by saying that in *Cooke* v *Head* he had suggested that 'whenever two parties by their joint efforts acquire property to be used for their joint benefit, the court may impose or impute a constructive or resulting trust'.

Lord Denning concluded by saying:

It seems to me that this conduct by Mr Eves amounted to a recognition by him that, in all fairness, she was entitled to a share in the house, equivalent in some way to the declaration of trust; not for a particular share, but for such share as was fair in view of all she had done and was doing for him and the children and would thereafter do. By so doing he gained her confidence. She trusted him. She did not make any financial contribution but she contributed in many other ways. She did much work in the house and garden. She looked after him and cared for the children . . .

In view of his conduct, it would, I think, be most inequitable for him to deny her any share in the house. The law will impute or impose a constructive trust by which he was to hold it in trust for them both.

In this case Lord Denning felt that he was able to use the statement of Lord Diplock to discover or impose a trust in the interests of fairness and justice. For completeness, it should be added that the rest of the Court of Appeal based their finding of a constructive trust on an understanding between the couple.

Criticisms of the new model constructive trust

A major objection to Lord Denning's new model constructive trust was uncertainty. The decision in any particular case would depend on the personal feelings and values of the particular judge.

The statement of Lord Diplock in *Gissing* v *Gissing* that was used as authority by Lord Denning was, many argue, taken out of context; and in his judgment in *Gissing* Lord Diplock emphasised that the trust imposed whenever it was inequitable for the legal owner to deny the claimant a beneficial interest would only arise 'if by his words or conduct he has induced the [beneficiary] to act to his own detriment in the reasonable belief that by so acting he was acquiring a beneficial interest in the land'. This reflects the conventional view of constructive trusts and is in line with the later statements of Lord Bridge in *Lloyds Bank plc* v *Rosset* discussed below.

In *Burns* v *Burns* [1984] 1 All ER 244, the approach of the Court of Appeal in general, and of Lord Denning in particular, was rejected and the law was stated in a much less flexible but far more certain form.

Burns v Burns [1984] 1 All ER 244

The facts of this case were very simple. A couple lived together, with the woman staying at home to look after the house and children but making no direct contribution to the purchase price of the house which was bought for them to live in. At one stage she did work but again did not contribute directly to the purchase of the house. She did pay some household bills and redecorated some of the house. The Court of Appeal held that she had no beneficial interest in the house which was in the sole name of the man.

Fox LJ stated:

If, therefore the plaintiff is to establish that she has a beneficial interest in the property she must establish that the defendant holds the legal estate on trust to give effect to that interest. That follows from *Gissing* v *Gissing* . . . For the present purposes I think that such a trust could only arise (a) by express declaration or agreement or (b) by way of a resulting trust where the claimant has directly provided part of the purchase price or (c) from the common intention of the parties. In the present case (a) and (b) can be ruled out . . . Her case, therefore, must depend upon showing a common intention that she should have a beneficial interest in the property. Whether the trust which would arise in such circumstances is described as implied, resulting or constructive does not greatly matter. If the intention is inferred from the fact that some indirect contribution is made to the purchase price, the term 'resulting trust' is probably not inappropriate. Be that as it may, the basis of such a claim, in any case, is that it would be inequitable for the holder of the legal estate to deny the claimant's right to a beneficial interest.

In determining whether such common interest exists it is, normally, the intention of the parties when the property was purchased that is important . . . It is necessary for the court to consider all the evidence, including contributions of the parties, down to the date of the separation (which in the case of a man and his mistress will generally, but not always, be the relevant date). Thus the law proceeds on the basis that there is nothing inherently improbable in the parties acting on the understanding that the woman 'should be entitled to a share which was not to be quantified immediately upon the acquisition of the home but should be left to be determined when the mortgage was repaid or the property disposed of, on the basis of what would be fair having regard to the total contributions, direct or indirect, which each spouse had made by that date' (see *Gissing v Gissing* . . . *per* Lord Diplock).

Fox LJ went on to say:

Looking at the position in 1963, I see nothing at all to indicate any intention by the parties that the plaintiff should have any interest in it. The price of the house was £4,900. Of that, about £4,500 was raised by the defendant on mortgage. The mortgage was in his own name; he assumed responsibility for the debt. The balance of the purchase price and the costs of the purchase were paid by the defendant out of his own moneys. The plaintiff made no financial contribution; she had nothing to contribute . . .

It seems to me that at the time of the acquisition of the house nothing occurred between the parties to raise an equity which would prevent the defendant denying the plaintiff's claim. She provided no money for the purchase; she assumed no responsibility in respect of the mortgage; there was no understanding or arrangement that the plaintiff would go out to work to assist with the family finances; the defendant did nothing to lead her to change her position in the belief that she would have an interest in the house . . .

I come then to the position in the year after the house was purchased . . .

So far as financial contributions are concerned, the plaintiff's position really did not change during the 1960s. She had no money of her own and could not contribute financially to the household. All the mortgage instalments were paid by the defendant alone.

Fox LJ then related how the plaintiff worked but she was not asked to use her income to pay household expenses; she was free to use her money as she wished. However, she did make some minor contributions to family expenses and, for example, paid some telephone bills and bought some domestic appliances and furniture but Fox LJ decided that none of this expenditure indicated the existence of a common intention that the plaintiff should have an interest in the house:

What is needed, I think, is evidence of a payment or payments by the plaintiff which it can be inferred was referable to the acquisition of the house. Lord Denning MR in *Hazell v Hazell* [1972] 1 All ER 923 thought that expression which appears in the speech of Lord Diplock in *Gissing v Gissing* . . . was being over-used. He said . . . that if there was a substantial financial contribution towards the family expenses that would raise the inference of a trust. I do not think that formulation alters the essence of the matter for present purposes. If there is a substantial contribution by the woman to family expenses, and the house was purchased on a mortgage, her contribution is, indirectly, referable to the acquisition of the house since, one way or another, it enables the family to pay the mortgage instalments.

Fox LJ went on to say that a payment could be said to be referable to the acquisition of a house if the payer (a) pays part of the purchase price or (b) contributes regularly to the mortgage instalments or (c) pays off part of the mortgage or (d) makes substantial contributions to the family expenses so as to enable the mortgage instalments to be paid.

Despite the fact that the approach of Lord Denning in the Court of Appeal has now been decisively rejected, it is interesting to note that the courts appear to have applied a more liberal, justice-seeking approach when deciding the size, as opposed to the existence, of an interest in property. In the case of constructive trusts, in theory, the size of the interest should reflect the terms of the common intention. However, in some cases the courts have made their decision on the basis of taking the 'fair view'. In *Stokes v Anderson* [1991] 1 FLR 391, for example, the Court of Appeal did not interfere with the decision at first instance that the parties had made their express common intention clear that the woman was to have a beneficial interest in the property and that she had acted to her detriment on the common intention. She had contributed £14,500 towards a house worth over £100,000. However, they had not agreed as to the quantification of the interest. Nourse LJ applied Lord Diplock's statement in *Gissing v Gissing* [1970] 2 All ER 780, where he said:

> And there is nothing inherently improbable in their acting on the understanding that the wife would be entitled to a share which was not to be quantified immediately upon the acquisition of the home but should be left to be determined when the mortgage was repaid or the property disposed of, on the basis of what is fair having regard to the total contributions, direct or indirect, which each spouse had made.

Nourse LJ said that the court must 'supply the common intention by reference to that which all the material circumstances have shown to be fair'. He opined that the allocation of the beneficial interest in *Eves v Eves* [1975] 3 All ER 768, a case where the woman made no financial contribution but did a great deal of work on the home, could only be explained on this basis. In that case, Lord Denning MR, in awarding the woman a quarter share, said 'one-half would be too much'.

But in *Stack v Dowden* and *Abbott v Abbott* (discussed below) some argue that the courts state that it is possible to impute an intention to the parties where none exists in order to find a constructive trust. To the extent that this is implemented in future cases, the wheel may have turned full circle. But after *Kernott v Jones* it seems imputation is possible only to quantify, not to establish, a beneficial interest.

The developing modern law

Objective 4

The modern law relating to disputes as to the ownership of the beneficial interest in a shared home has developed (mainly) through five cases: *Lloyds Bank plc v Rosset* [1990] UKHL 14, [1990] 1 All ER 1111 and *Stack v Dowden* [2007] UKHL 17 [2007] 2 All ER 729, which are both House of Lords cases; *Oxley v Hiscock* [2004] EWCA Civ 546, [2004] 3 All ER 703 which was decided by the Court of Appeal; *Abbott v Abbott* [2007] UKPC 53, [2008] 1 FLR 1451 which was a Privy Council case; and the Supreme Court decision in *Kernott v Jones* [2011] UKSC 53; [2011] 3 WLR 1121.

These cases follow on from the earlier, seminal, cases of *Pettitt v Pettitt* [1969] 2 All ER 385 and *Gissing v Gissing* [1970] All ER 780, in which the origins of the common intention constructive trust can be seen under which the rights of the parties are not based solely on their contributions to the purchase price of the property.

Unfortunately, the combined effect of these cases fails to resolve all the problems and predicting the result in a particular case is still uncertain, leading to potential expense and stress for those contesting the ownership of property. A particular difficulty is that the judgments in these key cases range wide and statements are made which clearly, strictly speaking, do not form part of the *ratio* of the respective cases.

For example, in *Stack v Dowden*, as the parties agreed that the claimant had an interest and the dispute was over the size of the interest, anything that the court said about establishing an interest is, strictly speaking, *obiter*.

Nevertheless, when eminent House of Lords/Supreme Court judges express their view, this will be taken as indicative of what the law is or should be. However, criticism has been voiced that some courts have regarded the judgment of Baroness Hale in **Stack v Dowden** as if it had statutory force.

One thing that has emerged from **Stack v Dowden** and **Kernott v Jones** is that the preferred tool for settling property disputes in the context of ownership of a shared, family home is the constructive trust based on the common intention of the parties, The use of the resulting trust was rejected by all but Lord Neuberger (in **Stack v Dowden**).

In **Stack v Dowden** Lady Hale said:

> These days, the importance to be attached to who paid for what in a domestic context may be very different from its importance in other contexts or long ago.

This was built on and re-emphasised by Lady Hale and Lord Walker in **Kernott v Jones**:

> Instead, the tool which equity has chosen to develop law is the 'common intention' constructive trust.

The constructive trust based on the common intention of the parties gives much more flexibility to the courts to take account of a range of factors, rather than, as with the resulting trust, simply deciding the ownership of the beneficial interest on a mathematical calculation based on the respective contributions of the parties to the acquisition of the property.

When dealing with disputes over the ownership of a home, the courts undertake a two-stage process.

- The first stage is to decide if the claimant has *some* beneficial interest.
- The second stage is quantifying that beneficial interest.

Where the property is in joint names and there is no declaration as to the ownership of the beneficial interest, after **Stack v Dowden** the starting point in claims to own a share of beneficial interest or the entire beneficial interest is the presumption that the beneficial interest will be owned equally. The court in **Stack v Dowden** and in **Kernott v Jones** proceeded, without a detailed explanation, on the basis that this alone establishes *some* share in the beneficial interest. So the first hurdle has been crossed.

Where the property is in the name of one of the parties, the starting point is that the other party has no interest at all. To establish a claim to a share, the claimant will need to show that there is evidence of a common intention constructive trust under which the claimant was entitled to *some* share. At this stage while the courts may find an express or inferred intention, imputing an intention is not permissible.

At the second stage the courts will again look for the intention of the parties. This intention may be expressed (if there is a clear agreement) or inferred from their conduct. But **Kernott v Jones** makes it clear that if it is not possible to find an express or inferred agreement the court can impute an agreement. Each party will be entitled to that share which the court considers fair, having regard to the whole course of dealing between them in relation to the property. This is in contrast to stage one where the intention must be objectively found to exist.

This two-stage approach is agreed to be correct but the edges sometimes become blurred. In some situations it is not always possible to decide if the remarks of a judge relate to stage one, stage two or both.

Although many, if not most, commentators agree that legislative reform is needed, the government has announced that no legislative reforms will be introduced in the current parliament. (See 'Reform' p. 389.)

Property in the sole name of one of the parties and no declaration of how the beneficial interest is owned

Stage one: establishing a beneficial interest under a common intention constructive trust

In *Kernott v Jones* Lord Walker and Baroness Hale developed the approach of Lady Hale in *Stack v Dowden*. In their joint judgment Lady Hale and Lord Walker said:

> The starting point is different [in sole name cases from cases where the legal title is in joint names] because the claimant whose name is not on the proprietorship register has the burden of establishing some sort of implied trust, normally what is now termed a 'common intention' constructive trust.

But does this starting point apply if the parties initially intended that the property would be transferred into their joint names but some 'external' factor intervened and the property was in fact transferred into the sole name of one of the parties?

This was one of the key issues in the recent Court of Appeal case *Thompson v Hurst* [2012] EWCA Civ 1752.

In the case a property was transferred into the sole name of Ms H although the parties had intended that the property would be in joint names. Ms H had two jobs but Mr T had not been working for the previous six months. The parties were advised that mortgage providers would look more favourably on an application by Ms H alone. Ms H applied successfully for a mortgage and the property was transferred into her sole name.

The relationship broke down and Mr T claimed a share in the beneficial interest.

Mr T claimed that the case should be decided using the law applicable to joint tenancy cases (see p. 373) as the parties *intended* the property to be in joint names. He argued that it was only the intervention of the 'external' factor of the mortgage application being made by Ms H alone that stopped the property from being transferred into joint names.

The leading judgment was given by Etherton LJ. He said:

> ... The transfer was not in fact into the joint names of the appellant and the respondent. There is, therefore, no scope for a legal presumption that the parties intended a joint tenancy both in law and equity. [Mr T's] argument amounts to a submission that there should be a legal presumption of joint beneficial ownership, not merely where the parties are indeed the joint legal owners, but where there is evidence that they would have liked to be joint legal owners but for one reason or another that was not practical or desirable. Neither **Stack** nor **Jones**, nor any other case, is authority for such a proposition. Indeed, the proposition is neither consistent with principle nor sound policy.

In *Kernott v Jones* Lord Walker and Lady Hale said:

> The first issue is whether it was intended that the other party have any beneficial interest in the property at all ... But their common intention has once again to be deduced objectively from their conduct.

So the claimant has first to prove that it was intended that they should have *some* share of the beneficial interest.

At this stage despite, and in the light of, the criticisms of the case, *Lloyds Bank v Rosset* still has *some* relevance.

In *Lloyds Bank v Rosset*, Lord Bridge attempted to summarise the law as it then stood and set out the ground rules for establishing a common intention constructive trust under which a claimant can establish a beneficial interest in property standing in the name of another.

Lord Bridge's statement – though subjected to criticisms – was accepted by many as the definitive guidance through this difficult area of law. But recently **Stack v Dowden** and **Kernott v Jones** have cast doubt as to the extent that Lord Bridge's statement can be regarded as 'good law' today. However, problems arise as these cases do not actually overrule **Rosset** – the courts simply saying that the law has moved on since **Rosset** was decided.

Lord Bridge set out two distinct situations relevant to settling disputes as to the ownership of the beneficial interest in property where common intention constructive trusts can arise.

Express common intention trusts

The first situation is where there has been an agreement based on express discussions between the partners. If there is an express agreement as to how the beneficial interest will be held, there may be problems relating to a possible lack of the evidence in writing required by the Law of Property Act 1925 s 53(1)(b). Unless a claim can be underpinned by detrimental reliance (an alteration of position in reliance on the agreement), thus raising the possibility of the court finding a constructive trust (or applying proprietary estoppel), the agreement will be unenforceable.

Lord Bridge said:

> The first and fundamental question which must always be resolved is whether, independently of any inference to be drawn from the conduct of the parties in the course of sharing the house as their home and managing their joint affairs, there has at any time prior to acquisition, or exceptionally at some later date, been any agreement, arrangement or understanding reached between them that the property is to be shared beneficially. The finding of an agreement or arrangement to share in this sense can only, I think, be based on evidence of express discussions between the partners, however imperfectly remembered and however imprecise their terms may have been. Once a finding to this effect is made, it will only be necessary for the partner asserting a claim to a beneficial interest against the partner entitled to the legal estate to show that he or she has acted to his or her detriment or significantly altered his or her position in reliance on the agreement in order to give rise to a constructive trust or proprietary estoppel.

Under this category, if a party alleges that an agreement exists, this must be based on express discussions between the parties. It is not possible to use in evidence the conduct of the parties in connection with 'sharing the house as their home and managing their joint affairs'.

In **Rosset** Lord Bridge identified **Eves v Eves** and **Grant v Edwards** as cases within this category, cases where the parties did arrive at an express agreement or common intention. In fact it is unrealistic to argue that there was any agreement. There certainly was no express agreement that the claimant should have an interest. In fact the only expression of intention was that the claimant would not have an interest. The only way that an agreement could be found was by inferring that although the defendant said one thing (that the claimant would not have an interest) he really meant something quite different (that the claimant would have an interest). Perhaps the explanation is better to be found in **Grant v Edwards**, where Mustill LJ thought that the basis might well be that the courts would not allow a defendant to deny an interest to a plaintiff when to do so would be to allow him to take advantage of his untruthful excuse.

Detrimental reliance

If an express agreement is alleged to exist, Lord Bridge said that there must be evidence of some action undertaken in reliance on the agreement. This is needed in order to avoid the problems of the Law of Property Act 1925 s 53(1)(b), which requires declarations of express trusts over land to be in writing. The court may declare a constructive trust on the basis of the reliance of one party and thus come within s 53(2), which does not require writing if the trust is implied, resulting or constructive. The type of action needed will not necessarily have to involve direct contributions to the purchase price but it is this reliance that, many argue, makes it unconscionable for the owner to be allowed to deny the claimant's interest.

In *Lloyds Bank plc v Rosset*, Lord Bridge said, in relation to the conduct needed to support an express agreement:

> [I]t will only be necessary for the partner asserting a claim to a beneficial interest against the party entitled to the legal estate to show that he or she has acted to his or her detriment or significantly altered his or her position in reliance on the agreement in order to give rise to a trust . . .

The precise type of conduct which would be acceptable to Lord Bridge is uncertain. The uncertainty is not helped by judicial statements at variance with each other.

Grant v Edwards [1986] 2 All ER 426

In this case, a cohabiting couple decided to buy a house which the man said should be conveyed into his name alone in order not to complicate the divorce proceedings of the woman. The woman contributed substantially to household expenses but the man paid the deposit and all the mortgage instalments. The Court of Appeal held that, on separation, the woman was entitled to half of the beneficial interest in the house.

Nourse LJ stated that where there was no written declaration or agreement, nor any direct contribution to the purchase price which could give rise to a resulting trust, a claimant must show that there was a common intention that such a beneficial interest should exist and that this intention had been acted upon by the claimant in order to establish a beneficial interest in property. If this common intention is shown to exist, and there is evidence of the act of the claimant, Nourse LJ said the court would construct a trust to give effect to the common intention.

Nourse LJ went on to say that there were rare cases where the parties may have come to an express agreement regarding the beneficial interest and where the parties have a common intention. He also said that, in *Eves v Eves*, the excuse put forward for not placing the property in joint names amounted to an agreement that the beneficial interest was to be shared. He said that the instant case also fell into this category. If this was not the intention, why was the excuse necessary? All that remained was to discover some conduct by the woman in reliance on the agreement which would enable the court to give effect to the agreement. It was considered that the financial contributions of the woman to the family expenses which enabled the man to pay the mortgage instalments was sufficient action on her part. The court was looking for conduct on the part of the woman upon which she could not reasonably be expected to embark except on the basis that she was to have an interest in the house.

In the same case, Browne-Wilkinson V-C said:

> Once it has been shown that there was a common intention that the claimant should have an interest in the house, any act done by her to her detriment relating to the joint lives of the parties is, in my judgment, sufficient detriment to qualify. The acts do not have to be inherently referable to the house.

Clearly, the view of Browne-Wilkinson V-C is wider than that of Nourse LJ. Browne-Wilkinson V-C suggested that the narrower view presented problems: 'In many cases . . . it is impossible to say whether or not the claimant would have done the acts relied on as a detriment even if she thought she had no interest in the house.' He went on to say that many acts (e.g. looking after the house, helping with bills) may be referable to mutual love and affection rather than to the belief that a plaintiff has an interest in the house.

In *Lloyds Bank plc v Rosset*, Lord Bridge appears to favour the wider rather than the narrower approach.

It should be noted that detrimental reliance is not mentioned in the judgments in *Stack v Dowden* or in *Kernott v Jones*. Is one to assume from this that the requirement no longer exists?

But the traditional view is that the claimant must have acted to her detriment in reliance on the common intention, this being vital in overcoming the lack of formality. Detriment would readily be found on the basis of a substantial contribution to a property which would not otherwise belong to the claimant at all.

Common intention constructive trusts inferred from conduct

The second situation where, on Lord Bridge's analysis, a common intention constructive trust arises is where there is no evidence to support a finding of an agreement or arrangement to share, and where the court must rely entirely on the conduct of the parties both from which to infer a common intention to share the property beneficially and as evidence of the conduct relied on to give rise to a constructive trust.

Lord Bridge said:

> In sharp contrast with this situation is the very different one where there is no evidence to support a finding of an agreement or arrangement to share, however reasonable it might have been for the parties to reach such an arrangement if they had applied their minds to the question, and where the court must rely entirely on the conduct of the parties both as the basis from which to infer a common intention to share the property beneficially and as the conduct relied on to give rise to a constructive trust. In this situation direct contributions to the purchase price by the partner who is not the legal owner, whether initially or by payment of mortgage instalments, will readily justify the inference necessary to the creation of a constructive trust. But, as I read the authorities, it is at least extremely doubtful whether anything less will do.

In the context of an inferred agreement, the conduct of the parties in making (direct) contributions to the purchase price is doubly important. First, the conduct will be evidence of a common intention that the beneficial interest should be shared and, secondly, it will constitute the detrimental conduct.

What the courts really seem to be doing, particularly in the case of the inferred agreement, is to look back at the way that the parties have behaved and then discover an agreement as to ownership which in reality was never made because the parties never had the issue of ownership in their minds. Some argue that this seems to be imputing, rather than inferring an agreement. But, in *Kernott v Jones*, Lord Walker and Baroness Hale made it clear that while imputation is permissible at the quantification stage it is not permissible at the stage of establishing *some* interest.

It is not every application of money towards the purchase price of property that will result in the provider of the money obtaining a share in the beneficial interest. For example, if X makes a gift of money to Y who then applies it towards purchasing a house, this will not result in X having an interest in the house. Also if Z lends money to Y to facilitate the purchase of a house, Z will not obtain a share in the equitable interest. If this was not the case, the providers of mortgage loans would obtain a share in the equitable interest of the property which was bought with the aid of the mortgage.

It is possible to argue that Lord Bridge was not absolutely ruling out all indirect payments. When he said he thought it 'extremely doubtful' whether anything less than direct contributions to the purchase price would be sufficient, it is possible to argue that he was not actually restricting acceptable conduct to direct contributions. However, the tenor of his remarks appears to be that he was intending to be restrictive in his approach. This approach leaves the woman who indirectly contributes, perhaps by paying other bills to enable the man to pay the mortgage, without an interest. As discussed elsewhere in this chapter, this rather restrictive approach has been criticised.

In *Stack* v *Dowden* Baroness Hale said:

> There is undoubtedly an argument for saying, as did the Law Commission in *Sharing Homes* (2002, *op cit*, para 4.23) that the observations, which were strictly *obiter dicta*, of Lord Bridge of Harwich in *Lloyd's Bank plc* v *Rosset* [1991] 1 AC 107 have set that hurdle rather too high in certain respects.

Also in *Stack* v *Dowden*, Lord Walker supported the argument that this restrictive approach was not appropriate:

> Lord Bridge's extreme doubt 'whether anything less will do' was certainly consistent with many first-instance and Court of Appeal decisions, but I respectfully doubt whether it took full account of the views (conflicting though they were) expressed in *Gissing* (see especially Lord Reid [1971] AC 886 . . . and Lord Diplock . . .). It has attracted some trenchant criticism from scholars as potentially productive of injustice . . . Whether or not Lord Bridge's observation was justified in 1990, in my opinion the law has moved on, and your Lordships should move it a little more in the same direction, while bearing in mind that the Law Commission may soon come forward with proposals which, if enacted by Parliament, may recast the law in this area.

But neither in *Stack* v *Dowden* nor in *Kernott* v *Jones* was *Rosset* overruled nor did Lady Hale or Lord Walker say what they thought the position should be.

The statement of Lord Walker perhaps implicitly approves of *Le Foe* (see p. 379 below).

A result of Lord Bridge's judgment is that his approach would inevitably lead to injustice and defeat the expectations of women. In a not untypical case, where a couple live together and the woman does not go to work but by agreement stays at home to look after the family, she would not be entitled to a share of the beneficial ownership of the home in the absence of an express agreement unless she made a direct contribution to the purchase price. Unless she had some private sources of finance, the very decision that she would stay at home would rob her not only of a career but also of the ability to contribute to the purchase of the home, and thus obtain a share in the beneficial interest. To some extent, this is relieved by the apparent ease with which the courts are prepared to find a common intention agreement from discussions etc. and so dispense with the need to find the agreement based on conduct. It may also be that in such cases the woman would be able to base a claim on proprietary estoppel.

In *Rosset*, Lord Bridge said that he considered the cases of *Pettitt* v *Pettitt* and *Gissing* v *Gissing* to be within his second class where (in the absence of an express agreement regarding the beneficial interest) in order to establish a beneficial interest the court must find evidence from which they can infer a common intention regarding the beneficial interest.

A general comment that may be made on this area of common intention trusts is that it ignores the realities of most relationships. In many, if not most, relationships the parties simply do not think about how the beneficial interest is to be shared. They may well assume (or hope) that the relationship will last for their lifetimes and so who owns what will never be a life issue and is never discussed, let alone agreed. In these cases a claimant will be forced to rely on an inferred common intention constructive trust to claim an interest where it is not absolutely clear that indirect contributions will be accepted by the courts and where performing 'domestic duties' will not suffice.

Stage two: quantification

After **Stack v Dowden** it was unclear whether or not the court could impute an intention to the parties and, if so, under what circumstances an imputation could be made and whether an intention could be imputed at stage one, stage two or at both stages.

It is now clear from **Kernott v Jones** that imputation is permissible but only at stage two – quantification – and even here the primary search is for the actual intentions of the parties, expressed or inferred. Imputation can only take place if this search fails.

Although **Kernott v Jones** concerned a property transferred into joint names, Lord Walker and Baroness Hale set out how quantification should proceed once *some* interest has been proved, and they said:

> 31. In deference to the comments of Lord Neuberger [in **Stack v Dowden**] . . . we accept that the search is primarily to ascertain the parties' actual shared intentions, whether expressed or to be inferred from their conduct. However, there are at least two exceptions. The first, which is not this case, is where the classic resulting trust presumption applies. Indeed, this would be rare in a domestic context, but might perhaps arise where domestic partners were also business partners . . . The second, which for reasons which will appear later is in our view also not this case but will arise much more frequently, is where it is clear that the beneficial interests are to be shared, but it is impossible to divine a common intention as to the proportions in which they are to be shared. In those two situations, the court is driven to impute an intention to the parties which they may never have had.

> 32. Lord Diplock, in **Gissing v Gissing** [1971] AC 886, 909, pointed out that, once the court was satisfied that it was the parties' common intention that the beneficial interest was to be shared in some proportion or other, the court might have to give effect to that common intention by determining what in all the circumstances was a fair share. And it is that thought which is picked up in the subsequent cases, culminating in the judgment of Chadwick LJ in **Oxley v Hiscock** [2005] Fam 211 . . . and in particular the passage in para 69 which was given qualified approval in **Stack v Dowden**: 'the answer is that each is entitled to that share which the court considers fair having regard to the whole course of dealing between them in relation to the property.'

> 33. Chadwick LJ was not there saying that fairness was the criterion for determining whether or not the property should be shared, but he was saying that the court might have to impute an intention to the parties as to the proportions in which the property would be shared. In deducing what the parties, as reasonable people, would have thought at the relevant time, regard would obviously be had to their whole course of dealing in relation to the property.

> 34. However, while the conceptual difference between inferring and imputing is clear, the difference in practice may not be so great. In this area, as in many others, the scope for inference is wide. The law recognises that a legitimate inference may not correspond to an individual's subjective state of mind. As Lord Diplock also put it in **Gissing v Gissing** [1971] AC 886, 906: 'As in so many branches of English law in which legal rights and obligations depend upon the intentions of the parties to a transaction, the relevant intention of each party is the intention which was reasonably understood by the other party to be manifested by that party's words or conduct notwithstanding that he did not consciously formulate that intention in his own mind or even acted with some different intention which he did not communicate to the other party.'

Lord Walker and Baroness Hale went on to say:

52 . . . The first issue is whether it was intended that the other party have any beneficial interest in the property at all. If he does, the second issue is what that interest is . . . [T]heir common intention has . . . to be deduced objectively from their conduct. If the evidence shows
a common intention to share beneficial ownership but does not show what shares were
intended, the court will have to proceed as at para 51(4) and (5) . . .

51 (4) In those cases where . . . is not possible to ascertain by direct evidence or by inference
what their actual intention was as to the shares in which they would own the property, 'the
answer is that each is entitled to that share which the court considers fair having regard to the
whole course of dealing between them in relation to the property': Chadwick LJ in *Oxley* v
Hiscock [2005] FAm 211, para 69. In our judgment, 'the whole course of dealing . . . in relation to the property' should be given a broad meaning, enabling a similar range of factors to
be taken into account as may be relevant to ascertaining the parties' actual intentions.

(5) Each case will turn on its own facts. Financial contributions are relevant but there are
many other factors which may enable the court to decide what shares were . . . fair . . .

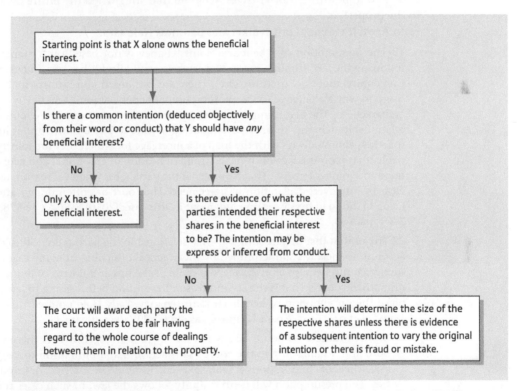

Figure 13.1 The shared home of X and Y. Purchased in the sole name of X. No declaration as to the
ownership of the beneficial interest

Property transferred into joint names but no declaration as to the ownership of the beneficial interest

Stage one: establishing a beneficial interest under a common intention constructive trust

The conclusions in Baroness Hale's opinion in **Stack v Dowden** were directed to the case of
a house transferred into the joint names of a couple, where both are responsible for any

mortgage, and where there is no express declaration of their beneficial interests. In such cases, she held that there is a presumption that the beneficial interests coincide with the legal estate: 'In the domestic consumer context, a conveyance into joint names indicates both legal and beneficial joint tenancy, unless and until the contrary is proved' (para 58). (Also, Lord Walker at para 33.)

In *Kernott* v *Jones* a house bought as a family home was transferred into the couple's joint names but there was no declaration as to how the beneficial interest was to be held.

Ms Jones (J) and Mr Kernott (K) met in 1981 and had two children together. In 1985 a house was bought which was intended to be their family home. The price paid was £30,000, with the £6,000 deposit paid exclusively from the proceeds of sale from J's previous home. The mortgage and upkeep on the house was shared between them. In 1986 they jointly took out a loan of £2,000 to build an extension. K did some of the work himself. The relationship deteriorated and in 1993 K moved out. From then onwards J lived in the property with the two children. In 1996 K bought his own house.

In 2007 J applied to the county court for a declaration under section 14 of the Trusts of Land and Appointment of Trustees Act 1996 that she owned the entire beneficial interest in the property.

In *Kernott* v *Jones*, Lord Walker and Baroness Hale said:

19 The presumption of a beneficial joint tenancy is not based on a mantra as to 'equity following the law' (though many non-lawyers would find it hard to understand the notion that equity might do anything else). There are two much more substantial reasons (which overlap) why a challenge to the presumption of beneficial joint tenancy is not to be lightly embarked on. The first is implicit in the nature of the enterprise. If a couple in an intimate relationship (whether married or unmarried) decide to buy a house or flat in which to live together, almost always with the help of a mortgage for which they are jointly and severally liable, that is on the face of things a strong indication of emotional and economic commitment to a joint enterprise. That is so even if the parties, for whatever reason, fail to make that clear by any overt declaration or agreement. The court has often drawn attention to this. Jacob LJ did so in his dissenting judgment in this case: [2010] EWCA Civ 578, [2010] 1 WLR 2401, para 90.

22 The notion that in a trusting personal relationship the parties do not hold each other to account financially is underpinned by the practical difficulty, in many cases, of taking any such account, perhaps after 20 years or more of the ups and downs of living together as an unmarried couple. That is the second reason for caution before going to law in order to displace the presumption of beneficial joint tenancy. Lady Hale pointed this out in *Stack* v *Dowden* at para 68 (see para 12 above), as did Lord Walker at para 33:

'In the ordinary domestic case where there are joint legal owners there will be a heavy burden in establishing to the court's satisfaction that an intention to keep a sort of balance-sheet of contributions actually existed, or should be inferred, or imputed to the parties. The presumption will be that equity follows the law. In such cases the court should not readily embark on the sort of detailed examination of the parties' relationship and finances that was attempted (with limited success) in this case.'

Without explaining why, the fact that a property was placed in joint names was assumed to lead to both parties having *some* share of the beneficial interest thus clearing the first hurdle, establishing that the claimant had *some* interest in the property.

Stage two: quantification

The current approach to quantifying the interest of a claimant who has proved that they are entitled to some share of the beneficial interest is to be found in *Stack* v *Dowden* (particularly the judgment of Lady Hale and *Kernott* v *Jones* (particularly the joint judgment of Lord Walker and Lady Hale).

In *Stack* v *Dowden* Lady Hale said:

69 In law, 'context is everything' and the domestic context is very different from the commercial world. Each case will turn on its own facts. Many more factors than financial contributions may be relevant to divining the parties' true intentions. These include: any advice or discussions at the time of the transfer which cast light upon their intentions then; the reasons why the home was acquired in their joint names; the reasons why (if it be the case) the survivor was authorised to give a receipt for the capital moneys; the purpose for which the home was acquired; the nature of the parties' relationship; whether they had children for whom they both had responsibility to provide a home; how the purchase was financed, both initially and subsequently; how the parties arranged their finances, whether separately or together or a bit of both; how they discharged the outgoings on the property and their other household expenses. When a couple are joint owners of the home and jointly liable for the mortgage, the inferences to be drawn from who pays for what may be very different from the inferences to be drawn when only one is owner of the home. The arithmetical calculation of how much was paid by each is also likely to be less important. It will be easier to draw the inference that they intended that each should contribute as much to the household as they reasonably could and that they would share the eventual benefit or burden equally. The parties' individual characters and personalities may also be a factor in deciding where their true intentions lay. In the cohabitation context, mercenary considerations may be more to the fore than they would be in marriage, but it should not be assumed that they always take pride of place over natural love and affection. At the end of the day, having taken all this into account, cases in which the joint legal owners are to be taken to have intended that their beneficial interests should be different from their legal interests will be very unusual.

70. This is not, of course, an exhaustive list. There may also be reason to conclude that, whatever the parties' intentions at the outset, these have now changed. An example might be where one party has financed (or constructed himself) an extension or substantial improvement to the property, so that what they have now is significantly different from what they had then.

Although Lady Hale said that 'cases in which the joint legal owners are to be taken to have intended that their beneficial interests should be different from their legal interests will be very unusual', in fact the court decided that this was an 'unusual' case and decided that Mrs Dowden was entitled to a 65 per cent share on the basis of what many argue are not really very unusual circumstances.

Ambulatory nature of constructive trusts

It is clear from a number of cases that the parties can make an agreement to change the original division of the beneficial interest. In joint names cases this is clear from *Kernott* v *Jones* and from *Aspden* v *Elvy* [2012] EWHC 1387 (Ch), [2012] All ER (D) 192 in sole names cases.

In *Stack* v *Dowden* Lady Hale said:

Furthermore, although the parties' intentions may change over the course of time, producing what my noble and learned friend, Lord Hoffmann, referred to in the course of argument as an 'ambulatory' constructive trust, at any one time their interests must be the same for all purposes. They cannot at one and the same time intend, for example, a joint tenancy with survivorship should one of them die while they are still together, a tenancy in common in equal shares should they separate on amicable terms after the children have grown up, and a tenancy in common in unequal shares should they separate on acrimonious terms while the children are still with them.

In *Kernott* **v** *Jones* the judgment of Lady Hale and Lord Walker it was stated:

> 14 It was also accepted (in **Stack v Dowden**) that the parties' common intentions might change over time, producing what Lord Hoffmann referred to in the course of argument as an "'ambulatory' constructive trust": Lady Hale, at para 62. An example, given in para 70, was where one party had financed or constructed an extension or major improvement to the property, so that what they had now was different from what they had first acquired. But of course there are other examples. The principal question in this case is whether this is one.

In *Aspden* **v** *Elvy* Behrens J (sitting as a deputy High Court judge) said:

> 93 The **Stack v Dowden** approach applies in a domestic context where two people buy property together and there is no express declaration of trust. As explained in **Jones v Kernott** the approach may be summarised as follows . . .

> 4. If the parties' intention changes subsequently the court is obliged to give effect to the changed intention. In such a case the court must first seek to ascertain the changed intention objectively and where possible give effect to that intention. Where that search proves fruitless the court is entitled to decide upon that intention by reference to what is fair.

While it is not absolutely certain it seems very likely that at stage one (establishing an agreement to vary the original shares) the agreement must be found objectively and cannot be imputed but at the second stage (quantification), if it is not possible to find an agreement, either express or inferred, the courts can impute an agreement to share on the basis of what is fair, taking account of the parties' whole course of dealings and conduct in relation to the property.

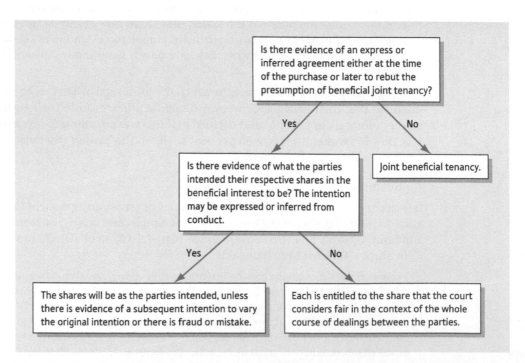

Figure 13.2 The shared home of X and Y. Purchased in the joint names of X and Y. No declaration as to the ownership of the beneficial interest

Issues that remain to be settled after Kernott v Jones

Do the principles in Kernott v Jones apply only to domestic property?

In both **Stack v Dowden** (Lady Hale) and **Kernott v Jones** (Lord Walker and Lady Hale) the judgments were directed to the case of a house transferred into the joint names of a married or unmarried couple, where both are responsible for any mortgage, and where there is no express declaration of their beneficial interests. In such cases, she held that there is a presumption that the beneficial interests coincide with the legal estate. For example in **Stack v Dowden**, Lady Hale said: '[I]n the domestic consumer context, a conveyance into joint names indicates both legal and beneficial joint tenancy, unless and until the contrary is proved'. (Para 58.)

There have been a number of cases on the establishment of common intention constructive trusts that are not the normal 'cohabiting couple sharing a home' cases.

In **Laskar v Laskar** [2008] 2 FLR 589 a mother and daughter bought a property intended as an investment and to produce income. It was conveyed into their joint names with no declaration as to how the beneficial interest was to be shared.

Lord Neuberger (sitting in the Court of Appeal) said:

> It is by no means clear to me that the approach laid down by Baroness Hale of Richmond in that case **Stack v Dowden** was intended to apply in a case such as this. In this case, although the parties were mother and daughter and not in that sense in an arm's length commercial relationship, they had independent lives, and, as I have already indicated, the purchase of the property was not really for the purpose of providing a home for them. The daughter hardly lived there at the time it was purchased, and did not live there much, if at all, afterwards, and the mother did not live there for long. The property was purchased primarily as an investment.
>
> Baroness Hale of Richmond's speech began by identifying the problem to be addressed as relating to 'a cohabiting couple' – see para [40] (and see para [14] of the speech of Lord Walker of Gestingthorpe). But a number of the remarks in the course of her speech indicate that her reasoning was intended to apply to other personal relationships, at least where the property is purchased as a home for two (or indeed more than two) people who are the legal owners – see especially at [the extract quoted above] with the reference to 'the domestic consumer context'. Accordingly I think His Honour Judge Behrens was right to conclude in **Adekunle and Ben v Ritchie** [2007] BPIR 1177 in the Leeds County Court that the reasoning in **Stack** applied to a case where a house was purchased by a mother and a son in joint names as a home for them both.

In **Geary v Rankine** [2012] EWCA Civ 555 the property was transferred into the name of one of the cohabiting parties only. Unlike **Stack v Dowden** and **Kernott v Jones**, the property was an investment property rather than a house bought as a family home. The property was bought to run as a guest house business. But the court applied **Kernott v Jones**.

Lord Justice Lewison LJ said:

> 18 . . . The applicable principles had been settled at the highest level in **Stack v Dowden** . . . and **Jones v Kernott** . . . The starting point is the legal title. In this case legal title was in Mr Rankine alone. Thus Mrs Geary has the burden of establishing some sort of implied trust; normally what is now termed a 'common intention' constructive trust. The burden is all the more difficult to discharge where, as here, the property was bought as an investment rather than as a home. The search is to ascertain the parties' actual shared intentions, whether express or to be inferred from their conduct . . .

Again in **Gallarotti v Sebastianelli** [2012] EWCA Civ 865 Arden LJ confirmed that, at least in broad terms, the principles from **Stack v Dowden** apply even in a situation where two male friends (not a cohabiting couple) bought a flat as a home. Arden LJ said:

6 In giving her reasons for the conclusion that the parties had equal shares in the Flat, the Recorder held that the onus of proof was on Mr Gallarotti. The Recorder held that the principles to be applied to a constructive trust were the same whether the parties were in a relationship such as that of husband and wife or were business associates, though the court might draw different inferences as to their conduct in the latter case. The Recorder held that 'in the light of the close relationship between the parties when the Flat was purchased' the analysis to be carried out 'is to be seen more in the domestic than in the commercial context' (Judgment, paragraph 106). I agree with all those points.

It remains to be seen to what extent, if any, the *Stack/Kernott* approach will be extended beyond the domestic setting, and how far and to what types of domestic settings it applies to. Certainly, in a commercial context it seems more likely that the application of resulting trust principles, where shares in the beneficial ownership reflect contributions to the purchase price, will provide solutions more in keeping with the probable intentions of the parties.

Do the principles in Kernott v Jones apply only where both are responsible for the mortgage?

In *Stack v Dowden* Lady Hale and in *Kernott v Jones* Lady Hale and Lord Walker said that the presumption that beneficial interest follows the legal estate applies where both parties are responsible for any mortgage. This leaves open two questions. First, will the *Stack/ Kernott* approach be applicable if there is no mortgage? Secondly, if there is a mortgage does it mean that if only one party is responsible for the mortgage the *Stack/Kernott* approach is not applicable? Would this be the case even if the other party made substantial contributions to the purchase and/or to the family expenses?

What is the current status of Rosset?

Despite criticisms of Lord Bridge's judgment in *Lloyds Bank v Rosset*, it is unclear to what extent, if at all, *Rosset* remains good law. Technically, neither *Stack v Dowden* nor *Kernott v Jones* overruled *Rosset*. But it would be naive to think that *Rosset* will now be slavishly followed.

Another issue relating to *Rosset* relates to the second limb of Lord Bridge's common intention trusts. Lord Bridge said, in the context of a common intention trust being inferred from conduct:

> In this situation direct contributions to the purchase price by the partner who is not the legal owner, whether initially or by payment of mortgage instalments, will readily justify the inference necessary to the creation of a constructive trust. But, as I read the authorities, it is at least extremely doubtful whether anything less will do.

Is Lord Bridge ruling out all other forms of contribution? Certainly, if he is purporting to exclude indirect contributions, this flies in the face of earlier cases and has been criticised in later cases.

An example of an indirect contribution would be where the woman goes to work and uses some of the money she earns to pay household bills, without which the man could not have made the mortgage payments.

In *Gissing v Gissing* [1970] 2 All ER 780 Lord Diplock said:

> Where the wife has made no initial contribution to the cash deposit and legal charges and no direct contribution to the mortgage instalments nor any adjustment to her contribution to other expenses of the household which it can be inferred was referable to the acquisition of the house, there is in the absence of evidence of an express agreement between the parties no material to justify the court in inferring that it was the common intention of the parties that

she should have any beneficial interest in a matrimonial home conveyed into the sole name of the husband, merely because she continued to contribute out of her own earnings or private income to other expenses of the household.

This can be interpreted as meaning that, if the wife had made an adjustment to her contributions to the other expenses of the household, Lord Diplock would have regarded it as a relevant contribution.

Burns v *Burns* [1984] 1 All ER 244 is another pre-*Rosset* case where the court accepted that indirect payments could suffice where they facilitated the other party making mortgage payments. In the case Fox LJ and May LJ considered indirect contributions to be sufficient. Fox LJ said:

> What is needed, I think, is evidence of a payment or payments by the plaintiff which it can be inferred was referable to the acquisition of the house . . . If there is substantial contribution by the woman to the family expenses, and the house was purchased by mortgage, her contribution is, indirectly, referable to the acquisition of the house, since, in one way or another, it enables the family to pay the mortgage instalments. Thus a payment could be said to be referable to the acquisition of the house, if for example the payer either (a) pays part of the purchase price or (b) contributes regularly to the mortgage instalments or (c) pays off part of the mortgage or (d) makes substantial financial contribution to the family expenses so as to enable the mortgage to be paid.

While not accepting that any payment/contribution, however small and/or irregular, would suffice, Fox LJ does approach the issue in a more liberal way than Lord Bridge.

Le Foe v *Le Foe* [2001] 2 FLR 970 is, potentially, an important case on indirect contributions to the purchase price in cases where there is no evidence of an express agreement as to how the beneficial interest would be held. The case is interesting both for the judge's view of Lord Bridge's judgment in *Lloyds Bank plc* v *Rosset* with respect to what type of conduct will, in the absence of evidence of an express agreement, justify the inference of trust and for the judge's approach to quantification of that interest.

Although this is a first-instance decision, it may well prove to be influential, and the approach of Nicholas Mostyn QC is mirrored in the conclusions of the Law Commission discussion paper, 'Sharing Homes' (see p. 387). The nub of the Law Commission paper is that a broader view should be taken of contributions etc. leading to the quantification of the size of any beneficial interest and that consideration should be given to indirect contributions to the purchase of property in considering whether a share in the beneficial interest has been established.

Simplifying the facts, H and W's house was in H's sole name. Although both H and W worked, H took responsibility for the mortgage and other outgoings relating to the house. W took responsibility for day-to-day domestic expenditure. W did make some payments from her own resources to cover, *inter alia*, mortgage arrears. There was no evidence that W's efforts or earnings enabled H to raise the mortgage or enabled him to make the mortgage repayments.

Later, a building society started possession proceedings. It was vital to W to establish that she was entitled to a share of the beneficial interest.

Nicholas Mostyn QC said that he had no doubt that the family economy depended for its function on W's earnings and that it was an arbitrary allocation of responsibility that H paid the mortgage, service charge and outgoings, whereas W paid for day-to-day domestic expenditure. He said that he clearly concluded that W contributed indirectly to the mortgage repayments, the principal of which furnished part of the consideration for the initial purchase price.

In situations where there is no evidence of an express agreement as to the sharing of the beneficial interest, Lord Bridge, in **Lloyds Bank plc v Rosset**, was generally thought to be stating unambiguously that only direct contributions to the purchase price or mortgage payments would suffice to create a constructive trust. In the instant case the claimant did not make any direct contributions but, the judge said, her assumption of the liability to pay some household expenses facilitated the making of the mortgage payments by the claimant's partner. This, the judge decided, amounted to an indirect contribution to the mortgage payments and this entitled her to a share in the beneficial interest.

In essence, Nicholas Mostyn QC stated that Lord Bridge, in **Lloyds Bank plc v Rosset**, was not saying that *only* direct contributions would suffice to establish a beneficial interest in the absence of an agreement as to how it should be shared. He was, the judge said, saying that it was only exceptionally that other behaviour would establish a share in the beneficial interest.

Nicholas Mostyn QC quoted the Lord Bridge statement, quoted above, in which he set out the two situations (express agreement and where there is no evidence of an agreement) that could lead to the finding of a shared beneficial interest and in which he said that, in the case where there was no evidence of an agreement, 'direct contributions to the purchase price by the partner who is not the legal owner, whether initially or by payment of mortgage instalments, will readily justify the inference necessary to the creation of a constructive trust. But, as I read the authorities, it is at least extremely doubtful whether anything less will do.'

Nicholas Mostyn QC then stated:

It is pertinent to note that in the final sentence of the passage I have quoted Lord Bridge of Harwich does not state the proposition he advances in absolute terms. In my view what Lord Bridge of Harwich is saying is that in the second class of case to which he is adverting, namely where there is no positive evidence of an express agreement between the parties as to how the equity is to be shared, and where the court has fallen back on inferring their common intention from the course of their conduct, it will only be exceptionally that conduct other than direct contributions to the purchase price, either in cash to the deposit or by contribution to the mortgage instalments, will suffice to draw the necessary inference of a common intention to share the equity.

I do not believe that in using the words 'direct contributions' Lord Bridge of Harwich meant to exclude the situation which obtains here. In **Gissing v Gissing** [1970] 2 All ER 780 Lord Diplock referred to just such a case. He said (at 795):

There is no suggestion that the wife's efforts or her earnings made it possible for the husband to raise the initial loan or the mortgage or that the relieving of the husband from the expense of buying clothing for herself and for their son was undertaken in order to enable him the better to meet the mortgage instalments or to repay the loan.

[Counsel] argued that because Lord Diplock was not addressing the scenario there mentioned I could not draw any conclusions as to what his decision would have been if he had. But I believe that Lord Diplock is saying quite clearly that if that was the situation, which I find to be the case here, then such would suffice to draw the necessary inference.

The same point was addressed by May LJ in **Burns v Burns** [[1984] 1 All ER 244].

[Counsel] has pointed to the fact that May LJ addresses indirect contributions to the mortgage only in the context of the claimant having made an initial direct contribution to the deposit. He says that in the next scenario, where that party has made no such contribution, the reference is only to direct contributions to the mortgage. I agree that May LJ does not directly address the position that we have here; namely where there was no initial cash contribution but only an indirect contribution to the mortgage. But I believe that a fair reading of his judgment is that such a state of affairs should suffice to enable the necessary inference to be drawn. Otherwise these cases would be decided by reference to mere accidents of fortune, being the arbitrary allocation of financial responsibility as between the parties.

I therefore conclude that by virtue of her indirect contributions to the mortgage I am entitled to infer that the parties commonly intended that W should have a beneficial interest in the former matrimonial home.

It is beyond doubt that if the woman simply performs family 'duties' such as looking after the house and the family this will not be treated as sufficient to entitle her to an interest. They do not amount to a contribution to the acquisition of the home. (See, e.g., *Gissing* v *Gissing* [1970] 2 All ER 780.) An illustration of this is to be found in *Windler* v *Whitehall* [1990] 2 FLR 505, where Millett J held that there was no evidence of an express common intention and there was no conduct referable to the acquisition of property. The woman had made no contribution to the purchase price. One of her arguments was that her interest derived from her performing housework and other domestic tasks. This was rejected.

Is detrimental reliance still necessary?

Lord Bridge in *Rosset* was clear that there must be detrimental reliance by the claimant, although he did not express with clarity what behaviour would amount to detrimental reliance.

In *Stack* v *Dowden* and in *Kernott* v *Jones* detrimental reliance was not mentioned. Does that mean that it was no longer a requirement?

Some recent Court of Appeal cases seem to assume that detrimental reliance is still needed. For example, in *Gallarotti* v *Sebastianelli* [2012] EWCA Civ 865 Arden LJ said:

> 5. . . . The Recorder relied for her conclusions on a common intention constructive trust, that is, a trust arising by operation of law where parties agree that beneficial ownership should be held in a particular way but do not follow the formalities required by law and where one of the parties has suffered detriment in reliance on the agreement . . .

How does imputed intention differ from inferred intention?

In *Stack* v *Dowden*, Lord Neuberger set out what is generally agreed to be an accurate definition of inference and imputation:

> 126. An inferred intention is one which is objectively deduced to be the subjective actual intention of the parties, in the light of their actions and statements. An imputed intention is one which is attributed to the parties, even though no such actual intention can be deduced from their actions and statements, and even though they had no such intention. Imputation involves concluding what the parties would have intended, whereas inference involves concluding what they did intend.

But in reality is there a difference between an inferred and an imputed intention? In *Kernott* v *Jones* the Justice's views on this point were not consistent.

Lord Walker and Lady Hale said:

> However, while the conceptual difference between inferring and imputing is clear, the difference in practice may not be so great. In this area, as in many others, the scope for inference is wide.

Lord Collins said:

> 65. That said, it is my view that in the present context the difference between inference and imputation will hardly ever matter (as Lord Walker and Lady Hale recognise . . .), and that what is one person's inference will be another person's imputation . . .

Lord Kerr said:

67. I agree that this appeal should be allowed. There are differences of some significance in the reasoning that underlies the joint judgment of Lord Walker and Lady Hale and that contained in Lord Wilson's judgment. I agree with Lord Collins that these are both terminological and conceptual. I am less inclined to agree, however, that the divergence in reasoning is unlikely to make a difference in practice. While it may well be that the outcome in many cases will be the same, whether one infers an intention or imputes it, that does not mean that the process by which the result is arrived at is more or less the same. Indeed, it seems to me that a markedly and obviously different mode of analysis will generally be required. Before elaborating briefly on that proposition, let me turn very shortly to the areas in which, as I see it, there is consensus among the other members of the court.

72. It is hardly controversial to suggest that the parties' intention should be given effect to where it can be ascertained and that, although discussions between them will always be the most reliable basis on which to draw an inference as to that intention, these are not the only circumstances in which that exercise will be possible. There is a natural inclination to prefer inferring an intention to imputing one. If the parties' intention can be inferred, the court is not imposing a solution . . . But the conscientious quest to discover the parties' actual intention should cease when it becomes clear either that this is simply not deducible from the evidence or that no common intention exists. It would be unfortunate if the concept of inferring were to be strained so as to avoid the less immediately attractive option of imputation.

In summary, therefore, I believe that the court should anxiously examine the circumstances in order, where possible, to ascertain the parties' intention but it should not be reluctant to recognise, when it is appropriate to do so, that inference of an intention is not possible and that imputation of an intention is the only course to follow.

74. The reason that I question the aptness of the notion of imputing an intention is that, in the final analysis, the exercise is wholly unrelated to ascertainment of the parties' views . . . In many ways, it would be preferable to have a stark choice between deciding whether it is possible to deduce what their intention was and, where it is not, deciding what is fair, without elliptical references to what their intention might have – or should have – been. But imputing intention has entered the lexicon of this area of law and it is probably impossible to discard it now.

Lord Wilson favoured imputation but even he said it was restricted to stage two. To extend it to stage one would, he said 'require careful thought'.

Having agreed that imputation is permissible at stage two in the absence of actual or inferred intention, the Justices could not agree if, in the case, it was possible to infer the intention of the parties or if the intention had to be imputed.

While Lord Collins agreed with Lady Hale and Lord Walker that in the case the changed intention of the parties could be inferred, Lord Wilson and Lord Kerr said they were unable to agree that an intention could be inferred but did arrive at the same result by imputing an intention.

So while inferring an intention and imputing an intention may be, in theory, distinct concepts, not all the justices agree that there is any real difference between the two.

Also, there was no agreement as to whether or not an agreement could be inferred in the case or if the decision should be based on an imputed decision. More uncertainty for claimants and would-be claimants.

Should a presumption of intention (e.g. of equality of ownership of the beneficial interest) be rebutted by an imputed intention?

It has been argued that a presumption should not be rebutted by an imputed intention. The argument continues, if there is not sufficient evidence of intention of the parties (express or inferred from conduct) the presumption of equity following the law should stand.

Improvements

It is clear from the cases that paying for or making minor improvements to property will not of themselves be sufficient to entitle the person responsible to a share of the beneficial interest. For example, in *Pettitt v Pettitt* [1969] 2 All ER 385, the man redecorated the home and had paid to have the garden improved. This was not sufficient to found a claim to part of the beneficial interest.

In the case of a married couple, s 37 of the Matrimonial Proceedings and Property Act 1970 states that where a spouse contributes money or money's worth to the substantial improvement of real or personal property they will, subject to any contrary agreement, be treated as having acquired, by virtue of the improvement, a share or an enlarged share in the beneficial interest as may seem just to the court in all the circumstances. This provision applies to any property real or personal and not merely to the matrimonial home. It does not matter whether the spouse paid for the improvements or did them themselves. In order for the section to apply, the improvement must be 'substantial'. This is a question of fact. The section applies whenever there are court proceedings and not merely to proceedings between the spouses.

The Civil Partnership Act 2004 s 65 contains similar provisions which apply where one of the civil partners makes a 'substantial contribution' to the improvement of property in which one or other of the partners has an interest.

Where these statutory provisions are not relevant (because the parties are not married or are not in a civil partnership), a claim to a beneficial interest might be based on a common intention trust (or perhaps estoppel – discussed below). However, it is clear that merely improving the property of another will not *per se* result in a share of the beneficial interest. In *Thomas v Fullerton-Brown* [1988] 1 FLR 237, the Court of Appeal restated the position that, in the absence of an express agreement or a common intention inferred from the conduct of the parties, the mere fact that improvements were made to property would not entitle the person effecting the improvements to an interest in the property. On the facts, the court decided that the work was, in fact, performed in return for rent-free accommodation.

Proprietary estoppel

It is possible for a spouse (or other claimant) to establish an interest in the family home under the doctrine of proprietary estoppel. Indeed, it has been argued that the distinction between proprietary estoppel and the constructive trust is now blurred and perhaps disappearing. Evidence of this may be found in the approach of Lord Bridge in *Lloyds Bank plc v Rosset* [1990] 1 All ER 1111. Support for this view can also be found, for example, in the judgment of Browne-Wilkinson V-C in *Grant v Edwards*.

In *Stack v Dowden* [2007] 2 All ER 729 Lord Walker expressed his view on the argument that (at least in the context of claims to shares in the 'family' home) the doctrines of proprietary estoppel and constructive trust should be assimilated. He said that proprietary estoppel consists of asserting an equitable claim against the conscience of the true owner. It is a 'mere equity'. It is satisfied by the minimum award necessary to do justice. This can sometimes result in nothing more than an award of a sum of money. However, a common intention constructive trust identifies the true beneficial owner(s) and the size(s) of their beneficial interests.

In order to invoke proprietary estoppel, the woman must establish that she has acted to her detriment on the faith of a belief, which was known to and encouraged by the other partner that she has been or is going to be given a right in or over property of that other partner. The court will not permit the other partner to insist on his strict legal rights if to do so would be inconsistent with her belief. If she satisfies the court that the requirements have been met, the object of the court will be to find a remedy which would be 'the minimum equity to do justice to the plaintiff': *Crabb* v *Arun* [1975] 3 All ER 865. This will not necessarily result in the woman being awarded the interest which would fulfil her expectation. The usual approach of the courts is to award that remedy which would reverse the detriment. This may result in the courts awarding an interest in the property (as in *Pascoe* v *Turner* [1979] 2 All ER 945) or perhaps a mere licence to occupy the house. The courts will not, however, make an order which in the context of the situation would be unworkable.

For example, in *Burrows* v *Sharp* [1991] Fam Law 67, a woman aged 77 lived in a council house caring for her handicapped daughter. She learnt of her right to buy the house at a discount. She agreed with her granddaughter and her (the granddaughter's) husband that she would buy the house and that they would pay the mortgage instalments. The tenant agreed that she would make a will leaving the house to the couple on the basis that they would live there, making a home for the handicapped daughter. She later executed such a will. It was initially planned that the couple would also keep paying the rent on their flat but it became clear that they could not afford to pay both the rent and the mortgage instalments. The three agreed that they would all live in the house, together with the handicapped daughter. The parties soon fell out. At first instance the judge ordered, reflecting the agreement, that the house be held on trust for sale for the woman, for life remainder to the couple as beneficial joint tenants. So long as the couple continued to pay the mortgage instalments all three would have the right to live there. The Court of Appeal said that, in view of the relationship between the parties, the order was unworkable. The court must be concerned to do justice, but in a manner which was workable. The fact that the judge at first instance tried to make an order reflecting the agreement of the parties was not, in this case, the correct approach. Basing the order on proprietary estoppel, the Court of Appeal decided that the couple should give up possession of the house and that the woman should pay them the relevant expenditure plus interest. These expenses were the cost of the instalments less the rent saved on the flat they formerly occupied, the conveyancing costs and other expenses relating to the house.

See 'Proprietary estoppel' in Chapter 12, p. 345, for the facts of *Matharu*.

In *Matharu* v *Matharu* [1994] 2 FLR 597, the dispute over ownership of the family home was settled using the principles of proprietary estoppel. In answer to a claim for possession by the husband, the wife claimed an interest in the property. The court did not award her an interest but did bar the husband's claim. This, in effect, gave her a roof over her head. The case did not even award her a licence to occupy. This may be thought rather a hard decision.

See Chapter 12 (p. 342) for more on proprietary estoppel.

Property other than a home

The cases establish that no special trust or property rules apply to the resolution of disputes regarding the ownership of the home. Therefore, the principles discussed above are as relevant to deciding the beneficial ownership of businesses, leasehold property or pure personalty as they are to determining the beneficial ownership of the 'family home'.

The particular problems arising in relation to joint bank accounts often occur. For example, a husband may decide to transfer a bank account that he opened with his own money into the joint names of himself and his wife. At a future date the question of the ownership of the funds in the account may arise. For example, there may be a dispute as to ownership if the couple split up or when one of them dies. In some cases the presumptions of resulting trust and advancement may provide a solution. If a husband transfers his account into joint names, the presumption of advancement will arise and, unless rebutted, the funds in the account will belong to the wife on the death of her husband. The presumption was rebutted in the case of ***Marshall*** v ***Crutwell*** (1875) LR 20 Eq 328.

In the case a husband transferred his bank account into the joint names of himself and his wife. He was very ill at the time and he thought it would be convenient if the wife could use the account to save him effort. All the cheques drawn by the wife were at his instruction and all were to pay for household expenses for which the husband was responsible. The court decided that the transfer had merely been made in order to allow the husband to run his financial affairs in a convenient manner. The husband had no intention of passing any beneficial ownership to his wife.

This case may be contrasted with ***Re Figgis*** [1968] 1 All ER 999, where the court decided that the presumption of advancement had not been rebutted. The court held that a bank account which the husband had placed in joint names some 50 years before he died was intended to provide for the wife and so on her death the funds in the account belonged to her.

Reform

Objective 5

Many jurisdictions acted ahead of England and Wales in giving cohabitants legal rights (e.g. Australia, Belgium, Canada, Denmark, Finland, France, Germany, Hungary, Iceland, the Netherlands, New Zealand, South Africa, Scotland, Spain and Switzerland, as well as some states of the USA).

In England and Wales, despite many calls for legislative reform from academics and judges, nothing has yet happened to address the key issues. There have been at least two non-government bills in the past few years that attempted to address the problems in this area but none has been passed into law. Any developments in the law have emerged from case law.

But one area where there has been reform is in the area of same-sex relationships, where the Civil Partnership Act 2004 has given same-sex partners who formally register their partnership many of the rights that married couples have in relation to property. (Civil partnerships are discussed at p. 356.) But although the same rules will apply to civil partners when their partnership is formally ended as apply to a married couple who divorce, in many other situations (for example, when one party dies or becomes bankrupt) the rules outlined above will apply, with all their uncertainty and attendant expense.

In England and Wales the key issues for debate included a wide range of homesharers, including same-sex couples, opposite-sex couples, those who share a home merely as 'friends', and children living in a parent's house in order to look after the parent.

It has been argued that any solution should not depend on judicial action, or at least not on judicial action alone. A number of statutory approaches are possible, it has been argued. One possibility is that the provisions of the Matrimonial Causes Act 1973 should be extended to cohabitees. This approach would involve difficulty of definition – who are cohabitees for the purpose of the legislation? Presumably, a very short period of cohabitation would not suffice? Would the test be: is the couple living as husband and wife? Would the fact that there were children of the couple make any difference to the decision? Would it cover same-sex couples? This may not be an ideal solution in many cases of cohabitation. It may be that a couple have decided not to marry, but to cohabit, because they have a positive wish not to be married and not to become 'bound' by the legal consequences of marriage. Additionally, this approach would not help in cases involving other types of homesharers, e.g. two friends who simply decide to live together in the same house and a house is bought, or cohabiting same-sex couples.

A second possible approach is via a statutory scheme under which the court was able to award the claimant financial redress rather than a share in the property, perhaps on the basis of reasonable expectation. This could allow a claim by a sharer who contributed to the family by looking after the house or family, perhaps having given up paid employment to do so.

Alternatively, the statutory scheme could include the possibility of a sharer being awarded a proprietary right, based on such contributions.

The Government's Consultation Document, 'Supporting Families', published on 5 November 1998, raised the possibility of pre-nuptial agreements (subject to some exceptions). (At the moment such contracts are not enforceable, but can have evidential weight in cases where the agreement is relevant to the issues. The justification that is normally used for unenforceability is that such agreements may be seen as undermining marriage, dealing as they do with what happens if the marriage breaks down.) These could be used to agree on the distribution of property, including a family home. Such contracts are common in other jurisdictions, especially within the USA. The suggestion is not without problems. First, in some relationships there is inequality of bargaining power and any agreement may well reflect that inequality. This would result in the 'weaker' party, the party that arguably the law should seek to protect, being treated disadvantageously. Many couples on deciding to marry do not consider the possibility of the marriage failing and so may in any case not make such an agreement. Any agreements that are made would need to be reviewed at regular intervals and whenever there is a significant change in their circumstances, e.g. the birth of a child, the purchase of a new home. If the original agreement is designed to cover the marriage however long it lasts, it would have to be drawn in the most general of terms and may be of little real use. As the initial agreement will in many cases have been prepared by a lawyer, any revision or new agreement will in many cases be drafted by a lawyer. This will cause expenses to be incurred. Will this put couples off making the agreements? Additionally, it is no doubt the case that on divorce or separation arguments may break out regarding possible undue influence, inequality of bargaining power, etc. The document does not deal with the issue of same-sex couples.

The Law Commission began to deliberate on the problems of homesharers many years ago and particularly announced in 1995 in its Sixth Programme of Law Reform that it would investigate the issues relating to the ownership of the family home in order to address the current uncertain, unfair and illogical state of the law.

In **Midland Bank v Cooke** [1995] 4 All ER 562, Waite LJ said:

> The economic and social significance of home-ownership in modern society, and the frequency with which such cases . . . are coming before the courts, suggest that the Law Commission's intervention is well-timed and has the potential to save a lot of human heartache as well as public expenditure.

Waite LJ also said:

> Equity has traditionally been a system which matches established principle to the demand of social change . . . There will inevitably be numerous couples married or unmarried, who have no discussion about ownership and who, perhaps advisedly, make no agreement about it. It

would be anomalous, against that background, to create a range of homebuyers who were beyond the pale of equity's assistance in formulating a fair presumed basis for the sharing of beneficial title.

After several false dawns, the much anticipated Law Commission paper was finally published in July 2002 – Law Commission discussion paper, 'Sharing Homes' (Law Com. No. 278). (Note it was a discussion paper, not a consultation paper.)

The discussion paper covered not only unmarried couples, but also same-sex couples, and friends, relatives and others who may be living together for reasons of companionship or care and support. It was greeted, in the main, with disappointment. The paper contained no real proposals for reform but rather restated the problems and issues, putting forward a framework for further public debate and consideration by the Government.

The paper did make a strong recommendation that all those entering into homeshares should seek legal advice and that the courts should relax their attitude towards the types of contributions that will lead to a share in the beneficial ownership. However, as has been noted elsewhere in this chapter, despite judicial advice couples on the whole tend not to contemplate the relationship breaking down and do not think about, let alone agree on, the ownership of the equitable interest in their home. But the overarching conclusion was that the Law Commission, while accepting the unsatisfactory state of the law, did not think that it was possible to devise a statutory scheme for ascertaining and quantifying beneficial interests across the range of homesharing situations.

This is in contrast, as the Law Commission accepted, to the approach in a number of other jurisdictions and with the ideas put forward in a paper published (also in July 2002) by the Law Society, 'Cohabitation: proposals for reform'.

The provisions also leave many 'homesharers' exposed to the problems outlined above. For example, opposite-sex cohabiting couples and those who simply decide to share a home will still be exposed to the vagaries of the existing law.

The Government stated that some unmarried opposite-sex couples were under the mistaken impression that they already had a legally recognised status as 'common law' husband and wife and restated the fact that there is no such status in England and Wales. This misconception, the Government conceded, can lead to difficulties – for example, one partner might be left financially vulnerable after the breakdown of their relationship because the partners had not made any clear arrangements or agreements about ownership of their shared property or property bought with joint funds. While the Government recognised this problem, it was stated to be a different situation from that of same-sex couples who want to formalise their relationship and cannot. The Government did not believe that the solution for those opposite-sex couples, who choose not to marry, is to offer them another way of entering into an equally formal kind of legal commitment to each other. This was, the Government decided, an entirely separate issue from the legal recognition of same-sex partnerships and no legislation was planned which would benefit unmarried opposite-sex couples. Also there were no plans to introduce legislation that would address the problems of other homesharers (siblings, flatmates, etc.).

In May 2006, following up on the discussion paper 'Sharing Homes' (Law Com. No. 278), the Law Commission published a consultation paper, 'Cohabitation: the financial consequences of relationship breakdown' (Consultation Paper 179).

Following on from the discussion paper and the consultation paper (above), on 31 July 2007 the Law Commission published its report, 'Cohabitation: the financial consequences of relationship breakdown' (Law Com. No. 307). The report deals only with cohabiting couples and not with others sharing housing, e.g. it does not apply to friends sharing a house, or to carers sharing a house with the person they care for, or to brother and sister (or other relatives) sharing a house. The proposals go some way to addressing the issues and uncertainties discussed in this chapter. However, unlike most Law Commission reports, it does not contain a draft bill. So, if its proposals are to be implemented, not only must the Government accept the proposals but also time and resources will have to be found to produce a bill. Some have argued that if the proposals are passed into law it may have the effect of encouraging people to cohabit rather than marry.

The proposals fall short of giving all cohabitees rights on the breakdown of their relationship and does not put those cohabitees who may have rights into the same position as spouses.

The proposals only give rights to cohabitees who have had a child together or who have cohabited for a minimum period of time.

It is possible to 'opt out' of the scheme.

The scheme applies only to applicants who have made 'qualifying contributions to the relationship giving rise to certain enduring consequences at the point of separation'.

The extract below is taken from the Executive Summary of the report:

Key Features of the Scheme: –

1.13 We do not think that all cohabitants should be able to obtain financial relief in the event of separation. We recommend that a remedy should only be available where:

- the couple satisfied certain eligibility requirements;
- the couple had not agreed to disapply the scheme; and
- the applicant had made qualifying contributions to the relationship giving rise to certain enduring consequences at the point of separation.

Eligibility requirements

1.14 The recommended scheme would apply only to cohabitants who had had a child together or who had lived together for a specified number of years (a 'minimum duration requirement'). The Report does not make a specific recommendation as to what the minimum duration requirement should be, but suggests that a period of between two and five years would be appropriate.

Disapplying the scheme

1.15 We reject an 'opt-in' scheme, which couples would be required to sign up to in order to be able to claim financial remedies on separation. Consultation confirmed our view that an opt-in scheme would not deal effectively with the problems of hardship created by the current law. Vulnerable individuals would be no more likely to protect themselves by registering than they are currently to marry. We are also aware that to introduce an opt-in scheme would effectively create a new status of 'registered cohabitant'. This would jeopardise the support of many who have expressed support for reform, but who are concerned to protect the institution of marriage, such as the Mission and Public Affairs Council of the Church of England.

1.16 Instead, we recommend that, as a default position, the scheme should be available between all eligible cohabitants. However, we understand the strongly held view that it is wrong to force cohabitants who have not chosen to marry or form a civil partnership into a particular legal regime against their will. We agree that it is very important to respect the autonomy of couples who wish to determine for themselves the legal consequences of their personal relationships.

We therefore recommend that a new scheme should allow couples, subject to necessary protections, to disapply the statute by means of an opt-out agreement, leaving them free to make their own financial arrangements.

Qualifying contributions and their consequences: the basis for remedies.

1.17 It would not be sufficient for applicants simply to demonstrate that they were eligible for financial relief and that the couple had not made a valid opt-out agreement disapplying the scheme. In order to obtain a remedy, applicants would have to prove that they had made qualifying contributions to the parties' relationship which had given rise to certain enduring consequences at the point of separation.

1.18 The scheme would therefore be very different from that which applies between spouses on divorce. Simply cohabiting, for however long, would not give rise to any presumed entitlement to share in any pool of property. Nor would the scheme grant remedies simply on the basis of a party's needs following separation, whether by making orders for maintenance or otherwise.

Despite all the calls for legislative reform and all the issues of uncertainty and expense that most accept exist in this area of law, the government seems unwilling to act. In March 2012 the government issued its annual report on the implementation of Law Commission proposals. On the proposals made, the report 'Cohabitation: the financial consequences of relationship breakdown' (LC 307) (31.07.2007) stated:

> 23 The Government considered the research on the impact of the Family Law (Scotland) Act 2006 along with the proposals set out in the Law Commission's report and announced in September 2011 that the recommendations for reform would not be taken forward in this Parliament. The Scottish legislation did not provide a sufficient basis for a change in the law and the family justice system is currently in a transitional period with major reforms on the horizon.

Subsequently Lady Hale made yet another judicial plea for reform. In the Scottish decision of **Gow v Grant** [2012] UKSC 29, a case on section 28 of the Family Law (Scotland) Act 2006, under which cohabitants in Scotland can apply to the court for financial provision when the cohabitation has ended otherwise than by death, Lady Hale (who delivered a concurring judgment) said that there were lessons to be learnt from the Scottish case in England and Wales. Lady Hale also supported the view of Law Commissioner, Professor Elizabeth Cooke, that reform should not be delayed until the next parliament.

The Liberal Democrat peer Lord Marks introduced a private members' bill – the Cohabitation Rights bill. But the 2013–14 session of parliament has prorogued and this bill will make no further progress. But without the support of the government it was always likely that the bill would only amount to another unsuccessful attempt to change to law.

The bill was based on the 2007 Law Commission recommendations, and proposed an 'opt out' system that would automatically bring cohabiting couples within scope unless they chose not to.

Under the draft bill, cohabiting couples would have fallen within the scope of the rules if they had lived together as a couple for two years or more, or if they had children. (The Law Commission did not specify the number of years required.) Cohabitants would have been given similar rights to married couples, although not as far reaching.

The court would have been able to make an order where the applicant has made a qualifying contribution resulting in him/her being at a disadvantage or the respondent retaining a benefit, and the court considers it just and equitable to do so.

There is more waiting and more couples are exposed to the existing, unsatisfactory, law.

Another related area where reform may be forthcoming is in the area of marital property agreements (pre-nups and post-nups). If such agreements became enforceable, it would avoid the need for a good many stressful, expensive and unpredictable property claims.

The Supreme Court in ***Radmacher* v *Granatino*** [2010] UKSC 42 recognised the potential legal effect of pre-nuptial agreements, but each agreement, under *Radmacher*, is considered on a case-by-case basis.

Currently pre-nuptial and post-nuptial agreements cannot be enforced as contracts and they cannot take away the powers of the courts to make property orders. The only option is to ask the court to make an order that reflects the terms of the agreement.

On 11 January 2011 the Law Commission published a consultation paper (Marital Property Agreements (Law Com. Consultation Paper No. 198) which reviewed the current law of marital property agreements (pre-nuptial and post-nuptial) and discussed options for reform. On 26 February 2014 the Law Commission report 'Matrimonial Property, Needs and Agreements' was published (Law Com. No. 343). The report recommends that legislation introduces 'qualifying nuptial agreements'. These would be enforceable contracts and would not be subject to the scrutiny of the courts. They would allow the parties to make binding agreements regarding the financial arrangements on divorce or dissolution.

Baroness Deech introduced the Divorce (Financial Provisions) Bill, in February 2014. But the 2013–14 session of parliament was prorogued without the bill passing through all the necessary stages to become law. As with almost all private members' bills, there was only a small chance of the bill being passed into law but it did, at least, give the issues some much needed publicity.

The bill covered a range of issues relating to financial provision on the divorce or dissolution of marriage of a couple. It also would have applied to civil partners. Under the bill pre- and post-nuptial agreements would have been binding, subject to certain safeguards.

If the law had been changed giving legal effect to such agreements, clearly it would have impacted greatly on the distribution of property on divorce or on the dissolution of a civil partnership.

Summary

- If relationships break down there may be competing claims to the ownership or beneficial ownership of a shared home but the issue of ownership may arise in a variety of other situations such as the death or bankruptcy of one of the parties.

- The courts have statutory powers exercisable on granting a divorce, a decree of nullity or a decree of judicial separation (or when a civil partnership is formally ended) under which the court can decide how property should be owned by the parties.

- Normally, where a conveyance or transfer expressly deals with both the legal and the beneficial interests in the property, this is conclusive.

- *Stack* v *Dowden* and *Jones* v *Kernott* have had an enormous impact and in particular have reinforced that the common intention constructive trust is the key to settling property disputes. There are different approaches where the legal title is in joint names as opposed to being in a sole name.

- It is widely agreed, particularly by the judiciary and academics, that there is an urgent need for reform. But despite various proposals for change, the current government is not willing to introduce legislation to reform the law.

Further reading

The Home

J Freeman, 'Presuming too much?' (2007) 151 (20) SJ 660.
Discusses the legal framework by which the courts resolve property disputes between unmarried cohabiting couples on the breakdown of their relationship in the light of *Stack v Dowden*.

K Fretwell, 'The cautionary tale of *Kernott v Jones*' (2012) 42 Fam Law 69.
Deals with *Kernott v Jones*, commenting on those areas where there was disagreement amongst the judges in relation to inferring and imputing an intention.

E Hicks and S Amin, 'Shared intentions' (2007) 157 (7279) NLJ 922.
Considers *Stack v Dowden*. Criticises the lack of guidance given by the Lords in the case and explains the importance placed on the intention of the parties in apportioning ownership where the property was in joint ownership. Considers the approach which would be taken where property is only in one name.

S Jones, 'A question of fairness?' (2011) 161 (7492) NLJ 1660.
Deals with the Supreme Court judgment in *Kernott v Jones* where there was no express declaration of trust and the house was in joint names. The issue of fairness is discussed together with the distinction between inferred and imputed intention.

J Lee, '"And the waters began to subside": imputing intention under *Jones v Kernott*' Lawyer Conv (2012) 5, 421–8.
Discusses the Chancery Division decision in *Aspden v Elvy* [2012] All ER (D) 192 (May) as to whether the claimant had a beneficial interest in a converted barn where he had originally owned the barn, but had transferred it into the sole name of the defendant, his former unmarried partner. He had contributed substantial amounts of physical work and finance towards its conversion into a house. The claimant alleged that the barn was intended to be for their shared occupation as a couple. Discusses how the court imputed the couple's intention as to their respective shares of the property, using the principles of the Supreme Court ruling in *Jones v Kernott*.

J Mee, '*Jones v Kernott*: inferring and imputing in Essex' [2012] Conv 2, 167.
Discusses the inference/imputation debate and if the decision in *Jones v Kernott* was, on the facts, correct. Deals with uncertainties remaining after the case.

F O'Sullivan, 'Securing greater rights for cohabitants' SJ (2013) 157(40) 15.
Discusses the Cohabitation Rights bill 2013. Considers factors that the courts would be required to take into account in deciding whether to make a financial provision order in favour of one partner in an unmarried couple whose relationship has broken down.

M Pawlowski, 'Beneficial entitlement – no longer doing justice?' [2007] Conv 354.
Discusses *Stack v Dowden* and the size of each legal owner's share of the equity in the family home. Looks at whether indirect financial contributions give rise to a beneficial interest under a constructive trust and notes the relevance of the doctrine of proprietary estoppel.

M Pawlowski, 'Joint ownership and beneficial entitlement: *Stack v Dowden*' [2007] Fam Law 606.
Explores the issue of the beneficial entitlement to the family home where the legal title is jointly owned, but where there has not been an express declaration of a beneficial joint tenancy. Discusses *Stack v Dowden*.

M Pawlowski, 'Constructive trusts and improvements to property' (2009) 39 Fam Law 680–6.
Examines the principles applicable when determining if a non-owning cohabitee has a beneficial interest over a property by way of a constructive trust due to the improvements made to the property.

M Pawlowski, 'Imputed intention and joint ownership – a return to common sense: *Jones* v *Kernott*' [2012] Conv 2, 149.
Discusses *Jones* v *Kernott* in the Supreme Court. Deals with the issue of imputing an intention and discusses the extent to which the case impacts on single and joint ownership cases.

M Pawlowksi 'Declarations of trust in the family home' TEL & TJ (2013) 145, April, 4–6.
Discusses the Court of Appeal judgment in *Pankhania* v *Chandegra* (2012) EWCA Civ 1438: does an express declaration of trust setting out the beneficial interests in a house rule out the possibility of interests based on contributions or improvements under a constructive trust?

R Probert, 'Cohabitants and joint ownership: the implications of *Stack* v *Dowden*' [2007] Fam Law 924.
Analyses the implications of *Stack* v *Dowden* on joint ownership of property by cohabiting couples. Examines the prevalence of joint ownership and express declarations of ownership by cohabitees. Questions whether a beneficial joint tenancy should be inferred from a legal joint tenancy.

J West, 'Redefining fairness' (2011) 161 (7490) NLJ 1571.
Discusses *Kernott* v *Jones* and concludes that this complex area of law has become a minefield.

J West and A Matheson, 'Love, life and the law' (2012) 156 (28) SJ 14.
Discusses case law, including *Kernott* v *Jones* and *Stack* v *Dowden*, relating the ownership and division of property. Questions the approach of the judiciary to developing the law.

M Yip, 'The rules applying to unmarried cohabitants' family home: *Jones* v *Kernott*', [2012] Conv 2, 159.
Considers if *Jones* v *Kernott* establishes a set of rules that can be applied when deciding the interests of cohabitees in the shared home. Also deals with the inference/imputation debate and the concept of ambulatory trusts.

14

The office of trustee: appointment, retirement and removal

Objectives

After reading this chapter you should be able to:

1. Understand and explain the role of trustees and understand that their position, duties and powers are governed by the terms of the trust, by a range of statutory provisions and by rules and principles developed by the courts.

2. Understand and explain the fiduciary position occupied by trustees and the impact of this on the ways in which they administer and manage the trust.

3. Understand and explain the general rule that trustees act without payment, and the common law and statutory exceptions to the rule.

4. Understand and explain how the common law standard of care expected of trustees has been modified under s 1(1) of the Trustee Act 2000 for a range of situations.

5. Understand and explain how a clearly worded provision in the trust documents can exclude or modify the liability of trustees for breaches of trust, including failure to carry out their prescribed duties or exceeding their powers.

6. Explain the methods of appointing trustees.

7. Understand and explain when and how a trustee's appointment may end or be ended.

Introduction

Objective
1

This chapter will examine the nature of the trustee and his office and will then proceed to discuss the appointment and removal of trustees. In many situations the legal principles and rules which will be discussed and which have been developed over a period of many years may be considered to be rather unsuited to the modern professional trustee.

Trustees occupy a pivotal and crucial role in a trust. The trust property is vested in the trustees and they are responsible for this property, the value of which may be a few pounds or many millions of pounds. Trustees must act absolutely selflessly: their sole object is to act in the best possible way for the beneficiaries. In their administration the trustees must not favour one beneficiary over another or one group of beneficiaries over another group.

In particular, the trustees must strike a balance between those beneficiaries interested in capital and those interested in income.

Example

If the trustees hold a fund on trust for Arthur for life and then for Ben absolutely, the trustees must be very careful when selecting investments not to choose investments which will unduly favour Arthur at the expense of Ben, or Ben at the expense of Arthur. They must not, for example, decide to invest all the trust fund in a very risky business which may bring in high income (benefiting Arthur) but which may well fail thus losing the capital invested (to the detriment of Ben). The trustees' powers and duties in relation to investment will be discussed in detail later.

See Chapter 16.

Chapters 15 and 16 cover trustees' powers and duties.

When administering a trust, trustees must be aware of their powers and duties.

These powers and duties may be set out in the trust documents and/or may be derived from the framework of powers and duties created by the law. These powers and duties initially were developed by the courts but gradually statutory provisions largely took over. In particular, powers and duties were included in the Trustee Act 1925 and the Trustee Act 2000.

The Law Reform Committee, 23rd Report ('The Powers and Duties of Trustees') (Cmnd 8733, 1982), (referred to as the 'Law Reform Committee Report' in this chapter) made a number of suggestions for change in the area of trustees' powers and duties, which will be discussed as and where appropriate in this chapter. Part II of the Trusts of Land and Appointment of Trustees Act 1996, which came into operation on 1 January 1997, made a number of important changes to the law relating to the appointment of trustees and their powers and duties. Unlike Part I of the Act, Part II applies to all trusts irrespective of whether the trust property is land, personalty or a mixture of the two. Again, the changes will be discussed as and where appropriate in this chapter.

See Chapter 15 for a discussion of trustees' powers and Chapter 16 for a discussion of trustees' duties.

Major changes to powers and duties followed from the Report of the Law Commission on Trustees' Powers and Duties (1999) LC 260. In particular, the report recommended changes to powers of delegation, powers to employ nominees and custodians, the power to buy land, the power to insure. The Trustee Act 2000 implemented, with some minor modifications, the changes recommended in the report.

The detailed changes are set out under the appropriate heading in this chapter. Perhaps the most important changes relate to powers of investment (these are discussed at p. 482).

Trustees' fiduciary position

Objective 2

It will be apparent that the trustees have an overriding responsibility towards their beneficiaries and that nothing must prevent or tend to prevent them from performing their duties solely in the best interests of their beneficiaries. In short, trustees are in a fiduciary relationship with their beneficiaries. They are under a duty to act in good faith towards the beneficiaries, who are in the position of relying on the trustees. (It should be noted that a trustee is only one example of a person occupying a fiduciary position. Other examples include solicitors, doctors, accountants and company directors.)

One aspect of this fiduciary position is the rule that a trustee must not place himself in a position where his personal interest and his duties towards his beneficiaries come into conflict. If such a situation exists, it is clear that the trustee may be tempted to act in his own interests rather than in the best interests of the trust and the beneficiaries. Any such conflict will not be allowed to prejudice the beneficiaries. The courts have traditionally taken a very firm approach, which is exemplified by the statement of Lord Herschell in *Bray* v *Ford* [1896] AC 44: it is 'an inflexible rule of a Court of Equity that a person in a fiduciary position . . . is not, unless otherwise expressly provided, entitled to make a profit; he is not allowed to put himself in a position where his interest and duty conflict'.

The 'no conflict' rule has been considered in a recent series of cases concerning pension trusts. (These are more fully discussed at p. 79.) In particular, *Re William Makin & Sons* [1993] OPLR 171, *British Coal Corporation* v *British Coal Staff Superannuation Scheme Trustees Ltd* [1993] PLR 303 and *Re Drexel Burnham Lambert UK Pension Plan* [1995] 1 WLR 32 are discussed.

The rule that a trustee must not profit from his trust and must not place himself in a position where his duty to the trust and his personal interest conflict does not apply if the trustee has been placed in this position by the creator of the trust rather than by his own conduct. So the rule would not be relevant if it was the settlor appointing the trustee who granted the trustee the conflicting interest.

In *Sargeant* v *National Westminster Bank plc* (1990) 61 P& CR 518, a testator owned freehold farms which were let to his three children. They farmed as a partnership, the assets being the tenancies. The testator appointed his three children as his executors under which the residuary estate was held on trust for sale, the capital being held for the three of them in equal shares. One of the children died intestate. His share in the partnership (which included the share in the tenancies) was bought by the other two children. The administrator of the intestate argued that the other children were under a fiduciary duty not to sell the interest in the partnership or the tenancies. This would have given rise to a conflict of interest flowing from their being both trustees and tenants of the trust property. They should, it was argued, have ended the tenancies. This would have ended the conflict of interest. The court held that to invoke the rule in this case would have led to an absurd situation. It was the testator who had created the conflict. He had appointed the children as his executors and granted the tenancies. It was the settlor and not the acts of the trustees which had created the conflict. The court decided that the rule was not applicable and it was no breach of duty to sell the freeholds subject to the tenancies.

The rule is that the fiduciary should not place himself in a conflicting position; here the fiduciary was placed in the position by the action of the testator.

The trustee may not purchase trust property – the rule against self-dealing

A trustee must dispose of any trust property in the most advantageous manner possible. It is obvious that, if a trustee was permitted to sell trust property to himself, there might be a temptation for him to sell on terms which were not the very best obtainable on behalf of the trust. Perhaps a higher price could have been obtained or more advantageous terms negotiated. It is clear that there could well be a conflict, and it is also clear that in many cases it would be very difficult to prove that the trustee had exploited his position. It is also possible that in deciding to buy or in setting the price or sale conditions the trustee used knowledge which he acquired in his capacity as trustee. Again, in these situations it would be very difficult to prove positively that the trustee had abused his position.

The rule is often stated in terms of the trustee being under a duty not to profit from his trust, but in *Tito* v *Waddell (No. 2)* [1977] 1 All ER 442, Megarry V-C described it as a rule against self-dealing, saying that, if a trustee purchases trust property from himself, any beneficiary may have the sale set aside *ex deito justiae*, however fair the transaction. He said that he regarded the law as putting the trustee under a disability.

Any purchase of trust property is voidable by any beneficiary so long as there is not an unreasonable delay between the sale and the attempt to set aside. The sale is voidable, however 'fair' the sale was, even if the price paid was the full market value and despite the fact that the beneficiary had full, independent legal or financial advice. Even if the sale was by public auction it may be set aside. The rule cannot be avoided by arranging a sale to the trustee's spouse or business partner.

There are also restrictions on a trustee purchasing property which at some time has been trust property. A trustee may not buy such property which was initially sold to a third party, unless the original sale was *bona fide* and there was no understanding that the trustee would later repurchase.

It is not possible to escape the rule by retiring as a trustee and then buying the property, because the possibility of abuse and of exploiting knowledge gained as a trustee is clearly still very strong. However, it is possible, if the retirement occurred a long time before the purchase, that it would be allowed to stand. In **Re Boles** [1902] 1 Ch 244, a trustee who had retired twelve years before purchasing trust property was allowed to keep the trust property, there being no evidence that he had taken any advantage of knowledge obtained as a trustee.

The case of **Holder v Holder** [1968] 1 All ER 665 must be regarded as unusual and perhaps may be thought of either as a one-off exception to the general rule or as questioning the validity of the rule itself. Alternatively, the case may have been wrongly decided.

In the case, a testator appointed his widow, a daughter and his son Victor as his executors. Victor was the tenant of a farm which formed part of the estate. He purported to renounce his executorship after taking a few minor steps towards the administration of the estate; however, these were in fact sufficient to prevent him from renouncing, as they amounted to acceptance of the office. Victor believed the renunciation to be valid. Victor subsequently bought the farm for a fair price at an auction. A beneficiary later tried to have the sale to Victor set aside. The Court of Appeal held that Victor was not prevented from buying the farm by his executorship.

The reasons for the rule were, according to Harman LJ, that a man may not be both a vendor and a purchaser, and there must never be a conflict of duty and interest. Neither applied to Victor, for he had not instructed the valuer nor arranged the auction, had never in reality assumed his duties as executor, nor had any influence on the other two executors. He made no secret of his intention to buy and had paid a good price for the property. The beneficiaries were not looking to Victor to protect their interests. In these special circumstances, the court refused to set aside the purchase.

Kane v J Radley-Kane [1998] 3 All ER 753 is an example where the self-dealing rule was invoked against a personal representative. A sole personal representative appropriated unquoted shares in her name in satisfaction of her statutory legacy of £125,000. The shares were later sold without the agreement of the beneficiaries. Section 41 of the Administration of Estates Act 1925 (which deals with appropriation) does not deal with this particular situation. Thus, it was assumed that the law remained as it was before 1925. Under the pre-1925 law, there was no objection to a personal representative taking assets *in specie*: for example, quoted stock, which was the equivalent of cash. But unquoted shares were not within this category. It was said that the self-dealing rule applied to personal representatives and, as the transaction had not been agreed either by the court or the beneficiaries, it was unlawful.

Purchase of a beneficial interest by a trustee – the fair-dealing rule

In *Tito v Waddell (No. 2)* Megarry V-C said:

> The fair-dealing rule is . . . that if a trustee purchases the beneficial interest of any of his beneficiaries, the transaction is not voidable *ex debito justitiae*, but can be set aside by the beneficiary unless the trustee can show that he has taken no advantage of his position and has made full disclosure to the beneficiary, and that the transaction is fair and honest.

There is clearly a danger that some exploitation of his position will occur if a trustee purchases a beneficial interest in a trust of which he is a trustee.

The court will treat such purchases with suspicion but they are not automatically voidable. They will, however, be voidable if the court feels there is any abuse of the trustee's position. In order to safeguard his purchase, the trustee should ensure that there has been a full disclosure of all information to the beneficiary and that the trustee gave full value for the interest. Additionally, the trustee would be wise to ensure that the beneficiary took independent legal advice.

The difference in the attitude of the courts to this situation and the purchase by the trustee of trust property is explained by Lord Eldon in *Ex p Lacey* (1802) 6 Ves 625:

> The rule I take to be this; not, that a trustee cannot buy from his *cestui que trust*, but, that he shall not buy from himself. If a trustee will so deal with his *cestui que trust*, that the amount of the transaction shakes off the obligation, that attaches upon him as a trustee, then he may buy.

Trustee must not compete with the trust

It will be recalled that the general rule is that a trustee must not put himself in a position where his duty as a trustee and his personal interest conflict or may conflict. This rule will prevent a trustee from conducting a business of his own which may compete with the business interests of the trust.

Re Thomson [1930] 1 Ch 203

This was a case in which a trustee was responsible for continuing to run a yacht-broking business which was part of the trust property. He wished to start a yacht-broking business of his own in the same town but was restrained by injunction from doing so because of the inevitable competition with the trust business. It was felt that the trustee's personal interest in maximising the profits of his own business might well conflict with his duty to ensure that the trust property (in this case, the yacht-broking business) was run in a way so as to ensure that the trust profited to the greatest possible extent.

This decision must not be thought of as preventing a trustee from having any personal business interests but only as preventing him from having those interests which bring his duty and personal interest into conflict. In *Re Thomson* (1930) the business was very specialised and the trustee's proposed business was in the same town. The decision might well have been different if the trustee's business was to be in another town some distance away or if the business were not so specialised. Again, the decision might well have been different had the trustee already been running his business when appointed as a trustee.

A trustee may not profit from his trust

The basis of this rule again lies in the duty of the trustee to administer the trust in the best interests of the beneficiaries, which would not be possible were the trustee able to make and keep profits from the trust. The existence of the rule is an attempt to prevent the trustee from placing himself in a position where his duty and personal interest come into conflict.

The rule is strictly applied and may be invoked irrespective of the honesty of the trustee. Of course, the rule may be modified by the terms of the trust. It does not matter that the trustee acted in the best interests of the trust or that the trust also benefited; the mere fact that the trustee has made a profit will allow the rule to be used to force him to discharge his gains. (See also p. 300.)

There are cases where a trustee has been allowed to obtain an indirect benefit, such as *Silkstone and Haigh Moor Coal Co v Edey* [1900] 1 Ch 167, in which a trustee sold trust property to a company in which he had shares. (Compare if the trustee was the major shareholder, or if he stood to make a substantial gain.)

Trustee must act without remuneration

Objective
3

This is another aspect of the general rule that a trustee's duty and personal interest must not conflict. It could well be very difficult to value the work of a trustee, but the reason for not allowing remuneration is that a trustee might be tempted to do work that was not necessary or work that did not result in a benefit to the trust. He might tend to conduct the trust business in a way that maximised his remuneration rather than in the way which was best for the trust and its beneficiaries. This rule does not, however, necessarily condemn a trustee to a great deal of unrewarded effort because, as discussed below, there is the possibility of delegating to others much of the 'routine' administration of the trust, leaving the trustee to make the decisions and to exercise any discretions. The trustee may pay the fees of such people out of trust funds.

There is, on the other hand, no objection to a trustee being reimbursed in respect of expenses properly incurred on behalf of the trust, and the Trustee Act 1925 s 30(2) provides statutory authority for such reimbursement. The section covers the properly incurred expenses of litigation. (For further discussion on the expenses of litigation, see p. 443.) However, there is no jurisdiction to award interest on the money laid out by the trustees on expenses: *Foster and Others v Spencer* [1996] 2 All ER 672.

There are a number of exceptions to the rule of no trustee remuneration.

Authority in the trust instrument

In many, if not all, professionally drafted trusts, there will be a charging clause under which trustees will be permitted to be paid for their work; indeed, no professional trustee would accept a trust unless there was an adequate charging clause. Even if the trustees are to be friends or relatives who will happily carry out their duties without reward, it is usually wise to include such a clause in case it becomes desirable to appoint professional trustees at a later stage. Charging clauses must be carefully drafted because in the past they have been rather strictly construed, and, unless widely drawn, a solicitor-trustee may find himself able to charge only for strictly professional duties.

Under the Wills Act 1837, a person who is a witness to the will cannot take any beneficial legacy or other gift under the will. Such gifts are 'utterly null and void'.

In the past in cases of trusts created by will, a charging clause in a will was regarded as a legacy and, as such, if the trustee acts as a witness to the will he would be prevented from claiming payment under the clause by virtue of s 15 of the Wills Act 1837: *Re Pooley* (1884) 40 Ch D 1.

The Trustee Act 2000 makes several important changes where a trustee acts as a witness to a will.

Section 28 deals with the situation where there is a charging clause and the trustee is either a trust corporation or is acting in a professional capacity. This section reverses the rule under which a charging clause is construed strictly and against the trustee (save where the provisions of the section are inconsistent with the terms of the trust):

(a) the trustee is entitled to payment even for services that could be provided by a lay trustee;

(b) any payment under a charging clause in a will is regarded as payment for service and is not regarded as a gift and so would not fall foul of s 15 of the Wills Act 1837, which prevents attesting witnesses from receiving gifts under a will. It is not uncommon for one who witnesses a will also to be appointed as a trustee.

A trustee is regarded as acting in a professional capacity if he acts in the course of a profession or business which consists of or includes the provision of services in connection with the management or administration of trusts (or a particular type of trust), or any particular aspect of the management or administration of trusts generally or any particular type of trust (s 28(4)).

Section 28 applies only to services provided after the commencement of the Act.

Contract with the beneficiaries

As long as all the beneficiaries are *sui juris*, of full age and absolutely entitled to the trust property, they may agree with the trustee that he shall be paid. Such contracts will be treated with suspicion by the courts.

If the agreement was made after the trustee had accepted his office, it is arguable that there might be no legally binding contract, as all the trustee would be offering by way of consideration would be the carrying out of his duties, which he is already bound to do. It may well be that this would be regarded as insufficient consideration and that the agreement would not be binding unless made by deed: *Stilk v Myrick* (1809) 2 Camp 317. However, in *Williams v Roffey Bros & Nicholls (Contractors) Ltd* [1990] 1 All ER 512, the Court of Appeal, although approving of *Stilk v Myrick*, decided that the performance of an existing obligation could provide sufficient consideration in appropriate cases. It may be argued that the policy underlying *Harris v Watson* (1791) Peake 102 (which was relied on by Lord Ellenborough in *Stilk v Myrick*) was the risk of economic duress if a party to a contract was able to 'persuade' the other party to give an enforceable promise to pay an additional sum for receiving merely what he had already contracted to receive. In *Williams v Roffey* there was no economic duress and the Court of Appeal held that the promise to perform the original contractual duty was enforceable.

Under court order

The court has an inherent power to allow a trustee (or other fiduciary) to be paid. It used to be said that this power would be exercised only in exceptional cases, perhaps where the trustee had performed unexpectedly onerous duties or had provided services which proved to be very beneficial to the trust. This attitude may be illustrated by the statement of Upjohn J in *Re Worthington (deceased)* [1954] 1 All ER 677 that 'the jurisdiction should be exercised only sparingly and in exceptional circumstances'.

Certainly, in the leading case of **Boardman v Phipps** [1966] 3 All ER 721, it could be argued that the situation was unusual and that the reward to the trust was great, but in the more recent case of **Re Duke of Norfolk's Settlement Trust** [1981] 3 All ER 220, a more liberal attitude may be detected in the Court of Appeal. An additional element in the latter case was whether the court had the power to vary the terms of an existing express charging clause, as well as allowing payment in the absence of any charging clause.

Boardman v Phipps [1966] 3 All ER 721

In this case, most of the funds of a trust were invested in shares in a family company which was unprofitable and not well managed. Boardman was a solicitor acting on behalf of the trust. He tried to persuade the trustees to buy additional shares in order to give them control of the company but they refused. Boardman then bought enough shares for himself to give him a controlling interest. He sold off assets of the company, making a good deal of money for himself and also for the trust, which still had a substantial holding in the company.

The House of Lords held that he must account to the trust for the profit he made, as the opportunity to make the profit arose because of his position as the trust's solicitor. This was a fiduciary position and his liability to account was similar if not identical to the position he would have been in had he been a trustee. However, the court decided that in the exercise of its inherent jurisdiction it would award him generous payment for his exceptional skill and work.

Re Duke of Norfolk's Settlement Trust [1981] 3 All ER 220

In this case, professional trustees were entitled to be paid under an express charging clause but applied to the court for the clause to be varied to give them the right to payment on a higher scale. The trustees also argued that the existing scale was so low that not only did it compare unfavourably with other charging clauses for similar trusts but, also, the trustees were operating at a loss. They also argued that they were doing extra and unforeseen work in relation to a redevelopment scheme, and that they were involved in additional work in connection with a reorganisation of the trusts to minimise capital transfer tax, and for this they claimed specific extra payment.

At first instance Walton J approved the extra payment in respect of the redevelopment but not in respect of the capital transfer tax reorganisation, saying that this was not beyond what trustees could reasonably be expected to do. However, Walton J did hold that the inherent jurisdiction did not extend to revising the existing scale fee in a trust instrument.

The trustees successfully appealed only on the issue of the revision of the scale fee. Brightman LJ said:

> If the court has an inherent power to authorise a prospective trustee to take remuneration for future services, and has a similar power in relation to an unpaid trustee who has already accepted office and embarked upon his fiduciary duties on a voluntary basis, I have some difficulty in appreciating the logic of the principle that the court has no power to increase or otherwise vary the future remuneration of a trustee who has already accepted office. It would mean that, if the remuneration specified in the trust instrument were lower than was acceptable, the court would have jurisdiction to authorise a substitute to charge an acceptable level of remuneration, but would have no jurisdiction to authorise the incumbent to charge precisely the same level of remuneration. Such a result appears to me bizarre, and calls in question the validity of the principle upon which it is supposedly based.

Brightman LJ went on to examine the two principles upon which the suggested rule, that the court has no inherent jurisdiction to vary the charges of a trustee as laid out in the trust instrument, was based. The first principle was that the right to remuneration is based on a contract and that the court has no power to vary the terms of the contract. Brightman LJ said that a trustee is under no contractual obligation to provide future services as he is able to express his desire to be discharged. If the rates of remuneration were to be changed by the court, this would merely amend for the future the terms of a contract which the trustee may, unilaterally, end. This could not be regarded as derogation from the contractual rights of the settlor or the beneficiaries, if they may be said to be entitled to the benefit of the contract.

The second principle which was put forward was that the remuneration amounted to a beneficial interest under the trust and the court has no inherent jurisdiction to vary beneficial interests, except in very rare cases [see p. 176]. Brightman LJ said that he did not accept that the remuneration constituted the trustee as a beneficiary under the trust.

Having disposed of the two arguments, Brightman LJ allowed the appeal, and as a consequence the scale charges of the trustees were varied.

It may be thought that this decision comes very close to a principle that a trustee, or at least a professional trustee, will always be entitled to reasonable payment.

In *O'Sullivan* v *Management Agency and Music Ltd* [1985] 3 All ER 351, a contract between a singer and his agent was set aside on the ground of breach of fiduciary duty and undue influence. The agent was awarded payment as he had assisted to a considerable extent in developing the career of the singer. It was held that the court was able to exercise this power despite the behaviour of the fiduciary.

However, an application for approval of remuneration was turned down by the House of Lords in *Guinness plc* v *Saunders* [1990] 1 All ER 652. Saunders was a director of a company which had initiated a takeover bid for another company. Three of the directors (including Ward) were appointed to see the takeover through. After the takeover, a company which Ward controlled sent an invoice for £5.2 million for the advice and services of Ward in relation to the takeover. Although payment was never authorised by the board of directors, one of the directors on the 'takeover committee' approved payment. It was claimed that the money was payable under an oral contract that Ward had made with the 'takeover committee' and that they had made the contract on behalf of the company. The terms of the contract, it was argued, entitled Ward to 0.2 per cent of the value of a successful takeover bid. The company denied that there was such a contract and argued that even if there was it would amount to a breach of the fiduciary duty of Ward as a director. The House of Lords held that on a construction of the articles of association of the company the 'takeover committee' had no power to enter the alleged contract on behalf of the company, so the contract was therefore void for want of authority.

Ward was not entitled to claim an allowance for his work because, by agreeing to provide services for a large fee (the size of which depended on the value of the bid), he had placed himself in a position where his duty as director (to negotiate the most advantageous deal for his company) conflicted with his personal interest (which would be maximised by his company paying a high price for the takeover).

It was considered that the courts would only award remuneration in cases where there was no possibility of encouraging a conflict between fiduciary duty and personal interest. It was doubted if the courts would exercise the power to award remuneration to a director when the articles of association of the company confided that power to the board of directors, as to do so would interfere with the company's administration of its own affairs. The House further held that the £5.2 million received by Ward was held by him on a constructive trust for the company.

The issue of payment for trustees was again considered by the court in *Foster and Others v Spencer* [1996] 2 All ER 672. In 1969 the plaintiffs were persuaded to become trustees of a cricket club. The club had become very run down, membership was declining and it was decided to sell the ground for development and to look for a new ground. There were considerable problems in selling. For example, the land was situated in a zone which had been specified by the local authority as an open space. If the land was to be sold at a good price, this specification needed to be altered and planning permission for development obtained. There were additional, more practical, problems, such as evicting some squatters and ensuring that the land was not invaded again. The land was eventually sold. Remuneration was sought for both past and future services. It was accepted that the services of two of the plaintiffs (a chartered surveyor and a building contractor who lived near the land) were particularly valuable. After referring to *Re Duke of Norfolk's Settlement Trust* (1981), the court held that they were entitled to payment for their services involving the sale of land. Judge Paul Barker QC decided that there were a number of decisive factors to support this decision. First, when they agreed to act as trustees they were not aware of the amount of work that they would be involved in and probably would not have agreed to act without remuneration. At the time of appointment, there were no funds out of which remuneration could have been made. If the trustees were not remunerated, it would result in the beneficiaries being unjustly enriched at the expense of the trustees. However, the judge decided that, as the future administration of the trust would not be too onerous and would not call for any special expertise, payment for future services would be refused. Should the future duties in fact prove onerous, the judge could not say that further application would be excluded.

Perotti v *Watson* [2001] All ER (D) 73 (Jul) involved an application for the award of fees to a solicitor for the administration of an estate. There was no professional charging clause. W (the solicitor) applied to the court to be paid for services provided to administer the estate of Mr Perotti (deceased). W was a solicitor who took instructions from the deceased to draft a will. Mr Perotti died and letters of administration were granted to the solicitor. It turned out that the administration of the estate was more complicated than was originally envisaged. Also, the claimant (P) had adopted an unreasonable attitude throughout. There were complaints about the way in which the administration had been handled. It had been held that, although there were shortcomings in the way that W had administered the estate, W was acquitted of dishonesty and the judge refused to remove him. In the instant case the issues were: did the court have the jurisdiction to grant W his legal fees; if so, should it be exercised; and at what level should remuneration be assessed?

The court held that it had jurisdiction to grant W the relief sought. (The case of *Foster and Others* v *Spencer* [1996] 2 All ER 672 was followed.) In the instant case more work was involved than was initially thought. This supported the court exercising its discretion. The court decided that, although W's conduct of the administration was criticised, this was not enough to mean that the court should totally refuse to exercise its discretion to award fees. The court, however, took the criticisms into account when assessing the level of the award and reduced the amount which otherwise would have been awarded.

Statutory provision

The provisions of s 29 in Part V of the Trustee Act 2000 make important changes to the rights of professional trustees to be paid, subject to contrary expression in the trust. These new provisions apply to trustees who are trust corporations (unless the trustee of a charitable trust). Such trustees are entitled to reasonable remuneration for any services that the trust corporation provides on behalf of the trust (s 29(1)).

Section 29(2) gives a similar right to reasonable remuneration to trustees who act in a professional capacity but who are not trust corporations, charitable trust trustees or sole trustees, provided that the other trustees have agreed in writing to the remuneration.

Under both subsections reasonable remuneration means, in relation to the services provided, such remuneration as is reasonable in the circumstances for the provision of the services by that trustee for that trust.

Under s 29(4) remuneration is payable even if a lay trustee could have provided the services.

Section 29(5) states that remuneration under this section is not payable if the trust instrument has a charging clause.

The remuneration of trustees of charitable trusts is covered by s 30.

As will be seen, there are specific statutory provisions regarding remuneration of the Public Trustee and judicial trustees. The Trustee Act 1925 s 42 provides that 'where the court appoints a corporation, other than the Public Trustee, to be a trustee . . . the court may authorise the corporation to charge such remuneration for its services as a trustee as the court may think fit'.

The rule in *Craddock* v *Piper*

Under the rule in ***Craddock*** v ***Piper*** (1850) 1 Mac & G 664, if a solicitor is acting as a trustee he is permitted to receive payment for work done in relation to litigation conducted on behalf of both himself and his co-trustees. There is a proviso in that recovery can be made only to the extent that the costs have not been increased by the solicitor acting for himself and his co-trustees. The rule is sometimes regarded as 'rather odd' and has been described by Upjohn J in ***Re Worthington (deceased)*** [1954] 1 All ER 677 as 'exceptional and anomalous and not to be extended'.

Trustees must act personally

A trustee's office is personal to him and the general rule is that the trustee must discharge his duties personally and may not delegate: *delegatus non potest delegare*. A settlor having specifically chosen a trustee to act is presumed to intend that particular individual to administer the trust personally. The settlor may have selected a particular person(s) because of their personal qualities, their sense of morality, their religious beliefs, etc. and the settlor would expect those values or beliefs to influence the way the trust was run. If someone else was delegated to deal with aspects of the administration of the trust, it may be that a quite different set of values and beliefs would be influential, resulting, perhaps, in decisions being made which the settlor would not have wished for or expected.

See Chapter 16 (pp. 457) for a more detailed discussion on powers to delegate.

There are several situations where delegation is possible, mainly the creation of statute. The Trustee Act 2000 has made important changes in this area.

Standard of care

Objective 4

The trustees must administer the trust property strictly in accordance with the terms of their trust. The general rule is that the trustees must carry out their duties personally and cannot simply sit back and delegate their responsibilities to others or allow their fellow trustees to administer the trust.

The trustees' duty to achieve the very best for their beneficiaries may involve them in acting in a way which is legally correct but which they feel to be immoral.

In ***Buttle* v *Saunders*** [1950] 2 All ER 193, the trustees had orally agreed to sell land to Mrs Simpson for £6,142, but before a written contract had been signed the trustees were offered £6,500 by Canon Buttle.

Wynn-Parry J decided that the trustees must accept the Canon's offer, although the trustees considered that they were morally bound to sell the property to Mrs Simpson. He said:

> It is true that persons who are not in the position of trustees are entitled, if they so desire, to accept a lesser price than that which they might obtain on the sale of property, and not infrequently a vendor who has gone some lengths in negotiating with a prospective purchaser decides to close the deal with that purchaser, notwithstanding that he is presented with a higher offer. It redounds to the credit of a man who acts like that in such circumstances. Trustees, however, are not vested with such complete freedom. They have an overriding duty to obtain the best price which they can for their beneficiaries.

The trustees are under a duty to protect and preserve the trust property and may in the course of carrying out this duty engage in litigation. This duty, although a continuing one, may be particularly relevant when a trustee is newly appointed. (This duty is discussed more fully on p. 417 under the heading 'Duties on appointment'.)

The office of trustee can be very onerous, involving difficult financial and administrative decisions, and discharging the duties may well occupy a great deal of time. The trustees will have duties which they will be under an obligation to discharge. They may also have powers and discretions and will have to decide if and how to exercise the powers and discretions vested in them.

Common law position

The trustees must discharge their duties, adopting the same standard of care as an ordinary prudent man of business would take in managing similar affairs of his own. The classic statement of this duty is to be found in the judgment of Sir George Jessel MR in ***Re Speight*** (1883) 22 Ch D 727 (affirmed in ***Speight* v *Gaunt*** (1883) 9 App Cas 1):

> It seems to me that on general principles a trustee ought to conduct the business of the trust in the same manner that an ordinary prudent man of business would conduct his own, and beyond that there is no liability or obligation on the trustee . . . It could never be reasonable to make a trustee adopt further and better precautions than an ordinary prudent man of business would adopt, or to conduct the business in any other way. If it were otherwise, no one would be a trustee at all.

When making investments, the trustee is subject to additional restrictions as he must not take the same risks as a prudent man of business might be prepared to take with his own money. The trustee must (applying the test objectively) take such care as an ordinary prudent man would take if he were investing for the benefit of people for whom he felt morally obliged to provide. In ***Learoyd* v *Whiteley*** (1887) 12 App Cas 727, Lord Watson stated the rule thus:

> As a general rule, the law requires of a trustee no higher degree of diligence in the execution of his office than a man of ordinary prudence would exercise in the management of his own private affairs. Yet he is not allowed the same discretion in investing the moneys of the trust as if he were a person *sui juris* dealing with his own estate. Business men of prudence may, and frequently do, select investments which are more or less of a speculative character but it is the duty of the trustee to confine himself to the class of investments which are permitted by the trust and likewise to avoid all investments of that class which are attended with hazard. So long as he acts in honest observance of those limitations the general rule already stated will apply.

In *Re Whiteley* (1886) 33 Ch D 347, Lord Lindley MR said:

> The duty of a trustee is not to take such care only as a prudent man of business would take if he only had himself to consider; the duty rather is to take such care as an ordinary prudent man of business would take if he were minded to make an investment for the benefit of other people for whom he felt morally bound to provide.

This restricts the freedom to invest that a man of business might have if he were investing for his own benefit. He would, in some cases, be prepared to take risks that would be unacceptable if he were investing with a view to discharging his moral responsibility towards another. Additionally, a trustee may only invest in investments either authorised by the trust or by statute. The duties of a trustee in relation to investment are covered by the Trustee Act 2000 (see p. 482).

If the trustee is a professional trustee, there will be a higher duty of care than is the case if a layperson acts. Such trustees may fall into one of two groups: they may either be banks etc. which claim to be professional trustees as such; or solicitors or accountants who might be described as possessing a professional qualification rather than holding themselves out as being 'specialist' trustees. In *Re Waterman's Will Trusts* [1952] 2 All ER 1054, Harman J said:

> I do not forget that a paid trustee is expected to exercise a higher standard of diligence and knowledge than an unpaid trustee and that a bank which advertises itself largely in the public press as taking charge of administration is under a special duty.

Such a trustee must exercise the special care and skill which it professes to have. Harman J regarded both types of professional trustees as coming within this principle. (See below, Trustee Act 2000 s 1(1).)

In *Bartlett v Barclays Bank Trust Co Ltd (No. 1)* [1980] 1 All ER 139, Brightman J, after having quoted the statement of Sir George Jessel in *Re Speight* (p. 404), regarding the standard required of trustees, went on to say:

> I am of the opinion that a higher duty of care is plainly due from someone like a trust corporation which carries on the specialised business of trust management. A trust corporation holds itself out in its advertising literature as being above ordinary mortals. With a specialist staff of trained officers and managers, with ready access to financial information and professional advice, dealing with and solving trust problems day after day, the trust corporation holds itself out, and rightly, as capable of providing an expertise which it would be unrealistic to expect and unjust to demand from the ordinary man or woman who accepts, probably unpaid and sometimes reluctantly from a sense of family duty, the burdens of trusteeship. Just as, under the law of contract, a professional person possessed of a particular skill is liable for a breach of contract if he neglects to use the skill and expertise which he professes, so I think a professional corporate trustee is liable for breach of trust if loss is caused to the trust fund because it neglects to exercise the special care and skill which it professes to have.

Despite the decisions discussed above, it has to be admitted that it is not completely clear whether or not the same standard of care applies to both professional and non-professional trustees. In *Nestlé v National Westminster Bank* [1994] 1 All ER 118, the Court of Appeal, in referring to the standards of the normal prudent man of business, appears to suggest that there is not a higher standard that applies to professional trustees, in that case the bank. The court decided that the bank was not guilty of a breach of trust in relation to the exercise of investment decisions despite behaving in a way that demonstrated 'symptoms of idleness and incompetence'. (This case is more fully discussed at pp. 477.)

Statutory standard of care: the Trustee Act 2000

Under the Trustee Act 2000 s 1(1), a duty of care is imposed on trustees in circumstances that come within Schedule 1. In general terms, the duty of care will apply to the exercise of a power to invest or to acquire land, when appointing agents, nominees or custodians under the provisions of the Act or when insuring the trust property.

Where this duty applies, the trustees are under the following duty of care:

1 Whenever the duty under this subsection applies to a trustee, he must exercise such care and skill as is reasonable in the circumstances, having regard in particular –

   (a) to any special knowledge or experience that he has or holds himself out as having, and

   (b) if he acts as trustee in the course of a business or profession, to any special knowledge or experience that it is reasonable to expect of a person acting in the course of that kind of business or profession.

This clearly imposes a higher level of duty of care on professional trustees in those situations where the provisions of the Act apply. But there is not one single expectation that flows merely from the fact that a trustee is a professional. The level of skill will relate to the particular profession carried on.

Restriction of liability

Objective
5

In fact, it may be purely academic if a higher standard of care applies to professional trustees. It is virtually inconceivable that such trustees would accept a trusteeship unless there was a broadly worded exemption clause. As discussed below, the current approach of the court is to interpret such clauses as exempting trustees from liability in many or most cases. So, unless either the courts or Parliament act to restrict the ability to exclude liability for breach of trust, whatever the standard of care of professional trustees, liability of the trustees will in most cases be severely restricted.

The extent (if any) that a trustee may be relieved from liability for breach of trust by virtue of an express clause in the settlement is debatable. The issue may be particularly relevant in the case of professional trustees, from whom a higher standard of care is expected, and who may well insist on some form of exemption clause being included in a trust before being willing to agree to act as trustee. It seems settled that exemption clauses will be construed strictly and against the trustee and that they will not exclude liability for fraud or intentional wrongdoing. It is probable that liability for gross negligence cannot be excluded.

It has been argued that if a clause is effective it should be subject to the reasonableness test of the Unfair Contract Terms Act 1977. But in *Baker v JE Clark & Co (Transport) UK Ltd* [2006] EWCA Civ 464, the Court of Appeal rejected the claim that a trustee exemption clause could be subjected to the reasonableness test in the Unfair Contract Terms Act 1977, the claimant having (rightly in the view of Tuckey LJ) conceded that a trust is not a 'contract' for the purpose of the Act.

The following cases give some guidance as to the extent to which it is possible to exclude or restrict the liability of trustees and the approach of the courts when interpreting exclusion or restriction of liability clauses.

In *Armitage v Nurse* (1995) *The Independent*, 3 July, Jacobs J decided that a clause which purported to exempt trustees from liability for loss or damage to the fund unless caused by their own actual fraud must be construed, even according to the *contra proferentem* rule, as exempting them from any liability for breaches of trust which were committed by wilfulness or recklessness provided the trustees were behaving honestly.

The case was appealed to the Court of Appeal ([1997] 2 All ER 705). The court decided that the words 'actual fraud' did not simply mean fraud but excluded constructive fraud and also equitable fraud and connoted simply dishonesty. Actual fraud involves an intention to deceive. If a trustee adopted a course of action that he knew was contrary to the interests of the beneficiaries or was recklessly indifferent as to whether or not the course of action was in their interests, there would be dishonest behaviour and thus actual fraud. Thus, a trustee was exempted from liability for loss or damage unless caused by his own dishonesty. It was irrelevant that he had been indolent, negligent, wilful or lacking in diligence. The court went on to say that a trustee acted dishonestly if he acted in a way that he did not honestly believe was in the interests of the beneficiaries whether or not he stood to gain personally. As it was not argued that the trustee had acted dishonestly, the trustees were absolved from liability. This restricted definition of fraud gave a very wide exemption to the trustees. There is a core of trust obligations which could not be reduced, such as the duty to act honestly and in good faith. However, the duty to act with care and prudence is not part of this core.

In common with a number of other judges, Millett LJ considered that legislative reform was needed, particularly where the trustees were professional trustees. He said:

> It must be acknowledged that the view is widely held that these clauses have gone too far, and that trustees who charge for their services and who, as professional men, would not dream of excluding liability for ordinary professional negligence, should not be able to rely on a trustee exemption clause excluding liability for gross negligence . . . If clauses such as [the clause under consideration in the case] are to be denied effect, then in my opinion this should be done by Parliament which will have the advantage of wide consultation with interested bodies and the advice of the Trust Law Committee . . .

Again, it may be argued that it should not be possible for paid, professional trustees to exclude or limit liability to the extent currently possible. (In the instant case one of the trustees was a solicitor.) There may be more justification in the cases of unpaid trustees.

Another Court of Appeal decision on trustees' exemption clauses is *Bogg v Raper* (1998) *The Times*, 22 April. Again, the decision was in favour of the trustee. Two trustees (one of whom was a solicitor) had helped a testator draw up his will, which contained a clause exempting them from liability for negligence. It was no wider than many clauses to be found in standard precedent books. It was argued that the trustees were in a fiduciary position to the testator and should not benefit from the clause unless the testator had full and independent advice about its effects.

This was rejected by the Court of Appeal. The clause did not bestow a benefit on the trustees but simply restricted their liability. The inclusion of the clause was not a transaction where the testator and those advising him had conflicting interests and where it would be expected that the testator would be separately represented. There was nothing to prevent a solicitor/draughtsman from benefiting from such a clause.

Millett LJ delivered the leading judgment as he had done in *Armitage v Nurse*. He again opined that there was a widely held view that such clauses had gone too far and referred to the possibility of legislative intervention.

In April 1999, the Court of Appeal heard yet another case involving a trustee exemption clause. In *Wight v Olswang* [1999] All ER (D) 436, the court decided that, if there was a doubt whether a trustee would be exempt from liability for a breach of trust, the doubt should be resolved against the trustee and a clause was construed so as not to protect him. In the case, the court was concerned with the correct approach when construing exemption clauses where a settlement contained two clauses: one (clause 11) was in general terms and the other (clause 18B), although covering the same basic issues, expressly, did not apply to paid trustees. In the particular case, the alleged liability might have been covered by either clause. The first clause would, the court decided, be construed as not applying to paid trustees. There was an obvious conflict between the clauses. Despite the general wording of clause 11, it must be construed as not applying to paid trustees: otherwise it would be repugnant to clause 18B.

Bonham* v *Fishwick [2008] EWCA Civ 373 is a Court of Appeal case on the application of a clause that exempted the trustees from liability except in the case of wilful and individual fraud or wrongdoing. The trustees claimed that they were not liable for wilful and individual fraud or wrongdoing as they had followed legal advice.

The key question was what was the legal advice given to and followed by the trustees. If they had not acted against legal advice from their counsel and solicitor, they would be entitled to rely on the exemption from liability.

Under the Trustee Act 2000 the duty of care applicable may be modified or excluded by the terms of the trust.

Following a widespread call for reform in this area, the Law Commission published a consultation paper 'Trustees Exemption Clauses' (No. 171) (2003) containing proposals to prevent professional trustees from relying on clauses excluding liability for negligence.

In brief, the paper set out a number of issues.

- The background, the problems and the issues to be addressed.

- It accepted that exemption clauses are currently often regarded as part and parcel of trusts and are in some cases a prerequisite to a professional trustee agreeing to act as a trustee.

- In many cases, professional trustees will be covered by liability insurance in any case. Lay trustees will often not know about such insurance, much less have such insurance.

After considering a number of possibilities and the issues involved, it was not thought appropriate to impose a blanket ban on trustee exemption clauses but it was thought that some changes were required. The 'main' proposal was that a distinction should be made between lay and professional trustees, although these definitions would have to be finalised.

In effect, lay trustees would still be able to benefit from exemption clauses, but professional trustees would not be able to shelter behind clauses that exclude liability for negligence. Professional trustees, it was thought, should be expected to act with reasonable care. The court should have the power to disapply trustee exemption clauses where reliance on the clause would be inconsistent with the overall purpose of the trust and it would be unreasonable in the circumstances for the trustees to be exempted from liability.

Alternative proposals were set out. One involved a judgment as to the reasonableness of the particular clause. The other alternative was that a trustee could not rely on a clause where it would not be reasonable so to do, in the light of all the circumstances, including the nature and extent of the breach of trust. Either of these solutions would, it suggested, introduce additional and unnecessary complexities into what is already a complex situation.

In 2006 the Law Commission published its 'Report on Trustee Exemption Clauses' (Law Com. No. 301). After considering the response to the earlier paper, the eventual recommendations were rather less radical than those set out in the consultation paper.

It recommended that an approach based on good practice – rather than legislation – should be the means to bring about reform of the conduct of trustees. The report recommended a rule of practice under which

> [a]ny paid trustee who causes a settlor to include a clause in a trust instrument which has the effect of excluding or limiting liability for negligence must before the creation of the trust take such steps as are reasonable to ensure that the settlor is aware of the meaning and effect of the clause.

This rule of practice, the Law Commission stated, represents 'the most appropriate and effective means of influencing and informing trustees so as to secure the proper disclosure of exemption clauses . . . Regulated persons would be required to adhere to defined good practice. Breach of this rule would not give rise in itself to liability in damages but would render the trustee open to disciplinary measures by the relevant governing body.'

The report stated that the Law Commission had spoken to a number of regulatory and professional bodies which 'would be prepared to introduce regulation of this sort into their own professional codes of conduct. The England and Wales region of the Society of Trusts and Estates Practitioners (STEP) was the first organisation to finalise such a rule . . .'

The report also stated that the Law Commission anticipated that the adoption of the rule will 'significantly ameliorate the problems associated with trustee exemption clauses'.

On 14 August 2010, the Parliamentary Under-Secretary of State for Justice (Mr Jonathan Djanogly) announced the Government's acceptance of the recommendations made in the Law Commission report. He went on to say that the Government will be promoting further uptake by writing directly to the relevant regulatory and professional bodies to urge them to adopt the approach recommended in the report.

This will not change the approach of the courts when interpreting exclusion or restriction of liability clauses and will not limit the ambit of such clauses, but will at least ensure that there is a greater prospect of settlors appreciating the presence and effect of such clauses.

Who can be a trustee?

Capacity

In general terms, anyone who has the legal capacity to hold property may be a trustee, including corporations. Clearly, there would have to be unusual circumstances before the appointment of a bankrupt or one who has been convicted of offences of dishonesty would be appropriate. Similarly, a person should not be appointed who, because of mental disorder or other relevant health factor, would not be able to carry out the duties of a trustee.

Minors

A minor is not capable of being a trustee of land, as the Law of Property Act 1925 s 1(6) prevents a minor from holding the legal estate in land. Although a minor may hold the legal estate in personalty, s 20 specifically provides that the appointment of a minor as a trustee shall be void. However, it appears that this prohibition only extends to express appointments.

In *Re Vinogradoff* [1935] WN 68, a minor was found to be a trustee under a resulting trust.

Re Vinogradoff [1935] WN 68

In 1926, Mrs Vinogradoff voluntarily transferred £800 of War Loan standing in her name into the joint names of herself and her granddaughter, aged four. Mrs Vinogradoff, however, continued to receive the interest from the War Loan for her own benefit. When she died, the question to be decided was whether her estate or her granddaughter was entitled to the War Loan. Farwell J held that her estate was entitled, applying the usual presumption that, where property is gratuitously conveyed to another, the recipient holds it on resulting trust for the donor. The result was that the four-year-old granddaughter held the property as trustee on the resulting trust.

The Crown

It is theoretically possible for the Crown to act as a trustee (*Penn v Lord Baltimore* (1750) 1 Ves Sen 444), or at least it can act as a trustee if it deliberately so chooses (see *Civilian War Claimants Association Ltd v R* [1932] AC 14, where Lord Atkin said (at 27): 'There is nothing so far as I know, to prevent the Crown acting as agent or trustee if it chooses deliberately to do so').

Number of trustees

In many trusts one trustee may be appointed and operate the trust, although there may be sound practical reasons for having more than one trustee. In a number of situations statute requires that there must be a minimum of two trustees or a trust corporation:

● capital money arising from land must be paid to, or at the direction of, at least two trustees or a trust corporation (Settled Land Act 1925 ss 18(1)(c) and 94(1); Law of Property Act 1925 s 27(2));

● except when the sole trustee is trust corporation, a valid receipt for capital money must be given otherwise than by a sole trustee (Trustee Act 1925 s 14(2)); and

● a conveyance or deed must be made by at least two trustees or a trust corporation to overreach any powers or interests affecting a legal estate in land (Law of Property Act 1925 s 2(1)(ii)).

Therefore, there would be no point appointing a single individual as the trustee to such a trust, as a second trustee would have to be appointed if the land is sold.

Section 7 of the Trustee Delegation Act 1999 deals with situations where the 'two-trustee rule' can and cannot be met and makes it clear that, so long as there are at least two trustees, the 'two-trustee rule' can be satisfied either by two people acting in different capacities or by two people acting jointly in the same capacity but not by one person acting in two capacities.

There is no upper limit to the number of trustees in a trust of pure personalty, although it may well be very difficult for a large number of trustees to work together. The Law Reform Committee 23rd Report ('The Powers and Duties of Trustees') (Cmnd 8733, 1982) recommended that, whatever type of property is involved, trustees should be limited to four unless the settlor makes a specific provision regarding the number of trustees. The recommendation was based on the increased delays and costs and administrative inconvenience flowing from larger numbers of trustees.

Where there is a settlement or a disposition creating a trust of land, the number of trustees may not exceed four (Trustee Act 1925 s 34). If the settlor names more than four to be trustees, the first four named who are ready, willing and able to act become the trustees. The other named will not become trustees unless they are appointed when a vacancy occurs. The number of trustees cannot be increased beyond four.

This restriction does not apply to land held for charitable, ecclesiastical or public purposes (Trustee Act 1925 s 34(2)).

Appointment

Initial trustees

Express appointment

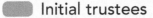

Objective 6

In the vast majority of cases the initial trustees will be appointed by the settlor either in the trust instrument or, in the case of **testamentary trusts**, in the will. In the case of an *inter vivos* trust the trustees will normally be parties to the deed creating the trust, and the trust will be constituted when the trust property is transferred to the trustees. Alternatively, the settlor can declare that he holds the property on specified trusts, in which case this declaration will name the initial trustee as the settlor and constitute the trust. If a trust is created by will, it is very common for the same people to be named both as executors and trustees of the trusts created by the will.

It is possible for the settlor expressly to give an individual or individuals the power to appoint the trustees. The precise scope of an express power in the trust to appoint trustees is a matter of construction. It is sometimes difficult to decide whether the person given such a power may appoint himself. This again is a matter of construction, but it may well be that if such a power exists it should be exercised with considerable caution.

In *Re Skeat's Settlement* (1889) 42 Ch 522, Kay J said: 'A man should not be a judge in his own case . . . he should not decide that he is the best possible person, and say that he ought to be the trustee.'

It is often thought unnecessary to include an express power of appointment as the statutory provisions are wide and will cover most situations.

If no trustee is appointed in respect of a testamentary trust, or all the named trustees refuse to act, or if all the named trustees die before the testator, or if for some other reason there is no initial trustee, the trust will not be allowed to fail for want of a trustee. There may be an express power to appoint trustees, in which case this may be used to fill the gap. In other cases the court will have the power to appoint under provisions discussed later. Until the appointment is made, the trust property will be held by the personal representatives of the testator as constructive trustees.

In the case of an *inter vivos* trust, if all the trustees disclaim, the property will vest in the settlor pending the appointment of new trustees. In other cases of failure of trustees in *inter vivos* trusts, the trust will fail. For example, if all the named trustees die before the trust documents are executed, or the proposed trustee is a corporation which is dissolved before the trust document is executed, the trust will fail. The difference between these two situations is that, if there are no trustees at all, then the attempted trust must fail as there will be nobody by whom the trust property can be held; whereas, if trustees disclaim, the theoretical position is that, until disclaimer, the trust property is vested in them and so the trust is properly constituted at that stage, and when the trustees later disclaim, the trust property reverts to the settlor, who will hold the property as trustee pending the appointment of new trustees.

Mallott v Wilson [1900–03] All ER Rep 326

In this case, Montague Fielden executed a deed in 1866 appointing William Carr as a trustee of a settlement which he declared in favour of his wife and children. In March 1867, Carr, who had not executed the original deed, disclaimed the trusts, whereupon Fielden executed a deed reciting that Carr had never accepted the trusts and declaring that the settlement was ineffective. In 1889 Fielden made a second settlement including all the property included in the 1866 settlement. The court was later asked to decide whether the 1866 settlement was still valid and binding, and the court said it was. The failure of the original trustee to assume the trusteeship did not destroy the trust; the settlor himself became trustee of the 1866 settlement in the absence of an original trustee.

There is one particular situation, however, where a new trustee may not be appointed and where the trust will fail for lack of a trustee. This is where, as a matter of construction, the settlor intends only the named trustee to act and no one else. In **Re Lysaght** [1965] 2 All ER 888, Buckley J said: 'If it is of the essence of the trust that the trustees selected by the settlor and no-one else shall act as the trustees of it and those trustees cannot or will not undertake the office, the trust must fail.'

It should be noted that the settlor has no power *qua* settlor to appoint a trustee once the trust has been established, although he may reserve himself the express power in the trust instrument.

By the court

If there is no express power of appointing trustees that can be used, the court may appoint initial trustees using the provisions of the Trustee Act 1925 s 41 (see p. 415).

Subsequent appointments

Express provision

The statutory powers to appoint trustees are wide and it is reasonably rare for an express power to be included in modern trusts. It is, however, common for the settlor to identify who is to exercise the statutory powers of appointment, discussed in the next section. As with an express power to make an initial appointment, discussed above, the precise scope of the power will be a matter of construction.

Statutory provisions

Trustee Act 1925 s 36(1)

This provision gives very wide powers of appointment, which are read into all trusts unless the trust instrument directs otherwise. It is generally agreed that, although most of the provisions of the 1925 Act apply equally to trustees and personal representatives, this sub-section does not apply to personal representatives. The provision can be used only if there is an 'outgoing trustee' who is being replaced.

When an appointment may be made
The wording of s 36(1) is reasonably clear and permits new trustees to be appointed in the following cases:

(a) **When a trustee is dead.** This provision permits the appointment of a new trustee where a trustee dies after assuming his office. It also covers a trustee, under a testamentary trust, who dies before the testator. It does not, however, cover the situation where, under an *inter vivos* trust, all the trustees die before the trust documents are executed.

(b) ***Prolonged absence of trustee.*** The power arises only after a trustee has been outside the United Kingdom for a continuous period of twelve months: any return, however brief, will break the period and the twelve-month clock will have to restart. (See ***Re Walker*** [1901] 1 Ch 259, where the power was held not to be available although the trustee had been outside the United Kingdom for more than twelve months, because the absence had been interrupted by a return to the United Kingdom for one week.) It does not matter that the trustee is 'accidentally' out of the United Kingdom for a period which exceeds the twelve-month limit; the power will still come into being. Therefore, the power will be available if the trustee goes overseas on holiday intending to be out of the country for only two weeks but is imprisoned and as a consequence is out of the United Kingdom for more than the twelve-month period.

(c) ***When a trustee desires to be discharged.*** Under this provision a trustee who wishes to retire may be replaced. This provides an opportunity for a trustee who would like to disclaim after acceptance to be released from his trusteeship. Also, it is possible for a trustee to retire from only part of the trust and continue to act in respect of the rest of the trust.

(d) ***When a trustee refuses to act.*** It is generally accepted that under this head a disclaiming trustee may be replaced.

(e) ***When a trustee is unfit.*** This will enable a trustee to be replaced who has become a bankrupt. For example, in ***Re Wheeler and De Rochow*** [1896] 1 Ch 315, Kekewich J held that bankruptcy rendered a trustee unfit but not incapable. It has been argued that bankruptcy should not always render a trustee unfit, particularly if no moral blame attaches to the trustee/bankrupt. A trustee will be unfit if he is convicted of a crime of dishonesty.

(f) ***When a trustee is incapable.*** It is generally agreed that this head will permit replacement of a trustee who is suffering from a mental or physical incapacity and as a consequence should be replaced in the best interests of the trust. It also may cover an enemy alien in time of war if the circumstances result in him being incapable of acting. It may be, for example, that the situation would prevent him from bringing actions in the English courts and thus he would be incapable of acting as a trustee. Section 36(3) specifically deals with a corporation which is dissolved and states that, as from the date of dissolution, the corporation will be deemed to be incapable of acting.

(g) ***When a trustee is an infant.*** The appointment of an infant as a trustee of an express trust is void, but it is possible for an implied, resulting or constructive trust to have a trustee who is an infant. Under the provision being discussed, such an infant trustee may be replaced.

Trustee's removal under an express power

In such a case a new trustee or trustees may be appointed to replace the removed trustee 'as if he were dead'.

Who can exercise the power?

Section 36(1) provides a list of those who are able to appoint new trustees, giving an order of priority:

1. Any person nominated to appoint new trustees by the trust instrument;

2. The surviving or continuing trustees;

3. The personal representatives of the last surviving or continuing trustee.

It does not matter if the nomination in the trust instrument does not specifically refer to s 36(1); so long as the power to appoint new trustees is given, the statutory provisions will apply. If there is no one on the statutory list who is ready, willing and able to exercise the statutory power, s 36(1) is unusable.

How the power is to be exercised

The only requirement is that the appointment must be in writing, but in most cases the appointment will be by deed in order to obtain the benefit of s 40 (see below).

Trusts of Land and Appointment of Trustees Act 1996

Section 19 of the Trusts of Land and Appointment of Trustees Act 1996, which came into force on 1 January 1997, introduced some important changes to the law in the area of appointment and retirement of trustees. Despite the name of the Act, these provisions apply to all types of trusts and not merely to trusts of land. These provisions apply where a number of requirements are met:

(a) all the beneficiaries must be of full age and capacity and (taken together) absolutely entitled to the property subject to the trust (s 19(1)(b)); and

(b) there is no person nominated for the purpose of appointing new trustees by the trust instrument (if any) creating the trust (s 19(1)(a)); and

(c) for express trusts, the provisions must not be excluded by the trust instrument or (for trusts created before 1 January 1997) they are not excluded by a deed executed by the settlor or surviving settlors (s 19(6)). Such a deed is irrevocable (s 19(7)).

Where these provisions are satisfied, the beneficiaries may unanimously direct, in writing, that either a trustee or trustees should retire from the trust (s 19(2)(a)), or the trustee or trustees for the time being (or, if there are none, the personal representatives of the last trustee) shall appoint, in writing, the person or persons specified in the direction to be a trustee or trustees. These may be replacement or additional trustees (s 19(2)(b)).

Section 19(3)(b) and (4) contain provisions relating to the protection of the trustee's rights. Section 19(4) lays down that, where a trustee retires under s 19(3), he and the continuing trustees shall (subject to any arrangements for protecting his rights) do all that is necessary to vest trust property in the continuing trustees (or the continuing and new trustees).

One way to ensure that the section is inapplicable is to include an express provision in the trust documentation which nominates those able to appoint new trustees.

The effect of s 19 on the type of situation in *Re Brockbank* [1948] 1 All ER 287 has been discussed (see p. 159). In the case the beneficiaries, who were all adult and of full capacity and who together were absolutely entitled to the trust property, were unable to direct the continuing trustee (who had the power to appoint new trustees under s 36(1) of the Trustee Act 1925) who to appoint as a new trustee. The only option open to the beneficiaries was to end the trust using the rule in *Saunders* v *Vautier* (1841) 4 Beav 115. From 1 January 1997, in such a case the beneficiaries may direct the trustees as to whom to appoint as a trustee, and direct that named trustees should retire provided the requirements of s 19 (outlined above) are met. As stated above, s 19 will be inapplicable if there is someone nominated for the purpose of appointing new trustees by the instrument creating the trust.

Section 20 of the Trusts of Land and Appointment of Trustees Act 1996 applies to enable a replacement trustee to be appointed where a trustee is incapable of exercising his functions as a trustee because of a mental disorder. There will be a problem in replacing him if there is no one who is both willing and able to make an appointment replacing him under s 36(1) of the Trustee Act 1925. Section 20 provides that, where there is no person who is entitled and willing to appoint a trustee in place of a trustee who is incapable of exercising his functions as a trustee under s 36(1), and the beneficiaries under the trust are of full age and capacity and between them are absolutely entitled to the trust property, the beneficiaries may give a written direction to either the receiver of the trustee, or to an attorney acting for him under the authority of a power of attorney created under an instrument which is registered under s 6 of the Enduring Powers of Attorney Act 1985, or to a person authorised for the purpose by the authority having jurisdiction under Part VIII of the Mental Health Act 1983. The direction will be to appoint by writing the person(s) specified in the direction to be trustee(s) in place of the incapable trustee.

A beneficiary may wish to withdraw from the direction given under s 19 or s 20 before it has been complied with. This is permitted, but if it happens the direction will no longer be unanimous and so will be ineffective because the legislation requires directions to be made unanimously by all the trustees (s 21(1)).

When these provisions are used, the normal restrictions imposed by statute apply. (See p. 410 for further discussion.)

Section 21(8) deals with the 'interaction' of the settlor's right to opt out if the trust was created before 1 January 1997 and the rights of the beneficiaries to direct appointment and/or retirement. Where an 'opt-out' deed has been executed, it does not affect anything done before its execution to comply with a direction under s 19 or s 20. So, on the basis of a valid direction given by the beneficiaries, if an appointment has already been made before the 'opt-out' deed is executed, the appointment is good. But where a direction has been given under either s 19 or s 20 but it has not been complied with, it shall cease to have any effect once the deed is executed. Thus, if the terms of the beneficiaries' valid direction have not been complied with, i.e. the retirement has not taken place and/or the appointments have not been made, the direction will cease to have any effect (and so cannot be acted upon) if in the meantime the 'opt-out' deed is executed.

Appointment by the court

The Trustee Act 1925 s 41 gives to the court a wide power, 'whenever it is expedient to appoint a new trustee or trustees, and it is found inexpedient, difficult or impracticable so to do without the assistance of the court', to make an order appointing one or more new trustees.

The requirement that it is 'expedient' for the courts to appoint was raised in *Re Weston's Settlement* [1968] 3 All ER 338. The lack of statutory guidance on 'expedient' was emphasised by Lord Denning MR who said, 'There being no guidance in the statutes, it remains for the court to do the best it can.' In other words Lord Denning claimed a wide discretion for the courts under s 41.

Section 41 may be used in cases where there is no one who is willing or able to exercise a power to appoint trustees. The power extends to appointing trustees as substitutes for existing trustees or as additional trustees. Also, the court can appoint in cases where there are no trustees. The section cannot be used simply to remove a trustee – a replacement trustee must be appointed.

The breadth of s 41 is shown by *Henderson v Henderson* [1940] 3 All ER 295 where a trustee was removed against his will. But Bennett J made it clear in *Henderson v Henderson* that this would not be done if there is any dispute about the facts, accepting the view of

Cotton LJ in *Re Combs* (1884) 51 LT 45. But in *Henderson* v *Henderson*, there was no dispute over the facts and a trustee was removed against her will. If there is a dispute about the facts, the courts may appoint under the inherent jurisdiction.

In *Re Tempest* (1866) 1 Ch App 485, Turner LJ set out the principles that the courts will use when appointing trustees, whether under s 41 or under the inherent power to appoint. Turner LJ said:

> First, the Court will have regard to the wishes of the persons by whom the trust has been created, if expressed in the instrument creating the trust, or clearly to be collected from it . . . Another rule which may, I think, safely be laid down is this – that the Court will not appoint a person to be trustee with a view to the interest of some of the persons interested under the trust, in opposition either to the wishes of the testator or to the interests of others of the *cestuis que trusts*. I think so for this reason, that it is of the essence of the duty of every trustee to hold an even hand between the parties interested under the trust. Every trustee is in duty bound to look to the interests of all, and not of any particular member or class of members of his *cestuis que trusts*.
>
> A third rule which, I think, may safely be laid down, is, that the Court in appointing a trustee will have regard to the question, whether his appointment will promote or impede the execution of the trust, for the very purpose of the appointment is that the trust may be better carried into execution . . .
>
> . . . but, on the other hand, if the continuing or surviving trustee refuses to act with a trustee who may be proposed to be appointed . . . I think it would be going too far to say that the Court ought, on that ground alone, to refuse to appoint the proposed trustee; for this would . . . be to give the continuing or surviving trustee a veto upon the appointment of the new trustee. In such a case, I think it must be the duty of the Court to inquire and ascertain whether the objection of the surviving or continuing trustee is well founded or not, and to act or refuse to act upon it accordingly . . .

In *Polly Peck International plc* v *Henry* [1999] 1 BCLC 407 the court refused to appoint as a trustee a person who lacked the expertise needed to carry out the trusts.

Appointment of additional trustees

It is possible to increase the number of trustees by using s 36(1), as this allows the appointment of one or more trustees (see p. 412).

Section 36(6) permits additional trustees to be appointed in writing, but the power is restricted. It could not be used if one of the trustees is a trust corporation, or to increase the number of trustees beyond four. From 1 January 1997 the position was altered by Schedule 3 paragraph 3(11) to the Trusts of Land and Appointment of Trustees Act 1996. The provision amends s 36(6) and allows an appointment where there is a trust corporation. The section (as amended) permits additional trustees to be appointed where there are not more than three trustees (irrespective of whether they are individuals or include a trust corporation).

The power under s 36 may be exercised by the person nominated in the trust instrument to appoint new trustees, or, if there is no such person who is ready, willing and able to act, the power is exercisable by the existing trustees. It would appear that s 36(6) gives the power to appoint 'another'; the person exercising the power cannot appoint himself.

The Trustee Delegation Act 1999 s 8 inserted four new subsections into s 36 (s 36(6A)–(6D)). These give an attorney of a trustee a new power to appoint new trustees on behalf of the trustee. The section applies where there is an enduring power of attorney or a lasting power of attorney registered under the Mental Capacity Act 2005.

Vesting property in new trustees

It is vital that trust property is properly vested in any new trustee. The property should be vested in the joint names of the new and continuing trustees. One method of achieving this is for the trustees in whose name the property stands to transfer it into the joint names of the new and continuing trustees. The form of the transfer will depend on the type of property involved, and the form appropriate to the property must be used. For example, if the trust property is unregistered land, it must be transferred by deed. If the trust owns shares, these must be transferred by the completion of a stock transfer form followed by entry in the books of the company. Personal chattels can be transferred by delivery.

However, the Trustee Act 1925 s 40 provides a convenient way of ensuring that property is vested in any new trustees. The section provides that if the appointment of the new trustee is made by deed the trust property will automatically vest in the new and continuing trustees as joint tenants. There is some property which is not covered by s 40 and this will have to be vested using an appropriate method of transfer as outlined above. Section 40 does not cover land held by way of mortgage, land held under a lease which has a covenant against assignment (unless the consent was obtained before the deed of appointment was executed), and stocks and shares, which must be formally transferred.

Duties on appointment

The trustee should examine all trust documents in order that he is aware of the details of the trust he is administering. He should identify the trust property and ensure that it is properly vested in himself and any co-trustees. He should analyse the investments which have been made to ensure they comply both with the terms of the trust and with the general law. He should also ensure that the investments are in the names of all the trustees.

The new trustee should check for breaches of trust committed before he assumes office. He will not be liable for these breaches committed by others, but he may be liable for his own breach if he fails to make a proper investigation or fails to take steps to remedy such breaches. Although the failure by a new trustee to investigate a prior breach of trust will itself be a breach of trust, new trustees are entitled to assume that there have been no breaches of trust prior to their appointment, unless there are suspicious circumstances indicating such a breach: *Re Strahan* (1856) 8 De GM & G 291.

Trustees are under a general duty to ensure that trust property is safeguarded. This duty may be particularly relevant when a new trustee is appointed. They will need to assess the situation and if, for example, trust property is outstanding, the trustee(s) must take steps to call it in.

If a trustee has been appointed to replace a trustee, he should ensure that no breaches of trust were committed by the former trustee with the continuing trustees.

Before appointment, a potential trustee should disclose any possible conflicts between his duty to the trust and his personal interests.

Ending trusteeship

Objective
7

The overriding principle is that the office of trustee is one that subsists for life. However, there are a number of ways in which the lifetime commitment may be cut short. In some cases it is the trustee who wishes for his office to end but in other situations the termination is imposed upon him.

Retirement

Express power

A trust instrument may provide expressly for the retirement of trustees, but this is unlikely as the statutory provisions discussed below are normally considered adequate.

Trustee Act 1925 s 36(1)

If a trustee 'desires to be discharged' he may retire, but s 36(1) applies only if he is being replaced by the appointment of another trustee or trustees. A trustee may retire from all or part of the trust.

Trustee Act 1925 s 39

If a trustee wishes to retire but there is not to be an appointment to replace him, s 39 may be used. However, the section contains a number of conditions which must be met if it is to be used to facilitate retirement. First, after the retirement at least two trustees or a trust corporation must remain. Secondly, the remaining trustees must agree to the retirement. Thirdly, the consent must also be obtained of anyone named in the trust instrument as having the power to appoint trustees. Fourthly, the retirement must be in the form of a deed. Unlike retirement under s 36(1), the trustee cannot retire from only part of a trust. He must either retire completely or stay on as a trustee.

There used to be a particular problem with s 39. As has been stated, the retirement is permissible only if after the retirement there will remain either a trust corporation or two individuals to act as trustees. The use of the word 'individuals' does not include corporate bodies. Where, before the retirement, there is a corporate trustee (not a trust corporation) and two individual trustees, it appears that s 39 does not permit one of the individuals to retire. This is because after the proposed retirement there would not be either a trust corporation or two individual trustees, although there would be two trustees. This is obviously not satisfactory and, from 1 January 1997, the position has been altered by Schedule 3 paragraph 3(13) to the Trusts of Land and Appointment of Trustees Act 1996. Section 39 has been amended so that 'persons' (a word which includes corporate bodies) has been substituted for the word 'individuals'. Thus, after 1 January 1997 the retirement of one of the individuals in the example above is permitted.

Trusts of Land and Appointment of Trustees Act 1996 s 19

See the discussion of s 19 of the Trusts of Land and Appointment of Trustees Act 1996 (at p. 414) under which trustees can be directed to retire.

Court order

The court may order the retirement of a trustee when exercising its powers under s 41. There is also an inherent power for the court to allow retirement. The court will not use this inherent power if it would result in the trust being left with no trustee (although in such a case the court could order the transfer of the trust property into court with the object that the trust will be administered by the court; this leaves the trustee in office but relieves him of all the problems of administering the trust).

Agreement of beneficiaries

If the trustee obtains the consent of all the beneficiaries who are entitled between them to the beneficial interest in the trust property, he may retire. It is, of course, necessary that the beneficiaries are all of full age and capacity. It is not clear what effect this will have on the co-trustees, although if they have agreed to the retirement they will be bound by it.

Removal

Express power

Although such a power is rare, it is open to the settlor to include in his trust instrument an express power governing the removal of trustees. Such powers are more common in commercial trusts as opposed to family and other private trusts. The power will name those who may exercise it and also state the situations when it can be exercised. As is normal, the exact scope of an express power will be a matter of construction.

Trustee Act 1925 s 36(1)

If a trustee remains out of the United Kingdom for more than twelve months, or is unfit to act, or refuses to act, or is incapable of acting, he can be removed and replaced by the court under s 36(1) (see p. 412).

Trustee Act 1925 s 41

If the court exercises its powers under s 41 (see p. 415), it may remove a trustee in the course of appointing a new trustee.

Trusts of Land and Appointment of Trustees Act 1996 s 19

See the discussion above. Trustees may be directed to retire, i.e. they can be removed.

Inherent power

In an action for the administration of a trust by the court, a trustee may be removed using the inherent powers of the court. The inherent power is rarely used, but, in *Clarke* v *Heathfield* [1985] ICR 606, the court removed the trustees of the funds of the National Union of Mineworkers because the trustees refused to return funds to the United Kingdom which, in contempt of court, had been transferred out of the country to escape sequestration.

Removal by the courts

In *Letterstedt* v *Broers* (1984) 9 App Cas 371 Lord Blackburn discussed the principles that should be applied when the court is deciding whether or not to remove a trustee. He said:

> It is not disputed that there is a jurisdiction 'in cases requiring such a remedy,' as is said in Story's *Equity Jurisprudence*, [section] 1287, but there is very little to be found to guide us in saying what are the cases requiring such a remedy; so little that their Lordships are compelled to have recourse to general principles.
>
> Story says, [section] 1289, 'But in cases of positive misconduct, Courts of Equity have no difficulty in interposing to remove trustees who have abused their trust; it is not indeed every mistake or neglect of duty, or inaccuracy of conduct of trustees, which will induce Courts of Equity to adopt such a course. But the acts or omissions must be such as to endanger the trust property or to shew a want of honesty, or a want of proper capacity to execute the duties, or a want of reasonable fidelity.' . . .

It is quite true that friction or hostility between trustees and the immediate possessor of the trust estate is not of itself a reason for the removal of the trustees. But where the hostility is grounded on the mode in which the trust has been administered, where it has been caused wholly or partially by substantial overcharges against the trust estate, it is certainly not to be disregarded . . .

As soon as all questions of character are as far settled as the nature of the case admits, if it appears clear that the continuance of the trustee would be detrimental to the execution of the trusts, even if for no other reason than that human infirmity would prevent those beneficially interested, or those who act for them, from working in harmony with the trustee, and if there is no reason to the contrary from the intentions of the framer of the trust to give this trustee a benefit or otherwise, the trustee is always advised by his own counsel to resign, and does so. If, without any reasonable ground, he refused to do so, it seems to their Lordships that the Court might think it proper to remove him; but cases involving the necessity of deciding this, if they ever arise, do so without getting reported.

In *Thomas & Agnes Carvel Foundation* v *Carvel* [2008] Ch 395 Lewison J reiterated that

[i]t is common ground that, in the case of removal of a trustee, the court should act on the principles laid down by Lord Blackburn in **Letterstedt v Broers** (1884) 9 App Cas 371, and that in the case of removing a personal representative similar principles should apply.

A case involving the removal of executors is **Angus v Emmott** [2010] EWCH 154. The deceased had died before a compensation claim had been finally settled. His executors could not agree as to how the claim should be handled and two of them would not agree to a particular document being submitted to the court. Richard Snowden QC (sitting as a deputy judge of the High Court) said, agreeing to the removal of executors, that in the case,

even without misconduct, a situation has been reached in which there is such a degree of animosity and distrust between the executors that the due administration of Mr Steel's estate is unlikely to be achieved expeditiously in the interests of the beneficiaries unless some change is made.

But a different decision was reached in **Kershaw v Micklethwaite** [2010] EWHC 506 (Ch). This case concerns removing an executor. Newey J, referring to the extract from Lord Blackburn's judgment in **Letterstedt v Broers** (above), said:

Similarly, I do not think that friction or hostility between an executor and a beneficiary will, of itself, be a good reason for removing the executor. On the other hand, a breakdown in relations between an executor and a beneficiary will be a factor to be taken into account, in the exercise of the court's discretion, if it is obstructing the administration of the estate, or even sometimes if it is capable of doing so. [Counsel] himself accepted in the course of argument that for a breakdown in relations to warrant an executor's removal, the breakdown must at least have the potential to cause difficulty in the administration of the estate. . . .

As I have already said, however, I do not consider that friction or hostility between an executor and a beneficiary is of itself a reason for removing the executor. [Counsel] suggests that, on the facts of this case, the hostility between [the executors] has the potential to create difficulties in the administration of the estate. While, though, it may well be that the administration of the estate could be carried out more quickly and cheaply were [the executors] to be on good terms, I do not think that the potential problems are such as to warrant the executors' removal. As I see it, the poor relations between the parties need not and should not either prevent or impede substantially the administration of the estate.

Perhaps the difference between **Angus v Emmott** and **Kershaw v Micklethwaite** is that in the former case the administration could not proceed until the disagreement was settled. The judge thought that there was no prospect of the executors coming to an agreement and so agreed to their replacement. However, in the latter case, while there was friction between beneficiaries and the executors, the executors were in full agreement as to how they should proceed with the administration of the estate.

In *Isaac* v *Isaac* [2005] EWHC 435 (Ch) Park J stressed that removal of a trustee is a very serious step to take. In the case, Park J said that the trustee whose removal was sought 'had not done anything to endanger the trust property and there was no maintainable allegation . . . of want of honesty, capacity or reasonable fidelity.' He went on to say that the applicants were not really dissatisfied with their welfare in their capacity as beneficiaries but were dissatisfied that they were unable to receive the advantages of personally owning substantial shareholdings in the company.

In his judgment, Park J took an orthodox approach to the question of removing trustees. As regards the general principle guiding the court in the exercise of its inherent jurisdiction, he quoted *Lewin on Trusts*, which referred to it as being

> the welfare of the beneficiaries and the competent administration of the trust in their favour. In cases of positive misconduct the court will, without hesitation, remove the trustee who has abused his trust; but it is not every mistake or neglect of duty or inaccuracy of conduct on the part of a trustee that will induce the court to adopt such a course . . .

Park J said it was 'a drastic step for the court to take' and one that should only be taken 'in a clear case' and that had removal been a live issue (the trustee had already decided to retire) he would not have ordered his removal.

Disclaimer

At any time before acceptance a trustee may elect to disclaim. The law is not so perverse as to force a trustee to accept the office against his will. It is most unlikely that an unwilling trustee would perform his duties satisfactorily. It is not possible to make a partial disclaimer: the choice is either to disclaim totally or act as trustee in relation to all the trust and all the trust property. Disclaimer may be express or may be implied from the conduct of the trustee. However, once the trustee has accepted the office, disclaimer becomes impossible. In some cases there has been considerable delay in the 'disclaimer' being made and there may be some argument as to the effect of this delay. One argument is that the delay could be construed as evidence that there has been an acceptance and so the 'disclaimer' is of no effect. A second argument is that a long delay coupled with inactivity *qua* trustee may actually be evidence that a disclaimer by conduct has been made.

It is often difficult to decide whether or not a trustee has accepted the office. Once accepted, the office cannot be disclaimed. In general, if the person concerned has purported to do acts which a trustee would normally do, or has taken control over the trust property, acceptance will have taken place.

Death

Trustees hold the trust property as joint tenants and so on any death the property automatically vests in the remaining trustees. They should, of course, ensure that all the trust property is duly registered in the names of the remaining trustees: for example, any shares must be placed in the names of the surviving trustees.

The office of trustee is also held jointly and will pass to the surviving trustees. (The Trustee Act 1925 s 18(1) states that when trusts are given to two or more trustees jointly, the same can be exercised by the survivors.)

On the death of the last surviving or sole trustee the trust property devolves on his personal representatives, who hold the property on the terms of the trusts. Section 18(2) allows, but does not compel, the personal representatives to exercise all the powers of the dead trustee. Once a new trustee is appointed the powers of the personal representatives end.

Special types of trustees

The Public Trustee

The Public Trustee is a corporation sole established by the Public Trustee Act 1906. He may act as a trustee either alone or jointly with others as a normal trustee, but he may not act as a trustee for a charitable trust, in relation to the administration of insolvent estates or as a trustee of a trust created under a deed of arrangement for the benefit of creditors. He may not usually accept a trust which involves running a business. He may refuse to act as a trustee but not solely on the ground of the small value of the trust property. The Public Trustee is often appointed as a last resort if there is no one else who is ready, willing and able to be a trustee. He may act as a custodian trustee, as a personal representative or as a judicial trustee.

The powers of the Public Trustee were explored in *Re Duxbury's Settlement Trusts* [1995] 3 All ER 145. The Public Trustee was appointed as a sole trustee replacing Barclays Bank Trust Company, who in turn replaced the three original trustees (who were individuals). Under clause 16 of the settlement it was stated that 'no discretion . . . shall be exercisable at any time when there are less than two trustees'. The court was asked to decide two questions: first, were the bank and the Public Trustee properly appointed and, secondly, could the Public Trustee exercise discretions under the settlement despite the wording of clause 16? At first instance, Rattee J held that, although the Public Trustee was properly appointed, the Public Trustee could not, alone, exercise the discretions. The fact that the court held that the appointment of the bank and then the Public Trustee were valid is interesting. In effect, it might be argued that, by appointing a sole trustee, this requirement could result in discretions not being exercisable, as clause 16 stated that discretions could not be exercised when there were less than two trustees. On appeal, the Court of Appeal held that the appointment was proper but also that the Public Trustee could exercise the discretions alone. The Court of Appeal stated that under s 5(1) of the Public Trustee Act 1906 the Public Trustee may be appointed in all cases as a sole trustee. Section 5(1) states: 'The Public Trustee may . . . be appointed to be a trustee of any . . . settlement or other instrument creating a trust . . . as if he were private trustee [and] although the trustees originally appointed were two or more, the Public Trustee may be appointed the sole trustee.' In *Re Moxon* [1916] 2 Ch 595, Sargeant J held that where the Public Trustee was appointed s 5 overrode a requirement in the trust instrument for there to be three trustees. The Court of Appeal applied a similar reasoning to the instant case and stated that if the Public Trustee may be appointed as a sole trustee it has to follow that he may act as a sole trustee, despite any express statement to the contrary in the settlement. It would be pointless appointing a trustee who was unable to act. Appointment and action are inseparable in this situation.

From 1 July 1995, the Public Trustee has a new role. Under s 14 of the Law Reform (Miscellaneous Provisions) Act 1994, the estate of an intestate vests in the Public Trustee until administrators are appointed. Formerly, the estate of an intestate vested in the

President of the Family Division of the High Court. Additionally, the Act states that the estate of a testator will vest in the Public Trustee where, at the date of the death or any time before probate is granted, there is no executor with the power to obtain probate. This latter provision will apply, for example, if all the executors named in the will predecease the testator or where all the named executors renounce probate. The legislation makes it clear that the Public Trustee will not obtain any beneficial interest in property vesting in him or come under any duty in respect of it. In the past, actions (e.g. possession proceedings) have been brought against the President of the Family Division. The provisions of the 1994 Act make it clear that it would not be appropriate to bring similar actions against the Public Trustee.

The Public Trustee and Official Solicitor are independent statutory office holders. Although the Official Solicitor and the Public Trustee have a number of separate functions their respective trusts, estates and deputyships are managed by the same team. Their office (OSPT) is an arm's length body of the Ministry of Justice that supports their work.

Judicial trustees

The Judicial Trustee Act 1896 permits the High Court to appoint a judicial trustee. The application can be made by the settlor, by the trustees or by a beneficiary and the appointment is at the discretion of the court. The court may appoint 'any fit and proper' person as a judicial trustee and in the absence of such a person may appoint an official of the court. The Public Trustee may be appointed as a judicial trustee. The idea behind the Act was to provide a middle course where the administration of a trust had broken down and it was not desired to put the estate to the expense of a full administration by the court. The judicial trustee will operate in close contact with the court and is subject to the court's control and supervision. The Act provides that a judicial trustee may be paid such sums as the court may order to cover any outlay and all his work.

Custodian trustees

This office was created by the Public Trustee Act 1906. The trust property and the trust documents of title (such as share certificates) are vested in the custodian trustee but the day-to-day management of the trust stays in the hands of the managing trustees, who also exercise any discretions and carry out any duties under the trust. Any money paid to or by the trust must be channelled through the custodian trustee. One advantage of this type of arrangement is that new managing trustees can be appointed without having to worry about vesting the trust property in them.

The Public Trustee may act as a custodian trustee, as may those corporations authorised under the Public Trustee Act 1906 and various statutory rules, including the Public Trustee Rules.

The Public Trustee Act 1906 authorises custodian trustees to charge fees for their work but the fee is limited to that which would be chargeable by the Public Trustee.

Trust corporations

It is becoming increasingly common to appoint professional trustees to administer a trust and in many cases the executor and trustee department of a bank will be used, which is an example of a trust corporation. Many insurance companies have trustee departments, which will also be trust corporations.

One of the advantages of appointing a trust corporation is, apart from the expert administration, that there need be no worries about the trustee dying and a replacement trustee having to be found. The major disadvantage is that trust corporations will charge for their services.

A trust corporation often has an advantage over an individual in that in some cases a single trust corporation can act whereas it requires at least two individuals. For example, a trust corporation can give a valid receipt for money arising from the sale of land; if the trustees were individuals the receipt has to be given by at least two trustees.

A definition of a trust corporation is in the Trustee Act 1925 s 68(18): ' "Trust corporation" means the Public Trustee or a corporation either appointed by the court in any particular case to be a trustee or entitled by rules made under subsection (3) of section four of the Public Trustee Act 1906, to act as a custodian trustee . . .'

The Public Trustee, the Treasury Solicitor and the Official Solicitor are trust corporations.

Also, corporations entitled to act as custodian trustees under the Public Trustee Act 1906 can act as trust corporations. These have to satisfy statutory criteria.

Trust corporations have no special right to be paid and in this respect are in the same position as other trustees. However, no trust corporation will accept a trusteeship unless there is an adequate charging clause, and the Trustee Act 2000 sections 28 and 29 now govern the right to remuneration.

Summary

- Trustees occupy a pivotal role and in many ways have an unenviable lot. Their position, duties and powers are governed by the terms of the trust and by a range of statutory provisions, in particular by the Trustee Acts 1925 and 2000, the Trusts of Land and Appointment of Trustees Act 1996 and the Trustee Delegation Act 1999. Additionally, in a number of areas, rules and principles have been developed by the courts.

- Trustees occupy a fiduciary position and thus must put the interests of their beneficiaries before any personal interests that they may have.

- The general rule is that trustees act without payment, but there are common law and statutory exceptions. In particular, the Trustee Act 2000 s 29 makes important changes to this general rule where the trustees are 'professional trustees'. In such cases the trustees are entitled to reasonable payment for the work that they do *qua* trustees. This provision can be excluded by the terms of the trust.

- The common law standard of care expected of trustees (the same standard of care as an ordinary prudent man of business would take in managing similar affairs of his own) has been modified under s 1(1) of the Trustee Act 2000 for a range of situations, providing for a 'statutory duty of care' which applies to a range of trustee activities. Where the provision applies, the trustees must exercise such care and skill as is reasonable in the circumstances. The expectations of trustees will be higher for professional trustees than for lay trustees.

- Despite a number of calls for reform, a clearly-worded provision in the trust documents can exclude or modify the liability of trustees for breaches of trust, including failure to carry out their prescribed duties or exceeding their powers.

- The initial trustees are normally named by the settlor in the trust documents, but there are underpinning statutory provisions and rules and principles created by the courts. The appointment of subsequent trustees is often dealt with in the initial trust documents again with an underpinning of statutory provisions and rules and principles created by the courts.

● A trustee's appointment may end or be ended in a wide variety of ways. This is sometimes dealt with in the initial trust documents. Also, there are underpinning statutory provisions and rules and principles created by the courts.

Further reading

Trusts of Land and Appointment of Trustees Act 1996

M Clements, 'The changing face of trusts: the Trusts of Land and Appointment of Trustees Act 1996' (1998) 61 MLR 56.
Wide-ranging survey of the Act and why it was needed, and also looks at some of the key provisions.

N Hopkins, 'The Trusts of Land and Appointment of Trustees Act 1996' [1996] Conv 411.
Wide-ranging review of the Act. Looks at the impact on the role of trustees.

Fiduciary position

F Barlow, 'Commentary on *Breakspear* v *Ackland* (2009) Ch 32', (2009) 5 PCB 327.
Discusses *Breakspear* v *Ackland* and whether to set aside appointments by the trustees because they were self-dealing transactions.

R Lee, 'Rethinking the content of the fiduciary obligation' (2009) Conv 236–53.
Discusses the fiduciary nature of trusteeship and in particular deals with the issue of conflict of duty and the non-profit rule.

E McCall '*Isaac* v *Isaac (No. 2)*: the court's jurisdiction to remove a trustee' (2009) 6 PCB 427.
Discusses *Isaac* v *Isaac (No. 2)* on the exercise of the court's inherent jurisdiction to remove a trustee in the interest of the beneficiaries.

Trustee Act 2000

T Harris, 'The Trustee Act 2000: plus ça change?' (2002) 152 (7037) NLJ 945.
Outlines the main provisions of the Act, covering the duty of care, investment, acquisition of land and appointing agents, etc.

Exclusion/restriction of liability clauses

S Bridge, 'Better regulation of trustee exemption clauses' (2006) 156 (7245) NLJ 1589.
Discusses the Law Commission report, 'Trustee Exemption Clauses', which proposes the introduction of a rule of professional practice rather than statutory reform.

A Hammerton, 'Trustee exemptions' (2005) 149 (32) SJ 976–7.
Discusses how successful trustee exemption clauses can protect negligent professional trustees.

F Quint 'Trustee exemption clauses: the alternatives' (2011) 2 PCB 84.
Discusses the Government's acceptance of the Law Commission's commendations and covers a range of protection for trustees in a variety of situations.

Special types of trustees

C Sanders, 'Public trustee reforms' (2002) 146 (25) Sol J 584.
The Public Trustee (Liability and Fees) Bill 2002 (now Act) changes the way the Public Trustee charges for providing a public sector trustee service of last resort.

15

Trustees' powers

After reading this chapter you should be able to:

1. Understand that the powers of trustees are often set out (at least in part) in the trust documents and that there is a range of underpinning statutory provisions, in particular those contained in the Trustee Acts 1925 and 2000 and the Trusts of Land and Appointment of Trustees Act 1996.

2. Understand and explain when the exercise of a discretion can be set aside under the rule in *Re Hastings-Bass*.

3. Understanding when the courts can (exceptionally) overturn the exercise of a discretion on the ground of mistake.

4. Understand the powers of trustees to sell trust property.

5. Understand the powers of trustees to insure trust property.

6. Understand the powers of trustees to maintain beneficiaries who are minors.

7. Understand and explain the power of trustees to allow capital to be used for the benefit of beneficiaries under the power of advancement.

Introduction

Objective 1

The next two chapters will deal with the powers and duties of the trustees. The general law (common law or statute), as supplemented by the terms of the trust, will impose on the trustees a wide range of duties which govern their administration of the trust. Some duties will relate to how the trustees deal with the trust property and others will cover their responsibilities towards the beneficiaries. The most important characteristic of a duty is that the trustee has no choice; the duty must be discharged.

The trustees will also have a number of powers relevant to the administration of the trust. Some of these will emanate from the general law while others will be expressly given by the terms of the trust. Some of the powers relate to the way that the trustees deal with the trust property, while others are concerned with the trustees' treatment of the beneficiaries. Trustees' powers are not mandatory; they merely provide a facility for the trustees.

They are not under an obligation to use a power and, if they do decide to use one of their powers, the manner in which they exercise it is entirely a matter for them. The powers are fiduciary powers and as such the trustees are under a duty to consider whether to exercise them or not, but having so considered there is no obligation to exercise. The general rule is that the court will not interfere with a decision to exercise or the manner of its exercise. (But see below.)

Every professionally drafted trust will have a number of express powers to supplement and, often, broaden out the powers given to all trustees by various statutory provisions.

The general rule is that trustees must discharge their role personally. Any powers that they may have must be exercised by the trustees and they must personally make the decisions in the course of administering the trust. However, there are several situations where trustees may delegate. Sometimes the delegation is simply the implementation of decisions made by the trustees, but in other cases the trustees are able to delegate the exercise of discretion/decision making. In particular, there are a number of statutory provisions.

This topic is dealt with in detail in Chapter 16.

The ambit of any express power or duty is a matter of construction, and obviously such powers must be carefully worded in order that the trustee is given exactly the power or duty which the settlor wishes to bestow. In order to find out what powers and duties a trustee possesses, and the extent of those powers and duties, it is necessary to read the terms of the trust instrument together with the provisions of the relevant statutes. It is always possible and sometimes desirable for the trustees to apply to the court, usually by an originating summons, for directions regarding their powers and duties relating to the management of the trust property.

The Trustee Act 2000 implements, with some minor modifications, changes to the powers and duties of trustees (primarily relating to duty of care, trustees' powers of investment and powers to appoint agents, nominees, etc.) recommended in the report of the Law Commission: 'Trustees' Powers and Duties' 1999 (Law Com. No. 260).

See Chapter 16.

The changes made by the Trustee Act 2000 (which came into effect on 1 February 2000) will be discussed at the appropriate points in this and a later chapter.

The Trusts of Land and Appointment of Trustees Act 1996, which became operative on 1 January 1997, created the concept of the trust of land. Under a trust of land, the ownership of the trust property is vested in the trustees. The Act redefines and widens the powers and duties of trustees of land. Section 6(1) grants to trustees of land all the powers of an absolute owner with respect to the land within their trust. The relevant provisions relating to powers and duties of trustees are covered in the appropriate sections of this chapter (powers) and Chapter 16 (duties).

Standard of care

See Chapter 14 (p. 403).

Setting aside the exercise of a discretion

Objective 2

The rule in *Re Hastings-Bass* [1974] 2 All ER 193 (as developed in subsequent cases) gave the trustees what is often called a 'get out of jail card'. It allowed trustees in many situations to exercise a power or discretion, discover that the results were not as they would have wished and have the exercise set aside using the rule in *Re Hastings-Bass* as developed in subsequent cases. Although the precise extent of the rule was not clear, it could enable trustees to escape liability for their decisions and could result in the beneficiaries being spared the adverse effects of the decisions. So everyone was a winner except, in many cases, HMRC. Many decisions that were set aside under the rule involved failed attempts by trustees to arrange the trust affairs so little or no tax was paid. If the trustees' decision was allowed to stand the failed attempt often would have resulted in tax or larger amounts of tax being paid than the trustees and the beneficiaries were planning for. When the decision was set aside under the rule the trustees could then reconsider their decision and put in place a new arrangement to save tax.

But in *Pitt v Holt and another; Futter v Futter* [2011] EWCA Civ 197; [2011] 2 All ER 450 the Court of Appeal reviewed the ratio of *Re Hastings-Bass* and decided that the rule as it had been developed was based on a misunderstanding of the case. In *Futter v HMRC; Pitt v HMRC* [2013] UKSC 26; [2013] 3 All ER 429 the Supreme Court dismissed the appeal in so far as it related to the rule, agreeing with the Court of Appeal that the rule in *Re Hastings-Bass* was a case on trustees acting in excess of their powers and was not a case on trustees exercising a power on the basis of inadequate or improper considerations.

The rule in Re Hastings-Bass before Pitt v Holt

In this section, 'the rule in *Re Hastings-Bass*' is used to mean the rule as developed in a number of cases heard before *Pitt v Holt and another; Futter v Futter*.

In the context of the exercise of a power, the rule in *Re Hastings-Bass* could be used to set aside the trustees' exercise of a power which did not achieve the end result that the trustees were intending.

As noted above, in many cases it was HMRC that suffered when trustees used the rule in *Re Hastings-Bass* to have their exercise of a discretion or power set aside.

Under the rule, the trustees' decision may be set aside if they (a) failed to take into account something which they ought to have taken into account or have taken into account something which they should not, and (b) would not have exercised the power in the way that they did had they taken account of the thing they have ignored or ignored the thing they should not have taken into account.

In *Re Hastings-Bass,* Buckley LJ said:

> Where by the terms of a trust . . . a trustee is given a discretion as to some matter under which he acts in good faith, the court should not interfere with his action notwithstanding that it does not have the full effect which he intended unless (1) what he achieved is unauthorised by the power conferred upon him or (2) it is clear that he would not have acted as he did (a) had he not taken into account considerations which he should not have taken into account or (b) had he not failed to take into account considerations which he ought to have taken into account.

In subsequent cases it was the second but not the first limb of Buckley LJ's statement that was developed and which became known as the rule in *Re Hastings-Bass*.

In *Re Hasting-Bass* Buckley LJ's formulation is in a negative form. In *Mettoy Pension Trustees Ltd v Evans* [1991] 2 All ER 513 Warner J set out the rule in a positive form.

> Where a trustee acts under a discretion given to him by the terms of the trust, the court will interfere with his action if it is clear that he would not have acted as he did had he not failed to take into account considerations which he ought to have taken into account.

In *Sieff v Fox* [2005] 3 All ER 693, Lloyd L J (sitting as a judge of the High Court) held that a decision of the trustees in the case could be set aside under the *Hastings-Bass* rule as they had failed to take account of the tax consequences of their decision, owing to the fact that they had been given incorrect tax advice and had they had the correct advice they would not have taken the decision. In *Sieff* v *Fox* Lloyd LJ restated the rule in *Hastings-Bass*. He said that the rule could be invoked to set aside a decision of trustees acting under a discretion where the trustees are 'free to decide whether or not to exercise the discretion' if the effect of the exercise of their discretion is different from what they intended, if it is clear that they would not have acted as they did had they not failed to take into account considerations which they ought to have taken into account or had taken into account considerations that they ought not to have taken into account.

In using the phrase 'free to decide whether or not to exercise the discretion' Lloyd LJ was distinguishing cases where the trustees are under an obligation to act from those where the trustees may decide whether or not they will exercise discretion.

Lloyd LJ said that, although the mistake related to fiscal consequences rather than being a mistake as to the substantive legal effect of a decision, this did not mean that the rule in *Hastings-Bass* was inapplicable. In many cases the tax consequences of a decision would be a relevant consideration.

In *Sieff* v *Fox*, Lloyd LJ said that he could not decide all the outstanding issues on the rule as it had developed and that the task would fall on the Court of Appeal when an appropriate case came before it. In the event, that case was *Pitt v Holt and another; Futter v Futter* in which the leading judgment was given by Lloyd LJ. (See below for a discussion of this case.)

There were at least three key issues raised by the cases developing the rule in *Re Hastings-Bass*.

First, was the effect of the rule to render the exercise of a discretion void or voidable? There appears to be no definitive decision on this and the view changes from case to case.

In *Abacus Trust Company (Isle of Man)* v *Barr* [2003] 2 WLR 1362 Lightman J, after having surveyed a number of cases, said that the effect was to render the decision voidable, not void. This is supported by *Sieff* in which Lloyd LJ said that, while in the instant case this issue was not relevant, he was attracted by the arguments that the rule made decisions voidable. This gives the courts some discretion and allows them to examine the facts of each particular case.

There have been some more recent decisions in which this point has been considered but there is no consistent view as to the effect of applying the rule.

- *Jiggens and English* v *Low and Low* [2010] EWHC 1566 (Ch). This is a first-instance decision in which the court said that the effect of applying the rule in *Re Hastings-Bass* was that the disposal was void.

- *Wyantt & others* v *Tyrrell & others* (2010) unreported. This is a first-instance decision on the application of the rule in *Re Hastings-Bass*. The court said that it was not necessary to decide if the effect of the application of the rule was to make the deed void or voidable, but that voidable seemed the appropriate solution.

Secondly, did the rule apply if the trustees *might* have come to a different decision or only if the evidence is that they *would* have come to a different decision?

There are were some cases where the courts have said that the rule applies if the trustees *might* have come to a different decision (e.g. *Stannard* v *Fisons Pension Trusts Ltd* [1991] Pensions LR 225 which is a case on a pension fund where the trustees were under a duty to act by appropriating an amount to be applied for the benefit of transferring employees though they had to decide, after consulting an actuary, what amount would be appropriate as being an amount that they decided was fair and equitable). But in *Sieff*, Lloyd LJ used '*would*'. But he sets out situations where *might* is correct (where the trustees are obliged to act). The question is whether the 'tightening' of the rule in e.g. *Stannard* is limited to pension trusts. Are there sufficient differences with pension cases to justify a difference between such cases and cases involving private trusts? Or is the key difference between *Stannard* and other cases that in *Stannard* the trustees were under a duty, whereas cases where the '*would*' approach is correct are cases where the trustees were simply exercising a discretionary power? There are some indications that the courts may have been moving towards tightening the rule in other types of trusts. For example, in *Breadner v Granville-Grossman* [2000] 4 All ER 705 Park J said:

> [I]t cannot be right, whenever trustees do something which they later regret and think they ought not to have done, they can say they never did it in the first place. It was not correct to suggest that whenever trustees do something which they later regret and think that they ought not to have done, then they can say that they never did it in the first place. However, the main ways at present open to the court to control the application of the principle are: (a) to insist on a stringent application of the tests as they have been laid down, (b) to take a reasonable and not over-exigent view of what it is that the trustees ought to have taken into account, and (c) to adopt a critical approach to contentions that the trustees would have acted differently if they had realised the true position.

Thirdly, what sort of mistake came within the rule? Can a mistake as to the consequences, as opposed to the effect, of a decision be set aside under the rule?

The rule was initially thought to be restricted to mistakes as to the effect of an act. But in *Abacus Trust Co v NSPCC* [2001] WTLR 953 and in *Green v Cobham* [2000] WTLR 1101 the rule was applied in the case of mistakes as to the consequences of a decision. This approach gains support from the judgment of Lloyd LJ in *Sieff*.

Pitt v Holt: review of the rule by the Court of Appeal

As stated above, in *Sieff v Fox*, Lloyd L J (sitting as a judge of the High Court) said that he thought that the rule in *Re Hastings-Bass* needed to be reviewed by the Court of Appeal. It was therefore a happy coincidence that one of the members of the Court of Appeal in *Pitt v Holt; Futter v Futter* [2011] EWCA Civ 197; [2011] 2 All ER 450 was Lloyd LJ. It was he who gave the leading judgment.

In both *Pitt v Holt* and *Futter v Futter* there was an application to reverse actions that had unintended or unconsidered tax consequences.

In *Pitt v Holt*, Mr Pitt suffered severe brain injuries. His receiver was his wife. Her advisers suggested settling sums received by way of damages on particular trusts. Neither the receiver nor her advisers considered the impact of inheritance tax but a large inheritance tax charge was triggered. It was sought to set aside the settlement, as IHT consequences had not been considered. It was claimed that she would not have entered into the transaction had she appreciated the tax consequences.

Pitt v Holt involved the person appointed by the Court of Protection as the receiver of a person severely injured in a road accident. The court said that the receiver was acting in a fiduciary capacity and it was accepted that the receiver could use the rule in *Re Hastings-Bass* if it was applicable in the case. Alternatively, relief was claimed in equity on the grounds of mistake. (See p. 435.)

In *Futter v Futter*, trustees were wrongly advised that exercising their discretions in a particular way would not attract a capital gains tax charge. There was no claim based on mistake. The only claim was based on the rule in *Re Hastings-Bass*.

Lloyd LJ analysed *Re Hastings-Bass* and its development in subsequent cases. His key finding was that the rule in *Re Hastings-Bass* as developed in subsequent cases was based on a mistaken view as to the ratio of the case. Thus the rule as developed needed to be reviewed and redefined.

Lloyd LJ identified what he saw as the error made in cases decided after *Re Hastings-Bass*. Lloyd LJ identified a paragraph in Buckley LJ's judgment which Lloyd LJ saw as an incorrect statement of the ratio of the case. (See p. 428 for the relevant paragraph.) In the paragraph, Buckley LJ covered two distinct issues. The first concerned actions that were beyond the powers of the trustees and the second concerned decisions which resulted from inadequate deliberation. In relation to the second issue Buckley LJ talked about trustees taking into account considerations which they ought not to have taken into account, and failing to take into account considerations that they should have taken into account. But Buckley LJ was referring to one of the submissions of the Revenue which was rejected. In fact, Lloyd LJ said, *Re Hastings-Bass* was a case where trustees had acted outside their powers. Lloyd LJ labelled these situations as ones where the trustees act '*ultra vires*'.

Lloyd LJ explained '*ultra vires*' acts. For example, a disposition by a trustee is *ultra vires* if it is a misapplication of property outside the four corners of the discretion, also a disposition of property to a non-object of the power is *ultra vires*. Such acts are void and have no legal or fiscal effect. Similarly, if the trustees used the wrong kind of document to achieve their desired effect or did not obtain necessary consents before acting, they would be acting *ultra vires*.

Most applications of the rule subsequent to *Re Hastings-Bass* were not '*ultra vires*' cases, but rather they were cases where the trustees were acting within their powers but made a decision which they later regretted and wished to overturn. These cases were not therefore strictly within the ratio of *Re Hastings-Bass* and so were, at best, questionable decisions. They were cases based on the rule as developed in subsequent cases, which were based on a misunderstanding of *Re Hastings-Bass*. These cases built on the second element in the paragraph of Buckley LJ's judgment (inadequate deliberation). So the development of the rule was based on a misunderstanding of the ratio of *Re Hastings-Bass*.

Lloyd LJ's position was problematical as *Re Hastings-Bass* was a Court of Appeal decision so he could not simply overrule it. It is arguable that it was open to the Court of Appeal to decide that the rule as developed, particularly in and through *Mettoy Pension Trustees Ltd* v *Evans*, was based on a mistake as to the ratio of *Re Hastings-Bass* and was thus *per incuriam* and could be overruled. What Lloyd LJ did do was to re-state the rule.

In situations where the trustees are not acting *ultra vires*, Lloyd LJ said that actions of trustees can only be set aside where the trustees act within their powers but act in a way that is in breach of their fiduciary duty. In these cases the action of the trustee was voidable.

Review of the law by the Supreme Court

In *Futter* v *HMRC; Pitt* v *HMRC* [2013] 3 All ER 429 the Supreme Court dismissed the appeal in so far as it related to the rule in *Re Hastings-Bass*. Lord Walker, who gave the only judgment, agreed with Lloyd LJ's views and arguments.

Lord Walker agreed with Lloyd LJ that the development of the rule by and through *Mettoy Pension Trustees Ltd* v *Evans* was based on a mistake or misunderstanding of the true ratio of *Re Hastings-Bass*.

Lord Walker said:

32 I respectfully agree with Lloyd LJ's view that the basis on which *Mettoy* was decided cannot be found in the reasoning which led to the decision in *Hastings-Bass*. It can claim to

be an application of Buckley LJ's summary statement of principle, but only if that statement is taken out of context and in isolation from the earlier part of the judgment. If the principle applied by Warner J [in *Mettoy Pension Trustees Ltd* v *Evans*] merits a name at all, it should be called the rule in *Mettoy*. But the rule as formulated by Warner J has given rise to many difficulties, both in principle and in practice.

Lord Walker set out three defects that might affect the exercise of a power by a trustee:

- Excessive execution (what Lloyd LJ called *ultra vires* acts in the Court of Appeal).
- Inadequate deliberations.
- Fraudulent appointment.

Excessive execution

This head covers a situation where the trustees have a power but their exercise is outside the terms of the power. It is clear that in this situation the exercise of the power is void.

Lloyd LJ in the Court of Appeal said:

92 It seems to me that Lightman J's analysis in *Abacus* v *Barr* points to the distinction between *Re Hastings-Bass* itself and the later cases in which the *Hastings-Bass* rule has been developed. In *Re Hastings-Bass* the issue was whether what the trustees had done was an exercise of the power of advancement under Section 32 at all. If it was not, then it was entirely void.

A simple example of excessive execution would be where trustees have the power to dispose of trust property to A or B but dispose of it to C.

Inadequate deliberations

A successful application to have the exercise of a power set aside must be based on a breach of fiduciary duty by the trustee.

Lord Walker said:

74 In my view Lightman J was right to hold [in *Abacus Trust Co (Isle of Man)* v *Barr* [2003] EWHC 114 (Ch)] that for the rule to apply the inadequate deliberation on the part of the trustees must be sufficiently serious as to amount to a breach of fiduciary duty. Breach of duty is essential (in the full sense of that word) because it is only a breach of duty on the part of the trustees that entitles the court to intervene (apart from the special case of powers of maintenance of minor beneficiaries, where the court was in the past more interventionist: see para 64 above). It is not enough to show that the trustees' deliberations have fallen short of the highest possible standards, or that the court would, on a surrender of discretion by the trustees, have acted in a different way. Apart from exceptional circumstances (such as an impasse reached by honest and reasonable trustees) only breach of fiduciary duty justifies judicial intervention.

If the trustees have taken and followed professional but incorrect advice, the trustees are unlikely to be in breach of their duty but the advisers are liable to be sued in professional negligence.

In both *Pitt* and *Futter* the fiduciaries had taken and acted on tax advice which was considered to be competent and so were not in breach of their fiduciary duty. So in neither case could the rule be used to set aside the decisions to adopt the supposed tax savings schemes.

Invoking the rule

Under the 'old' rule, it was the trustees who usually brought a friendly action to have their exercise of a power or discretion set aside. After *Pitt* v *Holt*, it will normally be the beneficiaries and not the trustees who will bring actions based on the rule. This is almost always bound to cause bad feeling between beneficiaries and trustees.

Lord Walker sounded a warning for trustees saying:

> 69 It is a striking feature of the development of the *Hastings-Bass* rule that it has led to trustees asserting and relying on their own failings, or those of their advisers, in seeking the assistance of the court. This was pointed out in no uncertain terms by Norris J in his first-instance judgment in *Futter* . . . There may be cases in which there is for practical purposes no other suitable person to bring the matter before the court, but I agree with Lloyd LJ's observation [in the Court of Appeal] that in general it would be inappropriate for trustees to take the initiative in commencing proceedings of this nature. They should not regard them as uncontroversial proceedings in which they can confidently expect to recover their costs out of the trust fund.

Under the 'new' rule, where successful applications by beneficiaries must be based on a breach of duty by the trustees, the actions may well become more 'hostile' and could well endanger the relationship between beneficiaries and trustees. Might one of the effects of the new rule be to make it more difficult to persuade people to act as trustees, at least where there is no wide exoneration clause?

Does the rule render the exercise of a power void or voidable?

As mentioned above there was some uncertainty as to whether under the rule the exercise of a power was void or voidable. In the Supreme Court, Lord Walker was very clear that the effect was to render the exercise voidable. So, unless and until the exercise of a power is set aside by the court it remains valid and effective.

Lord Walker said:

> 93 Counsel on both sides readily admitted that they had hesitated over this point, but in the end they were all in agreement that Lloyd LJ was right in holding . . . that,
>
> > 'if an exercise by trustees of a discretionary power is within the terms of the power, but the trustees have in some way breached their duties in respect of that exercise, then (unless it is a case of a fraud on the power) the trustees' act is not void but it may be voidable at the instance of a beneficiary who is adversely affected.'
>
> In my judgment that is plainly right, and in the absence of further argument on the point it is unnecessary to add much to it . . . We are in an area in which the court has an equitable jurisdiction of a discretionary nature, although the discretion is not at large, but must be exercised in accordance with well-settled principles.
>
> > The working-out of these principles will raise problems which must be dealt with on a case by case basis. The mistake claim in *Pitt* involves a problem of that sort. But it is unnecessary and inappropriate to prolong what is already a very long judgment by further discussion of problems that are not now before this court.

Exercising the discretion in tax avoidance cases

Lord Walker sounded a warning about the exercise of the court's discretion to set aside a voidable transaction where tax avoidance is involved. (See below at p. 437.) Although Lord Walker made the statement in relation to setting aside transactions because of mistake, it can be argued that the same approach could be taken by the courts when deciding whether or not to set aside a transaction when applying the rule in *Re Hastings-Bass.*

Exoneration clauses

In situations where there are professional trustees, there will often be exclusion clauses which might lead to trustees being protected from liability for their actions. Of course, all will depend on the wording of the exoneration clause. But in a well-drawn clause, the trustees may well escape liability for their breach, provided they have not acted dishonestly.

But what is the impact of such clauses on the applicability of the rule in *Re Hastings-Bass*?

Lord Walker set out HMRC's argument that such a clause does not prevent there from being a breach. It simply relieves the trustee from liability for the breach:

> 89 Even if a trustee is exonerated from liability to pay equitable compensation, he is still liable to injunctive relief to prevent a threatened breach of trust, and personal and proprietary remedies may be available against persons who receive assets distributed in breach of trust. Moreover an exoneration clause does not protect a trustee against removal from office by order of the court.

Unfortunately Lord Walker did not say whether or not he accepted the argument or whether an exoneration clause could ever exclude the applicability of the rule.

But he did go on to to say that:

> The *Futter No. 3* and *No. 5* settlements contain exoneration clauses in conventional terms, stating that 'in the professed execution of the trusts and powers hereof no trustee shall be liable for a breach of trust arising from a mistake or omission made by him in good faith'. I would not treat that clause as ousting the application of the *Hastings-Bass* rule, if it were otherwise applicable.

So we are left with the situation that, according to Lord Walker, exoneration clauses will not always exclude the applicability of the rule, but they may sometimes. This is not a very satisfactory state and it awaits future cases to refine the position.

To whom does the rule apply?

A question that is left open after *Futter* v *HMRC*; *Pitt* v *HMRC* is whether or not all fiduciaries are within the rule or not. In *Pitt*, Mrs Pitt was not a trustee. She was a receiver under the Mental Health Act 1983. At first instance HMRC had argued that the rule was only applicable to trustees. But this was not accepted by the court on the basis that the judge considered that there was no material difference between a trustee and a receiver exercising a power on behalf of a patient under the Mental Health Act 1983. Thus it remains to be seen if the courts will extend the rule to cover all or just some fiduciaries.

Would or might?

As set out above there was uncertainty as to whether the rule applied if the trustees *would* have acted differently or *might* have acted differently in cases where their deliberations have been inadequate. Lord Walker supplies no answer to this.

He said:

> To lay down a rigid rule of either 'would not' or 'might not' would inhibit the court in seeking the best practical solution in the application of the *Hastings-Bass* rule in a variety of different factual situations.

Good news? For whom?

This decision may well be good news for HMRC, as actions that trigger unexpected tax charges are less likely to be reversed than in the past. And perhaps good news for professional advisers, as trustees may well seek their advice more often, at the expense of the trust funds. On the other hand, they and their insurers will be anxious that a way of avoiding the consequences of bad advice has been removed.

Fraudulent appointment

In *Futter* v *HMRC, Pitt* v *HMRC* Lord Walker said:

> Lloyd LJ [in the Court of Appeal] then addressed the difficult question of how a fraudulent appointment (that is, an appointment ostensibly within the scope of a power, but made for an improper purpose) is to be fitted into the classification. The exercise of an equitable power may be fraudulent in this sense whether or not the person exercising it is a fiduciary. A well-known example of trustees exercising a power for an improper purpose is provided by *In Re Pauling* [1964] Ch 303, in which a power ostensibly exercisable for the benefit of young adult beneficiaries was used to distribute trust capital to be frittered away on their improvident parents' living expenses.
>
> There is Court of Appeal authority that a fraudulent appointment is void rather than voidable: *Cloutte* v *Storey* [1911] 1 Ch 18. In that case the appointee under an improper appointment had charged his equitable interest as security for a loan (and in doing so made two false statutory declarations as to the genuineness of the appointment). It was held that the lender had no security, even though it had no notice of the equitable fraud. It is an authority which has bedevilled discussion of the true nature of the *Hastings-Bass* rule. Lightman J found the judgment of Farwell LJ problematic ([*Abacus Trust Co (Isle of Man)* v *Barr* [2003] 1 All ER 763], para 31) and Lloyd LJ shared his reservations (para 98). So do I. It is hard to know what to make of Farwell LJ's observations [1911] 1 Ch 18, 31:
>
> > 'If an appointment is void at law, no title at law can be founded on it; but this is not so in equity: the mere fact that the appointment is void does not prevent a Court of Equity from having regard to it: eg, an appointment under a limited power to a stranger is void, but equity may cause effect to be given to it by means of the doctrine of election.'
>
> The decision in *Cloutte* v *Storey* may have to be revisited one day. For present purposes it is sufficient to note that a fraudulent appointment (that is, one shown to have been made for a positively improper purpose) may need a separate pigeon-hole somewhere between the categories of excessive execution and inadequate deliberation.

So having raised the issue as a difficult one, Lord Walker simply deferred any decision.

Setting aside the exercise of a discretion on the ground of mistake

Objective
3

In *Pitt* (but not in *Futter*), it was claimed that the actions of the trustees should be set, using the equitable jurisdiction to set aside voluntary transactions, aside on the ground of mistake.

In the Court of Appeal Lloyd LJ discussed the requirements for a transaction to be set aside on the ground of mistake. Lloyd LJ said that as well as the mistake being sufficiently serious it must be a mistake as to the legal effect rather than as to the consequences of the transaction. In the event the mistake was found to be as to the consequences rather than as to the legal effect of the transaction. Thus the transaction could not be set aside under this head. The court did not have to decide if the mistake was sufficiently serious.

In the Supreme Court Lord Walker reviewed the test and, having analysed the case law, decided that the difference between effect and consequences was not relevant. The key requirement was that the mistake had to be sufficiently serious. In the event the mistake

435

was considered to be sufficiently grave and the transaction was set aside on the basis of mistake. The gravity test is known as the *Oglivie v Littleboy* test.

It is probable that following the 'tightening' of the rule in *Re Hastings-Bass* the use of mistake as the basis of an attempt to set aside the exercise of discretions by trustees will become more common.

What is a mistake in this context?

In *Futter v HMRC; Pitt v HMRC* Lord Walker made it clear that the mistake must be one that would make it unconscionable for it not to be corrected. He went on to discuss the characteristics of a 'relevant' mistake.

Lord Walker said:

104 For present purposes a mistake must be distinguished from mere ignorance or inadvertence, and also from what scholars in the field of unjust enrichment refer to as misprediction . . . These distinctions are reasonably clear in a general sort of way, but they tend to get blurred when it comes to facts of particular cases. The editors of Goff and Jones, *The Law of Unjust Enrichment*, 8th ed. (2011) para 9–11 comment that the distinction between mistake and misprediction can lead to 'some uncomfortably fine distinctions', and the same is true of the distinction between mistake and ignorance.

Forgetfulness, inadvertence or ignorance is not, as such, a mistake, but it can lead to a false belief or assumption which the law will recognise as a mistake. The Court of Appeal of Victoria has held that mistake certainly comprehends 'a mistaken belief arising from inadvertence to or ignorance of a specific fact or legal requirement': Ormiston JA in *Hookway v Racing Victoria Ltd* [2005] VSCA 310, (2005) 13 VR 444, 450. That case was on the borderline between voluntary disposition and contract. It concerned prize money for a horse race which was paid to the wrong owner because the official in charge of prize money was ignorant of a recent change in the rules of racing (permitting an appeal against disqualification after a drugs test). He made a mistake as to the real winner.

The gravity test

In *Futter v HMRC; Pitt v HMRC* Lord Walker said:

126 The gravity of the mistake must be assessed by a close examination of the facts, whether or not they are tested by cross-examination, including the circumstances of the mistake and its consequences for the person who made the vitiated disposition. Other findings of fact may also have to be made in relation to change of position or other matters relevant to the exercise of the court's discretion. Justice Paul Finn wrote in a paper, Equitable Doctrine and Discretion in Remedies published in Restitution: Past, Present and Future (1998):

'The courts quite consciously now are propounding what are acceptable standards of conduct to be exhibited in our relationships and dealings with others . . . A clear consequence of this emphasis on standards (and not on rules) is a far more instance-specific evaluation of conduct.'

The injustice (or unfairness or unconscionableness) of leaving a mistaken disposition uncorrected must be evaluated objectively, but with an intense focus (in Lord Steyn's well-known phrase in *In Re S (A Child)* [2005] 1 AC 593, para 17) on the facts of the particular case.

Lord Walker said that when assessing the gravity of a mistake the court will take into account all the relevant facts which will include the consequences of the mistake and the circumstances under which the mistake was made. It does not matter if the mistake was due to the carelessness of the donor unless of course the donor decided to run the risk of being wrong. Although HMRC argued that tax consequences should be regarded as being in a different category the court did not accept the argument and decided that tax consequences could be relevant in deciding if the mistake was sufficiently grave.

Mistake and tax avoidance

Initially in *Futter* the only relief sought was by way of an application of *Re Hastings-Bass*. The Supreme Court refused to allow the appellants to raise for the first time the issue of mistake.

In *Pitt* the tax avoidance scheme was straightforward but in *Futter* the scheme was considered to be far more artificial. To what extent will the courts allow a mistake – even a serious mistake – as to the tax implications of a transaction to be grounds for setting the transaction? It seems that public opinion is hardening and that tax avoidance schemes are being increasingly viewed as 'unacceptable' both by the public and by (some) members of Parliament.

Lord Walker said:

135 Had mistake been raised in *Futter* there would have been an issue of some importance as to whether the Court should assist in extricating claimants from a tax-avoidance scheme which had gone wrong. The scheme adopted by Mr Futter was by no means at the extreme of artificiality . . . but it was hardly an exercise in good citizenship. In some cases of artificial tax avoidance the court might think it right to refuse relief, either on the ground that such claimants, acting on supposedly expert advice, must be taken to have accepted the risk that the scheme would prove ineffective, or on the ground that discretionary relief should be refused on grounds of public policy. Since the seminal decision of the House of Lords in *WT Ramsay Ltd* v *IRC* [1982] AC 300 there has been an increasingly strong and general recognition that artificial tax avoidance is a social evil which puts an unfair burden on the shoulders of those who do not adopt such measures. But it is unnecessary to consider that further on these appeals.

It is questionable if the role of the courts that Lord Walker is suggesting is an appropriate one. It is arguable that it should be the role of the legislature to set out the rules in such situations.

Applying *Pitt* v *Holt*

Although *Wright, Wright* v *(1) National Westminster Bank Plc and ors* (2014) Ch D, LTL 22/7/2014, is not a case on setting aside the exercise of a discretion, this first-instance case is one of the first to apply *Pitt* v *Holt*. The court set aside a discretionary trust on the grounds of mistake. On advice from the bank Mr Wright (H) transferred property into the trust. The beneficiaries were named as H, his wife (W), their children and remoter issue. When he created the trust H gave the bank a letter setting out his wishes to guide the trustee. The letter said that H's aim was to provide for his family in a tax-efficient manner, and that his intention was that the income from the settlement would be applied for the benefit of both his wife and children.

The settlor had made a mistake about the effect of the trust and believed that the income could be applied for the benefit of his wife during his lifetime. But in fact the terms of the trust stated that the bank (which was the trustee) could not exercise its power to apply any part of the income for the benefit of H or W. H said that had he realised that W could not benefit from the income of the trust he would not have set it up.

Norris J held that H had made a grave mistake and that it was just and appropriate for the court to exercise its discretion and set aside the trust. There had been a causative mistake that was so grave that it would be unconscionable to refuse relief. A mistake might be as to the legal character or nature of the transaction. The gravity of the mistake should be assessed on a close examination of the facts, including the circumstances of the mistake, its centrality to the transaction, and the seriousness of its consequences.

Power to sell

Express power

An express power to sell trust property is usually given in the trust instrument, and the precise extent of such a power will be a matter of construction. In the absence of an express power of sale, a statutory power will often exist.

Statutory powers of sale

Land

The 1989 Law Commission Report, 'Transfer of Land – Trusts of Land' (No. 181), made a number of far-reaching recommendations in relation to the powers of trustees of land. The trustees of land should, it was recommended, be put in much the same position as the absolute owner of land, although the powers should not be as readily exercisable. One consequence would be that the trustees would have the power to sell or retain the land and would have the power to apply the proceeds of sale to the purchase of land, including the purchase of a residence for a beneficiary. The powers recommended were wide but not unfettered, being subject to the general rule that trustees must exercise powers in the best interests of the beneficiaries. The Report is reflected in the provisions of the Trusts of Land and Appointment of Trustees Act 1996.

The Trusts of Land and Appointment of Trustees Act 1996, which came into force on 1 January 1997, creates the concept of the trust of land. Under a trust of land, the ownership of the trust property is vested in the trustees. Section 6(1) grants to trustees of land all the powers of an absolute owner with respect to the land within their trust. This, of course, includes the power to sell.

If land is settled under the Settled Land Act 1925, s 38(1) of that Act vests the power of sale in the tenant for life and the statute imposes very little limit on how the power of sale should be exercised.

Land could be held on a trust for sale which was either expressly created or which arose under a statutory provision.

Under the Trusts of Land and Appointment of Trustees Act 1996 no new Settled Land Act settlements can be created after 1996. Any attempt to do so will result in there being a trust of land. From 1 January 1997 all then existing trusts which contained land became trusts of land under s 1(1)(b) of the Trusts of Land and Appointment of Trustees Act 1996. The only exception is then existing Settled Land Act settlements which will continue to operate as strict settlements until all the land (or heirlooms) leave the trust. If an express trust for sale of land was created either before 1997 or after 1996, it will be a trust of land and a statutory power to postpone sale is implied into every such trust under s 4(1). This power to postpone cannot be excluded and the trustees are not liable in any way if they postpone the sale indefinitely.

An example of where property is held on a statutory trust with a power to sell occurs if a person dies without having made a will, i.e. intestate. Under Schedule 2 paragraph 5(2) to the Trusts of Land and Appointment of Trustees Act 1996, s 33 of the Administration of

Estates Act 1925 is amended and on the death, after 1996 of any person intestate as to any real or personal estate, that estate shall be held by his personal representatives with the power to sell it.

Formerly, under a trust for sale the land was vested in the trustees and they had the duty to sell but usually had a power to postpone that sale either under an express trust provision, under the terms of the statute imposing the trust or under the Law of Property Act 1925 s 25. But under the Trusts of Land and Appointment of Trustees Act 1996, from 1 January 1997 all trusts for sale became trusts of land, with the land vested in the trustees. Statutory trusts for sale are replaced by trusts with a power to sell. Trusts for sale of land which are created by a disposition are always subject to a power to postpone the sale, as noted above.

When land which is settled or which is held under a trust for sale is sold, the receipt of at least two trustees or a trust corporation is necessary.

Personalty

The position if chattels are held on a statutory or express trust for sale is that the trustees are under a duty to sell. The receipt of one trustee will give a purchaser a good discharge.

Personalty may also be subjected to an implied trust for sale, for example, under the rule in *Howe* v *Lord Dartmouth* (see p. 470). With respect to trusts created or arising on or after 1 October 2013, under s 2 of the Trusts (Capital and Income) Act 2013 the rule in *Howe* v *Lord Dartmouth* will only apply where settlors or testators expressly include the duty to apportion or expressly exclude the operation of the Act.

The Settled Land Act 1925 s 67 provides that where chattels (e.g. heirlooms) are held on a trust under which they will devolve with settled land, the tenant for life has the power of sale but must obtain an order of the court before selling. The proceeds from a sale are treated as capital and must be paid to the trustees.

Conduct of sales

The Trustee Act 1925 s 12 gives trustees wide freedom as to how sales are conducted. Trustees may sell or concur with others in selling all or part of the property. They may sell by private treaty or by way of auction. Land may be divided horizontally, vertically or any other way if the trustees decided that this would lead to sales which were more beneficial to the trust.

When a trustee sells trust property, he is under a duty to sell on the best possible terms and this usually means getting the highest possible price for the property. This duty even prevails against the trustees' sense of morality (see *Buttle* v *Saunders* [1950] 2 All ER 193, p. 385).

There is a balance to be drawn between getting the best possible price and steps needed to obtain it. For example, if the value of land might be increased by obtaining planning permission before the sale, trustees will not be in breach of their duty by selling without seeking planning permission, if it would be unreasonable to expect the trustees to become involved in speculative and expensive planning permission negotiations and applications and where the increase in value would only be marginal. (See *Page* v *West and others* [2012] All ER (D) 51 (JAN).)

Killearn v *Killearn and others* [2011] EWHC 3775 (Ch) illustrates the application of the principle that trustees should act to obtain the best price when selling. In the case the court decided (unlike in *Page* v *West* above) that certain steps by the trustees should be taken to obtain the best price. The court refused to approve of a sale of a Grade I listed seventeenth-century country house by trustees to a particular purchaser at a particular price. The trustees had not had the property marketed, as they argued that the sale needed to take place as soon as possible to save tax and because the house needed repairs. The court found that there was in fact no evidence of this urgency and that selling without a marketing campaign was inconsistent with the duty of the trustees to do everything for the benefit of beneficiaries and to sell at the best terms which would probably be obtained after a professionally conducted marketing campaign.

Power to buy land

See Chapter 16 (p. 484) for more on buying land.

See Chapter 16.

Power to partition

The Trusts of Land and Appointment of Trustees Act 1996 gives trustees of trusts of land the power to partition (s 7). Where the beneficiaries are of full age and are absolutely entitled in undivided shares to land subject to a trust, the trustees may partition the land, or any part of it. The trustees can split the land and convey individual parts to each beneficiary either absolutely or on trust.

Power to give receipts

The Trustee Act 1925 s 14(1) provides that the written receipt of a trustee for money, securities or personal effects will give the person paying or delivering a good discharge and will free him from any responsibility for any misapplication by the trustee of the money or property.

Section 14(2) of the Trustee Act 1925 (amended by the Trusts of Land and Appointment of Trustees Act 1996 Schedule 3 paragraph 3(3)) does not enable a sole trustee (except for a trust corporation) to give a valid receipt for the proceeds from the sale of land held under a trust for sale or for capital money arising under the Settled Land Act 1925 or under a trust of land.

The section applies to all trusts even if the instrument contains an express provision to the contrary. This provision ensures that third parties may pay money to trustees or transfer securities or other personal property with confidence that the trustees' receipt will be a sufficient discharge and also relieves the transferee from any responsibility for what the trustees do with the proceeds. Without this provision, trustees might encounter reluctance on the part of third parties to pay money or transfer property to them. See also the Trustee Delegation Act 1999, s 7.

Power to insure

The power

Objective 5

It is surprising that trustees are not under a duty to insure trust property (unless, of course, there is an express provision in the trust instrument). Under the Trustee Act 1925 s 19, there was a narrow statutory power to insure trust property against the risk of loss or damage by fire only. The section allowed cover up to three-quarters of the value of the property.

Section 34 of the Trustee Act 2000 provides for a new s 19 of the Trustee Act 1925.

The new s 19 is not restricted to insuring against fire and there is no restriction on the proportion of the value of the property that can be covered. Section 19(5) makes it clear that the trustees may take money to pay the premiums from capital or income. The statutory standard of care (p. 406) applies when trustees are exercising their power to insure whether it arises under s 19 or otherwise.

The new s 19(2) provides beneficiaries, who under a bare trust are absolutely entitled to the trust property (provided they are of full age and capacity) or who are together entitled to the trust property (provided they are all of full age and capacity), with the right to give the trustees directions regarding the insurance of trust property. This may include a direction that the property is not to be insured.

The provisions of s 34 apply to trusts created before or after the commencement of the Trustee Act 2000.

Although s 19 gives trustees the power (not the duty) to insure, it could be argued that it would be a breach of the trustees' general duty to preserve trust property if adequate cover was not arranged.

The proceeds

Section 20 of the Trustee Act 1925 deals with the application of the proceeds from insurance policies. The section provides that any money received by the trustees in respect of land which is settled land under the Settled Land Act 1925 shall be treated by the trustees as capital money.

Any proceeds received in respect of heirlooms which are settled within the meaning of the 1925 Act are treated in the same way as money arising on the sale of such property.

Proceeds received in respect of property held on trust for sale are held on the trusts arising upon a sale under the trust (s 20(3)(c) of the Trustee Act 1925). After 1996, Schedule 3 paragraph 3(5) to the Trusts of Land and Appointment of Trustees Act 1996 amends s 20(3)(c) so that the provisions cover land subject to a trust of land or personal property held on trust for sale.

In other cases, s 20 states that the insurance money shall be held on trusts which correspond as closely as possible to the trusts affecting the property in respect of which the money was payable.

The general effect of s 20 is, therefore, to treat the insurance moneys in a way which, as far as possible, leaves the interests of the beneficiaries unaffected.

Power to compound liabilities

The Trustee Act 1925 s 15 is important in that it provides trustees with the power to make sensible commercial decisions when dealing with disputes with third parties.

This provision gives to the trustees wide powers in relation to settling claims either made by or against the trust. If this power did not exist, the trustees would have to pursue every claim through the courts or risk being in breach of trust. In a commercial context, it is often better to settle a claim by means of an agreement and so avoid expensive, risky and time-consuming litigation. The provisions of s 15 give the trustees the power to enter into this kind of arrangement.

The section permits trustees to accept property before the time has arrived when it is transferable. They are also given the power to pay or allow debts on any evidence which they think is acceptable. This allows the trustees to pay debts which may in fact be doubtful if they think that there is enough evidence of the enforceability of the obligation.

It is often a sensible commercial decision to allow a debtor extra time to pay rather than initiating legal proceedings as soon as the debt becomes due. Section 15 gives trustees the power to allow a debtor additional time to pay. The trustees may enter into an agreement to accept any property in discharge of a debt owing to the trust.

Also, the section enables the trustees to compromise, compound, abandon, submit to arbitration or otherwise to settle a debt. This is a very wide power but, as with the other provisions of s 15, it must be used only in the best interests of the trust and the beneficiaries under it.

Section 15(2) gives the trustees some protection by providing that trustees using these powers will not be liable for any resulting losses arising from acts done in good faith.

Power to deal with reversionary interests

If the trust property includes property which is not vested in the trustees (or the proceeds of sale from such property) or things in action, the trustees are given some protection by the Trustee Act 1925 s 22. The trustees may agree a valuation for the property or accept authorised investments in full or partial satisfaction of the property or execute a release. If the trustees use these powers they will not be liable for any loss arising, provided they acted in good faith.

Additionally, s 22(2) reduces the obligations of the trustees before property falls into possession, by providing that the trustees are under no duty to place any *distringas* notices on the property out of which the interest is payable, or to take proceedings on account of acts or defaults of people in whom the property is vested. However, the subsection goes on to state that, if any beneficiary makes a written request, the trustees then come under a duty to take these actions.

This section does provide trustees with protection with respect to their dealings with property that is not in possession, but s 22(2) makes it very clear that nothing in s 22 releases trustees from the obligation to get in the interests as soon as possible after they fall into possession.

The statutory duty of care under s 1 of the Trustee Act 2000 applies to trustees exercising their powers under s 22 of the Trustees Act (Trustee Act 2000 Schedule 1 para 6).

Power to claim reimbursement for expenses incurred

As we saw earlier (at p. 398), there is no general power for trustees to claim payment for their work. However, there is a right to reimbursement from trust property for expenses properly incurred while administering the trust. The right to reimbursement was developed by the courts and is now to be found in the Trustee Act 2000 s 31 (replacing Trustee Act 1925 s 30(2)), which makes provision for trustees to be reimbursed out of trust funds for properly incurred expenses and makes it clear that the right continues even after the trustee has been appointed an agent, nominee or custodian. The provision obviously covers out-of-pocket expenses which the trustee incurs, such as postage and telephone calls. It will also allow the recovery of any insurance premiums which the trustee has paid and costs incurred in bringing legal actions on behalf of the trust.

Costs of litigation

The general rule is that trustees are entitled to be paid costs or indemnified out of trust funds for properly incurred expenses in litigation initiated for the benefit of the trust. This right is derived from s 31 of the Trustee Act 2000. If trustees commence litigation on behalf of the trust, they run the risk of the courts later deciding that such a course of action was not justified and the costs were not properly incurred.

The statutory right under s 31 provides for reimbursement from the trust property, and in most cases the individual beneficiaries have no personal liability. However, if the trustee holds property for a beneficiary who is *sui juris* and entitled to the entire beneficial interest, then the beneficiary is personally liable to reimburse the trustee (see ***Hardoon v Belilios*** [1901] AC 118, where Lord Lindley said that the personal liability of beneficiaries in this type of case was as old as trusts themselves).

Under the Rules of the Supreme Court 48.4:

> . . . where –
>
> (a) a person is or has been a party to any proceedings in the capacity of trustee or personal representative;
>
>   . . .
>
> (2) The general rule is that he is entitled to be paid the costs of those proceedings, insofar as they are not recovered from or paid by any other person, out of the relevant trust fund or estate.
>
> (3) Where he is entitled to be paid any of those costs out of the fund or estate, those costs will be assessed on the indemnity basis.

The trustees may decide to make a 'Beddoe' application, under which the court will determine whether or not the proposed litigation is the proper course of action. The proposed litigation may involve bringing or defending an action. If the court decides that the litigation is justified, the effect of the order is to protect the trustees against the beneficiaries and to remove the risk of not being reimbursed for expenses on the ground that the expenses of litigation were not properly incurred. (A 'Beddoe' application is derived from the case of ***Re Beddoe*** [1893] 1 Ch 547.)

Alsop, Wilkinson v Neary and Others [1995] 1 All ER 431

For further discussion of the Insolvency Act 1986 s 423, see Chapter 6, 'Setting trusts aside'.

In this case, the plaintiff applied to the court for an order setting aside a trust under s 423 of the Insolvency Act 1986.

The beneficiaries threatened the trustees with a breach of trust action if they (the trustees) did not defend the action. The trustees, as part of the same proceedings as the action to set aside the trust, made a 'Beddoe' application asking the court to decide if they should defend the action. Lightman J refused to give the trustees leave to defend. He said that in the instant case the dispute was between the beneficiaries and the plaintiff. The role of the trustee in such a case is to leave the two parties to the dispute to fight the action and to remain neutral in the action. Additionally, Lightman J said that 'Beddoe' applications should be brought in proceedings which are separate from the main action. This was both to ensure that the relevant parties to the application were in court and to avoid possible disclosure of confidential information to the other parties to the main action.

The Rules of the Supreme Court apply where a trustee takes part in litigation in his capacity of trustee. Reimbursement was refused in *Holding and Management* v *Property Holding and Investment Trust* [1988] 2 All ER 702. Maintenance trustee of a block of flats acted as agents of the landlord, collecting rent and organising maintenance. It levied contributions from tenants to build up a fund to be used for the maintenance of the flats. The trustee initiated repairs to the flats. The court was asked to decide whether a planned work (to be financed from the maintenance fund) was within the trustee's powers.

The tenants objected to the work, arguing that it amounted to improvements and not maintenance and was outside the powers of the trustees. The tenants also suggested a cheaper alternative.

A compromise was reached on the main issue and the trustees then applied for an indemnity from the maintenance fund for costs incurred. The court then refused to order an indemnity, saying that the litigation was brought not by the trustee *qua* trustee but in pursuance of the enforcement of the obligations of the tenants towards the landlord.

The dangers of participating in proceedings are illustrated by the case of *Singh* v *Bhasin* (1998) *The Times*, 21 August, in which the court considered a case where Bhasin had defended proceedings brought against an organisation of which he was a trustee, but he had not obtained a 'Beddoe' order in advance of the proceedings (see below). A member of an organisation (Singh) was suspended following a resolution passed at a general meeting. Bhasin, *qua* trustee, defended an action by Singh. The court decided that he defended the action at his own risk and at his own cost. On the facts, the trustee had acted unreasonably in defending the action. The defence was clearly bad as being in breach of the rules of the organisation and the rules of natural justice. The court would not have granted a 'Beddoe' authority to defend, had an application been made in advance of the proceedings.

It is possible, but unusual, for a trustee to seek an advance ruling as to whether or not he would be entitled to an indemnity against costs incurred in contemplated litigation. This happened in *Cripps Trust Corporation Ltd* v *Sands and others* [2012] EWHC 2229 (Ch). The court said that a trustee who acted reasonably and properly for the trust was entitled to an indemnity for his costs of conducting litigation. But the costs had to be reasonably and properly incurred. In order to decide that the trustee would be entitled to an indemnity, the court would have to be satisfied that it had all the information it needed to judge that the costs would be properly incurred. If after considering the available evidence there was doubt, it was probably the proper course for the court to leave the doubt to be resolved later, on all the proper facts. In the instant case there was doubt and the court refused to make the order that the trustee was seeking.

In most cases the reimbursement is made from the capital fund but it is possible for income to bear the cost. In fact, the trustee has a lien on all the trust property (capital and income) and this right takes priority over claims of third parties and beneficiaries. Technically, unless and until the trustee has been reimbursed, no one else will be able to claim under the trust. The right of the trustee was described by Lord Selborne in *Stott* v *Milne* (1884) 25 Ch D 710 as 'a first charge on all the trust property, both income and corpus'.

See Chapter 14 (p. 398) for a discussion of the payment of trustees.

Power to delegate

See Chapter 16 (p. 457) for a discussion of the duty of trustees to act personally.

The power of the trustees to delegate the administration of the trust to others is dealt with in Chapter 16.

Power to appoint agents, nominees and custodians

See Chapter 16 (p. 459) for a discussion of the powers to appoint agents, etc.

The power to appoint agents, nominees, etc. is covered in Chapter 16.

Power to apply to the court

Under the Trusts of Land and Appointment of Trustees Act 1996 s 14, the court has the power, on application by a trustee or someone having an interest in the land, to make a wide range of orders relating to the trustees' exercise of their functions relating to the land, including an order relieving the trustees of the obligation to obtain the consent of or to consult with any person in connection with the exercise of their functions. Section 15 of the Act lists factors which the court shall have regard to when determining an application for an order under s 14. The factors include the intention of the person creating the trusts, the purpose for which the property is held, the welfare of any minor who occupies or might reasonably expect to occupy the land as his home and the interests of any secured creditor of the beneficiary. The section is of wider application than the provisions of the Law of Property Act 1925 s 30 and, in particular, is not confined to cases where the trustees have refused to act. Under the section, the court can also declare the nature or extent of a person's interest in property subject to the trust. However, it is not possible, under this section, to make an order which relates to the appointment or removal of trustees (s 14(3)).

See also *Dear v Robinson* [2001] All ER (D) 351 (Oct) (see p. 86) where the court reversed an order for sale because of a change of circumstances.

Power to restrict the beneficiaries' right to occupy

Section 12 of the Trusts of Land and Appointment of Trustees Act 1996 gives beneficiaries who are beneficially entitled to an interest in possession of land the entitlement to occupy the land, subject only to the powers given to trustees by s 13 to exclude some (but not all) such beneficiaries. Section 12(1) does not give a right to occupy if the land is unsuitable or is unavailable for occupation (s 12(2)). The trustees must take account of the wishes of the settlor and the purposes for which the land is held when deciding matters of occupation under s 12 (s 13(1) and (4)).

Power to maintain a beneficiary

Objective
6

Example

Maurice, a minor, has an interest under the trust which is contingent on attaining the age of 18. It is no comfort to know that if and when he reaches 18 he will become entitled to the property if, in the meantime, there is little money to pay for his school fees and other expenses. The settlor may well not have directed what is to happen to any income arising under the trust until Maurice attains the age of 18 and his interest becomes vested. Here the statutory power of maintenance could be used to apply income towards paying the school fees and other expenses.

There are problems which would normally prevent the trustees from using the income generated under this trust to maintain Maurice. First, as Maurice is a minor he could not give the trustees a good receipt for any income paid over to him. Secondly, Maurice's interest is contingent, and, if he died before his interest had vested, the trustees could be asked to repay that income by those entitled to the property in the event of Maurice's interest failing to vest.

However desirable it may be, a power to maintain out of income will not be implied into a trust, but it may arise from statute, or as a consequence of an express provision in the trust instrument. The judges also have an inherent power to order maintenance for beneficiaries under the age of majority.

Express power

In professionally drafted trusts there may be an express power for the trustees to use income in this way, but in view of the statutory power under the Trustee Act 1925 s 31 (as amended) the draughtsman may well decide that the inclusion of such an express power is unnecessary. If there is an express power the precise ambit will be a matter of construction.

Inherent power to maintain minors

The court has an inherent power to allow the income from a trust to be used to maintain a minor. This power is based on the assumption that a settlor, having created a trust for children, would not intend to leave them unprovided for during their minority (see p. 177). The court has allowed capital to be used for the maintenance of minors in exceptional circumstances. Although the inherent power is usually exercised in favour of a minor, it can be used to maintain an adult: *Revel* v *Watkinson* (1748) 1 Ves Sen 93.

In *Douglas* v *Andrew* (1849) 12 Beav 310, Lord Langdale stated that, however large the fortune of the minor, the court will not permit the trust funds to be used for maintaining the minor if their father has the means to maintain, as the court would not allow the father to avoid discharging his duty towards his child and throw the burden onto the child.

Statutory power to maintain minors: s 31 of the Trustee Act 1925

The statutory power to maintain is contained in the Trustee Act 1925 s 31. In the Law Commission report 'Intestacy and Family Provision Claims on Death' (Law Com. No. 331), it was recommended that Section 31 of the Trustee Act 1925 should be amended and the Inheritance and Trustees' Powers Act 2014 implements the changes recommended. The Act came into force on 1 October 2014.

Extent of the power

Under s 31 the trustees may, at their sole discretion, apply or pay to the parent or guardian of the minor all or part of the income of the trust property for the 'maintenance, education or benefit' of the minor. If the minor is married, the trustees may make payments directly to him.

Section 31(1)(i) says that the trustees may make payments which may 'in all the circumstances, be reasonable'. Evidence was submitted to the Law Commission to the effect that this imposed an objective requirement of reasonableness whereas the section should reflect the fact that the trustees were exercising a discretion. If trustees improperly exercised this fiduciary power the beneficiaries could obtain redress through the courts.

This was accepted by the Law Commission and in the 'Intestacy and Family Provision Claims on Death' report it was recommended that this change should be implemented.

Section 8 of the Inheritance and Trustees' Powers Act 2014 amends s31(1) so that it is made clear that the exercise of the power is a matter for the discretion of the trustees. The phrase 'as may, in all the circumstances, be reasonable', is replaced by 'as the trustees may think fit'. This change applies to trusts created or arising after 1 October 2014 and where an interest under a trust is created or arises as the result of the exercise of a power under that trust after 1 October 2014.

The term 'maintenance' usually includes payments of a recurring nature to cover day-to-day expenses such as clothing, food, education, etc. However, the term 'benefit' has a much wider meaning and could include the provision out of income of advantages which would normally be regarded as advancements.

The statutory power applies to all trusts coming into operation after 1925, subject to contrary intention or modification by the settlor. A direction by the settlor that income is to be accumulated will show a contrary intention and render the statutory power unusable. In **Re Erskine** [1971] 1 All ER 572, the settlor stated that income was to be accumulated but the direction was held to be void as offending the perpetuity rule. The court decided that, despite the fact that the direction to accumulate was void, the settlor had expressed an intention to exclude the power of maintenance.

The power is available whether the trust was created by will or is an *inter vivos* trust, but it can only be exercised in favour of beneficiaries who are minors, i.e. under the age of 18 years.

Right to income

The trustees can only use income to maintain the minor if there is income available to which the minor has the right. One example of where income is not available is if property is held on trust for Ford for life, remainder to Maurice, who is a minor. Clearly, under the terms of trust, Ford is entitled to all the income generated and there will be no income available out of which to maintain Maurice. A beneficiary under a discretionary trust is not entitled to income and so the power of maintenance is not available: **Re Vestey** [1950] 2 All ER 891. Thus, the power can arise only if the interest of the minor, whether vested or contingent, carries with it the right to intermediate income. A vested interest normally carries the right to income. A contingent interest carries the right to income if the beneficiary is entitled to claim income generated from the time the interest is created up until the time the contingency happens and the interest becomes vested. This is described as the right to intermediate income. It is not always easy to decide whether an interest does carry the right to intermediate income as the rules are rather complicated. They are partly based on case law and partly found in statutory provisions, namely the Law of Property Act 1925 s 175 and the Trustee Act 1925 s 31(3).

As is usual, the basic rules as to entitlement are subject to the contrary intention of the settlor. If the settlor states in the trust that income arising before the interest becomes vested is to be paid to another, then this concludes the matter because obviously the interest of the beneficiary cannot carry the right to intermediate income as the settlor has specifically allocated that income to another. For example, if the settlor stated that the income from the property held contingently for Peter is to be paid to the settlor's daughter, Wendy, until Peter attains the age of 18, this will take away any right that Peter might otherwise have had to the intermediate income.

When does an interest carry the right to intermediate income? The following summarises the position for instruments coming into force after 1925 (subject to any contrary intention expressed by the settlor and subject to there being a prior interest, such as a prior life interest):

(a) A vested interest arising under a will or under an *inter vivos* gift will always carry the right to income.

(b) An *inter vivos* contingent gift usually carries the right to income.

(c) Gifts made by will present a rather more complicated problem:

    (i) A contingent gift of residuary personalty carries the right to income.

    (ii) A contingent or future specific gift of personalty or realty carries the right to intermediate income.

    (iii) A contingent pecuniary legacy does not carry the right to income in most instances.

The following exceptions have evolved to (c)(iii) above:

(a) where the testator was the father of, or *in loco parentis* to, the legatee;

(b) where the testator shows an intention to maintain;

(c) where the testator has separated the legacy as a separate fund for the legatee.

In these three exceptional cases, income is available to a contingent pecuniary legatee beneficiary. In fact, the Trustee Act 1925 s 31(3) refers only to the first of these exceptions, stating that, in this case, interest at the rate of 5 per cent p.a. shall be available for maintaining etc. a minor beneficiary. There has been some debate as to whether, by specifically referring to only one of the exceptional cases listed above, the section intends that the other two shall no longer apply. The general view is that all three of the exceptions do still apply and that in these cases intermediate income will be available for the maintenance of the beneficiary.

A contingent residuary devise of freehold land carries the right to intermediate income.

A contingent specific devise of freehold land carries the right to intermediate income.

Using the power

If the statutory power applies and the beneficiary is entitled to intermediate income, how should the power be exercised?

Section 31(1) contained a proviso which relates to the exercise of the power:

> [T]he trustees shall have regard to the age of the infant and his requirements and generally to the circumstances of the case, and in particular to what other income, if any, is applicable for the same purposes; and where the trustees have notice that the income of more than one fund is applicable for those purposes, then, so far as practicable, unless the entire income of the funds is paid or applied as aforesaid or the court otherwise directs, a proportionate part only of the income of each fund shall be so paid or applied.

In the Law Commission report 'Intestacy and Family Provision Claims on Death' it was recommended that Section 31 of the Trustee Act 1925 should be amended to delete the whole of the proviso.

The first section of the proviso which lists factors that trustees should take into account when deciding if and how to exercise the power was thought to be unnecessary as trustees would in any case need to consider the factors listed. Additionally there was no equivalent provision in s 32 (see below). Also, the provision is often expressly excluded in trusts and wills.

The second part of the proviso limits the income that can be used when the trustees have notice that there are other trust funds under which the income is applicable for the maintenance, education or benefit of a beneficiary. As far as it is practicable the trustees could only use a proportionate part of the income.

The Law Commission report stated that many of those responding to the earlier consultation thought that the requirement was too rigid and imposed a potentially costly administrative burden. Also, consultees said that it was very common for settlors to expressly exclude the provision.

Under Section 8 of the Inheritance and Trustees' Act 2014 the whole of the proviso is removed. This change applies to trusts created or arising on or after 1 October 2014 and where an interest under a trust is created or arises as the result of the exercise of a power under that trust on or after 1 October 2014.

Any application of income must result from a positive exercise of the power. In *Wilson v Turner* (1883) 22 Ch D 521, property was settled on trust for Mrs Wilson for life and after her death for her children, the trustees having the power to pay income for the maintenance or education of any minor child. After Mrs Wilson died, leaving a nine-year-old son, the trustees paid the whole income of the trust property to Mr Wilson, who maintained the child. They did not exercise any discretion in the matter but simply paid over the income as and when it arose. The court held that this was an improper exercise of their power to maintain and ordered that the money paid over be returned.

Surplus income

Section 31(2) provides that any income not used for the maintenance of a minor beneficiary is to be accumulated and invested. This accumulated income may be used in any future year to maintain the minor, as may income on the accumulated income.

Attaining the age of 18

Section 31(2) details what the position of a beneficiary is when he attains the age of 18, or on earlier marriage.

If a beneficiary has a contingent interest, as soon as he attains the age of 18 he will become entitled to future income as it arises, even though he may well have to wait some time for the contingency to happen and to become entitled to the capital. This entitlement to income is subject to the settlor expressing a contrary intention. The settlor could, for example, direct that the income was payable to another beneficiary until the interest vested.

The court has found a contrary intention from a direction to accumulate.

Re Turner's Will Trust [1936] 2 All ER 1435

In this case, the testator gave property on trust for beneficiaries, contingent on their attaining the age of 28 years. He gave the trustees an express power of maintenance and also a power to pay the income to any of the beneficiaries who attained the age of majority and directed that any surplus income was to be accumulated. The court decided that this direction to accumulate surplus income showed the necessary contrary intention and so those beneficiaries who attained the age of majority were not able to claim the income produced pending their reaching the age of 28 years.

Section 31(2) deals with the right of a beneficiary to previously accumulated surplus income on attaining the age of 18 or earlier marriage. Section 31(2)(i)(a) provides that if the beneficiary already has a vested interest then he will become entitled to past accumulations. Section 31(2)(ii) states that if at the age of 18 the beneficiary 'becomes entitled to the property from which the income arose in fee simple, absolute or determinable, or absolutely, or for an entailed interest' the surplus is payable to the beneficiary. The words 'fee simple, absolute or determinable' apply to realty and the word 'absolutely' applies to personalty. In **Re Sharp's Settlement Trusts** [1972] 3 All ER 151, Pennycuick J decided that where the beneficiaries were entitled to capital on attaining the age of 21, subject to an overriding power of appointment, they were not entitled 'absolutely' and so were not entitled to past accumulations of surplus income. The court stated that in the section the word 'absolutely' was used to denote complete beneficial ownership and dominion over property and was inapplicable to an interest which could be defeated by the exercise of a power. This gives rise to a rather odd situation. If a beneficiary has a determinable interest in realty he will be entitled to past accumulations of income; but a beneficiary who has a determinable (and so not absolute) interest in personalty will not. If at the age of 18 the interest is still not vested, then s 31(1)(ii) states that from the beneficiary's eighteenth birthday the trustees must pay over all income from the trust property to the beneficiary as and when it arises, but any income previously received which was accumulated remains as capital and the beneficiary is not entitled to it on attaining the age of 18, although he will naturally receive all future income generated by this accumulated income. When the beneficiary becomes entitled to the capital, he will receive the original trust capital together with the accumulated income.

Position if the interest does not vest

It may be that trustees use the power of maintenance to support a beneficiary who dies before his contingent interest becomes vested. The income cannot be recovered from the estate of the deceased beneficiary.

Power of advancement

Objective
7

The power of maintenance deals with the trustee's power to use generated income for the maintenance or benefit of a minor beneficiary. The power of advancement relates to the possibility of the trustees deciding to allow part of the trust capital to be paid to or used for the benefit of a beneficiary before his entitlement to the fund becomes vested.

If a settlor transfers property to the value of £50,000 to trustees for Arthur 'on attaining the age of 30', a power of advancement would allow the trustees to sanction the payment of part of the capital trust fund to or for the benefit of Arthur before he has attained the age of 30. It may be, for example, that Arthur is proposing to start a business and needs £10,000 to buy premises; he may request the trustees to exercise their power of advancement and transfer to him the £10,000. If the trustees agree to his request this would be an example of an advancement. A power of advancement would also be useful for making payments to a remainderman pending the death of the tenant for life, providing him with capital during the period before his interest becomes vested in possession.

Often the modern use of the powers is a product of seeking to use an opportunity to save tax rather than simply wishing to bestow a benefit on a beneficiary 'in need'. It may be thought desirable to transfer property out of the trust to one of the beneficiaries in order to attempt to reduce the impact of inheritance tax.

Express power

A trust may contain an express power of advancement, in which case its precise ambit will be a matter of construction. An express power may be contained in a trust where the settlor considers the statutory power of advancement to be too limited. For example, under the statutory power there is a limit on the proportion of a beneficiary's share in the trust property that can be advanced. A settlor may wish to give his trustees the power to advance a greater proportion to a beneficiary.

Inherent power of advancement to minors

The court has an inherent power to provide for minors and this can extend to ordering an advancement from capital.

Statutory power: s 32 of the Trustee Act 1925

The Trustee Act 1925 s 32 created a statutory power of advancement and this is now often relied upon, making express powers of advancement much less common in modern trusts than in trusts which came into effect before 1926. The statutory power under the Trustee Act 1925 s 32 is automatically exercisable under any trust coming into being after 1925, unless there is a contrary intention, express or implied (for an example of a contrary intention, see *Re Evans* [1967] 1 WLR 1294).

The power

Under the unamended s 32 trustees had the statutory power to pay or apply capital money for the 'advancement or benefit' of a beneficiary. This was clearly wider than the mere powers of advancement which were common before 1925, which were often restricted to giving the power to advance only, although it was not uncommon for express powers of advancement to be coupled with a power to apply capital for the 'benefit' of a beneficiary. The addition of the ability to use capital for the 'benefit' of a beneficiary went some way towards removing the traditional distinction between powers of advancement and powers of maintenance.

The statutory powers of maintenance and advancement are often considered together and there is good reason for this. The real difference under the powers is not for what purposes money may be allocated from trust funds, because both of the powers are worded widely and in particular contain the word 'benefit'. The real distinction is where the funds will come from. If an application from capital seems appropriate, then the power of advancement under s 32 will be used, whereas if it seems more apt to use some of the generated income the power of maintenance under s 31 will be resorted to. For example, it may be possible to use s 32 to 'advance' small, regular amounts of capital to provide for the accommodation or clothing etc. of a beneficiary. This would usually be regarded as 'maintenance' but can be achieved by using a power of 'advancement'.

In the Law Commission report 'Intestacy and Family Provision Claims on Death' (Law Com. No. 331), it was recommend that Section 32 of the Trustee Act 1925 should be amended so that the trustees have power to transfer or apply other property subject to the trust on the same basis as the power to pay or apply capital money to or for the advancement or benefit of a beneficiary. This recommendation has been implemented by Section 9 of the Inheritance and Trustees' Powers Act 2014. This change applies whenever the trust was created. This gives the trustees more flexibility and avoids the need for the trustees to put in place 'artificial' schemes to allow the transfer of capital other than money. Trustees could advance sums from capital money to the beneficiaries who could then use the money to buy the capital asset that the trustees wanted to pass to the beneficiary. The new provision makes it clear that these roundabout ways of transferring trust capital other than money need no longer be resorted to.

One point, however, should be noted: the statutory power of maintenance can be used only in relation to beneficiaries who are under age, so if the object is over 18 the trustees will not have a choice and will have to utilise capital under an exercise of the power of advancement.

Meaning of 'advancement or benefit'

The word 'advancement' means to establish someone in life or to make a permanent or long-term provision for them. Traditionally, this would include the purchase of a business. It was said by Malins V-C in *Re Kershaw's Trusts* (1868) LR 6 Eq 322 that 'advancement' was a concept appropriate to an early period of life, but it is now generally agreed that this is no longer the case and that advancements to individuals in middle age are now not uncommon. In *Re Kershaw* the court decided that a sum of money paid to set the beneficiary's husband up in business in order to try to keep the family together was an advancement. Although 'advancement' now has a wider meaning than previously, there are obvious limits. For example, the payment of a beneficiary's debts relating to day-to-day expenses would not normally be an 'advancement' (see *Taylor* v *Taylor* (1875) LR 20 Eq 155). But such a payment was held to amount to an advancement in *Re Blockley* (1885) 29 Ch D 250. See *Hardy* v *Shaw* [1975] 2 All ER 1052 for a discussion of 'advancement'.

The addition of the power to make payments for the 'benefit' of a beneficiary adds considerably to the scope for making payments. In *Pilkington* v *IRC* [1962] 3 All ER 622, Viscount Radcliffe said 'benefit' was a 'large' word and extended to a very wide range of situations. He considered that the power to make payments for the 'advancement or benefit' gave the trustees the ability to make any use of the capital which would improve the material situation of a beneficiary. This could cover the payment of routine, day-to-day debts which would not be an advancement but would be a payment for the 'benefit' of a beneficiary.

In *Pilkington* v *IRC* a beneficiary aged two years was not in need of any capital but the trustees of a settlement wished to exercise their statutory power of advancement in order that the capital advanced could be resettled. The object of the exercise was to save estate duty that would otherwise be payable in respect of the trust property and this would clearly be beneficial to the young beneficiary. The House of Lords decided that this would constitute a 'benefit' and thus be within the wording of s 32. It did not matter that the beneficiary was not in need, nor that other beneficiaries under the trust would benefit as a result of the saving of estate duty. In fact, the proposed resettlement was void as offending the perpetuity rules as they then stood, but this in no way affects the views of the House of Lords as to the meaning and effect of the phrase 'advancement or benefit'. Additionally, the court was quite happy to accept that, although the resettlement proposed was in fact void, there was no objection in principle to the power being used in order to resettle the capital advanced.

In *Re Clore's Settlement* [1966] 2 All ER 272, the court held that payments to charities constituted a 'benefit' as it relieved the wealthy beneficiary from making charitable contributions which he felt morally obliged to make.

Limits of s 32

The proviso to s 32(1) imposes certain limits on the power. For example, not more than one-half of a beneficiary's vested or presumptive share may be advanced. This limit may of course be expressly extended by a provision in the trust instrument and in practice often was.

If there was no express extension the flexibility of the trustees was limited. This restriction was particularly felt in the case of trusts with small amounts of capital.

Many considered that the limit created too much rigidity and could create burdens.

An example of the inconvenience caused by this limit is to be seen in *D (a child)* v *O* [2004] 3 All ER 780 when the Variation of Trusts Act 1958 was used to enable trustees to advance more than the 50 per cent limit imposed by s 32 of the Trustee Act 1925 in order to pay the school fees of an infant beneficiary. It was decided that such a variation would be for the benefit of the infant and that, if necessary, the whole of the capital could be used to pay the school fees. But the application obviously caused delays and incurred the costs of the court case.

The inflexibility of the limit is shown in *The Marquess of Abergavenny* v *Ram* [1981] 2 All ER 643 in which a beneficiary was advanced one-half of the value of his share of the trust property. Later, the value of the trust property increased but the court decided that the beneficiary was not entitled to any further advances. As the advancement was equal to the value of one-half of his share at the date of the advancement, this precluded any further exercise of the power in his favour.

In the Law Commission report 'Intestacy and Family Provision Claims on Death' (Law Com. No. 331) it was recommended that the power contained in Section 32 of the Trustee Act 1925 to pay or apply capital to or for the benefit of a trust beneficiary should be extended to the whole, rather than one-half, of the beneficiary's share in the trust fund.

The Law Commission considered that although it could be argued that this would increase the chance of fraud on the part of trustees, this possibility was outweighed by the advantages of more flexibility.

The change has been implemented by Section 9 of the Inheritance and Trustees' Powers Act 2014 which applies to trusts created or arising after 1 October 2014 and where an interest under a trust is created or arises as the result of the exercise of a power under that trust on or after 1 October 2014.

The one-half provision was considered in *The Marquess of Abergavenny* v *Ram*.

Additionally, under s 32, any advancement must be set against the eventual entitlement of a beneficiary. This is an example of hotchpot, an attempt by the courts to carry out the settlor's presumed intention.

Example

If £20,000 of property is held on trust for Albert and Betty equally subject to the contingency of attaining the age of 21 and Albert receives an advancement of £5,000, when the contingency is satisfied the amount of Albert's entitlement will be reduced by the value of the advancement. In other words, Albert will receive only a further £5,000 while Betty will receive £10,000. This will result in Albert and Betty benefiting to the same extent, that is by £10,000. This is presumed to be what the settlor would have wanted.

It has been suggested that the duty to bring advancements into account should be modified to make allowance for the effects of inflation and that trustees should calculate the fraction of the fund which was being advanced and that the beneficiary would be regarded as receiving a fractional share of his eventual entitlement. The present rule is that the property advanced is valued at the date of the advancement. Under the suggested modification, advancements would be thought of in fractional rather than cash terms.

The proviso to s 32 also states that if anyone exists who would be prejudiced by the exercise of the power, it cannot be exercised without the written agreement of that person. A straightforward example of this is where property is held on trust for Charles for life, remainder to Camilla. If the trustees exercised their power of advancement and transferred some of the trust fund to Camilla while Charles was still alive, this would clearly prejudice Charles as the value of the trust fund would be reduced, and thus the amount of income generated (to which Charles is entitled) would almost certainly go down. In this circumstance, the trustees could only exercise their power if Charles expressed his consent in writing. In *Henley v Wardell* (1988) *The Times*, 29 January, the court held that even though a trust instrument gave the trustees the 'absolute and uncontrolled discretion' to advance all of the capital, it did not release the trustees from the need to obtain the consent of the beneficiary entitled to the prior income. The court held that, as a matter of construction, the express provision was merely designed to increase the amount of capital that could be advanced from the statutory one-half rather than dispensing with the other requirements of the section.

There is a further limitation imposed by s 32(2) (as amended by the Trusts of Land and Appointment of Trustees Act 1996 Schedule 3 paragraph 3(8)), which states that the section does not apply to capital money arising under the Settled Land Act 1925.

Failure of an interest to vest

What would be the position if a beneficiary was entitled to a contingent interest and the trustees advanced a sum of money to him but the contingency was never satisfied and the interest never becomes vested? Would the advancement have to be repaid? The answer is no; the sum may be kept to the obvious prejudice of the trust fund and the other beneficiaries.

Trustees' responsibility to supervise

If the trustees exercise the power of advancement, to what extent are they under a duty to oversee the use of the funds advanced to ensure that they are used for the purposes for which the advance was requested? Section 32 gives the trustees the power to 'pay or apply' the money for the advancement or benefit of a beneficiary so they are free to become involved and to pay the money, not to the beneficiary, but to others in order to advance or benefit. It is also open to the trustees to pay the money to the beneficiary so that he will then have control of the money.

This problem fell to be considered in *Re Pauling's Settlement Trusts*.

Re Pauling's Settlement Trusts [1963] 3 All ER 1

In this case the trustees had an express power of advancement under a marriage settlement. The power was to advance to the children of the couple. The trustees advanced money, nominally to the children, but it was used to benefit the family as a whole. The family lived a very extravagant lifestyle. One of the sums advanced was used to buy a family home in the Isle of Man and other sums were used to reduce the wife's overdraft at her bank. In every case the consent of the wife was obtained according to the requirements of the express power, and sometimes legal advice was obtained before advancements were made. The children were of full age and never objected to the way in which the advancements were used, but they did know about the financial problems of the family. The trustees considered that they were exercising the power properly by paying the money to the children and thought that what the children did with the property advanced was not their ('the trustees') concern or responsibility. The Court of Appeal held that the power had been improperly exercised. The court said that when the trustees exercise a power of advancement, they may either make an out-and-out payment for the general benefit of a beneficiary (if they trust him to make proper use of the money and he is the type of person who can reasonably be trusted) or make a payment for a particular purpose. In the latter case the Court of Appeal said that trustees must not leave the beneficiary entirely free, legally and morally, to spend the money as he chooses. The trustees have a responsibility to inquire as to the application of the money. If the money was advanced for a particular purpose, the beneficiary is under a duty to use it for that purpose. If he does not, and the trustees know, it would be unsafe for the trustees to make further advances unless the trustees are sure that the money would be correctly used.

Summary

- The powers of trustees are often set out (at least in part) in the trust documents and there is a range of underpinning statutory provisions and in particular those contained in the Trustee Acts 1925 and 2000 and the Trusts of Land and Appointment of Trustees Act 1996.

- In most cases the courts will not interfere with the trustees' exercise of a discretion but the courts may set aside exercise of a discretion under the rule in *Re Hastings-Bass*. The rule has been re-stated in the Supreme Court in *Futter v HMRC; Pitt v HMRC*.

- The courts can (exceptionally) overturn the exercise of a discretion on the ground of mistake.

- Trustees have extensive though restricted powers to sell trust property which may extend to both land and personalty.

- The trustees have the power to insure trust property but surprisingly there is no duty to insure.

- The trustees may have the power to maintain beneficiaries who are minors. The statutory power under s 31 of the Trustee Act 1925 were amended by the Inheritance and Trustees' Powers Act 2014 which came into force on 1 October 2014.

- Trustees may have the power to allow capital to be used for the benefit of beneficiaries under the power of advancement. The statutory power under s 32 of the Trustee Act 1925 were amended by the Inheritance and Trustees' Powers Act 2014 which came into force on 1 October 2014.

Further reading

Setting aside the exercise of a discretion

M Firth, 'Monetary mistakes' Tax (2013) 171(4403) 14–17.
Discusses the Supreme Court decision in *Futter v HMRC, Pitt v HMRC*, particularly in the context of decisions made by trustees where there are adverse tax implications.

N Lee '*Futter v HMRC; Pitt v HMRC*: the rule in *Hastings-Bass* and of mistake reviewed' Conv (2014) 2, 175–85.
Reviews *Futter v HMRC; Pitt v HMRC* and the situations where the exercise of a discretion may be set aside under *Re Hastings-Bass*. Considers the situation where a trustee acts within his power but does so fraudulently.

S McKie 'Second thoughts: an eagerly awaited decision' PCB (2013) 4, 204–19.
Discusses the Supreme Court's decision in *Futter* v *HMRC; Pitt* v *HMRC*.

D Rees 'Whose mistake is it anyway? PCB (2014) 3, 149–56.
Discusses and criticises the Supreme Court ruling in *Futter* v *HMRC; Pitt* v *HMRC*.

J Toth and H Batten 'Trustees, mistake and *Hastings-Bass*' SJ (2013) 157(24) 10–11.
Discusses when trustees can rely on the rule in *Re Hastings-Bass*.

Conduct of sales

O Knowles and L Gregory, 'Doing the right thing' TEL & TJ (2012) 142.
Discusses *Page* v *West* on whether the trustees should sell the property as it was or seek planning permission for residential development which might have increased its value.

Power of advancement

D W M Waters 'The "new" power of advancement' [1958] Conv 413.
A wide-ranging survey of various provisions enabling 'advancement', including s 32 of the Trustee Act 1925. Examines the meaning of 'benefit' and 'advancement'.

16

Trustees' duties

Objectives

After reading this chapter you should be able to:

1. Understand and explain the general duty of trustees to act personally and the situations where delegation/appointment of agents is possible.

2. Understand and explain the extent of the duty to provide information and accounts to beneficiaries.

3. Understand and explain the duty to act impartially and the effect of the various rules of apportionment.

4. Understand and explain the duties relating to investment of trust property and, in particular, the main provisions of the Trustee Act 2000.

Standard of care

See Chapter 14 (p. 403) for more on standard of care.

See Chapter 14.

Duties on appointment

See Chapter 14 (p. 417) for more on duties on appointment.

See Chapter 14.

Duty to act personally

Objective 1

A trustee's office is personal to him and the general rule is that the trustee must discharge the duties personally and may not delegate: *delegatus non potest delegare*. A settlor having specifically chosen a trustee to act is presumed to intend that particular individual to administer the trust personally. The settlor may have selected a particular person because of their personal qualities, their sense of morality, their religious beliefs, etc. and the settlor would expect those values or beliefs to influence the way the trust was run. If someone else was delegated to deal with decision making or with aspects of the administration of the trust, it may be that a quite different set of values and beliefs would be influential, resulting, perhaps, in decisions being made which the settlor would not have wished for or expected.

It is the case that many if not most lay trustees lack the professional knowledge and skill to undertake the implementation of their decisions. For example, a lay trustee may be in a position to decide, after obtaining advice, to sell some land but he would almost certainly not have the ability to carry the transaction through. He would, in most cases, seek to appoint a solicitor to convey the property.

The origins of the statutory power to delegate lie in the willingness of equity to allow the appointment of agents to perform specific and specialist tasks: for example, the use of a solicitor to undertake the conveyance of land or accountants to produce the trust accounts. The scope of delegation was very limited. A trustee could only appoint an agent to act for him if the appointment either accorded with business practice or was reasonably necessary.

But, for example, an agent could not be appointed to perform a regular routine task which although tedious was within the ability of the trustee. The question to be asked was: would a reasonably prudent man of business appoint an agent in the circumstances? Even if it was justifiable to appoint an agent, the trustee had to ensure that the agent acted only within the usual scope of his business and the trustee had to exercise the care of a reasonable man of business when selecting an agent.

Fry v Tapson (1884) 28 Ch D 268

In this case, the trustees were empowered to invest trust funds in mortgages and they advanced £5,000 by way of mortgage on a freehold house and grounds in Liverpool valued, by a valuer, at between £7,000 and £8,000. The investment was suggested by the solicitor to the trust. The valuer was introduced by the solicitor and was an agent of the mortgagor. The valuer had no local knowledge and earned £75 commission for finding a lender. He overvalued the property which in fact was worth less than £5,000. The court held that the trustees were liable for the loss to the trust because they should have selected the surveyor personally.

If the trustee could show that the appointment was one that an ordinary prudent man of business would make and that the agent was appointed to act within his normal field, the trustee would not be held responsible for any loss caused by the agent's default provided he (the trustee) exercised proper supervision over the agent. It was, of course, never possible to delegate the exercise of discretions.

The Trustee Act 1925 s 23(1) created a statutory power to delegate in certain situations. The provision modified and extended the position under the 'ordinary prudent man of business' approach outlined above. Although the section undoubtedly altered the position of trustees greatly and freed them from having to perform all of the administration personally, there was an important reservation in that the subsection did not empower the delegation of the exercise of discretions but only allows the delegation of ministerial acts.

Additionally, there were continuing problems about the extent to which a trustee was liable for the defaults of an agent and the extent to which a trustee should oversee the actions of the agent. The decision in ***Re Vickery*** [1931] 1 Ch 572 was particularly problematical in that the court decided that a trustee was not liable for the default of an agent because the neglect to supervise the agent had not been deliberate.

The Trustee Act 2000 repealed s 23. The Trustee Act 2000 has made important changes in this area and there are now several situations where delegation is possible. There are two separate situations to deal with. The first is where an individual trustee wishes to delegate all or some of their powers and duties. The second is where the trustees collectively wish others to act for them.

Delegation by individual trustees

It is sometimes useful if an individual trustee can delegate at least some of his duties and responsibilities. Perhaps a trustee falls ill or is absent overseas.

Express power for an individual trustee to delegate

It is, of course, open to the settlor to specify that all or some of the trustee's responsibilities may be delegated. The express provision can either enlarge or restrict the ability to delegate given by the general law. The courts have the power to vary the express provisions. But, apart from where there is an express provision in the trust, the only delegation which can take place is within the limits of the statutory powers discussed below.

Statutory power for an individual trustee to delegate

Trustee Act 1925 s 25

Individual delegation is now covered by s 5 of the Trustee Delegation Act 1999, which provides a new s 25 of the Trustee Act 1925 in relation to delegation by powers of attorney granted after its commencement. This new section does give trustees the power to delegate.

In brief, the new s 25 permits delegation by individual trustees of powers and discretions for periods up to twelve months. A set period of up to twelve months may be specified. If no period is specified, the delegation will be for twelve months. The appointment must be in prescribed form, which is set out in the new s 25(6). The delegating trustee must give notice to the other trustees.

The new s 25(7) makes it clear that the donor of the power is liable for the acts and defaults of the donee (the attorney acting on behalf of the trustee) as if they were his own. This obviously encourages trustees to select the donee very carefully.

The power to delegate under s 25 applies to personal representatives as well as tenants for life and statutory owners (s 25(10)).

The new s 25(3) replaces the old s 25(2) but removes the prohibition on a sole co-trustee being the donee.

Additionally, s 6 of the Trustee Delegation Act 1999 repeals s 2(8) of the Enduring Powers of Attorney Act 1985. The consequence of this repeal is that an enduring power of attorney may be used under the new s 25 of the Trustee Act 1925. This enables power to be exercised after a donor has lost the mental capacity to make decisions for himself.

Statutory power of collective appointment by trustees

Part IV (ss 11–27) of the Trustee Act 2000

The Law Commission's Report, 'Trustees' Powers and Duties' (1999) Law Com. No. 260, recommended that trustees should have the power to delegate to agents, to vest trust assets in nominees acting in the course of their business and to deposit trust documents with custodians for safe keeping, provided that the custodian is acting in the course of its business. It was proposed that the same standard of care should apply to the exercise of the proposed statutory power and to the exercise of any express power (subject to contrary intention in the instrument creating the trust). Adopting these recommendations, Part IV (ss 11–27) of the Trustee Act 2000 changed the law regarding the collective appointment of agents, nominees and custodians by trustees to perform 'delegable functions'. It should be noted that this relates only to collective delegation by trustees. Delegation by individual trustees continues to be governed by s 25 of the Trustee Act 1925 as amended by s 5 of the Trustee Delegation Act 1999.

The powers are in addition to any contained in the trust instrument (s 26) and apply to trusts whether created before or after the commencement of the Trustee Act 2000 (s 27).

The powers to appoint agents and to delegate to them investment functions and to vest trust assets in nominees allow for a more 'modern', flexible and responsive approach to investment.

Under the pre-Trustee Act 2000 law the trustees had to retain the ownership of trust property and could not place trust property in the names of nominees. The power to vest trust property in nominees under the Trustee Act 2000 may be important in relation to investment processes. It is very common for investors to place their investments in the name of a nominee or custodian. A nominee is a person in whose name trust assets are vested. The Law Commission consultation paper, 'Trustees' Power and Duties' (1997) Law Com. No. 146, listed four situations where nominees could not be used under the then existing law but where their use would be very advantageous to trusts. These situations were also cited in the Report. First, the nominee may provide an administration service even where the portfolio is not managed by a discretionary fund manager. Secondly, if a portfolio is managed by a discretionary fund manager, it is normal to vest the title to the investments in a nominee to facilitate a more rapid transfer of securities. Thirdly, one way to deal with shares through the computerised CREST system is to vest the title to securities in nominees. Finally, investors may hold overseas shares which are dealt with in markets using a system similar to CREST and it may be convenient to deal via a nominee. Thus, vesting securities in a nominee may be seen as best practice in many situations. There are disadvantages, including the risk of misappropriation through forgery and fraud by the nominee.

A custodian is a person who undertakes the safe custody of assets or documents relating to assets.

Agents – Trustee Act 2000 ss 11–15

This section of the chapter deals with situations where the trustees as a body wish others to act for them. An example where this might be desirable is if all the trustees are elderly and perhaps finding the administration of the trust too onerous.

The provisions of the Trustee Act 2000 set out situations where the appointment of agents is possible and also prescribes the continuing liability of the trustees for any agents appointed. The powers to appoint agents apply unless there is contrary provision in the trust instrument.

Section 11 of the Trustee Act 2000 gives trustees wide powers collectively to appoint agents in the absence of express authority in the trust instrument. The trustees may not appoint a beneficiary under the trust as an agent. When selecting and supervising an agent, the trustees are exercising a fiduciary duty and are subject to the statutory duty of care.

A trustee's function may be delegated unless it appears in a list of 'non-delegable' functions which is set out in s 11(2).

Agents are subject to any restriction contained in the trust. Although agents are not subject to the statutory duty of care, they will have a duty of care under the law of agency.

11(2) In the case of a trust other than a charitable trust, the trustees' delegable functions consist of any function other than –

(a) any function relating to whether or in what way any assets of the trust should be distributed,
(b) any power to decide whether any fees or other payment due to be made out of the trust funds should be made out of income or capital,
(c) any power to appoint a person to be a trustee of the trust, or
(d) any power conferred by any other enactment or the trust instrument which permits the trustees to delegate any of their functions or to appoint a person to act as a nominee or custodian.

However, in the case of charitable trustees, functions are not delegable unless they appear on a list of delegable functions set out in s 11(3).

11(3) In the case of a charitable trust, the trustees' delegable functions are –

(a) any function consisting of carrying out a decision that the trustees have taken;
(b) any function relating to the investment of assets subject to the trust (including, in the case of land held as an investment, managing the land and creating or disposing of an interest in the land);
(c) any function relating to the raising of funds for the trust otherwise than by means of profits of a trade which is an integral part of carrying out the trust's charitable purpose;
(d) any other function prescribed by an order made by the Secretary of State.

Section 12 defines those who may act as agents and provides that the agent may be one of the trustees.

Section 13 states that, in the main, an agent to whom a function is delegated is subject to the specific duties attached to that function. The example generally given is, where an agent has powers relating to investment decisions, they are subject to the duties relating to investment under ss 4 and 5 of the Trustee Act 2000.

Section 14 sets out some restrictions on the terms that may (unless reasonably necessary) be included in the terms of any agency appointment.

The freedom given to trustees under s 14 is subject to a number of provisos, including the trustees being subject to the general duty of care (s 1 and Schedule 1).

Section 15 provides for some special requirements where trustees delegate 'asset management' functions. 'Asset management' functions are defined in s 15(5) as the functions of the trustees relating to (a) the investment of assets subject to the trust, (b) the acquisition of property which is to be subject to the trust, and (c) managing property which is subject to the trust and disposing of, or creating or disposing of an interest in, such property. Amongst the requirements is the need for writing or evidence in writing of the agreement to delegate and for the trustees to prepare a written policy statement guiding the agent's actions. The policy statement should be formulated with a view to ensuring that the functions will be exercised in the best interests of the trust.

Nominees and custodians – Trustee Act 2000 ss 16–20

Sections 16 and 17 of the Trustee Act 2000 cover the appointment of nominees and custodians. Nominees will have trust property registered or vested in their name. A custodian is one with whom trust assets or documents are deposited for safe keeping.

The appointment of a nominee or custodian must be in writing or evidenced in writing.

16. – (1) Subject to the provisions of this Part, the trustees of a trust may –
  (a) appoint a person to act as their nominee in relation to such of the assets of the trust as they determine (other than settled land), and
  (b) take such steps as are necessary to secure that those assets are vested in a person so appointed.
(2) An appointment under this section must be in or evidenced in writing.
(3) This section does not apply to any trust having a custodian trustee or in relation to any assets vested in the official custodian for charities.

Section 17 sets out provisions governing the appointment of custodians, i.e. people appointed to undertake the safe keeping of trust property.

17. – (1) Subject to the provisions of this Part, the trustees of a trust may appoint a person to act as a custodian in relation to such of the assets of the trust as they may determine.
(2) For the purposes of this Act a person is a custodian in relation to assets if he undertakes the safe custody of the assets or of any documents or records concerning the assets.
(3) An appointment under this section must be in or evidenced in writing.
(4) This section does not apply to any trust having a custodian trustee or in relation to any assets vested in the official custodian for charities.

Section 19 sets out the provisions relating to who may be appointed as a nominee or custodian. One of the main elements is that the person appointed must be either a corporate body controlled by the trustees or a person who carries on a business consisting of or including acting as a nominee or custodian.

Subject to this, the trustees can appoint one of their number, if that one is a trust corporation.

The terms of the appointment are regulated by s 20. They are similar to the provisions regulating the terms on which agents are appointed.

Section 32 sets out the right of agents, custodians and nominees to reimbursement for properly incurred expenses.

Managing the appointment and performance of agents, nominees and custodians

Acting in excess of powers

If trustees act in excess of their powers to appoint under the Act, s 24 states that this will not invalidate the appointment. This is important when appointees are dealing with third parties, who otherwise would need to investigate the detail of the appointment before feeling confident to deal with the appointee. Trustees would still be liable for the consequences of any appointment beyond their powers.

The need to review the arrangements relating to agents, nominees etc.

Section 22 sets out the responsibilities of the trustees to keep under review the arrangements under which the agent etc. acts and how the arrangements are being put into effect.

In essence, under s 22, the trustees must keep under review (and review at appropriate times) the arrangements under which the appointment was made and the manner in which the appointee is carrying out the duties, and whether the person appointed was and still is an appropriate person.

This duty of continuing review contrasts with the position in **Re Vickery** [1931] 1 Ch 572 (above) with regard to the duty to supervise under the now repealed s 23(1) of the Trustee Act 1925.

The trustee has a power of intervention, which covers giving directions to the agents etc. or removing an unsatisfactory appointee. If the agents etc. have been authorised to exercise asset management functions, the trustees also must consider if and when to change the investment policy statement, and whether or not the policy statement has been complied with.

Liability of trustees for acts of agents, nominees etc.

One key issue is the liability that trustees have for the acts of their agents, nominees and custodians. Section 23 covers this point. A trustee is not liable for any act or default of the agent, nominee or custodian unless he, the trustee, has failed to comply with the duty of care applicable to him, under paragraph 3 of Schedule 1 when appointing the agent etc. (s 23(1)(a)) or when carrying out the supervision required under s 22 (s 23(1)(b)).

Payment of agents, nominees etc.

Section 32 of the Trustee Act 2000 states that agents, custodians or nominees appointed under Part IV (other than trustees so appointed) may be reasonably remunerated, if engaged on terms that they will be so remunerated. Additionally, the trustees may reimburse the agent, nominee or custodian for properly incurred expenses.

Trusts of Land and Appointment of Trustees Act 1996 s 9

The Trusts of Land and Appointment of Trustees Act 1996 s 9 created new provisions under which trustees of a trust of land may as a body delegate their powers. Section 9 provides that the trustees of trusts of land may, by a power of attorney, delegate any of their functions which relate to the land to any beneficiary or beneficiaries who are of full age and beneficially entitled to an interest in possession in land which is subject to a trust. The delegation is made by all the trustees jointly by power of attorney (s 9(3)). Unlike the power to delegate by power of attorney under s 25 of the Trustee Act 1925, delegation under s 9 is not limited to periods of twelve months. Under s 9 the delegation may be for a definite period or it may be for an indefinite period (s 9(5)). Section 9(8) deals with the liability of the trustees for the acts or defaults of the beneficiaries to whom a function has been delegated. It provides that the trustees are jointly and severally liable for any act or default of the beneficiary (or any of the beneficiaries) if, and only if, the trustees did not exercise reasonable care in deciding to delegate the function to the beneficiary or beneficiaries. A delegation is revocable unless it is expressed to be irrevocable and given by way of security. It may be revoked by any one of the trustees and is automatically revoked if the beneficiary ceases to be a person beneficially entitled to an interest in possession in the land which is subject to the trust. Additionally, the delegation will be automatically revoked if a new trustee is appointed but not if a person ceases to be a trustee, for whatever reason, or if a trustee dies (s 9(3)).

Duty to act unanimously

One of the safeguards against trustees acting improperly is the rule that trustees must act jointly and unanimously when exercising powers and discretions. (See *Luke* v *South Kensington Hotel Co* (1879) 11 Ch D 121.) There is no possibility of a majority decision being valid or of the majority binding the minority. So, if one of several trustees enters a contract to sell trust property, the contract cannot be enforced against the trust estate. The need for unanimity is subject to a contrary provision in the trust instrument, or a court order.

For example, all of the trustees must join in the receipt for money (unless the trust provides to the contrary). In *Re Flower* (1884) 27 Ch D 592, Kay J stressed that the reason for this is that the trustees must not allow the trust money to get into the hands of one of their number. They must ensure that trust money is under the control of them all. If the trustees permit the funds to be under the control of one of their number, this will amount to a breach of trust on their part.

Under a trust for sale, therefore, if the trustees wish to exercise their power to postpone, this decision must be unanimous. If the trustees are in disagreement, the power to postpone cannot be exercised and the duty to sell must be complied with.

Re Mayo [1943] 2 All ER 440

In this case, three trustees held property on trust for sale with power to postpone. One of the trustees wanted to sell the property but the other two did not agree. Simonds J held that all the trustees must be in agreement to exercise the power of postponement. As there was no unanimity in the case, the two dissenting trustees were directed to take part in the sale under the duty to sell.

Obviously, this duty to act unanimously does not extend to the discharge of duties; duties have to be carried out and the fact that not all the trustees are agreeable is irrelevant.

The duty to act unanimously does not apply to the trustees of a charitable trust, where the majority may bind the minority: *Wilkinson* v *Malin* (1832) 2 Cr & J 636.

Duty to provide accounts and information

Accounts

Objective 2

In *Pearse* v *Green* (1819) 1 Jac & W 135, Sir Thomas Plummer MR said: 'It is the first duty of an accounting party whether an agent, a trustee, a receiver, or an executor . . . to be constantly ready with his accounts.'

A trustee must keep up-to-date and accurate accounts and allow beneficiaries to inspect them on demand. Strictly speaking, the beneficiaries are only entitled to keep copies if they pay for them.

There is no statutory duty to have the accounts audited, but the Trustee Act 1925 s 22(4) provides that, within limits, the cost of any audit that the trustees decide upon shall be paid from the trust property. The trustees may pay the costs out of capital or income as they see fit. The section provides that unless there are special circumstances this audit should take place not more often than once every three years. Section 13 of the Public Trustee Act 1906 permits any beneficiary or trustee to apply for the trust accounts to be investigated and audited. A copy of the report will be supplied to the trustees and to the applicant.

Beneficiaries' right to inspect trust documents

The trustees are also under a general duty to allow beneficiaries to inspect trust documents and to provide information regarding their administration of the trust.

There are three issues to be discussed. First, what documents are trust documents and so within any right of production? Secondly, what is the basis of the right to see trust documents? Thirdly, how is the apparent conflict resolved between the right of beneficiaries to see trust documents and the right of the trustees not to reveal reasons for their decisions?

What are trust documents?

There is no absolutely comprehensive definition of a trust document, but in *Re Londonderry's Settlement* [1964] 3 All ER 855, Salmon LJ identified a number of characteristics that trust documents have.

> The category of trust documents has never been comprehensively defined. Nor could it be – certainly not by me. Trust documents do, however, have these characteristics in common: (1) they are documents in the possession of the trustees as trustees; (2) they contain information about the trust which the beneficiaries are entitled to know; (3) the beneficiaries have a proprietary interest in the documents and, accordingly, are entitled to see them. If any parts of a document contain information which the beneficiaries are not entitled to know, I doubt whether such parts can truly be said to be integral parts of a trust document. Accordingly, any part of a document that lacked the second characteristic to which I have referred would automatically be excluded from the document in its character as a trust document.

This gives a flavour of what trust documents are, but is by no means a comprehensive answer to the problem of deciding what are and what are not, trust documents.

The basis of the right to see trust documents

In *O'Rourke v Darbishire* [1920] All ER 1, Lord Wrenbury stated that a beneficiary had the right to see trust documents because 'They are in a sense his own.' He argued that this right arose simply from the fact of being a beneficiary under the trust. The right, it was argued, was a proprietary right. Income beneficiaries are entitled to see all the accounts, but capital beneficiaries are entitled to see only the accounts which relate to capital transactions as only such transactions affect their interests. Trustees often keep some form of diary in which decisions and actions are recorded so that the information can readily be provided to the beneficiaries.

However, the view of Lord Wrenbury (that beneficiaries have the right to inspect trust documents) was rejected by the Privy Council in the case of *Schmidt v Rosewood Trust Ltd* [2003] 3 All ER 76. In the case a beneficiary under a discretionary trust applied for disclosure of trust accounts and information about trust assets. The trustees argued that the right to disclosure is a proprietary right and that discretionary beneficiaries do not have this right.

The Privy Council stated that the court has the jurisdiction to supervise the administration of trusts, including discretionary trusts, and that where appropriate the court could intervene in the administration. Additionally, it was said that the right to seek the assistance of the court does not depend on any entitlement to an interest under the trust and that a discretionary beneficiary was able to seek the intervention of the court. The Privy Council went on to state that no beneficiary has the *right* to the disclosure of trust documents. The court would assess and balance commercial and personal interests and confidentiality before making trust documents available. In doing this, the court was exercising part of its inherent jurisdiction to oversee and supervise trusts. The right to see documents was based on the fiduciary duties of the trustees, an element of which is the obligation to keep the beneficiaries informed. The courts have to balance the interests of beneficiaries in seeing documents with the interests of the trustees.

The conflict between the right of beneficiaries to see trust documents and the right of the trustees not to reveal reasons for their decisions

The trustees are not obliged to give the beneficiaries reasons for their decision as to whether or not to exercise a discretion. In *Re Beloved Wilkes' Charity* (1851) 3 Mac & G 440, the trustees of a charity were required to select a boy to be educated to become a minister of the Church of England, preference to be given to boys from four named parishes. The trustees chose a boy who did not come from one of these four parishes. The trustees refused to give any reasons for their decision and the court held that, in the absence of any evidence that the trustees had acted improperly, partially or dishonestly, the decision would not be interfered with nor would the trustees be called upon to provide an explanation. This puts beneficiaries in a rather difficult position. On the one hand, they can only expect the courts to interfere with the trustees' exercise of a discretion if there is fraud or other misconduct while; on the other hand, the ability of trustees to refuse to give reasons for their decisions makes it difficult for the beneficiaries to know if and when the exercise has been improper. It has been suggested that one way round this is for the beneficiaries to start an action and then to obtain discovery of the papers. However, the court may consider an exercise if the trustees in fact give reasons for their decisions. If the trustees do give reasons, the court will look at them and if they are inadequate the exercise may be set aside: *Klug v Klug* [1918] 2 Ch 67.

In some situations there may well be a conflict between the right of the beneficiaries to inspect trust documents and be provided with information and the trustees' right not to disclose their reasons for the exercise of a discretion. If the trust documents reveal why the decision to exercise a discretion was made, or the trust diary records these reasons, should these documents be available to the beneficiaries or not?

This was the issue in *Re Londonderry's Settlement*. The court decided that the right of the trustees not to reveal reasons for their decisions prevailed over the right of beneficiaries to inspect trust documents.

Re Londonderry's Settlement [1964] 3 All ER 855

The trustees of a family settlement had a power to appoint shares of capital to beneficiaries. They distributed all the capital in this way, bringing the settlement to an end. One of the beneficiaries asked the trustees for copies of the minutes of the trustees' meetings at which the decisions had been made and also for copies of letters between the trustees and beneficiaries. The trustees were not willing to do this as it would reveal the reasons why the decisions were made. The Court of Appeal held that the right not to disclose reasons for exercising a discretion prevailed over the right of the beneficiary to information. It was also decided that the letters were not trust documents and so the trustees did not, in any case, have to produce them for inspection by the beneficiaries.

Harman LJ said:

> I cannot think that communications passing between individual trustees and appointers are documents in which beneficiaries have a proprietary right . . . I do not think that letters to or from an individual beneficiary ought to be open to inspection by another beneficiary.

The Court of Appeal gave a number of reasons to justify the withholding of documents in the case which contain the reasons for exercising a discretion. Among them were: disclosure of reasons would embitter family feelings and the relationship between trustees and beneficiaries, and disclosure might make the lives of the trustees intolerable and might make it difficult to persuade people to act as trustees.

In *Breakspear v Ackland* [2008] EWHC 220 (Ch) the Court held that the principle established in *Re Londonderry's Settlement* [1964] 3 All ER 855 applied to family discretionary trusts. The process of the exercise of discretionary powers to dispose of property powers by trustees was confidential and the principle extended to letters that contained material which the settlor wished that the trustees should take into account when exercising their dispositive discretionary powers (sometimes called 'wish letters').

In *Wilson* v *Law Debenture Trust Corp plc* [1995] 2 All ER 337, the court was asked to decide whether the exception whereby trust documents may be withheld from beneficiaries if they reveal reasons for exercising discretions applies to pension trusts. A company was sold and all the employees of the company transferred their employment to the buyer. As part of the deal, the buyer was admitted temporarily as a participating employer in the pension scheme of the seller, until the buyer could set up a new pension scheme. When the new scheme was set up, all the employees joined the new scheme. At the time the old scheme was showing an actuarial surplus. The old scheme's terms gave the trustees the power to transfer to the new scheme such part of the assets as they determined to be appropriate, having taken advice. They transferred an amount which left a large part of the surplus in the old scheme. The plaintiffs (all former members of the old scheme) sought access to the documents which set out the reasons for the trustees' decision. It was argued that, unlike the beneficiaries in *Re Londonderry's Settlement*, here the beneficiaries were not volunteers and this should result in a greater duty of disclosure. It would not be reasonable for the beneficiaries, who had bought their entitlement, to be prevented from knowing the reasons for trustees' decisions and to be stopped from monitoring the exercise of discretions. Rattee J said that if different rules applied to pension trusts this change to the long-established principle should be made by Parliament, not by the courts.

To the extent that one of the justifications in *Re Londonderry's Settlement* for not revealing decisions is to prevent family discord, this is clearly not relevant in the instant case. Also, in relation to another reason in *Re Londonderry's Settlement* (to protect trustees from their lives being made intolerable if reasons were revealed), it can be argued that this should not apply in the case of professional trustees.

Duty to act impartially

Objective 3

It is the duty of the trustees to administer the trust for the benefit of all the beneficiaries and not to favour one beneficiary or one type of beneficiary at the expense of others.

Lloyds Bank plc v *Duker* [1987] 3 All ER 193

In this case, the court refused the request of a residuary beneficiary to take part of her entitlement *in specie*. She was entitled to 46/80 of the residuary estate and claimed 574 of the 999 shares in a company which were part of the residuary property. The court refused, saying that as 574 shares was a majority holding the value of those shares would be more than 46/80, the value of majority shares being greater than the value of minority shares. The court decided that in order to treat all beneficiaries fairly all the shares should be sold and the proceeds should be divided in the specified proportions.

The duty to act impartially is especially relevant in the context of investment. The trustees must not, for example, choose investments which are advantageous to the life tenant in terms of generating income while being disadvantageous to the remaindermen in that the capital value of the fund is put at risk and/or may not grow at a reasonable rate.

Capital v *income*

Key to discharging this duty is the definition of which receipts are classified as income and which as capital.

Currently there are two separate sets of 'rules', one governing receipts from companies and another covering other types of receipts.

In **Bouch v Sproule** (1887) 12 App Cas 385, the House of Lords set out the general rule for receipts from companies. Any profit that is distributed to trustee-shareholders by way of dividend is received as income. Shares received following capitalisation are capital. So if the company decides to distribute profit to shareholders by issuing them with additional shares, the trustee-shareholder will be regarded as having received capital. In other words, the classification of the receipt by the trustee-shareholder is determined by the decision of the company as to how it decides to distribute its profit. So, in a way, whether the trust receives capital or income is a matter of 'chance'. But this 'lottery' is of great significance if there are beneficiaries who would be entitled to income but not capital receipts or vice versa. Of course, any future dividends received on the shares would be income and so go to those entitled to income under the trust.

For the sake of completeness it should be noted that there are several exceptions to the rule.

In the Consultation paper ((2004) Law Com. No. 175) radical proposals were made under which all the existing classification rules for trustee-shareholder receipts would be abolished and replaced with a rule under which cash distributions (excluding payments made on liquidation or on unauthorised reduction of capital) or distributions which the trustees could have taken in cash should be classified as income and all other distributions from companies should be classified as capital.

Mainly because of taxation implications, rather less radical recommendations were made in 'Capital and Income in Trusts: Classification and Apportionment' (No. 315) published in 2009. The Law Commission Report proposed that shares distributed in a tax-exempt demerger should be classified as capital for trust law purposes. This would classify as capital those shares received as a result both of direct and indirect demergers. It was also recommended that when such a distribution is made, trustees should have a power to make a payment of capital to beneficiaries interested in income where otherwise there would be prejudice to those beneficiaries.

The Trusts (Capital and Income) Act 2013 gives effect, subject to minor modifications, to the recommendations of the Law Commission. Section 2 applies to the receipt by trustees of shares as a tax-exempt distribution on a demerger. Where such shares are currently classified as income, section 2 states that they will be classified as capital. Section 3 gives the trustees the power to compensate income beneficiaries where a tax-exempt distribution made by a corporate body is under section 2 treated as capital and the trustees are satisfied that, but for the distribution, there would have been a receipt of income for the purposes of the trust. These two sections of the Act apply whether the trust was created before or after the Act came into force (1 October 2013).

Rules of Apportionment

The courts and the legislature developed a number of rules of conversion and apportionment between capital and income which attempt to ensure that all beneficiaries are treated impartially.

In practice, in most well-drafted trust documents, these rules have been routinely excluded as their operation was often expensive, complicated and could lead to 'odd' results.

There are four main rules:

- Apportionment under s 2 of the Apportionment Act 1870.

- Rule in ***Howe v Lord Dartmouth*** [1775–1802] All ER Rep 24. This has two limbs. Under the first limb trustees are under a duty to sell certain property and convert the proceeds into authorised investments. Under the second limb trustees are under a duty, pending sale, to apportion income from unauthorised investments between capital and income.

- Rule in ***Re Earl of Chesterfield's Trusts*** (1883) 24 Ch D 643. This rule applies where part of the trust property which is subject to a duty to convert may consist of reversionary interests that have not fallen in and are thus not interests in possession.

- Rule in ***Allhusen v Whittell*** (1867) LR 4 Eq 295 which deals with apportioning the payment of debts between capital and income.

Reform of the Rules of Apportionment

The rules have been much criticised and there have been many suggestions for reform or even abolition.

The latest recommendations for reform were contained in the Law Commission Report, 'Capital and Income in Trusts: Classification and Apportionment' (No. 315) published in 2009. The Report recommended the abolition of the four main rules of apportionment set out above. The recommendations were, with minor changes, accepted by the government.

The following extract from the Summary of the Law Commission Report sets out the main (radical) recommendations for changes in the apportionment rules for non-charitable trusts and (in outline) the reasons for the recommendations. In essence it recommends the first rule in ***Howe v Lord Dartmouth*** (duty to convert), the equitable rules of apportionment and s 2 of the Apportionment Act 1870 as it applies to trusts should be 'abolished'.

29. These rules are the law's current rather archaic, and highly inconvenient, response to a number of factual situations in which investments do not give a balanced return to income and capital. We recommend reform that will prevent their automatic implication into trusts, without preventing settlors from incorporating them expressly.

30. We recommend that the first branch of the rule in ***Howe v Earl of Dartmouth***, requiring certain residuary personalty to be sold, be abolished. Underpinning this recommendation is the view that trustees should no longer be placed under a specific duty to sell the narrow range of investments to which that rule applies; rather, the sale and reinvestment of trust property ought to form part of a trustee's investment duties under the Trustee Act 2000. This recommendation would take effect for all trusts created after the implementation of our recommendations.

31. The [Law Commission Consultation Paper] provisionally proposed that all the equitable apportionment rules be abolished in their entirety . . . We have concluded that . . . there is no sensible alternative to the abolition of the rules of apportionment because of the practical problems to which they give rise. The fact that they are generally excluded in express trusts speaks for itself. Accordingly, we recommend that the equitable rules of apportionment should not apply to any future trusts, subject to any contrary provision in the trust instrument. It would remain open to future settlors to incorporate express provision in the trust deed if they wished to replicate the rules.

32. The statutory time apportionment rule contained in section 2 of the Apportionment Act 1870 is, likewise, routinely excluded in professionally drafted trust deeds, and when not excluded it is likely that trustees are either unaware of the rule or simply ignore it. Where it is applied, the rule operates against the interests of a life beneficiary, typically a widow or widower, and so in many cases the current default position would not accord with the wishes

of the testator and the needs of the beneficiaries. We therefore recommend that section 2 of the Apportionment Act 1870 should not apply to any future trusts, subject to any contrary provision in the trust instrument. Periodic payments such as dividends would therefore accrue to the income beneficiary at the date when they arise. In circumstances where it is important, settlors and testators can include a duty to apportion on a time basis.

The Trusts (Capital and Income) Act 2013 gives effect to the Law Commission recommendations, with some minor modifications.

The parts of the Act relevant here apply only to trusts created or arising on or after 1 October 2013 and to trusts created by will, or arising under the intestacy rules, in relation to a death on or after 1 October 2013. The Act calls trusts to which it applies 'new trusts'.

Section 1(2) disapplies the equitable rules of apportionment and s 1(1) says that s 2 of the Apportionment Act 1870 no longer applies to 'new trusts'. Section 1(3) states that where previously trustees were under a duty to sell property under the first limb of the rule in *Howe* v *Lord Dartmouth*, trustees will have a power to sell.

However, it is open to settlors or testators to expressly include the duty to apportion or to expressly exclude the operation of the Act.

Apportionment Act 1870 s 2

Trusts created before 1 October 2013

Under the Apportionment Act 1870 s 2 payments of income are treated as accruing daily and so, when appropriate, payments of income have to be apportioned on this basis. For example, S created a trust under which I is entitled to the income for life with remainder to R. Among the trust assets is a block of shares. To use the example given in the Explanatory Notes that accompanied the Trusts (Capital and Income) Bill, a dividend is declared on 1 February on the shares that last yielded a dividend on 1 December. I died on 1 January. Under section 2 of the Apportionment Act 1870, half the dividend is payable to R and half accrues to I's estate.

Trusts created on after 1 October 2013

The recommendation of the Law Commission to disapply the section has been implemented by s 1(1) of the Trusts (Capital and Income) Act 2013.

Under s 1(1) any entitlement to income under a 'new trust' is to income as it arises (and accordingly section 2 of the Apportionment Act 1870, which provides for income to accrue from day to day, does not apply in relation to the trust).

A 'new trust' is a trust created or arising on or after 1 October 2013 (and includes a trust created or arising on or after that day under a power conferred before that day).

This removes the need for trustees to undertake the task of apportioning income on the basis that it accrued on a daily basis and provides that the person entitled to the whole of any income receipt is the person entitled to income at the date that the payment arises.

Rule in *Howe* v *Lord Dartmouth* [1775–1802] All ER Rep 24

This rule has two elements:

- It may impose a duty to convert property from one form into another.
- It may impose a duty to apportion income pending actual conversion.

Trusts created before 1 October 2013

Duty to convert

Trustees may be under a duty to convert the trust assets into authorised investments. The duty may be derived from the terms of the trust (e.g. a trust for sale) or from statute. Since 1 January 1997, all trusts where the property includes land (except then existing Settled Land Act settlements) are trusts of land under which the property is held by the trustees subject to a power to sell. The rule in *Howe* v *Lord Dartmouth* will not apply to such trusts. In other cases the duty to convert may be imposed under the rule in *Howe* v *Lord Dartmouth*, which is an attempt to ensure that the trustees administer the trust in an even-handed way as between the life tenant and the remainderman.

Duty to apportion income

Both a duty to convert under an express trust and a duty under the rule in *Howe* v *Lord Dartmouth* carry with them a duty to apportion pending actual conversion.

The rule assumes that the life tenant may be advantaged at the expense of the remainderman if the trust property consists of wasting assets (e.g. a car) or hazardous assets (e.g. speculative, unauthorised investments). The assumption is that these types of investments may generate a high income or be otherwise beneficial to the life tenant but perhaps at a risk to the value of the capital when the remainderman's interest falls into possession. The rule is an attempt to compensate the remainderman. However, the rule applies only if there is no contrary intention and applies only to trusts of residuary personalty created by a will under which there are persons entitled in succession. The rule is clearly of relatively limited application, but where it applies the trustees are placed under a duty to sell the wasting or hazardous property and to invest the proceeds in authorised investments.

Apportionment pending conversion of unauthorised investments

If there is a duty to convert property into authorised investments, whether under the rule in *Howe* v *Lord Dartmouth* or under an express trust for sale, there will inevitably be a delay before the sale and reinvestment take place. What are the rights of the life tenant and the remainderman in the meantime? The courts have formulated a method of apportioning income generated pending conversion in order to hold the balance between the two interested parties.

The procedures are to be found, largely, in *Re Fawcett* [1940] Ch 402 and the same rules apply if there is a duty to convert under *Howe* v *Lord Dartmouth* or under an express trust for sale.

The first thing to be done is to value the property that must be sold. If the trustees have a power to postpone the sale, the property will be valued at the date of the testator's death. In other cases, property remaining unsold at the end of the executor's year (one year from the death) will be valued at that date. The proceeds of any property sold within the year will be taken as its value.

The next stage is to allocate to the life tenant what is considered to be a reasonable return on the assets. The return has for many years been set at 4 per cent, having been laid down in *Re Baker* [1924] 2 Ch 40 and *Re Beech* [1920] 1 Ch 40. It has been argued that a return of 4 per cent does not always represent a reasonable return in the light of the prevailing economic climate, and that perhaps the rate used should be that chargeable against trustees in respect of liability for breach of trust under the Administration of Justice Act 1965 s 6(1).

If the actual income produced exceeds the apportioned amount, the balance is added to capital. If the income produced is insufficient to cover the entitlement of the tenant for life, the shortfall can be made up from future income or from the proceeds when the unauthorised investment is sold. The tenant for life is not entitled to resort to unused income generated in past years to make good any current shortfall, as that unused income will have been added to capital and will no longer be regarded as having the character of income.

Once the sale and reinvestment have taken place, the tenant for life will be entitled to the actual income produced.

These apportionment rules apply unless there is a contrary intention. For example, if the settlor makes it clear that the life tenant is to receive the actual income pending conversion, this obviously rules out the need to apportion pending conversion.

Leases

There is some uncertainty as to whether the duty to convert under the rule in *Howe* v *Lord Dartmouth* and/or the apportionment rules apply to leases of land.

It is clear that there is no duty to convert leases exceeding 60 years as they are authorised investments under s 73(1)(xi) of the Settled Land Act 1925, but it is probable that the rule does apply to shorter leases of land. It is uncertain whether the duty to apportion applies to leases but the better view appears to be that it does not. It appears to be clear that there is no duty to apportion under an express trust for sale or a statutory trust for sale. The position seems to be the same if the duty to convert arises under the rule in *Howe* v *Lord Dartmouth*. This results from the provisions of s 28(2) of the Law of Property Act 1925, which provides that:

> Subject to any direction to the contrary in the disposition on trust for sale or in the settlement of the proceeds of sale, the net rents and profits of the land until sale . . . shall be paid or applied . . . in like manner as the income of investments representing the purchase money would be payable or applicable if a sale had been made and the proceeds had been duly invested.

By s 28(5) of the Law of Property Act 1925, 'land' includes 'land of any tenure'. The result of this is that the life tenant will be entitled to all the rent produced under a lease.

Trusts created on or after 1 October 2013

Section 1(2)(a) and 1(2)(b) of the Trusts (Capital and Income) Act 2013 disapplies both heads of the rule in *Howe* v *Lord Dartmouth* to trusts created on or after 1 October 2013.

With respect to trusts created or arising on or after 1 October 2013 the rule in *Howe* v *Lord Dartmouth* will only apply where settlors or testators expressly include the duty to apportion or expressly exclude the operation of the Act.

Given that trusts often operate for many years the rule will continue to be relevant for some time, both in relation to trusts created before 1 October 2013 and to trusts where the settlor has expressly included a duty to apportion under the rule.

Rule in *Re Earl of Chesterfield's Trusts* (1883) 24 Ch D 643

Trusts created before 1 October 2013

Part of the trust property which is subject to a duty to convert may consist of reversionary interests that have not fallen in and are thus not interests in possession. Until the interest falls in, it will produce no income for the life tenant. In theory, such an interest should be sold and the proceeds placed in authorised investments but in practice this is not always done. In many cases the trustees wait until the interest falls in. In either case, when the interest is sold or when the interest falls in, the trustees will be under a duty to make an apportionment in order to compensate the life tenant for the loss of income. The apportionment is carried out under the rule in *Re Earl of Chesterfield's Trusts*.

The rule states that the trustees should apportion the amount received by them between capital and income. They must allocate to capital that amount of money which, if invested over the intervening period at 4 per cent compound interest, would have produced the amount received by the trustees. The balance will be treated as income and be paid to the life tenant.

This same rule applies whenever the trust contains non-income-producing assets and there is a period during which the life tenant is deprived of income.

Under the Trusts of Land and Appointment of Trustees Act 1996, all trusts which include land will be trusts of land and the property will be held by the trustees subject to a power of sale. This means that the rule in *Re Earl of Chesterfield's Trusts* will not apply to such trusts.

Trusts created on or after 1 October 2013

Section 1(2)(c) of the Trusts (Capital and Income) Act 2013 disapplies the rule in *Re Earl of Chesterfield's Trusts* for trusts created or arising on or after 1 October 2013.

From this date onwards, the rule will only apply where settlors or testators expressly include the duty to apportion or expressly exclude the operation of the Act.

Given that trusts often operate for many years the rule will continue to be relevant for some time, both in relation to trusts created before 1 October 2013 and to trusts where the settlor has expressly included a duty to apportion under the rule.

Rule in *Allhusen* v *Whittell* (1867) LR 4 Eq 295 Trusts created before 1 October 2013

If the trustees under a will are called upon to meet debts (e.g. the funeral expenses), it would be very straightforward simply to take the money from the capital fund. However, this may be unfair as between the life tenant and the remainderman. The life tenant is entitled to any income generated by the estate after the death of the testator. As there will inevitably be delays between death and paying a debt, the tenant for life will receive income on that part of the capital which will go to the payment of the debt. The longer the delay, the greater the advantage to the tenant for life. For example, if the assets involved are £10,000 and the debt in question is £1,000 which is paid one year after the death, the tenant for life will be entitled to income on all the property, including the £1,000 until it is used to pay the debt. So for one year he receives income on £10,000 as compared to the net value of £9,000 which is what the remainderman will eventually receive.

The rule provides a method of apportioning the burden of debts and other liabilities between capital and income. The purpose is to ensure that neither income nor capital beneficiaries are advantaged.

Subject to a contrary intention, the trustees must calculate what sum of money would have to be invested from the death to the date the debt was paid, at the average rate of interest of the estate (less tax), so that when added to the income so generated it equals the amount needed to pay the debt. The debt will then be paid taking an amount equal to the notional income from the entitlement of the life tenant, the rest coming from capital.

This rule applies unless a contrary intention is expressed. In practice, the rule is expressly excluded in most professionally drafted trusts on the basis that it is complicated and expensive to administer and often leads to only small adjustments. In theory, when the rule applies, a separate calculation should be done for each debt that is paid. In many cases, where the rule is not actually excluded it is, in practice, ignored.

Trusts created on or after 1 October 2013

Section 1(2)(d) of the Trusts (Capital and Income) Act 2013 disapplies the rule in *Allhusen* **v *Whittell*** for trusts created or arising on or after 1 October 2013.

The rule will only apply where settlors or testators expressly include the duty to apportion or expressly exclude the operation of the Act.

Given that trusts often operate for many years the rule will continue to be relevant for some time, both in relation to trusts created before 1 October 2013 and to trusts where the settlor has expressly included a duty to apportion under the rule.

Duty to distribute to those entitled

The trustees are under a duty to distribute the trust property according to the terms of their trust. Any distribution to one who is not entitled will be a breach of trust even if the distribution has been made on the basis of legal advice. The other side of the coin is that a beneficiary can compel the trustees to transfer anything that he (the beneficiary) is entitled to under the trust, subject only to the proviso that the transfer will not adversely affect the interests of other beneficiaries under the trust. See ***Stephenson* v *Barclays Bank Trust Co Ltd*** [1975] 1 All ER 625.

If it is uncertain whether property should be transferred, perhaps because the wording of the trust is unclear or ambiguous, the trustees may apply to the court for directions.

One very common issue is identifying all the beneficiaries entitled under the trust. Is X still alive? Did Y die without issue?

One course of action for the trustees is to advertise in order to try to discover those who claim the right to trust property.

The placing of advertisements under the Trustee Act 1925 s 27 will provide the trustees with protection should, if after distributing property, other claims come to light. Advertisements must be placed in the *London Gazette* and in newspapers circulating in the area where land in the estate is situated, and other similar notices must be placed which the court would have directed. The notices must require people interested to send the trustees particulars of their claim. The notice must contain a time limit for claims, which must not be less than two months. When the time limit has expired, the trustees can distribute the trust property on the basis of the claims notified to them. The trustees will not be liable if this distribution turns out to be wrong: for example, if beneficiaries contact the trustees after the expiration of the time limit and after the property has been conveyed or distributed. This does not prevent these beneficiaries from trying to recover the wrongly distributed trust property but does protect the trustees from liability for breach of trust. The trustees may know that a particular beneficiary exists and has a claim to trust property, but it may be impossible to find the person or it may not be certain that he is still alive. In this type of situation the trustees could apply for an order. The court will direct the basis upon which the property should be distributed. The trustees are then protected if they distribute in accordance with the terms of the order. Trustees can also get some protection by obtaining a Benjamin order and proceeding to deal with trust property on the terms of the order. For example, leave can be given to distribute trust property on the basis that X is dead, or that Y died without issue. If there is an uncertainty as to the terms of the trust as the original documents have been lost, the court can give leave to deal with trust property on terms established by secondary evidence. If it later turns out that the basis on which the distribution was made is wrong (perhaps it later transpires that X is not dead), the trustees are protected from liability.

MCP Pension Trustees Ltd v *Aon Pension Trustees Ltd* [2010] EWCA Civ 377; [2012] Ch 1

> This case is a warning to trustees that they cannot blindly reply on the replies to a s 27 notice. In this case trustees had actual knowledge of the existence of some beneficiaries (X) but had forgotten about them. The beneficiaries did not respond to a s 27 notice that the trustees published. X were not included in the distribution of the trust property.
>
> The Court of Appeal held that the fact that the trustees had forgotten that they had notice was immaterial. Once actual notice was given, then in general it would persist and remain notice at the time of distribution. The fact that X had not responded to the s 27 advertisements did not affect their claim.

In *Re Benjamin* [1902] 1 Ch 723, a testator left his residuary estate to his children in equal shares. He had twelve children, one of whom had disappeared in September 1892, a year before the testator died. Inquiries were made but he could not be traced. Joyce J decided that in the absence of evidence that the son survived his father, the trustee should distribute the father's estate on the basis that the son died before his father. If the son later proved to be alive he would be able to trace his share into the hands of his siblings who had received his share. In such an eventuality, the trustees would be protected and would not be liable for a breach of trust. This decision has been used as the basis of orders in similar situations and the court orders are known as 'Benjamin orders'.

One drawback with applying for a Benjamin order, particularly if the trust is a small one, is that there will be costs incurred.

Trustees can seek an indemnity from all known beneficiaries should the missing beneficiary appear. But of course the beneficiaries may die or become bankrupt in which case the indemnity will be of little use.

The trustees could consider taking out insurance to cover their possible future liability and could also cover the liability of beneficiaries to whom trust property has been transferred.

It is always possible for the trustees to decide to set aside a fund against which any future claims can be set. But this is problematical. Known beneficiaries will be anxious to get their hands on the fund, and retaining the fund may extend the duration of the trust.

If there is a genuine problem regarding the identification or ascertainment of beneficiaries the trustees could, in the last resort, pay the funds into court as happened in *Re Gillingham Bus Disaster Fund* [1958] 2 All ER 749. The court decided that surplus funds collected after a number of Royal Marine cadets were killed and injured in a road accident were to be held on resulting trust for the contributors. Much of the money had been raised from street collections and other untraceable sources. That part of the surplus contributed by unidentifiable donors was paid into court by the trustees.

Duty to consult

In relation to the exercise of any of their functions relating to land, the trustees should, so far as is practicable, consult the beneficiaries of full age and beneficially entitled to an interest in possession in the land and, so far as is consistent with the general interest of the trust, give effect to their wishes or, if there is a dispute, to the wishes of the majority – according to the value of their combined interests (Trusts of Land and Appointment of Trustees Act 1996 s 11). These provisions do not apply, *inter alia*, where the disposition creating the trust excludes them or where the trust was created under a will made before 1997.

Duty to act without remuneration

See Chapter 14 (pp. 398–403) for more on the general duty of trustees to act without remuneration.

See Chapter 14.

Duty not to profit from the trust nor to act in a way whereby duty as a trustee and personal interest may conflict

See Chapter 14 (p. 394) for more on the fiduciary position of trustees.

See Chapter 14.

Duty to safeguard trust property

Trustees are under a general duty to ensure that trust property is safeguarded. This duty may be particularly relevant when a new trustee is appointed. They will need to assess the situation and if, for example, trust property is outstanding the trustee(s) must take steps to call it in.

Re Brogden (1883) 38 Ch D 546

In this case, trustees of a marriage settlement failed to sue to enforce the payment to the trust of £10,000 owed under a covenant. The failure was due to the view that the trustees took of the covenantor's family situation. They thought that his family could be threatened if the payment was made, particularly in the light of the current trade depression. The court stated that these were not factors that should influence the trustees and they were under a duty to sue to recover the £10,000. The Court of Appeal said that the only reason which would justify trustees not suing was if they had a well-founded belief that the litigation would not result in the trust property being recovered.

This very strict approach can also be illustrated bye *Buttle v Saunders* [1950] 2 All ER 193 (see p. 404).

The case of *Ward v Ward* (1843) 2 HL Cas 777n shows a rather more relaxed and, perhaps, more acceptable attitude of the courts. It was decided that the trustees were not in breach of trust when they failed to sue a debtor, who was also a beneficiary, on the grounds that the action could have ruined the debtor and would have made the lives of his children, who were also beneficiaries, very difficult.

To some extent the position of trustees, including newly appointed trustees, is helped by the powers to allow time for debts to be paid, to compound liabilities and to compromise doubtful claims under the Trustee Act 1925 s 15. Trustees are generally indemnified against the costs of litigation which are properly incurred. This right is derived from the Trustee Act 1925 s 30(2). If trustees commence litigation on behalf of the trust, they run the risk of the courts later deciding that such a course of action was not justified and the costs were not properly incurred.

Duty to invest

Objective 4

Trustees have a duty to preserve the trust property, and in discharging this duty they will usually need to invest the trust property.

When investing, the trustees must comply with their powers of investment, which may derive from the provisions of the trust instrument or from a court order or from statute (particularly from the Trustee Act 2000).

Trustees must always bear in mind their duty to treat their beneficiaries impartially and not to choose investments which will be more advantageous to one beneficiary or type of beneficiary than to others. For example, the trustees must not select investments that unduly favour those entitled to income at the expense of those entitled to capital or vice versa, although it may well be that the trustees should make their judgement on the basis of the total investments rather than on the basis of each investment separately.

The common law standard of care required of trustees when investing was laid down in *Re Whiteley* (1886) 33 Ch D 347. Lord Lindley MR said:

> The duty of a trustee is not to take such care only as a prudent man of business would take if he only had himself to consider: the duty rather is to take such care as an ordinary prudent man of business would take if he were minded to make an investment for the benefit of other people for whom he felt morally bound to provide.

Section 1 of the Trustee Act 2000 sets out the statutory duty of care that will apply (unless excluded under the terms of the trust) to the exercise of powers and duties relating to investment. The Act imposes a duty of care to exercise 'such care and skill as is reasonable in the circumstances'. The circumstances include any special knowledge the trustee holds himself out as having or, where the trustee is acting in the course of a business or profession, the level of skill and experience that is reasonable to expect of a person acting in the course of that profession or business. This duty of care is additional to the basic obligations of trustees, such as to act within the terms of the trust, to balance the interests of all beneficiaries, and not to act in a way that puts the personal interests of trustees into conflict with those of beneficiaries.

Schedule 1 to the Trustee Act 2000 specifically states that the new duty of care will apply to situations where the trustee is exercising either the general power of investment or a power of investment conferred by a trust instrument. It will also apply when the trustee is carrying out the duties under ss 4 and 5 (relating to the duty when exercising the power of investment or to the review of investments). Additionally, the duty of care will apply (under Schedule 1) to cases where the trustee is exercising the power given by s 8 to acquire land.

Nestlé v *National Westminster Bank plc* [1994] 1 All ER 118 appears to be a rather surprising case but it does show how difficult it is for beneficiaries to succeed in a claim against the trustees for mismanagement. Despite the court describing a professional trustee as incompetent or idle, it found that there was no breach of trust. A beneficiary claimed that the bank had committed a breach of trust in failing to adopt an appropriate investment policy. It was argued that if the trust fund had been managed correctly it would have been worth £1,000,000 rather than its actual value of £296,000. Four arguments were put forward as supporting the contention that there had been a breach of trust.

First, it was argued that the bank had failed to understand the scope of its powers of investment and, in particular, had not realised that it had the power to invest in shares outside the banking and insurance fields (the areas of the original trust investments). Additionally, this resulted in a failure to appreciate that the proceeds of sale of the family home could have been invested in equities. Secondly, it was argued that the bank had failed to conduct the regular reviews of its investments as it should have done. Thirdly, the plaintiff argued that the bank had failed to diversify the investments. Fourthly, it was claimed that the trustees had favoured the income beneficiaries over the capital beneficiary in the choice of investments.

Despite Staughton LJ saying that the bank had been incompetent or idle, the Court of Appeal held that the bank was not liable. The burden of proof was on the plaintiff to prove that she had suffered a loss from the alleged breaches of trust. She had failed to prove that such a loss had been suffered.

The court said that in order for the bank to have committed a breach of trust it must have failed to adhere to the usual standard of care, i.e. the ordinary prudent man of business investing for those to whom he owed a moral duty to provide: *Learoyd* v *Whiteley* (1887). This would involve two elements: first, a consideration of what the trustees did; and, secondly, proof that decisions were made which should not have been made or that decisions were not made that should have been made.

The Court of Appeal held that, although the bank had failed to review the investments regularly and had failed to appreciate the scope of its investment powers, that was not alone sufficient to give the plaintiff a remedy. The plaintiff would need to prove that the failure to diversify into equities had caused the loss. Although the bank had not been an effective investment manager, there was no breach shown which led to a proven loss. The court said that, despite the fact that a trustee is under a duty to act with prudence, no liability was incurred for decisions made on the wrong ground or for untenable reasons if later it became clear that there were good grounds for the decision. The beneficiary must show that, with respect to the conditions at the time, and not with the benefit of hindsight, the trustees would have made different investments. The court, having referred to Megarry V-C's statement in *Cowan* v *Scargill* (1984), where a trustee makes a decision on the wrong grounds but later it emerges that there were good grounds for the decision, held that the trustees were not liable. In the instant case, the trustees failed to invest the proceeds from the sale of the family home in equities because they assumed (without having taken legal advice) that they did not have the power so to invest. In fact, they had the power but the decision not to invest in equities was a correct one as at that stage about 75 per cent of the fund was already invested in equities. It must be shown that the trustee acted in a way that no reasonable trustee would have acted. Additionally, the court said that no *prima facie* loss flowed from the failure not to invest the proceeds of sale from the family home in equities. It could not be assumed that the property would not later have been sold by the trustees and the sale proceeds reinvested in tax-exempt gilt-edged securities in pursuance of the trustees' general policy of investing in such stock.

It may seem a little strange that the bank, a professional trustee, was exempted from liability when it failed to understand the terms of its investment powers and did not regularly review the investments. The argument was that the trustees had failed to diversify (all the investment in equities being in banking and insurance companies). Staughton LJ said that this was a very prudent approach but was not an approach which no prudent trustee would have followed.

Dillon LJ stated that the measure of compensation for a breach of trust which consists of a failure to act fairly or impartially is fair compensation and not just the least compensation for failing to follow the correct policy. Staughton LJ thought that the correct measure of compensation was the difference between the actual performance and that which would have been achieved (or was likely to be achieved) by a prudent trustee.

Perhaps one of the practical lessons to come out of the case is that in order to recover for an alleged breach of trust successfully a plaintiff must adduce evidence of actual losses.

The case is also interesting as it raises the general issue of the criteria that trustees must use in making investment decisions. It is usually said that the trustees have a duty to invest in a way that results in an equitable balance between the income and capital beneficiaries. Staughton LJ referred to the trustees' duty to act 'impartially, or fairly' as between beneficiaries, saying that he could see no significant difference between the two. He quoted Wilberforce J in *Re Pauling's Settlement Trusts (No. 2)* [1963] 1 All ER 857 at 862: 'The trustees would be under the normal duty of preserving an equitable balance . . .'

At first instance Hoffmann J had said the trustees must act 'fairly'. It may be argued that this 'fairness' test may well mean that a very different approach is required by trustees. The concept of 'fairness' may introduce factors which are personal to the beneficiaries, e.g. their relative wealth. It may be 'fair' in such a case to invest in a way that favours the poorer rather than the richer beneficiaries. Applying the 'equitable balance' principle would ignore these personal factors. In the Court of Appeal, Staughton LJ said he could not see any difference between the old duty and the 'fairness' test. However, Staughton LJ was prepared to allow the financial circumstance of the beneficiaries to be taken into account by trustees as well as the relationship between beneficiaries. He said, if the life tenant is living in penury and the remainderman has ample wealth, 'common sense suggests that a trustee should be able to take that into account, not necessarily by seeking the highest possible income at the expense of capital but inclining in that direction. However, before adopting that course a trustee should, I think, require some verification of the facts.' One issue that was not pursued, or at any rate not at length, was the relative standards of care expected of lay trustees, professional (e.g. solicitor) trustees and trust companies. The fact that the court quoted with approval the ordinary prudent man of business test from *Learoyd* v *Whiteley* (1887) does suggest that the court did not think that a different, tougher, test was applicable to professional trustees.

What is an investment?

Before the Trustee Act 2000 radically changed the law, trustees had to ensure that an investment was within one of the categories of authorised investments and was an appropriate investment of that type. The Trustee Act 2000 gave trustees a very wide power to investment; they have the same powers as an absolute owner of the trust property would have. But under the old law and the new law, the key questions for a trustee are: what is an investment, and is a particular investment appropriate to the trust being administered, and at what point should the investment be assessed for its continued suitability and sold if considered no longer suitable?

Before the Trustee Act 2000, the key identifier of an investment was that it was expected to provide an income. So buying property just to enjoy the ownership of it or because a capital gain was anticipated was not investing in this context. The only way that such property could, properly, be acquired, would be under an express power which permitted the purchase of such property. And it was not unusual for the trust instrument to permit trustees to buy a residence for a beneficiary.

In *Re Wragg* [1918–19] All ER Rep 233, Lawrence J said that to invest includes: 'to apply money in the purchase of some property from which interest or profit is expected and which property is purchased in order to be held for the sake of the income which it will yield'.

The Trustee Act 2000 did not take the opportunity to define 'investment', but it may be implicit that an investment involves the purchase of assets that will produce a return in terms of income or capital appreciation. There are several instances of the courts making pre-2000 statements that investment should include buying with a view to capital appreciation (e.g. Megarry V-C in *Cowan v Scargill* [1984] 2 All ER 750). Also, now that trustees have the same powers of investment as an absolute owner, it can be argued that an absolute owner would use the word 'investment' to include purchasing property with a view to capital appreciation.

In the Explanatory Note to the Trustee Act 2000, note 22 states:

> 'Investment' is not defined in the Act. The general power of investment permits trustees to invest assets in a way which is expected to produce an income or capital return.

The Explanatory Note has no legal status but it does indicate the thinking of those who drew up the Trustee Act 2000.

It should be noted that the purchase of a house for a beneficiary to live in would not have been an authorised investment under the pre-Trustee Act 2000 law as it would not produce income (see *Re Power* [1947] 2 All ER 282). Of course, the trust could contain an express provision authorising the purchase of a house, but in the absence of such a provision a house could not be purchased.

But, s 6(3) of the Trusts of Land and Appointment of Trustees Act 1996 gives trustees of land the power to purchase legal estates in land in England or Wales and section 6(4) allows this power to be used to buy land for investment, for occupation by any beneficiary or for any other purpose. This reverses *Re Power* in relation to trusts of land. Section 17(1) makes it clear that the power may be used even after all the original land has been sold and all that the trustees hold are the proceeds of the sale or property representing the proceeds of sale. As will be discussed later, the restrictions on investment contained in the Trustee Investments Act 1961 have been largely removed by the Trustee Act 2000. This removal will not permit trustees generally to buy houses for the occupation of beneficiaries, as such a purchase will still be covered by *Re Power* and may not be considered as an investment unless it can be argued that such houses are bought with a view to capital appreciation. Only under trusts of land will the trustees, by virtue of s 6(4), be able to make such a purchase.

The economic climate is sometimes such that purchasing assets with a view to capital appreciation may well be risky and, assuming that purchasing an asset with a view to capital appreciation is an investment, the trustees may well need to take particular care before making such a purchase and should also take care when selecting the person to give them advice on the purchase.

Types of investments

There is a bewildering range of investments available to trustees, some very safe, others extremely speculative. There are investments which promise a high rate of interest (often accompanied by some risk to capital), while others offer a lower rate of return but with less or no risk to capital. There are investments available which offer a fixed rate of interest and others that offer a variable rate. Some such investments have a fluctuating capital value. (Government stocks, where the prevailing 'price' depends on the relationship of the interest rate on the stock and the current general rate of interest, are an example. If the general rate of interest has increased since the stock was issued, the price of the stock will be reduced.) Debentures in companies are debts charged on the undertaking and its assets. The charge will be a floating charge, i.e. a charge on the assets of the company in order to permit the company to continue to deal with its assets. Preference shares give the owner the right to a dividend ahead of the owners of other types of shares in the company. This 'preference' gives the holder a better chance of receiving a return than, say, the holders of ordinary shares. This often results in such shares having a lower rate of return as the risk is lower. Of course, the holder of preference shares must hope that, even if the company makes too little profit to pay a dividend on its ordinary shares, it makes sufficient profit to pay out on the preference shares. Having a preference share is no guarantee of income.

One of the commonest ways of investing in a company is by purchase of ordinary shares or equities. The return could be entirely dependent on the profits of the company. If a company makes high profits, not only will this result in a high income through the declaration of good dividends but also the desirability, and thus the price, of the shares may well increase. Equities are a very rewarding investment when the company is performing well but can be a disaster if the company is performing badly.

It may be argued that the trustees should take into account the effect of inflation which not only will reduce the real value of capital over the years but also may eat into what was once a reasonable income. However, in *Nestlé* v *National Westminster Bank* [1994] 1 All ER 118, the court decided that trustees were under no duty to preserve the value of the trust fund in real terms.

Express investment powers

In many professionally drafted trusts there will be an express power of investment. Before the Trustee Act 2000 there were several reasons for this. First, the general powers of investment given to trustees by the Trustee Investments Act 1961 (see p. 482) were generally considered to be rather narrow and restrictive. Secondly, the provisions of the Trustee Investments Act 1961 imposed on the trustees expensive and complicated procedures which it was often thought desirable to avoid.

Part II of the Trustee Act 2000 has replaced the Trustee Investments Act 1961. It sets out wide powers of investment which, in brief, permit any investment that a trustee could make if he were absolutely entitled to the trust assets. So the need for an express power of investment has virtually disappeared. Perhaps the main use of an express investment section will now be where it is desired to restrict or even exclude the wide statutory powers of investment.

It is a matter of construction as to what types of investment are covered by any particular express investment clause. It may be that an express investment clause does not specifically give the trustees the power to vary the investments, in which case the power to vary will be implied.

In the past, the courts restrictively construed express investment powers and, for example, a power to 'invest in such securities as they might think fit' was held to allow trustees to select only from those securities which were authorised by the general law as being 'trustees' investments'.

This is no longer the approach that the courts take. In *Re Harari's Settlement Trusts* [1949] 1 All ER 430, Jenkins J held that a power to make such 'investments as to them may seem fit' allowed the trustees to make investments, including investments outside the range of authorised 'trustee investments'. He considered himself free to give the words of an investment clause their plain and ordinary meaning. Jenkins J said:

> There is a good deal of authority to the effect that investment clauses should be strictly construed and should not be construed as authorising investments outside the trustee range unless they clearly and unambiguously indicate an intention to that effect . . . It seems to me that I am left free to construe this settlement according to what I consider to be the natural and proper meaning of the words used in their context.

He went on to hold that the trustees had the power to make any investments which they honestly thought were suitable for the trust.

In any case, if the courts do restrict an investment clause to investments authorised by the law, the investment powers contained in the Trustee Act 2000 would mean that the trustees would still have very wide powers.

It is possible for the settlor specifically to instruct the trustees to make a particular investment. The trustees will then be under a duty to comply and they will not be liable for a breach of trust should the investment produce a loss. It is also possible for a settlor to instruct his trustees to invest all the trust funds in one particular investment: for example, in the shares of the settlor's own company. In such a case the trustees may need to take account of their general responsibility towards the beneficiaries and apply to the court for a variation of their powers of investment (see 'Variation of powers of investment', p. 488).

Statutory powers – the Trustee Act 2000

Until the Trustee Act 2000 came into force, trustees' powers of investment were governed by the Trustee Investments Act 1961. Almost as soon as the 1961 Act came into force, it was subjected to fierce criticism and it was argued that its provisions were in need of updating and simplification. Under the 1961 Act, as amended, trustees had to divide their fund into two parts. One part (one-quarter) had to be invested in 'safe' investments, such as building society shares etc. The other three-quarters could be invested in more risky investments, particularly in shares in companies. There were very elaborate rules applicable if additional funds accrued to the trust and complicated criteria that had to be met before shares in a company could be bought. In particular, newly formed and foreign companies were excluded. There were provisions regarding the need to take written advice before any but the safest investments were made. Additionally, complicated rules were applicable when funds were withdrawn from the trust.

In short, the statutory powers of investment under the Trustee Investments Act 1961 were subjected to an enormous amount of criticism as being outdated, overly complex, restrictive and expensive to comply with.

Authorised investments – the general power of investment

In one fell swoop s 3 removes most of the restrictions on investment and the complexities of the Trustee Investments Act 1961.

Section 3 of the Trustee Act 2000 states:

> 3. – (1) Subject to the provisions of this Part, a trustee may make any kind of investment that he could make if he were absolutely entitled to the assets of the trust.

(2) In this Act the power under subsection (1) is called 'the general power of investment'.
(3) The general power of investment does not permit a trustee to make investments in land other than in loans secured on land (but see also section 8).
(4) A person invests in a loan secured on land if he has rights under any contract under which –
    (a) one person provides another with credit, and
    (b) the obligation of the borrower to repay is secured on land.
(5) 'Credit' includes any cash loan or other financial accommodation.
(6) 'Cash' includes money in any form.

Investment criteria

The Trustee Act 2000 s 4 sets out the 'standard investment criteria' that a trustee must have regard to when exercising any power of investment, whether the power arises under the 2000 Act or in any other way.

Under s 4(3) the standard investment criteria, in relation to a trust, are:

(a) the suitability to the trust of investments of the same kind as any particular investment proposed to be made or retained and of that particular investment as an investment of that kind; and
(b) the need for diversification of investments of the trust, in so far as is appropriate to the circumstances of the trust.

The criteria retain the need for trustees to consider carefully before investing (or retaining an investment). It is not enough that a proposed investment is of itself a good one but it must also be of a kind that is suitable to the trust. The requirement to consider the need for diversification is retained by virtue of s 4(3)(b).

Advice

Section 5 states that, before exercising any power of investment, a trustee must obtain and consider proper advice about the way that the power of investment is exercised, having regard to the standard investment criteria. There is no requirement that the advice must be followed. Similar advice must be obtained and considered when a trustee is reviewing existing trust investments and whether or not they should be varied.

Proper advice is the advice of one who is reasonably believed by the trustees to be qualified to give the advice by reason of his ability in and practical experience of financial and other matters relating to the proposed investments (s 5(4)).

Unlike under the Trustee Investments Act 1961, there is no requirement that advice is in writing, although of course it may well be considered prudent to record such advice.

Jeffrey v Gretton and Russell [2011] WTLR 809 (Ch D)

This case is a warning to trustees that they must ensure that they take advice and actively review the property portfolio. Under a will the trustees held a valuable but dilapidated property. The trustees decided not to sell but to retain and refurbish the property. Leslie Blohm QC decided that the trustees acted in breach of trust as they had not taken professional advice and had not regularly reviewed the trust property portfolio. Although there was no duty to sell the property, the trustees were under a duty to ensure a portfolio that balanced the interests of a life tenant and the remaindermen. Their obligation was to consider their portfolio, take professional advice and to take reasonable care in assessing it and then decide whether to retain or sell property. But, in the event, the court found that the beneficiaries had not suffered any loss.

However, s 3 provides an exception where advice need not be obtained. This is where the trustee reasonably believes that in all the circumstances advice is unnecessary or inappropriate. This might be relevant where a trustee is proposing to make a 'standard' investment in a building society.

The folio theory of investment

Modern investors often take account of the folio theory. Under this approach, an investor looks at his entire holding as an entity rather than look at each investment separately. The success of the investor will be judged by the performance of the entire portfolio. Risk is assessed over the whole portfolio. The portfolio might include some risky investments as well as safer investments. Before the Trustee Act 2000, this approach could not be adopted. But the Trustee Act 2000, *seems* to have removed the objections.

Exclusion or restriction

Section 6 states that the general power of investment is additional to any power conferred on trustees otherwise than under the Act. But the power may be restricted or excluded by provision in the trust instrument or statute.

Existing trusts

The Trustee Act 2000 s 7 states that the general power of investment normally applies to all trusts whether created before or after the Act came into force. However, subsection (2) states that, although generally the terms of the trust can restrict the statutory powers of investment, this does not apply if the trust was created before 3 August 1961.

Buying land

One of the most obvious omissions from the 1961 Act was the power to invest in land, but trustees may be authorised to invest in land by an express power in their trust instrument or by statute.

Section 73(1)(xi) of the Settled Land Act 1925 permits trustees to invest the proceeds of sale of settled land in freehold land or leasehold land with at least 60 years of the lease to run. Trustees for sale of land are given similar power under s 28 of the Law of Property Act 1925. This latter power applies only if the trustees have not sold all the land within the trust.

As stated above, with respect to trusts of land, the situation regarding the purchase of a residence for a beneficiary was changed from 1 January 1997. Section 6(3) of the Trusts of Land and Appointment of Trustees Act 1996 gives trustees of land the power to purchase legal estate in land in England or Wales. Section 6(4) allows this power to be used to buy land for investment, for occupation by any beneficiary or for any other purpose. This reverses **Re Power** in relation to trusts of land. Section 17(1) makes it clear that the power may be used even after all the original land has been sold, and all the trustees hold are the proceeds of the sale or property representing the proceeds of sale.

Buying land under the Trustee Act 2000

Part III of the Trustee Act 2000 sets out wide powers of trustees to acquire freehold and leasehold land in the United Kingdom:

(a) as an investment;
(b) for occupation by a beneficiary; or
(c) for any other reason (s 8).

Thus, purchase of land may be possible for reasons other than investment. This section also modifies s 6(3) of the Trusts of Land and Appointment of Trustees Act 1996, which now refers to the power to acquire land given by the Trustee Act 2000 s 8.

For the purpose of exercising his functions as a trustee, a trustee who acquires land under this section has all the powers of an absolute owner in relation to the land.

Section 9 deals with restricting or excluding the power to buy land and states that the power is in addition to the powers conferred on trustees otherwise than by the Act, but that it is subject to any restriction or exclusion imposed by the trust instrument or by any enactment or any provision of subordinate legislation.

The power does not apply to trustees of existing trusts who, immediately before its commencement, have special statutory powers to invest or apply trust funds. (A power to invest or apply trust funds is a special statutory power if it is conferred by an enactment or subordinate legislation on trustees of a particular trust or a particular kind of trust.)

But, subject to this, the power applies in relation to trusts whether created before or after commencement.

May the trustees avoid certain types of investment?

The trustees' duty is clear: they must invest in the best interests of the beneficiaries and this almost always means in the best financial interests of the beneficiaries.

In most cases the trustees may take into account only factors which will maximise the financial benefits for the beneficiaries. The trustees may not take into account, for example, moral, political or religious factors in making investment decisions.

In the case of *Cowan v Scargill* [1984] 2 All ER 750, Megarry V-C was confronted with an argument by trustees as to whether non-financial factors should be taken into account when investment decisions were being made.

Cowan v Scargill [1984] 2 All ER 750

The mineworkers' pension fund was administered by ten trustees, some of whom were appointed by the National Union of Mineworkers. An investment plan was put to the trustees by their advisers but the trustees appointed by the Union objected on several grounds and, *inter alia*, wanted the plan revised to provide that there should be no increase in the amount invested overseas. They also wanted the plan to exclude the investment in any activity which would compete with coal: for example, in the oil industry. The court held that the trustees were in breach of their duties towards the beneficiaries in not adopting the investment plan.

Megarry V-C generally discussed the duties of trustees when exercising their powers of investment. He said:

The starting point is the duty of the trustees to exercise their powers in the best interests of the present and future beneficiaries of the trust, holding the scales impartially between the different classes of beneficiaries. This duty towards their beneficiaries is paramount. They must, of course, obey the law; but subject to that they must put the interests of their beneficiaries first. When the purpose of the trust is to provide financial benefits for the beneficiaries, as is usually the case, the best interests of the beneficiaries are normally their best financial interests. In the case of a power of investment as in the present case, the power must be exercised so as to yield the best return for the beneficiaries, judged in relation to the risks of the investments in question; and the prospects of the yield and capital appreciation both have to be considered in judging the return from the investment . . . In considering what investments to make the trustees must put on one side their own personal interests and views.

Megarry V-C went on to say that there may be cases when the selection of investments may involve non-financial factors. He emphasised that the duty of the trustees is towards the beneficiaries and in some cases the views of the beneficiaries may permit, or even compel, the trustees to take non-financial factors into account. Megarry V-C gave the example of a trust where all the actual and potential beneficiaries held very strict moral or social views: for example, condemning the use of alcohol or the sale of armaments. Such beneficiaries may well feel that it would be preferable for them to receive a lower rather than a higher return if the price of the higher return was investing the trust fund in investments of which they would not approve. In such a case, the trustees would be entitled to decide that 'benefit' had a meaning which is not always restricted to financial matters. In such a case, the trustees may well be not in breach of their duty if they decline to invest in companies producing alcohol or dealing in armaments, even if this reduces the income that could have been obtained. Megarry V-C said such cases would be rare and the burden would rest on those alleging that it would be for the beneficiaries' 'benefit' to receive less than would be the case if the funds were put into more profitable investments.

Martin v *City of Edinburgh District Council* (1988) SLT 329

The Council had decided, for political reasons, to sell all of the investments it held in South African companies. It did not consider the effect on the finances of the trust fund, nor whether it was in the best interests of the beneficiaries, nor did the Council take any professional advice. Lord Murray applied *Cowan v Scargill* and the court held this to be a breach of trust despite the fact that there was no loss to the trust.

So the overriding duty of trustees in almost all cases is to invest for maximum financial return. To what extent does this principle apply to charitable trusts? For example, are the trustees under a duty to maximise the financial return even if this means investing in companies whose activities conflict with the aims of the trust? In simple terms, may the trustees of a trust set up to fund research into a cure for cancer refuse to invest in shares in tobacco companies even if to adopt this policy would result in a loss of income? This issue was considered in *Harries* v *Church Commissioners for England*.

Harries v *Church Commissioners for England* [1993] 2 All ER 300

In this case the purpose of the Church Commissioners was to promote the Christian faith. The Bishop of Oxford claimed that the trustees should not invest in companies or activities whose activities were incompatible with the aim of promoting the Christian faith, even if this would result in the risk of a lower financial return. The court held that the basic rule remained and the trustees should in the vast majority of situations invest for maximum return.

Sir Donald Nicholls V-C refused the declaration, stating that in the vast majority of situations trustees would be discharging their duty by seeking the maximum financial return for the trust, consistent with financial prudence. It was not acceptable to deviate from this general rule save in a few, limited cases. Sir Donald said that one situation where deviation might be acceptable is where the trustees considered that an investment would conflict with the objects of the charity. But even here the trustees must ensure that their decision did not create significant financial risks. If the investment policy might hamper its work, for example, outrage sponsors or cause would-be recipients of its bounty to refuse to accept benefits, or where it was apparent to all (as opposed to the trustees or a majority of people) that the policy conflicted with its purpose, then financial risk could be justified. If even a minority of people thought that the objects of the charity could be carried out without taking the financial risk inherent in restricting the range of investments, the trustees had to give effect to that view.

Presumably, despite *Cowan* v *Scargill* and *Harries* v *Church Commissioners*, the trustees are free to make investments on an 'ethical' or 'moral' basis, provided they are able to demonstrate that their decision will not prejudice or put at risk the financial return or where the trust instrument contains a specific power so to do.

Pension fund investment

In its recent Report, 'Fiduciary Duties of Investment Intermediaries 2014' (Law Com. No. 350) the Law Commission clarified some aspects of the investment powers and duties of trustees of pension funds. There had been some uncertainty as to whether trustees had to invest with a view to short-term returns or whether investment for the long term should be their major aim. Also it was uncertain the extent to which trustees could take into account non-financial matters when making investment decisions.

The Report says that trustees do not have to 'maximise returns' in the short term at the expense of risks over the longer term. Also the Report states that trustees should take into account factors which are financially material to the performance of an investment. The Report states that while the pursuit of a financial return should be the main concern of pension trustees, the law is sufficiently flexible to allow other, subordinate, concerns to be taken into account. The law permits trustees to make investment decisions that are based on non-financial factors, provided that they have good reason to think that scheme members share the concern, and there is no risk of significant financial detriment to the scheme.

There appears to be nothing very surprising in the Report but at least trustees of pension funds should be clearer as to how they should discharge their investment duties.

Trustees who hold a controlling interest in a company

Assuming the trustees are authorised to invest in a company and they are justified in retaining the shares, what should the trustees do to oversee the conduct of the company? Are they entitled to sit back and allow the directors to run the company as they (the directors) see fit, or should the trustees take steps to use their controlling interest to ensure that the business is being run in the best interests of the beneficiaries? Should the trustees use their controlling interest to obtain representation on the board of directors?

In *Re Lucking's Will Trusts* [1967] 3 All ER 726, Cross J decided that in these circumstances the trustees should ensure that they are represented on the board.

This problem was addressed by Brightman J in *Bartlett* v *Barclays Bank Trust Co Ltd* [1980] 1 All ER 139. Brightman J held that the trustees must use the same care as an ordinary man of business would and obtain the fullest information regarding the operation of the company. The prudent man of business would act in response to knowledge that comes into his possession, suggesting that the company's affairs are not being conducted in the way they should be. But he would not rely on obtaining such information by chance, but will make inquiries of the directors. He would not be content with the information received by shareholders at a general meeting as this is often of a general nature only. He would use his power to ensure that he has sufficient information to enable him to make a decision as to whether or not he should intervene. Brightman J did not say that the trustees must ensure representation on the board and regarded Cross J in *Re Lucking* as merely proposing this as a convenient way in which the trustees could place themselves in a position to make informed decisions.

Variation of powers of investment

The trustees may consider that their powers of investment are too restrictive and need to be extended. It may be that the powers originate in an express investment clause drawn up many years ago when investment strategies and opportunities were very different, or the power to invest may be specifically restricted in ways that the trustees consider 'unworkable' or which impose other fetters on their ability to optimise trust investments.

If the trustees have a specific investment in mind which they are not empowered to make, they could consider applying to the court under the Trustee Act 1925 s 57 for a variation.

If the trustees wish for a more wide-ranging extension of their powers, then an application under the Variation of Trusts Act 1958 might be considered.

But in *Anker-Petersen* v *Anker-Petersen* (1991) 88/16 LS Gaz 32, Judge Paul Baker QC said that, where proposals to extend the trustees' powers of investment did not affect the beneficial interests, applications should normally be brought under s 57 of the Trustee Act 1925 rather than under the Variation of Trusts Act 1958. He said that, while there were doubts as to whether or not s 57 was available in cases of extending investment powers, he saw no reason to adopt a restrictive construction of the section. It was more convenient to use s 57 as the trustees were the natural persons to make the application, the consent of every beneficiary of full age was not essential and the court was not required to give consent on behalf of every category of beneficiary separately but would consider their interests collectively. These advantages would also lead to shorter and less expensive hearings.

When deciding cases under the pre-Trustee Act 2000 law, the usual attitude of the courts was that they would not grant investment powers beyond those conferred by the Trustee Investments Act 1961 unless special reasons can be proved. This is sometimes called the rule in *Re Kolb's Will Trusts* [1961] 3 All ER 811. It is not clear whether the courts would adopt the same approach to applications for variations after the Trustee Act 2000. And in any case it is debatable to what extent the *Re Kolb* rule still represents the state of the law. *Re Kolb* was decided about two months after the 1961 Act was passed, and it may not be surprising that the court took the view that the changes and additions to trustees' investment powers represented an acceptable and workable set of powers which ought, in the vast bulk of cases, to be sufficient for trustees. In later cases the courts took a more liberal approach and were more often willing to agree to variations. In *Mason v Farbrother* [1983] 2 All ER 1078, the court, while accepting that *Re Kolb* was still good law, said that it was very willing to discover 'special circumstances' in order to agree to the trustees' request for their powers of investment to be increased beyond those contained in the 1961 Act. The court held that the effect of inflation, and the fact that the application related to a trust of a pension fund 'with perhaps something of a public element to it', were 'special circumstances warranting the approval of the application'.

In *Trustees of the British Museum* v *A-G* [1984] 1 All ER 337, trustees applied to the court for an enlargement of their existing powers of investment which were contained in a scheme made in 1960. Megarry V-C considered the rule in *Re Kolb* and the circumstances when a court might agree to enlarging investment powers beyond those of the Act. He cited the recommendations of the Law Reform Committee, which proposed extending the powers under the 1961 Act. Clearly, Megarry V-C was not purporting to use the report as an authority, but was putting it forward as an illustration of how the provisions of the 1961 Act have been criticised as being in need of change, and of how those provisions should not be regarded as necessarily giving an acceptable or satisfactory degree of control and power to trustees. Megarry V-C referred to five matters that he suggested should be considered by the court, while emphasising that he was not proposing an exhaustive list. First, account should be taken of the provisions for the trustees to obtain advice and for exercising control over investment decisions. The wider the powers the more important these factors will be. Secondly, where the powers are wide it might be advisable to consider dividing the trust fund into parts, each with a different investment policy. For example, part might be placed in relatively safe investments, allowing the other part to be used in a more speculative manner. Thirdly, the court should judge the combined effect of width, division, advice and control, which all interact, in conjunction with the standing of the trustees. Fourthly, the size of the fund is important. A large fund may justify wider powers of investment than a small fund. In the case of a large fund, a wide power of investment would allow a spread of investments which might justify the risks that accompany a wide power. Fifthly, the objects of the trust may be material. In the instant case one of the objects of the trust was to achieve a capital growth in order to provide funds for the purchase of exhibits for the museum. This could well justify a wider power and greater risk in order to attempt to achieve the capital appreciation. Megarry V-C said that he would be unhappy to describe inflation as a special circumstance justifying a wide power of investment, as happened in *Mason* v *Farbrother*, as inflation was a very general circumstance. He opined that the best thing would be to say that the rule in *Re Kolb* had gone and with it any question of what is a special circumstance.

In *Steel* v *Wellcome Custodian Trustees* [1988] 3 All ER 726, the court took account of the size of the trust fund (£3 billion), the provisions regulating the taking of advice and the eminence of the trustees when agreeing to the extension of the powers of the trustees of a pension fund. In this case, the court granted very wide powers indeed – amounting to those that a beneficial owner would have. Hoffmann J, after applying Sir Robert Megarry's principle, that each case must be decided on its own merits, did make the point that the award of such wide powers was exceptional. For one thing, the need for diversification over the part of the fund to which the application related was clear, as over 90 per cent of the total fund was invested in the shares of one company. Hoffmann J considered that most of the trustees were not businessmen capable of managing a very large portfolio of shares, and made provision for the trustees to have the power to delegate the powers of investment over the whole fund, but he ensured that, as a matter of balance, the trustees would retain some liability for the acts of their delegates:

> The courts have always been reluctant to relieve paid trustees of liability for breach of trust. But I do not think it would be fair in a case like this, where delegation is a practical necessity, to insist that the trustees should be insurers of the acts of their investment advisers . . . On the other hand I think that paid trustees should be willing to accept responsibility for a higher standard of conduct than mere abstinence of bad faith.

The scheme, while allowing delegation, placed on the trustees the responsibility to supervise the acts of their agents and made them liable for negligence in choosing agents or for failure to take steps to remedy any breaches of trust of which they became aware.

With the extended powers of investment under the Trustee Act 2000, the need to seek to vary powers of investment will reduce, particularly as the Act applies to trusts created before and after the Act came into force. However, it may still be the case that the trust's express terms restrict the powers of investment and a variation to extend the powers may be desirable. It is arguable that, when making post-Trustee Act 2000 decisions on applications for variation, the courts would adopt the approach in *Re Kolb* and that the matters that were taken into account in *Steel* v *Wellcome* would be taken into account.

Summary

- Trustees are under a general duty to act personally but there are situations where delegation/appointment of agents is possible.

- Trustees have a duty to provide information and accounts to beneficiaries but there are limits to the information that has to be provided, particularly in those situations where there is a conflict between the duty to provide information and the right of trustees not to reveal reasons for their decisions.

- Trustees are under a duty to act impartially between beneficiaries. This becomes particularly important where some beneficiaries have an interest in the income that the trust produces while others have an interest in the capital of the trust fund. A number of apportionment rules have been developed aimed at ensuring fairness as between the various classes of beneficiaries. These rules, however, are routinely excluded in professionally drafted trusts. In any case, the impact of the rules has been severely restricted by the Trusts (Capital and Income) Act 2013.

- One of the most challenging duties of trustees is to invest the trust property. Again there may be a tension between investments that tend towards generating income and those that tend towards capital growth. Many trust documents will set out guidance or instructions as to how the duty to invest should be discharged. The main statutory provisions are contained in the Trustee Act 2000.

Further reading

Right of beneficiaries to information

W East, 'Letting the cat out of the bag: the law of trust disclosure' PCB (2013) 3, 106–12.
Discusses the law on the disclosure of trust documents to beneficiaries.

G Griffiths, 'Antipodean revelations? The beneficiary's right to information after "**Rosewood**"' [2005] Conv 93.
Considers the court's discretion to exercise its power to supervise the trust in the light of the Privy Council case of *Schmidt v Rosewood Trust Ltd*. Considers the New Zealand High Court case of *Foreman v Kingstone* [2005] WTLR 823 (NZ HC) to see what light it sheds on the duty to disclose.

P O'Hagan, 'Trustees' duty to disclose' (1995) 145 NLJ 1414.
Discusses the conflicting principles of the beneficiaries' right to see trust documents and the lack of a right of beneficiaries to see trust documents that reveal the reasons behind the trustees' decision to exercise a discretion or not.

M Pawlowski, 'Confidentiality or disclosure?' (2008) 96 TEL & TJ 12–14.
Discusses the discretion of the trustees to disclose the settlor's wishes to the beneficiaries of a family discretionary trust. Discusses the confidentiality principle relating to family discretionary trusts and whether a settlor's wish letter falls within the scope of that principle.

Liability for the acts of others

G E Dal Pont, 'Wilful default revisited – liability for a co-trustee's defaults' [2001] Conv 376.
The article discusses judicial interpretations of 'wilful default'. It discusses the topic in the context of the overall burdens on trustees and the strict duties placed on them.

Capital or income-classification

A Parry, 'A partial solution', (2009) 111 TEL & TJ 7.
Discusses the Law Commission Report 315, 'Capital and Income in Trusts'.
Examines the capital/income classification and the changes recommended. Also looks at the proposals to reform the rules of apportionment.

Apportionment

A Palin, 'Trusts (Capital and Income) Act' PCB (2013) 3, 101–5.
Discusses the provisions of the Trusts (Capital and Income) Act 2013 that disapply the apportionment rules. Discusses the background to the legislation.

Investment

N Convey, 'Ethics and trustee investment choice' (1990) LSG 87/23 17.
Discusses the general duty of trustees to maximise returns. Argues that it may be possible for a trustee to invest in competitive and morally sound investments using traditional criteria for choice.

A East, 'Keeping your balance' (2009) LEx April, 34.
Discusses the requirement for trustees to balance the competing interests of the capital and income beneficiaries. Deals with the duty of trustees to take reasonable care in the management of trust assets, to invest trust funds in accordance with their powers and to produce accounts.

G McCormack, 'Sexy but not sleazy: trustee investments and ethical considerations' (1998) Co Law 19(2) 39.
Examines the extent, if any, to which trustees are able to deviate from the goal of producing the maximum financial return for the trust in favour of furthering other aims and objectives.

R Nobles, 'Charities and ethical investments' [1992] Conv 115.
Discusses the extent, if any, to which trustees of a charity can adopt an investment policy that reflects the values and ideals of the charity rather than simply investing for the maximum financial return.

17

Remedies for breach of trust

Objectives

After reading this chapter, you should:

1. Understand the basis and measure of personal liability of trustees for breaches of trust and losses to the trust fund.

2. Be aware of the possible defences to personal liability and the contributions which may be claimed between trustees.

3. Be aware of the significance of statutory time limits on claims and when they may apply.

4. Understand in outline the duty of fiduciaries and others to account for gains.

5. Understand the nature of tracing, as a means of identifying and recovering property and the enforcement of other remedies.

6. Understand in outline the rules for and limitations on following property at common law.

7. Understand the rules which apply to tracing property in equity, including where property has been converted into something else, and where it has been mixed with other property or money and appreciate the advantages that equitable remedies provide over the common law.

Personal and proprietary claims

Objective
1

Where a trustee holds property for the benefit of another, that other, the beneficiary, has a proprietary remedy, that is the right to the property and its fruits, or the profit made from it, since a trustee may not profit from the trust. The trustee must administer the property solely for the benefit of the beneficiaries, and if the beneficiaries are adult and *sui juris* they can of course call for the property to be transferred to them. In the context of constructive trusts, some account has also been given of the situations in which receivers of property may also be expected to hold it on trust as constructive trustees.

See Chapter 12.

Where a trust exists, be it express, implied or constructive, the trustee is also personally liable to account for the profits made by him from the trust. He will also be personally liable for any losses arising from his breach of trust. Here the liability is for the value of the gains or losses rather than for specific property. It will also be seen that a proprietary

For claims under a constructive trust see Chapter 12. For trustees' duties see Chapter 16.

claim may be against not only the specific property but also its product. Since this chapter is concerned with remedies for breach of trust, reference should be made to the chapter on trustees' duties to determine when breaches have occurred.

It will be apparent to anyone reading this chapter that the remedies included, particularly the personal remedies, may be available in situations other than those where a trust exists. It is nevertheless appropriate to consider them in the trust context, always bearing in mind their application elsewhere.

Personal liability

A trustee is liable for breach of trust if he fails to do that which is required of him as trustee or if he does what he is not entitled to do as trustee.

Standard of care

The liability of a trustee for breach of duty is strict: there is no need to establish fraud or even carelessness on the trustee's part (though a trustee is on occasion spared liability if he is without fault, e.g. under the Trustee Act 2000 s 1). Where the loss arises from the exercise of discretionary powers, the general requirement should be borne in mind, as set out in *Re Speight* (1883) 22 Ch D 727, that the duty of the trustee is to conduct the business of the trust with the same care as an ordinary prudent man of business would extend towards his own affairs.

See also Chapters 14 and 16.

The measure of liability

In general, the trustee must account for profits made or replace losses caused to the trust. As was stated in *Re Dawson* [1966] 2 NSWR 211, by Street J:

> The obligation of a defaulting trustee is essentially one of effecting a restitution to the estate. The obligation is of a personal nature and its extent is not to be limited by common law principles governing remoteness of damage.

In *Target Holdings Ltd v Redferns*, the House of Lords considered the principles to be applied in determining the issues of causation and remoteness in cases of breach of trust.

Target Holdings Ltd v Redferns [1995] 3 All ER 785

In this case the defendants were solicitors acting for purchasers of certain property and for the plaintiffs, who were the mortgagees. On the understanding that the properties in question were to be purchased for £2 million, the plaintiffs loaned £1.5 million. In fact, the properties were purchased for £775,000. The £1.5 million was received by the defendants as trustees for the plaintiffs, to pay to the purchasers only upon completion of the necessary transfers of the property to them. In breach of trust, the defendants paid over the money before the transfers had been completed, and falsely represented that they had so been. The plaintiffs subsequently entered a contract to sell the property for £500,000. The defendants argued that their breach was a technical one only, and that the plaintiff had subsequently obtained the rights as mortgagees which they should have had. The fact that the property was not worth what it was supposed to be was not due to anything which the defendants had done: the true authors of the loss were fraudulent third parties who had persuaded Target to enter into the transaction in the first place. However, the Court of Appeal held that that causation argument was irrelevant: the trustees were in breach of their trust, and the plaintiffs had suffered loss, which the defendant trustees must make good.

The House of Lords allowed the solicitors' appeal. Lord Browne-Wilkinson considered the role of causation in equity and at common law:

> At common law there are two principles fundamental to the awards of damages. First that the defendant's wrongful act must cause the damage complained of. Second that the plaintiff is to be put 'in the same position as he would have been in if he had not sustained the wrong for which he is now getting his compensation or reparation'. Although . . . in many ways equity approaches liability for making good a breach of trust from a different starting point, in my judgement those two principles are applicable as much in equity as at common law. Under both systems liability is fault based: the defendant is only liable for the consequences of the legal wrong he has done to the plaintiff and to make good the damage caused by such wrong . . . the result reached by the Court of Appeal does not accord with those principles. Redferns as trustees have been held liable to compensate Target for the loss caused otherwise than by the breach of trust.

His Lordship acknowledged that equity proceeded on the basis of requiring the defaulting trustee to restore the estate, rather than by awarding damages, and, if trust property could not be returned, the trustee would be required to pay sufficient compensation to restore the trust estate. This was true even if the immediate cause of the loss was dishonesty or failure by some third party. Nevertheless, there must be some causal connection between the breach and the loss.

To some extent the amount of loss is a matter of speculation, but his Lordship concluded that equitable compensation for breach of trust must make good a loss in fact suffered by beneficiaries and which, using hindsight and common sense, can be seen to have been caused by the breach. Therefore, the appropriate date to assess the quantum of loss was the date of trial, not, as the Court of Appeal had thought, at the date of the breach.

Since the trust is entitled to any gain made from a breach of trust, this cannot be set off against a loss made from another breach, provided they are not part of the same transaction: in **Dimes v Scott** (1828) 4 Russ 195, unauthorised investments were retained too long but, when converted, enabled a much larger investment in authorised investments to be made than would have been possible if the conversion had taken place at the proper time. On the other hand, the interest yielded on the unauthorised investments was all paid to the tenant for life instead of being in part added to the capital. The executor was not permitted to set the capital gain against the loss of interest for, as Lord Lyndhurst said:

> With respect to the principal sum at whatever period [the unauthorised investment] was sold, the estate must have the whole amount of the stock that was bought; and if it was sold at a later period than the court required, the executor is not entitled to any accidental advantage thence arising.

As the measure of compensation is the loss to the fund, no question of tax liability need be considered. Though the beneficiaries' loss may be a loss net of tax, this arises only upon payment to the beneficiaries: the trust fund has lost the whole gross amount and must be compensated in full.

Interest

It was formerly clear that common law could only award interest in certain situations and then only simple interest, as provided by the Law Reform (Miscellaneous Provisions) Act 1934, as amended by s 35A of the Senior Courts Act 1981.

These statutory provisions make no such restriction on the powers of equity, however, and in situations where equity can award interest, that interest may be simple or compound as the situation demands. As Lord Denning stated in *Wallersteiner* v *Moir (No. 2)* [1975] 1 All ER 849:

> The reason is because a person in a fiduciary position is not allowed to make a profit out of his trust: and, if he does, he is liable to account for that profit or interest in lieu thereof. In addition, in equity interest is awarded whenever a wrongdoer deprives a company of money which it needs for use in its business. It is plain that the company should be compensated for the loss thereby occasioned to it . . . But the question arises, should it be simple interest or compound interest? On general principles I think it should be presumed that the company (had it not been deprived of the money) would have made the most beneficial use of it . . . Alternatively, it should be presumed that the wrongdoer made the most beneficial use of it. But, whichever it is, in order to give adequate compensation, the money should be replaced at interest with yearly rests, i.e. compound interest.

As this quotation implies, it is in the commercial sphere that compound interest would appear most appropriate, in the sense that it is in that sphere that property is most likely to have been used for profitable enterprise, or would have been had it not been wrongfully withheld.

Thus, in *Guardian Ocean Cargoes Ltd* v *Banco de Brasil* [1992] 2 Lloyd's Rep 193, Hirst J rejected the argument that compound interest was payable only in exceptional circumstances where the defendant is guilty of serious misconduct: 'the authorities I have cited make it clear that the award of compound interest is in no way punitive in character, but is related to the commercial circumstances'.

Accordingly, whereas in *O'Sullivan* v *Management Agency Ltd* [1985] 3 All ER 351 simple interest was appropriate because the defendant, a musician's manager, was not engaged in investment business, in *Guardian Ocean Cargoes*, the defendant recipient of the money was a bank, which 'must be presumed to have used the money for normal banking purposes as part of its working capital, and thus to have been in a position to earn compound interest'.

This raises the question of when equity has a jurisdiction to award interest. In *President of India* v *La Pintada Cia Navigacion SA* [1984] 2 All ER 773, Lord Brandon compared the position at common law and in equity:

> The Chancery courts, again differing from the common law courts, had regularly awarded simple interest as ancillary relief in respect of equitable remedies, such as specific performance, rescission and the taking of an account. Chancery courts had further regularly awarded interest, including not only simple interest but also compound interest, when they thought that justice so demanded, that is to say in cases where money had been obtained and retained by fraud, or where it had been withheld or misapplied by a trustee or anyone else in a fiduciary position . . . Chancery courts only in two classes of case, awarded compound, as distinct from simple, interest.

This passage was the object of much discussion by the House of Lords in *Westdeutsche Landesbank Girozentrale* v *Islington London Borough Council* [1996] 2 All ER 961. The majority view was that equity could only award compound interest in those two situations, i.e. fraud and misapplication of funds by a fiduciary. The majority also felt this conclusion was supported by the fact that Parliament, when passing the legislation referred to above in 1934 and 1981, had not seen fit to extend equity's powers in this respect. Accordingly, since the court concluded that the recipient of money paid under a void contract did not receive it in a fiduciary capacity, only simple interest could be awarded. (This case is discussed in detail below in the context of fiduciary relationships.)

This case was itself the subject of much comment, as well as strong dissenting judgments by Lords Goff and Woolf. Both agreed that no proprietary interest in the money existed for the bank, but both could see no reason why compound interest could not be awarded in the case of a personal claim and, furthermore, one at common law – i.e. in this case, a claim in restitution.

Subsequently, in *Sempra Metals* v *IRC* [2007] 4 All ER 657, the House of Lords decided by a majority that compound interest could be awarded on a common law restitutionary claim. In this case the claim concerned recovery of advanced corporation tax collected by the Inland Revenue. This practice was subsequently ruled to be illegal by the ECJ. The case thus has analogies with the case of *Westdeutsche Landesbank Girozentrale* v *Islington London Borough Council*, both involving a payment made under a mistake of law. It will be recalled that the issue in *Westdeutsche* was whether a fiduciary relationship existed between the bank and the council, since only if there was such a relationship could compound interest be awarded in equity, as it was assumed by the majority of the House of Lords that no compound interest could be awarded at common law. The assumption that compound interest can only be awarded where there is a fiduciary relationship has now been overturned and *Westdeutsche* distinguished. In the words of Lord Hope:

> Once it is accepted that losses caused by late payment are recoverable under the restitutionary remedy at common law irrespective of the position in equity, the problem that was addressed in *Westdeutsche* disappears.

Losses arising from breaches of duties of investment

Where trustees invest in unauthorised investments, they will be liable for any loss resulting when the investment is realised: *Knott* v *Cottee* (1852) 16 Beav 77. Similarly, if unauthorised investments are retained, the trustees will be liable for any fall in value between the time when the assets ought to have been realised and when they actually were: *Fry* v *Fry* (1859) 27 Beav 144. The question of duties to convert, under the rule in *Howe* v *Lord Dartmouth* [1775–1802] All ER Rep 2 or otherwise, should be borne in mind. If there is no duty to apportion, the remaindermen cannot seek to make the trustees liable for the fact that none of the income has been added to capital: their only claim will be to loss of capital value, if any, when the investment is realised. It should also be remembered that any loss incurred on the sale of authorised investments can only be recovered from the trustees if they are guilty of wilful default (*Re Chapman* [1896] 2 Ch 763), for if an investment is authorised it is a matter of discretion on the part of the trustee if, acting as a prudent man of business, he retains it. If trustees improperly realise authorised investments, they will be liable for the cost of replacing them or for the amount realised in selling them, whichever is the higher: *Re Massingberd's Settlement* (1890) 63 LT 296. Where the authorised investments are sold in order to purchase unauthorised ones, it will be irrelevant that the authorised ones were sold without loss: *Phillipson* v *Gatty* (1848) 6 Hare 26. It should also be noted that, under the rule in *Saunders* v *Vautier* (1841) 4 Beav 115, the beneficiaries may adopt any unauthorised investment.

Where trustees fail to invest at all they will be liable for interest: they have a duty to invest within a reasonable time. If they are specifically directed to make a particular investment, they will be liable for the cost of making that investment, so they will be liable for the extra cost if the price of the investment has risen meantime: *Byrchall* v *Bradford* (1822) 6 Madd 235. If they are directed to invest in a range of investments, it used to be thought that their failure to do so would make them liable only for interest, on the grounds that the loss is too speculative, but, in *Nestlé v National Westminster Bank* [1994] 1 All ER 118, the Court of Appeal held that if specific loss could be proved, then this would be the measure of the trustees' liability. Such loss may be very difficult to establish in practice, and, in that case, it was suggested that the trustees might be liable for fair compensation.

Where a continuing breach prevents an asset from being realised, the loss to the trust should be based on the highest value of the asset during the period when, but for the breach, it could have been realised: *Jaffray v Marshall* [1994] 1 All ER 143. This is true whether the asset is primarily an investment or not, and thus applied in this case to a house used as the residence of the life tenant.

Liability between trustees

Objective 2

Trustees are not vicariously liable for each other's breaches of trust. However, trustees are required to act jointly: there is no such thing as a sleeping trustee and any trustee who leaves the administration of the trust to others does so at his peril. If a breach of trust is committed, *prima facie* it is a breach by all the trustees. In the words of Kay J in *Re Flower* (1884) 27 Ch D 592: 'The duty of trustees is to prevent one of themselves having the exclusive control over the money, and certainly not, by any act of theirs, to enable one of themselves to have exclusive control over it.'

Likewise, no trustee should stand by while a breach of trust is being committed by his fellow trustees, or, having become aware of a breach of trust, take no steps to recover the trust's losses.

This general principle is, however, subject to statutory intervention: for example, the power of the court to relieve a trustee of liability under Trustee Act 1925 s 61.

Liability of trustees for breach of trust is joint and several, which means that if more than one is in breach the beneficiaries may recover the loss either in equal shares from all the trustees who are in breach or all of the loss from any one of them. Normally, where the latter happens, the trustee against whom the beneficiaries act to recover the loss may obtain a contribution from the other trustees who are in breach. Conversely, if all trustees are sued, the 'passive' ones are not entitled to an indemnity from the 'active' ones (remembering that passive trustees are equally liable with active ones if they permitted the breach). Thus, in *Bahin v Hughes* (1886) 31 Ch D 390, both active and passive trustees were equally liable and the passive one was not entitled to be indemnified by the active one.

Equity presumed equal contributions but this principle has been superseded by the Civil Liability (Contribution) Act 1978, which provides that any person liable in respect of any damage may recover from any other person liable for the same damage a contribution in an amount that the court finds just and equitable, having regard to the extent of that person's responsibility for the damage, even, in appropriate cases, to the extent of the full amount of the loss.

Trustees are entitled to be indemnified by a trustee who alone is guilty of fraud. In addition, under the rule in *Chillingworth v Chambers* [1896] 1 Ch 685, where one of the trustees in breach is also a beneficiary of the trust and intended to profit by the breach, the trustee-beneficiary must indemnify the other trustees to the extent of his beneficial interest.

It is also the case, under the rule in *Re Dacre* [1916] 1 Ch 344, that where a trustee-beneficiary is in breach of trust, he can receive no further benefit under the trust until the loss is made good. This, combined with the rule in *Chillingworth v Chambers*, means that the trustee-beneficiary's interest must be used up first in meeting the claim of the estate, and the other trustees who are in breach are only required to meet the loss in so far as it exceeds the trustee-beneficiary's interest. He is first to pay as trustee and last to be paid as beneficiary.

To summarise the position, then, where there is a breach of trust by more than one trustee, the beneficiaries may recover the loss from any one of the defaulting trustees or from all of them equally. If not all the defaulting trustees are pursued for the loss, those who are may seek a contribution from the other defaulters, that contribution now being determined by the court in accordance with the Civil Liability (Contribution) Act 1978. As against the beneficiaries, the trustees are all equally liable. As among themselves, they are liable in such shares as the court determines. There are, however, exceptional situations where one or more trustees may be liable to the beneficiaries in precedence to the others, remembering the statutory exemptions as well as the special rule relating to trustee-beneficiaries. There are also situations in which a trustee may have no liability to contribute to his fellows for their joint breaches.

Relief from liability

Statutory power

The Trustee Act 1925 s 61 provides:

> If it appears to the court that a trustee, whether appointed by the court or otherwise, is or may be personally liable for any breach of trust . . . but has acted honestly and reasonably, and ought fairly to be excused for the breach of trust and for omitting to obtain the directions of the court in the matter in which he committed such breach, then the court may relieve him either wholly or partly from personal liability for the same.

The predecessor of this provision, in the same terms, was discussed at length in *Perrins* v *Bellamy* [1898] 2 Ch 521 by Kekewich J, who pointed out that complete absence of dishonesty was a prerequisite for the operation of the section. Beyond that, he took the view that in general any trustee who acted reasonably ought to be relieved under the section. The burden of establishing reasonableness lies with the trustee: *Re Stuart* [1897] 2 Ch 583. In that case, Stirling J took one indicator of reasonableness to be whether the trustee would have acted the same way with his own money, as the matter concerned lending trust money on mortgage:

> I think that if he [the trustee] was – and he may well have been – a businesslike man, he would not, before lending his money, have been satisfied without some further inquiry as to the means of the mortgagor and as to the nature and value of the property upon which he was about to advance the money.

Accordingly, the trustee was not entitled to relief under the section.

The Court of Appeal recently considered the application of s 61 in two cases concerning firms of solicitors who were the victims of mortgage fraud: *Davisons* v *Nationwide BSc* [2012] EWCA Civ 1626, [2013] WTLR 393 and *Santander UK plc* v *RA Legal Solicitors* [2014] EWCA Civ 183.

Davisons v Nationwide BS [2012] EWCA Civ 1626, [2013] WTLR 393

In this case a firm of solicitors, D, had been instructed by the purchaser of a house, and by the building society which had agreed a mortgage on the property. In performance of their duties D paid over the mortgage advance to the vendor's solicitors, on the standard terms that the existing mortgage on the property would be discharged. However, the existing mortgage was not discharged, and it emerged that the mortgage advance had been paid by D to an imposter, who had placed a false address on the Law Society website. D paid the advance to this address, believing they were paying it to the vendor's solicitors.

The Court of Appeal held that D were in breach of trust. They were in a fiduciary position vis-à-vis the building society; they held the building society's money on trust and could only discharge the trust by paying the money to the right person and having the existing mortgage discharged, or by returning the money to the building society. Paying the money to someone else was a breach of trust. However, D had acted honestly throughout and had followed the Law Society rules for completion of the sale and were entitled to be relieved of liability under Trustee Act 1925 s 61, which required the party to have acted honestly.

It would thus appear that the duty of honesty overrode the trustee's absolute duty towards the beneficiary (in this case the building society). However, in *Santander* the Court placed more importance on the failure to follow long-established practice.

Santander UK plc v *RA Legal Solicitors* [2014] EWCA Civ 183, [2014] Lloyd's Rep FC 282

In this case a firm of solicitors, the defendants, had been duped by a fraudster (another firm of solicitors!) into releasing their client's purchase moneys without securing the conveyance of the property. The client's money was thus lost. The defendants had not established that they had acted reasonably, but the Court of Appeal held that even if they had, this would not absolve them since they had failed to follow well-established procedures which were intended to protect clients from loss. The failures were serious and the defendants could not reasonably expect to be absolved. Nor was this a case for relieving them of liability under the Trustee Act 1925 s 61. This case places the onus on the defendants to prove their reasonableness and honesty.

Consent by beneficiaries

Fletcher v *Collis* [1905] 2 Ch 24 is authority for the proposition that a beneficiary who knowingly consents to a breach cannot, provided he is of full age and capacity, complain of the trustees' conduct in committing the breach. In so far as his interest is affected, the consenting beneficiary cannot recover his losses resulting from that breach. According to *Holder* v *Holder* [1968] 1 All ER 665, it is not necessary for the beneficiary to know that what he is consenting to is a breach of trust, nor does the beneficiary have to derive any benefit from the breach, but the court must consider whether, in all the circumstances, it is fair and equitable that, having consented to the breach, the beneficiary should be allowed to sue the trustees. To avoid the risk of being sued, the trustees must put the beneficiaries fully in the picture, otherwise the court may not consider their consent sufficient to take away their right of action: *Boardman* v *Phipps*. Another relevant factor is the freedom with which the beneficiary gives his consent: it will afford the trustees no protection if it is given as a result of undue influence: *Re Pauling's Settlement Trusts* [1963] 3 All ER 1.

Impounding the beneficial interest

The difference between the following principle and that stated above of the trustee's immunity from action by the consenting beneficiary must be understood. Previously, the issue considered was that the trustee was not personally liable to the consenting beneficiary himself, whereas here the question is whether that consenting beneficiary must protect the trustee against liability to the other beneficiaries.

The court has an inherent jurisdiction to require the beneficiary to indemnify the trustees for any liability they may have as a result of a breach. For this jurisdiction to be invoked, however, it will be necessary to show that the beneficiary requested or instigated the breach or consented to it and derived a benefit from it. Once again, as with immunity above, the trustees will have to show that the beneficiary knew the facts which constituted the breach of trust, but it is not necessary to show that the beneficiary knew it was a breach (see *Raby* v *Ridehalgh* (1855) 7 De GM& G 104; *Re Somerset*, below).

The requirement of benefit to the trustee is removed, and the powers of the court enlarged in this matter, by the Trustee Act 1925 s 62, which provides:

> Where a trustee commits a breach of trust at the instigation or request or with the consent in writing of a beneficiary, the court may, if it thinks fit, make such order as to the court seems just, for impounding all or any part of the interest of the beneficiary in the trust estate by way of indemnity to the trustee or persons claiming through him.

It has been held in *Re Somerset* [1894] 1 Ch 231 that the powers to indemnify do not arise where the beneficiary has instigated acts which are not breaches of trust *per se*, but only become so because of the conduct of the trustees. Thus, a beneficiary may request the trustees to invest in authorised investments, and that is clearly not a breach of trust. If the trustees subsequently fail to exercise proper care in the management of those investments, so that loss is incurred, they are not entitled to be indemnified by the beneficiary. He did not instigate their breach and is entitled to expect them to exercise their discretions with proper care. The powers, both inherent and under s 62, can be exercised in favour of former trustees: *Re Pauling's Settlement Trusts (No. 2)* [1963] 1 All ER 857. In all cases, the indemnity is limited to the amount of the consenting beneficiary's interest under the trust.

Time limits on actions

Objective
3

The Limitation Act 1980 provides as follows:

Section 21. Time limit for actions in respect of trust property

(1) No period of limitation prescribed by this Act shall apply to an action by a beneficiary under a trust, being an action –
   (a) in respect of any fraud or fraudulent breach of trust to which the trustee was a party or privy; or
   (b) to recover from the trustee trust property or the proceeds of trust property in the possession of the trustee or previously received by the trustee and converted to his use

   . . .

(3) Subject to the preceding provisions of this section, an action by a beneficiary to recover trust property or in respect of any breach of trust, not being an action for which the limitation is prescribed by any other provision of this Act, shall not be brought after the expiration of six years from the date on which the action accrued.

For the purposes of this subsection, the right of action shall not be treated as having accrued to any beneficiary entitled to a future interest in the trust property until the interest fell into possession.

In general, the effect of these provisions is that if the beneficiaries are seeking a proprietary remedy, i.e. to recover trust property in the hands of trustees, their claim is not subject to any statutory time limit, whereas if they are seeking any other action against trustees for breach of trust it will be subject to a six-year time limit unless it concerns fraud by the trustee or fraud to which he was privy. Thus, most personal actions against trustees will be subject to the six-year limit.

For more on fiduciary duties of directors see Chapter 12 (p. 303).

In the context of the fiduciary duties of directors to their companies, two cases are illustrative. In *JJ Harrison (Properties) Ltd v Harrison* [2002] 1 BCLC 162 the claim was a proprietary one, to recover company property improperly obtained by a director and converted to his own use, so it falls within s 21(1)(b). The claim in *Gwembe Valley Development Corporation v Koshy (No. 3)* [2004] 1 BCLC 131 was a personal one, to account for profits, but as the judge had found K to be dishonest, the case fell within s 21(1)(a) as analogous to a fraudulent breach of trust.

A number of points may be noted. First, the provisions apply to all types of trustee, express, implied or constructive. However, the Supreme Court has held in *Central Bank of Nigeria v Williams* [2014] UKSC 10, [2014] All ER (D) 172 that the six-year time limit does apply in a claim against intermeddling strangers for knowing receipt. Such a stranger is not a trustee and the claim against him is for liability to account. *Novoship (UK) Ltd v Mikhaylyuk* [2014] EWCA Civ 908 states that the same will apply to an action for account against a stranger who dishonestly assists in a breach.

Potential liability of such strangers is considered in detail in Chapter 12 (p. 335).

Within the definition of trustees lie also personal representatives and some other fiduciaries. Secondly, time begins to run when the breach occurs as regards beneficial interests already in possession, but in the case of future interests it only begins to run when the future interest comes into possession; so, for example, if a breach occurs during the lifetime of the life tenant, the remaindermen will have six years from the time of the death of the life tenant in which to sue. Section 28 of the 1980 Act also provides that, where the person to whom the right of action accrues is under a disability (infancy or mental incapacity), time will only begin to run when the disability ends or the person dies, whichever is the earlier. This is subject to an ultimate maximum limit of 30 years. Section 32 provides that for any action based on fraud or where some fact relevant to the plaintiff's claim has been deliberately concealed from him, or the action is for relief from the consequences of mistake, time does not begin to run until the plaintiff has discovered the fraud, concealment or mistake. The section contains a provision protecting any interest acquired for valuable consideration by an innocent third party.

Cases outside the six-year rule

Reference has already been made to the position regarding proprietary claims for trust property in the trustees' hands. It may also be noted that, where the trustee is entitled beneficially to some of the trust property he holds, s 21(2) provides that his liability is limited to the excess over that entitlement. The reference to property received and converted to his own use has been held to mean some wrongful application of the funds to his own use: *Re Gurney* [1893] 1 Ch 590.

As regards actions for an account, s 23 implies that such actions are subject to the same time limit as the actions for breach upon which the duty to account is based. However, in *A-G v Cocke* [1988] 2 All ER 391, Harman J held that s 21(3) could not apply because the duty to account was not based upon breach of trust but simply upon the fiduciary relationship. Section 23 would appear, at least in most instances of the duty to account, to be based upon a false assumption that such a duty arises out of breach.

Actions in respect of fraud appear, according to **Thorne v Heard** [1895] AC 495, to require fraud by the trustee. Mere negligence in allowing the trust's solicitor to commit fraud was not in that case sufficient to satisfy the section.

Section 22 provides an alternative time limit in respect of claims to the personal estate of deceased persons. Here, twelve years rather than six is the limit, subject to the exceptions set out in s 21(1) and (2) (fraud and recovery of property). Unfortunately, it is not always clear which time limit applies because executors frequently act also as trustees.

No statutory time limit

Section 36 expressly provides that nothing in the Act shall affect any equitable jurisdiction to refuse relief on the ground of acquiescence or otherwise. In situations not covered by the Limitation Act 1980, the doctrine of laches may come into play. Equity has always exercised the right in appropriate cases to refuse relief where there has been unreasonable delay in pursuing a claim, and particularly where that delay, or other evidence, indicates acquiescence in the breach. The appropriate approach to whether the defence should apply was set out by Laddie J in **Nelson v Rye** [1996] 2 All ER 186, in which he stated:

> The courts have indicated over the years some of the factors which must be taken into consideration in deciding whether the defence (of laches) runs. Those factors include the period of the delay, the extent to which the defendant's position has been prejudiced by the delay and the extent to which the prejudice was caused by the actions of the plaintiff. I accept that mere delay alone will almost never suffice, but the court has to look at all the circumstances, including those set out above, and then decide whether the balance of justice or injustice is in favour of granting the remedy or withholding it. If substantial prejudice would be suffered by the defendant, it is not necessary for the defendant to prove that it was caused by the delay. On the other hand, the plaintiff's knowledge that the delay will cause such prejudice is a factor to be taken into account.

Liability to account for gains

Objective 4

See Chapter 12 in the context of constructive trust (p. 300).

A person in a fiduciary position is liable to account for any gains he makes from his fiduciary position, under the principle expressed by Lord Herschell in **Bray v Ford** [1896] AC 44: 'It is an inflexible rule of a Court of Equity that a person in a fiduciary position . . . is not, unless otherwise expressly provided, entitled to make a profit.' This has been considered in some detail in an earlier chapter, where the principle has been compared with the idea of proprietary liability for trust property. Chapter 12 also considers at length the duty to account for gains made by 'strangers': third parties who intermeddle in a breach of trust or fiduciary duty.

The duty to account is wider than the trust, in the sense that it may arise where no trust does. Where there is a trust, there may be little to choose in practical terms between a claim for an account and a claim to trust property, in that the claimant may obtain the same benefit. However, the claim to an account is a personal one; it does not depend on identifying particular property but, like all personal claims, it is only as good as the fiduciary's ability to pay; if the fiduciary is insolvent, the claim cannot be met. The claimant to an account enjoys no priority over other creditors. Furthermore, the claim to an account is subject to the time limits considered above.

Logically, the measure of the claim should be the amount of profit that the fiduciary has wrongfully obtained from his fiduciary position. It thus differs from a claim for compensation for loss caused by a breach of trust (though a trustee, as fiduciary, will also be subject to a duty to account where appropriate). However, in **Murad v Al-Saraj and Westwood** [2005] All ER (D) 503 (Jul) the defendant sought to argue that the measure should be compensatory.

Murad v Al-Saraj and Westwood [2005] All ER (D) 503 (Jul)

S and M entered into an agreement to buy an hotel, each contributing a share of the purchase price with the balance being borrowed from a bank. An agreement was made as to the division of the profits based on the contributions to the purchase price. The hotel was then sold for a profit of £2 million. It was held that S owed a fiduciary duty to M. S's fraud consisted of misrepresenting the source of his contribution to the purchase price, which he said would be in cash, whereas in fact it came largely from offsetting money owed to him in commissions by the vendor of the hotel. S claimed he should only be accountable for the extra profit which M would have made had they known this (they would have demanded a higher share of the profits had they known the true situation).

It was S's contention that the claimants were only entitled to compensation on the basis of their loss, as compared to the agreement that they would have made had they known the true facts.

The Court of Appeal, however, upheld the rule that S was accountable for the whole of the profits that he had made. The fact that he might have obtained M's consent to a different arrangement was irrelevant, since no actual consent was given, and M had been induced to enter the contract by S's fraud. In the words of Arden LJ:

> It has long been the law that equitable remedies for wrongful conduct differ from those available at common law. Equity recognises that there are legal wrongs for which damages are not the appropriate remedy . . . [T]he purpose of the account is to strip the defaulting party of his profit.

See Chapter 12.

There may be occasion when this rule operates harshly: see the discussion of **Boardman v Phipps**, where remuneration of the fiduciary was permitted.

The Court of Appeal discussed the nature of a claim for an account of profits in **Walsh v Shanahan and others** [2013] EWCA Civ 411, [2013] All ER (D) 180.

Walsh v Shanahan and others [2013] EWCA Civ 411 [2013] All ER (D) 180

In this case the court described the account of profits as the ordinary remedy against a fiduciary who breached his obligations and made a profit out of his trust. Nevertheless the award of an account of profits was a matter of discretion for the courts and an admitted breach of confidence in making unauthorised use of documents did not automatically entitle a claimant to an account of profits rather than an award of damages.

W and R were negotiating a property deal. W pulled out, but R went ahead and acquired the property. In the process R made use of confidential documents belonging to W. It was agreed that the information was confidential and the Court of Appeal held that the duty of confidence remained because R had used the information without W's informed consent. The trial judge had held that an award of profits would be disproportionate, since R would have been denied all the benefit of the deal, so the judge awarded damages, based on the likely cost of acquiring the confidential information, instead. The Court of Appeal upheld this decision, holding that any fiduciary duty ceased with the telephone conversation by which W had informed R that he was withdrawing from the deal. An important distinction was thus drawn between the duty of confidence in relation to the documents (which continued), and the fiduciary duty of agency to act exclusively for the benefit of the principle (which terminated with the telephone conversation).

Tracing, and the remedies which may follow

Introduction

Objective 5

The personal liability of trustees for breach of trust, and the personal liability of fiduciaries to account for profits, have been discussed and some of the limitations have been considered. Above all, any claim depends upon the trustee having sufficient funds to satisfy it: there is little point in seeking a personal remedy against an insolvent defendant, for the judgment creditor will have no greater right than any other creditors. In many situations, beneficiaries will have a more effective remedy if specific trust property can be identified in the hands of a trustee, for in such situations the trustee holds that property on trust and is liable to account for any profits made. Through the device of the constructive trust it is possible to extend this, first to benefits obtained by the trustee from his fiduciary position and secondly to others who may receive trust property through a breach of trust. The device of tracing further enhances this proprietary remedy because it allows a proprietary action to be brought not only against the original trust property but also against property into which the original property has been converted. If, for example, trust money has been used by the trustee to buy shares, then the shares, as the product of the trust money, are in effect the trust property. The greatest potential difficulty arises where trust property has been mixed with other property, but, fortunately, equity has devised rules in various situations for identifying the trust property from within the mixture.

The nature of tracing

There has been a tendency to confuse the process of tracing with the remedies which may be available after the tracing process. The term 'tracing claims' is misleading in this respect. In *Foskett* v *McKeown* [2000] 3 All ER 97, Lord Millett stressed that tracing is not a remedy but a process: it is merely the way you find the property that you wish to make the subject of a claim.

> Tracing is . . . neither a claim nor a remedy. It is merely the process by which a claimant demonstrates what has happened to his property, identifies its proceeds and the persons who have handled or received them, and justifies his claim that the proceeds can properly be regarded as representing his property. Tracing is also distinct from claiming. It identifies the traceable proceeds of the claimant's property. It enables the claimant to substitute the traceable proceeds for the original asset as the subject matter of his claim. But it does not affect or establish his claim . . . The successful completion of a tracing exercise may be preliminary to a personal claim or a proprietary one, to the enforcement of a legal right or an equitable one.

Foskett v *McKeown* is a fairly straightforward case of tracing in equity, so any comments by Lord Millett about the common law are, strictly speaking, *obiter*, so it will be necessary to wait and see what effect his view may have on tracing in common law. Nevertheless, it is submitted that the nature of tracing at common law is different from that in equity because of the nature of the remedies available at the end of the process.

Tracing at common law

Objective 6

A person who owns a chattel should be able to recover it or its value from anyone to whom physical possession passes, provided that legal ownership has not passed to that person. As the general common law remedy is damages, normally the legal owner will receive the value, though in some circumstances the court may make an order for specific recovery of the item itself. This right may be applied not merely to tangible assets but also to intangible ones such as choses in action. This common law right will also apply in limited circumstances where the chattel has been converted into something else, as was explained by Lord Ellenborough in *Taylor* v *Plumer* (1815) 3 M& S 562:

> It makes no difference in reason or law into what other form, different from the original, the change may have been made, whether it be into that of promissory notes for the security of the money which was produced by the sale of the goods of the principal . . . or into other merchandise, for the product of or substitute for the original thing still follows the nature of the thing itself, as long as it can be ascertained as such, and the right only ceases when the means of ascertainment fail, which is the case when the subject is turned into money, and mixed and confounded in a general mass of the same description.

It is the last point which limits the effectiveness of the remedy at common law. To assert a right of ownership at law, the owner must be able to identify the thing he owns. This is not a problem if the thing owned has been substituted by something else, but if it has been mixed with other property, and particularly with money, as a matter of evidence it cannot be identified as a separate item.

The problem of identification: mixing

In the common situation of money paid into a bank account, the limit of the common law right appears to be a case like *Banque Belge pour l'Etranger* v *Hambrouk* [1921] 1 KB 321, where it was possible to trace the plaintiff's money into a substantially unmixed bank account. However, as most accounts will be 'active', with money coming in from various sources and going out to various different purposes, common law will be no help in such situations. As was said in *Agip (Africa)* v *Jackson* [1992] 4 All ER 385: 'Money can be followed at common law into and out of a bank account and into the hands of a subsequent transferee, provided that it does not cease to be identifiable by being mixed with other money in the bank account derived from some other source.' Arguably, if property is converted into something else, to allow it to be followed at common law, the conversion must be a physical one. Thus, where money is paid into one branch of a bank and drawn out at another, the money is clearly physically different and, according to Millett J in *Agip* (above), cannot be seen as merely the product of the other: nothing passes from one branch to the other, except 'a stream of electrons', in the form of a telecommunication that the account has received additional funds. His Lordship was unable to accept that the money changed from money to electrons to new money. An alternative view on this, and one stressed subsequently in the Court of Appeal in *Agip*, was that to make the transfer to the other branch in this case, the money must have passed through the inter-bank clearing system, and thus have become mixed. It is thus said that 'tracing' (or 'following') at common law is essentially a physical process, which is defeated if that physical existence is compromised.

Retention of legal title

The crucial point in following at common law is the existence of the legal title in the hands of the follower/plaintiff. If the initial transaction, by which the follower lost possession, or any other subsequent transaction to which the goods have been subjected, has been effective to pass the legal title to another, then there can be no claim to follow that title: the former owner will be left only with personal remedies. If no such effective transaction has occurred, the original legal owner still has title, and can follow it as long as the goods remain in existence and unmixed, even though in a converted state.

It follows that someone with only an equitable interest cannot make a claim in law. In **MCC Proceeds v Lehman Brothers** [1998] 4 All ER 675 the Court of Appeal refused to allow the beneficiaries under a trust to pursue a claim at common law: they had no legal title, only an equitable one.

The remedies available

The kind of remedy available at common law will depend on the nature of the property involved. In the case of land, one may bring an action for its specific recovery, so this will truly be an action *in rem*, an action for the thing itself, and, furthermore, it will not be defeated by a *bona fide* purchaser. In the case of chattels the appropriate action may be under the Torts (Interference with Goods) Act 1977 for conversion. An asset may be followed into another's hands and, provided that none of the exceptions to the *nemo dat quod non habet* rule, which prevents a person who does not have good title himself from giving good title to another, applies, the true owner may, at the court's discretion, recover either the item or its value, and damages. Such an action does not apply to money, however; but, subject to the limitations indicated above, the person to whom the money belongs may have a restitutionary remedy. Thus, in **Lipkin Gorman v Karpnale** [1992] 4 All ER 512, the House of Lords recognised such a right of a firm of solicitors, where one of the partners in the firm had taken money from the firm's client account and had spent it gambling. In doing this, he had handed over the money to a gambling club under a void gaming contract. The right of the solicitors' firm was explained by Lord Goff:

> Before Cass [the gambling solicitor] drew upon the solicitors' client account at the bank, there was of course no question of the solicitors having any legal property in any cash lying in the bank. The relationship of the bank with the solicitors was essentially that of debtor and creditor; and since the client account was at all material times in credit, the bank was the debtor and the solicitors were its creditors. Such a debt constitutes a chose in action, which is a species of property; and since the debt was enforceable at common law, the chose in action was legal property belonging to the solicitors at common law.
>
> There is in my opinion no reason why the solicitors should not be able to trace their property at common law in that chose in action, or in any part of it, into its product, i.e. cash drawn by Cass from their client account at the bank. Such a claim is consistent with their assertion that the money so obtained by Cass was their property at common law.

The firm would not have been able to trace into the hands of anyone who had given good consideration, but in this case the court held that the gambling club had not done this: Cass had exchanged the money for gambling chips, but the court regarded these as merely money in another form.

In this case, the House of Lords accepted the principle of a defence of change of position, reversing previous cases on this point. This defence could apply in the case of an innocent volunteer, which the club was. They had changed their position by allowing Cass to gamble, taking the risk that he would win. In fact he did win some money, and the club were entitled to take that into account: they were only liable to the solicitor's firm to the amount of their *net* gain, i.e. after deducting the amount Cass had been paid in winnings, otherwise the club would have been out of pocket.

The concept of following money at common law, through the device of the chose in action of the legal owner, was later applied and extended by the Court of Appeal in *F C Jones & Sons v Jones*.

F C Jones & Sons v Jones [1996] 4 All ER 721

In this case the partners in F C Jones committed acts of bankruptcy and were adjudged bankrupt. This meant that legal title to the partnership's assets passed to the trustee in bankruptcy. In the meantime, one of the partners drew cheques on the partnership account totalling £11,700 and paid this money to his wife, Mrs Jones, who invested the money in potato futures. This proved a very successful investment and she received a total of £50,760 from it, which she placed in a separate bank account.

The money in the partnership account was represented by the chose in action, the right to sue the bank for the amount in the account, as in **Lipkin Gorman**. This chose in action belonged in law to the trustee in bankruptcy: Mrs Jones never acquired any legal title to it. Accordingly, it was possible to follow this legal property as a chose in action from the partnership account, into the investment and hence into the money now in Mrs Jones's account. No mixing had taken place and so following at law was not prevented.

The perhaps surprising thing about the case, however, is that the trustee in bankruptcy was entitled to claim not only the original £11,700, but the entire sum including the profits. This may seem fair: the money was never Mrs Jones's, and so any profit should belong to the owner of the capital. But one must remember the nature of this common law remedy (tracing in equity would not have been possible here: Mrs Jones was not the owner of anything of which she could have been a trustee, nor was she in a fiduciary position). Following is merely evidential: it shows the claimant where the money is which he seeks to recover, so that he may then exercise his legal rights. The Court of Appeal was not unanimous as to what legal rights were being exercised, and it is not clear that either an action in debt (*per* Millett LJ) or an action for money had and received (*per* Nourse LJ) should have given a right to more than the initial capital. It may be that the chose in action which Mrs Jones had against her own bank (i.e. for £50,760), was itself the product of the trustee in bankruptcy's property, and hence could itself be claimed to be 'owned' by the trustee.

No doubt, Mrs Jones would otherwise have been unjustly enriched, but that would imply a personal restitutionary liability, whereas here a proprietary claim was upheld (clearly more advantageous had Mrs Jones, for example, been bankrupt herself). Had it been possible to trace in equity, one would assume that the profits could also have been claimed. *Jones* is also interesting for Millett LJ's expression of the court's aim to ensure that the legal claimant should not be disadvantaged compared to the equitable one, to align legal and equitable claims, and to develop a rational and coherent law of restitution.

Application of claims to assert legal title in the case of trusts

Finally, it should be noted that the beneficiaries of a trust could oblige the trustee to assert his legal title and follow at common law, but *only* in cases where the trustee is not himself responsible for granting the property away. Thus, if the trustee has, in breach of trust, disposed of trust property, he cannot claim the legal title, on the principle of non-derogation of grant (he cannot derogate from the grant he has himself made). Only if, for example through theft or fraud, a third party has taken the property without the legal title, has the trustee a legal claim, which the beneficiaries could require him to assert.

Conversely, however, the fact that the trustee is in breach of trust does not prevent him from asserting such rights, as he may have as legal owner of the property, against the ultimate recipient of the property. Thus in **Montrose Investment Ltd v Orion Nominees Ltd** [2004] All ER (D) 500 (Jul) the Court of Appeal held that the ultimate recipient of sale proceeds of certain shares was accountable to the trustee for those proceeds (i.e. because in the particular situation they were 'owed' to the trustee), even though the trustee was in breach of trust in disposing of the shares in the first place.

Tracing in equity

Objective 7

It is submitted that the idea of tracing makes more sense in equity, where the claim is indeed to follow the property and to claim that property when found. According to Lord Millett in **Foskett v McKeown**, the tracing process is the same in law and in equity. However, the nature of the remedy is different: a proprietary remedy is available, depending upon the claimant asserting beneficial title to the property claimed. As was said by Millett J in **Agip (Africa) v Jackson** (above):

> The tracing claim in equity gives rise to a proprietary remedy which depends on the continued existence of the trust property in the hands of the defendant. Unless he is a *bona fide* purchaser for value without notice, he must restore the trust property to its rightful owner if he still has it.

As this quotation implies, the right to trace in equity depends upon the person tracing being the beneficial owner of an equitable proprietary interest in the property he is seeking to trace and, hence, the continued existence of the equitable property itself. We shall see that, as equity has a much more flexible view on the continued existence of such property (e.g. even when it is mixed with other property), the proprietary interest in equity can survive in situations where a legal interest would have vanished.

The existence of an equitable title

It is first necessary, though, to consider how the equitable proprietary interest has come into existence in the first place. The most obvious example would be by express trust, where the beneficiary has an equitable title to property which he will be able to trace into the hands of anyone except the *bona fide* purchaser of the legal estate without notice. Thus far, this is, apart from the more generous tracing rules outlined below, the exact parallel of the situation at common law. The plaintiff has an interest in property which is being misused or the possession of which has passed to some third party (which in this context usually means that the legal title has passed as well). The same analysis could apply where the plaintiff is a beneficiary under a resulting, as opposed to an express, trust.

A more difficult issue in regard to equitable tracing is whether any transaction can subsequently create an equitable interest where none existed before. This clearly appears to happen in some cases where a constructive trust is imposed, but the decision of the Court of Appeal in **Sinclair v Versailles** [2011] EWCA Civ 347, [2011] 4 All ER 335, appears to have significantly curtailed the number of situations where improper gains by fiduciaries will be regarded as held on trust and thus be available for proprietary remedies.

See Chapter 12 (p. 308).

The requirement of a fiduciary relationship

In the context of tracing, in order to establish the necessary equitable interest, it has long been held that a fiduciary relationship must exist. Recent statements confirming this are to be found, for example, from Millett J in **Agip (Africa) v Jackson**: 'The only restriction on the ability of equity to follow assets is the requirement that there must be some fiduciary relationship which permits the assistance of equity to be invoked', and from Goulding J in *Chase Manhattan Bank* v *Israel–British Bank* [1979] 3 All ER 1025: 'an initial fiduciary relationship is a necessary foundation of the equitable right of tracing'.

Where the proprietary interest depends upon the existence of a trust, either express, resulting or constructive, it is not clear that the requirement of a fiduciary relationship adds anything. It is clear that tracing trust property can take place, not only against the original 'fiduciary' (the trustee), but also against any third party, other than the *bona fide* purchaser, into whose hands the legal estate has passed. In the words of the Court of Appeal in *Re Diplock* [1948] 2 All ER 318:

> Equity may operate on the conscience not merely of those who acquire a legal title in breach of some trust, express or constructive, or of some other fiduciary obligation, but of volunteers provided that, as a result of what has gone before, some equitable proprietary interest has been created and attaches to the property in the hands of the volunteer.

The requirement of a fiduciary relationship has come in for criticism. In *Agip*, it was criticised as depending more upon authority than upon principle, and yet it may equally be said that it is unclear that there is any binding authority on the subject. To the extent that it is said to depend upon the House of Lords decision in *Sinclair* v *Brougham* [1914] AC 398, such arguments must now be seen in the light of *Westdeutsche Landesbank* v *Islington* (below).

Certainly, the courts have in the past been prepared to be generous in finding that the necessary fiduciary relationship existed. In particular, it has been held that the recipient of money paid by mistake has the necessary relationship to the payee. Thus, in *Chase Manhattan Bank* v *Israel–British Bank* (above), where money was paid under a mistake of fact, the court held: 'It is enough that, as in *Sinclair* v *Brougham*, the payment into the wrong hands gave rise to the fiduciary relationship.' It did not matter, therefore, that there had been no fiduciary relationship *vis-à-vis* the money prior to the payment. *Sinclair* v *Brougham* itself involved payments by depositors to a building society for purposes (banking) that were *ultra vires*. As was stated in *Re Diplock*: 'A sufficient relationship was found to exist [in *Sinclair*] between the depositors and the directors [of the building society] by reason of the fact that the purposes for which the depositors had handed their money to the directors were by law incapable of fulfilment.'

This generous view of the existence of a fiduciary relationship has, it would appear, received a severe setback from the decision in *Westdeutsche Landesbank* v *Islington London Borough Council*, so that those who receive money under a void or *ultra vires* contract will no longer be regarded as fiduciaries by reason only of that payment, and tracing will not therefore be possible against them.

Westdeutsche Landesbank v *Islington London Borough Council* [1996] 2 All ER 961

In this case the local authority (Islington) sought to reschedule its borrowing by entering into what is known as a 'rate-swap' agreement. Under this agreement it received several million pounds from the Westdeutsche Bank. Rate-swap agreements were subsequently ruled to be beyond the powers of local authorities, and thus void. The bank sought to recover its money. The issue in the case was whether the bank should also be awarded compound interest on this money. (The case is discussed in this context above.) In so far as it was relevant to their conclusions on the question of compound interest, all their Lordships declined to follow *Sinclair* v *Brougham*. Two of the majority,

> Lords Browne-Wilkinson and Lloyd favoured overruling it, while Lord Slynn agreed that it should be departed from. Accordingly, the local authority was not a trustee of, nor in a fiduciary relationship to the bank in respect of, the money. In Lord Browne-Wilkinson's words:
>
> > The claimant for restitution of moneys paid under an *ultra vires*, and therefore void, contract has a personal action at law to recover moneys paid as on a total failure of consideration; he will not have an equitable proprietary claim which gives him either rights against third parties or priority in an insolvency; nor will he have a personal claim in equity, since the recipient is not a trustee.

Accordingly, there may still be situations where mistaken payments might give rise to a fiduciary relationship, and hence tracing, and Lord Browne-Wilkinson was at pains to stress that their decision should not be taken as casting doubt upon the principles established in **Re Diplock**, where charities were liable to return moneys mistakenly paid out under a will. In the commercial sphere, however, their Lordships stressed that the courts should beware of importing trust principles which might have the effect of giving the payer an unfair advantage over other creditors of the payee.

Again, Lord Millett in **Foskett v McKeown** has condemned the need for the fiduciary relationship:

> Given its nature, there is nothing inherently legal or equitable about the tracing exercise. One set of tracing rules is enough . . . There is certainly no logical justification for allowing any distinction between them to produce capricious results in cases of mixed substitutions by insisting on the existence of a fiduciary relationship as a precondition for applying equity's tracing rules. The existence of such a relationship may be relevant to the personal nature of the claim which the plaintiff can maintain, whether personal or proprietary, but that is a different matter.

Certainly, the fiduciary requirement can present difficulties elsewhere. It is a curious circumstance that in many cases the absolute legal and beneficial owner of property cannot point to a fiduciary relationship upon which to base an equitable claim to trace. (In case of mistaken payments as in **Westdeutsche** (above), of course, legal title to the money had passed to the receiver, so the only proprietary claim which could have existed would have to have been an equitable one, which, as just explained, was also rejected.)

It will be remembered that in **Lipkin Gorman v Karpnale** (above), the claim before the House of Lords was a legal one, in that the solicitors still had legal title to the chose in action. Lord Goff commented: 'Of course there is no doubt that, even if legal title to money did vest in Cass [the guilty solicitor] immediately on receipt, nevertheless he would have held it on trust for the partners.' This was because Cass was a fiduciary *vis-à-vis* the solicitors' firm.

But the holder of a legal title who cannot establish a fiduciary relationship will be forced to rely on following the property at common law, with all the limitation of that remedy, while the holder of an equitable interest under a trust will, paradoxically, have a better remedy in equitable tracing. Lord Templeman in **Lipkin Gorman** suggested that, if property were stolen, the thief (who would not acquire legal title) might be regarded as holding the stolen property on trust for the legal owner, but this is surely stretching the concept of fiduciary to the limit. It is submitted, therefore, that while the fiduciary relationship may be useful in establishing liability in a constructive trust situation, there should be no need to seek such a fiduciary relationship in a case where the claimant already has equitable, or indeed legal, title.

Continued existence of the property claimed: conversion to another form

Equitable tracing, like that at common law, depends on the continued existence of the property alleged to be subject to the equitable rights. It follows that if the property has been destroyed or dissipated, it cannot be traced. If, however, the property has been converted into something else, the claimant can still trace it. In such a case, equity, according to *Re Hallett's Estate* (1880) 13 Ch D 696, allows the claimant either to take the property purchased with the 'trust money', or to have a charge on the property for the amount of the trust money. In Sir George Jessel MR's words:

> I will, first of all, take his position [i.e. the position of the beneficial owner] when the purchase is clearly made with what I will call, for shortness, the trust money . . . In that case, according to the now well-established doctrine of Equity, the beneficial owner has a right to elect either to take the property purchased, or to hold it as a security for the amount of the trust money laid out in the purchase; or, as we generally express it, he is entitled at his election either to take the property, or to have a charge on the property for the amount of the trust money.

In other words, the equitable remedy is proprietary here, in that the beneficial owner can actually recover the property, if it is still in its original form, or recover the property into which it has been converted. This may clearly be advantageous as compared to common law rights, which tend to be personal claims.

Continued existence of the property claimed: tracing and mixtures

The real advantage of equitable tracing, however, is that it is not defeated by the property having been mixed with other property. This right was recognised in *Pennell v Deffell* (1853) De M & G 372.

In a case where trust money and personal money have been mixed and the whole has been used to purchase property, there will be little difficulty in determining how much belongs to the trust and how much to the trustee, subject to the question of any increase in value. Difficulties arise, however, where only part of the mixed fund has been used to purchase the property: does it 'contain' trust and personal money in the same proportion as the mixed fund? Similarly, if the mixed fund is reduced by dissipation, is trust money dissipated in the same proportion? Equity makes certain presumptions about the expenditure of mixed funds, and the answers to these questions will depend upon a number of factors, including the source of the rest of the fund.

Mixing trust money and trustee's money

Where a trustee mixes trust money with his own, the basic rule is that the beneficiary is entitled to the first charge on the fund or any property purchased with it. It is also the case that where a trustee has mixed trust funds with his own, he is assumed to spend his own money out of the fund first, for, as was said in *Re Hallett*, the trustee 'cannot be heard to say that he took away the trust money when he had a right to take his own'. So in *Re Hallett* a solicitor had mixed trust funds with his own money in a bank account. He had then made various payments out of and into the fund. At his death the balance exceeded the amount of the trust moneys, but was not sufficient to meet his other debts as well. It was held that the beneficiaries were entitled to a charge for the full amount of the trust moneys ahead of the other creditors. Since the balance exceeded the trust moneys, the trustee was assumed to have left the trust money intact and spent only his own.

Where money from the mixed fund has been spent on property, there seems to be no particular distinction as far as the beneficiaries are concerned whether they seek to trace into the fund or the property. If either are sufficient to meet the charge, *Re Hallett* would seem to imply that they must proceed against the fund as *prima facie* the property has been purchased with the trustee's own money. If the fund is insufficient, then they must proceed against the property and in such a case it appears that the assumption that the trustee has spent his own money first will not be applied to the beneficiaries' detriment. Thus, in *Re Oatway* [1903] 2 Ch 356, the trustee first purchased some shares with money from the mixed fund, then dissipated the rest. The beneficiaries were entitled to trace into the shares.

If property has been purchased with trust money, or is in some other way the product of trust property, the beneficiary can assert a claim to it: it becomes trust property. This means that if it has increased in value, the beneficiary will keep that gain in value as well. This will apply if it was purchased with trust money directly, without mixing, or purchased with money out of a mixed fund which has been identified as trust money, applying the *Hallett* and *Oatway* rules above.

What if property is purchased with mixed funds (part trust's, part trustee's), so that it is itself 'mixed' property? Previous *dicta* in *Hallett* have been overturned in *Foskett* v *McKeown*, which makes it clear that the claimant is entitled to assert ownership in proportion to contribution of the trust money to the purchase price:

> Where a trustee wrongfully uses trust money to provide part of the cost of acquiring an asset, the beneficiary is entitled *at his option* either to a claim to a proportionate share of the asset or to enforce a lien upon it to secure his personal claim against the trustee for the amount of the misapplied money. (*Per* Lord Millett, following Scott V-C's *obiter* remarks in the Court of Appeal.)

In other words, the same rules apply as where the asset is purchased wholly with trust money: only here the claim is to a share and not the whole asset.

So, for example, an item costing £1,000 is purchased with £500 of trust money and £500 of the trustee's own money: if the item increases in value to £1,500, the beneficiaries are entitled to half the property, i.e. £750. If the asset had fallen in value to, say £800, the claimant would enforce a lien against the property for the amount of his loss, i.e. £500 plus interest.

Foskett v *McKeown* [2000] 3 All ER 97

The facts in this case were that the beneficiaries, Murphy's business clients, were trying to trace into the death benefit on a life insurance policy which Murphy's children had received on Murphy's death. Murphy had made five premium payments on the policy: three of his own money, and two of 'trust' money. The decision in the Court of Appeal was that the beneficiaries could claim only the amount of the premiums, plus interest. This was overturned in the House of Lords, applying the rule stated above, that the beneficiaries could claim a share proportionate to the amount that the trust money contributed to the purchase price.

The particular asset here was the death benefit paid out to Murphy's children on an insurance policy paid for partly with trust money. The House of Lords stressed that the money had been used to buy the policy. The policy was a bundle of various rights, one of which was the death benefit. In fact, because of the nature of the insurance policy, the value of the death benefit was not enhanced by the trust money payments. This led to some very complex reasoning in the Court of Appeal, but fortunately the House of Lords took a much more straightforward approach: the policy was in part the product of trust money, the death benefit was a product of the policy, so the beneficiaries could claim a share of the benefit *pro rata*. As in simple terms 40 per cent of the purchase money was trust money, the beneficiaries could claim 40 per cent of the death benefit. (Lord Millett's more complex approach to the share calculation was not followed by the other judges.)

The House of Lords stressed also that this was a proprietary claim. The claimants were the beneficiaries of a trust (money had been paid into a trust for the purchase of certain land). They therefore had an absolute proprietary interest in the money in equity and hence, via tracing, to the product of that money, i.e. the death benefit. The court distinguished this from any personal claim based on unjust enrichment.

Lord Browne-Wilkinson also distinguished this case from the one where trust money has been expended innocently on property belonging to another. In such a case the claim is, at most, to a proprietary lien to recover the money expended (i.e. no share in the property, or even in the enhancement in the value). Even this might not be allowed if it were inequitable to trace (see below).

In *Foskett* the money had gone to the family, who were innocent volunteers. Had it gone to Murphy himself, it might have been appropriate to deny him any gain on the ground of unjust enrichment. It should also be remembered that in the case of innocent volunteers, it might become unconscionable to trace into the asset at all, as implied in *Re Diplock* and *Lipkin Gorman* (see 'Loss of the right to trace', below) (see Figure 17.1).

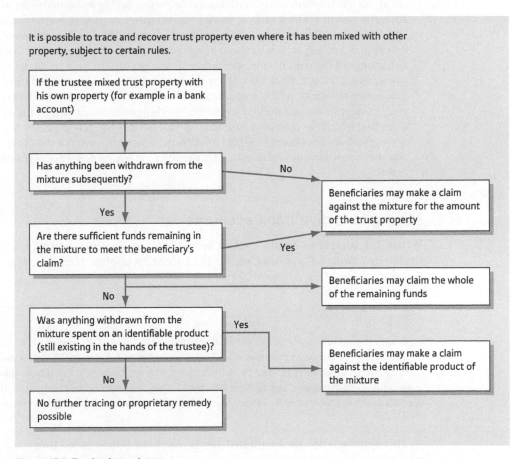

Figure 17.1 Tracing into mixtures

Mixing of money from different sources

In this situation there is no reason to give any claimant priority over any other since all are innocent: therefore, the rule is that they take *pari passu* (i.e. equally).

Example

If a mixed fund consists of £500 from trust A and £1,000 from trust B, and the whole of it is used to purchase, for example, shares, trust A will have a charge on the shares for £500 and trust B a charge for £1,000. Alternatively, the two trusts can agree to take the shares as trust property as tenants in common, one-third for trust A and two-thirds for trust B. If the shares fall in value to £750, then trust A will get £250 and trust B £500: they share the loss in proportion to the relative amounts of each trust's contribution to the purchase since none has any priority to the others. This rule applies equally to mixing of trust funds with funds of an innocent volunteer.

This rule, together with the reasons for it given by Lord Parker in *Sinclair* v *Brougham*, were spelt out in *Re Diplock* by Lord Greene MR:

> Equity regards the rights of the equitable owner as being 'in effect rights of property' though not recognised as such by the common law. Just as a volunteer is not allowed in equity . . . to set up his legal title adversely to the claim of a person having an equitable interest in the land, so in the case of a mixed fund of money the volunteer must give such recognition as equity considers him in conscience (as a volunteer) bound to give to the interest of the equitable owner of the money which has been mixed with the volunteer's own. But this burden on the conscience of the volunteer is not such as to compel him to treat the claim of the equitable owner as paramount. That would be to treat the volunteer as strictly as if he himself stood in a fiduciary relationship with the equitable owner which *ex hypothesi* he does not. The volunteer is under no greater duty of conscience to recognise the interest of the equitable owner than that which lies upon a person having an equitable interest in one of two trust funds of 'money' which have become mixed towards the equitable owner of the other. Such a person is not in conscience bound to give precedence to the equitable owner of the other of the two funds.

Mixing in 'active bank accounts'

Where the mixing takes place in an active banking account, however, a different rule, that to be found in *Clayton's Case* (1816) 1 Mer 529, applies. Here the approach is first in, first out.

Example

Thus, in the example given above of two trust funds mixed, if trust A's money were placed in a bank account on 1 January, and the money from trust B on 3 January, and then £250 were spent on shares, those shares would be presumed to be the product of trust A's money, as that was the first into the account. Furthermore, if, say, £750 of the account were dissipated by the trustee, this would be presumed to be all of trust A's money and £250 of trust B's money, again on a first in, first out basis.

This approach has been criticised, but it should be remembered that it is a presumption which may be displaced by the facts. It would not apply where the fund is not genuinely mixed, as, for example, where the trustee has shown evidence of keeping the money separate, as in *Re Diplock* (paying the money into a mixed fund but then paying the same amount into a separate account). Neither will it apply where the transactions in and out are so large and complex that no separation can be made.

Barlow Clowes International Ltd v Vaughan [1992] 4 All ER 22

This case considers the problems of distribution out of a mixed fund, and clearly indicates that the rule in *Clayton's Case* can be displaced in appropriate situations. In this case a large number of investors had, at various times over a period of several years, invested money in Barlow Clowes. As a result of misapplication of funds, the company was, at the time of the hearing, in liquidation and had far fewer assets than were necessary to meet investors' claims. The question arose, then, of how to divide what was left among those investors. There were three possibilities. First, it would be possible to apply *Clayton's Case* on a first in, first out basis. The effect of this would be that those who had invested latest would receive most, if not all, of the remaining funds, on the assumption that the earlier investors' money had been used up in the misapplications. The second possibility would be for division *pari passu* among all investors in proportion to the amount of their investments. The third was a rolling charge solution whereby each outgoing from the fund would be deemed to consist of amounts of the money from each investor who had money in the fund at the time in proportion to his share at that time.

Woolf LJ summarised the position by stating that the rule in *Clayton's Case* is the *prima facie* solution, but that its use is a matter of convenience and the court must consider whether it is impracticable or would result in injustice in the circumstances. In particular, the rule should not be applied if it is contrary to the presumed intention of the investors. The nature of the investment here – a common pool, created by Barlow Clowes without the knowledge of the investors – led the court to assume that, had they known their money was so held, they would have expected to have common rights, a 'shared misfortune'. Accordingly, a division *pari passu* was ordered. It was recognised that the fairest solution was probably the rolling charge approach but that, given the size and complexity of the fund, it was impracticable to apply this.

It appears increasingly likely that the rule will be displaced in the face of evidence of the parties' intentions and on the grounds of justice in general. Thus, in *Russell-Cooke Trust Co v Prentis* [2003] 2 All ER 478 the contributors in an investment scheme in this case were presumed to have expected their contributions (which went into a bank account) to form a common fund out of which investments would be made. 'First in, first out' was therefore inappropriate; all contributors ranked equally and a distribution *pari passu* of remaining money in the fund was ordered. In *Commerzbank Aktiengesellschaft v IMB Morgan plc* [2005] 1 Lloyd's Rep 298, Lawrence Collins J, applying *Barlow Clowes v Vaughan*, above, considered that the rule need only be applied when it was convenient and could do broad justice. As the amount of the claims far exceeded the sums in the accounts, the claimant beneficiaries would be paid *pari passu*, according to the amount of their contributions. The claimant-beneficiaries were the victims of a common misfortune and to apply the fiction of 'first in, first out' would be to apportion loss through a test that bore no relation to the justice of the case.

Loss of the right to trace

The right to trace in equity will be lost if one of the following happens.

First, if the property passes to a *bona fide* purchaser for value. This is obvious because an equitable owner is unable to assert his interest against such a person. Though purchase may involve a change of position, this is not crucial to the defence, which accordingly should be regarded as separate and based on different principles from the defence of change of position discussed below.

Secondly, if the property ceases to be identifiable. Whether mixed or not the property must continue to exist, so if the trustee dissipates the money or consumes it or uses it to pay a debt (which then, of course, itself disappears), then it ceases to be traceable. Where heterogeneous goods are mixed with others to produce a wholly new product, they are regarded as consumed and hence not traceable. In **Bishopsgate Investment v Homan** [1995] 1 All ER 347, the Court of Appeal ruled that there could be no equitable tracing into an overdrawn bank account, whether one which was overdrawn at the time of the payment in of the trust money, or one which subsequently became overdrawn. It is clear that in such a situation the trust property has disappeared, either because it has been used up in meeting some of the debt owed to the bank, or because it subsequently disappears as the money is used up in subsequent withdrawals.

Thirdly, where it would be inequitable to trace. In the context of innocent volunteers, **Re Diplock** took the view that this would include situations where the money was spent in improving the volunteer's land or where he used it to pay off his debts. Lord Browne-Wilkinson appeared to approve this in **Foskett v McKeown**:

> Cases where money of one person has been expended on improving or maintaining the physical property of another raise special problems. The property left at the end of the day is incapable of being physically divided into its separate constituent assets, i.e. the land and the money spent on it.

In any event, this defence may now be seen as part of the defence of change of position. It is clear, however, that the mere spending of the money is not a sufficient change of position for these purposes.

Lipkin Gorman v Karpnale [1992] 4 All ER 512

In this case, Lord Goff in particular stressed the importance of the defence of change of position. Here, where a solicitor embezzled money from his firm and used it for gambling at the Playboy Club, Lord Goff was of the opinion that the club had changed its position by allowing the solicitor to gamble, running the risk that he might win. They were therefore entitled to set any winnings by the solicitor against the claim by the firm for the money received by the club as bets by the solicitor, the club having acted in good faith throughout.

Lord Goff in **Lipkin Gorman** was not prepared to set the limits of this defence, but enunciated the principle that 'the defence is available to a person whose position has so changed that it would be inequitable in all the circumstances to require him to make restitution, or alternatively to make restitution in full'. His Lordship confirmed that such a defence could clearly never be available to anyone changing his position in bad faith: e.g. when he had known of the claimant's rights to restitution. Though speaking in the context of a common law remedy, restitution, it is also clear that his Lordship envisaged such a defence developing in the context of equitable tracing: 'while recognising the different functions of property at law and in equity, there may also in due course develop a more consistent approach to tracing claims, in which common defences are recognised as available to such claims, whether advanced at law or in equity'. The availability of such a defence in equity

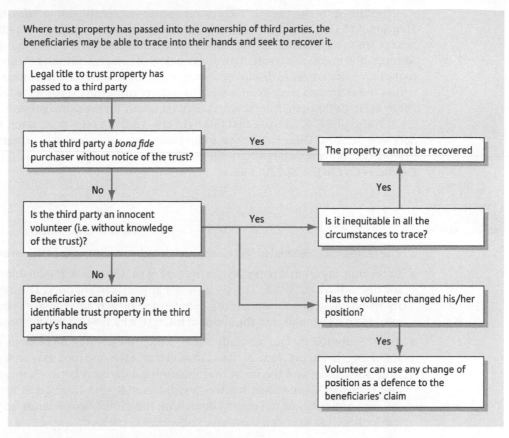

Where trust property has passed into the ownership of third parties, the beneficiaries may be able to trace into their hands and seek to recover it.

Figure 17.2 Tracing property into the hands of third parties

was clearly assumed by Millett LJ in **Boscawan v Bajwa** [1995] 4 All ER 769, in which he summarised the defences to a tracing claim thus:

> The defendant will either challenge the plaintiff's claim that the property in question represents his property (i.e. he will challenge the validity of the tracing exercise), or he will raise a priority dispute (e.g. by claiming to be a *bona fide* purchaser without notice). If all else fails he will raise the defence of innocent change of position.

It is clear that the defence of change of position is only available to a person acting in good faith. In a commercial context 'bad faith' has been held to include not only dishonesty, but also, in the words of Moore-Bick J in **Niru Battery Manufacturing Co v Milestone Trading Ltd** [2002] 2 All ER (Comm) 705 at 741 'failure to act in a commercially acceptable way and sharp practice of a kind that falls short of outright dishonesty as well as dishonesty itself.' This would include failure to make reasonable inquiries, where the recipient has concerns over the source the money received (see Figure 17.2).

Claims *in personam* under *Re Diplock*

Personal liability is usually limited to breaches by fiduciaries or those who dishonestly participate in such breaches. However, **Re Diplock**, as well as allowing a claim to trace against innocent volunteers, recognised a personal liability of innocent volunteers. This was confirmed by the House of Lords on appeal (under the name *Ministry of Health* v *Simpson* [1951] AC 251). The right applies to any unpaid or underpaid creditor, legatee or next of kin to recover from any person to whom the estate has been wrongfully distributed. 'Wrongfully' means as a result of a mistake of law or of fact. The limits of this right are: first, that of time limitation, as discussed above; secondly, that the claim is only for the amount which the claimants have been unable to recover from the executors, who are primarily liable; and thirdly, that, in any event, the claim is only for the principal sum, without interest. It is also probably the case that this right arises only in respect of claims to the estate of deceased persons. There have been some judicial pronouncements suggesting it may be extended to other fiduciary situations: *Butler* v *Broadhead* [1974] 2 All ER 401; *Re J Leslie Engineers Co Ltd* [1976] 2 All ER 85.

Summary

- The remedies considered in this chapter fall into two basic types: personal and proprietary.

- In relation to personal remedies, trustees are expected to take reasonable care in exercising discretions, but will be strictly liable for any breaches of duty. The measure of liability will depend upon a causal link between the breach and the loss, and the damages awarded may be subject to the award of interest, which will normally be simple interest.

- Trustees are jointly and severally liable, which means that a claimant may sue all of them together or only one of them, in which case the one sued may seek a contribution from the others, and the court may determine a division between them as seems just and reasonable. Individual trustees and fiduciaries who have acted honestly may be relieved of liability at the court's discretion. Individual beneficiaries may be unable to sue for breaches to which they have knowingly consented.

- Claims are subject to statutory time limits, which will apply except where there is fraud or the misuse of trust property.

- Trustees, fiduciaries and certain intermeddling third parties are also subject to personal liability to account for profits, which can be contrasted with claims to compensate for loss.

- Tracing is a process by which property misappropriated may be followed into other forms and into the hands of third parties. This may lead to personal or proprietary remedies, at common law or in equity, depending on the circumstances.

- Tracing at common law is essentially a physical process because of the nature of the common law remedies, and becomes impossible where the property or money sought to be traced has been mixed with other property.

- Equity is more flexible than the common law in this respect so, though following in equity requires the existence of some fiduciary relationship, property can be followed into mixtures. The right to trace in equity will be lost if the property is dissipated or falls into the hands of a *bona fide* purchaser.

- The rules for tracing into mixtures give priority to those having the better 'equity', that is those who are most innocent; beneficiaries will have priority over the trustee who has mixed their money with his own, but will be treated equally, and share gains and losses *pari passu* where several innocent beneficiaries' money has been mixed.

Further reading

Personal liability

M Conaglen, 'Strict fiduciary loyalty and accounts of profits' (2006) 65 CLJ 278.
Considers the arguments for and against a more flexible approach to fiduciary liability.

S B Elliott, 'Remoteness criteria in equity' (2002) 65 MLR 588.
Considers that rules for remoteness of damage should be the same for equitable claims as for contract or tort.

R Grantham and C Rickett, 'A normative account of defences to restitutionary liability' (2008) 67 CLJ 92.
Defences to unjust enrichment and the law of restitution.

J Mather, 'Fiduciaries and the law of limitation' (2008) 4 JBL 344.
Interpretation of the Limitation Act 1980, arguing for a six-year limitation period.

M McInnes, 'The account of profits for breach of fiduciary duty' (2006) 122 LQR 11.
Comments on *Murad* v *Al-Saraj* (2005).

C Mitchell, 'Recovery of compound interest as restitution or damages' [2008] MLR 290–302.
The significance of *Sempra Metals* v *IRC* (2007).

T Polli, 'Show me the money' (2010) 154 (46) SJ 12.
The causation rule as it may apply to breaches of fiduciary duty.

P Ridge, 'Pre-judgement compound interest' (2010) 126 LQR 279.
Considers whether compound interest should be available in cases of money paid by mistake.

I Samit, 'Guarding the fiduciary's conscience – a justification of the stringent profit-stripping rule' [2008] OJLS 763.
Arguments for the strict liability of fiduciaries to surrender profits.

Tracing and proprietary claims

D Fox, 'Vindicating property in substituted assets' [2001] LMCLQ 1.
Property rights in insurance moneys, after *Foskett* v *McKeown* (2001).

R Goode, 'Proprietary liability for secret profits – a reply' (2011) 127 LQR 493.
A reply to Hayton (article below), commenting on the availability of proprietary remedies as a means of denying a fiduciary improper gains.

R Grantham and C Rickett, 'Tracing and property rights: the categorical truth' (2000) 65 MLR 905.
Tracing and proprietary rights, as applied in *Foskett* v *McKeown* (2001).

D Hayton, 'Proprietary liability for secret profits' (2011) 127 LQR 487.

M Pawlowski, 'The demise of the rule in Clayton's Case' [2003] Conv 339.
Criticism in the light of *Barlow Clowes* v *Vaughan* (1992) and *Russell-Cooke* v *Prentis* (2002).

L Smith, 'Simplifying claims for traceable proceeds' (2009) 125 LQR 338.
Focuses *inter alia* on *Lipkin Gorman* v *Karpnale* (1991).

P Watts, 'Unjust enrichment and misdirected funds' (1991) 107 LQR 521.
Comments on *Lipkin Gorman* v *Karpnale* (1991).

18

The equitable doctrines

Objectives

After reading this chapter you should be able to:

1. Understand the doctrine of conversion and how it has been affected by the Trusts of Land and Appointment of Trusts Act 1996.

2. Understand the key requirements for the doctrine of election to apply and appreciate that it is based on the equitable doctrine that no one is allowed to blow hot and cold at the same time.

3. Understand that the doctrine of satisfaction is based on the maxim that equity imputes an *intention* to fulfil an obligation and that it may apply in a number of situations.

4. Understand that the doctrine of performance is based on the maxim that equity imputes an intention to fulfil an obligation and that under the doctrine an action is presumed to be done as a step towards satisfying an obligation.

Conversion

Objective
1

The doctrine of conversion is based on the equitable maxim, 'equity looks on that as done which ought to be done'. In a range of situations, equity will regard realty as personalty and personalty as realty. This can be important in some circumstances.

Example

Terry dies, leaving a valid will under which all of his personalty is left to Peter and all his realty to Robert. Terry entered into a legally binding contract to sell a piece of land to X but died before the sale was completed. This is a situation where the doctrine of conversion applies and, from the time that the contract was made, Terry is regarded as having an interest in the proceeds of sale-personalty. So Peter would be entitled to the proceeds of the sale when it is completed despite the fact that, at the time of his (Terry's) death Terry had not received the proceeds of sale and still had the legal estate in the land.

A classic statement of the doctrine (as it was before 1996) is found in *Fletcher* v *Ashburner* (1779) 1 Bro CC 497 where Sir Thomas Sewell MR said:

> [N]othing was better established than this principle, that money directed to be employed in the purchase of land, and land directed to be sold and turned into money, are to be considered as that species of property into which they are directed to be converted . . . The owner of the fund, or the contracting parties, may make land money or money land.

The Trusts of Land and Appointment of Trustees Act 1996, which became operative from 1 January 1997, made a number of changes to the application and operation of the doctrine of conversion in relation to land held on trust for sale or where personal property is held on trust to sell it and buy land with the proceeds.

But despite the side-note to s 3 of the Act to the effect that conversion has been abolished, the doctrine remains relevant in a number of cases.

The situations where the doctrine applies are outlined below.

Under an express trust

Before 1997, if a settlor or a testator directed trustees to convert realty into personalty (or vice versa) the doctrine of conversion would, subject to what is said below, have applied from the moment that the obligation took effect.

However, for the doctrine to apply, there needed to be an imperative direction to convert and there had to be someone who could enforce the conversion. If, for example, the settlor merely gave a power to convert, the doctrine did not apply and rights depended on the actual state of the property.

In all cases it was a matter of construction as to whether an imperative direction existed or not.

Normally, conversion took place as soon as the instrument imposing the obligation came into force. If the direction was contained in a will, the operative date was the date of death. If the obligation was contained in a settlement, conversion took effect as soon as the document was executed: *Griffiths* v *Ricketts* (1849) 7 Hare 299.

These rules applied even if the direction imposed a duty which only became operative at a future date.

Under the Trusts of Land and Appointment of Trustees Act 1996 any express *inter vivos* trusts for sale, whether created before 1997 or after 1996, become trusts of land (s 1). The section only applies to trusts created by will where the testator died after 1996. Under such a trust the property is held on trust with a power of sale. A power to postpone sale is implied into every express trust for sale of land and cannot be excluded.

Section 3 states:

(1) Where land is held by trustees subject to a trust for sale, the land is not to be regarded as personal property; and where personal property is subject to a trust for sale in order that the trustees may acquire land the personal property is not to be regarded as land.

(2) Subsection (1) does not apply to a trust created by a will if the testator died before the commencement of this Act.

(3) Subject to that, subsection (1) applies to a trust whether it is created, or arises, before or after that commencement.

So, despite the marginal note, 'Abolition of doctrine of conversion', the Trusts of Land and Appointment of Trustees Act 1996 does not abolish trusts for sale *per se*, but s 3 abolishes the doctrine of conversion in relation to trusts for sale.

The effect of s 3 is severely to restrict (but not to abolish) the application of the doctrine. The section applies both prospectively and retrospectively, i.e. it applies equally to trusts for sale whether created before or after 1 January 1997. The only cases where s 3 will not apply to a trust for sale, and so where the doctrine of conversion will continue to be relevant notwithstanding s 3, is where a trust for sale was created under a will of a testator who died before 1997.

Statutory trusts

There was a wide range of statutory provisions under which trusts for sale were imposed, particularly under the 1925 property legislation. The doctrine of conversion applied to these statutory trusts for sale unless the statute provided otherwise. In some cases the statute went even further and directed that an actual conversion would have no effect. For example, under the Settled Land Act 1925 s 75(5), capital money raised by the sale of settled land was treated as if it were still land.

The Trusts of Land and Appointment of Trustees Act 1996 made a number of amendments to existing statutory provisions, removing the imposition of a statutory trust for sale and substituting some other form of statutory trust without any duty to sell.

On an intestacy

Under s 33 of the Administration of Estates Act 1925, any property owned by one who died intestate was held by the personal representatives on trust for sale.

Paragraph 5 of Schedule 2 to the Trusts of Land and Appointment of Trustees Act 1996 replaced the provision in s 33(1) of the 1925 Act (which imposed a trust for sale) with the following: 'On the death of a person intestate as to any real or personal estate, that estate shall be held on trust by his personal representatives with the power to sell it.'

Thus the statutory trust for sale is replaced by a trust coupled with a power to sell. Irrespective of s 3 (above), the abolition of the former statutory trust for sale would have ensured that the doctrine of conversion no longer applied in this situation.

Two or more entitled to land

Under s 34 of the Law of Property Act 1925, a trust for sale was imposed whenever two or more people were entitled to land either as joint tenants or as tenants in common.

Section 34 has been amended by Schedule 2 paragraph 3 of the Trusts of Land and Appointment of Trustees Act 1996, which introduced a provision that the land will be held 'in trust for the persons interested in the land'. The abolition of the duty to sell under a statutory trust for sale would have been enough to ensure that the doctrine of conversion no longer applied, irrespective of the provisions of the Trusts of Land and Appointment of Trustees Act 1996 s 3.

Section 36 of the Law of Property Act 1925, which imposed a trust for sale where land was held by joint tenants, was amended by Schedule 2 paragraph 4 of the Trusts of Land and Appointment of Trustees Act 1996. The statutory trust for sale has been replaced with a provision that the land is held 'in trust for the persons interested in the land'. Again, the abolition of the statutory trust for sale would have ensured that the doctrine of conversion no longer applied to joint owners of land.

Partnerships

The Partnership Act 1890 s 22 provided that any land which is partnership property is regarded as personalty unless there is a contrary intention. This simply put in statutory form the then accepted equitable rule. The statute applied not only as between the partners themselves but also between those entitled to the property of a dead partner. The basis of the provision was the fact that when a partnership is dissolved the land would have to be sold and the proceeds of the sale distributed to the partners.

Section 22 of the Partnership Act 1890 was repealed by s 25(2) of the Trusts of Land and Appointment of Trustees Act 1996. However, the precise effect of this and the implications for the application of the doctrine of conversion after 1996 are unclear. It is possible that the repeal of s 22 simply restored the pre-Partnership Act 1890 position, i.e. the equitable rule that there was conversion in these cases. But this could only be argued if the basis of the equitable rule was an implied contract. If the rule was based on an implied trust, then it would appear that s 25(2) of Trusts of Land and Appointment of Trustees Act 1996 would operate to stop the doctrine from applying.

Court orders

The general rule is that if the court makes an order to sell property the doctrine of conversion operates from the date of the order.

Section 3 of the Trusts of Land and Appointment of Trustees Act 1996, which abolished the doctrine of conversion where land is held by trustees on trust for sale or personal property is held on a trust for sale in order that the proceeds of sale may be used to buy land, does not affect sales under court orders.

Contract to sell land

As soon as there is an enforceable, binding contract to sell land, there is a constructive trust under which the seller holds the property on trust for the purchaser.

Under the doctrine of conversion, the seller will be regarded as having an interest in personalty and the purchaser will be regarded as having an interest in realty. This conversion could be particularly important if one of the parties to the contract dies before completion. For example, if the seller dies before completion, his interest will pass to the person entitled to his personalty.

In *Hillingdon Estates* v *Stonefield Estates* [1952] 1 All ER 856, Vaisey J stated:

> Where there is a contract by A to sell land to B at a certain price, B becomes the owner in equity of the land, subject, of course, to his obligations to perform his part of the contract by paying the purchase money: but subject to that, the land is the land of B, the purchaser. What is the position of A, the vendor? He has, it is true, the legal estate in the land, but, for many purposes, from the moment the contract is entered into he holds as trustee for B, the purchaser. True he has rights in the land remaining, but those rights are conditional and limited by the circumstance that they are referable to his right to recover and receive the purchasemoney. His interest in the land when he has entered into a contract for sale is not an interest in land; it is an interest in personal estate, in a sum of money.

Again, the terms of the Trusts of Land and Appointment of Trustees Act 1996 s 3 leave the operation of the doctrine of conversion unaffected in this context.

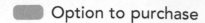 ## Option to purchase

The doctrine of conversion applies if an option to purchase land is created. Once the option is exercised, the doctrine applies and the property is regarded as personalty as far as the original owner of the land is concerned. But once the option is exercised, for the purposes of conversion, it operates retrospectively and equity regards the property as personalty from the date the option was granted.

Again, the terms of the Trusts of Land and Appointment of Trustees Act 1996 s 3 leave the operation of the doctrine of conversion unaffected in this context.

Lawes v *Bennett* (1785) 1 Cox 167

> This is the classic case on this aspect of the doctrine. Witterwronge granted a lease of a farm to Douglas, giving him an option to purchase the fee simple. Douglas assigned the lease and the option to Waller. Witterwronge died and left his real property to Bennett and his personalty to Bennett and Lawes equally. After the death Waller exercised the option and bought the farm. The court was asked whether, since at the date of death the farm was part of the testator's realty, the purchase money should be regarded as part of the real estate rather than as part of the personal estate. Sir Lloyd Kenyon MR held that it should be regarded as personalty. The exercise of the option operated to work a conversion from the date of the grant of the option even though the option was not exercised until after the testator's death. The fact that Waller could, in effect, choose whether the property should be realty or personalty was immaterial.

The important point to take from this case is the retrospective effect once the option is exercised.

The operation of the doctrine in this context is nothing if not complex. The theory is that conversion takes place only when the *option is exercised*, but once exercised it operates retrospectively back to the *date of the grant* of the option. This means that, if a testator dies leaving a will under which realty is left to Roy and personalty to Peter, a decision must be made as to the ownership of any of the testator's land which is subject to an option. The position seems to be that the land will pass to Roy but his interest will be defeasible in the event of the option being exercised. At that point the doctrine of conversion comes into play and the property will then be regarded as personalty from the date of the *grant* of the option, and so the proceeds of sale flowing from the exercise of the option will pass to Peter. However, between the death of the testator and the exercise of the option, any income or rent flowing from the land will be the property of Roy.

The general rule is subject to modification if the land which is subject to the option is contained in a specific devise. In such a situation, the cases suggest that, if the option existed when the will was made or if the granting of the option and the execution of the will were contemporaneous, then the rule in *Lawes* v *Bennett* may not apply. The argument is that when the testator executed the will he must have been aware of the option and would have wanted the devisee to take a benefit under the will, whether or not the option is exercised. If the option is granted after the will making the specific devise is executed, the devise will be adeemed by the exercise of the option: *Weeding* v *Weeding* (1861) 1 J & H 424. In such a case the rule in *Lawes* v *Bennett* applies.

The case of *Re Carrington* [1931] All ER Rep 658 demonstrates an extreme and arguably unwarranted application and extension of the doctrine. Carrington made a will in 1911 under which he specifically bequeathed 420 preference shares. In 1927 he granted an option to Hulme to purchase the shares, to be exercised within one month after his death.

Carrington died in 1930 and within one month Hulme exercised the option. The Court of Appeal reluctantly decided, using *Lawes* v *Bennett*, that the exercise of the option operated to adeem the specific legacy. The exercise of the option operated retrospectively and caused the shares to be regarded as personalty as from the date of the grant of the option.

In this case the doctrine operated in an unusual way. The normal effect of the doctrine is to cause property that is actually land to be regarded as personalty or vice versa. In *Re Carrington*, the doctrine operated to cause one type of personalty (the shares) to be regarded as a different form of personalty (money).

Conditional contracts

The terms of the Trusts of Land and Appointment of Trustees Act 1996 s 3 leave the operation of the doctrine of conversion unaffected in this context.

The rule in *Lawes* v *Bennett* has been subject to criticisms, but, in *Re Sweeting (deceased)* [1988] 1 All ER 1016, the court construed the rule as applying not only to cases involving options but also to cases involving conditional contracts. In the case, a testator made a specific devise of some land (the yard) which adjoined his house. Later, he exchanged contracts to sell both the yard and his house. The contract for the sale of the yard specified that its completion was conditional, *inter alia*, on the simultaneous completion of the contract for the sale of the house and in turn on the cancellation of a Class F land charge by the testator's wife, who was living in the house, and the releases being obtained from her of any legal or equitable rights she might have in the house. Neither contract was completed at the date of the testator's death, but his wife had given her consent to the sale. After his death both sales were completed. The issue was whether the specific devise of the yard was adeemed so that the proceeds of sale fell into residue. The argument put forward was that the rule in *Lawes* v *Bennett* was not restricted to options and could apply to conditional sales completed after death. If the rule did apply, the doctrine of conversion would apply and the property would be regarded as personalty (and not as the land) as from the date of the contract to sell and, thus, the specific devise would be adeemed. Nicholls J said, after hearing argument, that the rule was anomalous though well established:

> For my part I can see no rational basis for applying the rule in cases of an option but not applying it in the case of a contract of sale containing conditions such as those present in the yard contract and the house contract. If the rule applies where an option is not exercised until after the testator's death with the consequence that conversion and ademption occurs at that time, why should the rule not apply equally (or indeed *a fortiori*) where a contract exists at the death but subject to conditions which are subsequently fulfilled or waived? Moreover, I do not think that to apply the rule to such a conditional contract would be to extend the rule. Conversion and ademption may be worked by the existence at death of an uncompleted, specifically enforceable contract, or by the existence at the death of an option which is subsequently exercised: the existence at death of an uncompleted conditional contract which is subsequently completed falls somewhere between these two extremes.

Failure of conversion

There is said to be a failure of conversion when there are no beneficiaries for whose benefit the conversion was to take place. There can, however, be a partial failure of conversion as where some, but not all, of the beneficiaries do not exist.

To the extent that the Trusts of Land and Appointment of Trustees Act 1996 s 3 abolishes the doctrine of conversion, failure of conversion will be less important.

Total failure

In the case of a total failure of conversion, there will be no one who can enforce the conversion, and therefore the purpose for which the conversion was directed no longer exists. The consequence of this is that the property continues to be regarded as being in its original form.

> ### Example
>
> Blackacre was directed to be held on a trust for sale to hold the proceeds on trust for Peter and Ron, who both die before the trust comes into operation. There would be no one to enforce the conversion and the trust property would continue to be regarded as being land. This is an example of total failure of conversion. This could be very significant if the trust had been created in a will. The testator may well have left his personalty and realty to different beneficiaries. Blackacre would pass to the beneficiary entitled to the testator's land.

As already stated, the effect of total failure is that the conversion does not take effect and the property continues to be regarded as being in its original state. This remains the case even if there has actually been a conversion.

It does not matter whether the conversion was directed by a will or under an *inter vivos* trust; the effect of a total failure is the same. The only difference is the time at which it can be seen whether or not there has been a total failure. In the case of a will, the decision cannot be taken until death, whereas, with an *inter vivos* trust, the decision can be taken at the date when the trust was executed.

Partial failure

A partial failure of conversion occurs when only some of the beneficiaries for whom conversion was directed exist when the direction to convert comes into operation. The effect of partial failure is more complicated than the effect of a total failure. The cases draw a distinction between a partial failure under an *inter vivos* trust and a partial failure under a trust created under a will.

Partial failure under *inter vivos* deeds

In the case of a partial failure under a trust created by an *inter vivos* deed the position is clear. There will be a resulting trust in respect of the failure and the property will revert to the settlor in its converted form: *Clarke* v *Franklin* (1858) 4 K & J 257. The explanation of this is that there will remain a duty to convert despite the partial failure, and this will give rise to a notional conversion which will operate for all purposes in connection with decisions as to the nature or ownership of interests.

Partial failure under wills

If there is a partial failure in respect of a direction to convert contained in a will, there appears to be a further distinction to be drawn between directions to convert land into money on the one hand and directions to invest money in land on the other.

In the case of a direction to convert land into money, it is clear that the duty to convert still remains, as there will be some of the beneficiaries in existence for whose benefit the conversion was directed. Thus, as *Re Richerson* [1892] 1 Ch 379 illustrates, any interests will be considered to be interests in money. However, decisions regarding the devolution of the property will be resolved in favour of those entitled to the property in its unconverted state.

Example

The following may serve to illustrate this rather complicated area. If Terry devises land to trustees on trust for sale to hold the proceeds on trust for Ron and Peter, but Peter dies before Terry, who is entitled to Peter's lapsed share? If Terry's will gives Arthur the residuary personalty and Beatrice the residuary realty, Peter's lapsed share will pass to Beatrice, but she will take the property as personalty. The explanation of this apparently odd situation is simple. As the trust for sale was created to benefit Peter and Ron alone, it may well be wrong to allow the distribution of Terry's property among other beneficiaries to be affected by this trust for sale. In other words, for deciding the destiny of the trust property it should be regarded as land, except when considering the position of those for whom the conversion was directed. However, the trustees remain under a duty to convert, and so the interest will be regarded as being an interest in property in its converted state.

Ackroyd v *Smithson* (1780) 1 Bro CC 503

The testator directed that his real and personal estate should be sold and the proceeds used to pay his debts and certain legacies; any surplus was to be divided in fixed proportions between several residuary legatees. Two of these died and the question for the court was whether their shares were to devolve as realty or personalty. If the shares were realty they would pass under the intestacy rules to the testator's heir at law, whereas if the shares were personalty they would pass to the testator's next of kin. The court decided that the property should devolve to those entitled to the property in its unconverted state, as the trust for sale had been created to benefit the initial beneficiaries under the trust and not to affect the devolution of property among a wider group of beneficiaries. So, the real estate passed to the heir and the personal estate passed to the next of kin. However, the recipients took the property in its converted state. Therefore, although realty passed to the heir, he would obtain an interest in personalty.

This case illustrates the principle involved but it is a case decided before the intestacy rules were changed in 1925, and under the modern rules an intestate's property devolves without any distinction between realty and personalty.

In the case of a direction to convert money into land, it seems clear that the property will devolve to those entitled to the property in its unconverted form, but there is some uncertainty as to whether the interest will devolve as an interest in land (i.e. in its notionally converted state) or as one in money (i.e. in its original, unconverted state). It is clear that if the land has actually been bought, then the interest will be treated as an interest in land: *Curteis v Wormald* (1878) 10 Ch D 172. It is probable, but not certain, that if land has not been bought the interest devolves nevertheless as an interest in land. This was the view expressed in *Re Richerson* (above).

Reconversion

Reconversion takes place when a previous notional, equitable conversion is reversed and the property is again regarded as being in its original state.

Example

If trustees hold personalty on trust for sale and the whole equitable interest under the trust belongs to Ben (an adult), he can instruct the trustees not to sell, preferring the property to remain as land. If his instruction had no effect, the trustees could go ahead and sell the land. As absolute beneficial owner, he would be in a position to reverse immediately the action of the trustees in selling the land against his wishes. He could use the rule in *Saunders* v *Vautier* to demand that the trustees transfer the trust property (the proceeds of the sale) to him and he could use the money to buy back the land. This would be an absurd situation and thus in such a case the equitable doctrine of reconversion would apply. The decision of the beneficiary would bring about a reversal of the notional conversion which took effect on the creation of the trust for sale. Under the trust for sale there would be a binding obligation to sell the land, and so the doctrine of conversion would be applicable resulting in the property being notionally regarded as personalty. As soon as the beneficiary decides that he wants the land to be retained this notional conversion is reversed, and from that time onwards the property will be regarded as having been reconverted and will be treated once again as personalty.

The doctrine of reconversion is based on the principle that equity will do nothing in vain.

Reconversion results either from an act or by operation of law. To the extent that s 3 of the Trusts of Land and Appointment of Trustees Act 1996 abolishes the doctrine of conversion, reconversion will be less important.

Act of the parties

As the example above shows, a beneficiary who is an adult and who is absolutely entitled to the entire equitable interest is in a position to bring the doctrine of reconversion into operation. His decision will reverse the original notional conversion. The same will ensue if there are several adult beneficiaries who together are entitled to the entire beneficial interest and they all agree to the trustees not converting trust property.

Although the reconversion can be express or implied, the burden of proof is on those alleging that a reconversion has taken place. It seems that the courts will readily find an implied intention to reconvert in the case of land which is to be sold, but require rather stronger evidence in support of a claim that reconversion has taken place if the case is one where money is used to buy land.

Griesbach v *Freemantle* (1853) 17 Beav 314

The testatrix gave her estate, which included land and a mansion, to trustees on trust for sale to pay the proceeds of sale to her son. The son lived in the mansion for 16 years carrying out many improvements and paying for repairs. When he died the court decided that his conduct showed an intention to reconvert. He had, the court felt, shown an intention to take the property in its original, unconverted state, i.e. as land. The court said their decision might well have been different if the son had only been living in the mansion for a short time.

It was decided in *Re Pedder's Settlement Trusts* (1854) 5 De GM & G 890 that if money is to be used to buy land merely the receipt of the income from the money pending the purchase will not be sufficient evidence of an intention to reconvert.

If two people are co-tenants in property, can one of them acting alone effect a reconversion as regards his share of the property? The answer differs according to whether the trustees are under a duty to convert land into money or vice versa. If the trustees are under a duty to use money to buy land, then co-tenants are able to act unilaterally and to decide to take their share of the trust property in the form of money. The position is different if the trustees are under a duty to sell land. Here it is not possible for one of the beneficiaries to decide that he will take his share in the form of land and direct the trustees not to sell 'his share'. If this were possible, the trustees would discover that when they came to sell the land the rights of the electing tenant over the land would depress the market value of the part of the land that was to be sold, thus operating to the prejudice of the other beneficiary. It is accepted that an undivided share in land is far less saleable than the entire land, thus affecting its commercial value.

An example of an unsuccessful attempt by one of several beneficiaries to reconvert is to be found in **Lloyds Bank plc v Duker** [1987] 3 All ER 193, where one beneficiary was entitled to 46/80ths of the residuary estate, part of which consisted of a block of 999 shares in a company. The beneficiary wished to take part of her entitlement *in specie* and claimed 574 of the shares. The court said that, although the general rule was that a person entitled to an aliquot share of an estate was entitled to insist on a corresponding part of the estate property being distributed to him *in specie*, this would not apply if it would result in one beneficiary being favoured as against the others. In this case the court refused to apply the general rule. To allow the claim would result in a holding that would amount to a majority holding, and the value of each share which formed part of a majority holding would be more than the value of each share which formed part of a minority holding. The result would have been unfairness to the other beneficiaries. The beneficiary would have received a benefit greater than the 46/80ths she was entitled to. The court ordered that the shares should be sold and that the claimant would be entitled to 4680ths of the proceeds of sale.

What right has a remainderman to effect a reconversion? If land is held on trust for sale for Larry for life, remainder to Ron, can Ron elect and cause the doctrine of reconversion to come into play? It would clearly not be possible for any election by Ron to affect the position of Larry. But Ron is able to elect that, if when his interest falls in the property has not been actually converted, he will take in its unconverted state. The effect of this is that on the death of Larry an automatic reconversion will take place. This seems to be the situation whether the interest of Ron is absolute or contingent unless at the date of Ron's death the contingency is not satisfied, in which case the reconversion will fail to take effect.

There is no possibility of minors or people lacking the requisite mental capacity electing for a reconversion. However, in the case of minors the court can be asked to elect on their behalf if it is thought that such an election would benefit the minor. In the case of beneficiaries who lack the mental capacity to make an election, the Court of Protection can be asked to make the decision to reconvert on their behalf.

By operation of law

The most important example of reconversion by operation of law is where the property is said to be 'at home'.

In this case the reconversion is automatic. It occurs when property is held by two joint beneficial owners and one of them dies and causes the other to become absolutely entitled under the *jus accrescendi*. For example, if land was owned by two people as joint tenants, the Law of Property Act 1925 imposed a trust for sale under which the legal estate is held by the two for themselves as joint tenants of the equitable interest. When one of them dies, the other will automatically become entitled to the legal and equitable interest. At this time a reconversion will take place.

Re Cook [1948] Ch 212

Before 1926 a house was conveyed to John Cook and his wife as joint tenants. On 1 January 1925 a trust for sale was imposed under the Law of Property Act 1925 s 36. John died in 1944, his wife dying later in that same year. His wife left all her personal estate to her nephews and nieces. The question arose as to whether these beneficiaries were entitled to the house or whether it passed to those entitled to her real estate. The court held that the trust for sale imposed by the Law of Property Act ended on the death of John because at that time the entire estate, both legal and equitable, vested in the wife. The notional conversion under the trust for sale created by the Law of Property Act was reversed and the property formed part of her real estate and so did not pass under the gift of personalty to the nephews and nieces.

After 1 January 1997 the Trusts of Land and Appointment of Trustees Act 1996 removed the trust for sale.

Election

Objective 2

The equitable doctrine of election is based on the principle that no one is allowed to blow hot and cold at the same time. Another way of expressing this is to say that no one is permitted to both accept and reject an instrument. The doctrine demonstrates an attempt by equity to ensure that the wishes of a donor are not overridden.

Election usually arises in the context of gifts made by will but the same basic rules and principles apply to a gift by deed.

In **Re Edwards** [1958] Ch 168, Jenkins LJ said:

> The essentials of election are that there should be an intention on the part of the testator or testatrix to dispose of certain property; secondly, that the property should not in fact be the testator's or testatrix's own property; and, thirdly, that a benefit should be given by the will to the true owner of the property.

Example

Terry dies, leaving a will in which he states that £100,000 is to go to Ben and that Blackacre is to pass to Charles. In fact, Blackacre belongs to Ben. Ben will not be allowed to accept the legacy of £100,000 *and* insist on retaining Blackacre. It is assumed that the testator would not wish Ben both to take the benefit under the will and keep his own property.

Ben will have to decide what he wants to do.

If he wants to keep Blackacre Ben must elect to take *against* the will. He will keep Blackacre but he cannot also claim the full amount of the legacy as this will be used to compensate the 'disappointed' Charles for not receiving Blackacre. If Blackacre is valued at £100,000 or more, Ben will receive no part of the legacy as it will all be needed to compensate Charles (notice the maximum amount that Charles will receive is £100,000 and Charles cannot claim anything more even if the value of Blackacre exceeds £100,000). Put another way, it means that if Ben decides to keep his own property he will not be expected to pay for the privilege and at worst his financial position will be unchanged (he will still have Blackacre but will have received no benefit under Terry's will). However, if the value of Blackacre is less than £100,000, then Ben will be entitled to claim the balance remaining after Charles has been compensated for not receiving the land.

Ben may decide that he wishes to accept the legacy of £100,000. In this case, Ben must elect to take *under* the will. Ben will be able to claim the legacy in full *but* he must transfer Blackacre to Charles.

In most cases the decision will be made purely on financial grounds, and Ben will make the election which results in his benefiting to the maximum extent. However, it is possible to imagine situations when other factors will be taken into account. For example, if Blackacre has been in Ben's family for many years and has 'sentimental' value, then Ben may decide to elect to take against the will even though it would be financially more advantageous to claim the benefit under the will and to transfer Blackacre to Charles.

It is important to distinguish cases which call for an election from cases where the testator imposes a condition on the gift to the beneficiary. For example, the testator might say that the beneficiary is only to receive a gift under the will on condition that he (the beneficiary) transfers Blackacre to a third party. In such a case the doctrine of election does not apply. The situation is that the beneficiary can receive nothing under the will unless he complies with the condition and transfers Blackacre to the third party. If the beneficiary does not comply with the condition, his gift will fail and fall into residue. The result of this is that not only will the donee not receive any benefit, but also neither will the third party.

The basis of the doctrine of election is often said to be that the donor does not intend the donee to keep both the gift *and* his own property, and, while the donor cannot insist on the donee transferring his own property to the third party, the doctrine does ensure that if the donee decides to keep his own property the third party will not be left without any benefit at all. This is presumed to reflect what the donor would have wanted. In fact, in many cases it is difficult to argue that election is based on the intention of the donor, particularly in situations where the donor believes that the property that he purports to give to the third party is, in fact, his own. To the extent that many if not all cases of election arise because of a mistake, it may perhaps be argued that the problem might be better addressed by developing the power of the courts to 'correct' mistakes rather than relying on the doctrine which, as will be seen, sometimes leads to a result that the donor may well not have wanted (see Figure 18.1).

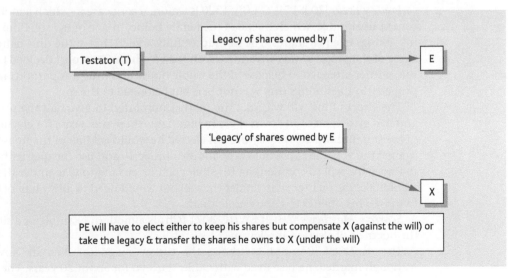

Figure 18.1 Election

Conditions for an election

There are a number of conditions that have to be satisfied before a beneficiary is put to an election.

(1) The donor must give some of his own property to the elector

In *Bristowe* v *Ward* (1794) 2 Ves 336 a testator had the power to appoint property among children who were entitled in default of appointment. It will be recalled that under a power of appointment those entitled in default are considered to be entitled to the property unless and until a valid appointment is made. In his will he appointed some of the property to the children but the rest to strangers. He gave none of his own property to the children. It was held that there was no case for election. Even though the testator had purported to dispose of property of the children to the strangers (the property over which the power of appointment existed and to which they were entitled in default of appointment), he gave none of his own property to them. (Compare this case with *Whistler* v *Webster*, below.)

(2) The donor must attempt to give some of the elector's property to a third party (X) in the same instrument

In *Whistler* v *Webster* (1794) 2 Ves Jun 367, John Whistler settled property on himself for life, and after his death to such of his children as he should appoint. In default of appointment their children were to take equally. By his will Whistler appointed the property not only to his children but also to other individuals. He left legacies to all his children. The court decided that the children were put on election. The children being entitled to the property in default of appointment were considered to be entitled to the property subject to the power being exercised, and so when the testator purported to appoint some of the property to strangers he was attempting to give the children's property to these 'appointees'. If the children elected to take under the will, they would take the legacies and surrender all claim to the property appointed to the strangers. If the children elected to take against the will, they would keep the property improperly appointed but would have to compensate the strangers out of the legacies.

Frear v *Frear* [2008] EWCA Civ 1320 is a more recent case in which a mother left 50 per cent of her residue, which included the family home, to one of her sons and 50 per cent to his siblings in equal shares. The son successfully argued that at the time of her death a half share of the property was already held on trust for him. The court decided that in her will the mother intended to dispose of the whole house and thus was purporting to dispose of property to the siblings that was not hers but belonged to the son.

The effect of the will was that the mother purported to give half the son's share away and had given half of her own share to him. Thus there was a case for election on the part of the son. But whichever way the son elected he would get half of the house. If he elected against the will, the son would keep his own property and use the quarter he was entitled to under the will to compensate his siblings. If he elected to take under the will, the son would take the quarter share under the will but would need to allow half of his own share to pass to his siblings to compensate them.

Scarfe v *Matthews* [2012] EWHC 3071 (Ch) is a modern example of a situation where the doctrine of election is relevant.

The deceased (Bernard Matthews the turkey magnate) died in November 2010. Although married, he had lived with Odile Marteyn for about 20 years. The deceased and his wife adopted three children and also had a natural son.

The deceased wanted to leave Odile Marteyn his villa France and made a French will which was intended to dispose of his immoveable property in France. The deceased was aware that, under French law, his children were entitled to 75 per cent of the villa on his death, so unless they gave up their rights, he was able to leave only 25 per cent of it to Odile Marteyn. Thus the will purported to leave to Odile Marteyn what under French law would be his children's property.

His English will left a £1 million legacy to Odile Marteyn, free of tax. The residuary estate was left to his natural son.

The deceased left a letter explaining his decision to give the villa to Odile Marteyn, and clearly hoped that his children would make it possible for Odile Marteyn to have the villa by waiving their rights to the French estate. The deceased's three adopted children decided not to give up their rights to the villa but his natural son decided to respect the wishes of his father and gave up his claim.

Under the English will, the administrators were obliged to pay all tax arising in consequence of his death, including French tax. The adopted children claimed that under the terms of the English will their liability for French inheritance tax should be paid by the administrator from the English estate. Odile Marteyn then claimed that the doctrine of election entitled her to be compensated by the adopted children. The issue was if the adopted children could take against the French will by enforcing their succession rights, at the same time still taking the benefit of the legacy of inheritance tax under the English will.

Although the case was decided on the basis of construing the wording of the will the judge said (*obiter*) that even if the issue was not determined by construing the will, in the circumstances, the doctrine of election applied and the adopted children were subject to an equitable obligation to pay to Odile Marteyn the amount which was equivalent to the amount paid by the administrator in respect of their liability to French inheritance tax.

Although the doctrine applies only if the gifts are contained in the same instrument, contemporaneous documents or two wills may suffice.

(3) Elector's property must be alienable

If the elector's property, which the donor purports to give away, cannot be alienated by the elector, no case for election arises. The essence of an election is that it is possible for the elector to transfer his property which the donor has purported to give to the third party. If such a transfer is not possible because the elector is unable to alienate the property concerned, then the elector cannot comply with the donor's wishes.

Re Lord Chesham (1886) 31 Ch D 466

In 1877 heirlooms, together with a manor house, were settled by a testator on trust for the benefit of Lord Chesham. In his will, made in 1878, the testator left the same heirlooms to Lord Chesham's two brothers and the residue of his estate to Lord Chesham. The court was asked whether Lord Chesham had to elect between the benefits given to him under the will and the heirlooms, and whether he would be liable to compensate his two brothers. The court held that he was only entitled to the heirlooms in conjunction with the manor house. He was not entitled to remove them from the house without committing a breach of trust. Therefore, he had no power to dispose of the heirlooms and so would not be able to transfer them to his brothers if he was put on election, and he elected to take under the will. Lord Chesham could not comply with the wishes of the testator and so there was no case for election. The result was that Lord Chesham was able to retain his property (the heirlooms) and claim the residue of the estate. He was under no obligation to compensate his brothers for their non-receipt of the heirlooms.

This case should be contrasted with *Re Dicey*.

Re Dicey [1957] Ch 145

Selina Dicey made a will leaving a house to her son Charles and 'my two freehold houses in Beresford Road' to her grandson. She did not own the freehold of these houses but was entitled to a life interest in them under a settlement which provided that, on her death, the houses were to be sold and half the proceeds for sale were to belong to Charles. The Court of Appeal decided that, although Charles did not have an absolute interest under the settlement, he did have a beneficial interest which he could transfer. Accordingly, he had to elect whether to take under the will, transferring his interest in the houses to the grandson, or against the will, compensating the grandson in respect of his disappointment in not receiving the property.

(4) Property given to the elector must be available to compensate third party

If the property given by the donor to the elector cannot be used to compensate a disappointed third party, there will not be a case for election. The classic example of this would arise if the donor gave property to the 'elector' on protective trusts. The nature of a protective trust is that if the principal beneficiary tries to alienate the property his interest determines. Thus, if the 'elector' is given property on protective trusts, he would not be able to use it to compensate a disappointed third party should he (the 'elector') decide to take against the instrument.

(5) Election is tested at testator's death

In the case of gifts by will, it is only if a case for election exists at the date of death that the doctrine applies.

Grissell v Swinhoe (1869) LR 7 Eq 291

The fund of a settlement belonged half to the testator and half to Elizabeth Swinhoe. The testator left all of the fund to his daughter, Charlotte, and Elizabeth's husband in equal shares. The testator died in 1855, Elizabeth a year later. Her husband became entitled on her death to her personalty. The court held that there was no case for election as at the date of the death of the testator the husband did not own the half share of the trust fund, and so at that date there was no property of the husband which the testator was purporting to transfer. If there had been a case for election, the husband would have had to elect to take under the will or against the will. In the former case, he would have been obliged to transfer 'his' share of the trust fund to Charlotte; and, in the latter case, he would have had to compensate her for not benefiting, using the testator's share of the trust fund.

(6) No contrary intention

It is important that the donor demonstrates an intention to give property to the donee and that the third party should receive a benefit. It does not matter that the donor mistakenly believed that the property he was 'giving' to the third party was his own, so long as his intention was that the third party should receive a benefit.

Elector dies without electing

There is often some confusion when the elector dies without having decided how he will elect. How does this affect those surviving him?

The problem is very simply resolved if all the property affected by the election devolves on the same person on the death of the elector. In such a case, the person in whom the property vests steps into the shoes of the elector and can decide whether to elect for or against the instrument: *Cooper* v *Cooper* (1874) 44 LJ Ch 6.

If the property concerned devolves on different people, the position is a little more complicated. For example, by his will a testator gives £10,000 to the elector and purports to give the elector's Blackacre to a third party. The elector dies before making any decision. In this case, Blackacre, the elector's own property, vests in Ron who is entitled to the elector's land. The gift to the elector of the donor's own property, the legacy of £10,000, vests in Peter who is entitled to succeed to the elector's personalty. However, the legacy is taken by Peter subject to an obligation to compensate the disappointed third party. The situation is as if the elector had elected to take against the will and to keep his own property.

Making the election

An election may be made expressly or impliedly, but in either case the court must be satisfied that the elector knew that an election was to be made and had all the knowledge necessary to elect. For example, he must know the relative values of the affected property. Also, the court must be satisfied that there was an intention to elect.

The enjoyment of property or receiving the income generated by property may well suggest an election which would result in the ownership of that property, but this conduct will not be so regarded unless there is full knowledge of all the facts.

Once an election is made, it relates back to the date of the will and this may mean that income received in the period before the election has to be accounted for.

Satisfaction

Objective 3

The doctrine of satisfaction is based on the maxim that equity imputes an intention to fulfil an obligation. An example may help illustrate the point.

Example

Terry owes Ben £10,000, the debt remaining outstanding at Terry's death. In his will, Terry leaves Ben £10,000. Can Ben claim the legacy *and* remain entitled to repayment of the debt from Terry's estate? In such a case equity may well consider that the legacy was intended by Terry to satisfy his obligation towards Ben, and so Ben will not be able to claim the repayment of the debt *and* the legacy. If Ben wishes to take the legacy, he must give up his claim to the debt.

There are a number of situations where the doctrine of satisfaction may be relevant and each will be considered in turn.

Satisfaction of debts by legacies

It is a general rule that a debt is presumed to be satisfied by a legacy of at least an equal amount. It is presumed that the debtor does not intend the creditor to both take the legacy and be repaid the debt. The doctrine does not apply if the debt was incurred after the will was made.

In *Talbott* v *Duke of Shrewsbury* (1714) Prec Ch 394, Sir John Trevor MR said:

[I]f one, being indebted to another in a sum of money, does by his will give him as great, or greater sum of money than the debt amounts to, without taking any notice at all of the debt, then this shall nevertheless be in satisfaction of the debt, so as that he shall not have both the debt and the legacy.

Re Haves [1951] 2 All ER 928

A husband, on his divorce, covenanted to pay his wife £3 a week charged on real property. By his will, he left her an annuity charged on the whole of his estate. The court held that this legacy satisfied the covenant.

However, the general rule can be displaced by a contrary intention on the part of the testator. An obvious example of a contrary intention would be if the testator, having left Ben a legacy of £10,000, said in his will that 'the debt of £10,000 to Ben is to be repaid'. A more general statement, for example, for the payment of all debts and legacies, will also mean that the doctrine will not apply. This is known as the rule in *Chancey's Case* (1717) 1 P Wms 408. This principle has been extended to cover a situation where a testator merely directs that his debts shall be paid without reference to the payment of legacies. (For an example, see *Re Manners* [1949] 2 All ER 201.)

In the vast majority of professionally drafted wills, there will be a direction to pay debts and so the effect of the rule in *Chancey's Case*, as extended, is that satisfaction rarely applies in this context.

Limits on the doctrine

The doctrine of satisfaction is subject to a number of limitations which the courts have created over the course of the doctrine's evolution.

The doctrine will not apply if the legacy is less than the debt, nor if the legacy is in any way less advantageous than the debt. If, for example, the legacy is contingent or conditional, or the amount is uncertain, the doctrine will not apply. If the will makes the legacy payable later than the due date for the debt, there will be no satisfaction. There is some conflict as to the application of the doctrine in a case where no date is specified for the payment of the legacy and the debt was due at the testator's death. The general rule is that legacies should be paid by the end of the executor's year (the year runs from the date of death). Until the year is up no legatee can demand his legacy, whereas the repayment of the debt can be insisted upon at the date of death. It has been argued, for example, in *Re Horlock* [1895] 1 Ch 516, that this makes the legacy less beneficial than the debt and so precludes the operation of the doctrine of satisfaction.

However, in *Re Rattenberry* [1906] 1 Ch 667, Swinfen Eady J put forward the contrary argument that, as a legacy carries interest from the date of death, this makes the legacy as beneficial as the debt.

The latter argument has much to support it. It also has the attraction that if the view in *Re Horlock* is adopted it would effectively mean that satisfaction would never apply to the debt/legacy situation.

The doctrine will not apply if the debt comes into existence after the will is made. It cannot be argued that the testator intended a legacy to satisfy a debt which did not exist when the will was made.

The doctrine does not apply if the gift in the will is one of land.

It should be noted that, if the debt pre-dates the will and the debt is repaid before the testator dies, the creditor cannot claim the legacy. When the debt is repaid, the legacy is adeemed as it is assumed that the only reason for the legacy is to satisfy the debt. There is some dispute as to whether this applies if the legacy is greater than the debt, but it is settled that it applies if the legacy is for the exact amount of the debt.

Satisfaction of legacies by legacies

If a testator leaves two gifts to the same person, can both of the gifts be claimed or is the beneficiary only able to receive one of them? It is, essentially, a matter of construction whether the beneficiary is intended to take one or both the legacies.

If the legacies are in different instruments, then the beneficiary will be presumed to be intended to take both unless the legacies are of exactly the same amount and the reason given for both legacies is the same. In other cases, the beneficiary may claim both legacies unless there is evidence (either from the will or from admissible external evidence) that this would defeat the intention of the testator.

However, if both legacies are contained in the same instrument, then it is far less likely that the beneficiary will be able to take both of them. If the legacies are of the same amount, and either the same motive is expressed for each or no motive is expressed at all, the presumption will be that only one of the legacies was intended. If the legacies are of different amounts, or if different motives are expressed, it will be presumed that the beneficiary was intended to take both of them.

Rule against double portions

The equitable principles applicable in this section are that equity imputes an intention to fulfil an obligation (i.e. the normal basis for satisfaction) and that equity presumes that a father would wish to deal fairly as between his children. It is presumed that a father would not wish his capital to be distributed in a manner which would favour some of his children at the expense of his other children.

Example

Jerry has two children, Elaine and Kosmo. Jerry gives Elaine £10,000 to help her to buy a muffin shop. Jerry dies and in his will he leaves Elaine and Kosmo a legacy of £10,000 each. The *inter vivos* gift to Elaine will almost certainly be considered to be a portion and so although Kosmo will be entitled to his legacy in full, it will be presumed that Jerry would not want to treat his children unequally and so Elaine will not be able to claim any part of her legacy. Thus they will both benefit equally. This is an example of the rule against double portions.

What is a portion?

It appears that the words 'portion' and 'advancement' bear the same meaning in this context. A portion is a provision for a child in discharge, or partial discharge, of the obligation to provide for that child. Often the gift is one of money but gifts of any asset may be classified as portions.

In *Re Cameron (deceased)*; *Phillips v Cameron and Others* [1999] 2 All ER 924 Lindsay J said that 'portion' is not a term of art but it seems to be something that a parent gives to establish a child in life or to make what is called provision for him.

Gifts made on the occasion of marriage or to set the child up in life or to make a permanent provision for the child are the types of transfers which may well be regarded as being portions or advancements (see *Hardy* v *Shaw* [1975] 2 All ER 1052).

Gifts made on marriage will usually be regarded as portions as will gifts made in a will, but in other situations the size of the gift will be important as the cases establish that the provision must be 'substantial'.

The size of the gift in relation to the assets of the donor is important, but in *Re Hayward* [1957] 2 All ER 474 Jenkins LJ stressed that the sum must, of itself, be substantial in order to be a portion. He went on to say that the fact that the gift is a very large proportion of the donor's estate is not by itself conclusive. The courts will say that gifts of small sums are not portions and there is no case in which the courts have added together a number of small gifts so that taken together they are a portion.

When deciding if a transfer is a portion or not, the intention of the parent must be to set the child up in life or to make provision for its future. So, for example, if the transfer is intended to be 'pure bounty' or if it is to satisfy a particular moral obligation there will be no portion.

The relevant question is, 'Was it the donor's intention that the gift is a portion?' Ideally a testator will expressly set out what his intentions are in the will but this is often not done. But in *Re Eardley's Will* (1920) 1 CH 397 it was said that the donor's intention does not need to be expressed; it may be 'irresistibly drawn from all the circumstances of the case'.

In *Kloofman* v *Aylen & Frost* [2013] EWHC 435(CH) the court decided that gifts of £100,000 made to each of two of his three children were not portions as his motives, in part at least, were to repay the daughters for money they had spent in taking care of their father and to finance his future care costs.

Re Cameron (deceased); *Phillips* v *Cameron and Others* [1999] 2 All ER 924 (see below) makes it clear that a payment *may* amount to a portion even though it is not directly received by that child. For example, if a grandfather (A) undertakes to pay the school fees of his grandchild (C), this could well be construed as a portion and as being a benefit to the grandfather's child (B) – the father of C – as it would relieve B of the responsibility for and expenses of providing C with education etc.

Importance of the relationship between the donor and the donee

A gift will not be a portion unless the donor is a parent of the donee or stands *in loco parentis* to the donee. (For more on loco parentis, see below and p. 276.)

Traditionally, portions were gifts by fathers but *Re Cameron (deceased)*; *Phillips* v *Cameron and Others* [1999] 2 All ER 924 establishes that the rule against double portions can apply to gifts made by mothers.

There is a presumption that a gift is a portion if it is made by a parent to her/his legitimate child. This appears not to have been affected by the Family Law Reform Act 1987. No presumption used to arise in the case of a father and an illegitimate child, but it is thought that either this is no longer the case or that very little evidence would be required in such a case to invoke the doctrine. The situation would be the same with a mother and her illegitimate child.

There is a presumption in the case of a gift by one standing *in loco parentis* to the donee. Proof of such a relationship requires evidence that the donor has undertaken to discharge the duty of financial provision that is normally the duty of the parent. The fact that the child's father is still alive, or indeed that the child is still living with its father, does not necessarily prevent another from standing *in loco parentis*. In *Powys* v *Mansfield* (1837) 3 My & Cr 359, a donee made payments for the education and maintenance of the children of his impecunious brother. The donee had arranged a marriage settlement for the brother's daughter. The court held that despite the fact that the daughter lived with her father until her marriage her uncle stood *in loco parentis* to her. It is easier to establish *loco parentis* where there is a (close) blood relationship between the parties.

Ademption of a legacy by a portion

This topic is often referred to as involving satisfaction but in fact the principles involved are those of ademption.

Ademption describes the situation where a testator leaves a specific bequest but the property bequeathed does not form part of his estate at his death – perhaps the property has been sold or has been given away. The general rule is that the gift will fail and the beneficiary will receive nothing, not even the proceeds, if the property has been sold.

If a testator makes a will giving his child a legacy and later gives a portion to the same child it is presumed that the portion was not intended to be in addition to the legacy, which will therefore be adeemed (see *Re Vaux* [1939] 4 All ER 703). If the portion was paid before the will was made, the child is entitled to both the portion and the benefit given by the will.

It is possible to have cases of ademption *pro tanto*. This occurs where the legacy in the will is larger than the amount given by way of the portion. The donee will be able to claim the balance under the will.

It has been decided that while the doctrine can apply to a gift of residue it does not apply if the gift in the will is one of land (see *Davys v Boucher* (1839) 3 Y & C Ex 93).

In *Re Cameron (deceased); Phillips v Cameron and Others* [1999] 2 All ER 924, an unusual question relating to double portions was in issue. The court decided that, for the purposes of the rule against double portions, a gift could be regarded as being for the benefit of a child of the donor even if the child of the donor did not receive it, and it was thus capable of being a portion. In other words, while the rule required there to be two portions which benefited the same person, a gift could be for a person's benefit even though it was not given directly to him and did not come into his hands.

The instant case involved a grandparent (A), one of his children (B) and B's child (C) – the grandchild of A. While he was alive the grandfather, A, paid the school fees of his grandchild, C. B was a residuary beneficiary under A's will. It was held that the *inter vivos* gift by a grandparent A for the benefit of a grandchild C could be taken to be for the benefit of the grandchild's parent, B, i.e. for the benefit of the donor's child. The justification for this is that the *inter vivos* gift will benefit the child, B, as it will, *pro tanto*, discharge the parent B's duty to maintain the grandchild, C, and to provide for his education. So the payment by the grandfather, A, of the school fees of the grandchild, C, and a gift of a share in the residue of the grandfather's will to the grandchild's father, B, gave rise to a double portion. The gift in the will and the *inter vivos* provision for the education of the grandchild, C, were such that it was possible to regard the donor, A, as likely to have regarded both gifts as making substantial provisions, both of which were intended to provide a substantial benefit to the same person, i.e. the donor's child, B. So, both gifts were portions in favour of the child, B, and the rule against double portions applied. As there was no evidence to rebut the rule, the *inter vivos* provision *pro tanto* adeemed the child's (B's) benefit under the will.

Race v Race (2002) LTL 9/7/2002 is a first-instance decision which is an example of the presumption against double portions and the satisfaction of a gift in a will by an *inter vivos* gift: in other words, the ademption of a testamentary provision by an *inter vivos* gift made after the execution of the will.

A key issue in the case was whether or not the rule against double portions applied to land. A father made a will providing that his daughter could live in his pub rent-free for as long as she wanted, after which it would be sold and the proceeds would be divided between the claimant (the testator's son) and the daughter equally. Subsequently, the father executed a deed of gift conveying the pub to himself and his daughter as beneficial tenants in common. The key question in the case was whether or not this subsequent, *inter vivos*, gift operated to adeem the daughter's half share in the residue under the will. It was held that both the gift in the will and the *inter vivos* gift amounted to 'portions'. This was as distinct from 'pure bounty' and 'giving as a present'. The rule against double portions depended on the presumed intention of the testator and was rebuttable. *Prima facie*, the rule against double portions would operate, under which rule the testamentary gift would be adeemed.

The judge (HH Judge John Behrens) considered that it was difficult to see why there should be any distinction between gifts of realty and gifts of personalty. There was, the judge considered, no rule of law that the rule against double portions did not apply to land. Thus, there was a presumption in this case that the deed of gift of land was an acceleration of the bequest in the will and the presumption had not been rebutted.

Satisfaction of a portion debt by a legacy

If a binding obligation to give a portion arises and the debtor later gives to the child a legacy of the same or of a greater amount, then a presumption will arise that the legacy was intended to satisfy the portion debt. The obligation may arise, for example, if the father enters into a covenant to make provision for a child. If the legacy is less than the debt, satisfaction *pro tanto* will take place.

In this situation, the child has a choice to make: he can either elect to enforce the portion debt or to take under the will.

Satisfaction of a portion debt by a later portion

If an obligation to give a portion arises, and the father later makes some other provision for that child, it is presumed that this latter provision is intended to be in satisfaction of the portion debt. If the latter provision is a portion, then the presumption against double portions will apply and the original debt is treated as having been discharged.

Strangers must not benefit

The doctrine will not be applied if to do so would benefit a stranger. The basis of the doctrine is that the children should all be treated fairly, and there is no question of a stranger being able to benefit from an application of the doctrine. Strangers are any people apart from those for whose benefit the doctrine was developed. In other words, satisfaction will not apply if it would work to the benefit of people other than a father's children or children to whom an individual stood *in loco parentis*. In this context, a stranger will include the wife of the donor or his grandchildren.

In **Re Heather** [1906] 2 Ch 230, a testator left £3,000 to his adopted daughter, Mary, and divided the rest of his property between Mary and another. The testator had made several gifts during his lifetime to Mary, including one of £1,000. The court held that the doctrine of satisfaction had no application in the case. First, the court decided that the £1,000 was not a portion. Secondly, even if it had been a portion, it would not have been satisfied by the legacy or the gift of residue. The result of applying the doctrine would have been to increase the benefits flowing to the other residuary beneficiary and the court thought that was not an appropriate application of satisfaction. The other beneficiary was a stranger, not one of those for whose benefit the doctrine was designed.

Rebutting the presumptions

The key question is always, 'What is the intention of the father?', and the presumption of satisfaction can be rebutted by either intrinsic or extrinsic evidence of the father's intention.

Performance

Objective 4

The equitable doctrine of performance is based on the maxim that equity imputes an intention to fulfil an obligation.

In **Tubbs v Broadwood** (1831) 2 Russ & M 487, Lord Brougham said: 'a person is to be presumed to do that which he is bound to do; and if he has done anything, that he has done it in pursuance of his obligation.'

Performance and satisfaction are often linked together and at first sight they do seem very similar concepts. However, there are important differences between them. Satisfaction deals with the possibility that a person may be intending to fulfil an obligation by doing something different, e.g. satisfying a debt by a legacy. Performance, on the other hand, deals with the possibility that an act was intended to constitute a step towards fulfilling an obligation. For example, if a husband has covenanted to settle property on his wife and he buys the property but does not transfer it into a settlement, then it may well be that under the doctrine of performance he will be considered to have bought the property as a step towards fulfilling his obligation. If this is the case, then the property will be bound by the covenant.

Obligation to purchase and settle land

This is one of the earliest applications of the doctrine and usually involves a husband entering into a covenant under which he promises to buy land which will be transferred to the trustees of his marriage settlement to be held on the trusts of that settlement for the benefit of the parties to the marriage and their issue. In the classic example, the land is bought but it is not transferred to the trustees. When the husband dies the problem to be solved is: to whom does the land belong?

Lechmere v *Lady Lechmere* (1735) Cast Talb 80

Lord Lechmere covenanted to pay out £30,000 to purchase and settle, within one year of his marriage, freehold lands in fee simple in possession. When Lord Lechmere died, he had not complied with the covenant but he had bought some land and had contracted to buy some more. Some of the property which he bought was freehold land and this was held to constitute a partial performance of the covenant and so was regarded as being within the settlement. The court decided that the doctrine of satisfaction applied even though the land had not been bought within one year of the marriage as promised. Additionally, freehold land which the husband contracted to buy after executing the covenant was held to be in satisfaction of the obligation. Other property which consisted of reversionary interests in freehold land and life interests in freehold land was not regarded as being bought in performance of the covenant. This was property of a different nature from fee simple land in possession, which was what Lord Lechmere had promised to settle. The court also held that the property owned by Lord Lechmere at the date of the covenant could not be regarded under the doctrine as being a performance of a covenant to buy future property.

A number of points may be taken from the case. First, it is possible for there to be *pro tanto* performance if part only of the property covered by the covenant is bought. Also, a covenant to buy and settle property of a specified nature, e.g. freehold land, will not be performed by the purchase of property of a different nature, e.g. leasehold land. A covenant to buy future property is not considered to be performed by the purchase or acquisition of property before the covenant was made. The non-compliance with a time limit will not prevent the doctrine from operating.

The doctrine also applies where the covenant requires the payment of money to trustees to be used to buy property and the covenantor buys property (of that description) himself.

Covenant to leave money by will

If a person enters into a covenant to leave property by will to an individual, what is the position if this is not done but the individual receives benefits on the intestacy of the covenantor? Is it possible for the individual to claim the property under the intestacy rules and enforce the covenant against the estate of the deceased? Usually, the covenant will be considered to have been performed *pro tanto* by virtue of the benefits obtained under the intestacy rules, and so the individual cannot claim both the benefit under the intestacy rules in full and enforce the covenant.

If the amount received is less than what was promised, this will be treated as performance *pro tanto*. This means that the balance can be sued for.

Blandy v Widmore (1715) 1 P Wms 324

A husband covenanted to leave his wife £620 in his will. He later died intestate. Under the intestacy rules the wife received more than £620. The court held that the wife was not entitled to the benefits under the intestacy rules and to enforce the covenant. The covenant was treated as having been performed.

However, the position is very different if the covenant has already been broken when the covenantor dies.

Oliver v Brickland (1732) cited 3 Atk 422

A husband covenanted to pay his wife a sum of money within two years of their marriage. He did not pay over the money and more than two years later he died intestate. The wife received benefits under the intestacy rules, which exceeded the amount the husband had promised to pay her. The court decided that there was no performance. The wife was entitled both to the benefits under the intestacy rules and to enforce the covenant. The reason for this was that before the husband died the covenant had been broken and at that time the wife acquired a debt.

Summary

- The doctrine of conversion is based on the maxim that equity looks on as done that which ought to be done.

- Where there is a duty to convert realty to personalty or vice versa, equity regards the property to be in its converted form as soon as the duty arises, whether or not the actual conversion has taken place.

- This doctrine has been significantly affected by the Trusts of Land and Appointment of Trustees Act 1996 which abolishes the application of the doctrine to a range of situations.

- The consequences of a failure of conversion vary according to whether the failure is total or partial.

- Reconversion takes place where a previous notional conversion is reversed and the property is then regarded as being in its original state.

- The doctrine of election is based on the equitable doctrine that no one is allowed to blow hot and cold at the same time.

- Election usually arises in the context of gifts by will but it can apply to *inter vivos* gifts. Election arises, for example, where the donor gives some of his own property to X and purports to give some of X's property to Y. It is presumed that the donor would not want X to both keep his own property and so disappoint Y and take the gift of the donor's property in full. X must elect to take either under or against the disposition.

- The doctrine of satisfaction is based on the maxim that equity imputes an intention to fulfil an obligation.

- The doctrine applies in a number of situations. For example, if a testator owes £X and makes a will leaving a legacy of £X to the creditor, it is presumed that the testator intends the legacy to 'pay off' or satisfy the debt. The creditor is not able to claim both the legacy and payment of the debt from the estate. The doctrine may also be applicable if the testator leaves two legacies to the same person. Satisfaction may also apply if a father makes an *inter vivos* provision for one of his children, having made a will leaving a legacy to that child. It is assumed that the testator would not intend the child to receive both the legacy and the *inter vivos* gift.

- The doctrine of performance is based on the maxim that equity imputes an intention to fulfil an obligation.

- Under the doctrine of performance an action is presumed to be done as a step towards satisfying an obligation.

Further reading

Election

E Bennett Histed, 'Election in equity: the myth of mistake' (1998) 114 LQR 621.
Discusses the difficulty in modern times to understand the true basis of the doctrine and its modern applications.

J Bird and E Saunders, '*Scarfe* v *Matthews*' PCB (2013) 1, 34–8.
Discusses *Scarfe* v *Matthews* and whether or not the doctrine of election applied.

A Bruce-Smith and J Summers, 'Election fever' (2009) 107 TEL & TJ 24–6.
Discusses *Frear* v *Frear* and reviews case law on election.

N Crago, 'Mistakes in wills and election in equity' (1990) 106 LQR 487.
Discusses the fact that in English law the doctrine can apply where the testator mistakenly thinks he owns the property he leaves to the beneficiary, and where he knows he does not own it. Also discusses the basis of the doctrine.

P J Millett, 'Response' (1990) 106 LQR 571; N Crago [reply by author] (1990) 106 LQR 572.
These two articles represent an exchange of views between Millet and Crago as to the relevance today of election based on mistake of the testator regarding his ownership of property.

Satisfaction

M Hodson, 'Ascertain the testator's true intentions' (2013) TEL & TJ 146, May, 14–17.
Discusses *Kloofman v Aylen & Frost* [2013] EWHC 435 (CH), on the presumption against double portions. Discusses the role of intention in rebutting the presumption.

19

Equitable remedies

Objectives

After reading this chapter, you should:

1. Have knowledge in outline of the different types of injunctions and the principles upon which they may be granted.
2. Understand the particular rules applying to interim injunctions.
3. Understand the range of defences that may be available to the granting of an injunction.
4. Be aware in outline of the types of interest that may be protected by an injunction.
5. Have detailed knowledge of the rules for the granting of search orders and freezing injunctions.
6. Understand the principles upon which damages may be granted in lieu of an injunction.
7. Be familiar with the basic principles for the granting of the decree of specific performance.
8. Be aware of the nature of rescission and the role of undue influence.
9. Have an outline knowledge of rectification.

The power of equity to act *in personam*, against the defendant, allowed the development of a range of remedies, more flexible than those of the common law, in the form of various orders addressed to a party and backed up by the threat of imprisonment for contempt if those orders were not obeyed. Such orders were imposed on the individual and as such were discretionary, dependent in particular on whether the conscience of the party was affected, and whether the plaintiff in turn 'deserved' the benefit of such an order. Such remedies may be final, representing the conclusion of the litigation, or may be interlocutory, holding actions pending trial, or may be ancillary, procedural devices in support of the substantive proceedings. The most important of these remedies are outlined below.

Injunctions

 ## Introduction

Objective
1

An injunction is a court order directing a person to do or refrain from doing a specified act. Injunctions may be granted by the High Court 'in all cases in which it appears just and convenient to do so' (Senior Courts Act 1981 s 37(1)). Under s 38 of the County Court Act 1984, as amended by the Courts and Legal Services Act 1990, the County Court is given the same powers as the High Court to make orders, save for certain specific exceptions. It may thus grant injunctions, with the exception of search (formerly Anton Piller) orders and freezing (formerly *Mareva*) injunctions, described below.

The power of the courts today to grant injunctions derives from the former jurisdiction of the Court of Chancery, and it is clear that, despite the wide wording of the Senior Courts Act 1981, referred to above, the jurisdiction may be exercised only on settled legal principles. It was held in the nineteenth century that the Judicature Acts 1873–75 had not given the new Supreme Court any wider jurisdiction than that which had previously been available in Chancery, or, by statute, in the common law courts. More recently, Lord Donaldson, in *Parker* v *Camden London Borough Council* [1985] 2 All ER 141, indicated that the modern court should not be hidebound by such a view:

> For my part I do not accept the pre-Judicature Act practices of the Court of Chancery or any other court should still rule us from their graves . . .
>
> As I see the matter the jurisdiction, as a jurisdiction, is quite general and, in terms, unlimited. Nevertheless it has to be exercised judicially and with due regard to authorities which are binding on the court.

After considering the authority on the particular point before him – which indicated that, where Parliament had imposed powers and duties on a particular body, the court should not be quick to assume those powers itself by, in this instance, appointing a receiver – he commented on the authority: '[I]ts reasoning does not depend on pre-1873 practices but on a clear view that parliamentary intentions so expressed should be respected.' It is submitted that these remarks, though made in a specific context, could serve as a guide to the exercise of jurisdiction to grant injunctions generally.

In *South Carolina Insurance* v *Assurantie Maatschappij* [1986] 3 All ER 487, Lord Brandon indicated that there were two basic situations where an injunction might be granted:

> The effect of these authorities, so far as is material to the present case, can be summarised by saying that the power of the High Court to grant injunctions is, subject to two exceptions to which I shall refer shortly, limited to two situations. Situation (1) is when one party to an action can show that the other party has either invaded, or threatens to invade, a legal or equitable right of the former for the enforcement of which the latter is amenable to the jurisdiction of the court. Situation (2) is where one party to an action has behaved, or threatens to behave, in a manner which is unconscionable.

Lord Goff, in the same case, took a more flexible view of the jurisdiction, however:

> I am reluctant to accept the proposition that the power to grant injunctions is restricted to certain exclusive categories. That power is unfettered by statute; and it is impossible to foresee every circumstance in which it may be thought right to make the remedy available.

Injunctions come in a number of forms: they may be prohibitory, that is to say forbidding certain conduct or ordering the defendant to cease certain conduct, or they may more occasionally be mandatory, ordering certain conduct, often ordering the undoing of something which interferes with another's rights, or they may be granted *quia timet*, to restrain conduct before it happens where it is expected to cause the claimant loss. They may be perpetual, that is final and permanent, or they may be interim, granted temporarily to restrain the defendant's conduct pending a full hearing of the matter. They may even, in cases of emergency, be granted *ex parte*, that is without the other party's case being heard, where there is not time to bring the matter even to an interim hearing.

Principles governing the grant of injunctions

Perpetual (final) injunctions

It is in the nature of an injunction, being an equitable remedy, that its grant is discretionary. Even if a legal right is infringed, the court may choose not to grant an injunction. It will be granted only where the common law remedies are inadequate, and in particular where damages would not be sufficient, in the sense that they will not provide adequate compensation, either because the loss cannot be quantified in money terms or perhaps where the damage is a continuing one which would require repeated claims. Neither will equity grant an injunction where it would be pointless to do so, as where the damaging conduct has already occurred and cannot be undone, as in a breach of confidence. The court may also choose in appropriate cases to delay the coming into effect of the injunction until the defendant has had time to remedy the conduct complained of.

Mandatory injunctions

These will be granted with particular discretion because they impose a duty of positive action on the defendant and often require constant supervision. Thus, in **Redland Bricks v Morris**, the House of Lords discharged the injunction.

Redland Bricks v Morris [1969] 2 All ER 576

In this case the defendants' clay diggings had caused a landslip which had removed a part of the plaintiff's land, which was used as a market garden, rendering it useless to the plaintiff. An injunction had been granted by the County Court, ordering the defendant to restore the land.

The House of Lords recognised the difference of approach between prohibitory and mandatory injunctions. As Lord Upjohn said: 'The grant of a mandatory injunction is, of course, entirely discretionary, and unlike a negative injunction can never be "as of course".'

This perhaps suggests that it is better for the defendant to go ahead and cause the damage, because the court is unlikely to order him to act positively to undo the damage, whereas, if he is sued before the damage occurs, a prohibitory injunction is very likely to be granted to stop his future behaviour. However, in this case the court was moved by the fact that the defendants, though acting wrongly, were merely negligent: they believed that their work would not cause damage, but it did. They had not set out deliberately or maliciously to cause the damage. If they had, Lord Upjohn said that a mandatory injunction might be granted, even if the cost of carrying it out was out of all proportion to the damage caused. Here, however, the defendants had not acted maliciously, so the cost to them of a mandatory injunction had to be considered. The likely cost of restoring the plaintiff's land was £30,000, whereas the land was worth only £12,000, and the damaged part only about £1,500. Also, the court felt that the injunction granted by the County Court judge was virtually open-ended: the defendants did not know exactly what they had to do. The court held that a mandatory injunction should be in such terms that the defendant must know precisely what he must do to comply.

Quia timet injunctions

Here no harm has yet occurred and so the court must be convinced that there is proof of imminent danger of substantial harm. As Lord Upjohn stated in **Redland Bricks v Morris** (above), the claimant must show a very strong probability that grave damage will accrue to him in the future.

This has been criticised as placing too high a burden on the plaintiff. Thus in **Hooper v Rogers** [1974] 3 All ER 417, though the risk of future damage was proved to be high, Russell LJ criticised the 'strong probability' requirement: 'It seems to me that the degree of probability of future injury is not an absolute standard: what is aimed at is justice between the parties, having regard to all the circumstances.' The injunction should not be sought prematurely, but as in that case no other step than to seek an injunction could be taken by the plaintiff, even though subsidence to the plaintiff's house might not occur for many years as a result of the defendant's removal of support, an injunction could have been granted in this situation. Thus damages could be awarded in lieu.

Interim injunctions

Objective 2

These were formerly known as interlocutory injunctions and are so described in many of the leading cases. The term 'interim injunction' has been adopted in the Civil Procedure Rules.

While the considerations set out in the previous section may be treated as of general application, it is apparent that further considerations must operate in the case of interim injunctions. Since they are granted at an interim stage, before the final determination of the rights of the case, it follows that nothing should be done, and that an injunction should not be granted, which will prejudice that final outcome or permanently damage the position of the parties at this early stage. Therefore, when considering whether to grant an interim injunction the court must first be satisfied, in the words of Lord Diplock in **American Cyanamid v Ethicon** [1975] 1 All ER 504, that there is a serious question to be tried. If there is, then the court must be satisfied that the balance of convenience is in favour of granting an injunction. The claimant will also be required to give an undertaking to pay damages to the defendant for any loss he suffers from the grant of the interim injunction if it turns out, at the full trial, that the claimant is not entitled to restrain the defendant's conduct in this way.

Some factors which should be taken into account in determining the balance of convenience were identified by Lord Diplock, and have subsequently been itemised by Browne LJ in **Fellowes v Fisher** [1975] 2 All ER 829 at 840:

1. As to that [i.e. the balance of convenience], the governing principle is that the court should first consider whether, if the plaintiff succeeds at trial, he would be adequately compensated by damages for any loss caused by the refusal to grant an [interim] injunction.

   If damages . . . would be adequate remedy and the defendant would be in a position to pay them, no [interim] injunction should be granted, however strong the plaintiff's claim appeared to be at that stage.

2. If on the other hand damages would not be an adequate remedy, the court should then consider whether, if the injunction were granted, the defendant would be adequately compensated under the plaintiff's undertaking as to damages.

    If damages in the measure recoverable under such an undertaking would be an adequate remedy and the plaintiff would be in a financial position to pay them, there would be no reason on this ground to refuse an [interim] injunction.

3. It is where there is doubt as to the adequacy of the respective remedies in damages . . . that the question of balance of convenience arises. It would be unwise to attempt even to list all the various factors which will need to be taken into consideration in deciding where the balance lies, let alone to suggest the relative weight to be attached to them. These will vary from case to case.

4. Where other factors appear to be evenly balanced it is the counsel of prudence to take such measures as are calculated to preserve the *status quo*.

5. The extent to which the disadvantages to each party would be incapable of being compensated in damages in the event of his succeeding at trial is always a significant factor in assessing where the balance of convenience lies.

6. [I]f the extent of the compensatable disadvantage to each party would not differ widely, it may not be improper to take account in tipping the balance [of] the relative strength of each party's case . . . This, however, should only be done when it is apparent on the facts . . . that the strength of one party's case is disproportionate to that of the other party.

7. [I]n addition to [the factors] to which I have referred, there may be many other special factors to be taken into consideration in the particular circumstances of individual cases.

In deciding whether to grant an interim injunction, then, it appears that the court should consider the interests of the two parties and whether they could be adequately compensated by damages if either an injunction is not granted and the claimant ultimately wins the case, or an injunction is granted but the claimant ultimately loses. Where this question is evenly balanced, then the court may look at all other relevant factors, including the strength of the parties' cases, if one is much stronger than the other, to see where the balance of convenience lies. If this too produces an even balance, then the general approach should be to maintain the *status quo*. This analysis is, however, subject to the presence of special factors in particular cases. The result of this approach has, however, been that cases are nearly always decided on the balance of convenience, with little if any consideration of the merits of the plaintiff's case. The matter was further considered by Laddie J in *Series 5 Software* v *Clarke*.

Series 5 Software v *Clarke* [1996] 1 All ER 853

This case concerned computer software. The plaintiff was a company involved in development of computer software. The defendants were employees of the company. One day they removed certain equipment from the plaintiff's premises, including a valuable software package, and the plaintiff's company accounts and client mailing lists. The defendants claimed they had not been paid and intended to hold the seized equipment and records etc. to force the plaintiff to pay them. The plaintiff claimed the defendants were plagiarising the software package and attempting to sell it direct to their customers, and sought injunctions forbidding the defendants from contacting any of the plaintiff's clients or revealing its trade secrets. The equipment was returned by court order, but Laddie J decided not to grant the plaintiff the injunction sought. He took the view that the strength of the plaintiff's case could not be ignored when deciding to award interim relief. Here the plaintiff's case that the defendants were plagiarising was weak and unsubstantiated. Also, it had delayed in taking proceedings and the balance of convenience did not justify awarding an injunction.

Recognising that the adequacy of damages will rarely settle the matter, and that the balance of convenience will have to be considered in most cases, he went on to reinterpret *Cyanamid* and concluded that Lord Diplock had not intended to make the radical change he is usually assumed to have made. In particular, Laddie J thought that Lord Diplock did not intend to exclude the court from considering the strength of the plaintiff's case. This issue is inherent in the balance of convenience; as he said: 'The courts would be less willing to subject the plaintiff to the risk of irrecoverable loss which would befall him if an [interim] injunction were refused in those cases where it is thought he was likely to win at the trial than in those cases where it is thought he was likely to lose.' Accordingly, Laddie J concluded that, in deciding whether to grant interim relief, the court should bear in mind: (1) the grant of an interim injunction is a matter of discretion and depended on all the facts of the case; (2) there are no fixed rules as to when an injunction should be granted. The relief must be kept flexible; (3) because of the practice adopted on the hearing of applications for interim relief, the court should rarely attempt to resolve complex issues of disputed fact or law; (4) major factors the court should bear in mind are (a) the extent to which damages are likely to be an adequate remedy for each party and the ability of the other party to pay, (b) the balance of convenience, (c) the maintenance of the *status quo*, and (d) any clear view the court may reach as to the relative strength of the parties' cases.

Similarly, the *Cyanamid* guidelines will not be appropriate in the case of mandatory interim injunctions, where, according to *Shepherd Homes v Sandham* [1970] 3 All ER 402, the court will have to feel a 'high degree of assurance' that the plaintiff will succeed in the full hearing before it will require the defendant to take positive action. This observation of Megarry J has been approved by the Court of Appeal in cases such as *Locobail International Finance v Agroexport* [1986] 1 All ER 901, where it was held not to be affected by the rule formulated in *American Cyanamid*.

Furthermore, even in the case of prohibitory interim injunctions, the court must be aware of the effect of the order. In most situations, as in *American Cyanamid* itself, the injunction is merely a holding action pending trial, but, where it has the effect of putting an end to the action altogether, the issue should be decided upon the broad principle: 'what can the court do in its best endeavour to avoid injustice' (*per* Eveleigh LJ in *Cayne v Global Natural Resources* [1984] 1 All ER 225). Consideration of the balance of convenience pending trial is clearly irrelevant if there is to be no trial.

Cambridge Nutrition v BBC [1990] 3 All ER 523

Cayne was cited in this later case, in which an interim injunction was sought to stop the BBC from broadcasting a programme about the plaintiffs, allegedly in breach of contract. The plaintiffs claimed that they had a contract with the BBC which included the term that the programme would not be broadcast until after the publication of a government report on medical aspects of a diet that the plaintiffs manufactured. The nature of the programme was such that it was only appropriate for broadcast before the publication. In other words, if the plaintiffs obtained an interim injunction, this would render the programme useless and 'kill the story'. In his judgment, Kerr LJ stressed this latter point. He stated that *Cyanamid* was only a set of guidelines; the only legal principle was the statutory power of the court to grant injunctions when it is just and convenient to do so. Citing *Cayne*, among other cases, Kerr LJ concluded that this was not an appropriate case for *Cyanamid* guidelines because 'the crucial issues between the parties do not depend on trial, but solely or mainly on the grant or refusal of [interim] relief'. An injunction was denied because the plaintiffs could not make out the *prima facie* case: in fact, it seemed unlikely that the contract the plaintiffs alleged had ever been made.

Fundamentally, therefore, the defendant should not be precluded by injunction from disputing the plaintiff's claim at trial, and accordingly an injunction will not be granted if it has this effect.

Injunctions and the Human Rights Act 1998

Since the coming into force of the Human Rights Act 1998 on 2 October 2000, the courts, when granting injunctions, or indeed any remedy, must have regard for the freedoms that the Act purports to uphold, i.e. those contained in the European Convention on Human Rights. Thus, in the context of injunctions restraining publication, the courts must have regard to the right of freedom of expression. Section 12 of the Act applies where the court is considering whether to grant any relief which, if granted, might affect the exercise of the Convention right to freedom of expression. Section 12(3) provides:

> No such relief is to be granted so as to restrain publication before trial unless the court is satisfied that the applicant is likely to establish that publication should not be allowed.

Section 12(4) further provides:

> The court must have particular regard to the importance of the Convention right to freedom of expression and, where the proceedings relate to material which the respondent claims, or which appear to the court to be journalistic, literary or artistic material (or to conduct connected with such material), to –
>
> (a) the extent to which –
>   (i)   the material has, or is about to become available to the public; or
>   (ii) it is, or would be, in the public interest for the material to be published;
> (b) any relevant privacy code.

These issues were considered in *Douglas v Hello! Ltd* [2001] 2 All ER 289, in which a film actor sought to restrain publication of photographs of his wedding on the grounds of privacy. The term 'likely' in s 12(3) has been interpreted to mean 'more likely than not' in *Cream Holdings Ltd v Banerjee* [2004] UKHL 44; [2005] 1 AC 253, and accordingly it is generally assumed that freedom of expression is paramount and hence an interim injunction will not be granted to protect privacy, unless the applicant convinces the court that he is more likely than not to win his claim for privacy at trial. This is clearly a higher standard than the normal 'serious case to be tried' requirement of *American Cyanamid*.

In *Greene v Associated Newspapers* [2004] EWCA Civ 1462; [2005] QB 972, however, the Court of Appeal rejected this test in libel cases and applied the older test; if the defendant asserts that he will prove the truth of his statement, then no interim injunction to prevent publication will be granted unless it is obvious that the defendant's claim will fail.

Defences to claims for injunctions

Delay

Objective 3

The court may refuse to grant an injunction if the claimant has delayed unreasonably in seeking the order. This may apply under the doctrine of laches even if the claim is not statute-barred. Obviously, the amount of delay which is acceptable for an interim injunction is likely to be much less than for a permanent one.

Delay in seeking a remedy was certainly one reason why it would have been oppressive to the defendant to impose an injunction in the case of *Jaggard v Sawyer* [1995] 2 All ER 189 (see below, 'Damages in lieu of injunction'), but, according to the Court of Appeal in

Mortimer v *Bailey* [2005] 2 P& CR 175, it is doubtful whether a person who did not seek an interlocutory injunction as soon as he knew that a building was being erected on neighbouring land, but who had made it clear that he objected to that construction as a breach of covenant, and who subsequently commenced proceedings, was barred from obtaining a final injunction.

Acquiescence

This very often occurs with delay, for delay may be evidence that the plaintiff has accepted the interference with his rights. Acquiescence may, however, occur even where there is no delay: evidence of acquiescence will be a matter of fact.

Hardship

Hardship to the defendant will be taken into account, particularly in the case of mandatory injunctions, and is likely to be of more importance in interim proceedings.

Plaintiff's conduct

For more on the effect of the claimant's conduct, see Chapter 3 (at p. 54).

As an injunction is discretionary, many factors may influence the court, one being whether the claimant deserves the remedy. The claimant must therefore come to court with clean hands, though uncleanness will necessarily have to be something relating to the matter for which the injunction is being sought and not merely general turpitude.

Public benefit

The use of injunctions is often criticised for offering undue protection to private rights at the expense of wider public interests, and the classic view of the courts is that to award damages instead is to allow the defendant to 'buy' the right to commit a wrong.

Thus, in ***Pennington* v *Brinscop Coal*** (1877) 5 Ch D 769 compliance with the injunction would force the defendant to close their business at a cost of over £190,000, whereas the loss to the plaintiff was, at most, £100 per annum. The case concerned pollution of the plaintiff's water by discharge from the defendant's mines. Having stated that the damage to plaintiff was 'by no means inconsiderable' Fry J continued:

> It has been suggested that there are no known modes of purifying the defendant's water, and that obedience to the injunction will be impossible, or possible only by stopping the defendant's works and throwing out of employment a large number of workmen. I cannot yield to these suggestions, nor can I find any such balance of convenience resulting from the granting of the injunction as would have induced me to refuse it.

Similarly, in ***Shelfer* v *City of London Lighting*** [1895] 1 Ch 287, the public interest in electricity generation was not allowed to override the private interest in quiet enjoyment of the plaintiff's premises.

In ***Kennaway* v *Thompson*** [1980] 3 All ER 329 it was argued that the issue of the public interest in watching or taking part in powerboat racing should be taken into account. Lawton LJ referred to Lindley LJ in ***Shelfer***:

> Neither has the circumstance of the wrongdoer being in some senses a public benefactor ever been considered a sufficient reason for refusing to protect by injunction an individual whose rights are being persistently infringed.

It is worth noting, though, that, although the court will not refuse an injunction, it may nevertheless qualify it in some way. Most often it may suspend its operation for a time, in order to allow the defendant to put his house in order. Thus, in *Pride of Derby* v *British Celanese* [1953] 1 All ER 179, the injunction against D to stop discharging effluent into the river was suspended for two years.

In *Kennaway* v *Thompson*, the injunction was granted, but on limited terms: the club was permitted to continue powerboat racing, but on very specific conditions: the number of boats was limited, as was the permitted decibel noise level, but a number of international, national and club competitions were permitted to be held, over a total of ten days, which were not subject to the other restrictions.

These kinds of restrictions have been described as: 'An uneasy compromise between the traditional fervour for the injunction as the appropriate remedy, and the realisation that an unlimited and immediate injunction may have undesirable effects' (Troman (1982) CLJ 87 at 95).

Though the injunction was qualified in *Kennaway*, Lawton LJ in that case took the opportunity to reassert the basic principle in *Shelfer*, which gives primacy to the individual interest. He considered the earlier case of *Miller* v *Jackson* [1977] QB 966, in which the Court of Appeal refused an injunction to stop the use of a cricket ground; Lord Denning's reasoning was arguably to give precedence to the public interest in that case, but he was in the minority. Cumming-Bruce LJ also felt that an injunction was inappropriate on more limited grounds, but he, along with Geoffrey-Lane LJ, recognised that the damage to the neighbouring gardens constituted a nuisance by the cricket club. Accordingly, no clear majority view emerged in *Miller* on the role of public interest in determining nuisance or the award of injunctions. Recently in *Coventry (t/a RDC Promotions)* v *Lawrence* [2014] UKSC 13; [2014] 2 All ER 622, the Supreme Court has recognised the importance of the public interest as a possible ground for refusing an injunction and granting damages instead (see further below at p. 570).

Situations where an injunction may be granted: the types of interest protected

Objective
4

It will, in general, be necessary for a private individual to show some legal or equitable right before the courts will grant an injunction to protect it. Such a right may arise not only in the English courts but also in the courts of other European Union members (see the Civil Jurisdiction and Judgments Act 1982, considered further below, under 'Freezing injunctions').

Where the plaintiff does not have some right recognised in either law or equity, the court cannot protect something it does not recognise. Thus, in *Paton* v *Trustees of British Pregnancy Advisory Service* [1978] 2 All ER 987, the court would not grant an injunction to a husband to prevent his wife having a legal abortion because he had no recognised right that was being infringed. At the same time, however, it is apparent that the law will develop to recognise new rights in particular cases. Many rights are already recognised and situations accepted where injunctions may be granted, and there is nothing to prevent the courts expanding these situations.

It appears that such rights must be private ones and that in general the private individual has no *locus standi* to seek an injunction to protect a public right, such as one protected solely by the criminal law. Here, however, the Attorney-General may seek an injunction. This may be upon the information of a member of the public: a 'relator action' such as may be taken, for example, in cases of public nuisance. Alternatively, the Attorney-General may act *ex officio* on his own initiative. The decision to seek an injunction or not in such a case is his alone, for which he is accountable to Parliament. It was established in *Gouriet* v

Union of Post Office Workers [1977] 3 All ER 70 that a private individual has no *locus standi* to challenge the Attorney-General's decision not to seek an injunction to prevent a breach of the criminal law: to lay the offender open to liability for contempt of court for disobeying an injunction, as well as criminal prosecution for the original offence creates an unacceptable double jeopardy and introduces civil standards of proof into what is essentially a criminal matter. Where the Attorney-General does act, however, an injunction will almost always be granted wherever the criminal sanction is inadequate or where an injunction is the only effective way to protect the public interest. Since it is public interests that are involved, it will not usually be necessary to consider balancing interests or the plaintiff's conduct.

The private individual, then, may seek an injunction in support of a wide range of private rights recognised either in law or equity. Among the wrongs he may prevent are breaches of contract, breaches of trust and torts. Some examples may be mentioned. In the case of *Lumley* v *Wagner* (1851) 1 De GM& G 604, an injunction was issued to restrain breach of the negative terms of a service contract, to the effect that the defendant would not sing for anyone else, though she could not be made to perform her positive undertaking to sing for the plaintiff. In *Waller* v *Waller* [1967] 1 All ER 305, a husband who was the legal owner of a house held on trust jointly for himself and his wife was restrained by injunction from breach of trust in selling the house without her agreement. In *Frank Reddaway & Co Ltd* v *George Banham & Co Ltd* [1896] AC 199, a *quia timet* injunction was granted to prevent the defendant using the name 'camel hair belting' to describe his product, a term which had come to mean exclusively the plaintiff's product, thus passing it off as the plaintiff's, to the plaintiff's potential loss. Injunctions may also be sought to prevent breaches of confidence: e.g. in *X* v *Y* [1988] 2 All ER 648, to prevent a newspaper from publishing details concerning doctors suffering from AIDS, the court being satisfied that the balance of public interest was in favour of restraint. Injunctions may also be available in family matters (e.g. to exclude one spouse from the matrimonial home), and against public bodies (e.g. to prevent unlawful expulsion from a trade union). Injunctions may even be brought to restrain judicial proceedings in the inferior courts, though not to restrain the legislative functions of Parliament.

Two particular uses of injunctions in procedural matters should also be noted: the search (formerly *Anton Piller*) order to prevent the destruction of evidence and the freezing (formerly *Mareva*) injunction to prevent assets being removed from the jurisdiction.

Enforcement of negative terms of contracts

The prohibitory injunction is regarded as the primary remedy for breach of a negative covenant: that is to say, it is the first choice, and damages will rarely be regarded as adequate. This was classically stated by Lord Cairns in *Doherty* v *Allman* (1878) 3 App Cas 709 at 720:

> [I]f there is a negative covenant, I apprehend, according to well settled practice, a Court of Equity would have no discretion to exercise. If parties, for valuable consideration, with their eyes open, contract that a particular thing shall not be done, all that a court of equity has to do is to say, by way of injunction that which the parties have already said by way of covenant, that the thing shall not be done; and in such a case the injunction does nothing more than give the sanction of the process of the court to that which already is the contract between the parties. It is not then a question on the balance of convenience or inconvenience, or the amount of damage or of injury.

However, enforcement of a negative covenant may have the effect of virtually enforcing the positive terms. The most obvious instance of this is the enforcement of negative covenants in contracts for personal services. Here, for example, enforcing a negative term that the party is forbidden to work for anyone else will have the practical effect of forcing the party to work under the contract, whereas it is clear that the courts will not normally grant specific performance to enforce the positive covenants in such a case.

The case of **Lumley v Wagner** has already been referred to above. Another classic case on this point is **Warner Bros v Nelson** [1936] 3 All ER 160 where the actress Bette Davis was under contract to Warner Bros to work exclusively for them for a period of three years. The court granted an injunction enforcing the negative undertaking not to work as an actress for anyone else. Branson J did not regard this as indirect specific performance, since there was nothing to prevent her from working elsewhere in other capacities than as an actress. 'She will not be driven, though she may be tempted, to perform the contract (i.e. go back to Warner Bros), and the fact that she may be so tempted is no objection to the grant of an injunction.'

Warner Bros v Nelson may be contrasted with cases in which the negative covenant was total: it prohibited the party from working at all, as opposed to merely not working in a particular capacity. In such cases the courts have refused to grant injunctions to enforce such absolute bans.

In **Warren v Mendy** [1989] 3 All ER 103, the plaintiff had a contract with a boxer, Nigel Benn, to manage him exclusively for three years. The action was actually against another manager for inducement to breach of contract, but the Court of Appeal felt that the same principles should apply as if an action for breach of contract was being brought against Benn himself. Would the court have granted an injunction to enforce the restrictive covenant? The court held not: to do so would in practice have forced Benn to perform his contract with the plaintiff. This was the real question: the court doubted **Warner Bros v Nelson** on the ground that in practice it was most unlikely that Bette Davis would take up other work, whereas if the contract imposed a shorter period of exclusivity it might not have had that effect. The length of restriction that might have been acceptable is a matter of debate, but clearly the three-year restriction in **Warren** would have forced Benn to continue his contract with the plaintiff, in other words, indirect specific performance.

In the context of contracts for the sale of goods, restrictive covenants sometimes exist by which a purchaser is obliged to purchase his goods from a certain supplier exclusively. Again, to grant a prohibitory injunction might be virtually equivalent to granting specific performance of the sale contract. This would not usually be granted in such cases as damages would be adequate.

Usually, however, the courts have not regarded granting a prohibitory injunction in such cases as equivalent to specific performance on the grounds that the defendant may still have the option of not buying/selling at all.

Thus in **Evans Marshall v Bertola** [1973] 1 All ER 992, the plaintiffs were sole agents for the sale of the defendant's sherry in the UK. They were granted an injunction to prevent the defendant breaking a term of a supply contract by which they had undertaken not to sell their sherry through another agency. The court regarded the injunction as 'encouraging' the defendant to keep their contract, not forcing them to do so (though their only alternative was not to sell their sherry in the UK at all).

By contrast, in **Fothergill v Rowland** (1873) 17 Eq 132, the defendant had contracted to sell all the coal from a particular seam to the plaintiff. The plaintiff sought an injunction to prevent the defendant selling it elsewhere, but this was refused on the grounds that it amounted to indirect specific performance. Sir George Jessel MR said he could not find any consistent judicial approach to this question, no clear line between cases where injunctions would be refused on the grounds that they amounted to indirect specific performance, and cases where they would be granted.

Injunctions to prevent tortious interference

Here the compelling remedy is the injunction in its various forms and, in particular, the final prohibitory injunction.

This is available to prevent the continuance or repetition of any tort which is capable of continuance or repetition. Thus it has been used to prevent trespass to the person, interference with contract, defamation, passing off, and most commonly in cases of nuisance and trespass to land.

In these two torts, the injunction is the primary remedy, that is to say it will be the first choice and will only be refused if damages are adequate. Thus in **Shelfer v City of London Lighting** [1895] 1 Ch 287 a pub lessee sought an injunction against an electric company whose generators were housed next door, to stop vibration and noise caused by these generators. The trial judge granted damages in lieu, but the Court of Appeal granted an injunction. AL Smith LJ stated that damages would only be granted in lieu:

> If the injury to the plaintiff's rights is small, and is one capable of being estimated in money, and is one which could be adequately compensated by a small money payment. And is one in which it would be oppressive to the defendant to grant an injunction.

Subject to these exceptional cases, then, a plaintiff is entitled to an injunction. As AL Smith LJ put it:

> A person by committing a wrongful act is not thereby entitled to ask the court to sanction his doing so by purchasing his neighbour's rights, by assessing damages on his behalf, leaving his neighbour with nuisance . . . In such cases the well-known rule is not to accede to the application, but to grant the injunction sought, for the plaintiff's legal right has been invaded, and he is *prima facie* entitled to an injunction.

He also stated that whether the interference is small is a matter of fact in each case, but in the facts before the court in **Shelfer**, the plaintiff was saddled with a 19-year lease, and if the nuisance continued he would be forced to put up with the noise and vibration for that time, the cracks in his house walls would get worse and his wife and daughter's health might continue to be affected. Such injury could not be regarded as small. And how could such damages be assessed to represent this continuing injury? To guess at them is not assessing them at all.

This case must, however, be read in the light of the comments of the Supreme Court in **Coventry (t/a RDC Promotions) v Lawrence** [2014] UKSC 13; [2014] 2 All ER 622 (discussed further below at p. 570). In that case the Supreme Court advocated a more flexible approach to the award of damages, whilst acknowledging that the injunction was still the primary remedy. In the words of Lord Neuberger PSC:

> First, the application of (A L Smith LJ's) four tests must not be such as 'to be a fetter on the exercise of the court's discretion'. Secondly, it would, in the absence of additional relevant circumstances pointing the other way, normally be right to refuse an injunction if those four tests were satisfied. Thirdly, the fact that those tests are not all satisfied does not mean that an injunction should be granted.

In **Kennaway v Thompson** [1980] 3 All ER 329, where an injunction was sought to prevent a powerboat club from racing on a reservoir to the annoyance of the plaintiff, the court cited AL Smith's comments with approval and felt that they did not apply; the harm was not trivial etc. An injunction was granted, though not an absolute one: racing was still permitted under restricted conditions.

Similarly, in **Pride of Derby v British Celanese** [1953] 1 All ER 179, the owners of a fishery sought an injunction to stop the defendants from discharging effluent and sewage into the river Derwent, which had killed all the fish and destroyed the fishery. An injunction was granted. The primacy of the injunction was reasserted by Lord Evershed MR:

> It is, I think, well settled that if A proves that his proprietary rights are being wrongfully interfered with by B, and that B intends to continue his wrong, then A is *prima facie* entitled to an injunction, and he will be deprived of that remedy only if special circumstances exist, including the circumstance that damages are an adequate remedy for the wrong that he has suffered.

It is clear that cases will exist where the court considers the harm to be trivial, though this will be a question of fact as AL Smith LJ recognised. Thus in **Armstrong v Sheppard & Short** [1959] 2 All ER 651 the court considered the interference trivial where it consisted of trespass to a narrow strip of the plaintiff's land by a sewer built by the defendants. No actual loss was established by the plaintiff, and nominal damages of 20 shillings were awarded.

A contrasting case, or perhaps one that shows that just because damage is trivial it does not mean that it will be sanctioned by the court, is **Anchor Brewhouse Developments v Berkley House** [1987] EGLR 173. Here an injunction was granted to prevent the defendant's cranes from swinging into the plaintiffs' airspace above their land, even though no harm was caused thereby. As Scott J stated:

> It would be possible for the law to be that the court should not grant an injunction to restrain a trifling trespass if it were shown to be reasonable and sensible that the trespass be allowed to continue for a limited period upon payment of substantial and proper damages. But I do not think it is open to me to proceed on that footing. The authorities establish, in my view, that the plaintiffs are entitled as of course to injunctions to restrain continuing trespasses.

Search orders (Anton Piller orders)

Objective
5

Search order is the new name adopted in the Civil Procedure Rules for what were formerly known as **Anton Piller** orders, after the case in which they were first introduced.

Anton Piller v Manufacturing Processes Ltd [1976] Ch 55

In this case, the plaintiffs believed that the defendants, who were in possession of confidential information from them, were selling it to the plaintiffs' competitors, but they were unable to establish this without access to the defendants' files. The Court of Appeal granted *ex parte* an order requiring the defendants to permit the plaintiffs on to their premises to inspect the relevant documents.

This kind of order was placed on a statutory basis by s 7 of the Civil Procedure Act 1997. This provides that the High Court may make an order for the purposes of securing, in the case of any existing or proposed proceedings in the court, (a) the preservation of evidence which is or may be relevant or (b) the preservation of property which is or may be the subject matter of the proceedings or as to which any question may arise in the proceedings.

The statute then provides for persons to be authorised to enter premises in England and Wales (the jurisdiction does not extend abroad or to Scotland) and, while there, to search for, inspect, photograph, sample or record anything described in the order, and to be provided with any information or article, and to retain for safe keeping any such article as is described in the order.

Placing the order on a statutory basis has removed the uncertainty regarding this jurisdiction. Previously, it had been supposed to be based on the controller of the premises granting permission to enter, but such permission was somewhat unreal in that failure to permit would have been contempt of court.

Such orders are clearly of great use in preventing the destruction of material useful to the other side in any legal dispute. Nevertheless, to prevent such destruction or removal, such orders are likely to be granted *ex parte*, so the first occasion on which the other side is made aware of the order is when a solicitor arrives on the doorstep. This lack of advance warning creates the danger of such an order being used oppressively. To prevent what might otherwise be a serious invasion of the defendant's rights, safeguards are required, both in limiting the court's jurisdiction, and in the manner in which the order is carried out.

In *Anton Piller* itself, Ormrod LJ stated that three conditions must be met if such an order is to be granted: the plaintiff must have an extremely strong *prima facie* case; he must show very serious actual or potential damage; and there must be clear evidence that the defendants have the incriminating documents and that there is a real possibility of their destruction before a normal application *inter partes* can be made, thus making a grant *ex parte* essential.

Furthermore, the potential harm to the defendant if the order is granted must not be excessive or out of proportion to the intended objective of the order.

There are also certain requirements regarding the carrying out of the order. These are now set out in the Practice Direction supplementing Part 25 of the Civil Procedure Rules which states that the order should be served by an experienced supervising solicitor (not of the firm acting for the applicant) accompanied only by those named in the order. Furthermore, where the premises at which the order is served are likely to be occupied by a woman alone, the supervising solicitor (if a man) should be accompanied by a woman, and applications should be dealt with in open court (previously applications to the Queen's Bench were heard by a judge in chambers). The standard form of the order explains its import and the supervising solicitor is required to explain the terms and effect of the order to the respondent and advise him of his right to seek advice, and of his rights of legal professional privilege and the privilege against self-incrimination (see below). To ensure access to legal advice, the order may only be served during normal working hours (Monday to Friday, 9.30 am–5.30 pm). The terms of the order also make it clear that the person who is served with the order is entitled to be present during the search and is entitled to a list of all documents and items removed under the order. The applicant must also undertake not to use the information obtained under the order for any purpose other than the legal proceedings, and must indemnify the defendant for any loss caused by the plaintiff's non-compliance with the order, if the court so orders.

This direction follows on the suggestions made by Sir Donald Nicholls V-C in *Universal Thermosensors* v *Hibben*.

Universal Thermosensors v *Hibben* [1992] 3 All ER 257

The plaintiff had obtained an order for the recovery of documents and equipment held by the defendants, its former employees who had set up a rival company, and an injunction preventing them using this confidential material. The defendants sued, claiming damages for the fact that the terms of the order were too wide, and for its faulty execution, though this last matter was settled out of court. No doubt, as the Vice-Chancellor pointed out, the documents would not have seen the light of day had less draconian steps been taken to recover them, but this result had been achieved at a high price. It is interesting to note also that the injunction, in forbidding the use of this information, had the effect of putting the defendants out of business. The order thus had the final effect which the plaintiff was seeking, and indeed the plaintiff had already disclaimed its intention to seek any further injunctive relief against the defendants.

The circumstances of the enforcement of the order in that case exhibit many of the problems subsequently addressed by the Practice Direction. In particular, the order was served in the middle of the night, on a private house occupied by a woman alone, and no officers of the defendant company were present when the search was made. The person served with the order was also prevented from communicating with any other person on the matter for a week: the Practice Direction states that such restriction shall be until the return date, or seven days, whichever is the lesser period, and, as stated above, does not prevent communication for the purposes of obtaining legal advice.

Protection against self-incrimination

It may be that information obtained as a result of a search order might provide evidence of criminal liability on the part of the defendants. Are they entitled to resist the order on the grounds of a privilege against self-incrimination?

Rank Film Distributors v *Video Information Centre* [1981] 2 All ER 76

In this case, the House of Lords reluctantly recognised such a privilege. Rank, who owned the copyright in films, obtained injunctions against those producing and selling illegal pirate videos, and an *Anton Piller* order against the respondents, who were suspected of selling them, requiring them to disclose the names of their suppliers and customers and all documents relating to the cassettes, and the whereabouts of all copies and masters known to them. The respondents sought to have the requirements of disclosure removed on the grounds that, if they were compelled to reveal the information, they would be laying themselves open to possible prosecution for offences under the Copyright Act 1956 and the Theft Act 1968 and for conspiracy to defraud. The House of Lords held that, because there was a serious possibility of the respondents being exposed to the serious charge of conspiracy to defraud, the privilege against self-incrimination should be upheld. There was no effective way to require the information to be revealed without this threat, since even an undertaking by the plaintiffs not to use the information for the purposes of prosecution could not prevent any third party pursuing the matter.

This privilege is specifically preserved by s 7(7) of the Civil Procedure Act 1997, which states that the section does not affect the right of any person to refuse to do anything on the ground that to do so might tend to expose him or his spouse to proceedings for an offence or the recovery of a penalty. Nevertheless, such a privilege could severely restrict the use of the order. Accordingly under the Civil Procedure Rules, the supplementary Practice Direction reiterates the basic privilege, but identifies certain specific situations where the privilege does not apply. These are (para 7.9):

(1) Intellectual Property cases in respect of a 'related offence' or for the recovery of a 'related penalty' as defined in section 72 Senior Courts Act 1981;
(2) proceedings for the recovery or administration of any property, for the execution of a trust or for an account of any property or dealings with property, in relation to –
    (a) an offence under the Theft Act 1968 (see section 31 of the Theft Act 1968); or
    (b) an offence under the Fraud Act 2006 (see section 13 of the Fraud Act 2006) or a related offence within the meaning given by section 13(4) of that Act – that is, conspiracy to defraud or any other offence involving any form of fraudulent conduct or purpose; or
(3) proceedings in which a court is hearing an application for an order under Part IV or Part V of the Children Act 1989 (see section 98 Children Act 1989).

The corollary to the removal of the privilege is, however, that any statement made, or in the case of a search order, any information revealed, is not admissible in evidence against the respondent or his spouse or civil partner. Witness, for example, the provisions of the Theft Act 1969, s 31:

(1) A person shall not be excused, by reason that to do so may incriminate that person or the spouse or civil partner of that person of an offence under this Act –

    (a) from answering any question put to that person in proceedings for the recovery or administration of any property, for the execution of any trust or for an account of any property or dealings with property; or

    (b) from complying with any order made in any such proceedings;

but no statement or admission made by a person in answering a question put or complying with an order made as aforesaid shall, in proceedings for an offence under this Act, be admissible in evidence against that person or (unless they married or became civil partners after the making of the statement or admission) against the spouse or civil partner.

The removal of the privilege in intellectual property cases was upheld in *Cobra Sports* v *Rata (No. 2)* [1997] 2 All ER 150. Here the order was ostensibly sought to obtain evidence of infringements of trade mark, even though it was clear that the plaintiff's main reason was to provide evidence of the defendant's contempt of court, and the defendant would have been entitled to invoke the privilege to protect himself against such an accusation. However, since the order was sought in an intellectual property situation no privilege was available, but the plaintiff would not be permitted to use the evidence, thus obtained, to prove contempt.

No such restriction applies, however, where the defendants may be exposed to a charge of conspiracy to defraud. This was recognised in *Sonangol* v *Lundquist* [1990] 3 All ER 283, where an order for discovery ancillary to a freezing injunction was successfully resisted on that ground. The defendants accordingly could not be required to reveal the amounts of their foreign assets, though they could still be asked to reveal their whereabouts. The substance of the test to be applied to determine whether the defendant can claim the privilege appears to be, in Staughton LJ's words, 'that there must be grounds to apprehend danger to the witness, and those grounds must be reasonable'. (In this context, for 'witness', read 'defendant', or the person who is the subject of the search or discovery order.) It was stressed, in *Tate Access Floors* v *Boswell* [1990] 3 All ER 303, however, that the privilege is against self-incrimination. No one can object to an order against a third party on the grounds that, if the third party is forced to reveal information, the objector himself may be incriminated. Thus, in *Tate Access Floors* an order was set aside against individual defendants, but not against corporate defendants, since these companies were separate entities and had not been shown to be the mere creatures of the individual defendants.

In *Tate Access Floors*, it was stated that where the privilege applies no search order should be made, at least not *ex parte* or in any way which might in practice preclude the defendant from raising the claim to privilege before the order is executed. This was distinguished, in *IBM* v *Prima Data International* [1994] 1 WLR 719, from an order which contains a proviso that expressly indicates that the defendant may claim privilege. In the words of Sir Mervyn Davies:

[T]he order means that the supervising solicitor must say to the defendant, 'I have a search order but I cannot execute it if you tell me that the search may result in disclosing matters showing that you have been involved in conspiracy.' It seems to me that the form of order adequately protects the defendant's privilege while at the same time allowing search if the privilege is not claimed.

Accordingly, an order was valid in this case because it effectively made the defendant's right to claim privilege clear to him. As he waived that right, the search made under that order was valid, though the court would need to be satisfied that the defendant did in fact understand that he had the right to refuse.

Finally, it may be noted that in *Bayer AG v Winter* [1986] 1 All ER 733, in support of a search order and a freezing injunction requiring the defendant to reveal documents and information about a fake insecticide, the Court of Appeal was prepared to grant an order preventing the defendant leaving the country, in order that he could be compelled, if necessary, to appear to answer questions on the matter.

It will be apparent from this last case, and from *Sonangol* above, that such discovery and privilege issues can also arise in the context of freezing injunctions, considered below.

Freezing injunctions

In the Civil Procedure Rules the term 'freezing injunction' has been adopted for the *Mareva* injunction, previously named after the leading case.

In *Mareva Cia Naviera SA v International Bulkcarriers SA* [1980] 1 All ER 213n, it was held that an injunction could be granted to prevent the defendant to an action from removing assets from the jurisdiction. In *Rasu Maritima v Pertambagan* [1977] 3 All ER 324, Lord Denning indicated the situation in which this jurisdiction might need to be invoked:

> A plaintiff has what appears to be an indisputable claim against a defendant resident outside the jurisdiction, but with assets within the jurisdiction which he could easily remove, and which the court is satisfied are liable to be removed unless the injunction is granted. The plaintiff is then in the following difficulty. First he needs leave to serve the defendant outside the jurisdiction, and the defendant is then given time to enter an appearance from the date when he is served, all of which usually takes several weeks or even months. Secondly, it is only then that the plaintiff can apply for summary judgment . . . with a view to levying execution on the defendant's assets here. Thirdly, however, on being apprised of the proceedings, the defendant is liable to remove his assets, thereby precluding the plaintiff in advance from enjoying the fruits of a judgment which appears irresistible on the evidence before the court. The defendant can then largely ignore the plaintiff's claim in the courts of this country and snap his fingers at any judgment which may be given against him. It has always been my understanding that the purpose and scope of the exercise of this jurisdiction is to deal with cases of this nature. To exercise it *ex parte* in such cases presents little danger or inconvenience to the defendant. He is at liberty to apply to have the injunction discharged at any time at short notice.

In the modern age of international companies this is a common problem: the jurisdiction of a court, in so far as it is territorial, may be frustrated by a party moving his assets outside that territorial jurisdiction. Here equity, acting *in personam*, may intervene against that party. As was pointed out in an earlier chapter (see Chapter 2), this *in personam* jurisdiction is not territorially limited, but may operate anywhere in the world. As Dillon LJ stated in *Derby v Weldon (No. 6)* [1990] 3 All ER 263 at 272:

> The jurisdiction of the court to grant a freezing injunction against a person depends not on the territorial jurisdiction of the English court over assets within its jurisdiction, but on the unlimited jurisdiction of the English court *in personam* against any person, whether an individual or corporation, who is, under English procedure, properly made a party to proceedings before an English court.

This is confirmed by the wording of the Senior Courts Act 1981 s 37(3):

> (3) The power of the High Court under subsection (1) to grant an interlocutory injunction restraining a party to any proceedings from removing from the jurisdiction of the High Court, or otherwise dealing with, any assets located within that jurisdiction shall be exercisable in cases where that party is, as well as in cases where he is not, domiciled, resident or present within that jurisdiction.

Thus, the original scenario envisaged for freezing injunctions was their use to prevent assets from being removed from the jurisdiction prior to trial. As will be seen below, this scope has been considerably widened. Such injunctions may now be used to prevent any misuse of assets designed to defeat the plaintiff's claim. This problem may arise either before the plaintiff has obtained judgment or afterwards, when he is seeking to enforce the judgment he has obtained. To that end, he may obtain a search order and a freezing injunction together, to enable him both to identify and freeze the defendant's assets.

It should be noted that this jurisdiction is exclusive to the High Court: under the County Court Remedies Regulations 1991, the County Court has power to grant such injunctions only in very limited situations.

The freezing injunction is interlocutory: it is not an end in itself but the means to prevent the defendant removing assets: while a plaintiff must take the risk that a defendant against whom he has a successful action may not have the assets to meet his claim, the courts can intervene to prevent the defendant acting unfairly to bring this about by moving his assets outside the jurisdiction. In the words of Lord Donaldson in *Derby* v *Weldon (No. 2)* [1989] 1 All ER 1002 at 1006:

> The fundamental principle underlying this jurisdiction is that, within the limits of its powers, no court should permit a defendant to take action designed to ensure that subsequent orders of the court are rendered less effective than would otherwise be the case. On the other hand, it is not its purpose to prevent a defendant carrying on his business in the ordinary way, or if an individual, living his life normally pending the determination of the dispute, nor to impede him in any way in defending himself against the claim. Nor is its purpose to place the plaintiff in the position of a secured creditor. In a word, whilst one of the hazards facing a plaintiff in litigation is that, come the day of judgment it may not be possible for him to obtain satisfaction of that judgment fully or at all, the court does not permit the defendant artificially to create such a situation.

It is clear from Lord Donaldson's words, however, that the court must not allow this principle to be used oppressively against the defendant. Thus, a set of guidelines has developed which should be followed when the jurisdiction is invoked. These were set out by Lord Denning in *Third Chandris Shipping* v *Unimarine* [1979] 2 All ER 972 at 984:

> Much as I am in favour of the freezing injunction, it must not be stretched too far lest it be endangered . . . These are the points which those who apply for it should bear in mind. (i) The plaintiff should make full and frank disclosure of all matters in his knowledge which are material for the judge to know. (ii) The plaintiff should give particulars of his claim against the defendant, stating the ground of his claim and the amount thereof, and fairly stating the points made against it by the defendant. (iii) The plaintiff should have some grounds for believing that the defendant has assets here . . . (iv) The plaintiff should give some grounds for believing that there is a risk of the assets being removed before the judgment or award is satisfied . . . (v) The plaintiffs must, of course, give an undertaking in damages, in case they fail in their claim or the injunction turns out to be unjustified . . .

We shall take each of these points in turn.

Disclosure

The detailed requirements and considerations of the court in the matter of disclosure were examined at some length by Ralph Gibson LJ in **Brink's-Mat Ltd v Elcombe** [1988] 3 All ER 188:

> In considering whether there has been relevant non-disclosure and what consequence the court should attach to any failure to comply with the duty to make full and frank disclosure, the principles relevant to the issues in the appeal appear to me to include the following: (i) The duty of the applicant to make 'a full and frank disclosure of all the material facts'. (ii) The material facts are those which are material for the judge to know in dealing with the application as made; materiality is to be decided by the court and not by the assessment of the applicant or his legal advisers. (iii) The applicant must make proper inquiries before making the application. The duty of disclosure therefore applies not only to material facts known to the applicant but also to any additional facts which he would have known had he made such inquiries. (iv) The extent of the inquiries which will be held proper, and therefore necessary, must depend on all the circumstances of the case including (a) the nature of the case which the applicant is making when he makes the application, (b) the order for which the application is made and the probable effect of the order on the defendant, and (c) the degree of legitimate urgency and the time available for the making of the inquiries. (v) If material non-disclosure is established the court will be 'astute to ensure that a plaintiff who obtains . . . an *ex parte* injunction without full disclosure is deprived of any advantage he may have derived by that breach of duty'. (vi) Whether the fact not disclosed is of sufficient materiality to justify or require immediate discharge of the order without examination of the merits depends on the importance of the fact to the issues which were to be decided by the judge on the application. The answer to the question whether non-disclosure was innocent, in the sense that the fact was not known to the applicant or that its relevance was not perceived, is an important consideration but not decisive by reason of the duty on the applicant to make all proper inquiries and to give careful consideration to the case being presented. (vii) Finally it is not for every omission that the injunction will be automatically discharged. A *locus poenitentiae* may sometimes be afforded. The court has a discretion, notwithstanding proof of material non-disclosure which justifies or requires the immediate discharge of the *ex parte* order, nevertheless to continue the order, or to make a new order on terms: 'when the whole of the facts, including that of the original non-disclosure, are before it, the court may well grant such a second injunction if the original non-disclosure was innocent and if an injunction could properly be granted even had the facts been disclosed.

It is clear from this statement that the duty of disclosure includes an obligation on the claimant to make appropriate inquiries. It is also apparent that, though the sanction for non-disclosure may be draconian, the court should consider all the relevant facts before deciding what sanction to impose, and may in appropriate cases regard the non-disclosure as not material and may leave the injunction in place.

The claimant's claim

While the requirements under this head are in general self-evident from Lord Denning's statement, it is of course essential that the claimant should actually have some substantive claim against the defendant, independent of the claim for the injunction itself. This should follow from the interlocutory nature of the remedy, as stated by Lord Diplock in *The Siskina* [1977] 3 All ER 803 at 824:

> A right to obtain an interlocutory injunction is not a cause of action. It cannot stand on its own. It is dependent on there being a pre-existing cause of action against the defendant arising

out of an invasion, actual or threatened, by him of a legal or equitable right of the plaintiff for the enforcement of which the defendant is amenable to the jurisdiction of the court. The right to obtain an interlocutory injunction is merely ancillary and incidental to the pre-existing cause of action. It is granted to preserve the *status quo* pending the ascertainment by the court of the rights of the parties and the grant to the plaintiff of the relief to which his cause of action entitles him, which may or may not include a final injunction.

The requirement that the claimant be able to establish an arguable case has been reiterated in *Polly Peck International v Nadir (No. 2)* [1992] 4 All ER 769, an application for a freezing injunction against a bank alleged to hold assets placed there by the first defendant. Scott LJ emphasised that a freezing injunction could never be justified unless a fair arguable case for liability could be shown. On the facts he regarded the plaintiff's claim as 'no more than speculative'. This issue had to be taken, he felt, in conjunction with the effect of the injunction on the defendants if granted, and on the plaintiffs if discharged. To impose an injunction upon a bank would seriously interfere with its business and might lead to a run on it. Accordingly, it was only in unusual circumstances that a freezing injunction would be granted against a bank, and here the facts did not justify it (though a more limited injunction was granted in respect of assets held in its London branch).

One effect of the *Siskina* principle was that the freezing injunction could not be issued to support a substantive claim in a foreign jurisdiction where the English court did not have jurisdiction over the substance of the claim. So a litigant in a foreign court suing a defendant who had assets in England could not obtain an order to control those assets, which might be required to meet the litigant's claim. This situation was much criticised but was nonetheless confirmed in *Mercedes Benz v Leiduck* [1995] 3 All ER 929. This has, however, been substantially modified by the Civil Jurisdiction and Judgments Act 1982 s 25, and by the Interim Relief Order 1997, made under that Act. The effect of this legislation is that, since 1 April 1997, the English courts have had jurisdiction to grant freezing injunctions in support of proceedings, commenced or to be commenced, in any foreign country. A similar provision has been introduced in respect of foreign arbitrations by s 2 of the Arbitration Act 1996. However, s 25(2) of the 1982 Act states that the courts may refuse to grant such an injunction where the fact that they have no power to grant other than under the Act 'makes it inexpedient' to do so. Where such an injunction is granted, it may be of purely domestic or worldwide application as appropriate, in the same way as an injunction in support of a claim in England may be (see further below).

The courts have in the past taken the view that the grant of freezing injunctions to support claims in foreign jurisdictions will be exceptional, and particularly so if the injunction is to apply to assets abroad, because of the danger that the courts in several different countries might all make criss-crossing orders, possibly contradictory, in respect of the defendant's assets throughout the world. The principles to be applied in such cases were considered by the Court of Appeal in *Crédit Suisse Fides Trust SA v Cuoghi*.

Crédit Suisse Fides Trust SA v Cuoghi [1997] 3 All ER 724

In this case the plaintiff was making its claim in the Swiss courts against a defendant who was domiciled and resident in England. The defendant appealed against the granting of a worldwide freezing injunction on the grounds that the court should be satisfied that the circumstances were wholly exceptional before granting such an injunction. The Court of Appeal dismissed the appeal, clearly indicating that a more flexible approach should be taken in the future, and that such orders should not be viewed as exceptional. The English courts should be willing to grant such an order in support of substantive proceedings in a foreign court unless the circumstances made it inexpedient.

In particular, they should be willing to grant it where the assets were not within the foreign court's jurisdiction, but were within that of the English courts, and should not be deterred from granting such an order just because the foreign court itself had no power to make such an order. As regards the *in personam* effect of the order, against the defendant himself, where the assets were not within the English courts' jurisdiction, but the defendant was, the English courts should have regard to the domicile of the defendant and the likely reaction of the foreign court: if the foreign court had refused an order (as opposed to not having power to grant one), the English courts should not interfere. The English courts should not generally refuse to grant a freezing injunction where this refusal would interfere with or hamper the hearing of the substantive case in the foreign court.

See Chapter 11 for the facts of *Walsh*.

In ***Walsh* v *Deloitte & Touche*** [2001] All ER (D) 326 (Dec) the Privy Council in this case stated that it was a 'commonplace' that the most convenient forum for trial of the issue might not be the place where it was desirable to issue a freezing injunction. A company, Bre-X, had become bankrupt and Deloitte had been appointed trustee. Deloitte were seeking to make W liable for possible breaches of his fiduciary duties as founder and principal shareholder of Bre-X. The trial of the issue was to take place in Ontario, Canada, where Bre-X had been based, but it was perfectly proper for a worldwide freezing order to be granted by the courts in the Bahamas, where W had resided prior to his death. The most appropriate place for an order to be made was where the defendant was amenable to the *in personam* jurisdiction of the court if he disobeyed.

Banco Nacional de Comercio Exterior SNC* v *Empresa de Telecomunicationes de Cuba SA [2007] 2 All ER 1093 is a case in which the issue of a worldwide order was deemed inexpedient.

A domestic order (applying to the defendant's assets in England) and a worldwide order were granted in support of a judgment of a court in Turin, the relevant contract between the two parties being within that court's exclusive jurisdiction. The Court of Appeal set the worldwide order aside. In this case, there could be no doubt that it would be inexpedient to grant the claimant a worldwide freezing order. Any assets within the jurisdiction would be protected by the domestic order. The worldwide order was directed only at assets outside the jurisdiction. There was therefore no connecting link at all between the subject matter of the measure sought and the territorial jurisdiction of the court. It was not suggested that the worldwide order should be made in order to assist the Italian court or any of the other courts of the member states which had been involved in enforcement proceedings. Furthermore, it was not the policy of the Italian court to grant worldwide freezing orders. Given the multiplicity of enforcement proceedings in other member states, there was a danger that an English worldwide freezing order would give rise to disharmony or confusion and/or risk conflicting, inconsistent or overlapping orders in other jurisdictions. The case also turned on the application of Art 47 of Council Regulation (EC) 44/2001 concerned with enforcement of commercial judgments within the EU.

Belief that the defendant has assets within the jurisdiction

Lord Denning pointed out that in most cases the claimant will not have precise information about whether the defendant has such assets: he will not know the extent of the assets, but merely have indications of them. This, together with the amount of the claimant's claim, will have implications for the nature of the order granted and the extent to which the defendant's assets should be tied up, which is discussed further below. The extent to which possession of assets within the jurisdiction is still a requirement is also considered further below.

Belief that the assets will be dissipated

When the freezing injunction first came into being, it was largely as a result of concern that assets to meet the claimant's claim in the English courts might be removed from the jurisdiction of those courts. Thus, statements in early cases considered the kind of evidence that might lead to this conclusion. For example, in *Montechi* v *Shimco* [1979] 1 WLR 1180 Lord Bridge stated:

> It seems to me that the basis of the freezing injunction is that there has to be real reason to apprehend that, if the injunction is not made, the intending plaintiff in this country may be deprived of a remedy against the foreign defendant whom he seeks to sue.

Lord Denning indicated in *Third Chandris Shipping* v *Unimarine* that such grounds would not be provided by the mere fact that the defendant was abroad, but he posited the case of the company registered abroad in a country of convenience:

> But there are some foreign companies whose structure invites comment. We often see in court a corporation which is registered in a country where the company law is so loose that nothing is known about it, where it does no work and has no officers and no assets. Nothing can be found out about the membership, or its control, or its assets, or the charges on them. Judgment cannot be enforced against it. There is no reciprocal enforcement of judgments. It is nothing more than a name grasped from the air, as elusive as the Cheshire cat. In such cases the very fact of incorporation there gives some ground for believing there is a risk that, if judgment or an award is obtained, it may go unsatisfied. Such registration of such companies may carry many advantages to the individuals who control them, but they suffer the disadvantage of having a freezing injunction granted against them. The giving of security for a debt is a small price to pay for the convenience of such a registration.

It is now clear that the freezing injunction serves a wider purpose than this, and that any dissipation of assets should if possible be prevented. At the same time no such order should be so prescriptive as to be damaging to the defendant's business, bearing in mind that the defendant has, in most cases, yet to be found liable. It is thus normal to qualify the order with the proviso that the defendant should not be prevented from dealing with his assets in the normal course of business. A balance must be struck, but there must always be concern that that ordinary course of business might be a cloak for dissipation. Such was the issue in *Perry* v *Princess International Sales & Services Ltd*.

Perry v *Princess International Sales & Services Ltd* [2005] EWHC 2042 (Comm)

In this case the defendant's real property was subject to a freezing order. He wished to use this property as security to borrow money for speculative investments and the concern was raised that this might lead to its loss. The fundamental question, according to Clarke J in deciding whether an order should be continued, was whether there was 'sufficiently solid evidence of a real risk of dissipation of assets'. The court concluded that, though each case had to be judged on its facts, such investment could be within the ordinary course of business, even if there was a 'substantial degree of risk or speculation', and so the defendant would not be breaking the terms of the order by using the property as security in this way. Such dealings could be distinguished from those which were improper or unjustifiable, in that their primary object was to dissipate assets and thus defeat the possible claim. The court also concluded that the risk of dissipation of real property assets was inherently less, at least on the facts of the case.

The claimant's undertaking in damages

The claimant's undertaking in damages is a requirement for all interim proceedings. As such proceedings do not determine liability, but are merely based upon the claimant making out a strong case, it follows that the claimant may eventually lose, and in the meantime the defendant may have been put to cost and inconvenience. Therefore, the claimant must be prepared to indemnify the defendant against that risk.

The effect on third parties

The freezing injunction, like all injunctions, is said to operate *in personam* against the conscience of the party injuncted. However, to the extent that it freezes the assets of that party, it may have significant effects on third parties and their dealing with those assets. To the extent that it binds the defendant's property, it may be said to operate *in rem*.

Lord Denning so described a freezing injunction in *Z Ltd v A* [1982] 1 All ER 556, comparing the freezing injunction with the arrest of a ship. Since the injunction is a method of attaching the asset itself, any third party who has notice of it and who deals with the asset, or assists the defendant in doing so, is liable for contempt of court. Giving the example of a freezing injunction granted against the defendant's bank account, Lord Denning stated the position to be as follows:

> As soon as the bank is given notice of the freezing injunction, it must freeze the defendant's bank account. It must not allow any drawings to be made on it, neither by cheques drawn before the injunction nor by those drawn after it. The reason is because, if it allowed any such drawings, it would be obstructing the course of justice, as prescribed by the court which granted the injunction, and would be guilty of a contempt of court.
>
> I have confined myself to banks and bank accounts. But the same applies to any specific asset held by a bank for safe custody on behalf of the defendant, be it jewellery, stamps, or anything else, and to any other person who holds any other asset of the defendant's. If the asset is covered by the terms of the freezing injunction, that other person must not hand it over to the defendant or do anything to enable him to dispose of it. He must hold it pending further order.

The potential effect of a freezing injunction on innocent third parties required that certain safeguards be provided for such parties. The claimant should indemnify the third party for any expenses and liabilities which he incurs as a result of the injunction. The claimant should identify as precisely as possible the asset held by the third party which is the subject of the injunction. In the case of a bank, he should identify the relevant account. If he asks the bank to undertake a search to identify the defendant's assets, he must undertake to pay the costs of this. The judge to whom application for the injunction is made should be informed of all the third parties upon whom it is intended to serve notice of the injunction. Though it is now customary to fix the maximum amount to be restrained, this may create particular problems in the case of third parties. If possible, however, a maximum sum should be fixed in relation, for example, to a particular bank account. The defendant should also be allowed to spend a fixed sum on normal living expenses where appropriate. Lord Denning also stressed the importance of fixing an early date for hearing *inter partes*.

It is clear that the effect of freezing of assets must be carefully considered. Freezing the account in *Z v A* did not, in the Court of Appeal's view, prevent the making of payments to honour obligations to third parties, e.g. payments under letters of credit or under a bank guarantee. Neither, in the view of the majority, did it prevent payment of cheques supported by credit or cheque cards.

Assets abroad

In its original form, the freezing injunction was intended to prevent the removal of assets from the United Kingdom to places outside the jurisdiction. It is now clear, however, that it is not so limited, and can be applied to assets which the defendant has outside the jurisdiction.

This was confirmed by Lord Donaldson in *Derby* v *Weldon (No. 2)* [1989] 1 All ER 1002, where he stated that the normal form of the freezing injunction order should be confined to assets within the jurisdiction because most defendants operate nationally rather than internationally, but that once the court was dealing with an international operator, the position might well be different. He stressed the underlying rationale of this type of injunction:

> In my judgment, the key requirement for any freezing injunction, whether or not it extends to foreign assets, is that it shall accord with the rationale on which freezing relief has been based in the past. The rationale, legitimate purpose and fundamental principle [is] . . . that no court should permit a defendant to take action designed to frustrate subsequent orders of the court. If for the achievement of this purpose it is necessary to make orders concerning foreign assets, such orders should be made subject, of course, to ordinary principles of international law.

Where a defendant does have sufficient assets within the jurisdiction, that will be a good reason for confining the order to those assets, but where he does not, then the greater is the necessity of taking protective measures in relation to assets outside it. Nevertheless, the court, in granting such an injunction, should be mindful of special factors which would then come into play.

First, the court must consider whether an order against foreign assets was enforceable, since equity does not act in vain. In this case, the defendants were two companies, one based in Luxembourg and one in Panama. Lord Donaldson considered that sufficient enforceability was to be found in the fact that, if the injunction was disobeyed, the court would bar the defendants from defending the action:

> This is not a consequence which they could contemplate lightly as they would become fugitives from a final judgment given against them without their explanation having been heard and which might well be enforced against them in other courts.

Secondly, the court must be satisfied that the order does not conflict with the ordinary principles of international law, in that it should not infringe the exclusive jurisdiction of the courts of other countries. The freezing injunction does not do this, as it operates solely *in personam*.

There remains the impact on third parties, the general nature of which is considered above. This is recognised as a problem in foreign asset cases. A third party wholly within the jurisdiction is in contempt if he knowingly aids the defendant in disobeying the order. If he is wholly outside the jurisdiction, he is either not in contempt or at least cannot be punished. The situation is more complex where a corporate third party, such as a bank, is partly within and partly outside the jurisdiction.

This problem was recognised in *Babanaft International Co* v *Bassatne* [1989] 1 All ER 433, where Kerr LJ stated:

> Unqualified freezing injunctions covering assets abroad can never be justified, either before or after judgment, because they involve an exorbitant assertion of an *in rem* nature over third parties outside the jurisdiction, of our courts. They cannot be controlled or policed in our courts, and they are not subjected to the control of the local courts . . . In consequence . . . any purported assertion of such jurisdiction is unworkable and merely gives rise to problems and disputes.

It was recognised that freezing injunctions must therefore take account of these problems by containing an appropriate proviso. Lord Donaldson in *Derby* v *Weldon (No. 2)* concurred with the need for a proviso of some sort, though he was unhappy with the use of the term *'in rem* effect' and the view that that effect was direct. In his view, an injunction operated in two ways: first, directly against the defendant, and secondly, indirectly against third parties in that they cannot give effect to instructions given to them by the defendant to do or concur in acts which would breach the order. He continued:

> I have no doubt of the practical need for some proviso, because in its absence banks operating abroad do not know where they stand and foreign banks without any branch in England who are thus outside the jurisdiction of the English courts may take . . . offence at being, as they see it, 'ordered about' by the English courts.

Accordingly, he proposed that an injunction operating against foreign assets should contain the proviso that, in so far as it is intended to have extra-territorial effect, no person should be affected by it until and only to the extent that it is declared enforceable by the relevant foreign court, unless they are the person to whom the injunction is addressed, or a third party who is within the jurisdiction of the English court and who has notice and is able to prevent breaches of the order. This principle is now provided for in para 19 of the Practice Direction annexed to the Civil Procedure Rules, Part 25.

Damages in lieu of injunction

Objective 6

This jurisdiction, which derives from the Chancery Amendment Act 1858 and is now to be found in the Senior Courts Act 1981 s 50, enables the court to award damages in situations where no damages are available at law. In other situations, where common law damages are available, the court may, if it has jurisdiction to award an injunction, decide to award damages instead. In both situations it appears that the same considerations will operate.

The first requirement is, of course, that the court has jurisdiction to award an injunction, whether or not it might withhold it in the exercise of its discretion. The decision to award damages may then be made in accordance with the conditions laid down in *Shelfer* v *City of London Lighting* [1895] 1 Ch 287. Under this case, damages were awarded in lieu of an injunction only if (a) the injury to the plaintiff is small, (b) the injury is capable of being estimated in monetary terms, (c) the injury would be adequately compensated by a small payment, and (d) the case is one where it would be oppressive to grant an injunction. These guidelines were accepted as a good working rule in *Jaggard* v *Sawyer*, but both the Master of the Rolls and Millett LJ stressed that the underlying issue is whether it would in the circumstances of the case be oppressive to the defendant to grant the injunction to which the claimant is *prima facie* entitled.

Jaggard v *Sawyer* [1995] 2 All ER 189

In this case, the defendants had obtained planning permission for, and had begun to build, a new house behind their existing one. To create access to this new house, they wished to build a driveway over the front garden of the existing house, and had obtained planning permission for this. The front garden was, however, subject to a covenant for the benefit of the other houses in the cul-de-sac, that it was only to be used as a garden. The plaintiff, a neighbour, sought an injunction to enforce the covenant, but only began the action after the building of the new house was well advanced. Millett LJ pointed out that, in most cases of this type where an injunction is sought, a building had been constructed in breach of restrictive covenant: though there was a *prima facie* right to an injunction, to force the building owner to demolish it would cause a loss to him out of all proportion to the plaintiff's loss if it were refused. To grant an injunction in such a case would deliver the defendant to the plaintiff bound hand and foot to be subjected to any extortionate demand the plaintiff might make: the defendant would be willing to give anything rather than demolish the building, and could thus be blackmailed by the plaintiff. So it was in this case: the house would have been left 'landlocked' (i.e. with no access other than through the existing house), and thus practically useless. Accordingly, the trial judge had been right to refuse an injunction.

The *Shelfer* principles were strictly applied by the Court of Appeal in *Regan* v *Paul Properties Ltd* [2007] 4 All ER 48 in the context of injunctions for the enforcement of rights to light. Mummery LJ held that the infringement of a legal right can *prima facie* be restrained by an injunction. The loss to the claimant (a reduction of about £5,000 in the value of his property) was not considered small, nor was it considered oppressive to require the defendants to spend £35,000 removing work already completed and to suffer a loss of £175,000 in the expected value of their property. It was not appropriate to balance these losses; the defendants had taken a calculated risk in proceeding when they knew of the claimant's objections, even though they did so believing (on the basis of incorrect advice) that he had no claim.

This and other preceding cases must now be seen, however, in the light of the Supreme Court's decision in *Coventry (t/a RDC Promotions)* v *Lawrence* [2014] UKSC 13; [2014] 2 All ER 622, which appears to undermine the authority of *Shelfer* considerably.

Coventry (t/a RDC Promotions) v Lawrence [2014] UKSC 13; [2014] 2 All ER 622

This case concerned a claim for nuisance by noise. The claimant, L, and another, purchased a bungalow near Cambridge. They became concerned about the noise from a nearby motor racing stadium and sought an injunction against the racing on the grounds that it constituted a nuisance.

Having determined that the noise from the motor racing stadium did constitute a nuisance, the Supreme Court considered the appropriate remedy. Whilst the majority of the Court regarded an injunction as the primary remedy, they nonetheless felt that a more flexible approach should be adopted to the award of damages, rather than the 'mechanical' approach they perceived in cases such as *Regan*. In the words of Lord Neuberger PSC:

> The court's power to award damages in lieu of an injunction involves a classic exercise of discretion, which should not, as a matter of principle, be fettered, particularly in the very constrained way in which the Court of Appeal has suggested in *Regan* . . . And, as a matter of practical fairness, each case is likely to be so fact-sensitive that any firm guidance is likely to do more harm than good.

His Lordship nonetheless recognised the importance of the public benefit of the activity as one factor, and, linked with that, the fact that the appellant had planning permission for their activities.

Accordingly, though the trial judge's award of an injunction was restored, the claimants were given liberty to seek to have it set aside and damages awarded instead.

As to the measure of damages, since an injunction prevents future loss, the measure should be essentially compensatory for any future loss to the plaintiff. Following *Wrotham Park Estate* v *Parkside Homes* [1974] 2 All ER 321, the appropriate measure in *Jaggard* v *Sawyer* was a figure equivalent to that which the plaintiff might reasonably have been able to ask to give up her rights; the 'value' to her of the restrictive covenant. In *Lunn Poly* v *Liverpool and Lancashire Properties* [2006] All ER (D) 264 (Mar), Neuberger LJ identified three methods of calculation: first on compensatory principles (assessment of actual loss); secondly on a negotiation basis, what the parties would have reasonably agreed in hypothetical negotiations (as applied in *Jaggard* v *Sawyer*); and thirdly, in some cases where account should be taken of any benefit derived by the infringing party. At first instance, the judge had decided that the 'negotiating' approach should be taken and this was not challenged in the Court of Appeal. After all, the tenants had indicated that they agreed to the landlords' breach of covenant (the moving of a fire door), subject to the payment of a suitable sum. The Court of Appeal stated that the sum should normally be calculated as if the hypothetical negotiations had taken place at the time of the breach.

In *Horsford* v *Bird* [2006] All ER (D) 79 (Jan), the Privy Council applied the approach adopted in *Wrotham Park Estates* v *Parkside Homes* as to the appropriate measure of damages, that is the sum which the trespasser would reasonably have paid for the trespass. In this case the respondent encroached on neighbouring land when constructing a building. The land was vacant undeveloped land with a small price, but clearly it was worth a great deal more to the respondent since it enabled him to complete a major building project. The question to be asked, according to Lord Scott, was:

> how much the appellant could reasonably have sought from the respondent . . . as the price of the appellant's land that the respondent had incorporated into his garden.

Accordingly damages were not to be assessed merely on the value per square foot of the undeveloped land, but rather on the amenity value to the respondent, who had been able to build a more attractive garden and swimming pool as a result of his trespass. The Privy Council therefore doubled the amount of damages awarded. The appellant was also entitled to mesne profits (for the use of the land during the trespass). The Privy Council did not, however, think this a case for aggravated damages, despite the fact that the respondent had apparently made no attempt to discover the ownership of the land on which he proposed to trespass.

Enforcement of injunctions

The order of the court has authority ultimately because of the sanctions available to the court if it is disobeyed. Disobedience of an injunction is contempt of the court for which the sanctions available are as set out in Order 45, rule 5 of the Rules of the Supreme Court (now contained in Schedule 1 to the Civil Procedure Rules):

(1) Where:
    (a) any person required by a judgment or order to do an act within the time specified in the judgment or order refuses or neglects to do it within that time . . . or,
    (b) a person disobeys a judgment or order requiring him to abstain from doing an act,

    then, subject to the provisions of these rules, the judgment or order may be enforced by one or more of the following means, that is to say –

    (i) with the permission of the Court, a writ of sequestration against the property of that person;
    (ii) where that person is a body corporate, with permission of the Court, a writ of sequestration against the property of any director or other officer of the body;
    (iii) subject to the provisions of the Debtors Acts 1869 and 1878, an order for committal against that person or, where that person is a body corporate, against any such officer.

It will be immediately apparent that this provision covers any remedy, not merely injunctions, which fall most obviously within (1)(b). Where imprisonment is resorted to, then, under the Contempt of Court Act 1981, this is limited to a fixed period not exceeding two years. The courts have wide powers to suspend the imprisonment or make it dependent upon compliance with certain conditions.

Specific performance

Objective
7

An order for specific performance is an order to a contracting party that he carry out his obligations under the contract.

By its very nature, an order for specific performance cannot be granted unless there is a binding contract to enforce. It is important to note that equity will only recognise contracts for which consideration has been given: as has already been established in an earlier chapter (see Chapter 4 on constitution), equity will not assist a volunteer and further gives no special status to contracts under seal. Specific performance also presupposes that there is something left under the contract to perform; the contract must in that sense be executory.

For enforcement of covenants see Chapter 4.

That the plaintiff must have some legal or equitable right to enforce has been stressed in the case of *Re C (A Minor)* [1991] 2 FLR 169. In that case, a local authority sought to enforce an undertaking by an independent school to provide a place for C. The trial judge considered whether specific performance could be applied to the facts. He posed the question:

> Will the court exercise its jurisdiction to make a mandatory injunction, forcing an outside party to assume an active continuing role in relation to the ward, simply on the basis that, after weighing the rights of the outside party in the balance, it considers that in the ward's interest it should do so?

He concluded:

> I have come unhesitatingly to the conclusion that, in the present situation, the court will decline to exercise its jurisdiction otherwise than in accordance with the normal rule which requires an injunction to be founded upon a legal or equitable right. However much the court may be persuaded that the ward needs to be cared for by a particular person or educated at a particular school, and however small the perceived prejudice to the person or school in having to care for him or educate him, the court will not force such a role upon the latter unless he or she is compellable under principles of law.

Wardship jurisdiction made no difference to that general principle.

The Court of Appeal concurred with this view, Sir Stephen Brown P doubting that the undertaking by the school could be regarded as creating a contract.

Principles for granting specific performance

As with all equitable remedies, specific performance is discretionary and in particular will be granted only where damages are not an adequate remedy for the breach. Thus, in the area of sale contracts, there may be an assumption that if the thing sold can easily be obtained elsewhere, then damages will be adequate, and hence specific performance should not be granted. The claimant can use the damages to buy the thing elsewhere, and the measure of damages is, *prima facie*, the price of the replacement.

Contracts for the sale of land are thus invariably specifically enforceable since the land is generally regarded as unique. In *Sudbrook Trading* v *Eggleton* [1982] 3 All ER 1, Lord Diplock expressed the view that damages would 'constitute a wholly inadequate and unjust remedy for breach. That is why the normal remedy is a decree of specific performance . . .'

In contracts for the sale of goods, on the other hand, it follows that specific performance would only be available if the goods were unique and could not be obtained elsewhere. Traditional examples would be old master paintings, or rare antiques. The same approach has been taken to contracts for the sale of ships, which may often have unique qualities.

Such contracts, though, will be comparatively rare; normally, the buyer can go out and buy the same thing in the marketplace, so damages equivalent to the price of so doing will be adequate.

Nevertheless, on occasion the courts have granted specific performance even for non-specific or unascertained or future goods on the grounds of what has been called commercial uniqueness, that is where goods could not, in the circumstances, be obtained elsewhere.

In *Sky Petroleum* v *VIP Petroleum* [1974] 1 All ER 954, the fact that the goods (petrol), though unascertained (the contract was just for petrol, not any specific petrol), were practically unobtainable anywhere else, so that if the claimant did not receive supplies from the defendant he would go out of business, was justification for granting specific performance of the supply contract.

(The remedy granted was actually an interlocutory injunction, but for these purposes the rules are the same.)

This case, had it been followed, might offer a major exception to the adequacy of damages rule, or lead to it being overridden in many commercial cases. However, a note of caution was sounded by the Court of Appeal in *Société des Industries Metallurgiques* v *Bronx Engineering* [1975] 1 Lloyd's Rep 465. Here the court took the view that, even if the sellers of certain machinery were in breach of contract, it was very unlikely that specific performance would be granted to the buyers. This despite the fact that, as in *Sky Petroleum*, the buyers were faced with severe disruption of their business if the machinery supply contract was not performed, since it would take them nine to twelve months to obtain alternative machinery (and here, the machinery was specific and ascertained).

There are clearly sale of goods contracts where the loss to the buyer is not merely the cost of replacing the goods, which could in most cases be adequately compensated with damages, but also disruption of his business. In such a case, the evaluation of that disruption may prove difficult, which in itself might be a good reason for granting specific performance.

Similarly, damages may not be adequate where the measure would be nominal but measurable loss has occurred. Thus, in *Beswick* v *Beswick* [1967] 2 All ER 1197, where the contract was to pay a pension to Peter Beswick for the rest of his life and thereafter to his widow, Lord Denning took the view that damages would not be adequate. The action was by the estate of Peter, which had lost nothing by the breach and hence would receive only nominal damages, which would not in fact compensate for the loss to the widow.

It is not, however, necessary to show that the plaintiff has a right to damages, for the right to specific performance may arise independently of a breach of contract, which must, of course, be established if damages are to be claimed. Thus, it appears that the fact that the plaintiff has no right to damages may itself be a ground for granting specific performance: *Wright* v *Bell* (1818) 5 Price 325.

It is frequently said that the court will not grant specific performance of contracts which require some continuous acts in their performance by the defendant, for that would require the court to make constant supervision of the contracts. In *Ryan* v *Mutual Tontine* [1893] 1 Ch 116 a tenant sought specific performance of his landlord's contractual duty to provide a resident porter 'constantly in attendance'. Specific performance was refused on the ground referred to above. Lopes LJ stated:

> In order to give effect to (the contract), the court would have to watch over it and supervise its execution. But it is a recognised rule that the court cannot enforce a contract by compelling specific performance where the execution of the contract requires such watching over and supervision by the court.

It is submitted that the real issue here is whether the terms of the contract are sufficiently clear for the courts to enforce them. In *Posner* v *Scott-Lewis* [1986] 3 All ER 513, the relevant considerations were said to be: Was there a sufficient definition of what was to be done in order to comply with the order of the court? Would enforcing compliance involve the superintendence by the court to an unacceptable degree? What were the respective prejudices or hardships that would be suffered by the parties if the order was or was not made?

The requirement of continuous supervision was also a factor in refusing specific performance in *Re C* (above). As Stuart-Smith LJ indicated:

> The court will not specifically enforce a contract in which one party is bound by continuous duties, the due performance of which might require constant supervision by the court. While the child is at school, the school exercises its quasi-parental control. If the school will not co-operate with the parents, it seems to be that there is a risk that they would not discharge their duties properly; plainly that is not something that the court could supervise.

It is clear that the courts regard damages as the normal remedy for breach, and only in special cases will they interfere by granting specific performance. Their discretion to do so is governed by fixed and settled rules. The court will take account of the plaintiff's conduct: he must come to the court with clean hands and he must have performed or be prepared to perform his side of the bargain.

As regards the requirement of 'clean hands' (a principle discussed generally in Chapter 2), it has been stressed in *Quadrant Visual Communications* v *Hutchinson Telephones* (1991) 136 SJ 32(LB) that the maxim's application is entirely in the court's discretion, so that any attempt to exclude it by the terms of the contract cannot be effective; to hold otherwise would, in Stocker LJ's view, turn the court into a mere rubber stamp.

Ordinarily, a plaintiff is not prevented from seeking specific performance because of his delay. The reason for this, and the exceptions, were set out by Browne-Wilkinson V-C in *British and Commonwealth Holdings* v *Quadrex Holdings* [1989] 3 All ER 492:

> In equity, time is not normally of the essence of a contractual term . . . However, in three types of case time is of the essence on equity: first, where the contract expressly so stipulates; second, where the circumstances of the case or the subject matter of the contract indicate that the time for completion is of the essence; thirdly, where a valid notice to complete has been given.

Thus, the court may on occasion take account of the delay in seeking the order, though there is no statutory limitation period. What will be considered a reasonable delay will depend upon the subject matter of the contract, so where, in *Glasbrook* v *Richardson* (1874) 23 WR 51, the subject matter was a colliery, 'a property of an extremely speculative character, approaching a trade', a delay of three months was considered too much. More recently, the view has been expressed, by Megarry V-C in *Lazard Bros & Co Ltd* v *Fairfield Properties Co (Mayfair) Ltd* (1977) 121 SJ 793, that delay *per se* should not prevent the remedy being granted if, between the plaintiff and defendant, it was just that it should be.

The court, in determining whether to grant a decree of specific performance, may take into account whether the contract is a fair one or whether specific performance would cause undue hardship, either to the parties or to a third party. Thus, for example, in *Spiller* v *Bolton* (1947) 149 EG 450, specific performance was refused of a contract to purchase land for building, because the auctioneer had not made it clear that the land was being considered for local authority controls which would have made building impossible. Lack of fairness may arise also because of inequality of the parties' bargaining power, and it may also take into account the interests of a third party, as where ordering specific performance would necessarily interfere with a pre-existing contract with a third party: *Willmott* v *Barber* (1880) 15 Ch D 96.

Thames Guaranty Ltd v *Campbell* [1984] 2 All ER 585

This case illustrates that hardship to a third party may sometimes justify refusal of specific perform-ance. In this case, a husband had obtained loans on the security of his share in a house jointly owned by himself and his wife. The wife was unaware of the arrangement, though the loan company, at least in the latter stages, was aware that she had an interest in the house. The security of the loan was to be a charge on the husband's share in the house. The loan company sought to require the husband to create an equitable charge on the property as he had undertaken to do. The creation of this charge would enable the loan company to apply for sale of the property under s 30 of the Law of Property Act 1925. This would not of itself necessarily deprive the loan company of its right to specific performance, but in the circumstances this would seriously prejudice the wife, who was an innocent third party. As Slade LJ stated (at p. 599):

> [W]hen the competing equities are considered, the hardship that Mrs Campbell, as an innocent third party, would suffer if an order were made for partial performance of the agreements for a charge would far outweigh the hardship that the plaintiffs would suffer if such an order were refused. They have been largely the architects of their own misfortune, in failing to require Mr Campbell to perfect the charge which he had agreed to give them, after they had acquired full knowledge of his wife's interest.

Mutuality

It is commonly said that, if specific performance could not be granted to one of the parties, then, it should not be granted against that party. In the words of Buckley LJ in *Price* v *Strange* [1977] 3 All ER 371:

> the court will not compel a defendant to perform his obligations specifically if it cannot at the same time ensure that any unperformed obligations of the plaintiff will be specifically performed, unless, perhaps, damages would be an adequate remedy to the defendant for any default on the plaintiff's part.

Typical cases where contracts are not mutual are where the plaintiff's lack of capacity prevents his side of the bargain being specifically enforced or where the plaintiff's obligations are of such a nature that the court would not grant specific performance to enforce them. *Price* v *Strange* established that mutuality at the time of the making of the contract was not always a bar to specific performance. In that case, although the plaintiff's obligations to repair were not specifically enforceable at the time of the contract, nevertheless the plaintiff had performed most of those obligations subsequently and the defendant's obligation to renew the lease became enforceable, subject to compensation for repair work carried out by the defendant.

Mistake and misrepresentation

Mistake and misrepresentation may be grounds for rescission of contracts. They may also be a ground for refusing specific performance. This has most frequently arisen in cases of unilateral mistake by the plaintiff, especially where that has resulted from the defendant's fault.

Denny v Hancock (1870) 6 Ch App 1

In this case, due to an error in the vendor's ground plan of land offered at auction, the defendant believed that the land he was buying was other than it actually was. The court refused to grant specific performance against him. By contrast, in **Malins v Freeman** (1836) 2 Keen 25, due to no fault of the vendors, the defendant's agent made an unreasonable mistake and bid for the wrong land. Specific performance was granted against him.

Contracts for personal services

It is generally considered inequitable to award specific performance of contracts for personal services, such as employment contracts. In the words of Fry LJ in **De Francesco v Barnum** (1890) 45 Ch D 430: 'the courts are bound to be jealous, lest they should turn contracts of service into contracts of slavery'.

The reasoning behind this, as well as the inequity of forcing people to work together, is that such contracts would be very difficult to police by the threat of committal for contempt. Thus, in the famous case of **Lumley v Wagner**, referred to above in the context of injunctions, the court refused specific performance to make Miss Wagner sing for Mr Lumley. Only in exceptional circumstances will the courts depart from this rule (**Hill v Parsons** [1971] 3 All ER 1345). That this principle applies to all personal contracts, and not merely to employment contracts, is clear from **Re C**, referred to above. In this case, where the contract, if one existed, was to provide schooling for C, the school was unwilling, to say the least, to provide that schooling. Stuart-Smith LJ considered this crucial when balancing the interests of C:

> The real difficulty, as it seems to me, is the personal nature of the relationship between the parties. The courts are reluctant to force parties to enter into, and continue in, a personal relationship against the will of one of the parties. Despite all that has happened, the parents still seem anxious that the boy should attend this school. They say he is happy there, getting on well and the staff treat him sympathetically. But it is plain the school are unwilling to take the boy at any price. However unjustified such an attitude may be, it is a fact. In exercising its discretion, the court has to balance a number of factors, and it is plain that in exceptional cases the court will enforce the contract, notwithstanding the personal nature of the relationship.

His Lordship considered that the interests of the boy, C, were something that the court was entitled to take into account, and concluded:

> If I were convinced that it was entirely in the boy's interest to be educated at this school, then I would hold that the [trial] judge was wrong and that this was one of those rare cases where the court would enforce the contract notwithstanding the personal nature of it. But having regard to the hostile attitude of the school and the governors, both to the boy and in particular to the parents, I am left in very considerable doubt whether it is in his best interests he should go to this school.

This gives an indication of the factors that the court will have to weigh in such cases.

The effect of a decree of specific performance

In *Johnson* v *Agnew* [1980] AC 367, the defendant argued that once the plaintiff had obtained specific performance he had irrevocably elected for that remedy and had forfeited all rights to damages. The House of Lords rejected this, but made it clear that the plaintiff had no right to termination of the contract and damages. Once an order for specific performance had been made, the court would not make an order dissolving the specific performance and terminating the contract and awarding damages instead, if the court did not feel it just to do so.

Rescission

Objective 8

A party to a contract may have the right to rescind, that is to say, the right to set the contract aside and be restored to his former position if the contract contains some inherent flaw rendering it voidable in equity. While a court may make an order to this effect, rescission is really the act of one party declaring that he no longer considers himself bound. It may then be necessary to seek the assistance of the court in restoring any property since the parties are entitled to restitutio in integrum, i.e. to be put into the position they would have been in had the contract not been entered into. Alternatively, the court may have to act to refuse to allow the other party to enforce.

Grounds for rescission

Misrepresentation

A contract may be rescinded where it has been induced by a misrepresentation, whether fraudulent or innocent. If the representation was fraudulent, the innocent party was also entitled to set the contract aside in law and obtain damages. The right to obtain damages was extended at common law to negligent misrepresentations by *Hedley Byrne* v *Heller* [1963] 2 All ER 575, and the position has been substantially altered by the Misrepresentation Act 1967 which, as well as extending the right to damages to negligent misrepresentations, also allows under s 2(2) that damages may be awarded in lieu of rescission wherever the court thinks it would be equitable to do so, which means that damages can be awarded in lieu of rescission even in cases of innocent misrepresentation.

Mistake

There is significant difficulty in this area as to the relative ambit of common law and equity. A contract may be void for mistake at common law, in which case equity has no role to play. However, in certain cases of common mistake, i.e. a mistake shared by the parties, rescission has been granted. Thus, in *Cooper* v *Phibbs* (1867) LR 2 HL 149, the parties agreed on the lease of a salmon fishery, both of them believing that it was not the subject of an entail when in fact it was. The potential tenant was granted rescission of the contract. Though the topic of mistake in contracts is a complex one and, furthermore, one more appropriately dealt with in works on contract, it should be clear that for equity to intervene the mistake must be mutual, because other forms of mistake would tend to prevent agreement in the first place and hence there will be no contract which can be rescinded, though misrepresentation may be a relevant issue.

Undue influence

The common law can provide a remedy if a transaction is entered as a result of duress or physical pressure, but equity may intervene if the transaction was the product of undue influence. If the court finds undue influence the transaction may be rescinded.

The concept of undue influence is very difficult to define but is generally agreed to involve the exercise of unacceptable pressure as a result of the dominant position of the influencer.

Usually, an allegation of undue influence will relate to activities connected with a particular transaction, but occasionally it will be argued that the influence flows from the general domination of one party over the other.

Presumption of undue influence

In *Bank of Credit and Commerce International* v *Aboody* [1992] 4 All ER 955, the Court of Appeal classified undue influence into two basic categories, actual and presumed. The House of Lords in *CIBC Mortgages* v *Pitt* [1993] 4 All ER 433 has subsequently overruled *Aboody* in one respect and held that in cases of actual undue influence, once the influence is established, the plaintiff need not prove that the transaction was manifestly disadvantageous, for, as Lord Browne-Wilkinson stated: 'Actual undue influence is a species of fraud. Like any victim of fraud, a person who has been induced by undue influence to carry out a transaction which he did not freely and knowingly enter into is entitled to have it set aside as of right.'

In *Daniel* v *Drew* [2005] All ER(D) 84, the Court of Appeal highlighted the distinction between actual and presumed undue influence. Actual undue influence was something that had to be done to twist the mind of a donor, whereas in cases of presumed undue influence it was more a case of what had not been done, namely ensuring that independent advice was available to the donor. The critical question was whether the persuasion or the advice had invaded the free volition of the donor to accept or reject the persuasion or advice or withstand the influence. The donor might be led but she must not be driven and her will must be of her own volition. In determining this, it was important to consider the vulnerability of one party in the analysis, likewise the forcefulness of the personality of the other.

In cases of presumed undue influence, it will be necessary for the complainant to prove that there was a relationship of trust and confidence between complainant and wrongdoer of such a nature that it is fair to presume that the wrongdoer abused that relationship in procuring the complainant to enter the impugned transaction. In other words, it is not necessary to prove actual influence, merely the existence of the confidential relationship. Such a relationship may be established in two ways: first, certain relationships, such as that between solicitor and client, as a matter of law raise the presumption of influence; and secondly, even where the relationship is not one of those, the complainant may be able to establish the *de facto* existence of such a relationship by showing that he generally reposed trust and confidence in the wrongdoer.

Situations where *de facto* confidential relationships have been found are numerous.

Allcard v *Skinner* (1887) 36 Ch D 145

In this case, a woman joined an order of nuns and, having taken a vow of poverty, gave all of her property to the mother superior of the sisterhood. The rules of the order prevented her from obtaining independent advice. The relationship gave rise to a presumption of influence, strengthened by the lack of advice.

Cheese v Thomas [1994] 1 All ER 35

More recently, in this case, the judge at first instance found undue influence in a case of an elderly man and his great-nephew who bought a house together, with the intention that the elderly man should live in it for the rest of his life, and that thereafter the house would belong to the great-nephew:

It was common ground that the relationship was a confidential one: they were close, Mr Thomas was considerably younger, and had business experience and a degree of actual influence over Mr Cheese. Undue influence was therefore to be presumed (*per* Sir Donald Nicholls V-C in the Court of Appeal).

According to the Court of Appeal in *Macklin v Dowsett* (2004) 34 EG 68, the issue was not whether the transaction was to D's manifest disadvantage, but whether the transaction was not readily explicable by the relationship of the parties and whether an ascendancy relationship had existed.

The principles for rebutting an assumption of undue influence were considered by the Court of Appeal in the case of *Pesticcio v Huet* [2004] All ER (D) 36 (Apr). P was the sole owner of a house, which he shared with his mother. He was mentally and physically disadvantaged. Whilst in hospital following an accident, he was visited several times by a solicitor, T, who had been contacted either by N (P's sister) or her daughter. P signed a form for enduring power of attorney in favour of N and he executed a will appointing N and her daughter as executors. Some time after, P made a gift of the house to N who then sold the house to her daughter's boyfriend. Thereafter, P's brother was appointed as P's receiver and litigation friend. He brought proceedings to set aside the deed of gift.

The Court of Appeal held that the presumption of undue influence could be rebutted by showing that the transaction had been entered into after the nature and effect of the transaction had been fully explained to the donor by an independent qualified person, following *Inche Noriah v Omar* [1929] AC 127. The court had to be satisfied that the advice given by the independent qualified person was relevant and effective. It had to free the donor from the impairment of the influence on his free will. Importantly, it had to give the donor the necessary independence of judgement to make choices with a full appreciation of what he was doing. In the instant case, the judge found that the advice given by T was inadequate and wanting in several respects. Her advice could not be equated to that which a competent adviser would have given if acting solely for P: accordingly the deed of gift was set aside.

The Court of Appeal has subsequently stressed, in *Smith v Cooper* [2010] EWCA Civ 722, that, once the situation is one where undue influence is presumed, even the fact of the claimant having received professional advice does not automatically rebut the presumption. The issue which must be addressed is whether the claimant in fact entered into the transaction of his or her free will, free from the defendant's influence.

Misrepresentation, cohabiting guarantors and third-party rights

Barclays Bank v O'Brien [1993] 4 All ER 416

In this case, a husband was granted an overdraft facility by his bank, secured against the matrimonial home, which was owned jointly by himself and his wife. The wife signed the necessary documents without reading them, since the bank's instructions to its employees that she should be made fully aware of the effect of the documents and be advised to obtain independent advice were not carried out. She was persuaded to agree by the husband falsely representing to her that the guarantee was for a much smaller amount than was actually the case, and that it was only for a limited period. The bank later sought to enforce the guarantee against her. Under ordinary principles, the bank as a third party to the misrepresentation was bound by it in certain circumstances. In the words of Lord Browne-Wilkinson:

> Her right to set aside that transaction will be enforceable against third parties if either the husband was acting as the third party's agent or the third party had actual or constructive notice of the facts giving rise to the equity.

This is the rule which would apply in any case of misrepresentation. Are wives in any special position? In particular, is the bank in this case to be regarded as having constructive notice of the misrepresentation because of the relationship of confidence which may exist between husband and wife? The court made it clear that the relationship of husband and wife is not one of those where there is a presumption, as a matter of law, of undue influence. Nevertheless, the law contains what has been referred to as an 'invalidating tendency' towards married women, because even today many wives repose confidence and trust in their husbands in relation to their financial affairs. Therefore, when a wife offers to stand surety for her husband, as happened here, the creditor is put on inquiry by a combination of two factors: first, that the transaction is not on its face of any financial advantage to the wife; and secondly, that there is a substantial risk in transactions of this kind that in procuring his wife's agreement, the husband has committed some legal or equitable wrong.

> It follows that, unless the creditor who is put on inquiry takes reasonable steps to satisfy himself that the wife's agreement to stand surety has been properly obtained, the creditor will have constructive notice of the wife's rights [i.e. the right to have the transaction set aside].

His Lordship made it clear that the same approach should be applied to all other cases where there is an emotional relationship between cohabitees, since in any such cases there was the underlying risk of one cohabitee exploiting the trust of the other.

Crédit Lyonnais v *Burch* [1997] 1 All ER 144

This case makes it clear that there need be no emotional or sexual relationship involved. Here the defendant, Miss Burch, was a relatively junior employee of a travel agency. Mr Pelosi, a senior official of the agency, whom Miss Burch trusted and on whom she relied heavily, persuaded her to give an unlimited guarantee of the agency's overdraft, secured by a second mortgage on her flat. The Court of Appeal was of the opinion that the fact that the transaction was so disadvantageous to Miss Burch should have put the bank on notice of undue influence: in such circumstances they could not presume that she would have received advice. In the words of Millett LJ:

> they must have known that no competent solicitor could advise her to enter into a guarantee in the terms that she did.

The third party's notice of the misrepresentations means that the agreement is wholly unenforceable by the third party: in *TSB* v *Camfield* [1995] 1 All ER 951, the Court of Appeal made it clear that the third party is not entitled to enforce the agreement even partially to the extent of the amount to which the wife believed the surety was limited.

Dunbar Bank plc v Nadeem [1997] 2 All ER 253

If the guarantor has in fact derived a benefit from the guarantee, she will only be able to have the guarantee set aside upon making restitution for the benefit received. On the facts of **Nadeem**, the wife had guaranteed her husband's debts, on the strength of which the bank advanced a sum of money which was used, *inter alia*, to purchase a leasehold property in the husband and wife's joint names. To have the guarantee set aside (and the facts were clear that the bank had constructive notice of the undue influence on the wife), she had to reimburse the bank with the value of the amount of the loan used to acquire her share in the leasehold.

The procuring of independent advice may remove undue influence, but here the issue has to be seen from the point of view of the third party. Thus, a third party may avoid constructive notice of the undue influence, and hence the wife's equity, by taking reasonable steps to ensure that she receives what reasonably appears to them to be independent advice. The matter thus becomes one of the interrelationship of the third party, the legal adviser and the guarantor: in practice, the bank, the solicitor acting for the wife, and the wife herself.

In *Royal Bank of Scotland* v *Etridge (No. 2)* [2001] 4 All ER 449, the House of Lords stressed the general principle that he who alleges undue influence must prove it. Thus, where a wife had acted as surety for her husband's debts, and now wished to avoid liability on the grounds of her husband's undue influence over her, *prima facie* it was for her to prove the influence. A transaction where a wife guaranteed her husband's business debts was *not* one where undue influence was presumed unless the contrary was proved, 'though there might be cases which call for an explanation'.

In cases where the wife wishes to stand surety, the bank, as creditor, is put on inquiry, as there is a risk that the husband may have committed a legal or equitable wrong entitling the wife to set the transaction aside. In other words, the bank should realise that the husband in such cases may have misled his wife or concealed the true nature of the transaction, and if this were true the wife would be able to avoid her liability as surety.

Given that the bank is put on inquiry, the House stated that the bank need do no more than take reasonable steps to satisfy itself that the practical implications of her standing surety had been explained to the wife. This could normally be done by relying on confirmation from the solicitor acting for the wife that he had advised her appropriately. If the bank actually knew that the solicitor had not in fact advised the wife, then it would not have fulfilled the requirement to take reasonable steps, but ordinarily it could rely on the solicitor's statement. If the solicitor had failed to give proper advice, but had told the bank he had, this would be a matter between the solicitor and the wife, but the wife could not set aside the transaction *vis-à-vis* the bank, and would be liable as surety.

The House also set out in some detail the obligations on the solicitor in such a case and the level of advice and information he should give, including explaining the nature of all the documents and the intended transaction, the extent of her potential liability and which of her assets might become liable. The solicitor should also explain the consequences of his informing the bank that he has explained the matter to her. Above all, the solicitor should stress that the decision to act as surety was the wife's, alone and independently. All this should be explained at a face-to-face meeting between the wife and the solicitor, not in the presence of the husband.

Although, based on the facts of the cases, it is assumed that the husband is the debtor and the wife is the surety, these principles would equally apply where the roles of the spouses were reversed, or where the partners were unmarried, heterosexual or homosexual (bearing in mind that in such cases the property used as security is usually the home which they co-own and in which they cohabit).

All of this cannot, however, interfere with the free will of the guarantor. If the guarantor chooses to proceed with an unwise transaction, against the advice of their solicitor, then, as in *Banco Exterior International* v *Thomas* [1997] 1 All ER 46, the transaction is valid, even though the bank was informed of the solicitor's advice. What matters is whether there is undue influence, not whether the transaction is unwise, unless, as suggested in *Etridge* (above), the nature of the transaction is itself suggestive of undue influence (which in *Banco Exterior International* v *Thomas* was rebutted by the proven fact of independent legal advice).

Bars to relief

Affirmation

If the party who is entitled to rescind the transaction is found to have affirmed it, the right to rescind will be lost. A contract will be affirmed if the party takes benefits under it knowing that the right to rescind exists.

Laches

Unreasonable delay with knowledge of the right to rescind will be a bar to obtaining the remedy. In *Allcard* v *Skinner* (1887), there was a delay of five years after the woman left the sisterhood. She had been advised by her solicitor of her right to seek rescission and her delay barred her claim to rescind. Delay may also be treated as evidence of affirmation.

Third-party rights

If the subject matter of the transaction has been acquired by a third party who had no notice of the undue influence, and who provided value, the right to rescind will be lost.

Restitutio in integrum

It is usually said that the courts will not order rescission if the parties cannot be restored to their original positions. The courts do not insist on exact restoration, particularly in cases of fraud, but aim at achieving practical justice, rather than precise restoration. The problem of restoring the parties was discussed in *Cheese* v *Thomas*, referred to above. The Vice-Chancellor stressed that the principle is one of restitution, not damages.

> Damages look at the plaintiff's loss, whereas restitution is concerned with the recovery back from the defendant of what he received under the transaction. If the transaction is set aside, the plaintiff also must return what he received. Each party must hand back what he obtained under contract.

This is straightforward in a simple contract of sale: if the contract is set aside, the vendor returns the money and the purchaser returns the item purchased. In the ordinary way, it does not matter that the item has subsequently fallen in value: the purchaser may lose financially, but the court is not concerned with compensation here.

Cheese v Thomas [1994] 1 All ER 35

The facts of this case were different, in that both parties had contributed, in differing amounts, to the purchase of a new item, a house. Furthermore, one of them had raised the money by way of mortgage, most of which was still owing. The house was sold at a loss, and the question was how this loss was to be shared. The mortgagor took priority, recovering the full amount of the debt, and only a small amount remained. Simply to hand this to the plaintiff, Mr Cheese, who had put in capital, would be unfair to him, in that he would bear all the loss, and Mr Thomas, whose mortgage liability had been met, would suffer none. The court ordered that the sale value before deduction of the mortgage should be divided between them in proportion to their contributions to the purchase. Accordingly, £55,700 was divided between them in shares of 43 to 40, or £28,700 to Mr Cheese and £26,700 to Mr Thomas: Mr Cheese thus received the net proceeds of £17,667 and a further £11,033 from Mr Thomas.

The court emphasised that decisions as to restitution in these cases are essentially discretionary, with the ultimate object of achieving practical justice:

> The basic objective of the court is to restore the parties to their original positions, as nearly as may be, consequent upon cancelling a transaction which the law will not permit to stand. That is the basic objective. Achieving a practically just outcome in that regard required the court to look at all the circumstances, while keeping the basic objective firmly in mind. In carrying out this exercise the court is, of necessity, exercising a measure of practical justice in the particular case.

The behaviour of the parties is clearly a factor. As Fox LJ stated in *O'Sullivan* v *Management Agency and Music Ltd* [1985] 3 All ER 351: 'where there has been dishonesty or surreptitious dealing or other improper conduct then . . . it might be appropriate to refuse relief; but that will depend on the circumstances'.

Rectification

Objective 9

Rectification is a power of equity to correct a document so that it reflects accurately the agreement of the parties. This is not to be confused with the power, both at common law and in equity, to correct errors which are obvious on the face of the document, for rectification entails a party presenting extrinsic evidence of the agreement and seeking to bring the document in line with it. Denning LJ stated the preconditions for rectification in *Frederick E Rose (London) Ltd* v *William H Pim Jnr & Co Ltd* [1953] 2 All ER 739:

> In order to get rectification, it is necessary to show that the parties were in complete agreement on the terms of their contract, but by an error wrote them down wrongly . . . If you can predicate with certainty what their contract was, and that it is, by a common mistake, wrongly expressed in the document, then you can rectify the document.

It is important to remember that the court is concerned with their actual agreement, even if that was reached as a result of a shared mistake, rather than what they would have agreed if they had not been mistaken. So, in *Rose* v *Pim*, the parties agreed to buy and sell horsebeans, which both believed to be the same as feveroles. It was not subsequently open to them to say that they had meant to buy and sell feveroles as distinct from horsebeans.

583

It follows from the requirement of agreement that rectification will not normally apply where there is a unilateral mistake, i.e. a mistake made by only one party where the other knows he is mistaken, because in that case it cannot be said that both parties are agreed that the document is wrong. One party may no doubt say that it does not represent the agreement as that party understood it, but he cannot say that they both understood it in this way. However, if one party is mistaken and the other guilty of fraud, the court may order rectification so that the document actually says what the innocent party thought it said.

This last issue was considered in *Riverlate Properties v Paul* [1974] 2 All ER 657, where the Court of Appeal refused to allow rescission of a lease for unilateral mistake, the party who was not mistaken being unaware of the mistake. Russell LJ posed the question:

> Is the plaintiff entitled to recission [sic] of a lease on the mere ground that it made a serious mistake in drafting of the lease which it put forward and subsequently executed, when (a) the defendant did not share the mistake, (b) the defendant did not know that the document did not give effect to the plaintiff's intention, and (c) the mistake of the plaintiff was in no way attributable to anything said or done by the defendant? . . . In point of principle, we cannot find that this should be so. If reference be made to principles of equity, it operates on conscience. If conscience is clear at the time of the transaction, why should equity disrupt the transaction?

Accordingly, the lease would not be rescinded, either with or without the option to the defendant to accept rectification to cure the plaintiff's mistake, the defendant not being guilty of anything approaching sharp practice in relation thereto.

Burden of proof

The party wishing to have the document rectified is under a very heavy burden to show that it does not in fact represent the parties' intentions. He must, in the words of Russell LJ in *Joscelyne v Nissen* [1970] 1 All ER 1213, produce 'convincing proof'. As Brightman LJ stated in *Thomas Bates & Son Ltd v Wyndham's (Lingerie) Ltd* [1981] 1 All ER 1077:

> [A]s the alleged common intention *ex hypothesi* contradicts the written instrument, convincing proof is required in order to counteract the cogent evidence of the parties' intention displayed by the instrument itself. It is not . . . the standard of proof that is high, so differing from the normal civil standard, but the evidential requirement needed to counteract the inherent probability that the written instrument truly represents the parties' intention because it is a document signed by the parties.

A subjective or objective test?

In *Chartbrook v Persimmon Homes* [2009] UKHL 38; [2009] 1 AC 1101, the House of Lords applied an objective test to the interpretation of the contract; in other words, what would the reasonable person have understood the parties to have meant. It thus ignored details of the pre-contract negotiations as evidence of the parties' actual intention, following long-established court practice.

Deeds, wills and settlements

The cases considered above are concerned with agreements and contracts, where the issue is whether the terms as recorded coincide with the agreement as the parties understood it.

Rectification can also apply, however, to other types of documents, such as wills and settlements, which are by their nature unilateral; there is no question of parties being at cross-purposes. In the case of a trust settlement, for example, the issue will be whether the trust deed records the intentions of the settlor. Again, 'convincing' proof must be provided that it does not, if rectification is to be granted. It is important to distinguish between the settlor's intentions as to what the trust deed should say, and what the wider implications, for example on tax liability, might be. Rectification will not be granted just because it turns out that the settlement as planned and drafted did not have the tax advantages that were expected. Nor is it an opportunity to draft a wholly new settlement to achieve those advantages. As stated by Rimer J in *Allnutt v Wilding* [2006] EWHC 1905 (Ch); [2006] WLTR 1317:

> [R]ectification is about setting the record straight. In the case of a voluntary settlement, rectification involves bringing the trust document into line with the true intentions of the settlor as held by him at the date when he executed the document.

Defences

Rectification will not be granted where there is undue delay or where the contract has been performed in its mistaken form, or is no longer capable of performance. Neither will it be granted where a *bona fide* purchaser has acquired an interest under it.

Administration of Justice Act 1982 s 20

This provides for rectification of wills in certain circumstances. Section 20 states:

(1) If a court is satisfied that a will is so expressed that it fails to carry out the testator's intentions, in consequence
    (a) of a clerical error; or
    (b) of a failure to understand his instructions,
it may order that the will shall be rectified so as to carry out his intentions.

The section also provides that an application to rectify under this section may not normally be brought more than six months after the grant of representation. Personal representatives will not be liable for distributing the estate after six months on the assumption that no application will be made outside that time, but any rights the beneficiaries may have to recover the property wrongly distributed is preserved.

Summary

- Equity is the principal source of the compelling remedies in English law, that is to say, those which enforce obligations or prevent breaches of them, as opposed to awarding compensation for those breaches once they have occurred.

- Such remedies have, however, traditionally been regarded as subordinate to common law damages, and are only awarded at the discretion of the court. They may be withheld if the court feels that the claimant does not 'deserve the remedy because of his own unconscionable conduct or because of unreasonable delay in seeking the remedy.

- Injunctions may be granted to prohibit certain behaviour by the defendant which infringes the claimant's rights. They may also be sought to oblige the defendant to take positive action to restore the claimant's rights, but this is less likely due to the possible burden on the defendant.

- Injunctions may be granted as the final remedy in a case, or they may be obtained at an interim stage, to prevent loss to the claimant pending a full trial of his claim. In a claim for an interim injunction the court will consider the balance of convenience to the claimant and defendant.

- Injunctions may be granted to protect a range of legal or equitable interests of the claimant, for example in contract or tort, or for the protection of property rights.

- Injunctions may also be granted to allow the claimant to search the defendant's, or a third party's, premises or records to look for evidence which may be relevant to his claim.

- Injunctions may also be granted to freeze the assets of the defendant to prevent him disposing of them, so they will be available to meet the claimant's claim for financial reparation, should he win his case.

- Where an injunction is in principle available to protect the claimant's legal or equitable rights, the court may nevertheless, at its discretion, withhold the injunction and grant damages instead.

- The decree of specific performance may be granted to enforce the terms of a contract in cases where damages would not be an adequate compensation.

- The remedy of rescission allows a contract or agreement to be set aside where a party to it has been subject to undue influence or has not been free to make an informed decision when entering the agreement. This may affect any third party rights under the agreement.

- Rectification allows documents, such as deeds and written contracts, to be amended if they do not reflect the true intention of the parties.

Further reading

Interim injunctions

A Keay, 'Whither *American Cyanamid*?: interim injunctions in the 21st century' (2004) 23 CJQ 133.
A review of developments since *American Cyanamid*.

J Phillips, 'Interlocutory injunctions and intellectual property: a review of *American Cyanamid* v *Ethicon* in the light of *Series 5 Software*' [1997] JBL Sep 486.
Contrasting the two cases.

Defences to injunctions

R A Buckley, 'Injunctions and the public interest' (1981) 44 MLR 212.

A Casenote on *Kennaway* v *Thompson* (1980).

G Watt, 'Building at risk of injunction' [2005] Conv 460.
Examination of the *Shelfer* principles as applied in *Mortimer* v *Bailey* (2004).

Enforcement of employment contracts

H McLean, 'Contract of employment – negative covenants and no work, no pay' (1990) 49 CLJ 28.
An examination of *Warren* v *Mendy* (1989).

Search orders

B Andoh, 'The search order and the privilege against self-incrimination' (2005) 26 Bus LR 6.
A review of the rules for search orders and a critique of the privilege.

K Reece-Thomas and M Dockray, '*Anton Piller* orders: the new statutory scheme' [1998] CJQ 272.
The effects of the Civil Procedure Act 1997.

Freezing injunctions

D Capper, 'The trans-jurisdictional effects of *Mareva* injunctions' (1996) 15 CJQ 211.
Application of freezing orders in respect of assets abroad and in support of cases in other jurisdictions.

L Collins, 'The territorial reach of the *Mareva* injunction' (1989) 105 LQR 262.
Application to assets abroad.

P McGrath, 'The freezing order; a constantly evolving jurisdiction' (2012) 31 CJQ 12.
Application in five recent cases, including application to trust assets.

A Zuckerman, '*Mareva* and interlocutory injunctions disentangled' (1992) 108 LQR 559.
Looks at orders against banks, *Mareva* injunctions and tracing.

Damages in lieu of injunction

Z Bhaloo and M Marsh, 'A game of chance' (2006) 0629 EG 124 & 0630 EG 95.
Examination of the discretionary approach to the grant of injunctions.

M Dixon, 'The sound of silence' [2014] Conv2, 79–84.
A discussion of *Coventry* v *Lawrence* (2014).

D Halpern, 'Damages in lieu of an injunction: how much?' [2001] Conv 453.
Principles for quantification of damages in such cases.

M Warwick, 'Final injunctions' (2005) 149 (27) Sol J 823.
Comparison of *Jaggard* v *Sawyer* (1995) with *Mortimer* v *Bailey* (2004).

Specific performance

G Jones, 'Specific performance of a contract of service' (1987) 46 CLJ 21.
Specific performance of covenants: examination of *Posner* v *Scott-Lewis* (1987).

Undue influence and rescission

R Bigwood, 'Undue influence in the House of Lords, principle and proof' (2002) 65 MLR 435.
The general principle of the court's power to relieve for undue influence.

D Capper, 'Undue influence and unconscionability: a rationalisation' (1998) 114 LQR 479.
Whether the two doctrines could be merged.

J Devenney, L Fox-O'Mahony and M Kenny, 'Standing surety in England and Wales: the sphinx of procedural protection' [2008] LMCLQ 513.
Legal protection for non-professional sureties guaranteeing family loans.

L Mason, 'Undue influence and testamentary dispositions: an equitable jurisdiction in probate law?' [2011] Conv 115.
Considers the different situations where undue influence may be an issue, and in particular the contrast between testamentary and *inter vivos* instances.

J Mee, 'Undue influence, misrepresentation and the doctrine of notice' (1995) 54 CLJ 536.
Future application of the doctrine as set out in *Barclays Bank* v *O'Brian* (1994).

M Oldham, 'If at first . . . undue influence and the House of Lords' (2002) 61 CLJ 29.
The requirements for advising sureties, in light of *Royal Bank of Scotland* v *Etridge* (2001).

H Tjio and A Phang, 'The uncertain boundaries of undue influence' [2002] LMCLQ 231.
Operation of undue influence doctrine in the light of *Royal Bank of Scotland* v *Etridge* (2001).

Rectification

P Davies, 'Rectifying the course of rectification' (2012) 75 MLR 412.
Explains the uncertainty arising from the House of Lords' application of an objective test for common mistake in *Chartbrook Ltd* v *Persimmon Homes Ltd* (2009).

G McMeal, 'Interpretation and mistake in contract law: "The fox knows many things . . . "' [2006] LMCLQ 49.
Traditional and modern techniques of constructing and interpreting contracts.

E Palser, 'Rectification for unilateral mistake: how heavy is the burden of proof?' [2006] LMCLQ 139.
Power to rectify in cases of unilateral mistake.

Glossary

Note: This glossary is not a substitute for a legal dictionary. In particular the brief definitions of words and phrases that it provides are those which apply in the context of equity and trusts. There may often be other meanings for these words in other legal contexts.

ab initio from the beginning.

absolute owner one who owns all of the rights in property – both legal and equitable.

absolute title ownership of all of the rights in property – both legal and equitable.

acquiescence a term describing the behaviour of a claimant who, knowing of his legal right, allows the defendant to act in breach of that right. This will usually prevent the claimant from seeking a remedy in equity.

ademption ademption describes the situation where property mentioned in a specific bequest in a will is not part of the testator's property at the time of death. The bequest fails and the person named as the beneficiary will receive neither the particular property nor anything representing it.

administrator one who administers (winds up) the estate of a person who has died not leaving a valid will.

advancement an advancement (certainly historically) describes a sum of money or other benefit given to (usually) one's child to set the transferee up in life. In most cases the sum of money would tend to be larger rather than smaller and the beneficiary would tend to be younger rather than older – though normally not a minor. An example could be a payment to buy a child of the transferor an interest in a business. (Note 'child' could be, and normally would be, over 18 years of age.)

advancement (presumption) the presumption that transfers between certain people are intended as gifts. For example, from a father to his child, from a husband to his wife and from a person to

one he stands *in loco parentis* to. This presumption was abolished when s 199 of the Equality Act 2010 came into force.

agent a person who has entered into an agreement to act on another's behalf (the other person being known as the principal). This is a fiduciary relationship, giving rise to a fiduciary duty on the agent not to make personal gains from his position

Anton Piller order *see* 'search order'.

apportionment trustees have a duty to be even-handed as between beneficiaries and between beneficiaries with different types of interest under the trust (for example, some beneficiaries may be entitled to income, others to capital).

The Trusts (Capital and Income) Act 2013 disapplies the rules of apportionment for trusts created or arising on or after the day on which the Act came into force and to trusts created by will, or arising under the intestacy rules, in relation to a death on or after 1 October 2013. Settlors or testators can expressly include the duty to apportion. Also settlors can expressly include a duty to apportion on or after 1 October 2013.

bailment an example of a bailment is the deposit of a piece of property for a particular purpose. For example, where goods are lent, hired out or deposited for safe custody, there is a bailment.

bare trust a trust in which the property is held on trust absolutely for the beneficial interest of an individual(s), who is/are competent to wind up the trust at any time. The trustees (normally referred to in this context as nominees) act under his/their direction and control.

beneficiary principle the principle that a trust must have a human beneficiary or beneficiaries, on whose behalf the courts may order the trustees to act in managing the trust property; the trustees cannot be said to act under any obligation if there is no beneficiary who can enforce the trust. The main exception to this is the charitable trust (*see* 'charitable trusts' and 'purpose trusts').

beneficiary under a trust the one for whom the trust is set up. The beneficiary is the owner of the beneficial interest in the trust property.

bequest gift made under a will.

bona vacantia goods belonging to nobody. If no one has a good claim to the ownership of property under a trust, it will pass to the Crown as *bona vacantia*.

breach of contract a breach of contract occurs where one of the parties fails to carry out his duties or promises under a valid contract.

breach of trust any failure by the trustees to carry out the terms of the trust. A distinction should be drawn between trustees' duties, which are compulsory, and their powers where they have some discretion, subject to their general duty of care.

cestui que trust old-fashioned synonym for a beneficiary under a trust.

charitable incorporated organisation (CIO) a new form of structure available to charities from 2013, whereby they may organise themselves as a corporation, which has a separate legal personality, limiting the liability of the directors and allowing the organisation to hold charity property and to enter into contracts, without the need to be registered as a company under the Companies Acts.

charitable trusts trusts where property is held on trust for the fulfilment of purposes which are recognised by law as charitable. Sometimes referred to as 'public trusts'.

chose in action intangible property such as a debt.

consideration the giving of something of value in return for a promise. This is a requirement for an enforceable contract, and the same applies to covenants to settle property; equity will not enforce (by an order for specific performance) a promise to settle property on trust on behalf of those who have not given consideration for the promise (known as 'volunteers'), hence the maxim, 'equity will not assist a volunteer'.

constructive trust a trust recognised by the courts in situations where justice and good conscience require it, as opposed to being expressly created by a settlor or where his intention to create a trust is implied by his conduct. Numerous examples exist, of which the most common arise from misuse of trust assets by a fiduciary, or from situations where an innocent party has acted to his detriment in the belief that property is, or will become, his.

contingent interest an interest which is subject to some condition which may not happen. Thus the potential beneficiary may never receive the interest because the condition may not be satisfied.

covenant a promise contained in a deed. This has no special status in equity, but parties to a covenant may have common law remedies (damages) for breach of it.

cy-près term from Norman French which means as near as possible. It is used e.g. where the objects of a charity have become 'impossible' to perform and the funds are applied to another charity with similar objects.

deed a document under seal (carrying a seal, or, in modern law, expressed to be by deed). The method of conveyance of unregistered land. The terms of an express trust are normally (but need not necessarily be) set out in a deed. *See also* 'covenant'.

devise a gift of real property (land) by will.

devisee one to whom a gift of land is made in a will.

discretionary trust a trust where the trustees have a power of appointment, that is, typically, to determine who amongst a class of beneficiaries shall receive trust property and in what shares.

donationes mortis causa (DMC) gifts made in contemplation of death (not necessarily imminent death but death from a specific cause).

en ventre sa mère this refers to a child conceived but not born and means 'an unborn child inside the mother's womb'.

equitable interest an interest of a beneficiary under a trust is an example of an equitable interest, i.e. an interest recognised (originally) by the court of equity as opposed to the common law courts.

estoppel the principle whereby an individual may acquire an equitable right or interest because he has relied to his detriment on the promise of another that the promisor will not enforce his rights against the promisee.

executor one who administers the estate having been appointed in a valid will.

fiduciary duty certain relationships, such as that of trustee and beneficiary or director and company or agent and principal, are described as fiduciary. The fiduciary must act in utmost good faith, and is not permitted to act in such a way that his personal interest and his fiduciary duty conflict. Thus, for example, a trustee must not (normally) acquire trust property for himself.

fixed trust a trust in which the beneficial interests are fixed: that is, set out in definite terms by the settlor, as opposed to being determined at the discretion of the trustees.

freezing injunctions an injunction ordering a party to litigation (or potential litigation) not to remove assets from the court's jurisdiction, or otherwise deal in them, to defeat the claim of a potential claimant.

imperfect gift one where the necessary formalities for the transfer of the property have not been completed. In such a case, equity will not perfect such a gift by treating the intended donee as the beneficiary under a trust (though there are exceptions).

in personam literally this means 'in person'. An action or remedy is *in personam* where it is only available against a person who owns property which is the subject matter of an action.

in rem a right *in rem* is a right to property and thus will attach to that property whoever has possession of it, subject in the case of equitable rights to the *bona fide* purchaser principle.

injunction a court order, originally from the Court of Chancery, ordering a person to refrain from doing some act (a prohibitory injunction) or, more occasionally, ordering the performance of some act (a mandatory injunction). For example, an order to stop some activity which causes the plaintiff to suffer a nuisance.

intangible property this is property, like a bank account, that lacks a physical existence.

intellectual property choses in action such as patents, copyrights, etc. These are forms of intangible property.

inter vivos a transaction taking effect during life.

interim injunction an injunction issued at a preliminary stage, before there has been a full trial of the matter. For example, where a claimant alleged that a defendant was selling a product in infringement of the claimant's patent pending a full trial to determine the patent rights, the defendant is prevented by interim injunction from continuing to sell the product.

intestacy the state of dying without leaving a valid will.

intestate one who dies without leaving a valid will.

laches delay; the doctrine of laches enables the court to refuse an equitable remedy to a claimant who has delayed so long in seeking a remedy that it would be unconscionable to impose it on the defendant. Often linked with 'acquiescence'.

legacy a gift of personalty under a will.

legatee one to whom a gift of personalty is made in a will.

letters of administration letters of administration are granted by the court to a person(s) under the intestacy rules (the administrator). The grant enables them to deal with the intestate deceased's assets and distribute to those entitled under the intestacy rules.

life in being this relates to the perpetuity rules. A life in being is a human being who is alive at the effective date of a disposition. A child conceived but not born also qualifies as a life in being for this purpose, provided that they are in fact born alive. The concept of lives in being is not relevant to trusts governed by the Perpetuities and Accumulations Act 2009.

limitation period the period of time set down by law, after which an action cannot be brought.

Mareva **injunction** *see* 'freezing injunctions'.

mere powers a power given to an individual, usually not a fiduciary, to determine the distribution of property among a class. Contrasted with a trust in that a mere power is purely discretionary and cannot be enforced by anyone who might benefit from its exercise.

next of kin the nearest blood relative(s) of a deceased who is/are alive at the date of the death, or the spouse/civil partner of the deceased. The intestacy rules specify the deceased's 'closest' relatives for the purpose of distributing the intestate's estate.

perpetuity period, rules against the period to which trusts are limited, preventing the creation of trusts which last for ever, and preventing the creation of contingent interests which may not vest within the period provided for by the law.

personal property property which is not land or an interest in land.

personal representative one who handles the estate of a dead person. The term covers executors and administrators.

power of appointment the power to select who, from among a class, will receive property.

preamble the term commonly applied to the preamble to the Statute of Elizabeth (the Charitable Uses Act 1601), which set out a list of purposes which were charitable and formed the basis of the definition of charity.

principal a person to whom an agent owes his fiduciary duty and to whom he is accountable for any gains made as a result of his fiduciary position.

probate (grant of) a grant of probate issued by the court (through the Probate Registry) enables the executor to prove their right to deal with the testator's property.

promissary estoppel a form of 'estoppel' where a party makes a promise not to enforce the terms of a contract. This is normally not supported by consideration and so should not be enforceable. However, the promisor is prevented from going back on the promise because the other party has relied on it. It differs from most estoppel in that it does not give rise to a property right.

proprietary remedy a term applied to remedies which recognise that a claimant has ownership (usually equitable ownership) in property which is ostensibly owned by another. Thus a constructive trust may be imposed on property held by a fiduciary, so that the person owed the fiduciary duty is able to claim the property and trace into any gains or profits made on it.

public benefit the requirement that a charitable trust, to be valid, must be for the benefit of the public at large, or a sufficient section of the public, as opposed to being limited to a class of individual beneficiaries.

purpose trusts trusts for the fulfilment of a purpose, as opposed to containing interests for individual persons. Normally not possible, unless the trusts are charitable.

quia timet literally 'because he fears'. A term applied to injunctions where the remedy is sought before any actual harm has occurred but where the claimant fears it will happen in the future, and can produce evidence to support this fear.

real property land.

rectification the process by which a document can be corrected if it fails to reflect accurately the agreement of the parties.

remainderman a beneficiary under a trust who is entitled to the capital from the trust fund after the death of the tenant for life.

rescission the equitable remedy whereby a contract may be set aside due to some flaw, such as a misrepresentation by one of the parties, e.g. as to the nature of the goods which are the contract's subject matter.

restitutio in integrum the recovery of rights or property completely, without loss. This may be lost if, for example, the subject matter of a contract has been destroyed or changed.

restitution an area of law concerned with the right of recovery from the defendant of gains by which he has been unjustly enriched (as opposed to a measure based on the claimant's loss). Distinguished from property rights which may be enforced regardless of such enrichment.

resulting trust a trust where the equitable interest returns to the settlor.

search order court order, similar to an injunction, by which the court may give a potential litigant the right to search the premises of parties to litigation, or third parties, to look for information or material relevant to potential litigation, such as company records, patented designs, etc.

secret trust/half-secret trust a trust set up to avoid the consequences of a will being a public document. A fully secret trust is used where a testator does not wish to reveal in his will the fact that he has set up a trust, its terms and who the beneficiaries are. A half-secret trust is used where the testator reveals on the face of the will that T takes as a trustee, but the will does not reveal the terms of the trust and who the beneficiaries are.

settlement although this term has a technical meaning in some taxation contexts, in most situations it is a synonym for a trust.

settlor one who sets up (creates) a trust. The term is used most often in relation to express trusts.

specific performance an equitable remedy by which a party to a contract is ordered to perform his obligations under the terms of the contract. Normally available only where the common law remedy of damages would be inadequate.

subrogation the equitable remedy under which a claimant's rights are transferred to another, typically to his insurer, who will be entitled to enforce those rights for his own benefit because he has already met the claimant's claim under the insurance policy.

tenant for life the beneficiary under a trust who has an interest limited to their lifetime. This normally entitles them to the income from the trust fund, but not the capital.

testamentary trust a trust created under the terms of a will.

testator one who makes a valid will.

tracing the process by which trust property which has been removed from a trust can be followed into the hands of third parties or, when converted, into other form of property. Once the property has been identified, the claimant may then seek a remedy to recover it. It is possible to follow

property at common law, but this is severely limited and the use of the equitable charge makes the process in equity much more flexible.

undue influence a person may not be bound by an agreement or transaction if he was induced to enter into it because he was under the undue influence of another. There is a presumption of undue influence in fiduciary relationships, and it may be found as a fact in other relationships, such as marriage. This presumption may be rebutted by proof that independent advice was given. Thus in recent cases where a husband has sought to put a charge on the matrimonial home to secure his debts, it will be necessary to show that the wife received independent advice before she agreed to the charge, otherwise the chargee (e.g. a bank or other creditor) will not be able to enforce the charge against her, or the home.

unincorporated association an organisation not run as a company or corporation. Examples include clubs and societies. Such organisations do not have a separate legal personality but exist as associations of individuals. Issues arising from this include the way in which an association holds property; normally this is held on trust by a treasurer on behalf of the members, subject to the club's rules and constitution.

unjust enrichment the principle which, according to some authors, underlies the award of restitutionary remedies. Such remedies are designed to remove improper gains from the defendant. The constructive trust and its fiduciary duty to account for profits are sometimes considered restitutional for this reason.

use in effect the forerunner of the trust.

vested interest an interest under a trust to which the beneficiary is definitely entitled (i.e. not subject to some condition which may not occur), even though the property may not fall into his possession until a later date (a future interest).

vesting property effectively transferring property to a person (including one who is a trustee).

volunteer someone who has not given consideration for a promise, which is therefore not enforceable in equity by him (*see* 'consideration').

will a document that satisfies the relevant statutory provisions (mainly those contained in the Wills Act 1837). The will must be in writing, **signed** by the **testator**, or by someone else at his direction and in his presence. The will must be signed, or the signature acknowledged, in the presence of two or more witnesses, present at the same time and each witness must attest and sign, or acknowledges, his signature in the presence of the testator.

A will can do a variety of things but is mainly used to state who will receive the testator's property on their death.

witness (to a will) one who signs a will in the presence of the testator (or acknowledges an existing signature), the testator having signed or acknowledged an existing signature in the presence of the witnesses.

Index